Teaching Health Science

Teaching Health Science

Elementary and Middle School

FOURTH EDITION

STEPHEN J. BENDER, HSD, MPH
Professor of Health Science
San Diego State University
San Diego, California

JAMES J. NEUTENS, PhD, CHES
Professor and Director of Education in Obstetrics and Gynecology
The University of Tennessee Graduate School of Medicine
Knoxville, Tennessee
AND
Adjunct Professor, Department of Health Studies
The University of Tennessee
Knoxville, Tennessee

SELENE SKONIE-HARDIN, MPH, CHES
Teacher
Liberty Bell Middle School
Johnson City, Tennessee

WALTER D. SOROCHAN, HSD, MPH
Professor of Health Science
San Diego University
San Diego, California

JONES AND BARTLETT PUBLISHERS
Sudbury, Massachusetts
BOSTON TORONTO LONDON SINGAPORE

Editorial, Sales, and Customer Service Offices
Jones and Bartlett Publishers
40 Tall Pine Drive
Sudbury, MA 01776
508-443-5000
info@jbpub.com
http://www.jbpub.com

World Headquarters

Jones and Bartlett Publishers
40 Tall Pine Drive
Sudbury, MA 01776
978-443-5000
info@jbpub.com
www.jbpub.com

Jones and Bartlett Publishers Canada
P.O. Box 19020
Toronto, ON M5S 1X1
CANADA

Jones and Bartlett Publishers International
Barb House, Barb Mews
London W6 7PA
UK

Previous editions published by Addison-Wesley Publishing Company.

Library of Congress Cataloging-in-Publication Data
Teaching health science : elementary and middle school / Stephen J. Bender . . . [et al.]. — 4th ed.
p. cm.
Rev. ed. of: Teaching elementary health science / Stephen J. Bender, Walter D. Sorochan. 3rd ed. c1989.
Includes bibliographical references and index.
ISBN 0-7637-0256-0 (hardcover)
1. Health education (Elementary)—United States. 2. Health education (Middle school)—United States. I. Bender, Stephen J. II. Bender, Stephen J. Teaching elementary health science. III. Title.
LB1588.U6T43 1997
372.3'7'0973—dc20 96-36806
CIP

Acquisitions Editor: Joseph E. Burns
Production Manager/Coordination: Judy Songdahl
Manufacturing Manager: Dana L. Cerrito
Design: Deborah Schneck
Editorial Production: Helyn Pultz
Typesetting: Graphic World Inc.
Cover Design: Hannus Design Associates
Cover Printing: Henry S. Sawyer
Printing and Binding: Courier

Cover Photo: Mary Kate Denny/Tony Stone Images
Photo Credits: p. 3 © Michael Siluk—The Picture Cube, Inc.; p. 9 © Michael McGovern—The Picture Cube, Inc.; p. 16 © Robert Finken—The Picture Cube, Inc.; p. 24 © Frank Siteman 1994; p. 30 David S. Strickler—The Picture Cube, Inc.; p. 33 © Michael Siluk—The Picture Cube, Inc.; p. 38 © Jeff Dunn—The Picture Cube, Inc.; p. 41 © Emilio Mercado—The Picture Cube, Inc.; p. 53 © Michael Siluk—The Picture Cube, Inc.; p. 62 © Richard S. Orton—The Picture Cube, Inc.; p. 74 © Meri Houtchens-Kitchens—The Picture Cube, Inc.; p. 78 © Bob Kramer—The Picture Cube, Inc.; pp. 85, 86 © Michael Siluk—The Picture Cube, Inc.; p. 97 © Richard S. Orton—The Picture Cube, Inc.; p. 107 © Michael Siluk—The Picture Cube, Inc.; p. 116 © Spencer Grant—The Picture Cube, Inc.; p. 122 © Rafael Millán; p. 125 © J.D. Sloan—The Picture Cube, Inc.; p. 136 © Frank Siteman—The Picture Cube, Inc.; p. 146 © Spencer Grant—The Picture Cube, Inc.; p. 148 CLEO Photo—The Picture Cube, Inc.; p. 156 © Bob Kramer—The Picture Cube, Inc.; pp. 168, 182 © William Thompson—The Picture Cube, Inc.; p. 192 © Frank Siteman; p. 195 © Steven Ferry; p. 198 © David S. Strickler—The Picture Cube, Inc.; p. 218 © Robert Finken—The Picture Cube, Inc.; p. 224 © John Coletti—The Picture Cube, Inc.; p. 231 © Spencer Grant—The Picture Cube, Inc.; p. 241 © John Nordell—The Picture Cube, Inc.; p. 243 © Rafael Millán; pp. 257, 259 © Frank Siteman; p. 269 © Janice Fullman—The Picture Cube, Inc.; p. 272 © James Neutens; p. 276 © Rafael Millán; p. 290 © Emilio Mercado—The Picture Cube, Inc.; p. 301 © Steven Ferry; p. 303 © L.S. Stepanowicz—The Picture Cube, Inc.; p. 309 © Michael Siluk—The Picture Cube, Inc.; p. 317 © Steven Ferry; p. 321 © Sandra Johnson—The Picture Cube, Inc.; p. 324 © Bob Kramer—The Picture Cube, Inc.; p. 333 © CLEO Photo—The Picture Cube, Inc.; p. 335 © Lora Askinazi—The Picture Cube, Inc.; p. 344 © William A. Todd—The Picture Cube, Inc.; p. 354© Robert Finken—The Picture Cube, Inc.; p. 357 © Herb Smitzer—The Picture Cube, Inc.; p. 358 © Steven Ferry

Printed in the United States of America
01 00 99 98 10 9 8 7 6 5 4 3 2

To my elementary-school daughters, Elizabeth and Emily,
two of the best teachers I have ever had,
and to Mary for her unrelenting patience and support

J.J.N.

■ ■ ■ ■ ■

To my parents, who taught me that I could achieve any
goal I set, and my husband, who has supported me
in all the attempts

S.S.H.

■ ■ ■ ■ ■

To all those prospective teachers who will, we hope,
benefit from this book

S.B. and W.S.

CONTENTS

PREFACE

Since the third edition of *Teaching Elementary Health Science,* much has changed in health education, not the least of which are National Health Education Standards. The Standards take both health-education content and high-risk behaviors into consideration, with the goal being health-literacy for all school children. In addition to development of the Standards, several commissions have met, polls have been conducted, and research completed, all emphasizing the interdependence of education and health. These positive events were taking place at a time when childhood health problems seemed to be increasing, especially with regard to violence, drugs, and communicable diseases. Close examination of the issues revealed that middle-school children were at particular risk, and this edition was developed with this reality in mind. Consequently, the original title has been expanded to *Teaching Health Science: Elementary and Middle School* to reflect the changing needs of teachers, parents, and children.

New to the Fourth Edition

The basis for change in this edition is not only the changing climate of health education but also the comments of many reviewers of the third edition. Current and potential users evaluated that edition to provide a wide range of new ideas. Elementary and middle-school teachers were also consulted as the draft for the fourth edition was being developed. Their ideas and comments were synthesized to form this new edition, which, as a result, is almost an entirely new text.

This edition is divided into two interrelated parts. Part One covers health science foundations, including the relationship between education and health (Chapter 1), the meaning of comprehensive school health (Chapter 2); curricular approaches (Chapter 3), learning strategies (Chapter 4), and instructional accountability (Chapter 5). The emphases, as seen in the first chapter, are on the newly forged partnership between education and health and how this is brought together through the National Health Education Standards. Part One also includes a new section on teaching controversial issues (Chapter 4).

Part Two contains eleven chapters, each of which is divided into three sections. The first section provides an epidemiologic background of the topic, describing incidence, prevalence, and related matters. The second section provides content support for teachers. Of course the content has been updated and made specific for elementary and middle-school students as well as the university community. The third section, teaching strategies, contains new activities that are divided by grade level, related to the National Health Education Standards, and skill-oriented. The chapter order in Part Two of this edition has been changed to reflect both importance to school children and how most health education courses are being taught today. The chapter covering illness and disease (Chapter 8) now contains a section on AIDS. A chapter on violence (Chapter 13) is new to this edition, and addresses violence both in and outside the school setting. Also, the chapter covering the human body (Chapter 16) now has sixteen color plates of human anatomy, which can make learning much more fun.

The appendices contribute greatly to the text. Appendix A reprints the National Health Education Standards for Students. Appendix B lists the names and addresses of a number of organizations that can be contacted for updated news on health issues. Appendix C provides current World Wide Web sites that disseminate information relevant to health education.

We sincerely hope that both teachers and students will benefit from this text.

Acknowledgments

This fourth edition, like the previous three editions, depended upon the contributions of many people. We would like to acknowledge the comments and suggestions of the users of previous editions. Their comments were heeded and placed into the final version. We are also indebted to the many reviewers who evaluated the manuscript at different stages of development: Mary Bonstrum, University of Minnesota; Eileen Clifford, University of Minnesota; Jean Denney, California State University at Chico; Dorothy Downey, West Texas State University; Kathie Garbie, Kenneshaw College; June Gorski, University of Tennessee; Onie Grosshans, University of Utah; Debbie Miller, University of Charleston; Frank Schnabe, Iowa State University; Thomas Timmerick, California State University at San Bernardino; David White, East Carolina University; E.D. Wilkens, Lemoyne-Owen College; and Clay Williams, Bowling Green State University. The final draft was reviewed and greatly improved by the comments of David Lohrmann, Academy for Educational Development; James McGuire, West Georgia College; David R. Stronck, California State University at Haywood; and David White, East Carolina University.

Special thanks to Paige Cruise, University of Tennessee Graduate School of Medicine, for her invaluable assistance and expertise throughout the maturation of this project. Our warmest thanks to Joseph Burns and Suzanne Crane at Jones and Bartlett for their editorial expertise and ability to maintain communication between the authors and the many experts involved throughout the process. Thank you to Helyn L. Pultz for her detailed editing. Finally, we thank our friends and family, who displayed on-going support and patience throughout this enterprise.

S.J.B.
J.J.N.
S.S.H.
W.D.S.

PART ONE

Health Science Foundations

1

Education and Health
A Natural Relationship

Upon completion of this chapter, you should be able to:

- *Explain the interrelationship between education and health*
- *Identify the rationale for the school as a focal point of health promotion*
- *Describe the health status of children*
- *Define and differentiate among high-risk behaviors*
- *Explain health and health education*
- *Offer examples of the health challenges facing elementary and middle school teachers*

Education and Health

> Today our youth face many public health, educational, and social challenges not experienced at such epidemic levels by previous generations of young people . . . . Schools are in a unique position to improve not only the educational status but also the health status of young people throughout the nation *(David Satcher, Director, Centers for Disease Control).*

The School as the Center for Health Promotion and Education Efforts

Schools, according to many, should be at the center of health promotion and education efforts (Lain, Cheaper, Well, 1992). Others, however, argue that schools cannot do everything or that they are not a panacea for the social ills of the nation. While it is readily admitted that this is true, nonetheless schools must address students' health needs when they directly affect learning.

About 90 percent of all children are healthy at birth. Preschoolers and kindergarten children generally arrive at school eager to learn, drug-free, and healthy. Yet, as children prepare for and move through our educational system, too many develop health deficits that obstruct educational progress. Somewhere along the line they make choices—or have them made for them—to adopt behaviors that frequently expose them to multiple risks for injury, ill health, and inadequate school performance.

Ask any teacher about children's learning ability when they are healthy as compared to when they are not. Any health problem—from a common cold, to poor vision, deafness, hunger, alcohol abuse, and child abuse—can impede learning (National Health/Education Consortium, 1990). Similarly, any anguish and mental health problems brought on by a faltering home life can thwart learning through chronic distraction, ill-preparedness, and truancy.

Research reveals that the pattern of poor health obstructing learning ability begins early in life. Newman & Buka (1990) documented seven such preventable conditions in children from birth to age five: prenatal exposure to drugs, prenatal alcohol exposure, maternal smoking, low birthweight, lead poisoning, child abuse/neglect, and malnutrition. Unfortunately, many infants and children experience more than one of these risk factors to learning. The result is that 12 percent of children—450,000 additional each year—enter school with a hampered ability to learn, a disadvantage that would not exist without the risk factors. As teachers can testify, these problems are often exacerbated by poverty or other social problems.

Knowledge of the link between education and health has existed for many years, and today we generally accept the fact that education can have a positive bearing on health. Increases in knowledge about HIV (human immunodeficiency virus), for example, have helped many to take action to reduce the likelihood of contracting it. And appreciation of the importance of seat belts and infant car seats prevented many injuries. In other words, history shows us that *education affects health.*

Recently, however, we have also come to understand that *health affects education.* Unhealthy behaviors, according to several investigations into health and academic functioning, are highly associated with failure in school. For example, young adolescents who smoke, do drugs, or practice early and unprotected sexual activity are prone to academic insufficiency (Carnegie Council on Adolescent Development, 1989). And school failure may be a precursor to an adult life of unemployment, dependency, and perhaps crime. This is a sad prediction for even one child, let alone the thousands we are dealing with on a daily basis.

While the schools obviously do not cause these risk behaviors and consequent health deficits, they are in a unique position to address them. About 47 million children attend K–12 grades every school day. Approximately 6 million adults staff those schools. In total, these two groups comprise almost one-fifth of the U.S. population (Green & Kreuter, 1991)—and these numbers do not include the thousands of day care centers, preschools, and higher education facilities. In addition, school health-promotion programs can impact not only students but also teachers, administrators, food service workers, custodial staff, and others. Thus no other institution is so uniquely suited to increase knowledge and develop decision-making skills concerning health, which in turn assists schools in reaching both their short-term and long-term goals.

Since educational failure is a common thread running through many behavioral problems, it is natural for schools to help with these problems. Academic achievement can be enhanced when schools serve as a hub for collaborative delivery systems—health care, mental health, child protective services, and the like. While such collaboration is important at all grade levels, it may be especially important at the middle and junior high school levels (Carnegie Council on Adolescent Development, 1990). Admittedly, teaching at the elementary or middle school level is complex and demanding. Nonetheless, every such teacher must realize that he or she has at least as much influence on the overall development of the youngster as any other immediate forces within the child's environment.

Thus there is no doubt ". . . that education and health are inextricably intertwined" (National Commission on the Role of the School and the Community in Improving Adolescent Health, 1990, pp. 4–5). The importance of this interweaving was officially recognized by the federal government in 1994, when the Secretaries of Education and Health and Human Services distributed a joint statement (Box 1.1) underscoring the cooperation between their departments to improve the health of children (Riley & Shalala, 1994).

Prevention versus Inaction

Underachievement and school failure brought about by unhealthy behavior and attendant health deficits come at a high cost for local communities as well as for the nation as a whole. In their review of existing data, the Carnegie Council on Adolescent Development (1990) reported that each year's school dropouts, over their lifetimes, cost the United States approximately $260 billion in lost earnings and taxes. About 46 percent of teen girls who give birth go on welfare within four years, and of those who are unmarried and give birth, 73 percent are on welfare in the same time period. More than $19 billion in payments is spent each year to support teen families. Furthermore, it has been estimated that alcohol and drug abuse in 1980 cost the United States $136 billion in treatment, crime, and reduced productivity (Carnegie Council on Adolescent Development, 1990). Just think of what the schools could do with all that money.

It appears that prevention is the key if both education and health outcomes are to be realized and costs are to be reduced. An investment of $1 in prenatal care saves $3 in the baby's first year of life by reducing the need for costly remedial care. There is a $10 return on every dollar invested in child immunization as evidenced by reductions in childhood illness and death from disease. For pregnant women enrolled in Medicaid, there is a $2 savings within the first 60 days of a baby's life for every dollar spent on prenatal food supplements. This return on the investment occurs because the chance of having a low birthweight baby is reduced. Similarly, poverty-stricken children who receive comprehensive primary and preventive health care spend about 10 percent less annually on health care than those who do not have or use such care (Children's Defense Fund, 1991). And there is a 35 percent reduction in the likelihood of welfare dependency in adulthood for each added year of high school education. Recognizing these costs, corporate America has begun several initiatives in support of family systems, improved prenatal care, and early childhood education. Such businesses know their investment will reap large dividends (Children's Defense Fund, 1991).

Not everything can be quantified in economic terms, however. On the intellectual, emotional, and

BOX 1.1

JOINT STATEMENT ON SCHOOL HEALTH BY THE SECRETARIES OF EDUCATION AND HEALTH AND HUMAN SERVICES

Health and education are joined in fundamental ways with each other and with the destinies of the Nation's children. Because of our national leadership responsibilities for education and health, we have initiated unprecedented cooperative efforts between our Departments. In support of comprehensive school health programs, we affirm the following:

- *America's children face many compelling educational and health and developmental challenges that affect their lives and their futures.*

  These challenges include poor levels of achievement; unacceptably high drop-out rates; low literacy; violence; drug abuse; preventable injuries; physical and mental illness; developmental disabilities; and sexual activity resulting in sexually transmitted diseases, including HIV, and unintended pregnancy. These facts demand a reassessment of the contributions of education and health programs in safeguarding our children's present lives and preparing them for productive, responsible, and fulfilling futures.

- *To help children meet these challenges, education and health must be linked in partnership.*

  Schools are the only public institutions that touch nearly every young person in this country. Schools have a unique opportunity to affect the lives of children and their families, but they cannot address all of our children's needs alone. Health, education, and human service programs must be integrated, and schools must have the support of public and private health care providers, communities, and families.

- *School health programs support the education process, integrate services for disadvantaged and disabled children, and improve children's health prospects.*

  Through school health programs, children and their families can develop the knowledge, attitudes, beliefs, and behaviors necessary to remain healthy and perform well in school. These learning environments enhance safety, nutrition, and disease prevention, encourage exercise and fitness; support healthy physical, mental, and emotional development; promote abstinence and prevent sexual behaviors that result in HIV infection, other sexually transmitted diseases, and unintended teenage pregnancy; discourage use of illegal drugs, alcohol, and tobacco; and help young people develop problem-solving and decision-making skills.

- *Reforms in health care and in education offer opportunities to forge the partnerships needed for our children in the 1990s.*

  The benefits of integrated health and education services can be achieved by working together to create a "seamless" network of services, both through the school setting and through linkages with other community resources.

- *GOALS 2000 and Healthy People 2000 provide complementary visions that, together, can support our joint efforts in pursuit of a healthier, better educated Nation for the next century.*

  GOALS 2000 challenges us to ensure that all children arrive at school ready to learn; to increase the high school graduation rate; to achieve basic subject matter competencies; to achieve universal adult literacy; and to ensure that school environments are safe, disciplined, and drug free. Healthy People 2000 challenges us to increase the span of healthy life for the American people, to reduce and finally to eliminate health disparities among population groups, and to ensure access to services for all Americans.

In support of GOALS 2000 and Healthy People 2000, we have established the Interagency Committee on School Health co-chaired by the Assistant Secretary for Elementary and Secondary Education and the Assistant Secretary for Health, and we have convened the National Coordinating Committee on School Health to bring together representatives of major national education and health organizations to work with us.

We call upon professionals in the fields of education and health and concerned citizens across the Nation to join with us in a renewed effort and a reaffirmation of our mutual responsibility to our Nation's children.

Source: From R. W. Riley & D. E. Shalala, Joint statement on school health, *Journal of School Health* 64, 4(1994):136. Reprinted with permission.

moral levels we can understand the need for reducing high-risk behaviors and avoiding damage to our children. Today citizens as a whole as well as people who work with children live in fear of youth in our homes and schools and on our streets. We are unsettled to discover that 70 percent of the nation's fifty largest school districts have installed metal scanners to detect firearms. We are disheartened by the number of teenage pregnancies. We are alarmed by the percentage of students who abuse drugs and alcohol. We are dismayed at the of number of deaths resulting from unintentional injuries. We are sorrowful when we learn of a student's suicide or involvement in a homicide.

In short, the stakes are high. Professional educators and health care professionals must work in concert to take advantage of the education–health interrelationship to the fullest. As Hewlett noted some time ago, "No matter how much money you pump into schools, no matter how well you pay the teachers, fine-tune the curricula, or enrich the programs, you do not address the critical needs of a substantial segment of students unless you also concern yourself with nutrition, health care, housing, and family functioning—the factors that determine the early development of the child. If children are hungry or abused, if their minds are paralyzed by fear, or if they live in cramped squalid tenements, it is unlikely they will do well in school" (1985, pp. 219–220). The costs of inaction are also high. But prevention strategies through school intervention work (Connel & Turner, 1985; Pigg, 1989; Allensworth, 1994; Opuni et al., 1994).

Health Status: An Overview

Examination of data, as well as the personal experience of teachers and health care providers, illustrates the tremendous shift in the health profile of American children over the last several decades. At one time, preschool and school children lived under the dominating threat of polio, pneumonia, measles, whooping cough, scarlet fever, and other infectious diseases. While not eliminated altogether, such threats have been reduced greatly through widespread immunization so that they are no longer the leading causes of death among infants and children. But 6 percent of the adolescent population—about 2 million in number—continues to suffer from serious, chronic medical and psychiatric disorders (American Medical Association, 1990).

The new threats to health and learning, coined *social morbidities*, stem from behavior and social environment and are generally viewed to be preventable. For example, the leading cause of death in childhood, unintentional injury, is also one of the most preventable dangers to health. Other preventable social morbidities among children and

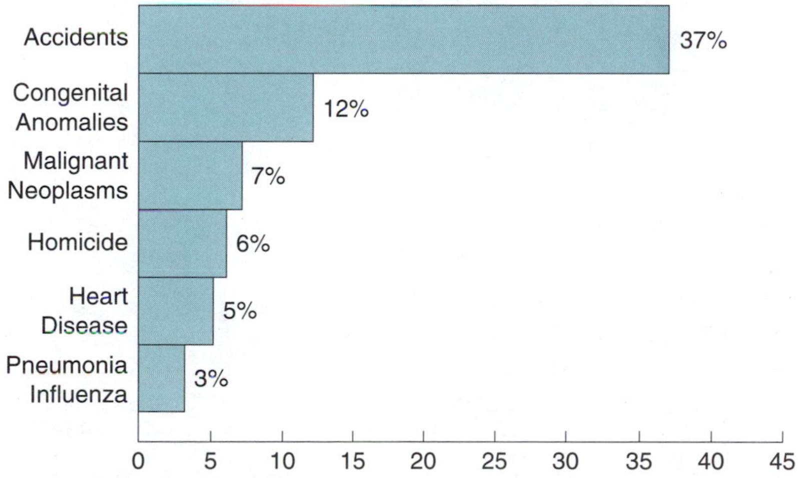

FIGURE 1.1 Leading Causes of Death for Ages 1–4 by Percent (*Source: Statistical Abstract of the United States,* 1994)

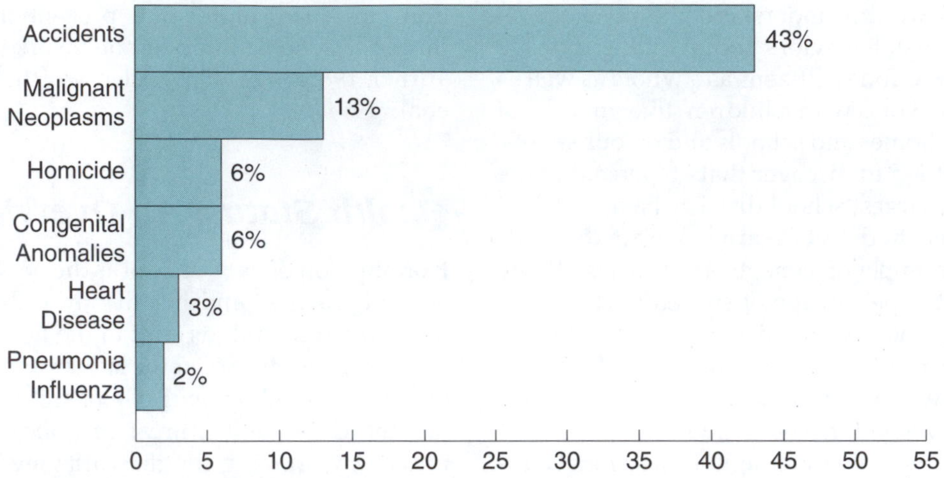

FIGURE 1.2 Leading Cause of Death for Ages 5–14 by Percent
(*Source: Statistical Abstract of the United States,* 1994)

youth that cause death or poor health include homicide, suicide, child abuse and neglect, lead poisoning, developmental problems, sexually transmitted diseases, and human immunodeficiency virus (HIV) that can lead to acquired immunodeficiency syndrome (AIDS) (U.S. Department Health and Human Services, 1990). These problems account for the majority of health deficits today (Figures 1.1, 1.2, and 1.3).

Perhaps the best way to grasp the realities of what confronts all of us is to look at health status by age group. While this overview may be considered a description, it is best to think about it as prescription for what must be done.

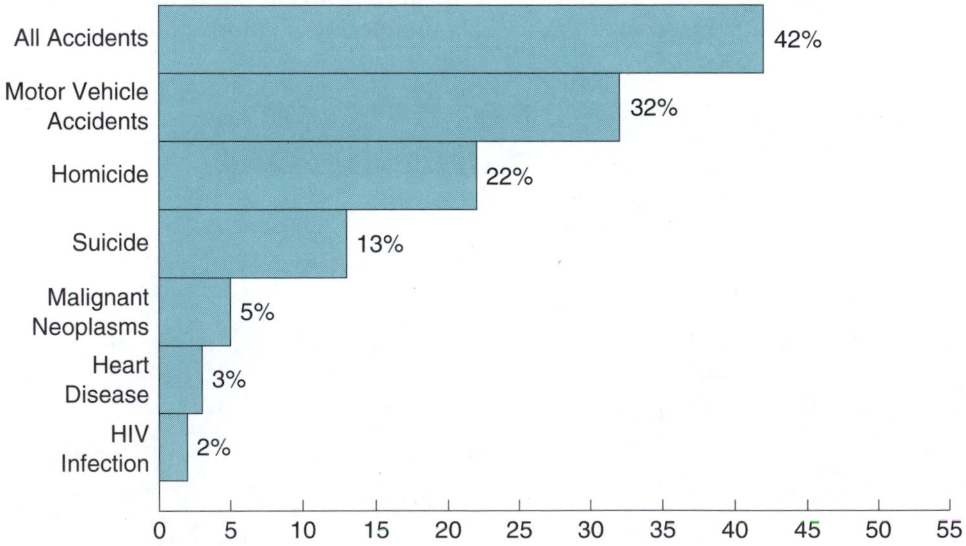

FIGURE 1.3 Leading Cause of Death for Ages 15–25 by Percent
(*Source: Statistical Abstract of the United States,* 1994)

Many of the health deficits that affect infants and carry through to school age can be prevented with good prenatal care.

Health Status of Infants

The health status of infants is very important to teachers because many of the health problems encountered this early in life continue into the school years and oftentimes into adulthood. Some of the major issues are as follows (U.S. Department of Health and Human Services, 1991):

- About 50 percent of pregnancies in the United States are unintended—mistimed or unwanted. Unintended pregnancies are associated with both low birthweight and infant death.
- Low birthweight babies are about two times more likely to suffer from severe congenital anomalies or developmental delays.
- Low birthweight babies stand a significantly greater chance of experiencing long-term disabilities, including autism, cerebral palsy, developmental disabilities, hearing impairments, mental retardation, and vision problems.
- Rates for babies born with HIV infection and cocaine addiction are rising, with inestimable long-term sequelae.
- Infant mortality rates are on the decline, yet of those who live many have been harmed, some irreparably, during the prenatal and neonatal periods.
- The infant mortality rate among African-Americans is about double that for Caucasians.

Many of these health deficits can be reduced with improved prenatal care and education. Unintended pregnancy, for example, may be due to lack of knowledge, failure to employ that knowledge, or inadequate family planning services. Sexually active people should know the risks, consequences, and the means to prevent tragedy. This can be done through education on several fronts, including the schools. Prenatal education and services must be more readily available to those who do become pregnant if the cycle is to be broken.

Health Status of Children

Anyone who has or works with children 1 to 14 years of age is well aware that this time in life is critical for healthy development. Children are dependent upon others for the basics of life—food, shelter, clothing—and they are very vulnerable to the behavior patterns of those around them. This places them at special risk for accidental injury, child abuse and neglect, homicide, and developmental problems. More often than not, these problems are preventable. Yet, according to the U.S. Department of Health and Human Services in 1991,

- About one-half of childhood deaths result from unintentional injuries, with about one-half of these stemming from motor vehicle accidents.
- Other injury-related causes of death are drowning, falls, poisoning, and fire.
- The number of childhood (ages 1–14) homicides rose by 21 percent overall from 1980 to 1990. The rate is higher among African-American children.
- More than 1 million children are demonstrably harmed by abuse or neglect (1986 data).
- The most common kind of neglect is educational, followed by physical and emotional.
- Emotional and psychological learning disorders are on the rise.
- Hearing and speech impairment and other chronic conditions are rising in frequency, with low-income children at greatest risk.
- The overall death rate for African-American children is much higher than for Caucasian children.
- Between 1985 and 1990, the child death rate decreased in thirty-eight states, stayed the same in three, but rose in eight (predominately rural) states—Alabama, Kentucky, Missouri, Nebraska, Nevada, New Hampshire, North Dakota, and South Dakota—and the District of Columbia (Center for the Study of Social Policy, 1993).

Improving the health of children living in the United States requires a wide range of interventions, several of which may be offered by the school through health services. Nonetheless, other social and economic steps must be taken if intervention is to succeed. It is well known that seventh grade is often the pivotal point for establishing behavior patterns that direct students for the remainder of their lives. Thus the intertwining of education and health may be most needed in the upper elementary and middle school years.

Health Status of Adolescents and Young Adults

The number of behavior models witnessed by children expands proportionately as their world widens during adolescence and young adulthood (15–24 years of age). Navigation through the myriad risk factors—alcohol, tobacco, drugs, physical activity, diet, safety, and sexual behavior—is influenced by several factors. That is, the successful road to adulthood depends on formal and informal support systems, the safety of the neighborhood, economic opportunities, and of course, the quality of the schools. An overview of the preventable problems in this age group are as follows (U.S. Department of Health and Human Services, 1991):

- Over the last decade, the percentage of teens completing high school has decreased. And on average, dropouts can expect to earn about one-third less each year than those who graduate.
- Hispanic teenagers are less likely to complete high school on time than are either African-American or white teens (Center for the Study of Social Policy, 1993).
- There is a three times greater likelihood of dropping out of school for students from poor families versus affluent families.
- A large percentage of teens have no productive role in society in that they are not in school, nor the military, nor the labor force, nor are homemakers. African-American teens are two and one-half times, and Hispanic teens two times, as likely as white teens to be in this category.
- The two most preventable health problems are injuries/violence and adoption of unhealthy lifestyles.
- The leading causes of death are injuries, homicide, suicide, cancer, and heart disease. The last two are greatly overshadowed by the others.
- Unintentional injuries account for about 50 percent of all deaths, with three-quarters of these being motor vehicle accidents and one-half of those involving alcohol.
- Homicide is the second leading cause of death for all adolescents. Although the rate among

African-American males is seven times higher than for white males, the difference is largely due to socioeconomic conditions rather than racial differences. Approximately 50 percent of homicides involve alcohol.

- Suicide is the second leading cause of death among white males 15 to 25 years of age, and the rate is increasing. White males are twice as likely as African-American males to commit suicide.
- The use of tobacco products, particularly snuff and chewing tobacco, is on the rise.
- Pressure for earlier and earlier sexual activity makes young adolescents susceptible to HIV, AIDS, STDs, and of course, pregnancy. Rates for gonorrhea and syphilis are higher among 15 to 19 year olds than all other age groups in the nation.
- The juvenile-crime arrest rate has increased dramatically in the last ten years.

The most striking change in health status for 15 to 24 year olds as compared to children is the escalation of violence. While the roots for such behavior are no doubt established early on, they are exhibited most greatly in this age group. But another very important issue is the increasing percentage of teenagers who fail to finish high school. The implications for educational intervention and comprehensive school health programs during the elementary and middle school years cannot be overstated.

The New Morbidities and High-Risk Behavior

For the first time in the history of this country, young people are less healthy and less prepared to take their places in society than were their parents *(National Commission on the Role of the School and Community in Improving Adolescent Health, Executive Summary, 1990, p. 2).*

The preceding quote, from the report *Code Blue,* represents the major education-health dilemma confronting us today. That is, a growing number of children are at high risk of never becoming responsible adults (Dryfoos, 1990, 1994). The risks they face revolve around the new, social morbidities mentioned earlier—violence, unprotected sex, depression, drugs, and related problems. Unlike the morbidities of earlier generations (pneumonia, polio, whooping cough, etc.), the new morbidities arise from children and youth making decisions that could jeopardize their health and undermine academic achievement. In other words, the social morbidities compel children to decide whether or not to partake in risky behavior—risky to them educationally as well as to their personal health.

Risk behaviors are those actions that increase the *probability* of children suffering negative consequences such as poor health and school failure. Examples of risk behaviors include running into the street without looking, smoking cigarettes, engaging in sexual intercourse, and fighting. Each risk behavior possesses short-term and/or long-term negative consequences. Running into the street and being struck by an oncoming car can have both immediate and long-term effects. Smoking cigarettes may display no immediate negative consequence but does hold some very significant long-term effects.

High-risk behaviors place a child in greater jeopardy—increase the odds of suffering negative consequences—than does lower-risk behavior. When a child rides in a pick-up truck without a seat belt, he or she is at risk of injury. However, riding in the open back of a pick-up, unbelted, places the child at a much greater risk of injury. The adolescent who engages in unprotected sexual intercourse is at much higher risk for STDs, HIV, unintended pregnancy, and emotional sequelae than is the adolescent who employs an effective contraceptive technique.

Risk conditions or situations are circumstances in which children live, or are placed, that increase the likelihood or probability of negative consequences occurring. These conditions could be a student's peer group, the degree of violence in the community, the availability of alcohol and drugs, living in a home without running water, having nonsupportive parents or guardians, and the like.

From an educational-health perspective, it is important to identify those children and youth that have the personal, social, or demographic characteristics that predict vulnerability. That child or group of children should become the target for intervention strategies, that is, prevention.

Who Is at Risk?

The High-Risk Social Environment

As is the case with health status, the last several decades have ushered forth tremendous changes in almost all the social institutions that affect children. The "old" family model of Mom at home, Dad at work, and two children in school is long gone. Today one in four children lives in a single-parent family, which is double what it was only two decades ago (Center for the Study of Social Policy, 1993). Minority children are most likely to live in a family with one parent; over one-half of African-American children and almost one-third of Hispanic children do so. This increase reflects both rising divorce rates and out-of-wedlock births. As might be expected, women are the heads of most single-parent homes. While many such families succeed, the road is a difficult one. In terms of dollars and cents, the average income of families headed by women is 60 percent less than those headed by men. Missing work to meet teachers or to go to a physician's office is at best a burden, at worst an impossibility.

Today two-parent families often struggle to get by economically, too. Seventy-five percent of all mothers of school-age children are in the labor force. So much time and money are spent on health insurance, health care, housing, and the like that there is little left over to meet their children's other needs (USDHHS, 1993). The 1980s were a testament to increasing poverty, with more than 14 million children—22 percent of all children—in families that were living below the poverty line. In the past, it was the elderly who were the most disadvantaged group; today it is the youngest people in our society.

Each year the United States is producing millions of new, vulnerable families (Center for the Study of Social Policy, 1993), that is, families in which at least one of the following conditions exists: (1) the mother has not completed high school when she has her first baby, (2) the mother is not married to the father when the baby is born, or (3) the mother is still in her teens—still a child herself—at the time of the birth of her first baby. Research reveals that 45 percent of new families in 1990 began with one of these risk factors; 24 percent had two risk factors; and 11 percent experienced all three risk factors. As shown in Figure 1.4, these percentages increase dramatically if we consider only those children in poverty between the ages of 7 and 12 years. The educational repercussions in these vulnerable families are immense. Observing children who are in the lower half of their class, it was found that 58 percent were born into families that had all three risk factors; 53 percent born into families having two of the risks; and 47 percent experiencing one risk factor (Figure 1.5). While outcome is not preordained, these three factors place families at greater risk of dependence on public aid, instability, and eventual break-up.

Besides grades, our educational systems provide tremendous evidence of the growing difference between the "haves" and the "have-nots." Kozol's (1991) investigation into rich and poor schools revealed glaring dissimilarities. In East St. Louis he visited a school that had recently been flooded with raw sewage from the city's antiquated sewage system. The high school physics class had no water for the lab. And not far from the school is a large chemical plant and a very large toxic-waste incinerator. All this is despite the fact

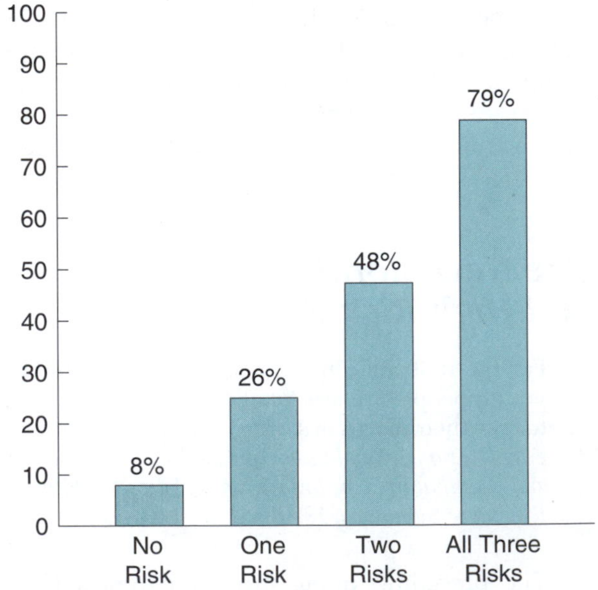

FIGURE 1.4 Children in Poverty by Number of Risk Factors, Ages 7–12, 1988 (*Source:* Center for the Study of Social Policy, p. 13)

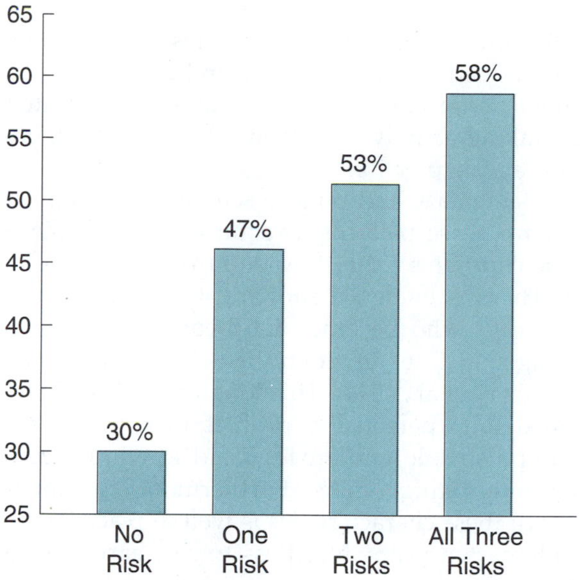

FIGURE 1.5 Children in Lower Half of Class by Number of Risk Factors, Ages 7–12, 1988 (*Source:* Center for the Study of Social Policy, p. 13)

that East St. Louis is one of the highest-taxed school districts in Illinois (Scherer, 1993). Camden, New Jersey, and dozens of other school districts endure similar taxation along with deteriorating schools. The only rays of hope are some of the excellent teachers and courageous administrators found in these systems. Living and going to school in such conditions place resident children—and indeed all who live there—at very high risk.

Perhaps the most dramatic sign of our degenerating social environment is the 225,000 to 500,000 children who go to sleep homeless (Pawlas, 1994). The fastest growing segment of the homeless population is families (Select Committee on Children, Youth, and Families, 1987), which now comprise one-third of the total homeless (Mihaly, 1991). Research shows that homeless children are likely to experience a multitude of problems that can lead to school failure. Some of these are physical abuse, eating and sleeping disorders, low self-esteem, attention deficit disorder, withdrawal, speech delays, regressive behaviors, immature motor behavior and peer interaction, and aggression (Reinherz & Gracey, 1982; Coe et al., 1991; Pawlas, 1994). Once again the interrelationship between health and education is underscored.

Knowledge of the high-risk environment is important to the teacher, not only for predicting who is most likely to experience health and education problems but also to direct attention away from making high-risk children into victims. That is, knowing the social setting of students should help teachers understand that certain children are often at risk because they live in high-risk environments (Panel on High-Risk Youth, 1993).

High-Risk Personal Antecedents

While it is important to understand that a child's environment is a predisposing factor for academic ability and health status, it is equally important to recognize other markers of high or low risk. These include unique characteristics and demographic descriptors—gender, age, and so forth.

In a search for such markers, Dryfoos (1990) investigated four problem behaviors of 10 to 17 year olds: delinquency, substance abuse, adolescent pregnancy, and school failure and dropping out. Her belief was that if antecedents—conditions or events taking place before the problem behavior occurs—could be identified, then prevention programs could address the factors that put children at risk rather than the problem behaviors themselves. Although each problem behavior yielded several antecedents, six were common to all of the problem behaviors investigated. Two of them, parental role and neighborhood quality, lie within the social environment and have already been discussed. The other four antecedents are more personal or individual in nature:

Age: The earlier a child or adolescent begins any behavior—sexual, substance abuse, low grades, delinquency—the more likely he or she is to have "heavy involvement" in the behavior, and more negative consequences.

School performance and expectations: Students' expectations for education and school grades are another antecedent. Low academic achievement is associated with all four problem behaviors and generally leads to dropping out.

General behavior: Examination of general behavior revealed that conduct disorders—

acting out, truancy, and antisocial behavior—play a predictive role in all the problem behaviors.

Peer influence: Low peer resistance or associating with friends who exhibit risky behaviors is a predictor for risk behavior, too. This comes as no surprise to anyone who works with children and youth.

It is vital to grasp the strong interrelationship among all six of these antecedents. Early initiation to alcohol consumption and smoking has been shown to lead to even greater usage and experimentation with other drugs. Of course substance abuse interferes with academic achievement and is linked to delinquency, which in turn is associated with early sexual behavior, pregnancy, and dropping out. Early sexual activity is aligned with the use of cigarettes, alcohol, and other illicit drugs, not to mention lower grades, dropping out, and delinquency. In sum, early involvement with one problem often leads to involvement with others.

In differentiating among young people, Dryfoos (1990, 1994) estimates that about 10 percent of adolescents aged 10–17 are at very high risk, that is, they do it all (or almost all). Another 15 percent are at high risk, often participating in behaviors similar to those at greater risk, but usually with less frequency and fewer consequences. In other words, while their delinquent offenses are less serious they still use large amounts of alcohol, cigarettes, and marijuana, and engage in unprotected intercourse. It goes without saying that this group is behind in school. The moderate risk group, making up about 25 percent of the 10 to 17 year olds, is known as the experimenters. Youth and adolescents in this group are generally involved in only one risk behavior. The remaining 50 percent of youth and adolescents are in the low-risk group, with few, if any, negative behaviors and consequences.

Much evidence exists to support the clustering of risk-taking behaviors as a central concept in understanding morbidity and mortality in the childhood and adolescent populations (Zabin et al., 1984; Mittelmark et al., 1987; Mott et al., 1988; Orr et al., 1991; Santelli & Beilenson, 1992). In an examination of sexual behavior, fertility, and sexually transmitted diseases, Santelli and Beilenson (1992) uncovered eight biopsychosocial risk factors: poverty, race/ethnicity, religiosity, peers, school performance, family, puberty, and related risk-taking activity. (These are discussed in more detail in Chapter 10.)

Elementary and middle school teachers must look for these patterns as soon as possible since some children start getting into trouble very early on. There is evidence showing that about 3 out of 5 boys who become "hard-core" delinquents by age 13 can be identified in kindergarten (Tremblay et al., 1994). This longitudinal study revealed their personality profiles in kindergarten as impulsive, low in anxiety, and low in concern about upsetting others. Furthermore, the interplay of these characteristics is well in place by the kindergarten years. Needless to say, early recognition of these antecedents is necessary if risk reduction and health-enhancing interventions are to take place.

In summary, today's children live in a world that requires them to make decisions that directly affect their health. Their decision-making is greatly influenced by several risk conditions at social-environmental and personal levels. About 1 in 4 children and adolescents engage in high-risk behavior—truancy, falling behind in school, using drugs, and/or having unprotected sexual intercourse. This means that 7 million youngsters may never become productive, healthy citizens. The positive light in this picture is that the education-health interrelationship is a means to increase knowledge and acquire skills so that healthful decisions can be made.

Putting the Health in Education

The three major ways health is put into education are through *comprehensive school health programs, comprehensive school health education,* and *integration of* the first two with other subject matter. The remainder of this chapter provides an overview of the three avenues of putting health into education. (Chapters 2 and 3 cover these topics in greater detail.)

Improving the health status of children requires a wide range of interventions, several of which may be offered in the school environment.

What Is Health?

A concept of health is necessary if teachers, students, parents, or friends are to achieve it—or help others attain it. Most of us have a mental image or idea of health; however, putting that conception into the words of a good definition is difficult. This holds true for health professionals and laypersons alike.

One definition of health is that of the World Health Organization (WHO, 1947): "Health is a state of complete physical, mental and social well-being and not merely the absence of disease or infirmity." Although this definition is a good starting point, it fails to reflect current thoughts about health, such as:

- Health is not a state, but a dynamic, ever-changing process.
- Health status fluctuates through a continuum ranging from death to optimal well-being.
- Health comprises a spiritual component in addition to the physical, mental-emotional, and social ones.
- All health components are inseparable, interdependent parts of the whole.
- Health components are affected by many determinants, including heredity, physical and social environment, personal choice and lifestyle, the health care system, and political/economic reinforcements, to influence health status (i.e., where it is on the continuum).

Dunn (1961) and Hoyman (1975), recognizing these phenomena, developed levels of wellness and an ecological model of health, respectively. Figure 1.6 illustrates how health status can move up and down the wellness "ladder." It implies that level of well-being may fluctuate from time to time.

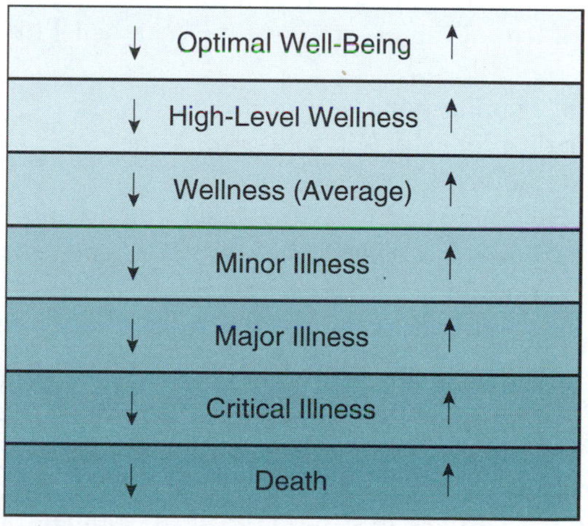

FIGURE 1.6 Levels of Wellness

In the ecological model of health, the components of health can be characterized as the following (incomplete list of) characteristics:

1. Physical (function of body systems and processes)
   a. Efficient functioning of body systems and organs
   b. High level of immunity
   c. Adequate regular diet
   d. Adequate muscular strength
   e. Adequate neuromuscular coordination, balance, and flexibility
   f. Appropriate body density and weight
2. Mental-emotional (feelings, thoughts, identity, functioning)
   a. Coping successfully with stressors
   b. Feeling good about self (self-image)
   c. Feeling good about others
   d. Accepting reality
   e. Maintaining self-discipline and control
   f. Maintaining of emotional stability
   g. Accepting responsibility for age-appropriate behavior and social roles
   h. Establishing and maintaining commitments
3. Social (interacting with others)
   a. Having an appropriate number of intimate friends
   b. Socializing with friends, relatives, and others
   c. Accepting appropriate responsibility for others
   d. Making new friends
   e. Having friends of all ages
4. Spiritual (inner strength to live; a belief in something)
   a. Having hope
   b. Having the will to live and do
   c. Aspiring for excellence
   d. Having ambition to achieve and accomplish
   e. Having a belief in something greater than oneself
   f. Having the courage to take calculated risks and face the unknown

Although these health components are written here as separate entities, generally they are inseparable, interdependent parts of the whole. For example, an athlete in superb physical health but low in social or spiritual health is unable to reach optimal well-being, or even high-level wellness. By comparison, a physically challenged student who has good mental-emotional health, gets along well with others, and aspires for excellence may be healthier. All four components complement one another, and all are responsible for contributing to health status (i.e., placement on the wellness continuum). In other words, health cannot be neatly divided into parcels but rather must be seen from a holistic viewpoint. To attain high-level wellness (*optimal* well-being may be unachievable) requires a conscious effort to harmonize the components of health. Needless to say, this is difficult. Success on the road to high-level wellness is dependent upon the ability to harness the many determinants that affect one's health.

Figure 1.7 highlights how our health components can be affected and thereby influence our placement on the wellness ladder. Six major determiners that affect the four health components are:

- Genetics. This can play an immediate or long-term role in our health. A poor genotype may have little influence on our health, such as mild allergies, or a major influence, such as Huntington's chorea, which can cause death.
- Physical environment. Food, shelter, pollution, and the like can serve to enhance or detract from our health status.
- Social environment. Family interaction, poverty level, cultural beliefs and health habits, and the like can have a tremendous influence in placing someone at risk.
- Personal lifestyle. The decisions we make about how to live produce positive or negative consequences. Unwise decisions—smoking, substance abuse, unprotected intercourse, not eating well, failing to brush our teeth—are likely to lower our health status on the wellness scale.
- Health care system. Access to health care providers, facilities, and pharmaceuticals along with appropriate health insurance has a definitive effect on our health.
- Political and economic reinforcement. The nature of local as well as national legislation, health policy, and available financial resources can affect our health components. For example, a health insurance policy may require you to see a physician who is many miles away even though another physician lives in a neighboring county only a few miles away.

Negative Determiners	Wellness Scale	Positive Determiners
Poor heredity, inherit weak immune system	Optimal well-being	Good genotype, positive maturation and aging
Inadequate physical environment, pollution	High-level wellness	Healthy physical environment, shelter, food, water
Negative social environment, dysfunctional family, poverty	Wellness (average)	Sound family environment, good schools, not impoverished
Unhealthy habits, smoking, drinking, fighting, making poor decisions to jeopardize health	Minor illness	Making decisions that enhance health, choice of friends, doing well in school
Engaging in several unhealthy behaviors, early sex activity, drugs, truancy, acting out in school	Major illness	Reducing risk by increasing health knowledge, developing positive attitudes, and acquiring skills to enhance health
No access to adequate health care, medications, insurance	Critical illness	Immediate access to health care, medications, hospitals, insurance available
Legislation and political policy that inhibits education and health through lack of funding	Death	Political and economic conditions support health care, health education, general education

FIGURE 1.7 Determiners of Wellness Levels

Teaching at the elementary and middle-school levels provides a teacher with many opportunities to reinforce healthy behaviors and to change unhealthy ones. In reflecting on Figure 1.7, it is important to be positive rather than negative and avoidant in teaching about health. Students want to learn about themselves and their own health; they need to be guided in a direction that moves them upward on the wellness scale.

Figure 1.8 illustrates how health knowledge combined with appropriate skills in decision-making can add to quality of life. Person A displays the norm—a good life overall and a gradual decline in the older years. Person B, on the other hand, lacked either the knowledge or skills necessary for life quality and suffered the consequences of low life and health quality for several years before dying. Person C acquired the necessary health knowledge and skills, thereby adding quality years to her life.

What Is Health Education?

Comprehensive school health education is one of eight components of a comprehensive school health program. In some instances, health education may play a minor role in program efforts, while in others it may be the leading edge.

Health education has been defined many ways by many people. As the field of health education has evolved, so too have the definitions. The following are some examples:

> Health education attempts to close the gap between what is known about optimum health and that which is actually practiced (Griffiths, 1972).

> Health education is a process which bridges the gap between health information and health practices. Health education motivates the person to take the information and do something with it—to keep him[or her]self healthier by avoiding actions that are harmful and by forming habits that are beneficial *(Report of the President's Committee on Health Education, 1973).*

> Health education is any combination of learning experiences designed to facilitate voluntary adaptations of behavior conducive to health *(Green et al., 1980).*

> The health education field is that multidisciplinary practice which is concerned with designing, implementing, and evaluating educational programs that enable individuals, families, groups, organizations, and communities to play active roles in achieving, protecting, and sustaining

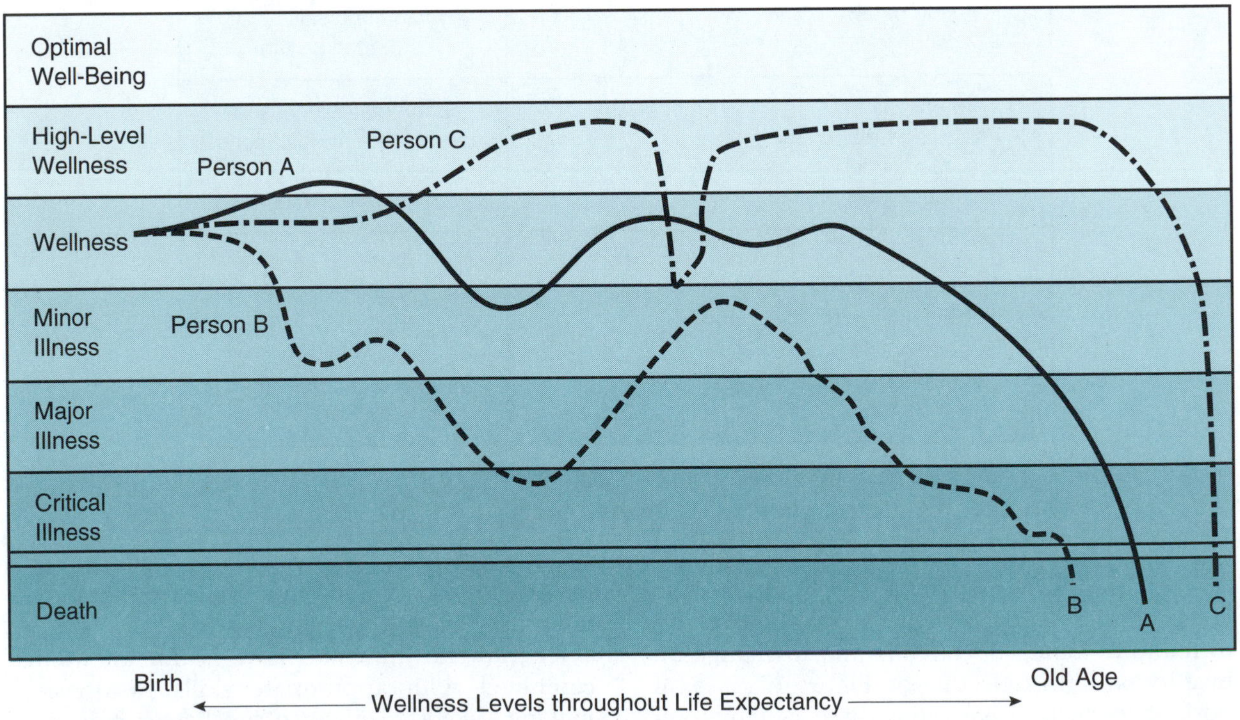

FIGURE 1.8 Knowledge, Decisions, and Quality of Life

health (Report of the Joint Committee on Health Education Terminology, 1990).

While these definitions vary, the common theme throughout is that health education is related to health behavior as well as to knowledge and attitude. In other words, health education operates within all three educational domains—cognitive, affective, and practice. Health education is provided at all stages of life, even before birth when offered to pregnant women. Similarly, it takes place in several settings—schools, communities, work sites, health care settings, and the consumer marketplace.

In the school setting, according to the National Professional School Health Education Organizations (1984), health education includes:

1. A planned, sequential, prekindergarten to grade 12 curriculum based on students' needs and current health concepts and societal issues
2. Instruction intended to motivate health maintenance and promote wellness, not merely to prevent disease
3. Activities to develop decision-making skills and individual responsibility for one's health
4. Opportunities for students to develop and demonstrate health-related knowledge, attitudes, and practices
5. Integration of the physical, mental, emotional, and social dimensions of health as the basis for the study of ten content areas: growth and development, personal health, prevention and control of disease, consumer health, community health, environmental health, family life, nutritional health, safety and accident prevention, and substance use/abuse
6. Use of program planning, formative and summative evaluation, effective management systems, and resources.

Unlike the "old" days, when health education meant rainy-day activities or the passing along of information, state-of-the-art school health education today addresses the modification of health behavior (Allensworth, 1994). This goal is especially important given the health status of children and the fact that an unhealthy lifestyle accounts for 50 percent of premature illness and death (USDHEW, 1979).

Since early childhood habits often endure throughout life, health-education intervention during the elementary and middle-school years is crucial. The Centers for Disease Control identified the areas of nutrition, physical fitness, injury prevention, alcohol and other drug prevention, and reproductive health as critical to reduce premature illness and death (Kolbe, 1990). The nearly 300 organizations involved in writing *Healthy People 2000: National Health Promotion and Disease Prevention Objectives* (USDHHS, 1989) expanded this list to include the following themes: conflict resolution, prevention of HIV and other sexually transmitted diseases, tobacco, alcohol, and other drugs, human sexuality, and exercise and fitness. (Each of these issues is addressed in separate chapters later.) In short, the charge to education is to focus on the priority behaviors that most influence health. This mission ties together (1) the interrelatedness of education and health, (2) the health status of children, (3) the acquisition of knowledge and development of skills to reduce high-risk behaviors, and (4) the concept of health.

Given this charge and this mission, health education is in a state of evolution. (The changing nature of health education is discussed in detail in Chapter 2.)

Meeting the Challenge: Education and Health Reform

In recent years, the educational and health care systems in the United States have come under tremendous scrutiny and fire. On the educational front, business, political, and even educational leaders have criticized student performance, calling for broad and deep reform. The business community has found that students no longer have the knowledge or skills necessary to be productive members of our ever-increasingly technological world. As a result, policymakers are examining all factors impeding effective learning. While educators are becoming aware that students with serious health problems (physical, mental, emotional, or social) are less likely to reach their academic potential, business and governmental leaders are simultaneously recognizing that these health problems threaten our competitiveness in the global marketplace (Lohrmann, 1993). Lower productivity by some segments of the American workforce is brought about by lack of knowledge, but it can also be brought about by illness and higher absenteeism. From a business perspective, the latter two lead to premature disease onset and higher costs for health treatment, with consequent lower profits and fewer resources for marketing, research and development, and training.

The themes of poor preparedness and little return on investment are evident in the health care system, too. Although the United States spends a larger share of its resources on medical care than any other nation in the world, little benefit in the form of improved health care has been shown (Kassberg, 1992). In addition to the rising costs, public outcry has focused on the large number of uninsured and underinsured. Approximately 25 percent of those lacking health insurance are children (Brindis, 1993). Both high cost and lack of insurance reduce access to appropriate health care, thereby contributing to spiraling costs, lowered health status, and diminished academic ability.

Once again, the interconnectedness between education and health is evident. However, this interdependence goes well beyond the school years. The challenge to the country is to dovetail reform in both the education and health arenas so that children can grow up to lead healthy, productive lives. The common ground in to both systems, as we have seen, is the high-risk behaviors based upon personal choice and social environment. We must put the health in education with an emphasis on prevention if we are to meet the challenge.

Implications for Elementary and Middle-School Teachers

Summary Issues

1. Education affects health and health, in turn, affects the ability to learn. The two are inextricably intertwined.
2. The pattern of poor health obstructing learning ability begins early in life.
3. Preschoolers and kindergarten children usually arrive at school eager to learn, drug-free, and healthy. Somewhere along the line, they make individual choices regarding health-risk behaviors, and frequently their decision-making exposes them to multiple risks for injury, ill health, and inadequate school performance.
4. One fifth of U.S. population is connected to schools. No other institution is so uniquely suited to increase health knowledge and develop health-conducive decision-making skills, both of which assist schools in reaching their short-term and long-term goals.
5. Academic achievement can be enhanced when schools serve as a hub for collaborative delivery systems—health care, mental health, child protective services, and the like.
6. Underachievement and school failure brought about by unhealthy behavior and attendant health deficits come at a high cost for local communities as well as for the nation as a whole.
7. The new threats to health and learning, social morbidities, stem from behavior and social environment and are generally viewed to be preventable.
8. Risk behaviors are those actions that increase the *probability* of children suffering negative consequences such as poor health and school failure. Each risk behavior possesses short-term and/or long-term negative consequences.
9. Risk conditions or situations are circumstances in which children live, or are placed, that increase the likelihood or probability of negative consequences occurring.
10. Knowledge of high-risk environmental and personal antecedents is necessary to the teacher, not only in prediction of who is most likely to experience health and education problems but also to direct attention away from making certain children victims.
11. Today's children live in a world that requires them to make the most serious decisions that can affect their health. About one in four children and adolescents engages in

several high-risk behaviors such as truancy, falling behind in school, using drugs, or having unprotected sexual intercourse. Another 25 percent experiment with unhealthy behavior. Much evidence exists to support the clustering of risk-taking behaviors as a central concept in understanding morbidity and mortality in the childhood and adolescent populations.

12. Health comprises several interrelated dimensions—physical, mental, social, and spiritual—which are affected by many determiners, so that health and wellness fluctuate on a continuum from optimal well-being to death.
13. Health education operates within all three educational domains: cognitive, affective, and practice.
14. Since early childhood habits often endure for years, health-education intervention during the elementary and middle-school years is crucial.
15. School health education addresses the modification of health behavior. This is especially important given the health status of children today and the fact that an unhealthy lifestyle accounts for 50 percent of premature illness and death.
16. In recent years, the educational and health care systems in the United States have come under tremendous scrutiny and fire. While educators are becoming aware that students with serious health problems (physical, mental, emotional, or social) are less likely to reach their academic potential, business and governmental leaders are simultaneously recognizing that these health problems threaten our competitiveness in the global marketplace.
17. The interconnectedness of education and health goes well beyond the school years, it continues for a lifetime. The nation's challenge is to dovetail reform in both the education and health arenas so that children can grow to lead healthy, productive lives. The thread common to both systems is the high-risk behaviors based upon personal choice and social environment. We must put the health in education by emphasizing prevention if we are to meet the challenge.

Teacher Ramifications

The information presented in this chapter holds the following ramifications for the elementary and middle-school classroom teacher. As a teacher you should:

1. Have an understanding of the education-health interrelationship in order to improve academic performance, enhance student health status, and produce graduates who will have a positive impact at local and global levels
2. Comprehend the tremendous importance of the classroom teacher in this interrelationship, rather than leaving the issues to the national or even state level
3. Accept responsibility for not only increasing knowledge but also reinforcing or modifying behavior so that it is conducive to health and education goals
4. Attempt to identify students with a clustering of moderate-to-high behaviors and take steps to intervene in a positive fashion
5. Understand the goals of health education and how they fit into your overall educational goals
6. Address your needs as they relate to teacher preparation for putting the "health" into education and educational reform.

References

Allensworth, D. D. The research base for innovative practices in school health education at the secondary level, *Journal of School Health* 64, 5(1994): 180–187.

American Medical Association. *America's Adolescents: How Healthy Are They?* Department of Adolescent Health, Profiles NLO126690, Chicago, 1990.

Brindis, C. Health policy reform and comprehensive school health education: The need for an effective partnership, *Journal of School Health,* 63, 1(1993):33–37.

Carnegie Council on Adolescent Development. *Turning Points: Preparing American Youth for the 21st Century.* Task Force on the Education of Young Adolescents, Waldorf, MD, 1990.

Carter, J. E. The challenge of education for health in America's schools, *Journal of School Health* 60, 4 (1990):129.

Center for the Study of Social Policy. *Kids Count Data Book: State Profiles of Child Well-Being*. Annie E. Casey Foundation, Washington, DC, 1993.

Children's Defense Fund. *The State of America's Children 1991*. Washington, DC, 1991.

Coe, J., Salamon, L., & Monar, J. *Homeless Children and Youth*. Transaction Publishers, New Brunswick, NJ, 1991.

Connel, D. B., & Turner, R. R. The impact of instructional experience and the effects of cumulative instruction, *Journal of School Health* 55, 8(1985): 324–331.

Dryfoos, J. G. *Adolescents at Risk*. New York, Oxford University Press, 1990.

Dryfoos, J. G. *Full-Service Schools*. San Francisco, Jossey-Bass, 1994.

Dunn, H. L. *High-Level Wellness*. Mt. Vernon Printing Company, Washington, DC, 1961.

Green, L. W., Kreuter, M. W., Deeds, S. G., & Partridge, K. B. *Health Education Planning: A Diagnostic Approach*. Mayfield, Palo Alto, CA, 1980.

Green, L. W., & Kreuter, M. W. *Health Promotion Planning: An Educational and Environmental Approach*. Mayfield, Palo Alto, CA, 1991.

Griffiths, W. Health education definitions, problems, and philosophies. *Health Education Monographs*, 31(1972):12–14.

Healthy People 2000: National Health Promotion and Disease Prevention Objectives. U.S. Department of Health and Human Services PHS 91-50212, Washington, DC, 1989.

Hewlett, S. A. *When the Bough Breaks: The Cost of Neglecting our Children*. HarperCollins, New York, 1991.

House of Representatives Select Committee on Children, Youth, and Families. *Crisis in Homelessness: Effects on Children and Families*. U.S. Government Printing Office, Washington, DC, 1987.

Hoyman, H. S. Rethinking an ecologic system model of man's health, disease, aging, and death, *Journal of School Health* 45, 9(1975):509–518.

Kassberg, M. Health care reform: How will it affect you? *Pediatric Management* 45, 10(1992):23–38.

Kolbe, L. J. An epidemiological surveillance system to monitor the prevalence of youth behaviors that most affect health, *Health Education*, 21, 6(1990): 316–321.

Kozol, J. *Savage Inequalities*. Crown, Chicago, 1991.

Lain, A. T., Cheaper, G. R., & Well, K. S. Creating an agenda for school-based health promotion: A review of 25 selected reports, *Journal of School Health* 62, 6(1992):212–228.

Lohrmann, D. K. Overview of curriculum design and implementation. In B. S. Mahoney and L. K. Olsen, eds., *Health Education Teacher Resource Handbook*. Kraus International Publications, Millwood, NY, 1993.

Mihaly, L. *Homeless Families: Failed Policies and Young Victims*. Children's Defense Fund, Washington, DC, 1991.

Mittelmark, M. B., Murry, D. M., Luepker, R. V., et al. Predicting experimentation with cigarettes: The childhood antecedents of smoking study (CASS), *American Journal of Public Health* 77(1987): 206–208.

Mott, F. L., & Haurin, R. J. Linkages between sexual activity and alcohol and drug use among American adolescents, *Family Planning Perspectives* 20(1988):128–136.

National Commission on the Role of the School and the Community in Improving Adolescent Health. *Code Blue: Uniting for Healthier Youth*. National Association of State Boards of Education, Alexandria, VA, 1990.

National Health/Education Consortium. *Crossing the Boundaries between Health and Education*. National Commission to Prevent Infant Mortality, Washington, DC, 1990.

National Professional School Health Education Organizations. Comprehensive school health education, *Journal of School Health* 54, 8(1984):312–315.

Newman, L., & Buka, S. L. *Every Child a Learner: Reducing Risks of Learning Impairment during Pregnancy and Infancy*. Education Commission of the United States, Denver, 1990.

Opuni, K. A., Smith, P. B., Arvey, H., & Solomon, C. The Northeast adolescent project: A collaborative effort to address teen-pregnancy in Houston, Texas, *Journal of School Health* 64, 5(1994):212–214.

Orr, D. P., Beiter, M., & Ingersoll, G. Premature sexual activity as an indicator of psychosocial risk, *Pediatrics* 87(1991):141–147.

Panel on High-Risk Youth, Commission on Behavioral and Social Sciences and Education. *Losing Generations: Adolescents in High Risk Settings*. National Academy Press, Washington, DC, 1993.

Pawlas, G. E. Homeless students at the school door, *Educational Leadership* 51, 8(1994):79–82.

Pigg, R. M. The contribution of school health programs to the broader goals of public health: The American experience, *Journal of School Health* 59, 1(1989):25–30.

Reinherz, H., & Gracey, C. A. *The Summons Checklist: Technical Information*. Simmons School of Social Work, Boston, 1982.

Report of the Joint Committee on Health Education Terminology 1990. *Journal of School Health* 61, 6(1991):251–254.

Report of the President's Committee on Health Education, Public Affairs Institute, New York, 1973.

Riley, R. W., & Shalala, D. E. Joint Statement on School Health, *Journal of School Health* 64, 4(1994):135–136.

Santelli, J., & Beilenson, P. Risk factors for adolescent sexual behavior, fertility, and sexually transmitted diseases, *Journal of School Health* 62, 7(1992):271–279.

Satcher, S. *Journal of School Health* 65, 6(1995):289.

Scherer, M. On savage inequalities: A conversation with Jonathon Kozol, *Educational Leadership* 50, 4(1993): 5–9.

Seffrin, J. R. The comprehensive school health curriculum: Closing the gap between state-of-the-art and state-of-the-practice, *Journal of School Health* 60, 4(1990):151–156.

Tappe, M., Telljohann, S., Nolte, A., & Lohrmann, D. K. National health education standards: A forum for review and comment by ASHA members. Paper presented at the American School Health Association annual conference, Houston, 1994.

Tremblay, R. E., Pihl, R.O., Vitaro, F., & Dobkin, P. L. Predicting early onset of male antisocial behavior from preschool behavior, *Archives of General Psychiatry* 51(1994):732–739.

U.S. Department of Health, Education, and Welfare, Public Health Service. *Healthy People: The U.S. Surgeon General's Report on Health Promotion and Disease Prevention*. USDHEW, Washington, DC, 1979.

U.S. Department of Health and Human Services. *Child Health USA '92 0–16–036247*. U.S. Government Printing Office, Washington, DC, 1993.

U.S. Department of Health and Human Services. *Healthy People 2000: National Health Promotion and Disease Prevention Objectives* (Summary Report S/N 017–001–00473–1). U.S. Government Printing Office, Washington, DC, 1990.

U.S. Department of Health and Human Services. *Healthy Children 2000: National Health Promotion and Disease Prevention Objectives Related to Mothers, Infants, Children, Adolescents, and Youth*. Jones and Bartlett, Boston, 1991.

World Health Organization. *Chronicle of the WHO*, WHO, New York, 1947.

Zabin, L. S. The association between smoking and sexual behavior among teens in U.S. contraceptive clinics, *American Journal of Public Health* 74(1984):261–273.

2

The Teacher and Comprehensive School Health

Upon completion of this chapter, you should be able to:

- *Identify the eight major components of a comprehensive school health program*
- *Synthesize and explain how the eight components of a comprehensive school health program interact to address priority behaviors or outcomes*
- *Briefly describe the history of health education and how it is currently changing*
- *Summarize and appraise the responsibilities and competencies necessary for health instruction at the elementary-school level*

The Need for Comprehensive School Health Programs

The health and education issues confronting students, teachers, and parents are formidable and many in number. Unhealthy lifestyles account for 50 percent of premature illness and death, and the environment contributes an additional 20 percent (U.S. Dept. of Health, Education, and Welfare, 1979). These facts, combined with the reality that schools involve at least one-fifth of our population, indicate that schools ". . . could do more perhaps than any other single agency in society to help young people, and the adults they will become, to live healthier, longer, more satisfying, and more productive lives" (Allensworth & Kolbe, 1987, p. 409).

To meet this challenge, Kolbe (1986) expanded the original concept of a comprehensive school health program from simply school health services, school health education, and the school environment to include school physical education, school food service, school counseling, school-site health promotion programs for faculty and staff, and integrated school–community health promotion efforts. Given the complexity of the issues facing us, Kolbe reasoned that a coordinated effort to address a specific behavior could be of greater benefit. For example, efforts in physical education classes united with those of school food services may do more for weight reduction and control than any effort by either domain alone. Similarly, school health education programs to reduce teen pregnancy are likely to be more effective when linked with school health services (contraception education and services), school health environment (policies), school counseling (interpersonal relations and risk-taking), and integrated school–community health promotion efforts (education and access to needed services). Figure 2.1 illustrates the comprehensive school health program model.

In addition to showing integration of the eight program components, Figure 2.1 illustrates the key interrelationship between health and education in regard to *outcomes.* While immediate outcomes reflect *health-related behaviors,* both short-term and long-term outcomes involve *health status, cognitive performance,* and *educational achievement.* The theory is that the healthy student learns and performs better than does the unhealthy student.

Guidelines for each of the eight program areas have been established by the American School Health Association (1994; 1987). They are as follows:

School Health Services

The purpose of school health services is to support the educational process (Oda, 1987). The need for support is evident due to the growing number of special-needs students, mainstreamed students, and problems requiring a health-care professional's intervention. In addition to the conventional first aid and triage activities, professional nurses and other health-care professionals conduct one-on-one education and screening and early intervention activities, provide special health care needs as required by law or as defined in the school health services plan, and maintain health records for each student. In short, school health services amount to more than a first-aid station.

School Health Education

This program area has evolved from a "rainy-day activity" to a planned, sequential, prekindergarten through grade 12 curriculum that focuses on priority health behaviors via ten content areas. School health education is discussed in detail later in this chapter.

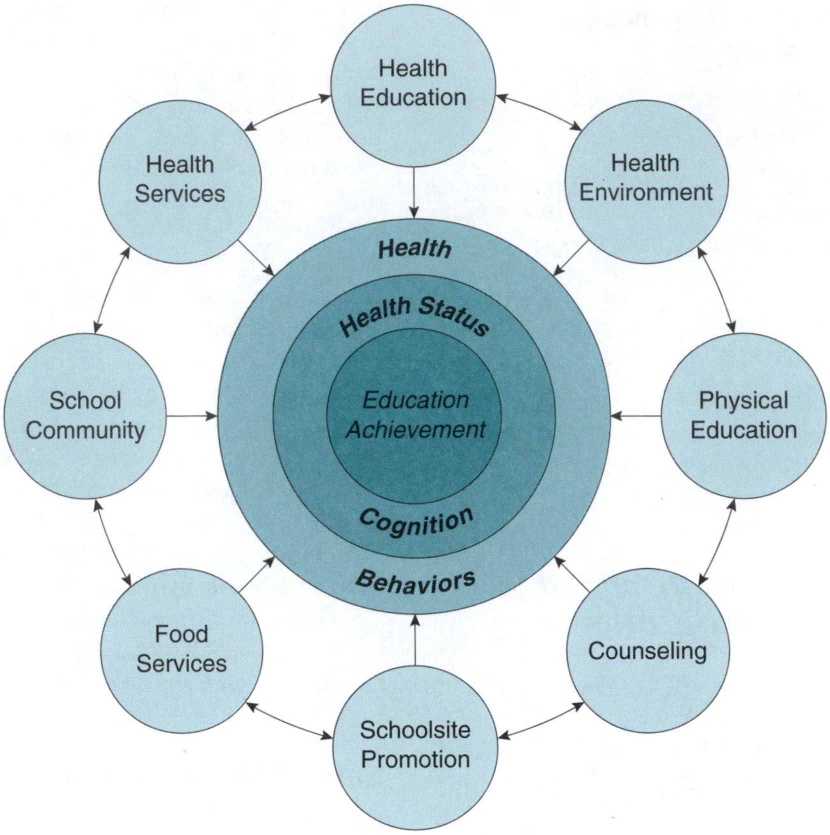

FIGURE 2.1 Comprehensive School Health Program

School Health Environment

Both physical and psychological surroundings are included in the school health environment. Physical conditions, such as "sick building" syndrome, ventilation, heating, air-conditioning, safety, noise, drinking water, and lighting impact the students and those who work in the school. But everyone in the school is also affected by the psychological environment, those interrelated emotional, social, and physical aspects of the environment. Academic achievement may be lower in schools with an unhealthy environment. School environment is often established by formal and informal policies (Allensworth & Kolbe, 1987). For example, developing self-esteem among teachers and students can be policy-driven if a school officially recognizes and rewards teaching excellence as well as student achievement. Similarly, a policy prohibiting smoking in the teacher's lounge makes a strong statement in support of related health-education efforts.

Integrated School–Community Health Promotion Efforts

Integration of school and community efforts is a logical step in promoting the health of children. Schools cannot be islands separated from the community (Gonder, 1981), nor is learning synonymous with schooling since much of what we learn is outside the classroom (Silberman, 1976). Furthermore, health-enhancing behaviors are much more likely to be adopted when messages from sources external to the school (home or parents, TV personalities, agencies, and physicians) are consistent with those given in the school (health education professionals) (Pentz, 1986). Finally, the health status of students can be enhanced when school health services are linked to community personnel (speech pathologists, pediatricians, etc.) and resources (Killip, 1987).

Thus interdisciplinary school health teams comprising teachers, nurses, parents, students, school psychologists, and other community personnel foster excellent coordination, communication, and integrated support in addressing priority health behaviors. School-based clinics throughout the United States have shown that much can be accomplished with such combined efforts (U.S. Dept. of Health and Human Services, 1993).

School Physical Education

Instruction in physical education involves all aspects of physical health: intellectual, social, and emotional. With appropriate planning, activities in physical education can do the obvious by promoting cardiovascular and respiratory efficiency and improving balance, strength, endurance, and flexibility. However, a good program can also cultivate positive self-esteem, appropriate body image, and social expression. With a shift from a sports-skills orientation to a fitness orientation, contributions to the health of all children are realized.

School Food Service

To safeguard the health of the nation's children, the National School Lunch Act was passed in 1946. The purpose was to provide nutritious, reasonably priced lunches to school children and residents in child care institutions. In 1977, the Nutrition Education and Training Program was created to teach children healthy dietary habits via positive classroom and lunchroom experiences. As part of the overall school health program, school food services provide a "living" environment in which children can learn proper nutrition. School health education comes to life when children reach the cafeteria. Poor nutrition not only fails to support health education, but it also reduces the chances of reaching long-term outcomes—educational achievement in any subject.

School Counseling

School counseling and psychology is an important part of the comprehensive school health program. Educational and health interventions are often based upon psychological screenings. Students with negative health behaviors can seek assistance from this avenue if it is available to them. Counselors or psychologists can play a role in drug and alcohol programs as well as teen pregnancy, suicide, and other problems. Of course part of their task is also to implement Public Law 94–142, the Education for All Handicapped Children Act. In this regard, schools must identify, assess, offer educational plans, and reevaluate all students who are challenged in ways that handicap learning.

School-Site Health Promotion for Faculty and Staff

The school is an excellent site for health promotion in terms of its facilities and personnel. A gymnasium can be used for fitness classes in the late afternoon, evening, or early morning before school starts. School nurses and health educators can conduct health fairs, including basic medical screenings. Such activities can save the school district money via less absenteeism due to illness, fewer health care claims, and less use of substitute teachers. Productivity and teacher morale may be increased, too. From a teaching perspective, faculty and staff who participate in a wellness program serve as excellent role models to students.

Comprehensive School Health Programs and Outcomes

Comprehensive school health programs provide a multifaceted means to address health behaviors pertinent to school aged children. For many years, these programs, including the health education component, have worked toward behavioral outcomes as well as the traditionally academic cognitive and affective outcomes. As illustrated in Figure 2.1, the health behavior modification or reinforcement outcomes serve the educational outcomes (i.e., higher achievement).

The following examples show how the eight components of a comprehensive school health program (CSHP) can be coordinated to deal with physical fitness, injury prevention, and nutrition outcomes.

Physical Fitness

Outcome: To increase the level of physical fitness among students by 50 percent

Target group: Students in grades 3 through 8

School health services: Work with physical education program to screen students for physical fitness and medical fitness.

School health education: Develop several classroom activities dealing with the positive aspects of physical fitness and how it relates to all other aspects of health and educational achievement.

School health environment: Establish policies allowing students, faculty, and staff to use school facilities outside regular school hours for fitness purposes.

Integrated school–community: Through physical education, health education, or special workshops, bring in "big name" coaches to talk about physical fitness, a hospital pathologist to talk about what happens to your body when you are not physically fit, local organizations such as Kiwanis to sponsor fitness games with prizes, rehabilitation centers to coordinate wheelchair races on school grounds, or the like.

School physical education: Classes can be fitness-oriented rather than sports-skill oriented; fitness assessment is a major role. Plan the programs and play a lead role in coordinating activities with community organizations.

School food service: Carry out education in the classroom and cafeteria showing what foods are beneficial for growth and fitness, and monitor the foods eaten, with a prize to the student(s) who stick to the fitness-foods program the longest.

School counseling: Assess morale, attitudes toward fitness, self-esteem, and the like prior to, during, and at the end of the program. Conduct some group sessions to discuss the role of fitness for special-needs students, disadvantaged students, and even students who "ride" everywhere in cars.

School-site health promotion: All teachers can have posters in their rooms depicting some type of physical activity and fitness. Teachers and staff can work out with students or participate in group discussions. Games of fitness with faculty and students can be scheduled on the school grounds. Parents can be brought in to enter such contests, too—or at least to watch.

Injury Prevention

Outcome: To increase bicycle safety and the use of bicycle helmets

Target group: Grades 1 through 6

School health services: Compile statistics on children injured at home or school in bicycle-related accidents and publish them for teachers and students. Show the nature of the injuries, where/how they occurred, the time missed from school, and so forth. School nurses can discuss the seriousness of some injuries, a neurologist could address severe head injuries, and vision screening can also be conducted.

School health education: Lessons need to be injury prevention–oriented, with activities encouraging the use of bicycle helmets. Appropriate learning-theory models need to be applied.

School health environment: Publicize policies regarding the riding and parking of bicycles on school property and the safety of bicycle stands. Create bicycle paths.

Integrated school–community: Hold a biking spree at the school sponsored by a local hospital and conducted by the police department. Students would have to pass riding tests to get their license. Bicycle repair shops could inspect bikes and give them a passing or failing grade. Machine shops can work with teachers and counselors to equip wheelchairs or make new inventions for special-needs students.

School physical education: Include activities for balance, hand-eye, and leg-eye coordination as well as strength exercises for handling and pedaling bicycles.

School food service: Make special desserts for those who "earn" their bicycle license or whose bikes pass inspection.

School counseling: Let the desires of special-needs students be known in regard to transportation, and work with the bicycle-spree team to make arrangements for wheelchairs or specialized bicycles. Help students who do not own bikes by ensuring that they play a role, perhaps as observers, helping to inspect bikes, or printing the licenses.

School-site health promotion: Faculty can lead a bike-a-thon around the school or at a local track. Money could be raised by having students and/or parents sponsor a faculty member with so much money per lap. Parents could enter the bike-a-thon, or perhaps provide expertise on racing, mountain biking, or even dirt biking. Faculty and staff can talk with students about how biking keeps them physically fit and/or how biking is an excellent recreational activity and/or family activity.

Nutrition

Outcome: To increase the selection of low-sodium foods for meals and snacks

Target Group: African-American school students (among whom the problem is greater), kindergarten through grade 3

School health services: Address the medical consequences of hypertension, particularly as it derives from high salt intake; conduct screenings.

School health education: Sequence lessons through all four grade levels with appropriate outcomes at each level. Cognitive, affective, and behavioral objectives must be measurable on a regular basis.

School health environment: Establish policies regarding snack food machines to include reducing or prohibiting high-sodium snacks. Placement of these vending machines is crucial for success of the program.

Integrated school–community: Parents need to play a special role to achieve the outcome. Literature can be sent home regarding hypertension, food selection, and food preparation. Conduct workshops at the school for parents on these topics as well as the medical aspects of hypertension. The local hospital could sponsor a hypertension screening clinic for all parents. Managed care organizations (such as HMOs) could have special screening and referral days during the "campaign."

School physical education: Discuss the role of nutrition in physical activity as well as teaching exercises that help control hypertension. Life-long activities need to be learned.

School food service: Play a major role through classroom instruction at all levels as well as workshops for parents, faculty, and staff. Display posters made in art or health education classes in the cafeteria and hallways. Mark food in the cafeteria for sodium levels (low, medium, or high). From the screening program in health services or community organizations, nutritionists can formulate dietary plans of action for students.

School counseling: Be available to help students with concerns about hypertension in themselves or in family members.

School-site health promotion: Faculty and staff can demonstrate how to read labels on snacks or set-up a display of healthy, low-sodium snacks. They can role-model a "swap-snack" day in the cafeteria in which they swap snacks with one another, and the person who is left with the highest-sodium snack gets a nutritious booby prize.

In 1993, the Public Health Service published a list of findings from evaluated school health programs demonstrating program component interaction. This document gives information about evaluated programs involving all of the comprehensive school health program areas. The information explains the purpose, the targeted grade level, the population studies, the program setting, the health components involved, the date of the evaluation, agency involvement, and a contact person. For example, the Exeter-Andover project is outlined in the food services section. According to the document, the purpose of the program is to "modify dietary intake of sodium and fat through environmental intervention" (p.VI-1). It goes on to explain that it is intended for a high school audience and the program setting is the school cafeteria.

Comprehensive School Health Education

Background

Health education in the schools has been around a long time. Historically, it dates back to the 1800s under the title of hygiene. Harvard University offered the first course in this subject matter, and in 1823 the first health education textbook was published (Cortese, 1993). In 1850, publication of Lemuel Shattuck's "Report of the Sanitary Commission of Massachusetts" provided even greater impetus for public health education, and by 1890, several states required teaching about the "evils" of alcohol and tobacco, with the drive for such education coming from the Women's Christian Temperance Union (WCTU).

Columbia University graduated the first school health-education major in 1924. Then the American Association of Secondary School Administrators published *Health in the Schools* in 1942. Eight years later, the Department of Elementary School Principals of the National Education Association issued *Health in the Elementary School.*

The concept of health education in the school dates back to the 1800s, and has evolved significantly since the days of these children in the early '50s.

Both reports showed the importance of health in the schools. In 1955, the White House Conference on Education was convened and comprised personnel in both education and medicine. The link between the two fields was recognized; each of the major educational goals set forth included health. In the late 1950s, health, safety, and physical education were identified as important to elementary and secondary education by the Education Policies Commission of the States (1959).

Nonetheless, while health educators have espoused healthy school environments and health education for years, an investigation of 17,000 students in the early 1960s revealed that health education was sorely lacking (Sliepevich, 1963; Mahoney & Olsen, 1993). Identified problems ranged from poor teaching to lack of parent and community involvement, little administrative support, and inadequate facilities. In 1967, the results of a major study, the School Health Education Evaluation Study, were released. This landmark work provided a superb conceptualization of health education for grades K through 12. It took the needs of the community into consideration as well as those of the school and students. The ten principal concepts it developed still serve as the basis for many curricula today.

In the late 1970s, 600 kindergarten students in two New York school districts became an experimental group in the Primary Grades Health Curriculum Project. From kindergarten through grade 3 these students received a special health curriculum. Researchers administered both a pretest and a posttest. Results after grade 3 showed that the students in the experimental group had less exposure to alcohol than their friends, did not smoke cigarettes like the control group, and had more positive attitudes about health. Even a significant number of parents of the children in the experimental group modified their smoking habits as a result of the program (Andrews & Hearne, 1984).

In the early 1980s, another significant research effort into the effects of health education was begun, the School Health Education Evaluation Study. Four curricula were investigated in twenty states, involving 1071 classrooms and 30,000 children in grades 4 through 7. Over a three-year period, information was gathered regarding knowledge, attitudes, and practices. Altogether, six volumes of information were collected. In short, this research, sponsored by the Centers for Disease Control and the Office of Disease Prevention and Health Promotion, showed that health education works. If carried out well, health education can increase knowledge, improve attitudes, and most importantly, modify behavior so that it is health-enhancing rather than health-detracting (American School Health Association, 1985).

Following shortly after this research, more evidence showing the effectiveness of health education was released in 1988 (Harris). This examination of 4738 grade 3 through 12 students in 199 schools supported the hypothesis that students' positive health habits, health knowledge, and attitudes increased proportionate to the number of years of health instruction received. For example, students with three years of health education drank alcohol less than those with just one year of such instruction. This held true for other drug usage, too. And exercise was greater among students who had more health instruction than those who had less.

By the mid- to late 1980s, research in health education was claiming some success behaviorally and substantial success cognitively and affectively. The ingredients for effective health education at that time, according to the National Professional School Health Education Organizations (1984), were: (1) a pre-K to grade 12 curriculum offered in a planned sequence and based on student needs and societal issues, (2) instruction that went beyond disease prevention to health and wellness promotion, (3) development of decision-making skills for self-responsibility in health, (4) activities to demonstrate knowledge, attitudes, and practices in health, (5) integrated physical, mental, emotional, and social health dimensions as a basis for ten content areas—growth and development, personal health, prevention and control of disease, nutrition, safety and accident prevention, substance use and abuse, consumer health, environmental health, family life, and community health—and (6) program planning, including appropriate evaluation, for effective management and resource utilization.

Despite the successes, educators today believe health education can reach an even greater potential (Seffrin, 1990; American Public Health Association, 1987; Botvin, 1986). The call for further change, combined with the otherwise evolving educational landscape, has placed health education in a state of flux.

Challenges and Changes

The recent call for change has, in part, derived from past successes. Behavioral scientists are steadily discovering what works and advocating the use of "what works" in all programs to prevent high-risk behaviors (Allensworth, 1993; Kumpfer, 1989). Policymakers such as the National Association of State Boards of Education and the American Medical Association (1989) champion a "new" health education that is multifaceted, more sophisticated, and moves well beyond basic hygiene, exercise, and the usual food groups. Such change is welcomed by administrators and educators who face students coming to school with serious emotional, physical, social, and family problems that impede educational achievement and negatively impact the school environment for all students (Sullivan & Bogden, 1993). The business world is encouraging change, too, so that future workers will have the necessary skills to compete in the marketplace.

Allensworth (1993; 1994) recommends the following changes in health education:

1. *Focus on priority behaviors, those that most influence health.* As discussed in Chapter 1, some problem behaviors can be labeled "priority" because they have a greater detrimental influence on health and education than do others (Dryfoos, 1990; Kumpfer, 1989). Remember that, according to the U.S. Public Health Service, 50 percent of premature death and illness result from unhealthy lifestyles; heredity accounts for 20 percent, environment for 20 percent, and the health-care delivery system for 10 percent. The Centers for Disease Control (Kolbe, 1990) see the critical issues as intentional and unintentional injury, alcohol and drug prevention, nutrition, physical fitness, reproductive health. *Healthy People 2000* (U.S. Dept. of Health and Human Services, 1989) identifies the

most important areas as injury prevention and control, alcohol and other drugs, nutrition, conflict resolution, human sexuality, sexually transmitted diseases, and HIV. Although the current focus on priority behaviors is a shift from the ten content areas recommended earlier, the two approaches are very compatible.

2. *Schedule sufficient programming to elicit behavioral change.* Data from the School Health Education Evaluation Study (1985) show that a minimum of forty to fifty hours of classroom health education is needed to modify behavior. Unfortunately, most states fail to meet this minimum. Fifty hours at each elementary and middle-school grade are recommended by the American School Health Association (1988). This instruction is especially important, since many habits, good and bad, are developed during these age levels.
3. *Replace the health instruction model with a health promotion model, emphasizing multiple strategies based upon multiple theories.* Activities "as usual" must be replaced with a well-planned series of strategies. Three strategies, at minimum, are needed for each priority behavior. Examples of strategies include social support, role-modeling, direct intervention, policy mandates, environmental changes, and media and community efforts. Theories used in health education strategies are social learning theory, theory of reasoned action, the health belief model, and multiattribute utility theory.
4. *Coordinate the entire school program to provide a variety of interventions.* Messages that are delivered in a consistent fashion and from several sources (teachers, parents, school staff, peers) are more effective in changing behaviors. Thus integrating curricula (discussed fully in Chapter 3) to focus on priority behaviors is essential.
5. *Coordinate health-promotion activities throughout the schools and community.* While parents are having more input into the school, the school can reach out to community agencies and organizations for collaborative efforts. These could include dissemination of information, clinical services, planning, monitoring, training, and advocacy.

BOX 2.1 ■ ■ ■ ■ ■

BARRIERS TO COMPREHENSIVE SCHOOL HEALTH EDUCATION

Although the importance of comprehensive school health education is being recognized more and more, there are several barriers to its implementation. Butler surveyed the Council of Chief State School Officers to get their perception of the greatest barriers. She had the Council members rank-order perceived barriers, with (1) being the greatest barrier. Findings showed the barriers in the following order:

1. Lack of local administrative commitment
2. Lack of adequately prepared teachers
3. Lack of time in the school day/year
4. Lack of money/funds
5. Health education's lack of credibility as an academic subject
6. Lack of community/parental support and controversial topics

The top three barriers were seen as the most significant. Recommendations to address them included inviting administrators to workshops and conferences dealing with effective comprehensive school health education, conducting quality in-service programs, and marketing to school administrators and professors of education.

Adapted from S.C. Butler, Chief state school officers rank barriers to implementing comprehensive school health education, *Journal of School Health* 63, 3(1993):130–132.

6. *Promote student involvement by using teaching strategies that match educational goals.* Just as strategies should be varied, it is also important that they align with goals. If awareness is the goal, then lectures, posters, and the like are appropriate. However, if decision-making is the goal, something like problem based learning should be employed. In other words, "filler" activities will not get the job done. Student participation is central to changing behavior.
7. *Incorporate the necessary basic skills that can address a variety of health problems and issues.* Teachers, including professionally certified health educators, should understand that several generic skills can effectively promote the adoption of health-enhancing behavior: decision-making, problem-solving, refusal skills, communication, media analysis, stress management, assertiveness, and goal-setting (Fetro, 1992). Use of such skills helps students address multiple health and educational concerns. But they need assistance in developing each skill and, just as importantly, time to practice the skills and feedback on their progress. Of course the skills can be practiced in different content areas. For example, refusal skills can be practiced in the alcohol and drug area as well as the family life area.

Some programs have already taken action on these recommendations. At the national level, curricular changes have taken place to include generic concepts and health education standards for grades 4, 7, and 11. (These are discussed in detail in Chapter 3.)

The Teacher and Comprehensive School Health

Central to both comprehensive school health programs and school health education is the teacher. While all programs have potential, that potential can only be achieved through teacher participation. Consequently, ". . . elementary [and middle-school] teachers should be able to communicate the concepts and purposes of health education; assess health instruction needs and the interests of elementary school students; and plan, implement, and evaluate school health instruction" (Olsen & Mahoney, 1993, p. 30). If absent from teachers' preservice professional preparation, in-service education programs should be offered.

The Association for the Advancement of Health Education (AAHE) and the American School Health Association (ASHA) formed a joint committee to help address these issues (AAHE & ASHA Joint Committee, 1992). Given that a framework had already been developed to prepare health educators for the higher grades, the committee developed a list of minimal responsibilities and competencies for elementary classroom teachers. Figure 2.2 displays the five areas and related competencies. They are in the order in which they are likely to be learned or practiced, not in order of priority. It is generally believed that these can be learned by teachers in one course. However, such a professional preparation course would need to be supplemented by another course providing background information on modeling healthy behavior and teaching the ten content areas of comprehensive school health education.

Since the estimated lifespan of a health fact is five years, in-service programs are necessary to keep abreast of changing health knowledge. Health education journals, videos, software, and conferences are other ways to keep up with dis-

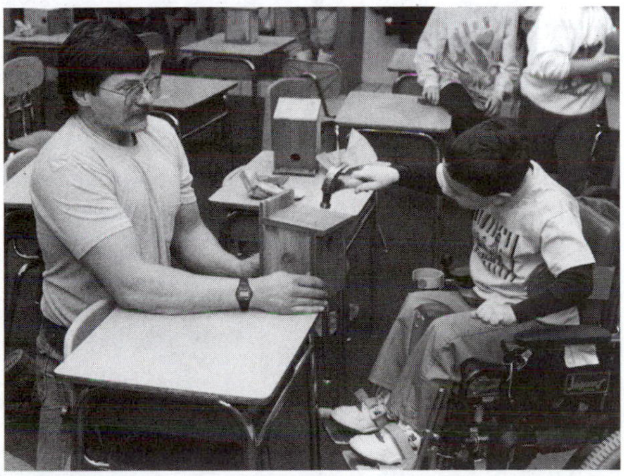

The teacher is the key to success for any comprehensive school health program.

Responsibility I—Communicating the concepts and purposes of health education.

Competency A: Describe the discipline of health education within the school setting.

Subcompetencies:

1. Describe the interdependence of health education and the other components of a comprehensive school health program
2. Describe comprehensive school health instruction, including the most common content areas.

Competency B: Provide a rationale for K-12 health education.

Competency C: Explain the role of knowledge, skills, and attitudes in shaping patterns of health behavior.

Competency D: Define the role of the elementary teacher within a comprehensive school health education program.

Subcompetencies:

1. Describe the importance of health education for elementary teachers.
2. Summarize the kinds of support needed by the K-6 teacher from administrators and others to implement an elementary school health education program.
3. Identify available quality continuing education programs in health education for elementary teachers.
4. Describe the importance of modeling positive health behaviors.

Responsibility II—Assessing the health instruction needs and interests of elementary students.

Competency A: Utilize information about health needs and interests of students.

Competency B: List behaviors and how they promote or compromise health.

Responsibility III—Planning elementary school health instruction.

Competency A: Select realistic program goals and objectives.

Competency B: Identify a scope and sequence plan for elementary school health instruction.

Competency C: Plan elementary school health education lessons which reflect the abilities, needs, interests, development levels, and cultural backgrounds of students.

Competency D: Describe effective ways to promote cooperation with and feedback from administrators, parents, and other interested citizens.

Competency E: Determine procedures which are compatible with school policy for implementing curricula containing sensitive health topics.

Responsibility IV—Implementing elementary school health instruction.

Competency A: Employ a variety of strategies to facilitate implementation of an elementary school health education curriculum.

Subcompetencies:

1. Provide a core health education curriculum.
2. Integrate health and other content areas.
3. Incorporate topics introduced by students into the health education curriculum.
4. Utilize affective skill-building techniques to help students apply health knowledge to their daily lives.
5. Involve parents in the teaching/learning process.

Competency B: Incorporate appropriate resources and materials.

Subcompetencies:

1. Select valid and reliable sources of information about health appropriate for K-6.
2. Utilize school and community resources within a comprehensive program.
3. Refer students to valid sources of health information and services.

Competency C: Employ appropriate strategies for dealing with sensitive health issues.

Competency D: Adapt exisiting health education curricular models to community and student needs and interests.

Responsibility V—Evaluating the effectiveness of elementary school health instruction.

Competency A: Utilize appropriate criteria and methods unique to health education for evaluating student outcomes.

Competency B: Interpret and apply student evaluation results to improve health instruction.

FIGURE 2.2 Health Instruction Responsibilities and Competencies for Elementary (K–6) Classroom Teachers (*Source:* From Joint Committee of AAHE and ASHA (J. Ellis, chairperson), Health instruction responsibilities and competencies for elementary (K–6) classroom teachers, *Journal of School Health* 62, 2(1992):77. Reprinted with permission.)

coveries in the health field. Staying current not only makes comprehensive school health dynamic, it boosts morale and, most importantly, allows the school to invest in both the health and education of our children simultaneously.

Implications for Elementary and Middle-School Teachers

Summary Issues

1. Unhealthy lifestyles account for 50 percent of premature illness and deaths in the United States.
2. Approximately one-fifth of our population is involved in the school system, which makes it an ideal place to address health and education issues.
3. The eight major components of a comprehensive school health program (CSHP) are: health services, health education, health environment, physical education, food services, counseling, health-promotion programs for faculty and staff, and integrated school–community health-promotion efforts.
4. All of the components of a comprehensive school health program (CSHP) can be coordinated to bring about immediate health-related outcomes such as behavior change.
5. Short-term and long-term outcomes from CSHPs include health status, cognitive performance, and educational achievement. The assumption is that a healthy student learns and performs better than an unhealthy student.
6. School health services go beyond first aid and triage to one-on-one education, screening, and early intervention activities conducted by well-trained nurses and other professionals.
7. The school health environment involves both physical and psychological surroundings.
8. Integrated school–community health promotion allows for interagency teams and consistent messages regarding a target behavior or outcome.
9. Physical education offers a variety of approaches to health and health-related problems, including body image, self-esteem, and social expression.
10. School food services are much more than the cafeteria and can play an instrumental role in several health-promotion efforts.
11. School counseling can provide psychological screening as well as services in many target behaviors, such as suicide prevention, drug and alcohol programs, and mental health.
12. School-site health promotion for faculty and staff is an excellent opportunity for role-modeling, morale-boosting, and health cost containment.
13. School health education continues to change as a result of research and practice successes and failures.
14. The ten content areas of health education are community health, environmental health, personal health, injury prevention, nutrition, substance use and abuse, illness and disease prevention, family life, consumer health, and growth and development.
15. Today's educators need to focus on priority behaviors via multiple strategies and generic skills, with high student involvement and assistance from both the educational and lay communities.
16. There are five responsibilities in health instruction that apply to elementary school teachers.

Teacher Ramifications

In regard to comprehensive school health programs and comprehensive school health education, the elementary and middle-school teacher should:

1. Realize that the teacher is the key to success. He or she must be able to carry out the health instruction responsibilities and competencies for elementary and middle school.
2. Focus on priority behaviors via multiple strategies and generic skills and attain high student involvement and assistance from both the educational and lay communities.
3. Attend in-service workshops to enhance skills to the degree that he or she can actively participate in a comprehensive school health program.

4. Be able to explain the relationship between comprehensive school health and health-educational outcomes.
5. Help meet the following objective from *Healthy Youth 2000* (American Medical Association, 1990):

   #8.4. Increase to at least 75 percent the proportion of the nation's elementary and secondary schools that provide quality planned and sequential kindergarten through grade 12 school health education.

References

Allensworth, D. D., & Kolbe, L. J. The comprehensive school health program: Exploring an expanded concept, *Journal of School Health* 57, 10(1987):409–412.

Allensworth, D. D. Health education state of the art, *Journal of School Health* 63, 1(1993): 14–20.

Allensworth, D. D. The research base for innovative practices in school health education at the secondary level, *Journal of School Health* 64, 5(1994): 180–187.

American Association of Secondary School Administrators. *Health in the Schools,* twentieth yearbook. AASSA, Washington, DC, 1942.

American Medical Association. *Healthy Youth 2000.* AMA Department of Adolescent Health, Chicago, 1990.

American Public Health Association. Criteria for the development of health promotion and education programs, *American Journal of Public Health* 77(1987):89–92.

American School Health Association. Results of the school health education evaluation, *Journal of School Health* 55, 8(1985):295–355.

American School Health Association. The comprehensive school health program—Exploring an Expanded Concept (Special Issue), *Journal of School Health* 57, 10(1987).

American School Health Association. Year 2000 health objectives for the nation—Recommendations for the school health program. Testimony presented to the U.S. Public Health Service, San Francisco, March 12, 1988.

American School Health Association. *Guidelines for Comprehensive School Health Programs* 2d ed. ASHA, Kent, OH, 1994.

Andrews, R. & Hearne, J. Effects of the primary-grades health curriculum project on student and parent smoking attitudes and behavior, *Journal of School Health* 54, 1(1984):18–20.

Association for the Advancement of Health Education and American School Health Association Joint Committee. Health instruction responsibilities and competencies for elementary (K-6) classroom teachers, *Journal of School Health* 62, 2(1992):76–77.

Botvin, G. Substance abuse prevention research: Research developments and future directions, *Journal of School Health* 56, 9(1986):369–374.

Connell, D. B., Turner, R. R., & Mason, F. F. Summary of findings of the school health education evaluation: Health promotion effectiveness, implementation, and costs, *Journal of School Health* 55, 8(1985):316–321.

Cortese, P. Accomplishments in comprehensive school health education, *Journal of School Health* 63, 1(1993):2123.

Department of Elementary School Principals of the National Education Association. *Health in the Elementary School,* National Education Association, Washington, DC, 1950.

Dryfoos, J. G. *Adolescents at Risk.* Oxford University Press, New York, 1990.

Fetro, J. *Personal and Social Skills: Understanding and Integrating Competencies across Health Content.* ETR Associates, Santa Cruz, CA, 1992.

Gonder, P. O. Exchanging school and community resources. In D. Davies, ed., *Communities and Their Schools.* McGraw-Hill, New York, 1981.

Harris, L. *An Evaluation of Comprehensive Health Education in American Public Schools.* Metropolitan Life Foundation, New York, 1988.

Killip, D. C., Lovick, S. R., Goldman, L., & Allensworth, D. D. Integrated school and community programs, *Journal of School Health* 57, 10(1987):437–444.

Kolbe, L. J. An epidemiological surveillance system to monitor the prevalance of youth behaviors that most affect health, *Health Education* 21, 6(1990):40–43.

Kolbe, L. J. Increasing the impact of school health promotion programs: Emerging research perspectives, *Health Education* 17, 5(1986):47–52.

Kumpfer, K. L. Prevention of alcohol and drug abuse: A critical review of risk factors and prevention strategies. In D. Shaffer, I. Phillips, & N. B. Enzer, eds., *OSAP Prevention Monograph 2: Prevention of Mental Disorders, Alcohol and Other Drug Use in Children and Adolescents.* Office of Substance Abuse Prevention, Rockville, MD, 1989.

Lohrmann, D. K., Gold, R. S., & Jubb, W. H. School health education: A foundation for school health programs, *Journal of School Health* 57, 10(1987): 437–444.

National Commission on the Role of the School and the Community in Improving Adolescent Health. *Code Blue: Uniting for Healthier Youth.* National Association of State Boards of Education, Alexandria, VA, 1989.

National Education Association and American Association of Secondary School Administrators, Educational Policies Commission. *An Essay on Quality in Public Education.* National Education Association, Washington, DC, 1959.

National Professional School Health Education Organizations. Comprehensive School Health Education, *Journal of School Health* 54, 8(1984):312–315.

Oda, D. School health services, *Journal of School Health* 57, 10(1987):437–444.

Olsen, L., & Mahoney, B. S. Current trends. In B. S. Mahoney & L. K. Olsen, eds., *Health Education: Teacher Resource Handbook for K-12.* Kraus International Publications, Millwood, NY, 1993.

Pentz, M.A. Community organizations and school liaisons: How to get programs started, *Journal of School Health* 56, 9(1986):382–388.

School Health Education Evaluation Study. *Health Education: A Conceptual Approach to Curriculum Design,* 3M Educational Press, St. Paul, MN, 1967.

Seffrin, J. R. The comprehensive school health curriculum: Closing the gaps between the state-of-the-art and the state-of-the-practice, *Journal of School Health* 60, 4(1990):151–156.

Silberman, C. The Carnegie study of education of educators: Preliminary statement of intent. In L. Cremin, ed., *Public Education,* Basic Books, New York, 1976.

Slipcevich, E. *Health Education: A Conceptual Approach to Curriculum Design.* 3M Education Press, St. Paul, MN, 1967.

Slipcevich, E. M. Foreward. In C. H. Veenker, ed., *Synthesis of Research in Selected Areas of Health Instruction.* National Education Association, Washington, DC, 1963.

Sullivan, C., & Bogden, J. F. Today's education policy environment, *Journal of School Health* 63, 1(1993): 28–32.

U.S. Department of Health, Education and Welfare, Public Health Service. *Healthy People: The U.S. Surgeon General's Report on Health Promotion and Disease Prevention.* USDHEW, Washington, DC, 1979.

U.S. Department of Health and Human Services. *Healthy People 2000: National Health Promotion and Disease Objectives.* USDHHS, Washington, DC, 1989.

U.S. Department of Health and Human Service, Public Health Service. *School Health: Findings from Evaluated Programs.* USDHHS, Washington, DC, 1993.

3

The School Health Education Curriculum

Upon completion of this chapter, you should be able to:

- *Explain why traditional health curricula are inadequate*
- *Explain why the National Health Education Standards were developed*
- *Identify the structure of the National Health Education Standards*
- *Synthesize and explain the relationship between the National Health Education Standards and health content, CDC adolescent risk behaviors, and curriculum scope and sequence*
- *Develop learning assessments*
- *Organize health units and lessons using the National Health Education Standards*
- *Appraise different ways to teach health education in an integrated fashion*
- *List ways to increase parental involvement in health education*

The Elementary–Middle School Curriculum

Teaching at the elementary–middle school level is no easy task. The skills required are both complex and demanding. But in fact, the elementary–middle school teacher has at least as much influence on the overall development of each youngster as any of the immediate forces in his or her environment. Unfortunately, many teachers do not realize their profound influence on the children they teach.

The extent of influence on students has implications for elementary–middle school health education. Theoretically, the primary responsibility for the health of the school child rests with the parents and the school's role is to supplement their efforts. However, in all too many instances, the role of the school becomes primary. This reality is especially important when it comes to dealing with health behaviors that can be detrimental to children in their early years and/or much later in their lives.

The teaching of elementary–middle school health education can be thought of as a process to influence youngsters' health practices, attitudes, and knowledge. In theory, health education is developed much in the same manner as any of the other traditional subjects of the curriculum. But perhaps the key difference between health and other subjects is the expected outcomes. The teaching of health is aimed at assisting the youngster to develop intelligent self-direction in health matters. However, what is so easily said is not so easily accomplished. The process of health education is a complex art; many factors ultimately bear on the quantity, quality, and effectiveness of the instruction. The teacher should ponder the following questions:

- What can I hope to accomplish by providing health instruction for my students?
- What should I teach about?
- What is the most effective way for me to teach health?
- When should I teach it?
- What materials or resources would enhance my instruction?
- How far can I go with the difficult or controversial areas of health education?
- How can I evaluate my health instruction?

Education that is motivating, relevant, timely, and provides for student and teacher involvement requires careful planning and organization. Health education is no exception to this rule. The quantity and quality of health instruction in the classroom are direct reflections of motivation, planning, and organizational skills. Haphazard education is often misguided. Thus, a teacher who desires to be effective in health instruction should make a conscious effort to fulfill several prerequisites:

1. Appropriate qualifications, including training in health education via classes or in-service programs.
2. For curriculum planning, thorough understanding of the concept of developmental tasks and their relationship to the needs, interests, and maturational stages of youngsters.

3. For planning and implementing an instructional program, insight into the bases of health behavior.
4. The capacity to employ a variety of strategies to build skills and effect behavioral change.
5. The ability to develop concepts.
6. The ability to construct attainable outcomes.
7. Knowledge of how to carry out evaluation of instruction.

These prerequisites are compatible with the health instruction responsibilities and competencies shown in Figure 2.2.

Because health instruction is complicated, it should be approached with a great deal of forethought and planning so that it can foster development of healthful behavior on the part of the students. When approached in this manner, everyone benefits—including the teacher, who can have fun implementing the curriculum.

Traditional Curriculum Design

Health curricula have employed several designs over the years. Most of them have been organized around the ten content areas of health instruction discussed in Chapters 1 and 2. Lohrmann (1993) and Pollock (1987) noted five different traditional curriculum approaches. First is the body system design, in which the body is the central theme of the curriculum. The advantage of this approach, of course, is that it generates interest among students. However, more often than not, it fails to deal with issues that are not physiological. A second traditional design is that of health problems. This approach emphasizes prevention and skill-learning, but often ignores the generic skills that are applicable to many different kinds of problems. The third traditional design, the health content design, has been one of the most popular since it provides comprehensive coverage, easy implementation, and some national consistency. On the other hand, content design emphasizes facts at the expense of skills. The fact approach is a definite drawback today because the number of facts seems to be doubling yearly. The health topic design, the fourth traditional design, is similar to the content design but includes subareas related to lifestyle choices. This approach can severely limit the content covered. The fifth traditional approach has focused on concepts, shifting away from content, per se, toward powerful ideas. It provides an effective means of organization since it employs major themes running throughout the entire curriculum as content changes from grade to grade. The drawback of this approach is that it requires a very well-prepared health educator who knows how to apply the conceptual model to the classroom.

Recognizing that each of these approaches has disadvantages, it was then suggested that health curricula be framed around the six high-risk behavior areas identified by the Centers for Disease Control (Kolbe, 1990). The disadvantage of this approach, however, is that health education could become too narrowly focused in some communities and that teachers might have difficulty designing methods to teach skills regarding the specified behaviors.

A New Curriculum Framework: Health Education Standards[1]

Although traditional approaches to health curricula have much to offer, they have many shortcomings, too. Health educators, like specialists in other subject matter areas, came to recognize that the needs of learners were changing. Moreover, in this era of educational reform, it was seen that generic skills must be acquired if students are to become responsible family members and citizens. These generic skills include "problem-solving, decision-making, critical thinking, communication, literacy, and numerical skills" (National Health Education Standards, 1995, p. 3).

[1]Much of this section is adapted from the work of the Joint Committee on National Health Education Standards. Copies of *National Health Education Standards: Achieving Health Literacy* can be obtained through the American School Health Association, Association for the Advancement of Health Education, or the American Cancer Society.

A focus on health education and the teaching of generic thinking skills produces healthy children who grow up to be healthy productive adults.

The necessity of a new curriculum was based on the premise that healthy students will become healthy adults who will help the nation's economic competitiveness and well-being, by (1) becoming effective workers, (2) having fewer work absences due to illness, (3) engaging in preventive behaviors thereby using high-cost medicine less, and (4) needing fewer health insurance benefits. And indeed, a Gallup poll conducted in 1993 showed that the American public agrees health education should be a national priority.

The major findings of the National Health Education Standards (1995) are as follows:

- Nearly 9 in 10 adolescents believe that health information and skills are of equal or greater importance than other school subjects.
- Eighty-two percent of parents of adolescents believe that health education is at least as, if not more, important than other subjects taught in school.
- Parents embrace teaching generic skills like problem-solving, decision-making, and other skills applicable to health.
- Administrators concur with parents and students that health education is equal to or of greater importance than other things adolescents are taught in school, and they believe that more health education should be taught.

Given this interest in health education, the Joint Committee for National Health Education Standards met in 1993 to begin work. Two years later, in May 1995, the National Health Standards and Opportunity-to-Learn Standards were released for implementation. According to the committee, "National Health Education Standards improve student learning across the nation by providing a foundation for curriculum development, instruction, and assessment of student performance" (p. 5). In addition, the Standards provide goals for professional preparation and continuing education of teachers.

The overall goal of the Standards is to increase *health literacy.* Health literacy is defined as the capacity of individuals to obtain, interpret, and understand basic health information and services, and the competence to use such information and services in ways that enhance health. The health-literate person demonstrates the following four principal characteristics:

1. *Critical thinker and problem solver.* The health-literate person identifies health problems and addresses them creatively.

Utilizing several credible resources, decision-making skills are combined with creative skills to achieve goals conducive to health.

2. *Responsible, productive citizen.* Health-literate people are responsible, productive community members who meet their obligations for a safe, secure, and healthy quality of life for all citizens. They apply democratic and organizational principles in order to maintain individual, family, community, and world health.
3. *Self-directed learner.* The need to be a self-directed learner is more evident every day and the health-literate person possesses a command of the health promotion and disease prevention knowledge. The self-directed learner uses numerical and critical-thinking skills to gather, analyze, and apply health information as needs and priorities change throughout life. Interpersonal and social skills are used to learn from others.
4. *Effective communicator.* Health-literate individuals are effective communicators. They organize and transmit beliefs, concepts, and information about health through a variety of means—verbal, written, artistic, and/or technological. These individuals are strong health advocates regarding policy, programs, and positions.

The four components of health literacy are interwoven throughout the Standards.

The Structure of the National Health Education Standards

The publication *National Health Education Standards: Achieving Health Literacy* (1995) is made up of three components: (1) each standard itself, (2) a corresponding rationale statement, and (3) performance indicators for that standard. Curriculum committees or individual teachers may choose to add a fourth component, learning assessments.

The *Health Education Standards* identify what knowledge and skills students should know and be able to achieve. However, the means to accomplish these are left to teachers since they are the ones implementing them. The Standards are broad and flexible to accommodate the strengths and needs of students, families, and local communities. In other words, even though the Standards are national, there is latitude for local variation in implementation.

The *rationale statement* provided with each Standard provides clarity and enables teachers and others to understand the intent of the Standard.

The *performance indicators* are a series of specific concepts and skills students should know and be able to do by the end of grades 4, 8, and 11 for each Standard. They are written in a fashion similar to behavioral objectives, but they can be used to organize student assessment, also. The four themes in health literacy are reflected in the performance indicators as well as the Standards.

Learning assessments can be constructed by teachers to refine or emphasize performance indicators as well as to incorporate content. Like performance indicators, they describe what students will know and be able to do. Learning assessments go beyond performance indicators in that they provide detail to both the student and the teacher. Learning assessment may be used either after completing a prescribed unit of instruction or in conjunction with performance indicators at the end of any sequential period. They are of particular importance when it comes to evaluation.

Listed below are the seven National Health Education Standards with their corresponding rationale statements, an example of a performance standard for the end of grade 4, and an example of a learning assessment to correspond with the performance standard. The content area of substance use/abuse, specifically smokeless tobacco, is used as an example. The complete set of Standards with their accompanying rationales and performance indicators are reprinted in Appendix A.

> *Health Education Standard 1:* Students will comprehend concepts related to health promotion and disease prevention.
>
> *Rationale:* Basic to health education is a foundation of knowledge about the interrelationship of behavior and health, interactions within the human body, and the prevention of diseases and other health problems. Expe-

riencing physical, mental, emotional, and social changes as one grows and develops provides a self-contained "learning laboratory." Comprehension of health-promotion strategies and disease prevention concepts enables students to become health-literate, self-directed learners, which establishes a foundation for leading healthy and productive lives.

Example Performance Indicator: As a result of health instruction in grades K–4, students will be able to:
Describe relationships between personal health behaviors and individual well-being.

Example Learning Assessment: Students will be able to:
During a class discussion, verbally list three negative effects of using smokeless tobacco.

Health Education Standard 2: Students will demonstrate the ability to access valid health information and health-promoting products and services.

Rationale: Accessing valid health information and health-promoting products and services is important in the prevention, early detection, and treatment of most health problems. Critical thinking involves the ability to identify valid health information and to analyze, select, and access health-promoting services and products. Applying skills of information analysis, organization, comparison, synthesis, and evaluation to health issues provides a foundation for individuals to move toward becoming health-literate and responsible, productive citizens.

Example Performance Indicator: As a result of health instruction in grades K–4, students will be able to:
Explain how the media influence the selection of health information, products, and services

Example Learning Assessment: Students will be able to:
Given a magazine advertisement for smokeless tobacco, explain why it is appealing to children

Health Education Standard 3: Students will demonstrate the ability to practice health-enhancing behaviors and reduce health risks.

Rationale: Research confirms that many diseases and injuries can be prevented by reducing harmful and risk-taking behaviors. More importantly, recognizing and practicing health-enhancing behaviors can contribute to a positive quality of life. Strategies used to maintain and improve positive health behaviors will utilize knowledge and skills that help students become critical thinkers and problem-solvers. By accepting responsibility for personal health, students will have a foundation for living a healthy, productive life.

Example Performance Indicator: As a result of health instruction in grades K–4, students will be able to:
Demonstrate strategies to improve or maintain personal health

Example Learning Assessment: Students will be able to:
Explain the risk of choking on chewing tobacco during athletic activities.

Health Education Standard 4: Students will analyze the influence of culture, media, technology, and other factors on health.

Rationale: Health is influenced by a variety of factors that coexist within society. These include the cultural context as well as media and technology. A critical thinker and problem solver is able to analyze, evaluate, and interpret the influence of these factors on health. The health-literate, responsible, and productive citizen draws upon the contributions of culture, media, technology, and other factors to strengthen individual, family, and community health.

Example Performance Indicator: As a result of health instruction in grades K–4, students will be able to:
Describe how culture influences personal health behaviors

Example Learning Assessment: Students will be able to:
Provide three reasons why smokeless tobacco use is so prevalent among professional baseball players and not among tennis players

Health Education Standard 5: Students will demonstrate the ability to use interpersonal communication skills to enhance health.

Rationale: Personal, family, and community health are enhanced through effective communication. A responsible individual will use verbal and nonverbal skills in developing and maintaining healthy personal relationships. The ability to organize and convey information, beliefs, opinions, and feelings are skills that strengthen interactions and can reduce or avoid conflict. When communicating, individuals who are health-literate demonstrate care, consideration, and respect for self and others.

Example Performance Indicator: As a result of health instruction in grades K–4, students will be able to:
Describe some characteristics needed to be a responsible friend and family member

Example Learning Assessment: Students will be able to:
In a role-playing situation, demonstrate the ability to explain to a friend why he or she should not use smokeless tobacco

Health Education Standard 6: Students will demonstrate the ability to use goal-setting and decision-making skills to enhance health.

Rationale: Decision-making and goal-setting are lifelong skills essential to implementing and sustaining health-enhancing behaviors. These skills make it possible for individuals to transfer health knowledge into healthy lifestyles. When applied to health issues, decision-making and goal-setting skills will enable individuals to collaborate with others to improve the quality of life in their families, schools, and communities.

Example Performance Indicator: As a result of health instruction in grades K–4, students will be able to:
Set a personal goal and track progress toward its achievement

Example Learning Assessment: Students will be able to:
Write out their goal in regard to using smokeless tobacco

Health Education Standard 7: Students will demonstrate the ability to advocate for personal, family, and community health.

Rationale: Quality of life is dependent on an environment that protects and promotes the health of individuals, families, and communities. Responsible citizens, who are health-literate, are characterized by advocating for and communicating about positive health in their communities. A variety of health advocacy skills are critical to these activities.

Example Performance Indicator: As a result of health instruction in grades K–4, students will be able to:
Identify community agencies that advocate for healthy individuals, families, and communities

Example Learning Assessment: Students will be able to:
Demonstrate the ability to telephone the local chapter of the American Cancer Society or American Lung Association and ask questions about smokeless tobacco

Note that two types of knowledge are incorporated into the Standards. The first is health content, which is carried throughout the Standards and emphasized in Standard 1 (comprehension of health promotion and disease prevention) and Standard 3 (practice health-enhancing behaviors and reduce risks). The second involves processes and skills for healthful living. While this, too, is implied in all the Standards, it is concentrated in Standard 2 (access valid health information), Standard 4 (impact of culture, media, technology), Standard 5 (goal-setting and decision-making), Standard 6 (interpersonal communication), and Standard 7 (healthy advocacy).

Relationship among Standards, Health Content, and Risk Behaviors

As noted previously, the traditional health curriculum was content driven but recently shifted to revolve around the six high-risk behavior areas demarcated by the Centers for Disease Control. The National Health Education Standards provide a curriculum framework with health topics derived from both the content areas and risk behaviors. Content and risk behaviors should be based upon the needs of the local community. Figures 3.1 and 3.2 illustrate the relationship

Health Education Content Areas	National Health Education Standards	Centers for Disease Control and Prevention Adolescent Risk Behaviors
Community Health Consumer Health Environmental Health Family Life Mental and Emotional Health Injury Prevention and Safety Nutrition Personal Health Prevention and Control of Disease Substance Use and Abuse	Students will comprehend concepts related to health promotion and disease prevention. Students will demonstrate the ability to access valid health information and health-promoting products and services. Students will demonstrate the ability to practice health-enhancing behaviors and reduce health risks. Students will analyze the influence of culture, media, technology, and other factors on health. Students will demonstrate the ability to use interpersonal communication skills to enhance health. Students will demonstrate the ability to use goal-setting and decision-making skills to enhance health. Students will demonstrate the ability to advocate for personal, family, and community health.	Tobacco use Dietary patterns contribute to disease Sedentary lifestyle Sexual behaviors that result in HIV infection/other STDs and unintended pregnancy Alcohol and other drug use Behaviors that result in intentional and unintentional injury

FIGURE 3.1 Relationship of the Health Education Content Areas and Adolescent Risk Behaviors to the National Health Education Standards (*Source:* This represents the work of the Joint Committee on National Health Education Standards. Copies of *National Health Education Standards: Achieving Health Literacy* can be obtained through the American School Health Association, Association for the Advancement of Health Education, or the American Cancer Society)

among the Standards, health content, and CDC-identified behaviors.

Relationship among Standards, Scope, and Sequence

Scope is the what to teach, whereas *sequence* is the when to teach. The Department of Education in each state provides guidelines for scope and sequence for health education by grade level. In regard to scope, the National Health Education Standards and performance indicators provide an excellent framework as to what should be taught to produce a health-literate student. The health content areas and Centers for Disease Control adolescent risk behaviors can be incorporated into the scope. The sequence framework in the Standards is established through the specific grade-level performance indicators for grades K–4, grades 5–8, and grades 9–11. Figure 3.3 shows the relationship among scope, sequence, standards, and performance indicators using Standard 1 as an example.

Of course scope and sequence can be refined further through the use of learning assessments, which can be administered at each grade level. Either the curriculum committee or individual teacher can interweave the behavioral objectives of the present state curriculum into the new framework by means of learning assessments.

Content Standards	Sample Topics for Curriculum Development: 4th Grade	8th Grade	11th Grade
1. Students will comprehend concepts related to health promotion and disease prevention.	CH, EH, FLE, PCD, PH, INJ, GD, NUT, NH, CM, FIT, TOB, SUA, ALC, EMH	FLE, GD, PCD, PH, CH, EH, S, INJ, ALC, NUT, NH, CM, FIT, TOB, SUA, EMH	GD, PH, PCD, NUT, FIT, TOB, ALC, S, INJ, NH, CH, EH, CLE, CM, SUA, EMH
2. Students will demonstrate the ability to access valid health information and health-promoting products and services.	CH, CM, FLE, PH, EH, PCD, INJ, GD, ALC, NUT, FIT, TOB, SUA, NH, EMH	CH, CM, PH, EH, FLE, PCD, INJ, GD, ALC, S, NUT, FIT, TOB, SUA, NH, EMH	CH, CM, PH, EH, FLE, PCD, INJ, GD, ALC, S, NUT, FIT, TOB, SUA, NH, EMH
3. Students will demonstrate the ability to practice health-enhancing behaviors and reduce health risks.	FLE, GD, NH, PCD, PH, SUA, EMH, NUT, FIT, TOB, ALC, S, INJ, CH	FLE, GD, NH, PCD, PH, SUA, EMH, NUT, FIT, TOB, ALC, S, INJ, CH	CM, FLE, GD, NH, PCD, PH, SUA, EMH, NUT, FIT, TOB, ALC, S, INJ, CH, EH
4. Students will analyze the influence of culture, media, technology, and other factors on health.	CH, CM, FLE, PH, EH, PCD, INJ, GD, ALC, S, NUT, NH, FIT, TOB, SUA, EMH	CH, CM, FLE, PH, EH, PCD, INJ, GD, ALC, S, NUT, NH, FIT, TOB, SUA, EMH	CH, CM, FLE, PH, EH, PCD, INJ, GD, ALC, S, NUT, NH, FIT, TOB, SUA, EMH
5. Students will demonstrate the ability to use interpersonal communication skills to enhance health.	FLE, PH, TOB, ALC, INJ, CH, EH, PCD, GD, S, NUT, FIT, SUA, NH, EMH	FLE, PH, TOB, ALC, INJ, CH, EH, PCD, GD, S, NUT, FIT, SUA, NH, EMH	CM, FLE, GD, NH, PH, SUA, NUT, FIT, TOB, ALC, S, INJ, CH, EH, PCD, EMH
6. Students will demonstrate the ability to use goal-setting and decision-making skills to enhance health.	FLE, GD, PH, INJ, ALC, TOB, SUA, EMH	CM, FLE, GD, PH, S, INJ, ALC, TOB, SUA, EMH	CM, FLE, GD, PH, S, INJ, ALC, TOB, SUA, EMH
7. Students will demonstrate the ability to advocate for personal, family and community health.	CM, EH, FLE, PH, INJ, CH, NH, NUT, FIT, TOB, SUA, ALC, GD, PCD, EMH	CM, FLE, PH, EH, S, INJ, CH, NH, NUT, FIT, TOB, SUA, ALC, GD, PCD, EMH	CM, EH, FLE, PCD, PH, INJ, CH, NH, NUT, FIT, TOB, SUA, ALC, GD, S, EMH

Key: CH = Consumer Health; EH = Environmental Health; FLE = Family Life Education; PCD = Prevention and Control of Disease; PH = Personal Health; INJ = Intentional and Unintentional Injury; EMH = Emotional/Mental Health; GD = Growth and Development; ALC = Alcohol and Other Drugs; S = Sexuality; NUT = Nutrition; CM = Community Health; FIT = Fitness; TOB = Tobacco; SUA = Substance Use and Abuse; NH = Nutritional Health

FIGURE 3.2 Relationship of the Health Education Content Areas and Adolescent Risk Behaviors to the National Health Education Standards (*Source:* This represents the work of the Joint Committee on National Health Education Standards. Copies of *National Health Education Standards: Achieving Health Literacy* can be obtained through the American School Health Association, Association for the Advancement of Health Education, or the American Cancer Society)

Scope Suggested by Standard and Performance Indicators		
Standard 1: Students will comprehend concepts related to health promotion and disease prevention.		
Sequence Suggested by Performance Indicators		
As a result of health instruction in Grades K–4, students will:	As a result of health instruction in Grades 5–8, students will:	As a result of health instruction in Grades 9–11, students will:
1. Describe relationships between personal health behaviors and individual well-being	1. Explain the relationship between positive health behaviors and the prevention of injury, illness, disease, and premature death	1. Analyze how behavior can impact health maintenance and disease prevention
Scope Suggested by Content/Risk Behaviors Used to Teach toward the Performance Indicators and Standard		
1. Substance use and abuse; tobacco, specifically smokeless tobacco	1. Injury prevention; specifically protective equipment when playing, e.g., skateboarding and roller blades	1. Family life; sexual behavior to prevent STDs

FIGURE 3.3 Relationship of Scope and Sequence to National Health Standard 1 and Performance Indicators

Organization of Health Instruction Using the Standards

The change from memory-centered learning of content to acquisition of knowledge and skills requires a well-conceived plan of educational experiences. This can begin with a unit plan. The health education unit plan consists of standards, performance indicators, learning assessments, content, learning experiences, evaluation procedures, and resources. Although there are several forms for presenting a unit plan, we have found that the horizontal-row form possesses considerable merit (see Figure 3.4).

Unit Title

The title of the unit should be short, clear, and concise. Every effort should be made to convey to the reader the nature of the topic to be covered. The title may reflect the overall standard, the performance indicator, or even the learning assessments.

National Health Education Standard

The standard(s) serves as the framework for the unit plan. As such, it is the focal point for the development of the remainder of the unit and the entire instructional process. Together, they act as guides to the performance indicators and assessment criteria. As a general rule, all seven standards should be addressed in every unit in age and developmentally appropriate ways.

Performance Indicators and Learning Assessments

The unit plan should include statements that clearly describe what students will know and be able to do after completing the unit of instruction. The performance indicators and the learning assessments add direction to the instructional process. They suggest what should be taught and how. The learning assessments refine or "fine-tune" the performance indicators to the degree that they can be used for evaluation purposes. Moreover, they may be directly linked to areas of

Unit Title ______________________ Grade Level ______________________

Time Period ______________________ Instructor ______________________

National Health Education Standard(s)

1.
2.
Etc.

↕

Performance Indicator(s)

1.
2.
Etc.

↕

Learning Assessment(s)

1.
2.
Etc.

↕

Content

Content should go beyond facts to support learning assessments, performance indicators, and national health education standards.

↕

Learning Strategies or Experiences

1.
2.
Etc.

↕

Evaluation Techniques

1.
2.
Etc.

↕

Resources

1.
2.
3.
4.
Etc.

FIGURE 3.4 Suggested Format for a Unit Plan

health content, unlike the national performance indicators.

Developing Learning Assessments

Learning assessments provide detail to both the student and the teacher. Like performance indicators, they are molded after behavioral objectives. The latter have been around for a long time and teachers who have written them before will have no difficulty in developing learning assessments. Also, like behavioral objectives, learning assessments provide direction in terms of what should be taught (including content), how it should be taught, and whether or not that which is taught is actually learned.

More specifically, teachers and students benefit from learning assessments in the following ways:

1. Given clearly defined learning assessments to work toward, teachers can design instructional experiences specifically to achieve them. They can also evaluate the effectiveness of such strategies according to whether the learning assessments are achieved.
2. Students can be examined prior to instruction to ascertain both their level of readiness and level of achievement in the past.
3. Each student can be evaluated on mastery of the learning assessments. In this way, every student can be required to master all the learning assessments.
4. Where appropriate, content can also be evaluated if there are learning assessments written specifically for it.

Learning assessments should be very detailed so that both students and teachers know exactly what is required. Needless to say, detail is good in providing direction, but especially important when used for evaluation. The following are the details that should be incorporated into learning assessments:

1. *Who* is expected to perform the required task or behavior. The who refers to students or learners.
2. The *behavior* to be demonstrated. Use action verbs such as "write," "explain," and "identify."
3. The *content* or result of the student's behavior that will be evaluated to determine the student's level of performance. In content areas, this is what the student is able to define, discuss, and so forth. In skills areas, the student may demonstrate, illustrate, select, translate, and the like.
4. The *conditions* under which the student is to perform the task or behavior. For example, on a test or in a role-playing situation.
5. The *standards* that will be employed to ascertain whether the student has achieved the learning assessment. These standards could be written as "90% accuracy," "three out of five," and so on.

Using a learning assessment presented above, let us look at the elements.

Students will be able to:

During a class discussion, verbally list three negative effects of using smokeless tobacco

Who: students

Behavior: verbally list

Content: negative effects of using smokeless tobacco

Condition: during a class discussion

Standard: three

Often a learning assessment may be simplified by being worded like a performance indicator. That is, the learning assessment would contain all of the elements except the conditions and standards. In this case, the learning assessment above would read as:

Students will be able to:

Verbally list some of the negative effects of using smokeless tobacco

Written in this fashion, the three key elements are the who, the desired observable behavior, and the content. The greater the clarity of these elements, the greater the probability that the learning assessment will clearly communicate to the student what he or she is to learn and do.

Shown below are lists of terms that can be used in learning assessments. The first list fails to offer direction or serve as a basis for fair evaluation. The second is much more precise.

Less precise terms (many interpretations)

Know	Value
Realize	Comprehend
Enjoy	Desire
Believe	Feel
Understand	Respect
Appreciate	

More precise terms (fewer interpretations)

Define	Interpret
Distinguish	Describe
Recall	Name
Recognize	Construct
Demonstrate	Compare
Apply	Translate
Organize	State
Discuss	Illustrate
Identify	Summarize
List	Classify
Diagram	Select
Acquire	Order

Content

The content section of the unit plan outlines the subject matter to be used in teaching toward the learning assessment, then to the performance indicator, then to the National Health Education Standard. The content should be carefully selected to enhance the development of the desired knowledge and skills.

Content is a collection of facts and other information. To be useful, facts must be relevant to the learning assessments, performance indicators, and of course the standards. It may be difficult for a child to assimilate and categorize numerous facts. Indeed, a child may forget the details of the content in a few minutes, before it even enters long-term memory.

But teachers can make the content meaningful to children by providing appropriate learning experiences. They should help their students understand and remember the content and lead them toward the performance indicator and standard. In selecting content, the teacher should start out at the student's level and then select and present content in a progressive manner.

Learning Experiences or Strategies

In order to teach effectively, that is, foster motivation, internalization of information, and acquisition of skills, suitable instructional methods must be chosen. The teacher should consider such issues as class differences, strengths, weaknesses, and time allotment. It may be necessary to develop more than one learning strategy for any particular lesson. (Chapter 4 is devoted to learning strategies to be used in the classroom.)

Evaluation Procedures

It is important to implement some form of measurement and evaluation of instruction. Such accountability can take on many forms: knowledge tests, attitude scales, practice inventories, checklists, rating scales, observations, oral and written reports, and so on. The learning assessment developed at the beginning of the unit should serve as the evaluation criterion. Making students aware of the learning assessments *prior* to doing the unit is fair, since evaluation should not be a guessing game of "What does the teacher want us to know?" In fact, prior knowledge of learning assessments can only assist students and teachers in achieving the performance indicators and Standards. (More information on evaluation is provided in Chapter 5.)

Resources

This section of the unit plan lists materials, supplies, and aids necessary to the instructional process. Videotapes, projectors, screens, models, specimens, transparencies, overhead projectors, VCRs, computer software, slides, and slide projectors are all teaching aids and resources. A list of references is very appropriate, too. One list could be for teachers and another for students, the latter providing exact page numbers if necessary. Problem-based learning lends itself to the use of references to acquire several skills.

The Daily Lesson Plan

Once the unit plan is complete, the daily lesson plans must be made. They provide the day-by-day progression toward the established objectives of the unit. Effective lesson-planning requires that the instructor have a clear understanding or overview of the total learning package presented in the unit. With that understanding in mind, the teacher carefully separates the unit into the separate daily lesson plans.

A lesson plan may extend beyond more than one class period. It may also be designed for completion in one class period but have to be extended into another due to miscalculation of time it will take. Either way, the daily lesson plan should clearly convey a sense of continuation from one class period to the next and ultimately realize the learning assessments, performance indicators, and Standards. Figure 3.5 shows a suggested format for the daily lesson plan.

The daily lesson plan should be structured so that each component reinforces the others. In addition to the components depicted in Figure 3.5, the daily lesson plan might include the following:

1. Key questions for review, to help children internalize content and acquire skills
2. Key words important to the standard or performance indicator
3. References for students and the teacher
4. Teaching aids and resources
5. Evaluations, such as quizzes before and after the lesson or observations of behavior
6. Time allotted for each learning experience

Health instruction, like the practice of medicine, is both a science and an art. It is a science in that it has interdisciplinary content and relies on the principles of educational and developmental psychology. In terms of employing a body knowledge, techniques, and methods, it is similar to medicine. Knowing which techniques to use and how to use them, however, is an art in medicine, as it is in teaching. The art of medicine is in diagnosing, prescribing, and treating. The art of health instruction is in selecting appropriate learning strategies to attain learning assessments and performance indicators—decision-making—as well as manipulating human behavior. Teaching is an art because a teacher is a social engineer, having students evolve new health habits and behaviors. Dealing with children to attain the National Health Education Standards is an art. Thus developing the lesson plan uses a scientific approach, and executing it is an art.

Curriculum Approaches

As schools restructure and curricula change, so too do opinions about approaches to teaching elementary health education. There are currently two theories. The first is that health education, as a discipline, can be taught via direct instruction; it is a stand-alone specialty. The second is that health education, as with many other subjects, should be integrated into the overall curriculum. The following discussion is intended to help you form your own opinion.

Direct Instruction

Direct health instruction is scheduled, planned, and directed toward the fulfillment of pupils' health needs and interests. The major advantage of direct instruction is that teachers are used to it, therefore they find implementation easy. Another is that textbooks are written with direct instruction in mind and this is especially important at the elementary level since scope is often based on the textbook (rather than needs, problem areas, etc.). A third advantage is that the many commercial curricula available support direct teaching, not integrated approaches. The same holds true for most state Department of Education curricula.

Some of the advantages, however, could be considered disadvantages. For example, a curriculum directed by a commercial package or textbook may fail to meet the needs of local students. Not all 4th graders across the nation are alike. Another disadvantage is that health is seen as separate from other life events.

Other issues related to the effectiveness of direct instruction include the degree of administrative support, the amount of time available, the background preparation of the teacher, and the

National Health Education Standard: ____

Performance Indicator(s): ____

____

____

Learning Assessment(s): ____

____

____

Content	Time Allocated	Learning Experiences	Teaching Aids
1. (*NOTE:* Record WHAT it is you are going to disseminate to the students.) 2. 3. 4. Etc.		1. (*NOTE:* Record HOW you are going to convey the content. Learning experience number 1 should be correlated to content number 1, etc.) 2. 3. 4. (*NOTE:* "Key words and key questions" can be listed under the learning experience where appropriate.)	1. (*NOTE:* Record all essential materials, supplies, and aids necessary to carry out the instructional process.) 2. 3. 4. Etc.
		Evaluation Procedures	
		1. (*NOTE:* Some form of measurement and evaluation is important to determine whether established objectives have been attained.) 2. Etc.	**References** (*NOTE:* List sources that substantiate the validity of your content.)

FIGURE 3.5 Suggested Format for a Daily Lesson Plan

In order to learn effectively, students need to see both the relevance of what they are being taught and a connection between subjects.

potential for appropriate sequencing of material throughout the elementary years.

Where direct instruction is permissible, it is recommended that twenty minutes per day be devoted to health education in the early elementary years. In the middle-school years, students should receive daily health education for at least one semester. If this is not possible, the minimum should be one full class period each week for the entire school year.

Integration or Interdisciplinary Instruction

In the last few years, the integrated approach to teaching many subjects has been gaining popularity. The reasons for this, according to Jacobs (Brandt, 1991) are fourfold:

1. *Knowledge explosion:* The school year is not long enough to fit in everything that needs to be covered. As a result, much of the newest knowledge is omitted.
2. *Relevancy:* Too many children are bored with school, mentally dropping out because they don't see the relevancy of what they are learning. Children need to see the connection between subjects.
3. *Common sense:* Life is not made up of separate and distinct parts, nor should education be. Topics should be supportive of one another.
4. *Teacher collaboration:* Integration requires teachers to work together rather than in isolation. Respect for the subject matter and colleagues usually increases.

Willis (1992) claims that integration brings order to the curriculum and is "life-like," since pieces of information can be unified by a common principle, problem, or theme. Such unification can bring meaning to learning. As teachers work together toward integration too, flexibility and creativity can flourish (Reynolds, 1993). In many middle schools, this atmosphere has led to teaming in which groups of teachers from different areas collaborate to make up instructional units.

From the perspective of health education, acquisition of generic skills may be best learned through an integrated approach. The Standards encourage integration of the ten content areas in health education anyway and taking integration one step further may be of benefit. The National Health Education Standards may be able to be aligned with many of the standards developed in other elementary school areas, including math, language arts, and social studies (*Education Week*, 1995). And "Curriculum integration can be a pragmatic use of the disciplines" claims Jacobs (Brandt, 1991).

In addition, publishers can correlate the National Health Standards with their textbooks (Figure 3.6). Doing so would facilitate direct teaching as well as the integration of standards and teaching materials.

Parent involvement can be enhanced by an integrated curriculum, too. Allensworth (1993) believes that parents can play a role in "providing information, service, advice, planning, research monitoring, training, and advocacy."

Integration at the elementary school level can be fairly easy since students usually remain with the same teacher for all subjects. In middle school, or whenever this no longer occurs, integration is more challenging. To develop an interdisciplinary curriculum on a grand scale, Jacobs (Brandt, 1991) suggests an action plan at the school district level. Her action plan has four phases over three years. Phase 1 involves internal and external research. The former is curriculum mapping, in which the interdisciplinary team plots month by month the topics taught. The latter involves going to conferences, other sites, and such. Phase 2 is proposal development, taking about two to four months. In the first effort, "most schools decide to upgrade an existing unit of study through collaboration between disciplines" (p. 27). Phase 3 comprises implementing and monitoring a pilot program. Phase 4 is the adoption of the program. The lesson to be learned here is that integration is more than simple correlation; to be successful, it takes much effort and planning.

A starting point could be the selection of a unifying theme, called a *web*. The theme should be broad enough to stretch across the curriculum but not so broad as to be useless. Themes should incorporate the components of *interactions, argument and evidence, communities, change, dependence and independence, systems,* and *power* (Reynolds, 1993). The following questions can assist in theme selection (Kovalik in Willis, 1992):

1. What is so important about this theme that it will promote future learning?
2. Does it have substance and application to the real world? (E.g., Dinosaurs are dead.)
3. Are relevant materials readily available?
4. Is it meaningful and age-appropriate?
5. Does it tie into other units, enabling students to make generalizations and gain greater understanding? (I.e., themes must relate to one another. It is a mistake to think "You do fish for one month, then simple machines for one month.")
6. Is it worth the time needed to create and implement it?

The interdisciplinary wheel, developed by Jacobs (1989) and Palmer (1991) and applied to health education by Allensworth (1993), illustrates integration using smoking as the theme (Figure 3.7).

There are several ways in which health education can be integrated at the elementary and middle school levels. The following list is an adaptation from Reynolds (1993) combined with our own suggestions:

Social Studies

- Look at careers in health care by inviting in guest speakers representing the medical, paramedical, and nurse-practioner (PA) fields.
- Examine different cultures, especially those that are represented in the classroom.
- Address how diets and food preparation are unique to cultures and how the differences impact health.
- Talk about the pathway of food from the field to the grocery store. If possible, arrange a field trip to a farm, food-processing plant, or grocery store.
- Trace family heritage, looking at the definitions of families over the years.
- Examine how food labels, cosmetic labels, and over-the-counter medicine labels have changed in the last ten years.
- Trace the history of violence in the United States or in schools.

Standard 1: Students will comprehend health promotion and disease prevention concepts.

Performance Indicators	Discover: Decisions for Health (Green)	Discover: Decisions for Health (Red)	Healthy Sexual Development
By the end of grade 8, students will:			
1. Explain the relationship between positive health behaviors and the prevention of injury, illness, disease, and premature death.	Ch 1: Lessons 1, 2, 3 Ch 3: Lessons 1, 2 Ch 4: Lessons 1, 2, 3, 4, 5 Ch 5: Lessons 1, 2, 3	Ch 1: Lesson 2 Ch 3: Lessons 1, 2 Ch 4: Lessons 1, 2, 3, 4, 5, 6 Ch 5: Lessons 1, 2, 3	Chapter 5
2. Describe the interrelation-ship of mental, emotional, social, and physical health during adolescence.	Ch 1: Lessons 1, 4 Ch 2: Lessons 1, 2	Ch 1: Lesson 2 Ch 2: Lessons 1, 2, 3	Chapters 2, 3, 4
3. Describe how body systems are interrelated.	Ch 1: Lessons 2, 3 Ch 4: Lessons 1, 3	Ch 1: Lessons 1, 2, Ch 4: Lesson 1	Chapter 2
4. Describe how the family and peers influence the health of individuals.	Ch 1: Lessons 4, 5 Ch 2: Lesson 3	Ch 1: Lessons 3, 4 Ch 2: Lessons 1, 2	Chapters 4, 5, 6
5. Analyze the interrelationship between the environment and personal health.	Ch 7: Lessons 1, 2, 3	Ch 1: Lesson 3	
6. Identify ways to reduce risks related to health problems of adolescents.	Ch 1: Lessons 1, 2, 3 Ch 5: Lessons 1, 2 Ch 4: Lessons 1, 2, 3, 4, 5	Ch 1: Lessons 2, 4 Ch 4: Lessons 1, 2, 3, 4, 5, 6 Ch 5: Lessons 1, 2 Ch 6: Lessons 1, 4	Chapters 5, 6
7. Recognize that many causes of premature death can be prevented by positive health practices and appropriate health care.	Ch 1: Lesson 3 Ch 3: Lesson 1 Ch 4: Lessons 3, 4, 5 Ch 5: Lessons 1, 2, 3, 4	Ch 1: Lesson 2 Ch 3: Lesson 1 Ch 4: Lessons 2, 4, 5, 6 Ch 5: Lessons 1, 2, 3, 4 Ch 6: Lesson 1	Chapters 5, 6

FIGURE 3.6 Textbook Correlation with National Health Education Standards. This example illustrates Health Education Standard 1 for three different textbooks. (*Source:* From R.D.K. Powell, National health standards correlated to *Discover: Decisions for Health* (Jr. High/Sr. High) and *Healthy Sexual Development* (Jr. High/Sr. High School) (Circle Pines, MN: American Guidance Service, Inc., 1995). Reprinted with permission.)

- Examine the differences and similarities between the genders in regard to health roles.
- Discuss the role of women as health care specialists in their families.
- Trace how media messages on health issues have changed over the last five years.
- Discuss the evolution of the public health movement.

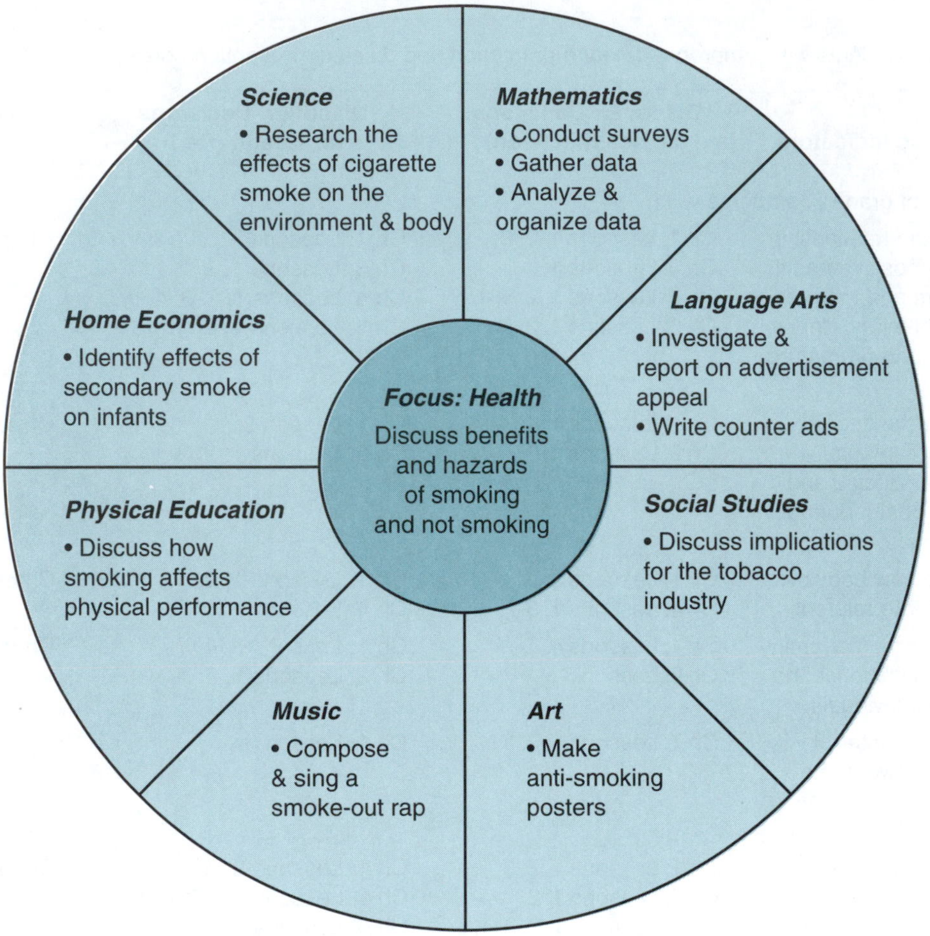

FIGURE 3.7 Integration Planning Wheel (*Source:* Adapted from D. Allensworth, Health education: State of the art, *Journal of School Health* 163, 1, (1993):16.)

- Talk about our changing health care system and how it impacts students now.
- Study the history of medical practices for common illnesses, including a discussion of medical myths.
- Talk about the eradication of smallpox.

Science

- Discuss the role of the sun, including its impact on health (skin cancer and protection).
- Talk about the impact of personal health and hygiene on good health.
- Research the effects of medicines, alcohol, caffeine, and tobacco on the body and mind.
- Discuss how the common cold is spread.
- Show how the scientific approach to problems can be applicable to making decisions about health behavior.
- Apply science-inquiry skills to current health problems.
- Do experiments to show the effects of pollution on health.
- Arrange a field trip to a polluted body of water or downtown area and discuss the effects on local residents.
- Address the safety issues in laboratory work and relate them to working with infectious diseases (including HIV) in a laboratory.

- When discussing anatomy (e.g., muscles), talk about the role each organ system plays in health.
- Discuss the effects of weather and climate on health and disease.
- Have a guest speaker address the problem of sanitation as it relates to recycling.
- Study air-conditioning and heating systems, relating them to health problems.
- Select a childhood disease and follow its evolution, or follow the history of childhood immunizations.

Language Arts

- Have the class make a two page newspaper with a column or two about health issues pertinent to elementary school students.
- Originate a poster contest on various health concerns.
- Have students write letters to local elected officials about health matters such as violence in the schools.
- Develop skits in which students can role-play communicating health information or refusal skills.
- Skim through magazines to find pictures of children with varying facial expressions, then discuss what the expressions might mean and the feelings that might accompany them.
- Encourage students to write out personal health goals in a journal.
- Have students learn some American Sign Language so that they can communicate with the hearing-impaired.
- Arrange for students to move around the school in wheelchairs so that they identify the difficulties, frustrations, and joys of being physically-impaired.
- Create a large poster of the food pyramid and have students paste pictures of their favorite foods (including candy and ice cream) in the appropriate spot.
- Have students read stories or articles about someone who has a debilitating disease (e.g., heart disease, cancer, AIDS) and discuss the implications it has for the family as well as the feelings everyone might have about it.
- Use health terms in spelling contests or exercises.
- In teaching about libraries, select a health problem to learn about health resources.
- Have a debate on a local health issue, such as whether to have snack vending machines in the school.
- Analyze a magazine ad depicting a health product for children.

Mathematics

- Use food measurements to learn about numbers and fractions.
- Employ local health data for simple addition and subtraction.
- Explore local mortality and morbidity rates for childhood injuries, drownings, and the like.
- When using money to study numbers, employ the figures for health costs, including the purchase of medicine.
- For graphs, use the stages of human growth.
- Compare two or more sources of pollution, such as automobile emissions and factories.
- Calculate the amount of money spent on smoking one-half pack a day, three packs per day, and not smoking at all.

Physical Education

- Emphasize safety precautions in exercising as well as around play equipment.
- Discuss common athletic injuries and how to care for them.
- Determine the gender differences in sports.
- Talk about responsibility for the health and safety of others.
- Address how individual physical differences play a role in physical activities.
- Promote personal hygiene.
- Discuss the relationship between nutrition and physical activity.
- Discuss the importance of physical activity as it relates to mental health.
- Have the students talk about fair play and cooperation through sports and physical activity.
- Discuss boy-girl relationships in recreational activities.

Music

- Discuss why mouthpieces should be cleaned.
- Look at differences in voice control as they relate to lung capacity, abdominal muscles, and other physiological factors.
- Examine how voices change at puberty.
- Debate whether to share wind instruments.
- Explain how music classes can detect hearing problems.
- Talk about the effect of posture and breathing on singing.
- Create songs that have health messages.

Art

- Discuss the need for proper lighting for health as well as drawing.
- Explain how color impacts mood.
- Construct posters about various health issues or campaigns.
- Make colored graphs depicting health data relevant to children.
- Use (clothed) models for drawing and discuss human anatomy.
- Talk about the proper mixing of paints from the standpoints of safety and appropriate disposal of waste.

Parent Involvement in the Curriculum

The involvement of parents in the school curriculum has been an issue for years. As every teacher knows, there are some parents who schedule conferences and attend every parent-teacher meeting, while others avoid the school at almost any cost. Given the nature of health education, parent involvement should be encouraged, both to reduce misperceptions and enhance student learning. And all efforts to enhance parental involvement in the schools should foster a meaningful dialogue rather than the usual monologue.

Schurr (1992) recommends the following steps to engage parents in the school curriculum:

1. Inform parents of the school's intentions early in the year, including how parents can get involved and perhaps notations from individual teachers. In health education, parents could be asked to share stories or present problems to be addressed by students, or share their feelings about personal health issues.
2. Assess school policies regarding the presence of parents; make sure administrators welcome them to the classroom.
3. Establish a parent center, resource room, or lounge to serve as a gathering place to socialize with school personnel, display agency information, and share wisdom and experiences.
4. Spend the time to get school issues out into the community via public service announcements, community bulletins, newspapers, and other media. Arrange for school displays in hospitals or malls.
5. Create and disseminate a handbook of tips and guidelines for parents.
6. Have an evening or weekend public-information fair to educate parents about all aspects of schooling as well as how they impact students and the school.
7. Develop a parent and student exchange day so that parents can develop an appreciation for what a teacher's day is really like. (More often than not, they see the teacher arriving in the morning and leaving in mid-afternoon—and the summers are free!)
8. Award extra academic credit to students whose parents demonstrate involvement of some kind in their children's education. Make sure the choices are feasible and equitable, since both parents work outside the home in many families.
9. Sponsor an old-fashioned family night at the school wherein students present something they did, display posters they have made, and so on. Keep the atmosphere relaxed.
10. Develop a system in which teachers contact parents at least three times during the school year, whether by phone call, written message, or face-to-face visit. Or publish a monthly parent newsletter.

11. Send home a small journal at the beginning of the year with the suggestion that parents can jot down any issues, concerns, or positive points they have about the class or their child, then send the journal back to the teacher for comment. Parents are under no pressure to comply; this is a matter of convenience for busy people.
12. Have local elected officials, such as the mayor, issue a proclamation for "Parent Appreciation Day" or the like. The school should do the leg work.
13. Develop monthly help or home-achievement packages. Because parents often look for help, these should contain brief but pertinent information such as how to read to children, how to listen, how to improve study skills or to make a work center, how to say no, or how to get the most out of a parent-teacher conference. If affordable, an audio- or videotape of simple information or instructions could be included in the package.
14. Home visits can develop unique bonds between teachers and families. These must be done by invitation and scheduled, the school administration must support them in all ways, substitute teachers should be included, and compensation must be arranged if done on a weekend day. The purpose of the visit should be centered around education. Obviously, the teacher may gain some insights.
15. Create a schoolwide homework policy to eliminate unfair, unequal, and inappropriate homework assignments. The inability of a student to complete homework can be stressful on all family members, and needless or unfair homework only creates stress. Develop innovative homework assignments, such as parent-student tasks, group activities, roulette homework challenges, and student-generated lessons.
16. Institute a school "welcome wagon" or "meet and greet" program for newcomers to the community and school. A "bag of goodies" given to parents or students might include coupons that could be cashed in to meet key people in the school or visit the parent lounge or resource center, as well as information about programs.

Implications for Elementary and Middle-School Teachers

Summary Issues

1. Traditional health curriculum design includes body system design, health problem design, health content design, health topic design, and conceptual design.
2. Curriculum designed around high-risk adolescent behaviors *only* can fail to address other needed areas and concerns.
3. Health education receives wide support from parents, students, and administrators, with more than 80 percent wanting more in the schools.
4. National Health Education Standards emphasizing knowledge and acquisition of skills were published in 1995.
5. The overall goal of the National Health Standards is to increase health literacy. The health-literate person is a(n): (1) critical thinker and problem-solver; (2) responsible, productive citizen; (3) self-directed learner; and (4) effective communicator.
6. There are seven National Health Education Standards, each having a rationale statement and performance indicators.
7. The performance indicators are a series of specific concepts and skills students should know and be able to do by the end of grades 4, 8, and 11.
8. Learning assessments can be written by the teacher or a team of teachers to refine or emphasize the performance indicators. They may include content.
9. The Health Education Standard and its performance indicator(s) and learning assessment(s) should be in concert with one another.
10. The National Health Education Standards incorporate the ten content areas of health education as well as the six CDC risk behaviors.

11. Scope and sequence can be established using the National Health Education Standards and accompanying performance indicators. The learning assessments can be used to provide more detailed information about both scope and sequence.
12. The well-conceived unit of instruction consists of a title, the National Health Education Standard(s), performance indicator(s), learning assessment(s), content, learning strategies, evaluation procedures, and resources.
13. Learning assessments can contain all of the following elements: who, behavior, content, conditions, and standards. They may also be abbreviated to include only the who, the desired observable behavior, and the content.
14. Lesson plans should be built around the standards, performance indicators, and learning assessments.
15. The two major curriculum approaches are direct instruction and integrated or interdisciplinary instruction.
16. Interdisciplinary approaches require much preparation and planning and mean more than correlation. A central theme, or web, needs to be woven throughout all participating disciplines.
17. Parent involvement in school matters, particularly curriculum, is important and may be encouraged in many ways.

Teacher Ramifications

In regard to health curriculum matters, a teacher should:

1. Review the present curriculum, including the state Department of Education and commercial products, in light of the National Health Education Standards.
2. Read the National Health Education Standards and performance indicators thoroughly to understand the knowledge and skills to be acquired by students.
3. Develop learning assessments where appropriate.
4. Apply existing scope and theory to the National Health Education Standards.
5. Reorganize present curriculum on the basis of the National Health Education Standards.
6. Examine the present curriculum approach and consider alternative approaches.
7. Find means to involve parents more.
8. Assist in meeting the following *Healthy Children 2000* objectives:

#2.19. Increase to at least 75 percent the proportion of the nation's schools that provide nutrition education from preschool through 12th grade, preferably as part of quality school health education.

#3.10. Establish tobacco-free environments and include tobacco-use prevention in the curricula of all elementary, middle, and secondary schools, preferably as part of quality school health education.

#4.13. Provide to children, in all school districts and private schools, primary- and secondary-school educational programs on alcohol and other drugs, preferably as part of quality school health education.

#5.8. Increase to at least 85 percent the proportion of people aged 10 through 18 who have discussed human sexuality, including values surrounding sexuality, with their parents and/or have received information through another parent-endorsed source, such as youth, school, or religious programs.

#7.16. Increase to at least 50 percent the proportion of elementary and secondary schools that teach nonviolent conflict-resolution skills, preferably as part of a quality school health education.

#8.4. Increase to at least 75 percent the proportion of the nation's elementary and secondary schools that provide planned and sequential kindergarten through 12th grade quality school health education.

#9.18. Provide academic instruction on injury prevention and control, preferably as part of quality school health education, in at least 50 percent of public school systems grades K–12.

#18.10. Increase to at least 95 percent the proportion of schools that have age-appropriate HIV education curricula for students in grades 4 through 12, preferably as part of quality school health education.

#19.12. Include instruction on prevention of the transmission of sexually transmitted diseases in the curricula of all middle and secondary schools, preferably as part of quality school health education.

References

Allensworth, D.D., & Kolbe, L.J. The comprehensive school health program: Exploring an expanded concept, *Journal of School Health* 57,10(1987): 409–412.

Allensworth, D.D. Health education: State of the art, *Journal of School Health* 63, 1(1993):14–20.

Boyett, J.H., & Conn, H.P. *Workplace 2000: The Revolution Reshaping American Business.* Dutton, New York, 1991.

Brandt, R. On interdisciplinary curriculum: A conversation with Heidi Hayes Jacobs, *Educational Leadership* 49(1991):24–26.

Education Week. A Special Report on Standards Containing a List of Standards for All Disciplines (April 12, 1995).

Healthy People 2000: National Health Promotion and Disease Prevention Objectives (PHS 91-50212) U.S. Department of Health and Human Services, Washington, DC, 1989.

Jacobs, H.H. Planning for curriculum integration, *Educational Leadership* 49(1991):27–28.

Joint Committee on National Health Education Standards. *National Health Education Standards: Achieving Health Literacy.* (No. 95–50M–No. 2027), American Cancer Society, Atlanta, GA, 1995.

Kolbe, L.J. An epidemiological surveillance system to monitor the prevalance of youth behaviors that most affect health, *Health Education,* 21, 6(1990): 40–43.

Lohrmann, D.K. Overview of Curriculum Design and Implementation. In B.S. Saxton and L. Olsen, eds. *Health Education: Teacher Resource Handbook.* Kraus International Publications, Millwood, NY, 1993.

Monson, M.P., & Monson, R.J. Who creates curriculum? New roles for teachers, *Educational Leadership* 51, 2(1993):19–21.

O'Neil, J. Turning the system on its head, *Educational Leadership* 51, 1(1993):8–13.

O'Neil, J. Aiming for new outcomes: The promise and the reality, *Educational Leadership* 51, 6(1994): 6–10.

Pollack, M. *Planning and Implementing Health Education in Schools.* Mayfield, Mountain View, CA, 1987.

Rash, J.K., & Pigg, R.M. *The Health Education Curriculum.* Wiley, New York, 1979.

Reynolds, S.T. Main topics and integration. In B.S. Mahoney and L.K. Olsen, Eds. *Health Education: Teacher Resource Handbook.* Kraus International Publications, Millwood, NY, 1993.

Schurr, S.L. Sixteen proven ways to involve parents, *From Schools in the Middle* 2(1992):3–9.

Secretary's Commission on Achieving Necessary Skills: *What Work Requires of Schools: A SCANS Report for America 2000.* U.S. Department of Labor, Washington, DC, 1991.

U.S. Department of Health and Human Services. *Healthy Children 2000: National Health Promotion and Disease Prevention Objectives Related to Mothers, Infants, Children, Adolescents, and Youth.* Jones and Bartlett, Boston, 1991.

Willis, S. Interdisciplinary learning: Movement to link the disciplines gains momentum. *Curriculum Update.* Association for Supervision and Curriculum Development, Alexandria, VA, 1992.

4

Learning Strategies and Controversial Issues

Upon completion of this chapter, you should be able to:

- *Explain the importance of strategies to health education*
- *Integrate strategies and health knowledge, attitudes, and behavior*
- *Define the role of personal and social skill-building activities*
- *Justify the need for the skills in problem-solving, decision-making, refusal, communication, behavior-contracting, media analysis, and conflict resolution*
- *Use several approaches in the classroom illustrating different skills*
- *List strategies to prevent or ameliorate controversy in school health education*

Learning Strategies

To see
To hear
To touch
To feel
To Wonder?

To do
To discover
To understand
To learn . . .

To be
To feel good
To be well
To live
To be happy!

This poem suggests the nature and purpose of this chapter. The first part has to do with the natural ability of children to learn and the body senses they use to receive messages from the teacher as well as to practice skills. The middle part suggests how the message (information) is internalized through learning experiences. Note that the "to do" component is essential for skill-building, for example, refusal skills regarding any unwanted behavior such as drugs or sexual relations. What does the last part suggest? All three parts of the poem are involved in the learning process.

Teaching is both a science and an art. Teachers apply science in selecting relevant content, materials, and methods and in projecting expected performance indicators as part of a curriculum standard. But the effective blending of these into an educational recipe to ensure continuing progress of children toward optimal well-being and more abundant living is an art. This chapter provides suggestions on how elementary and middle-school teachers may develop greater skill in the art of teaching for health. The value of suggested methods depends on the way they are used. Methods should motivate children to discover understandings and feelings and to build necessary skills. Some methods work better than others, but methods alone are not enough. They need to be reinforced by materials and visual aids. Thus the medium of the method is enriched by the materials and becomes a message in itself. The teacher blends methods and materials so that children may internalize a message. Out of such learning experiences should emerge health literacy.

The Challenge to Teaching Methods

There was a time when teaching was accepted as the act of delivering priceless pearls of wisdom to a captive audience of learners. It was also assumed that the mere telling of things to be learned fulfilled the obligation of the teacher. Today this misconception is seldom found among elementary school teachers. The emphasis in teaching for health today is on behavior rather than on the imparting of facts and information.

Kolbe et al. (1981, p. 24) noted two phases of health education activities:

> The first phase of activities should be designed to enable the individual to decide competently whether, in fact, he or she should adopt the behavior. The second phase of health education activities should then enable, support, and indeed elicit the occurrence of that behavior. . . . The function of the first phase of health education activities would be to increase the competencies of

> individuals to make decisions about behaviors conducive to health. . . . The function of the second phase of health education activities would be to increase the skills and inclinations required by individuals who decided to engage in the health-conducive behaviors.

It is important to remember, first, that individuals make choices about their health behavior. This requires teaching about decision-making. The second part requires health education teachers to enhance student skills such that they can carry out their health-producing behaviors. For the preschool child, this may mean making a decision about brushing teeth. For those who decide to do so, the skills to complete the behavior must be taught cognitively and practice opportunities should be given. Similarly, the seventh grader who is deliberating about drug use must be shown the choices in order to make a decision and provided with occasions to practice the skills to prevent drug abuse. Of course both the cognitive and skills processes are more complex at this level.

Several curricula are built around behavioral theories and their teaching methods are a part of their theoretical structure. But researching successful health education programs, Fetro (1992) found that personal and social skill-building activities were common to all of them.

Bandura's (1986) social learning theory is conducive to building these skills. For example, Bandura would suggest that the 7th grader who is contemplating drug use must: (1) understand what must be done to avoid it, (2) believe that he or she will be able to use the method, (3) believe that the method will actually work, and (4) anticipate a benefit after achieving the behavior. Social learning theory posits that students can learn these concepts, in part from watching others, and with practice can develop the necessary skills required for any particular behavior.

A related theory is McGuire's (1964) social inoculation theory, which suggests that people become socially "inoculated" just as they become physically inoculated. In social inoculation, when people recognize different forms of pressure, have a great desire to resist the pressure, and begin practicing resistance to weak forms of the pressure, they will eventually develop resistance to the pressure.

Both Bandura's and McGuire's themes are evident in the cognitive-behavioral prevention model developed by Kirby (1992). Three components of this model are (1) activities to personalize information about health, (2) training in decision-making and communication skills, and (3) practice in applying what has been learned.

The key focus for teachers is to select learning strategies that provide background information, assist in decision-making skills, support personal and social skill-building, have proven effective in the past, can be modeled or role-played, and allow opportunities for practice. Needless to say, one activity is unlikely to fulfill all of these qualifications, so careful planning is required to accomplish the task. In other words, activities should not be "fillers." They must be purposeful, and this is particularly true if national standards are to be met.

Nature and Application of Methods

Beginning teachers are often fixated on teaching strategies. That is, they are more concerned about how to teach than about what or where to teach. This is a good example of putting the cart before the horse. Before the horse is harnessed to the cart, we must have a load for it to pull and we must know where the barn is—where we want to go. The analogy of the horse/cart and teaching is illustrated in Figure 4.1. The load of hay may be thought of as the cognitive material and skills to be taught, the horse as the vehicle or method of teaching, and the barn as the performance indicator or standard. Methods are like the horse; they help the teacher to communicate the information and the student to practice the skills, but they are not the substance (the hay).

Communication of cognitive material and skills requires sharing and participating. The teacher, as a speaker, only starts the process; the student, as a hearer, must complete it. Whether the teacher has information, an idea, an attitude, a feeling, or an undertaking to share with pupils, the process of transmitting and receiving responses constitutes communication, which may be verbal, nonverbal, or both. Thus the teacher should con-

FIGURE 4.1 Importance of Body Senses to Learning

tinually adapt the teaching method on the basis of feedback from the pupils.

Selecting the best way to communicate with children is most important. Perhaps the first thing for the teacher to keep in mind is how people, of course including children, receive information: through our senses. Table 4.1 summarizes the relative importance of the different body senses in learning. Another thing to remember is that most health (and living) experiences are sociological in nature, so the reactions of others play a significant role in how we behave.

Table 4.1 Relative Importance of the Body Senses to Learning

Sense	Importance (in education) (Victor, 1970, p. 6)	Estimated importance in health science instruction
1. Sight	75%	52%
2. Hearing	13	13
3. Touch	6	6
4. Smell	3	3
5. Taste	3	3
6. Balance	—	3
7. Kinesthetic	—	—
8. Feeling (emotions)	—	20

The implications for teaching are many. The nature of a topic and the behavior expected may call on one of the lesser-used senses far more than the table indicates. This may be especially true when children are unable to read. Teaching through multiple senses becomes very important at this level. When peer-group pressure to conform behavior becomes important, especially in the intermediate grades, the sense of feeling becomes important. Educators in general have failed to recognize the potential of this sensory area. Thus the teacher must always be conscious to:

1. Use those senses most important to the child in relation to the specific lesson at hand
2. Stimulate senses as often as possible for retention of learning
3. Employ as many senses as possible

We have all probably heard a sentence or word that recalled a song; a phrase that made us recall a poem; a familiar scene, an event; an exercise, a good physical feeling; a smell, a process; a touch, a material; a social occasion, a wonderful feeling of belonging and happiness; or a taste, a good or poor product. Stimulating a special sense, or more than one, gives the student an additional dimension to learning and recalling. The senses are the receivers of communication.

Many teachers use more learning activities than are necessary. Doing so tends to prolong a unit unnecessarily, slow down learning, and dull pupils' interest. The experienced teacher employs learning activities wisely and economically, realizing that sometimes one activity is enough. Occasionally one good activity can provide an understanding of more than one concept or develop more than one skill. Other times, when a concept is abstract or the skill difficult, more than one activity may be necessary. Slow learners usually learn better when more than one activity is used.

Grade level may also influence the number of learning experiences needed. In the lower grades, children's attention span is short, and their ability to think abstractly is not well developed; therefore, more than one activity is often necessary to obtain satisfactory understanding. A teaching strategy may have to be repeated several times, or another strategy may have to be introduced. However, in the upper grades one well-chosen activity is usually sufficient. In all cases, the best procedure is for the teacher to use as many—but *only* as many—activities as are necessary to ensure satisfactory learning. Teachers should choose and modify methods in light of specific situations with the understanding that learning experiences should impart both knowledge and essential health-related skills. In practice, no method can or should remain static; all of them yield to the purposes and procedures of particular classes. Method is a process, not a predetermined formula. The effective teacher does not select a method, but instead develops a flexible procedure that is applicable to a particular situation. Effective teaching and learning do not come as a result of merely using the visual method, or a field trip, or a discussion. Progress in social learning is the result of the blending of the elements that constitute growth and development.

Learning Experiences for Health Instruction

Owing to the nature of elementary school children, the subject matter with which they deal, and the educational goals established for them, some learning experiences are more appropriate than others. Appropriate experiences for primary children include storytelling, puppet shows, skits and plays, simulation or acting out, demonstrations, problem-solving, and discussions. Others include exhibits and displays, health fairs, field trips, surveys, guest speakers, debates, panels, lectures, programmed instruction, cooperative learning, portfolios, and contract teaching. Learning experiences at the intermediate level may include all of the primary experiences, as well as cardboard games, experiments, role-playing, and computer-assisted health education.

The learning experiences discussed below are appropriate for elementary school children. Since they have great potential for helping children to discover concepts and apply them to everyday living, they are explored in some depth.

The following criteria can be used to determine whether a particular learning experience is appropriate:

1. Does the learning experience contribute to pupils' attainment of *expected behavioral objectives, performance indicators,* or *standards*?
2. Does the learning experience impart both knowledge and health-related skills?
3. Does it help children to evolve and discover the *topic concept*? (This discovery occurs only through the learning experience.)
4. Is it *action-oriented* instead of listening-oriented? That is, learning experiences that contribute to developing affective behaviors should take precedence over those focusing primarily on cognitive behaviors. Likewise, learning experiences that evolve or modify health habits and behavior should take precedence over those that focus on cognitive and/or affective behavior.
5. Does it *teach through two or more sense organs?* A learning experience that communicates through two or more body sense organs—eyes, ears, nose, tongue, skin, glands (emotions), muscles (neuromuscular system)—is more effective, clearer, and more enduring than one that communicates through just one sensory organ. The information picked up by one sense organ should be reinforced by another. Thus the ears can be complemented by the eyes. If a

third sensory organ is added, the effect on the student is stronger and more enduring. More important, it helps a student more readily discover a health concept. The more sense organs involved in recording and decoding information, the more meaningful the information.

6. Is it economical in terms of time and cost (materials and visual aids)?
7. Is it appropriate for the subject matter as well as for the expected standard?
8. Is it age-, developmentally, and culturally appropriate?

Problem-Based Learning

Use of problem-solving methods in education has been around for a long time. However, more often than not, the problems are unlike real-life situations or are given to the students after they have been bombarded with facts and principles. When problems lack relevance, students do not invest any effort in them. Even when real-life situations are used, if they are given to students at the end of a lesson the teacher is missing opportunities to exploit several skills simultaneously.

Problem-based learning (PBL), which has its roots in science education and medical education, avoids these drawbacks (Barrows & Tamblyn, 1980; Aspy et al., 1993). PBL is being recognized as a meaningful approach in K-12 education in both the classroom and textbooks (Neutens, 1994; Stepien & Gallagher, 1993). It capitalizes on students' natural inquisitiveness for solving problems. Students, like the rest of us, face problems every day and need to find workable solutions. Problems may range from how to brush teeth properly to how to avoid abuse.

Problem-based learning should not be simply the presentation of problems to students as a focus for learning or as an example of what has just been learned. It is a rigorous, structured approach to learning that is tailor-made for health education (Neutens, 1993/1994). Some of the major advantages of PBL are the following:

- PBL can be used to learn subject knowledge (drugs, sexuality, nutrition) and/or skills, including critical thinking, decision-making, analysis, assertiveness, refusal, communication, conflict resolution, and of course problem-solving. In other words, like the standards, PBL reflects both cognitive and behavior learning components.
- It is a stimulus for active learning.
- It is student-oriented.
- It uses real-life situations, making it relevant to students.
- PBL assignments can be developed for individuals, small groups, or the class as a whole.
- Problems can be designed to be very simple, dealing with only one content area, or they can be designed to embrace several content areas simultaneously, just as do real-life problems.
- PBL can be made transdisciplinary to function in integrated curricula.
- It can combine theory and practice.
- PBL can be used in conjunction with other strategies such as role-playing.
- PBL can be evaluated to ascertain strengths and weaknesses in different skills and knowledge.

The following are the steps involved in the PBL process:

Step 1: Presentation of the Problem. The problem is presented to the students before anything else. The problem must be written in a very structured, concise format if it is to lead them toward the desired behavioral objective, performance indicator, and standard. It can be large or small (the small ones are called *post-hole problems*). The decision expected depends on the amount of time available and/or deemed appropriate for the particular problem and content area. For example, more time would probably be spent on the problem behaviors identified by the Centers for Disease Control than some other behaviors. The problem must be relevant and realistic to simulate real life.

Evaluation at this step assesses students' ability to recognize and define a problem. If the problem is data-based, such as a graph or table, evaluation may be more along the line of data perception and interpretation. If a student has difficulty with this step, it may explain why he or she engages in some unhealthful behavior, and remediation is advised.

Step 2: Generate Possible Solutions or Hypotheses. Individually, in groups, or as a whole class, several hypotheses can be developed. A hypothesis is an assertion or proposition put forth as *possibly* being true, based upon our current knowledge about the problem, yet requiring further investigation. In other words, the students can suggest solutions to the problem based on the information they currently possess. This is similar to brainstorming but must be focused.

Evaluation of the ability to see options and potential solutions occurs at this step. Teachers may have students who identify the problem readily but are unable to think of any options and need help in developing this set of skills.

Step 3: Inquiry Skills. Students use the resources at their disposal to verify, refine, or refute the hypotheses or posited solutions. Resources could include a teacher handout, textbooks, videos, the library, other teachers, and so on. The amount of time available often dictates the resources to be used. The National Health Education Standards that may fit into this step include: (1) Students will comprehend health promotion and disease prevention concepts, and (2) Students will demonstrate the ability to access valid health information and appropriate health products and services.

Evaluation of inquiry strategy consists of assessing the type and sequence of actions taken by the student regarding the hypotheses. More often than not, students can recognize a problem and even offer tentative courses of action but have no idea how to check out their ideas. Teachers can assist them in acquiring skills and identifying resources that can be used over and over.

Step 4: Application of Information Gathered Back to the Problem. As the students gain information, they must apply it back to the problem. Given enough time and resources, students can see the "big picture" as well as the specific problem. They employ critical thinking skills, analytical skills, and decision-making skills during this part of the process. The National Health Education Standards that fall into this step are (3) Students will demonstrate the ability to practice health-enhancing behaviors and reduce health risks, and (4) Students will analyze the impact of culture, media, technology, and other factors on health.

Evaluation of the application of information includes considering all the pertinent factors that impinge upon the health issue in the problem. If role-playing or the like is involved at this step, then demonstrated abilities can be evaluated also. Some students can gather all kinds of information but fail to put the puzzle together. Help with these skills may be all that is needed to allow these students to become problem solvers.

Step 5: Review, Synthesis of What Has Been Learned, and Evaluation. The possible solutions are reviewed and synthesized in order to select the "best" solution to the problem. Obviously decision-making and critical thinking skills are learned at this juncture. Discussion may pursue (a) the steps involved in the process, (b) the "best" solution and why it was selected, and (c) how what has been learned can be applied to other problems. In regard to the National Health Standards, this step addresses (5) Students will demonstrate the ability to use effective interpersonal communication skills which enhance health, (6) Students will demonstrate the ability to use goal-setting and decision-making skills that enhance health, and (7) Students will demonstrate the ability to advocate for personal, family, and community health. Standards 5 and 7 can be specifically addressed if the teacher has the students role-play, write out, or say (versus explain) exactly what the character in the problem should say. (An example of this step is provided later in this chapter.)

Evaluation at this step will vary according to the nature of the problem and the Health Education Standards used in its formulation. Decision-making skills are always involved, however, and evaluation at each of the steps thus far can ascertain overall reasoning abilities.

Step 6: Putting It All Together. The information learned and the skills used are combined with each student's personal style and mode of expression. For example, some students are less assertive than others in communicating refusal. Thus the solution selected may have to be tailored to fit the student.

Evaluation can be of students' ability to integrate the skills into their personal behavioral repertoire. Some students may move through all the previous steps, and agree with them, but end by saying, "Gee, I don't think I could do that." The teacher may need to work with such students to instill confidence or practice the skills.

Let us look at a specific example using the PBL process. Since PBL can be applied to both content and skills, our illustration uses the National Health Education Standards and refusal skills. Note that the Standards and performance indicators involved are specific so that direction remains focused. It is easy to get off track otherwise.

Prior to Step 1, the teacher selects the standards and performance indicators as focal points or end points for the exercise:

Standard 2: Students will demonstrate the ability to practice health-enhancing behaviors and reduce health risks.

Performance Indicator

A. Explain the importance of assuming responsibility for personal health behaviors

Standard 5: Students will demonstrate the ability to use effective interpersonal communication skills which enhance health.

Performance Indicators

A. Demonstrate effective verbal and nonverbal communication skills to enhance health

B. Demonstrate refusal and negotiation skills to enhance health (The teacher may add assessment skills or behavioral objectives to focus the exercise even more.)

Content Area: Tobacco.

Step 1: Presentation of the Problem. The teacher writes a short, concise problem on a single sheet of paper:

> Jon, a middle school student, walked home with his two best friends, Sean and Walker, after school. Upon arriving home, he found a note from his mother saying that she wouldn't be home for another hour. The three of them were sitting outside the back door when Sean reached into his backpack and pulled out a pack of cigarettes. Walker immediately took one. Sean then offered one to Jon. Jon didn't know what to do.

Step 2: Generation of Things Jon Could Say or Do. The students suggest the following potential solutions to Jon:

- Take one and smoke it.
- Take one but don't inhale the smoke.
- Tell Sean he might have one later.
- Explain that his mother would "kill" him if she found out, so no thanks.
- Let Sean and Walker know they are crazy to be smoking and that he is not going to smoke.

Step 3: Checking Out the Suggestions. The students have had no information as yet about tobacco (since the problem is presented first), so they need to check out

- Basic information about the health effects of tobacco.
- The effects of smoke on the mouth if it isn't inhaled.
- Various aspects of peer pressure.

In this case, there is ample time allotted to the PBL exercise, so the teacher may offer resources to the students:

- A video on smoking
- A video on refusal skills
- Reading material
- Other teachers
- Voluntary organizations

The purpose of this exercise is not just to teach some content but to enhance skills as denoted in the Standards and performance indicators.

The format used in this step could be:

- The class as a whole
- Small group discussion
- Collaborative learning groups
- Independent study, possibly including a "home activity" (taking the work home and getting ideas from parents).

The teacher also evaluates the students' inquiry skills at this step.

Step 4: Fitting the Information into Jon's Problem. The students apply the information they have accumulated as follows:

- Smoking has the long-term potential consequence of lung cancer, so Jon shouldn't smoke on a regular basis.
- Second-hand smoke also has health consequences, so not inhaling does not eliminate Jon's risks.
- There are ways to handle peer pressure, so Jon has the option of saying no.

They use several skills in applying the learned information back to the problem:

- Refusal skills
- Communication skills

Here those students who do not know how to make gathered smoking information applicable receive specific help.

Step 5: Reviewing the Suggestions, Selecting One, and Evaluating. The teacher has several students role-play Jon, saying exactly what they think he should say. Two other students play the roles of Sean and Walker. The students select the option of telling Sean no and add the fact that smoking is harmful. In the class discussion afterward, they address the issues of personal responsibility, effective verbal and nonverbal communication, and refusal skills.

The teacher uses the standards and performance indicators for health literacy as guides for evaluating the students' decision-making.

Step 6: Putting It All Together. During the discussion, it becomes apparent that students differ in their approach to the problem even if the intended result is the same. Some are more diplomatic than others in their use of refusal skills. The teacher reinforces the most appropriate aspects of each student's response.

Writing Vignettes for Problem-Based Learning

Developing and writing cases for PBL are not simple tasks. Recall that a vignette must be highly structured if it is to produce maximum benefit. The steps for writing vignettes are as follows:

1. Identify the Health Education Standard(s), performance indicators, and related behavioral objectives. These should be specific since they automatically become part of the evaluation process.
2. Select a vignette to highlight the Standards, indicators, and objectives in step 1. The selection may include a content area. At this stage of development, the vignette is still an idea of a story. The most important point is that the vignette be real to the students.
3. Determine the format of the problem. The format for presentation and discussion dictates the vignette to some degree. A brief or post-hole problem is generally handled in one class period, so they must be very focused, with specific content. A post-hole problem may be an end in itself or an entry point to a more demanding one. In contrast, a *progressive disclosure problem* requires more than one class period. While also focused, its degree complexity is greater, demanding that information be given to students in segments. (This is discussed more fully in step 6 of the writing process, and examples are given at the ends of some chapters later in the book.)
4. Determine the level of detail for the problem. The driving force here is student ability and of course the nature of the problem. A general rule of thumb is to provide only the necessary information, to keep the students on track toward the objectives, performance indicators, and health education Standards.
5. Write the story or vignette. There should be no hidden surprises in the vignette. Keep an eye on detail so that you can keep the discussion focused. But remember, many children will go over every word looking for clues and something esoteric will throw them, and you, off base.
6. If necessary, break up the vignette for teaching purposes. In a post-hole vignette there is no break, but, with a progressive

disclosure vignette breaks are required. Understand that wherever you stop in the story places emphasis at that point. For example, using the Centers for Disease Control risk behavior of unintentional injury as a focal point, the vignette may begin with a second-grade student at home with a babysitter. The sitter falls unconscious to the floor. Breaking at that point emphasizes that the second-grader must do something now. Students should seek more information, such as: Are neighbors nearby? Is there an older sibling in the house? Is 911 available? Once these issues have been raised, the teacher or facilitator gives students the second part of the progressive disclosure vignette. It should answer their questions and lead them to the next part. Using our example, we find that no older sibling is present, no nearby neighbors are at home, and that 911 is available. Now what should the second-grade student do? This story can be carried to the point of having students role-play calling 911, including what they would say and following appropriate first aid instruction (e.g., checking the airway).

7. Prepare questions from the objectives, performance indicators, and Standards. These should be turned into questions to assist students in working through the problem, and they may follow each segment of the vignette. In our progressive disclosure example, a behavioral objective could be, "The student will be able to talk with 911 personnel in a deliberate fashion, presenting all the appropriate information." As a guiding question, this could read as, "What information should be told to the 911 operator?" Questions such as these are especially helpful to students in the lower grades.
8. Identify resources for the students. Let them know where they can go for help regarding this particular problem. Even if the problem is about accessing health information, some guidelines should be offered.
9. Prepare a teaching or facilitating guide. This should provide (a) suggestions for teaching this problem, (b) information regarding commonality of the problem, (c) the necessary answers to the questions. Doing so allows almost anyone to use the PBL vignette, including substitutes.
10. Review the vignette with colleagues and/or a few students. This is essential to be certain that the story is focused, relevant, and divided for emphasis in the correct places. If the vignette deals with data or the human body, consensus with colleagues may be critical.

Tips for PBL Facilitators

Since PBL is relatively new to many teachers, the following tips are offered:

- Guide the group toward the level of understanding needed for their learning level.
- Bring students back to the vignette if they wander off the subject.
- Allow for errors, and help students learn through the errors.
- Provide frequent feedback to individuals and the group regarding progress.
- Guide subtly rather than directly (will vary by grade level).
- Help all students become valued members of the group.
- Assist in evaluating ideas and the reasoning process.
- Share expertise in a limited fashion.
- Communicate enthusiasm and demonstrate motivation for problem-solving.

Discussion and Questioning

These two methods of effective learning are employed in all classrooms. Both are used as follow-ups to other learning experiences. Questioning students about the topic at hand is the teacher's chief means of directing discourse. Students also question the teacher and one another about the topic. Questions prompt thinking about specific subjects.

A good classroom discussion, however, requires (1) an emotionally favorable classroom environment, which permits students the appropriate freedom of expression; and (2) participants with sufficient information to discuss a topic sensibly. The first condition results from the teacher's general spirit or attitude. He or she should avoid ridicule and in general regard any sincere response as a useful contribution to the discussion. The second condition is important in order to avoid the rambling and unproductive "pooling of ignorance." Therefore, discussions are usually more successful after students have done some reading or viewed a film, a puppet show, skit, role-play, demonstration, or experiment.

Discussion usually centers on the teacher; that is, the teacher directs the questioning. However, if the teacher wants more participation from pupils, it can be achieved through small-group discussions, or *buzz sessions.* In this method, three to five children are organized into a group, and a leader and recorder may be appointed. The theme or goal of the group is written down. After ten to twenty minutes of buzzing—researching ideas, sharing feelings, suggesting alternative solutions, and so on—the recorder of each group makes a brief oral report. The teacher, as mediator, entertains questions from the class, allows the pupils to answer, and at the end, summarizes the discussion. Buzz sessions sensitize students to the feelings of their peers as well as to health issues.

Perhaps the greatest challenge facing the teacher in regard to questioning is to encourage students to question both the teacher and one another. Students' questions should arise from a desire to understand both the topic at hand and the position taken by other participants.

Cooperative Learning

Cooperative learning is an instructional method that encourages students to work together in order to maximize learning. It is used extensively in disciplines other than health education—reading, language arts, mathematics, social studies, and science. Cooperative learning engages students in active learning, requiring them to work together as equals to achieve something important to all group members.

Specifically, a student learning team is made up of four to six heterogeneous members—high, middle, and low achievers; boys and girls; varying ethnicities; and so forth. The groups may be *informal,* in that they meet just for one class period; *formal,* or focusing on a topic/problem for several class sessions or weeks; or a *base* cooperative learning group, or one that remains together for a long period of time (e.g., a semester). A base group provides stable membership and thus can serve as a support group for each member. Research has shown that cooperative learning can have beneficial effects on several academic outcomes: skills, attitudes, achievement, retention, and motivation (Slavin, 1989/1990; Johnson & Johnson, 1989/1990; Solomon et al., 1990; Hayes & Brickle, 1991).

Cooperative learning is generally adjunct to initial instruction and provides the opportunity to pursue higher-order skills, such as analysis, synthesis, and evaluation (Cinelli et al., 1994). This method of social learning also requires students to depend on rewards from each other. Usually, team scores are based on academic improvement over the past performance (Hawkins et al., 1992). The key is that each student, no matter what his or her ability, is involved in peer teaching and in so doing, contributes to the welfare of the group. According to Cinelli et al. (1994), the following elements should be used to frame successful cooperative learning groups:

1. *Positive interdependence.* Assign mutual group goals with a fair division of tasks, information, materials, resources, and rewards. For example, one pencil to be shared, one report to be submitted, or one bit of information given to each group member so that all must educate the others.
2. *Face-to-face interaction.* Passing notes is replaced by actual conversation and eye-to-eye contact.
3. *Individual accountability.* This implies that individual learning is important. Individual mastery should be monitored in addition to the achievement of group goals.
4. *Interpersonal and small-group skills.* These must be taught and learned if the group is to be effective. Skills include decision-making, leadership, communication, trust-

building, conflict management, and so forth.

5. *Group process.* This allows students to see how groups can be successful or unsuccessful. Teachers can have students list three group members' actions that made the group work well and what else could have been done to achieve the goal. Teachers can monitor group skill acquisition.

The cooperative learning approach can be valuable in helping students acquire several skills. For effective implementation, you would need to (1) ascertain group and academic objectives, (2) determine group size and assign students to the groups, (3) make the classroom conducive to communication, (4) supply the necessary materials, (5) assign student roles and job descriptions (recorder, manager, coach, communicator), (6) explain the task, criteria for success, and what you want in the way of behaviors, (7) monitor and provide feedback as a facilitator, (8) teach social skills as needed, and (9) evaluate learning according to the objectives and give the group feedback on achievement (Johnson et al., 1991).

Cooperative learning is quickly catching on in health education. Hayes & Brickle (1991) showed how cooperative learning can be used to integrate math concepts into health instruction on sexuality and HIV. Dorman et al. (1989) employed this technique in AIDS education, and Cinelli et al. (1994) provide an example of cooperative learning for nutrition education. There is no doubt that this approach complements health instruction, particularly since it relates to many different outcomes.

Experiments

Experiments are procedures undertaken to discover suspected truths or to prove (or disprove) a specific point. Experimentation is generally used to demonstrate how things are done, how they work, or what the truth is. It employs precise controls so as to achieve valid results. The purpose of an experiment is to illustrate the particular content or concept under consideration. Experiments can help children to internalize information, investigate health phenomena, and weigh and sift evidence. This process also enables them to develop their own concepts.

The following are the basic steps in conducting experiments:

1. Define the problem to be solved.
2. Select the methods or procedure to be used.
3. Identify and assemble necessary materials and apparatus.
4. Conduct the experiment.
5. Collect and record data.
6. Select, organize, and interpret data.
7. Prepare conclusions.
8. Discuss the outcomes of the experiment and what was learned. Identify key concepts and relate them to everyday living.

Experiments may be demonstrated for the class by the teacher or a pupil, or conducted individually by each pupil. They are an excellent way of arousing interest in a health topic and solving problems. Like demonstrations (see below), experiments provide excellent opportunities to help the slow learner while challenging the rapid learner. The elementary school teacher should continually involve the children when doing experiments. However, if the procedure involves a hazard or risk of accident, the teacher should perform an experiment alone, or avoid it altogether. The wise teacher keeps experiments simple but stimulating enough to encourage children to think, and uses them to help children answer a question or understand an idea.

Demonstrations

A demonstration is similar to an experiment, but it illustrates what is already known, whereas an experiment is a way of finding out a fact. A demonstration is a process of graphic explanation of a selected idea, fact, relationship, or phenomenon.

Demonstration is visual. And children like to be entertained; they like to see things done before their eyes, especially if there is an element of mystery involved. Demonstrations may be conducted by the teacher, a pupil, or the whole group. Any demonstration requires planning to be effective.

Plays are fun and appropriate learning experiences for elementary and middle-school children.

Sociodramas

Children like to play. They like to pretend, to imagine, and to imitate others. Play is part of growing up socially, and to the child, it is real. Through play, learning takes place and life takes on social meaning. Thus by use of sociodrama and simulation games, children learn about living. Children play house, school, doctor and nurse, cowboys and Indians, cops and robbers, and other life roles. Pretending at play is part of being young. Pretending is an interesting learning experience, trying out various real or fantasy characters. By pretending to be a firefighter, the child sees or dreams about what it is like to be a firefighter. Dramatic play of this sort may be used by elementary school teachers not only to gain insight into their pupils but to help the children discover the art of living for themselves. Types of sociodramas having a natural appeal to children are simulation, role-playing, puppets, plays and skits, storytelling, and health games.

Most sociodramas may be used effectively through the following procedures:

1. *Select the situation.* The situation should be a fairly simple one, involving one main idea or issue. It should also involve personalities. The issues should be those that arise because people have different desires, beliefs, hopes, and aspirations, or ones that come about from the inability of people to understand the point of view of others.
2. *Think out a series of questions* to guide discussion after the sociodrama.
3. *Choose participants.* When first trying out role-playing, the teacher should select students who are fairly well informed about the issue to be presented and who are imaginative, articulate, and self-assured. After students have become familiar with the technique, the teacher should ask for volunteers.
4. *Prepare the audience.* Just before the sociodrama, the teacher should direct the class to observe for certain feelings, behaviors, and events.
5. *Act out the situation.* The teacher should allow children to be as actively involved as possible. As the director, the teacher should, when necessary, remind the students of their role in the sociodrama and

then withdraw and become a member of the audience. The sociodrama should be challenging, mentally stimulating, and fun for everyone.

6. *Follow-up.* First the teacher should express pleasure at how well the players performed. A good sociodrama generates interest and arouses comments and questions, so follow-up has to do with effective completion of the learning process. The valuable concepts conveyed through sociodramas need to be nailed down by means of reviews, discussions, and question-and-answer sessions. (This kind of follow-up is a part of all good learning experiences.) An attempt should be made to identify main ideas and emotional reactions, and to stimulate class involvement through questions, comments, and observations. At the end, the key points should be summarized. Ideally, students will be able to internalize the main idea of the sociodrama. With slow learners and, especially, primary school children, follow-up activities might include creative writing and drawing.

Role-Playing

Role-playing is the unrehearsed acting out of a situation or a problem. It is a form of improvisation in which participants assume the identity of other persons and imitate a role model's behavior in a particular set of circumstances. Such on-the-spot acting can portray a concept or dramatize problem-solving. Two or more people may participate, and ordinarily a short time is allowed for planning. This learning experience has great potential to increase awareness and modify attitudes. It may also be used to introduce a health topic, give students an opportunity to use what they have learned by applying some principle to the solution of a problem, or illustrate the influence of tradition, values, or social pressure on individual behavior. Role-playing differs from standard drama in that no script, memorization, or rehearsal is needed. In fact, the value of role-playing as a teaching device lies in its spontaneity of presentation. The action comes directly from the individual's creative use of his or her own experience.

The problem should be relevant to the health topic under study, deal with a significant idea or issue and involve personalities in a real-life situation. Use caution if a role-play requires students to try to get other students to participate in unhealthy behaviors. That theme could convince them to do so. The problem should elicit feelings and attitudes rather than convey straight factual information.

A certain amount of planning is necessary. The problem and the roles to be acted out need to be identified. Specific roles and limited background regarding the personalities and attitudes to be projected should be briefly described on slips of paper. The duration of the play should be short—one to three minutes. Two to five players are usually needed for a single episode. The roles assigned to students may be either congruent with or opposite to their real-life feelings. In either case, the roles should be portrayed as the children perceive them and as the plot develops. The role-playing should be stopped at the end of a specified time, when the idea or point has been reached, or when the dramatization begins to lag. The teacher should thank the participants for their performances and allow them to discuss the play. The teacher should then follow up the role-playing by pointing out the main ideas and emotional reactions presented.

Plays and Skits

A play is carefully rehearsed dramatization that involves a script, props, and scenery. It can be extremely useful in portraying important social concepts. Play scripts may be obtained from professional organizations or developed as a class project. The latter has the advantage of student involvement and the discovery and application of knowledge to individual and group problems.

A skit or playlet is a relatively brief dramatic presentation that is often satirical or comic. It too may be planned, but it requires little rehearsal. It has great appeal to primary school children, for it is short and may be used to help them explore problems in human relations. It may be presented in the classroom by simply providing scripts to students and asking them to act out what they read.

The emphasis in both plays and skits should be on attaining and maintaining healthful living, not on dramatization. Humor and mild ridicule in a script may be used to influence student behavior. Plays, which are probably more appropriate for the intermediate grades, should last five to ten minutes, whereas skits may last from three to five minutes and be used at both the primary and intermediate levels. Intermediate-grade pupils should be encouraged to write a skit or play and present it to primary-grade children or their own class. After the presentation, the class can analyze the skit or play and its relationship to them, their needs, and their lives.

Puppets

Puppets are fascinating to most children. Puppets can make statements that will be remembered longer than those made by a teacher. Interest may be maintained at an even higher level when the puppets are made by the class and spontaneous dialogue added. Puppets have great attitudinal effect on primary children as well as allowing for creativity.

Puppet shows may be presented very effectively by the pupils; the teacher merely facilitates the process. A health theme or situation should be selected by the class and teacher for dramatization. A variety of methods may be used in the construction of the puppets, for example, hand puppets, stick puppets, paper-bag puppets, sock puppets, *papier-mâché* figures, or one- and two-string marionettes. The characters assumed by the puppets may be taken from *Sesame Street* or other familiar television shows as well as favorite storybook situations. The stage may be a sheet or blanket stretched out as a curtain with the puppet manipulators behind the curtain, the puppets above it, and the audience on the other side, or a large cardboard box with a curtain as a stage. The extended sheet as a curtain has appeal because it is quick and easy to rig up and implies a relaxed and informal setting. An added advantage is that it provides space for mass participation of the pupils. One group can manipulate the puppets, another can hold the curtain, and a third provide the dialog. Puppets provide an ideal opportunity for creativity and subject correlation of health science with art, English, and drama. As with all sociodramatic techniques, follow-up is necessary.

Storytelling and Reading Stories

Storytelling has been used by the world's greatest teachers. Jesus used it, as did Plato, Confucius, and other great philosophers. It has great appeal to primary school children because it lets them hear living language, language that communicates at a level above and beyond that of everyday usage. People tell stories to children to:

1. Entertain and charm them. Life is made rich by sharing the adventures of others, finding new solutions to old problems, and seeing the familiar in a new way.
2. Explain human nature. As children identify with the characters, they learn to recognize their own feelings about health topics.
3. Give reassurance that life is good. Since news stresses the exceptional (crime, violence, accidents), children, especially, need reassurance that most people are kind and thoughtful, that most people have only good intentions, or that most people feel the same about work, play, and well-being.
4. Give meaning to the big ideas of life. The good, the true, and the beautiful are learned concepts. Storytelling creates a concrete situation in which ideas and judgments can be tested and applied to personal experiences.
5. Give children a sense of competence to face each day, an appreciation of our environment, or an understanding of the self.
6. Encourage the development of good listening skills and provide aesthetic enjoyment.
7. Stimulate the imagination and provide opportunities for creative expression.

A storyteller should be honest and relaxed and tell the story in a sincere manner. The story should possess substance and involve content related to the topic under study. The beginning storyteller should explore the children's collection in the library for suitable stories and review the story in detail so as to know it well but avoid rote memorization. The storyteller uses his or her own personality as a teller—

that is, his or her own choice of words, voice, pace, gestures, facial expressions, and so on—sending it to the ears and imagination of the listeners. Visual aids can be used to stimulate imagination, but not to the point that they distract from or interfere with the story. They need to create a visual picture of the story, project into its character, and take into account ways in which its effectiveness might be enhanced. The teller selects and arranges supplementary materials. Pictures are an important aid in helping primary children to understand stories. Visual aids and supplementary materials should be set up at the children's eye level. The storyteller should also arrange the seating so that there is closeness and a relaxed atmosphere.

The class needs to be motivated to listen attentively to the story. One way of doing this is to use an eye- or ear-catching technique to gain initial attention and create a warm emotional climate. The teller then unfolds the story by dramatizing it enthusiastically. He or she should avoid interrupting the story unnecessarily but allow for some student reaction and response. With storytelling, too, there is a need to provide follow-up activities.

Health Games

Many commercial board games, from Monopoly, Concentration, and checkers, to Ludo and Fox and Geese, are available and familiar for adults and children. Thus the format and process of playing board games may be adapted to health instruction. Children in the intermediate grades are mature enough to play and learn from such games. Health games should be designed to help children become more knowledgeable, clarify misconceptions, reinforce positive attitudes, and develop constructive health habits (see Figure 4.2). A good health game has a main theme, such as drug misuse, ecology, water or air pollution, or disease control. Tokens, symbols, or colors may represent the players on the board. The players take turns, throwing dice, spinning an arrow, moving marked staves, or using some other chance technique. The game should provide for risk-taking and acknowledge the consequences of good and bad

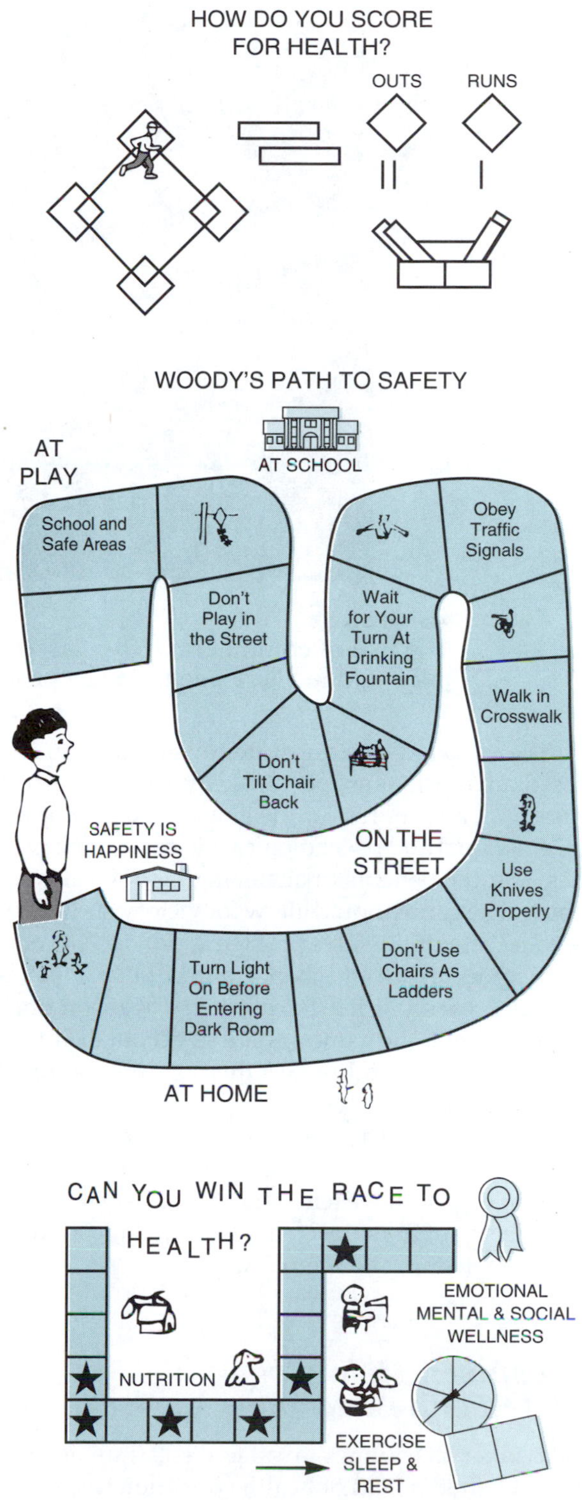

FIGURE 4.2 Teacher/Student-Made Health Games Allow for Student Participation and May Be Used as Bulletin Boards or Adapted for Groups of Four or Five Students

The use of computers in the classroom allows children to learn at their own pace and facilitates learning by providing immediate feedback.

decisions. Good decisions are rewarded with success; bad decisions are penalized by loss of reward or disaster. The progress of the game should be based on emotional and psychological factors, cultural values, and the benefits of achievinging optimal well-being. The game should allow for victory, success, or reward; attempt to solve problems; provide for varying degrees of skill and chance; and be bound by simple rules that allow it to be completed in a short time. While playing the games, children act out their feelings and wishes and project their understanding of social and health issues.

Teachers and pupils should create their own games. The quality of a game will depend on the psychology of the teacher and his or her creativity, knowledge of the subject matter, acquaintance with gamesmanship, and interest in games.

Computer Technology and Health Education

Like other disciplines, available software, including CDs, in the field of health education has grown rapidly. Computer-assisted health education may be classified on the basis of how pupils use the software and computer. Available software can provide learning experiences that:

1. Provide information
2. Analyze data, behaviors, and habits
3. Predict high risks because of health habits; appraise risks
4. Stimulate real-life situations with many choices
5. Develop skills for managing time, stress, and so forth
6. Keep records and monitor progress
7. Perform statistical analysis and other math functions

Health education software can enhance health lessons. It can be fun to use, mentally challenging, help with problem-solving, and increase the attention span of children through use of color, graphics, animation, and sound. Computers can facilitate learning and promote better health by providing immediate feedback. They allow pupils to learn at their own pace and provide reinforcement for attitude or behavior modification.

Health education computer programs often

request that the student respond with a choice provided by the computer, or provide personal information which is then used by the program to analyze individual behavior and make recommendations for change.

As with other learning resources, teachers should clearly identify their lesson objectives first and then select the appropriate software. If software is to provide a positive learning experience, it must be used correctly. This requires good judgment by the teacher. Computer-assisted health education provides the teacher with an advantage over other learning resources only when it performs better than the teacher could do without the computer.

Although more and more education software is becoming available, according to the Educational Products Information Exchange (Dorman, 1992) only 5 percent of programs can be noted as exemplary and only 25 percent meet their minimal standards. About 99 percent are not evaluated prior to marketing. Listed below are six criteria that may be beneficial in selecting software (Buckleitner, 1995).

1. Be sure it is easy to install. Most companies have help lines to offer assistance. However, if that fails, it is best to return the product.
2. It should be easy to use. Introductions should be short and probably verbal. The student should be able to jump right into the substance of the program.
3. Check that it has a good response time. When the mouse is clicked or key pressed, children lack patience to wait very long for a response. The program must respond quickly to hold their attention.
4. It should be childproof. Children are curious and will click on anything to see what happens. The program must be durable enough to withstand this type of abuse. If programs lock-up easily or send cryptic error messages, don't buy them.
5. The program should be challenging and fun. Children like mazes, puzzles, and drawings that challenge them on several levels. Lacking these traits, a program soon becomes boring.
6. Make sure it is educational and not just entertaining. Programs to fill time are not suitable.

An evaluation form specifically for health education software is depicted in Figure 4.3. In addition to the obvious, educational software should document the learning theory used as a basis for the program. Learning principles employed in the software should be denoted, also. In making decisions about health education software, Dorman (1992) recommends:

- Applying the characteristics of your own students to the software program capability
- Evaluating the software in terms of standards, goals, objectives, and content
- Requesting a demonstration whenever possible
- Asking for pilot-test or similar data regarding the software program
- Checking on the need for additional software or hardware to run the program
- Assessing technical merits such as sound, color, and graphics
- Considering ease of use
- Not using software if another teaching methodology is more motivational or sound

Relationship between Methods and Materials

Materials and teaching aids are part of methodology, but it is often difficult to distinguish between the two. For example, a film, by itself, is a teaching aid. It becomes a part of a methodology when children discuss what they saw and heard after seeing it. Likewise, cut-out pictures of foods may be used with a flannel board or bulletin board as teaching aids. But when these items are used to demonstrate a balanced daily diet, they structure an organized teaching method.

Materials may facilitate a method. They should make the method more meaningful. Good teachers use a variety of materials and methods. Perhaps it is wise to think of both methods and materials as contributing to effective learning. Use of both helps children to make well-being a dynamic and valued force in their lives.

Title of Program: ______________________ **Version:** ____________
Distributor: ______________________ **Copyright:** ____________
Address: ______________________ **Cost:** ____________

Phone for technical support: ____________ **Serial # or site license agreement #:** ____________
License restrictions: ☐ **no copies allowed** ☐ **backup copy only** ☐ **multiple copies allowed** ☐ **site license in effect**
Estimated Operating Time: ______

Hardware/Software Required:

Computer brand:	☐ IBM	☐ Macintosh	☐ Apple	☐ Tandy	☐ Other ________
Printer Type:	☐ Laser	☐ Dot-matrix	☐ Letter quality		
Other:	☐ Mouse		☐ Graphics required		☐ Color monitor required

Amount of memory: ____________ Version of DOS required: ____________

Target Population:

Age group: ____________

Grade:	☐ Elementary	☐ Middle	☐ High School	☐ Secondary	☐ Adult
Ability:	☐ Advanced	☐ Average	☐ Low	☐ Remedial	
Grouping Requirements:		☐ Individual	☐ Pairs	☐ Small Group	

Accompanying Instructional Materials:

Content Evaluation:

☐ Objectives stated clearly
☐ Content presented accurately
☐ Free from stereotypes and bias
☐ Content covers curricular needs
☐ Appropriate reading level
☐ Free from grammar/punctuation/spelling errors

Technical Evaluation:

Check program features:

☐ graphics	☐ music	☐ time display
☐ color	☐ voice	☐ score display
☐ sound	☐ windows	☐ modem

☐ Display screens legible
☐ Help screen available
☐ Teacher can control or alter the content
☐ Evidence the product has undergone revision
☐ Learner input errors handled effectively
☐ Can the rate of presentation be altered
☐ Re-enter the program at last page of exit
☐ Level of skill is required for the instructor

Instructional Evaluation:

☐ Level of the learner assessed
☐ Record kept of learner progress
☐ Learner practice or examples provided
☐ Personalization provided
☐ Requisite skills stated
☐ Branching based upon individual needs
☐ Positive feedback provided to the learner
☐ Post text provided
☐ Instructions provided

Documentation:

☐ Documentation included
☐ Results of pilot testing given in documentation
☐ On-screen documentation provided
☐ Technical support provided
☐ Documentation easy to use
☐ Suggestions of time allotments and use of courseware provided
☐ Instructor's manual provided
☐ Student manual provided

Description of the Program:

Health Content Area(s):

☐ aging	☐ exercise/fitness
☐ accidents	☐ mental health
☐ community health	☐ nutrition
☐ consumer health	☐ personal health
☐ disease prevention	☐ sexuality
☐ environmental	☐ substance abuse
☐ other ____________	

Reviewed By: ______________________ **Date:** ______________________

FIGURE 4.3 Health Education Software Evaluation Form (*Source:* From S.M. Dorman, Evaluating computer software, *Journal of School Health* 62,1(1992):36. Reprinted with permission.)

Controversial Issues in Health Education Instruction

Controversy about what is being taught and how it is being taught has been around for at least 150 years (Rippa, 1984). In many ways, this is not surprising. According to Van Patten (1994, p. 746), "It has been said that education is the most important function of state and local governments, and diverse groups want to shape that function." Comprehensive school health education is not immune from such pressure. Although surveys at local, state, and national levels continually reveal majority support for health education in the public schools, some organizations have gone to great lengths to oppose certain aspects of it.

These groups, often members of or supported by well-financed national religious organizations, generally have good intentions but tolerate little or no diversity in any form. It is important to understand that opposition, in and of itself, is neither good nor bad. Rather, the motivation behind the opposition is what is important. In many groups, the real motivation is concealed behind a screen of, "We only want to improve our schools." Hostile opposition often takes the form of interference by (a) causing confusion, (b) forcing staff to waste precious time and resources to defend themselves, and (c) attempting to alienate staff and teachers from one another or from the administration. Van Patten (1994) provides as an example "The Michigan Experience," in which comprehensive school health education was attacked at both local and state levels. The opposition organizations were well financed and distorted information to incite others. For example, the DADS Foundation and the Rutherford Institute, a conservative religious foundation, claimed that the stress-reduction exercise of calm breathing was in fact a practice of Eastern religions and placed their children in a state of altered consciousness. As a result, they wanted the entire program scrapped. But opposition can come from many different directions, depending upon the nature of the group.

Sources of Controversy

Comprehensive school health education deals with problem behaviors. Among professionals, these behaviors are viewed from a health perspective; however, others may have different outlooks (Neutens, 1992). The inclusion of any of the following topics raises ire in some communities: addictive behaviors, teen suicide, teen pregnancy, contraception, violence, diseases like HIV/AIDS, child abuse, sexual abuse, sexuality education, relaxation exercises, pregnancy termination, homosexuality, and even some aspects of nutrition. Using the state of Michigan as an example of what is wrong with health education again, one group found the following wrong with the Michigan Health Education Model (Van Patten, 1994; Bell, 1991):

- It uses problem-solving with people (PSP) as a means to change children's values.
- It teaches about "responsible" use of drugs rather than abstinence.
- It has an antifamily bias.
- It attempts to place children in an altered state of consciousness by means of "calming" exercises.
- It invades family privacy.

As might be expected, groups with such objections are very much against decision-making skills and student autonomy. They believe the curriculum should be authoritarian, if not dictatorial, and that certain unquestionable rules should apply.

Preventing Controversy

To avoid needless or nonproductive controversy, steps can be taken at both the administrative and teacher levels. The most basic concept applying to the prevention of false allegations and needless legal action is the development of community trust in school policies and personnel. This is attainable if the community has appropriate input into school curriculum, programs, and policies. School districts and boards should be prepared to demonstrate the following:

1. Written policies and procedures for curriculum and material selection
2. Written plans of the policies, curricula, and materials for educators, parents, and community members to review and comment on as they are being developed

3. Written procedures to address complaints and concerns from community members

Note that these three steps are seen as important for sexuality education but not for other areas of health education. But remember that in today's world almost any part of the curriculum can be held hostage by a small but vocal pressure group. Local districts and state boards of education must act in concert in their efforts to educate our children.

To help schools avoid controversy, the National PTA (1987) recommends the following actions to address extremism:

1. Hold meetings to discuss the effects of extremism on the school and the community.
2. Have a committee investigate and present information about the tactics used by extremist groups.
3. Arrange meetings to debate important issues.
4. Urge school boards to have written policies.
5. Offer PTA representation on all selection, retention, and complaint committees for school curricula, programs, and libraries.
6. Emphasize the importance of sticking with school policies when choosing materials for classrooms or libraries, at least until complaints are processed.
7. Stress the importance of First Amendment rights.
8. At all PTA meetings, be certain that all voters are members in good standing and that a full democratic debate is conducted before a vote.
9. Have school board–candidate nights so that the PTA membership can hear what the candidates have to say and what (or who) they represent.

Of course, all the policies in the world won't be of benefit if the classroom teacher fails to take his or her own preventive steps. Suggestions for teachers include the following:

1. Follow all written school policies and guidelines pertaining to your program, especially those on material selection.
2. Be prepared to teach. In other words, have an adequate background in the subject area in relationship to the grade level.
3. Understand and apply health *science* to health education when teaching epidemiological, database, anatomical, and physiological information.
4. Communicate on a regular basis with the principal or other administrator as to what is happening in the classroom, particularly in regard to methods and homework assignments.
5. Always preview materials—computer instruction, videos, games.
6. Select guest speakers judiciously, and know their theme and content.
7. Do not let personal values or biases replace school policy or guidelines.
8. Employ appropriate language, and set a positive example for children.
9. Answer questions to the best of your ability but within the guidelines established by the school. Make referrals to others if necessary.
10. Do not set up "secret" meetings with a small group of students to discuss things that are pertinent to them but not the whole class.
11. Be fully aware of multicultural and gender differences as they apply to your teaching area so as not to inadvertently offend anyone.
12. Personal experiences should remain just that: personal.
13. "Conducting research" to find out what students think, feel, or do must be approved, including the specific questionnaire to be used.
14. Keep accurate records on a situation that could be questioned at a later date.
15. Be prepared for opposition, and know what steps are to be taken by yourself, the administration, and the school district.

When controversy does arise, it can be emotionally troubling to all involved. As a teacher, it is important to remain as calm as possible and to know that you have followed school policies. Even when you try your best, understand that

> There are people who cannot accept positions outside of their own religious code, tolerate diversity, or accept a school health education program that results in developing personal responsibility. They reject the use of scientific knowledge within age-appropriate levels of health information. They oppose providing students with knowledge about sexual matters, certain diseases, abuse avoidance (physical and substance), and the use of their decision-making capabilities *(Van Patten, 1994).*

And try to keep in mind that controversy can be used to improve programs.

Implication for Elementary and Middle-School Teachers

Summary Issues

1. Teaching is both a science and an art. Science is applied in selecting content, materials, and methods and in assessing expected performance indicators in regard to the curricular standard.
2. The first phase of health education activities is to assist the student in deciding whether or not to adopt a health-enhancing behavior.
3. The second phase of health education activities is to provide the necessary skills to carry out the health-enhancing behavior once it is adopted.
4. Learning theory should be the cornerstone of learning activities. Social learning theory, social inoculation theory, and cognitive-behavioral approaches have been successful in health education.
5. There should be a clear relationship among cognitive material, skills, methods, and performance indicators.
6. Children, like adults, learn through their senses, with sight and hearing paramount.
7. Criteria should be used to evaluate the appropriateness of a learning activity.
8. Problem-based learning can be used to learn both subject matter and skills, including critical thinking, decision-making, analysis, assertiveness, refusal, communication, and conflict resolution.
9. In problem-based learning, the vignette or case is always presented first, before disseminating any information, just like in real life.
10. Problem-based learning is a focused, highly structured activity rather than presentation of a problem for discussion or to fill time.
11. Computer software should be evaluated prior to purchase or use.
12. Educational software should have a basis in learning theory and address specific performance indicators or learning assessments.
13. Comprehensive school health education, by its nature, is open to controversy from several groups. Controversy can be beneficial to a program, depending upon the motivation underlying it.
14. Steps can be taken by school districts, school boards, and PTAs to prevent or reduce the likelihood of harmful controversy in school health education programs.
15. Teachers can take at least fifteen actions to prevent unwanted controversy from their classroom.

Teacher Ramifications

In regard to teaching strategies and controversial issues, a teacher should:

1. Select strategies with deliberate speed based upon a written set of criteria developed by a committee that represents community as well as school interests.
2. Allow other educators and community members to preview, assess, and comment on all materials that are to be used in the classroom.
3. Follow all written policies regarding the teaching of health education and related areas.
4. Establish written guidelines for referral of students for questions that are considered

"too controversial" to be handled in the classroom.

5. Know the potential sources of controversy in the curriculum and have a good understanding of how some groups attempt to sabotage education in order to obtain control and place their agenda into the system.
6. Use educational strategies that are fun, motivating, and appropriate for student age and health standards.

References

Aspy, D.N., Aspy, C.B., & Quinby, P. What doctors can teach teachers about problem-based learning, *Educational Leadership* 50,7(1993):22–24.

Bandura, A. *Social Foundations of Thought and Action.* Prentice-Hall, Englewood Cliffs, NJ, 1986.

Barrows, H.S., & Tamblyn, R.M. *Problem-Based Learning: An Approach to Medical Education.* Springer, New York, 1980.

Bell, R.K. *Improving the Michigan Model.* RKB Associates, Novi, MI, 1991.

Buckleitner, W. Six ways to develop a sixth sense about software, *Home PC* 2,5(1995):143–144.

Cinelli, B., Symons, C.W., Bechtel, L., & Rose-Colley, M. Applying cooperative learning in health education practice, *Journal of School Health* 64,3(1994):99–102.

Dorman, S.M., Small, P.A., & Lee, D.D. A cooperative learning technique for AIDS education, *Journal of School Health* 59,7(1989):314–316.

Dorman, S.M. Evaluating computer software for the health education classroom, *Journal of School Health*, 62,1(1992):35–37.

Fetro, J. *Personal and Social Skills: Understanding and Integrating Competencies across Health Content.* ETR Associates, Santa Cruz, CA, 1992.

Hawkins, J.D., Catalano, R.F., Morrison, D.M., et al. The Seattle social development project: Effects of the first four years on protective factors and problem behaviors. In J. McCord and R. Tremblay, eds., *The Prevention of Antisocial Behavior in Children.* Guilford, New York, 1992.

Hayes, D.M., & Brickle, H.W., Using cooperative learning to integrate math concepts into health instruction on sexuality and HIV education, *Journal of School Health* 61,4(1991):178–180.

Johnson, D.W., & Johnson, R.T. Social skills for successful group work. *Educational Leader* 47, 4(1989/1990):29–33.

Johnson, D.W., Johnson, R.T., & Smith, K. *Active Learning in the College Classroom.* Interaction Book Company, Edina, MN, 1991.

Kirby, D. School-based programs to reduce sexual risk-taking behavior. *Journal of School Health* 62,7(1992):280–287.

Kolbe, L.J., Iverson, D.C., Kreuter, M.W., Hochbaum, G., & Christensen, G. Propositions for an alternate and complementary health education paradigm, *Health Education* 12(1981):24–30.

McGuire, W. Inducing resistance to persuasion. In L. Berkowitz, ed., *Advances in Experimental Social Psychology.* Academic Press, New York, 1964.

National Parent Teachers Association. *National PTA's Guide to Extremism* (Pub No. 1610187–15). Chicago, IL, 1987.

Neutens, J.J. Sexuality education in comprehensive school health programs: Surviving the "moral smog," *Journal of School Health* 62,2(1992):74–75.

Neutens, J.J. From where I sit. *Family Life Educator* 12,2(1993/1994):16–17.

Neutens, J.J. *Healthy Sexual Development* (Middle school/junior high edition). American Guidance Service, Circle Pines, MN, 1994.

Rippa, S.A. *Education in a Free Society.* Longman, White Plains, NY, 1984.

Slavin, R.E. Research on cooperative learning: Consensus and controversy. *Educational Leader* 47,4(1989/1990):52–54.

Solomon, D., Watson, M., Schaps, E., et al. Cooperative learning as part of a comprehensive classroom program designed to promote prosocial development. In S. Sharon, ed., *Current Research on Cooperative Learning.* Praeger, New York, 1990.

Stepien, W., & Gallagher, S. Problem-based learning: As authentic as it gets, *Educational Leadership* 50,7(1993):25–28.

Van Patten, M.M. Dealing with controversy in the school health program. In P. Cortese and K. Middleton, eds., *The Comprehensive School Health Challenge* vol. 2. ETR Associates, Santa Cruz, CA, 1994.

Victor, E. *Science for the Elementary School.* Macmillan, Toronto, 1970.

5

Instructional Accountability

Upon completion of this chapter, you should be able to:

- *Explain the meaning of and discern the differences between evaluation, measurement, and testing*
- *Explain the interrelationship between National Health Education Standards, performance indicators, learning assessments, and evaluation*
- *Justify the use of the National Health Education Standards in the everyday classroom*
- *Compare and contrast several ways to test students*
- *Explain several nontest evaluation measures*
- *Critically appraise and explain how problem-based learning strategies can be used to evaluate skills acquisition and accumulation of knowledge*

Evaluation: An Overview

Accountability is an integral part of the educational process, especially as it pertains to the evaluation of students. One of the most important points about evaluation is that it is *not* something to be "tacked on" at the end of a unit or course. Moreover, it is *not* confined to measurement of cognitive knowledge retained. Finally, it is *not* restricted to paper-and-pencil tests or computer quizzes.

Now that we know what evaluation is not, let us take a look at what it is. In a sentence, *evaluation* is a comprehensive, on-going process involving a variety of techniques and inextricably linked to learning goals, that is, standards, performance indicators, learning assessments, or objectives. Evaluation is much more than testing. Many of the decisions you make as a teacher are based on observation in the classroom. Class discussion may reveal a misunderstanding to be corrected immediately; Johnny may need help with his math problems; Paige might need assistance in identifying the problem in a problem-based learning vignette; Tun may require help in expressing or asserting himself in a role-play situation. In short, you make decisions about students based on oral comments, statements of knowledge, actual performance, physical behavior, and even tone of voice. All of these methods are informal but nonetheless indispensable.

Formal evaluations supplement the informal ones. That is, tests and related procedures are simply a systematic, comprehensive, and objective means to obtain more information. Both approaches procure data about students and require interpretation by the teacher. Both serve as evaluation evidence in the decision-making process.

To this extent, evaluation is far more complex than either testing or measurement alone. Compared with measurement, evaluation refers more to

Proper student evaluation involves much more than occasional testing; it is a comprehensive, on-going process that the teacher participates in on a daily basis.

value and quality. Evaluation deals with questions and judgments of worth rather than amount. Evaluation should be thought of as a much more inclusive process whereby quantitative statements are incorporated en route to ultimate value judgments.

Measurement answers the question How much? Essentially, it assigns numerals to a criterion according to a preconceived set of rules. Functions such as ranking, classification, comparison, description of status or change, and prediction are all types of measurement. A multitude of techniques and instruments may be employed to fulfill these functions, such as rating scales, score cards, systematic observation, and measure achievement. When all is said and done, measurement is probably best thought of as a condition of quantity. For example, a score of 95 percent on a multiple choice nutrition test is a measurement.

Testing is the process of using tests, though emphasis is usually placed on the instrument used in the process. Such tools as observation, checklists, inventories, questionnaires, rating scales, and interviews are used. The administration of a twenty-five–question multiple-choice test on nutrition to a fifth-grade class is a typical example of testing. Table 5.1 illustrates the interrelationships among testing, measurement, and evaluation.

Evaluation is not an easy task; however, it is a very important one. In health education, it is essential that evaluation be conducted in both the cognitive and behavioral realms in order to meet the challenges placed upon the discipline and the teacher of health education. One thing is for sure: As a prospective teacher, you are destined to confront your share of difficulties related to evaluation. Most likely you will change your personal philosophy about evaluation numerous times as you progress through your neophyte years of teaching.

Purposes of Evaluation

The following are some of the reasons why teachers evaluate health instruction:

1. Perhaps one of the most important purposes is to assist in the *diagnosis* and/or *classification* of pupils who need special help. Evaluation might also determine the specific kind of help needed by a youngster.

The health services of the school health program provide an excellent analogy. A youngster failing to meet minimum standards for the Snellen Eye Test (most often administered by the school nurse as a screening device) is referred for a more comprehensive eye examination. Let us say that the youngster is found to be nearsighted and needs glasses.

But diagnosis can also be viewed in another way. The teacher may want to use an examination to introduce a unit of study in order to determine just what the class already knows and does not know about a particular topic. Data of this nature can be helpful in determining where the greatest

Table 5.1 Interrelationship of Testing, Measurement, and Education

Term	Definition	Concept	Point of Reference
Testing	Procedure of systematizing observations, e.g., a 25-question multiple-choice nutrition examination for fifth graders.	Instrument (tool)	Tests, checklists, rating scales, observation, etc.
Measurement	Assigning symbolic significance, e.g., a score of 95 percent.	Score (quantity)	Rank, status, classification, comparison, etc.
Evaluation	Determining the worth of measurement, e.g., the number of scores above 95, the mean score for the test.	Value (quantity)	Goals, objectives, expected outcomes

amount of instructional emphasis should be placed. Periodic evaluation of this nature can also be helpful to updating a course of study.

2. Evaluation can be thought of as *accountability.* Without some form of accountability, we can never be sure whether our objectives have been attained. With reference to health education, we are concerned about whether our students are improving their health behavior or skills acquisition, attitudes, and knowledge. The dedicated teacher wants to know if his or her teaching has been effective. Thus meaningful evaluation of instruction can be helpful in providing a valid indication of the effectiveness of the teacher's effort.

The task is assessing pupils' progress. But true appraisal of changes in health knowledge, attitudes, and practices or skill acquisitions resulting from organized classroom learning experiences is no easy task. Building on the concept of evaluation as diagnosis, the teacher could administer the same test at both the beginning and the end of a unit and compare the results. There is no question that such an approach lends itself in a more realistic fashion to the cognitive domain. (Objective measurement of changes in attitudes and behavior is more difficult, and is addressed later.)

3. For those operating within a traditional numerical grading system, sound tests of knowledge provide *objective information on which to base grades.* This particular approach to evaluation has come under the greatest criticism of late at the elementary school level. Today there appears to be a strong trend away from the categorical approach of grading at the elementary level. Instead, more and more emphasis is being placed on descriptive analysis of each child's academic progress. However, it is still necessary to measure cognitive progress if any meaningful descriptive evaluation is to be achieved. So, although letter grades may be eliminated, testing may very well continue to play a large role in the evaluation process.

4. Some educators steadfastly assert that evaluation instruments (tests) are excellent *motivational devices* for students. Certainly tests can be challenging and educationally rewarding for many students—perhaps all students under the right conditions. However, wrongly used, tests can be a most deadening influence. Needless to say, then, this purpose of evaluation is highly controversial. All too often, a teacher's opinion is influenced by his or her own success with educational measurement. It is indeed sad to see a teacher who attempts to use testing as the prime motivating force for his or her students. If tests were taken away from this type of teacher, what control would she or he have over the class? A misguided rationale such as this on the part of a teacher is most unprofessional.

5. Although it seems obvious, evaluation is a way to *inform parents* about their children's progress. When evaluation is used objectively and consistently, parents value a teacher's comments.

In summary, evaluation should be thought of as a means to an end, not an end in itself. The greatest value of evaluation lies in the use to which it is put. Properly implemented evaluation in health education can be diagnostic, provide for accountability, used as a basis for letter-grade assignment if necessary, and perhaps even be motivational if realistically approached. Keep in mind, however, that evaluation in health education is far more than *how much* a child knows.

Just as important is how a child feels and what he or she does about health matters. This is what makes meaningful evaluation of health education such a difficult task. Although most teachers easily develop the ability to measure students' health knowledge, much skill is required to develop effective techniques that can validly measure health practices and attitudes.

Knowledge of good health practices has long been considered a basis for healthful behavior. Proponents of this theory argue that what a child knows will have a strong bearing on how she or he feels and will act in health matters. No doubt, someone adhering to this philosophy would place a great deal of emphasis on how much the students know about health. However, there is little evidence to support such a theory. Knowledge is just one of the many influential factors affecting health behavior. And given the multitude of avoidable health problems clearly evident in our enlightened society today, one wonders how important it is.

Just as important are how a youngster feels and behaves. Ideally, we should strive to evaluate students' health practices and attitudes as conscientiously as we do their health knowledge.

Evaluation and National Health Education Standards

The National Health Education Standards (discussed in Chapter 3) describe the skills and knowledge necessary for health literacy. While the Standards are neither a federal mandate nor a national curriculum, they do provide a framework for a health knowledge and skills curriculum, and "provide a basis for assessing student achievement and progress" (Joint Committee, 1995, p. 9). The performance indicators in the National Health Education Standards are ". . . intended to serve as a blueprint for organizing student assessment" (Joint Committee, 1995, p. 10).

To refine, to emphasize, and to incorporate content, learning assessments can be developed. Learning assessments, as discussed in Chapter 3, describe what students will be able to do and know after completing a prescribed unit or course of instruction. They go beyond performance indicators in providing detail to both the student and the teacher. Like performance indicators, they are molded after behavioral objectives. As such, learning assessments provide direction in terms of what should be taught (including content), how it should be taught, and whether that which is taught is learned. In other words, learning assessments add a third level of specificity, and are thereby useful in clarifying standards and performance indicators.

Specifically, teachers and students benefit from learning assessments in the following ways:

1. Given clearly defined learning assessments to work toward, teachers can design instructional experiences to achieve them, and can evaluate the effectiveness of such strategies according to whether the learning assessments are achieved.
2. Students can be examined prior to instruction to ascertain their level of readiness and how much they have achieved already.
3. Each student can be evaluated on the mastery of learning assessments. In this way, every student can be required to master all learning assessments.
4. Where appropriate, content can be evaluated when the learning assessments are written specifically for it.

Figure 5.1 illustrates the relationship of the National Health Education Standards, performance indicators, and learning assessments to evaluation. Note that the Standards encompass a variety of performance indicators and that the performance indicators, in turn, can encompass several learning assessments. The key is to relate evaluation procedures as closely as possible to the learning assessments and/or performance indicators. In other words, evaluation techniques should be chosen or constructed to provide the best evidence possible concerning the attainment of knowledge and/or skills (i.e., learning assessments and/or performance indicators).

Figure 5.2 shows how this works using

National Health Education Standards
(Direct teaching toward health literacy)

↕

Performance Indicator
(Specific concepts and skills for health literacy)

↕

Learning Assessment
(3rd level of specificity to clarify performance indicators and standards)

↕

Evaluation Techniques
(Methods to provide evidence of student knowledge and skills as described in learning assessments, performance indicators, and the National Standards)

FIGURE 5.1 Relationship of Evaluation to National Health Education Standards (*Source:* Adapted from N.E. Gronlund, *Measurement and Evaluation in Teaching* 5th ed. (New York: Macmillan, 1985), p. 47.)

National Health Education Standard 3: Students will demonstrate the ability to practice health-enhancing behaviors and reduce health risks. The content area in this case is nutrition, and the Centers for Disease Control risk behavior is dietary patterns contributing to disease. The performance indicator is listed as a primary number (1, 2, or 3), and the learning assessments are subnumbered (1.1, 1.2, 2.1, 3.2, etc.). Note how the learning assessments clarify the performance indicator, allowing both students and the instructor to know what is expected and how and on what students will be evaluated.

Relating Test Items to National Health Education Standards

To make the relationship between test items and the National Health Education Standards meaningful, the items must match the performance in-

Standard 3: The student will demonstrate the ability to practice health-enhancing behaviors and reduce health risks.

Grade: 6

Content Area: Nutrition

CDC Risk Behavior: Dietary patterns contributing to disease

Performance Indicator and Learning Assessments	*Evaluation Technique (Number corresponds with learning assessment)*
1. *Explains* the importance of assuming responsibility for personal health behaviors	
1.1 *Classifies* foods according to the food groups in the Food Pyramid	1.1 Objective test
1.2 *Describes* the role of each food group in a health-enhancing diet	1.2 Short-answer essay
2. *Analyzes* a personal health assessment to determine health strengths and risks	
2.1 *Conducts* a three-day eating habits assessment	2.1 Anecdotal records
2.2 *Submits* a three-day record of food and drink consumed to the teacher	2.2 Dietary report, observation
2.3 *Identifies* the food and drink consumed by food group	2.3 Observation
2.4 *Draws conclusions* from the data regarding the health-enhancing or health-detracting aspects of personal eating habits	2.4 Anecdotal records, verbal report in class
3. *Demonstrates* strategies to improve or maintain personal and family health	
3.1 *Designs* a plan to improve personal diet based on things he/she can control (e.g., selection from what is offered in cafeteria, or snacks, etc.)	3.1 Dietary report, observation, checklist
3.2 *Performs or carries out* the design, keeping a dietary record for one week	3.2 Anecdotal records
3.3 *Distinguishes* between improvement or status quo in nutritional status	3.3 Checklist or rating scale

FIGURE 5.2 Example of Evaluation Using National Health Education Standard 3

dicators and subsequent learning assessments. If a learning assessment requires identification, for example, then the test item must supply what needs to be identified. On the other hand, if a student must supply an answer, then the item must be written in a fashion to have answers supplied rather than selected. If something must be performed, then the items should require actual performance rather than having a student tell how to do it.

The following examples illustrate the relationship of evaluation to the National Health Standards and, in particular, the importance of matching items as closely as possible to learning assessments. The first two learning assessments are taken from Figure 5.2; the others are separate examples.

Learning assessment: Classifies foods according to the food groups in the Food Pyramid

1. Popcorn is sorted into which of the following food groups?
   A. Bread, cereal, rice, pasta
   B. Vegetables
   C. Fruit
   D. Milk, yogurt, cheese
   E. Meat, poultry, fish, dried beans, nuts

Learning assessment: Describes the role of each food group for a health-enhancing diet

In three or four sentences each, describe how each of the major food groups contributes to our health.

Learning assessment: Define the common terms used in discussing nutrition.

In one or two sentences, define each of the following terms:

1. Macronutrients
2. Kilocalories
3. Lipids
4. Anorexia nervosa

Learning assessment: Distinguishes between nutritional fact and myth

Read each of the following statements. If you believe it is a fact, circle the *F*. If you think the statement if a myth, circle the *M*.

F M Children having nothing to fear from cholesterol.

F M Everyone should take vitamin supplements.

F M Sugar is a good source of energy and is good for us.

F M Soft drinks are a good nutritional substitute for water.

Learning assessment: Draws valid conclusions from given nutritional data

Read the paragraph below and then answer the questions.

> Emily, a sixth grader at Riverton, bought three bacon, tomato, egg, and cheese biscuits at her favorite fast-food restaurant. To be healthy, she ordered a large glass of whole milk. After eating her food, she got a medium strawberry ice cream cone to eat on her way home.

Circle *F* if you believe the statement to be false or *T* if you believe it to be true.

T F Emily ate something from each food group.

T F Emily's meal is high in lipids.

T F If Emily continues to eat in this fashion, cholesterol levels could become a problem.

Relating Nontest Items to National Health Education Standards

As shown in Figure 5.2, there are several situations in which testing procedures are inappropriate. Rather, to evaluate performance skills such as refusal skills, communication skills, inquiry skills, and critical-thinking skills, teachers need to let the student perform and then judge the effectiveness of the performance. Such assessment is not new to education; the disciplines of physical education, art, shop, and home economics have been doing it for years.

The fundamental point, as with testing procedures, is to align the observational or nontest items with the learning assessments and performance standards. The nontest procedures include checklists, rating scales, conferences, and self-

Rating Scale Item

Learning assessment: Distinguishes between improvement or status quo in nutritional status

My efforts in the bread, cereal, rice and pasta group reflect a

1	2	3	4	5
Large deficiency	Small deficiency	Same as before	Small increase	Large increase

Selected Checklist Items

Learning assessment: Designs a plan to improve personal diet based on things he or she can control

Item	*Yes*	*No*	*No Need to Change*
1. Eating breakfast	✓		
2. Selecting "dietary meal of the day" in cafeteria		✓	
3. Avoiding foods with high cholesterol			✓
4. Eating more fruit	✓		

FIGURE 5.3 **Examples of a Rating Scale and Checklist**

evaluations. Examples of a rating scale and checklist are shown in Figure 5.3. The particular learning assessment based upon the performance indicator specifies the characteristics to be observed. Both the rating scale and checklist offer a convenient method of recording performance.

Summary

The National Health Education Standards provide a curriculum framework as well as an evaluation blueprint for health education instruction. Each Standard is clarified by performance indicators, which are suggested for grades 4, 8, and 11. Learning assessments can be developed to add a third level of specificity. The learning assessments can be used to incorporate content and CDC risk behaviors into evaluation, too. Moreover, the learning assessments can be constructed for separate units and/or grade levels to further refine the performance indicators.

The selected method of evaluation should be in concert with the learning assessment and performance indicator, and the Standard from which the learning assessment was derived. Health education instruction involves both the measurement and evaluation of cognitive performance and behavioral skills. Both test and nontest evaluation methods are applicable to the National Health Education Standards.

Methods of Appraising: Test Procedures

The assessment of health knowledge presents far less of a problem than does the challenge of evaluating health attitudes and practices. It is in the cognitive domain that the teacher can be most effective in evaluating. However, the basic philosophical question is, How useful and meaningful is evaluation in this area? We have already discussed the argument that knowledge alone does not necessarily motivate students to practice wise health behavior. Then again, no one has yet proved that knowledge is not a prerequisite to an intelligent decision regarding health behavior. For example, it is logical to assume that if a person does not know about a vaccine for polio, he or she may never be immunized or see that his or her children are. This outcome is as unfortunate as the one for the person who knows better but fails to act. Keeping in mind the ultimate goal of health education (health literacy), it follows that students should acquire certain basic knowledge that will influence health behavior favorably. Thus acquisition of knowledge is an objective of health education and should be subjected to evaluation as are the other areas. The point of importance is that the evaluation of health knowledge is only one aspect of health education evaluation. Actually, it should be thought of as sharing "equal billing" with the evaluation of health practices and attitudes.

Constructing Teacher-Made Tests

Teacher-made paper-and-pencil tests are the most common approach to evaluating pupil health knowledge. Examinations developed on the basis of recognized principles of test construction can be an effective means of evaluating both knowledge and understanding. Since entire textbooks and courses are devoted to test construction, only an overview of the various methods is presented here.

There are two time-consuming procedures involved in examinations. The first is the construction of the exam, and the second is the grading of it. The general rule of thumb is that the easier the examination is to construct, the more difficult it is to grade, and vice versa. For example, while essay examinations can be developed in minutes, they take hours to grade. In contrast, multiple-choice examinations take hours to make—the rate for an expert is five-to-ten items per hour—and only minutes to grade. For this reason (among others) selecting the types of questions is very important.

Short-Answer and Completion Items

Short-answer and completion items are supply-type questions. The answers may range from a single word, number, or character to a few sentences. These types may be particularly good in the early years of elementary school. Examples are as follows:

Short answer: What is the name of the substance made by the endocrine glands? (Hormones)

Completion: Endocrine glands make substances called (hormones).

Short answer: At what age can a baby hold up its head if its back is supported? (4 months)

Completion: A baby can hold up its head at about (4 months) of age if its back is supported.

The short-answer item can be used to evaluate terminology, facts, methods or procedures, and even interpretation of data. Some examples are:

Interpretation of Data

How many food groups are pictured in the Food Pyramid? (6)

Terminology

The part of the body that joins the mouth to the stomach is called the (esophagus).

Knowledge of Methods or Procedures

What technique is used in emergencies to help someone breathe? (Artificial respiration)

The advantages and disadvantages of short-answer items are as follows.

Advantages

1. Easy to construct, since it has simple learning outcomes
2. Students must supply the answer, thereby reducing guessing

Disadvantages

1. Primarily used to measure facts or memorized information
2. Unsuitable for complex learning tasks
3. Can be difficult to score unless item is worded very carefully

Before supplying answers, students must know if partial or total points will be deducted for spelling errors. The teacher needs to determine the purpose of the test. Of course, if spelling is not counted, the teacher may have difficulty reading or understanding what a student put down on the paper.

Alternative-Response or True-False Items

These items generally involve the ability to identify the correctness of something—facts, defini-

Directions: Read each of the statements. If the statement is true, circle the *T.* If the statement is false, circle the *F.*

T F 1. Alcohol is a depressant drug.
T F 2. Nicotine is a chemical found in cigarettes.

Directions: Read each of the following statements to distinguish fact from opinion. If the statement is a fact, circle the *F.* If the statement is an opinion, circle the *O.*

F O 1. Carbohydrates are essential nutrients for the body.
F O 2. Cereals are the best way to obtain carbohydrates.

Directions: In each of the following statements, both parts of the statement are true. You are to decide whether the second part explains *why* the first part is true. If it does, circle *Yes.* If it does not, circle the *No.*

Yes No 1. Brushing teeth is important *because* it helps prevent tooth decay.
Yes No 2. During pregnancy, a woman's breasts become larger *because* the mammary glands are getting ready to make milk.

Directions: Read each sentence below. If the statement is true, circle the *T.* If the statement is false, circle the *F* AND change the underlined word to make the statement true. Place the new word in the blank space after the *F.*

T F ________________ 1. The body system responsible for creating offspring is called the lymphatic system.
T F ________________ 2. The nerve cells in the nervous system are call neurons.

FIGURE 5.4 Examples of Alternative-Response and True-False Items

tions, or principles. They can be used to distinguish between fact and opinion and, on occasion, to recognize cause-and-effect relationships. Some examples of their usage are shown in Figure 5.4.

The last example is a combination of true-false and supply. For these items, it is important to underline or mark the words to be changed so that students do not rewrite the entire sentence.

The advantages and disadvantages to alternative-response items are:

Advantages

1. Simple to construct for an experienced teacher
2. Can cover a wide range of topics

Disadvantages

1. Mainly limited to cognitive knowledge areas
2. Many subject areas do not lend themselves to true-false items (e.g., facts).
3. Students have a 50 percent chance of getting the item right, and if it's poorly written, perhaps an 80 percent chance.

Matching Items

The matching item has two columns. The column on the left has a word, number, or symbol that has to be matched with a word, phrase, or sentence in the right column. The student is to recognize the relationship between the items. The items in column A should be homogeneous. Those in column B should be plausible for each item in column A. Examples are shown in Figure 5.5.

The examples illustrate two very important points. First, there are more items in column B than are needed to match items in column A. Second, any item in column B may be used more than once. Constructing the test in this way prevents matching the final pair by process of elimination.

Directions: Column A lists four different drugs. Column B lists the effects of taking drugs. Write the letter of the drug effect from Column B in the space to the left of the drug in Column A that matches that effect.

Column A	*Column B*
______1. Anabolic steroids	A. Can cause slurred speech, dizziness, and death by suffocation
______2. Alcohol	B. Increases body weight and muscle strength
______3. Inhalants	C. Mimics adrenaline, producing extra energy
______4. Tobacco	D. Causes a few minutes' "high" and then depression
	E. A depressant that can cause digestive and liver problems
	F Can cause emphysema and lung cancer
	G. Excites the central nervous system and distorts perceptions

FIGURE 5.5 Examples of Matching Items

The advantages and disadvantages of matching items are:

Advantages

1. Compact way to cover a lot of course content
2. Fairly easy to construct but must be careful (in practice, many items are poorly constructed)

Disadvantages

1. Restricted to factual information
2. Difficult to find homogeneous material

Multiple-Choice Items

Multiple-choice items are made up of a problem and potential solutions. The problem statement is called the *stem,* and list of solutions contains words, phrases, symbols called *alternatives.* One of the alternatives is the *correct answer* and the other alternatives are called *distractors,* or *foils.* As the name implies, their purpose is to distract those students who are unsure of the correct response.

In creating a multiple-choice item, the stem can be written as either a question or a statement. The question format is probably the best for younger students. As for the alternatives, two options are available. On the one hand, all the choices can be wrong except for one. This is called the *correct-answer* type. On the other hand, the *best-answer* type of question offers alternatives that are all acceptable, except that one is more acceptable than the others. As you would expect, the best-answer type is more difficult since it requires finer discrimination. Some examples are shown below.

Correct-Answer, Question Format

Which phrase best describes the disease of arthritis?

A. Brings about high blood sugar
B. A seizure disorder
C. Causes stiffness and pain in the joints
D. Causes difficulty in breathing

Best-Answer, Question Format

What is the first thing you should do in an emergency situation?

A. Call for professional help (e.g., 911)
B. Take care of life-threatening conditions
C. Check the victim's airway, breathing, and circulation
D. Start rescue breathing

Multiple-choice items are very versatile in that they can measure any learning, from simple to complex. The typical uses of these items are to measure knowledge of terminology, facts, principles, methods, and procedures. At a more complex level, multiple-choice items can be used to measure understanding and application. Two examples are:

Best-Answer, Incomplete-Statement Format, Cause-and-Effect Relationship

The best reason for setting limits early in a relationship is because

A. They remove gray areas from situations with no rules
B. It gives you the opportunity to think about your own values
C. It will help you avoid behaviors inconsistent with your values
D. You can identify risks you wish to avoid

Best-Answer, Question Format, Application of Facts and Principles

At a party one night, Reggie's friends were encouraging him to drink beer, but he does not want to. What is the first step for Reggie to take to say no to his friends?

A. Say "no" in a clear manner
B. Communicate his decision in a diplomatic and honest way
C. Make a decision about what to do if such a situation before it happens
D. Suggest alternative activities to drinking beer at the party

The advantages and disadvantages of multiple-choice items are listed below.

Advantages

1. Can measure simple to complex levels of knowledge
2. Choice of alternatives makes it better than short-answer items
3. Less chance of guessing the answer correctly
4. Greater reliability than true-false items
5. Do not need homogeneous material as matching items do
6. Relatively free from response sets
7. Students who choose certain distractors let teachers know where corrections are needed
8. Easy to grade

Disadvantages

1. Difficult to construct
2. Time-consuming to construct
3. Measure verbal-level learning
4. Do not measure problem-solving skills very well
5. Difficult to find adequate distractors
6. May be inappropriate for very young ages

Essay Questions

The essay question can be either an *extended-response type* or a *restricted-response type.* The *extended-response type* gives students almost free reign in answering the question. In contrast, the *restricted-response type* limits the length, organization, or nature of the answers.

Examples:

Extended-Response Type

What do you think the role of the school should be in promoting the health of eighth graders? Include classroom and nonclassroom activities.

Restricted-Response Type

Write out two advantages and two disadvantages of living a healthy lifestyle.

As can be seen above, extended-type questions requires students to decide what is most pertinent, how to organize the answer, and how much to write. This is good if the teacher wishes to evaluate content, organizational ability, expression of ideas, and the like. However, as a measure of factual material, essay questions are poor. Essay questions are also difficult to grade. Although the restricted type of essay question reduces these both of these limitations, it lacks the capability for organizational, expression, and coherency skill measurement. In other words, each has its own strengths and weaknesses, which are almost opposite one another. Therefore, selection depends largely on the nature of the learning assessment and/or performance objective.

The comparative advantages of essay and objective questions are shown in Table 5.2.

Methods of Appraising Nontest Procedures

If you were asked to name the most popular form of evaluation used by teachers today, what would your answer be? If it is paper-and-pencil knowledge tests, you are right. In many instances, this is the only form of evaluation used by teachers. Such an inflexible approach is unacceptable in health education. Health is a way of life, and knowledge is only one aspect of the health-educated person. To do the topic justice, it is necessary to assess student health practices and attitudes as well as knowledge. Following are several suggested approaches to the evaluation of health education at the elementary level.

An alert teacher can learn a great deal about a student by observing behaviors and reactions.

Table 5.2 Comparative Advantages of Essay and Objective Tests

Variable	Essay Test	Objective Test
Measurement ability	Good for complex learning, e.g., thinking skills. Inefficient for measuring factual knowledge. Good for abilities of selection, organization, writing and expression, problem-solving	Difficult to construct for measurement of complex learning. Efficient for measuring knowledge. Inefficient for organization, writing, expression, some problem-solving
Preparation	Easy	Difficult if done well
Course content sampling	Limited; only so many questions can be asked	Extensive; many questions covering many areas can be asked
Pupil flexibility in answering	Lots of flexibility in both how and what	Very restricted, prevents bluffing or digression from topic
Learning influence	Makes student think in broad terms, often going beyond immediate subject matter, including skills acquisition	Student thinks more about facts and knowledge; capable of making fine discriminations
Scoring	Difficult; recommend reading all answers and then starting reading over to assign grades	Easy
Reliability	Usually low	Generally very high if well designed

Source: Adapted from N.E. Gronlund, *Measurement and Evaluation in Teaching* 5th ed. (New York: Macmillan, 1985), p. 131.

Observation and Anecdotal Records

One of the easiest yet most meaningful forms of evaluation is observation. Actions do speak louder than words, and the observant teacher can perceive a great deal about a youngster's health practices and attitudes. The creative teacher also can foster situations that provide the opportunity to observe students' health behavior. By critically observing typical situations, teachers can determine if instruction has had any significant impact on students' health behavior.

The implications of this approach are far-reaching. Whenever beginning a health unit, the teacher decides what he or she will regard as a satisfactory change in student health behavior after the unit has been completed. Since the expected outcomes for each lesson plan are for the most part behaviorally stated, they offer the direction needed to determine the observable behavior for which the teacher might watch.

Let us consider a practical example. A teacher is undertaking a unit of study in nutrition with his fourth-grade class. One of the expected outcomes of a day's lesson is "Is capable of selecting a balanced meal." Once the instruction is complete, the teacher merely observes the quality of the eating practices exhibited by the students in the lunchroom. But due to the fact that cafeteria lunches purchased children are already balanced, it would be advantageous to reserve evaluation for the days when the youngsters bring their own lunches.

The possibilities for evaluation of this sort are unlimited. Every content area of elementary health education offers an opportunity for observation and evaluation. Perhaps the only drawback of observation is that it is subjective, thus prone to error and bias. However, effort can be made to clarify and define observation by knowing precisely what one is looking for. By adhering to the principles of evaluation and maintaining a critical and precise approach to what is being observed, the elementary school teacher can ascertain a great deal about the health practices of his or her students.

Anecdotal records are excellent in that they depict actual behavior. However, to make them worthwhile, it is recommended that the teacher (Gronlund, 1985)

1. Confine observations to behavioral areas that cannot be evaluated in other ways
2. Limit observation of all the students at any given time to just a few behaviors
3. Limit extensive observation of behavior to those pupils who need help the most.

Portfolios

As elementary and middle-school education shifts from traditional learning to skill-based and performance-based outcomes, different evaluation approaches are needed. Thus use of portfolios has been increasing. In essence, a portfolio is a learning résumé containing evidence of what a student knows and what he or she can do. As such, it fits nicely with the acquisition of health skills, attitudes, and knowledge.

The first task for a teacher is to determine the specific purpose of the portfolio. Then the teacher must clarify what constitutes appropriate evidence. Collins (1991) proposes four types of evidence or documentation. *Artifacts* are one type. In elementary or middle school, these could be a collection of magazine articles or pictures revolving around a specific health problem. The artifact should be an actual sample of the student's work.

A second type of evidence is reproductions of a usual classroom event, for example, a picture of a bulletin board completed by the student, or perhaps of a poster presentation. It could also be a videotape of student(s) cleaning up the environment.

Attestations, as evidence, comprise documents written about a student's work by a "third party." For example, a community agency may write a letter of thanks or congratulations to the student who participated in the environmental clean-up. A teacher could write a letter of commendation for the student's efforts in peer teaching.

The fourth source of evidence is productions prepared specifically for the portfolio to document knowledge and skills. A student could write about the trials and joys of serving on the school cafeteria committee, or as a member of Students Against Drunk Driving (SADD). Each document should have a caption explaining what the document is and how it demonstrates the skill or knowledge acquired. In other words, the caption justifies the inclusion of the document in the portfolio, and is necessary for proper evaluation. Cleary (1993) suggests that students could document something from each health education unit studied. Of course a similar approach could be used to document fulfillment of performance standards and learning assessments for the National Health Education Standards.

The use of portfolios is evolving. Consequently, some teachers find them to be of great value while others see them as busy work. Some of the concerns raised about portfolios are (Herman, 1992): How are different reports, videos, or pictures weighted and compared? How does one measure student reflections or journal entries? Is the portfolio rated overall or as individual pieces of evidence? Are teachers trained to evaluate this way? Such pitfalls can be overcome with careful planning and forethought. To assist teachers, a private software company worked with the Michigan Department of Education to create the Electronic Student Portfolio (1992). Its documents can be digitized and scanned for export to diskettes. The Grady Profile (1991) is another computerized software program capable of storing text, sound, and images, including video clips.

It is recommended that a portfolio team be established, and consist of the school health educator, school nurses, and appropriate supervisory personnel to ensure broad input (Cleary, 1993). The portfolio can be valuable in assessing selected skills and knowledge. However, it is not intended to stand alone, so it should be combined with additional approaches (tests) to arrive at overall evaluation.

Conferences

A one-to-one conference can be most effective for learning about a youngster's health attitudes and practices. A warm, empathic teacher is capable of establishing rapport with students, becoming both friend and confidant. Such a relationship is conducive to learning about students' health behavior. It also provides an excellent opportunity to determine if there are any hidden problems. Often a student refrains from discussing his or her feelings or behavior in front of the class for fear of being embarrassed. Likewise, teachers should be careful not to raise any question about a student's health behavior in front of the class if it might prove embarrassing for the youngster. Such inquiries are better left to individual conferences. The teacher's job is to assist young people in developing their maximum health potential. If individual conferences can contribute to this goal, they are worthy of implementation. Based on the results of such a conference, the teacher will, ideally, be able to evaluate any problems and proceed accordingly.

Self-Evaluation

Student input is becoming more of an issue with each passing day, and rightfully so. A student who is allowed to be a part of the evaluation process cannot help getting involved. When measurement is developed by each student or as a result of a group endeavor, it is likely to be much more meaningful to the students.

Primary-grade children are entirely capable of developing simple checklists or rating scales for evaluating individual or group health behavior. The teacher simply acts as the class facilitator in this case. Once the instrument is developed, the students complete it, rating their own health behavior.

Intermediate and junior high school students find it more challenging to develop their own expected outcomes, learning experiences, and accountability techniques. Much to the amazement of many teachers, students are often tougher on themselves than the teacher would have been. Motivation can also be greatly enhanced. Care should be taken when such an approach is pursued, however, that students build in feasible and attainable accountability factors. It is easy for students to become overzealous and set their sights too high. The teacher's role is one of mediator and guide.

Do not be surprised if your first attempt at introducing self-evaluation falls far short of your expectations. This will be true especially if the students have never attempted it before. Keep in mind that students are trained to expect direction from the teacher. When the roles are reversed, most students are overwhelmed at first and respond rather erratically.

However, the more students practice such an approach, the more proficient they become with self-evaluation. In the long run, the benefits in terms of motivation and personal satisfaction far outweigh the detriments of any initial confusion and uncertainty. Modern psychology and democratic social values both hold that important educational strides can be achieved by eliciting student participation in evaluation. The present trend in education will continue to place more and more responsibility on students for evaluating their own achievement. If such endeavors are taken seriously by both the teachers and students, and every effort is made to make them as valid as possible, there is no question that self-evaluation can be most desirable.

Checklists and Rating Scales

Checklists and rating scales are excellent tools of evaluation, especially when used to supplement self-evaluation. In this case, they serve as self-administered inventories and can easily be developed to assist in the evaluation of health practices. Use of a checklist or rating scale makes assessment more objective. Hence order and continuity are added to the evaluation process.

Health checklists and rating scales are similar in nature. Both are designed to seek an indication of the quality and quantity of a student's health behavior. The main difference lies in degrees of measurement. More precisely, the checklist requires only a simple yes or no answer. That is, the respondent either is or is not performing a particular health practice. Rating scales allow more latitude in responding. The factor of degrees of behavior is introduced. Often a straight yes or no response cannot completely or correctly answer a question. Thus rating scales attempt to address such a possibility by adding more response categories. A traffic safety education rating scale for the primary grades shown in Figure 5.6 is an example.

	Always	Usually	Seldom	Never
1. I cross streets only at marked crosswalks and refrain from jaywalking.	______	______	______	______
2. When I do cross at a marked intersection, I am sure that all traffic is stopped and that I can make the entire crossing safely.	______	______	______	______
3. I obey "walk" and "don't walk" signals.	______	______	______	______
4. I obey the safety patrol and traffic officers.	______	______	______	______
5. I walk my bicycle across intersections.	______	______	______	______
6. I do not play in the street.	______	______	______	______
7. I enter and get out of cars on the curb side.	______	______	______	______
8. If I must walk in the road, I do so facing traffic.	______	______	______	______
9. If I am out at night and near traffic, I wear white or carry a light.	______	______	______	______

FIGURE 5.6 Example of a Rating Scale for Traffic Safety Education

If all of the statements in a rating scale are expressed positively, numerical values can be assigned to the response alternatives. This quantitative aspect can be helpful in the evaluation process. The category "always" can then be assigned three points; "usually," two points; "seldom," one point; and "never," zero. A total scale can then be determined by simply adding up the values for each response. With "always" being the most desirable response, the best possible score is 27 points. Teachers and students together can establish the ranges for evaluation purposes. Using the traffic safety example, they might look something like this:

> A perfect score of 27 points: Excellent traffic safety practices
>
> 22 to 26 points: Good traffic safety practices, but room for improvement
>
> 21 and below: You are an excellent candidate for an accident; you will probably have one unless you quickly improve your traffic safety practices.

Although the uses of checklists and rating scales are most important, only the most naive teacher would ask students to engage in them and then use the results for grading purposes. Such an approach would only encourage students to be dishonest in their responses, and both students' and teacher's time would be wasted. Thus, students should be made well aware of the fact that checklists and rating scales will not be graded (except, perhaps, for completion credit) and that they are designed to assess personal health practices so that students can benefit from recognition of their level of well-being. However, teachers can derive some input in terms of secondary evaluation by taking note of the responses of the students. That is, the results do reflect on the effect of the teaching that has preceded the checklist or rating scale.

Any evaluation should be twofold. First, the teacher can ascertain the status of certain of the students' health practices. In light of these findings, future instruction can be altered if necessary. Second, each child is afforded an opportunity to evaluate his or her own health practices and, ideally, make adjustments where necessary.

Evaluation and Problem-Based Learning

As discussed in Chapter 4, problem-based learning (PBL) is applicable to skill acquisition as well as knowledge aquisition. Since, if done properly, it is a highly focused strategy, specific learning assessments can be written for it. Consequently, progress toward completion of the performance indicator(s) and learning assessments can be measured—both knowledge acquisition and skill acquisition. From a knowledge standpoint, appropriate test items need to be constructed. From a skill perspective, if not measurable by test means, then an observation grid could be constructed. Figure 5.7 illustrates a generic grid for evaluating some basic problem-solving skills.

If a teacher's intention is to be highly specific or evaluate several different learning assessments, a grid can be designed for these purposes. For example, remember Jon, the middle-school student who didn't know whether to smoke a cigarette offered by his friend Sean? (See Chapter 4.)

The National Health Education Standards and performance indicators for this problem-based strategy were Standard 3 with performance indicator 1, and Standard 5 with performance indicators 1 and 6, all at the grades 5–8 level. The learning assessments are listed on the evaluation grid in Figure 5.8. Note that different skills are being evaluated in this grid than those in the more generic grid in Figure 5.7.

With such a grid, the teacher can use observation and anecdotal records to ascertain strengths and weaknesses for individual students as well as for the class as a whole. Since it is unlikely that all students could role-play the part of Jon in this scenario, data would be accumulated over several PBL exercises to develop a "picture" of each student. Depending upon the grid used, information can be collected on specific skills (decision-making, critical thinking, assertiveness, refusal, communication, conflict resolution, problem-solving, inquiry, and related others) and on content.

In summary, problem-based learning is an appropriate means to evaluate the acquisition of skills. Based upon the learning assessments, the teacher determines which skills are to be observed and then keeps a record of strengths and weak-

Date:____________ Grade:______

National Health Education Standard #______

Performance Indicator(s): Grade______ Numbers ______, ______, ______, ______,

Learning Assessment(s):

____

____

____

Scoring Key: 1 = Needs improvement; 2 = Average; 3 = Very good; 4 = Excellent

Name/ assessment area	Ability to recognize the problem	Ability to generate possible solutions	Ability to use inquiry skills	Ability to apply information to problem	Ability to synthesize	Ability to put it all together
Teresa T.						
Willie W.						
Paige C.						

FIGURE 5.7 Generic Evaluation Grid Using Problem-Based Learning Strategies

nesses. In this fashion, teaching can be modified to address the class as a whole, or an individual or individuals, depending on the results of the evaluation.

Implications for Elementary and Middle-School Teachers

Summary Issues

1. Evaluation is a comprehensive, on-going process involving a variety of techniques, and is linked to Standards, performance indicators, and learning assessments.
2. Measurement answers the question, How much? and involves assigning numerals (or letters) to criteria according to a preconceived set of rules.
3. Testing is the process of using tests.
4. There are several reasons for evaluation in health education instruction. Some are diagnosis or classification, accountability, grading, motivation, and feedback to parents and students.
5. The National Health Education Standards, performance indicators, and teacher-constructed learning assessments are an integral part of evaluation in health education.
6. The National Health Education Standards provide a framework for health knowledge and skills; the performance indicators serve as a blueprint; and the learning assessments refine the performance indicators and can be used to incorporate content areas and CDC risk behaviors.
7. Test procedures include short-answer items, alternative-response items, matching items, multiple-choice items, and essay questions.
8. The nontest evaluation methods reviewed are observation and anecdotal records, conferences, self-evaluation, checklists, and rating scales.
9. Problem-based learning lends itself to the evaluation of both knowledge and skill acquisition.

Date: ____________________ Grade: 6

National Health Education Standards #3, #5 Content area: Tobacco Smoking

Performance Indicator(s): Grades 5–8 Numbers 3(1), 5(1, 6)

Learning Assessment(s):

1. Explains the adverse effects of smoking and how he/she feels about it
2. Through role-playing, communicates information and feelings clearly
3. Says "no" clearly in role-play
4. Looks firm (body language) to support what he or she is saying in the role-play scenario
5. In role-playing, suggests an alternative behavior to smoking
6. Communicates desire to remain friends

Scoring Key: 1 = Needs improvement; 2 = Average; 3 = Very good; 4 = Excellent

Name	Explains Adverse Effects of Smoking and Feelings about It	Communicates (Smoking Effects) Clearly in Role-Play	Says No Clearly in Role-Play	Body Language Supportive of Verbal Communication	Suggests Appropriate Alternative Behavior	Clearly Indicates Continuance of Friendship
Teresa T.						
Willie W.						
Paige C.						

FIGURE 5.8 **Example of an Evaluation Grid Using a Problem-Based Learning Strategy**

Teacher Ramifications

In regard to evaluation, a teacher should:

1. Acquire the skills for test construction either through in-service training or by completing a class on test construction
2. Relate the developmental skills of students to evaluation techniques and select the techniques most appropriate for the students
3. Use evaluation for improvement in students, teaching, and the program
4. Employ the National Health Education Standards in evaluation
5. Write learning assessments to specify what students should know or be able to do
6. Use grading in a positive, rather than punitive, way
7. Evaluate the acquisition of skills as well as cognitive learning

References

Cleary, M.J. Using portfolios to assess student performance in school health education *Journal of School Health* 63,9(1993):377–381.

Collins, A. Portfolios for biology teacher assessment, *J Sch Pers Eval Educ* 5,2(1991):147–167.

Electronic Student Portfolio. Technical Edge, Swartz, MI, 1992.

Grady, E.L. *The Real Picture: Portfolio-Based Assessment.* Aurbach and Associates, St. Louis, 1991.

Gronlund, N.E. *Measurement and Evaluation in Teaching* 5th ed. Macmillan, New York, 1985.

Herman, J.L., Aschbacker, P.R., & Winters, L. *A Practical Guide to Alternative Assessment. Association for Supervision and Curriculum Development,* Alexandria, VA, 1992.

Joint Committee on National Health Education Standards. *National Health Education Standards: Achieving Health Literacy.* 1995. Copies may be obtained through the American School Health Association, Association for the Advancement of Health Education, or the American Cancer Society.

PART TWO

Content, Strategies, and Skills

CHAPTER 6
Growth, Development, and Personal Health and Fitness

CHAPTER 7
Nutrition

CHAPTER 8
Illness and Disease

CHAPTER 9
Safety, Injury Prevention, and Emergency Care

CHAPTER 10
Emotional Well-Being and Stress Reduction

CHAPTER 11
Alcohol, Tobacco, and Other Drugs

CHAPTER 12
Family, Relationships, and Sexuality

CHAPTER 13
Violence Prevention

CHAPTER 14
Consumer Health

CHAPTER 15
Environmental Conservation

CHAPTER 16
The Human Body

6

Growth, Development, and Personal Health and Fitness

Upon completion of this chapter, you should be able to:

- *Identify appropriate developmental tasks*
- *Explain the terms and principles of growth and development*
- *Describe the physical, mental, social, and moral development of students during their elementary and middle-school years*
- *Explain the role of responsibility in personal health*
- *Identify symptoms of vision, hearing, dental, posture, and sleep problems and offer suggestions to ameliorate them*
- *Identify the implications of child growth, development, and personal health for the teacher*

Holistic Development—An Overview

Elementary school children develop in many ways—physically, emotionally, socially, and morally. Gradually, barring any major problems, they mature into healthy adults. Teachers are fortunate to be able to help children structure the foundations of life. Watching and helping children develop into unique, well-adjusted, successful beings have to be among the greatest rewards and joys of being a teacher.

While the rewards are inherent, however, observing development is demanding on the teacher. It requires sensitivity and keen awareness since the physical, emotional, social, and moral aspects of development occur simultaneously and quickly. From a purely educational perspective, each one of these developments is crucial in determining lesson content, teaching methodology, and the like. Missing the target by being too high, too wide, or too low reduces learning opportunities. From a health standpoint, recognition of development is important in order to ascertain susceptibility and vulnerability to risk factors. Table 6.1 illustrates some of the growth and development characteristics of children, specifically, physical, emotional, social, and intellectual characteristics.

As teachers observe children's growth and development, they note that children get sick less and less as they progress into late childhood. They take better care of themselves also, as they learn safe ways to live. When problems do arise, they can often be readily corrected with early acknowledgment and intervention.

During their elementary school years, boys and girls try out their abilities and interests and begin to gain self-confidence. Although they still need and count on the friendly care and backing of their parents and family, they manage more and more of their own affairs. Teachers should remember that although their students become more and more self-reliant, they still need attention, love, and sympathy.

Children love to play. Play not only makes friends but also expresses self, maintains physical fitness, and clarifies the values of life. It is through physical activities and play that children acquire the good balance, coordination, gracefulness, muscular strength, and physical stamina that are the foundations of adult health and life. Children can't get enough of games that emphasize physical alertness—chasing, climbing, dodging. Swinging, whether from a safe swing or a rope, gives children a chance to feel and identify their kinesthetic senses. Tag and other games in which there is a chance to avoid capture appeal to children. Turning handsprings; balancing on a beam; bouncing a ball; and catching, throwing, and batting a ball are all physical skills demanding control of big skeletal muscles.

When playing, children create their own rules and insist on playing by their rules. They enforce the moral virtues of honesty and fair play much more harshly than a teacher does. Their play entails trying out values by which to play and live. These games and trying-out experiences are critical, for they have great developmental meaning and pay-offs in maturation.

Once children, especially those in the primary grades, have acquired good control over their bodies, they have a great deal of energy for learning and social skills. Their efforts in learning to read and write demand exact adjustments of the smaller muscles and the development of hand-eye coordination.

School-age children delight in putting their hands to work. With initiative and fervor, children

Table 6.1 Growth and Development Characteristics of Children

Grades K–3, Ages 5–8

Physical Characteristics	Needs
Growth relatively slow. Increase in large-muscle coordination, beginning of development of small-muscle control. Bones growing. Nose grows larger. Permanent teeth appearing or replacing primary teeth; lower part of face more prominent. Hungry at short intervals; may overeat and become fat. Enjoys active play—climbing, jumping, running. Susceptible to fatigue and limits self. Visual acuity reaches normal. Susceptible to respiratory and communicable diseases.	To develop large-muscle control through motor skills. To have play space and materials. To use instructional tools and equipment geared to stage of development. To establish basic health habits: toileting, eating, covering nose and mouth with cough, etc. To have snack time and opportunity to develop social graces. To have plenty of sleep and rest, and exercise interspersed with rest. To have health examinations and follow-up. To have visual and auditory checks. To have dental attention.
Suggested Activities: Vigorous games emphasizing outdoor play with basic movement patterns and skills as well as singing games and rhythms.	

Emotional Characteristics	Needs
Self-centered, desires immediate attention to his/her problem—wants to be first. Sensitive about being left out. Sensitive about ridicule, criticism, or loss of prestige. Easily aroused emotionally. Can take responsibility but needs adult supervision. Parent image strong; also identifies with teacher. Expresses likes and dislikes readily. Questioning attitude about sex differences.	To receive encouragement, recognition, ample praise, patience, adult support. To express inner feelings, anxieties and fears. To feel secure, loved, wanted, accepted (at home and at school). To be free from pressure to achieve beyond capabilities. To have a consistent, cooperatively planned program of classroom control. Must have guidance. To develop self-confidence. To have some immediate desirable satisfactions. To know limitations within which he or she can operate effectively. To develop realistic expectations of self.

Social Characteristics	Needs
Lack of interest in personal grooming. Engages in imitative play. Friendly, frank, sometimes aggressive, "bossy," assertive. Generally tolerant of race, economic status, etc. Gradually more socially oriented and adjusted. Boys and girls play together as sex equals, but aware of sex differences.	To have satisfactory peer relationships; receive group approval. To learn the importance of sharing, planning, working and playing together—both boys and girls. To have help in developing socially acceptable behavior. To learn to assume some responsibility; to have opportunities to initiate activities, to lead. To work independently and in groups. To accept sex role. To develop an appreciation of social values, such as honesty, sportsmanship, etc.

continued

Table 6.1 Growth and Development Characteristics of Children–*continued*

Grades K–3, Ages 5–8—continued

Intellectual Characteristics	Needs
Varied intellectual growth and ability of children. Interested in things that move, bright colors, dramatizations, rhythmics, making collections. Interested in the present, not the future. Learns best through active participation in concrete, meaningful situations. Can abide by safety rules. Wants to know "why." Attention span short.	To experience frequent success and learn to accept failure when it occurs. To have concrete learning experiences and direct participation. To be in a rich, stable, challenging environment. To have time to adjust to new experiences and new situations. To learn to follow through to completion. To develop a love for learning. To learn without developing feelings of hostility. To communicate effectively.

Grades 4–6, Ages 8–11

Physical Characteristics	Needs
Growth slow and steady. Girls begin to forge ahead of boys in height and weight. Extremities begin to lengthen toward end of this period. Muscle coordination improving. Continued small muscle development. Bones growing, vulnerable to injury. Permanent dentition continues. Malocclusion may be a problem. Appetite good, increasing interest in food. Boundless energy. Tires easily. Visual acuity normal. Menarche possible toward end of this period.	To develop and improve coordination of both large and small muscles. To have plenty of activities and games which will develop body control, strength, endurance, and skills-stunts (throwing, catching, running, bicycles, skates). To have careful supervision of games appropriate to strength and developmental needs; protective equipment. To have competitive activity with children of comparable size. To have sleep, rest, well-balanced meals. To have health examinations and follow-up. To have visual and auditory checks. To have dental attention.

Suggested activities: More formal games with emphasis on body mechanics.

Emotional Characteristics	Needs
Seeks approval of peer group. Desire to succeed. Enthusiastic, noisy, imaginative, desire to explore. Negativistic (early part of period). Begins to accept responsibility for clothing and behavior. Increasingly anxious about family and possible tragedy. Increasing self-consciousness. Sex hostility. Becomes "modest" but not too interested in details of sex.	To begin seriously to gain a realistic image of self and appreciate uniqueness of personality. To be recognized for individual worth; to feel self-assurance and self-esteem. To receive encouragement and affection; to be understood and appreciated. To exercise self-control. To talk about problems and receive reasonable explanations. To have questions answered.

Grades 4–6, Ages 8–11—continued

Social Characteristics	Needs
Learns to cooperate better in group planning and group play and abides by group decisions. Interested in competitive activities and prestige. Competition keen. Begins to show qualities of leadership. Developing interest in appearance. Strong sense of fair play. Belongs to a gang or secret club; loyal to group. Close friendships with members of own sex. Separate play for boys and girls.	To be recognized and accepted by peer groups; receive social approval. To have relationships with adults which give feelings of security and acceptance. To assume responsibilities, have increased opportunities for independent actions and decisions. To develop appreciation for others and their rights. To learn to get along with others and accept those different from self.

Intellectual Characteristics	Needs
Likes to talk and express ideas. High potential of learning—in science, adventure, the world. Eager to acquire skills. Wide range of interests; curious, wants to experiment. Goals are immediate. Demands consistency. Generally reliable about following instructions. Attention span short.	To experiment, explore, solve problems, challenges, use initiative, select, plan, evaluate. To receive individual help in skill areas without harmful or undue pressure. To have opportunities for creative self-expression. To have a rich environment of materials and the opportunity to explore it. To participate in concrete, real-life situations. To be able to accept one's self with strengths and weaknesses.

Grades 7–9, Ages 11–14

Physical Characteristics	Needs
Accelerated, uneven growth. Individual differences most prominent; girls continue rapid growth, are taller and heavier than boys in early period. Muscular growth toward adult size begins toward end of period. Variable coordination. Bones growing, vulnerable to injury. Onset of puberty generally at the beginning of this age range for girls and at the end for boys. Dental caries common. Permanent dentition—28 teeth. Malocclusion may be present. Appetite ravenous but may be capricious. Enjoys vigorous play. Tires easily, particularly girls. Visual problems increase. Variations in development of secondary sexual characteristics. Menarche. Skin problems, voice changes, etc. Reproductive organs growing.	To have adequate nourishment for growth spurt and daily energy. To understand developmental changes of adolescence. To recognize wide physical differences as normal. To have good protective equipment in games. To have physical activity interspersed with rest. To have health examinations and follow-up. To have visual and auditory checks. To have dental attention.

Suggested Activities: Competitive games with only moderate fatigue or emotional stress, yet involving quickness and skill.

continued

Table 6.1 Growth and Development Characteristics of Children–*continued*

Grades 7–9, Ages 11–14—continued

Emotional Characteristics	Needs
Emotional instability; sudden and deep swings in mood. Strong feelings of like and dislike, negative and positive attitudes. Sensitive, self-critical but cannot take criticism. Overanxious about health; thinks s/he has a gruesome disease. Over-concerned about physical and emotional changes. Striving for independence from adults. Hero worship. Searching for sensational emotional experiences. Self-conscious. Shows growing restraint in expressing feelings. Unique sense of humor.	To express volatile emotions, grief, anger, disappointment, likes, dislikes. To assume responsibility for own conduct. To achieve more independence. To feel secure, wanted, loved, trusted, adequate, capable. To have privacy respected. To exercise self-discipline. To experience success, receive individual recognition. To identify with a friendly adult (teacher, parent, older friend). To be alone occasionally. To feel the support, firm guidance and assurance of an adult. To differentiate between reality and fiction, fact and fiction.

Social Characteristics	Needs
Interested in competitive sports as participant and spectator. Developing good sportsmanship. Socially insecure. Very peer-conscious. Desires freedom with security. Argues against authority but wants it. Sensitive to appearance (clothes, skin). Imitative fads in clothing, speech, etc. Wishes to conform to clearly defined pattern of good school citizenship. Assumes responsibility for personal and group conduct. Beginning to discriminate right from wrong. Aware of opposite sex, chivalry, rivalry, teasing. Separating into groups by sex: boys into large groups, girls into small groups, then gradually mixed groups.	To see one's self as a socially accepted, important person. To relate to members of the same and opposite sex. To receive recognition from and acceptance by peers. To work and play with different age groups. To recognize the importance of leadership as well as being a follower. To have congenial social settings.

Intellectual Characteristics	Needs
Eager to learn, curious, alert exploring. Reads widely. Wider range of abilities and interests. Wants to succeed. Wants precise assignments and meaningful experiences. Skeptical, demands facts. Unrealistic in passing judgment. Overconfident in own information. Increasing span of attention and concentration.	To determine individual motives, goals, standards and ideals. To satisfy curiosity, desire to know; to experiment. To express one's self verbally, manually and through activities such as dance, music, clubs, debate, etc. To appreciate the value of work and products of work. To know the satisfaction of achieving to the extent of one's ability.

Source: From J. W. Lochner, Growth and development characteristics, *A Pocketguide to Health Problems in School,* Physical Activities (Kent, OH: American School Health Association, 1981).

construct things—carts, kites, airplanes—weave, tie knots, and cut out paper dolls, with varying degrees of success. Intermediate-level children are very industrious. They like to work and to do things, finding it emotionally satisfying to accomplish things with their minds and bodies. It is through work that children discover how to become successful, feel good about themselves, and feel confident enough to try again. In both work and play, they learn that losing isn't the end of the world.

Children try out new things. Experimentation challenges them to try out all their senses. They discover the tastes of new foods and sweet grass, and the scents of perfume, flowers, and pine needles. They burrow into snow and haystacks and fling themselves down slides. They enjoy going barefoot and feeling mud squish between their toes. They attack novel computer games and lessons with reckless abandon, leaving adults in a state of wonderment.

Children observe parents, teachers, and adolescents taking medicines, smoking tobacco and marijuana, drinking alcoholic beverages, fighting, and ending relationships. Such observations arouse their curiosity, often motivating them to discover for themselves what it's like to engage in such behavior. Teachers must distinguish between behavior based on natural curiosity and that which is high-risk behavior that leads to education and health deficits.

Children's holistic development is founded on their need to (1) fulfill biological, safety, social, ego, and intellectual needs; and (2) develop skills that allow them to fulfill these basic needs. In essence, children attain optimal well-being when they develop skills that allow them to fulfill these basic needs. Conversely, children unable to develop skills to fulfill most of their basic health needs suffer from minor illnesses and personality disorders. They are unable to become effective learners or succeed in adult life.

Developmental Tasks

The preceding generalizations about the development of elementary and middle-school children reflect a holistic developmental perspective. Holistic development is affected by not only a child's nutrition, genetic potentials, physical activity, and physical environment, but the social milieu, too. Social and peer group pressures greatly influence children's behavior and habits. One such behavioral conditioner is the sociocultural environment. A culture creates aspirations: the urges or inclinations to learn to read and write, ride a bicycle or skateboard, use a computer, play team sports, drink soft drinks, chew gum, drink beer, smoke cigarettes, and so on.

As children grow and develop on all fronts, they must complete certain developmental tasks. According to Havighurst (1953, p. 12), "A developmental task is a task which arises at or about a certain period of time in the life of the individual, successful achievement of which leads to his [or her] happiness and to success with later tasks, while failure leads to unhappiness in the individual, disapproval by society, and difficulty with later tasks."

The developmental tasks of elementary and middle-school children can be summarized as follows:

1. Learning necessary physical skills for ordinary games and activities
2. Building wholesome attitudes toward oneself as a growing organism
3. Learning to get along with peers
4. Learning appropriate masculine or feminine roles
5. Developing fundamental skills in reading, writing, and calculating
6. Developing concepts necessary for everyday learning
7. Developing a conscience, morality, and a scale of values
8. Achieving personal independence
9. Developing attitudes toward social groups and institutions

Developmental tasks arise from (1) the physiological process of maturation, (2) social expectations, and (3) the child's personal values and aspirations. Some tasks arise mainly as a result of physical maturation, such as learning to walk, control elimination, skip, throw and catch a ball, and write. Other tasks develop mainly from cultural pressures: learning to read, participate as a responsible citizen in society, and assume appropriate gender roles. Still others grow out of personal values, for example, choosing and preparing for a vocation. Most, however, arise from all three forces working together.

Growth and Development: Terms and Principles

Definition of Terms

Three terms—growth, development, and maturity—are often used synonymously to describe the progress of a child toward adulthood. In fact, the terms are different but inseparable; none takes place alone.

Growth refers to quantitative changes, or increases in size and structure. It indicates actual increase in size of either a part of the body or the whole organism. A child grows in height and weight, and his or her brain increases in size.

Development, by contrast, refers to changes that are qualitative in nature. Development, as an organization of all the parts that growth and differentiation have produced, implies the overall process of change. An increase in height is growth; an increase of small-muscle coordination in the fingers is development. Development depends in part on physical maturation—growth. But development may also refer to emotional and social behavior.

Maturity marks the end of growth and development. However, when applied to children, it is used to connote potential. It is most often used to identify that process of inner growth and development (called *maturation*) by which an individual moves toward the attainment of his or her uppermost physical, emotional, intellectual, and social potentials. It can be likened to ripening. Maturity also refers to growth and development that have reached their ceiling or that are greater than expected for a child at a given age. Thus a five-year-old child who resembles a seven-year-old in behavior is said to be "mature for his or her age." The term may be used to describe either growth or development at any stage. For example, a child's ability to control elimination is dependent on development of the sphincter muscles. When these are fully developed, at about 3 years, a child can begin to control elimination like other individuals.

The complex processes of growth, development, and maturation should be viewed as products of heredity, environment, self-concept, and cultural expectations. When a child is mature enough physically, emotionally, and socially, she or he is also ready to learn. Learning occurs most efficiently when a child is sufficiently mature for a particular learning experience.

Principles of Growth and Development

All growth and developmental processes in children, when studied in detail over a long time, follow basic patterns. These patterns reflect the physical, emotional (psychological), social, intellectual, and behavioral traits of the whole child. All normal children tend to follow a general sequence of growth and development, which is characteristic of the species of human beings in general and their cultural group in particular. Development follows a pattern that is little influenced by experience. That is, a child matures when he or she is ready to mature. Such general developmental patterns are referred to as *principles*.

Teachers should use these principles as guidelines for understanding children, their growth and development, what to expect of them, and when to expect it, as well as for handling children effectively. The following principles should be helpful to teachers:

1. *Growth is patterned.* Although some children mature early and others late, each child has a unique pattern that unfolds at a characteristic rate.
2. *Growth is sequential.* Growth follows an orderly and predictable sequence, which in general is the same for all individuals. When age differentials are ignored, the growth pattern for boys and girls is the same. One stage leads to the next. Deviations from the sequence provide clues to growth difficulties.
3. *Growth is cyclic.* Rapid growth is usually followed by a period of slow, steady

growth and development. These cycles are readily apparent in the curve of the growth of the body as a whole. Human life proceeds by stages. Each stage can be distinguished by a dominant feature that gives the period its unity and its uniqueness.

4. *Developmental rates vary.* Developmental rates are different for boys and girls. After age ten, the growth rate for girls changes, becoming about two years ahead of that for boys. The tempo of development is uneven. The feet, hands, and nose, for example, reach their maximum developmental level early in adolescence, whereas the lower parts of the face and shoulders are slower in reaching theirs. Likewise, the heart, liver, and digestive systems grow slowly in childhood but rapidly during the early adolescent years.
5. *Developmental patterns show wide individual differences.* Each child's growth and development are unique. Children reach puberty at different ages. Because of genetic influences, each part of the body has its own particular rate of growth and development. Each child follows a predictable pattern in a way and at a rate that are unique. Physical development depends partly on heredity and partly on environmental factors, such as food, emotional stress, and so on. Personality development is influenced by attitudes and social relationships.
6. *Each stage of development has characteristic traits.* Each body system develops at its own rate. Each body trait has its own unique developmental rate and characteristics, helping to identify a child's behavioral, chronological, and maturational levels. A developmental pattern is affected not so much by what the child can accomplish as by the way in which he or she behaves.
7. *Development is a product of the interaction of the child with his or her environment.* Growth and development are genetically, socioculturally, and environmentally determined.
8. *The body tends to maintain a state of equilibrium,* called homeostasis. The body strives to maintain a constant internal environment despite changing conditions, whether internal or external.
9. *There is unity in growth patterns.* The child grows physically, emotionally, socially, morally, and intellectually as a whole being. All aspects of the child's development are interrelated. The stage of maturity of one trait affects the development of others. There is a marked relationship between sexual maturing and patterns of interest and behavior.
10. *Development is continuous.* Cellular growth continues from conception to death. Likewise, emotional, social, spiritual, cultural, creative, and intellectual potentials all exist and may be developed to high levels approaching self-actualization. Because development is continuous, what happens at one stage has an influence on the stage that follows.
11. *Development proceeds from the general to the specific.* A baby sits before she or he walks. A child learns words that are abstract, like *doggie,* before he or she calls the dog a specific name, like *Brownie.*
12. *Development comes from both maturation and learning.* Development of physical, emotional, and intellectual traits, for example, comes partly from an intrinsic maturing of those traits and partly from exercise and experience on the part of the child.

Physical Development and Growth Cycles

Growth in height and weight reflects general physical progress in the development of body systems and processes. It is an indication of progress toward the child's optimal well-being and maturity. But height and weight are only outward indicators of growth and development, for there is no correlation between body size and well-being. At the

Rate of physical maturity is an individual process, as exhibited by this group of middle-school girls at recess.

same time, the organs and body systems within the body are also increasing in size and developing their unique functions at their own speed.

Increases in height and weight progress at a slow rate for ages 6 to 12. Weight increases average approximately four to seven pounds a year, whereas height increases two or more inches a year (Figure 6.1). From ages 5 to 10 years, boys are generally taller than girls. Then there is a short period, from ages 10 to 14, when girls exceed boys in height. In general, children show a much steadier rate of gain in height than they do in weight.

Growth and development are rhythmic, not regular. A child does not gain a given number of pounds annually, or grow a given number of inches. Studies of growth and development have revealed that there are four distinct periods of growth, two characterized by slow growth and two by rapid growth. From birth to 2 years, there is rapid growth. This is followed by a period of slow growth up to puberty, or sexual maturing, which usually begins between the eighth and eleventh years. From then until 15 or 16 years, there is once again rapid growth. This is turn is followed by a period of fairly abrupt tapering off of growth until full adult maturity.

Increments of Growth and Development

The measurement of various body organs at regular intervals during their periods of growth and development reveals certain trends in the rate of change common to all normal children. Such measurements have been plotted on a graph, shown in Figure 6.2, to provide a visual summary of the growth and development of the various parts of the body.

Four types of growth curves—A,B,C,D—are illustrated in the figure. Curve A represents growth and development of the lymphoid type (thymus, tonsils, adenoids); curve B, that of the central nervous system (brain, nerves); curve C, that of the general type (body as a whole, respiratory, digestive, muscular, skeletal, excretory, and cardiovascular systems); curve D, that of the reproductive, or genital, system. The growth curves for height and weight resemble curve C in the figure.

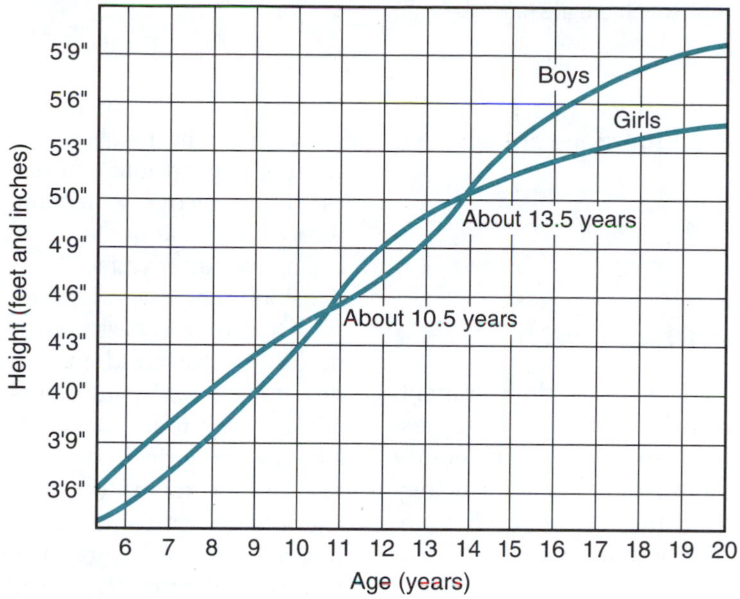

FIGURE 6.1 Average Height of 6- to 19-Year-Old Boys and Girls

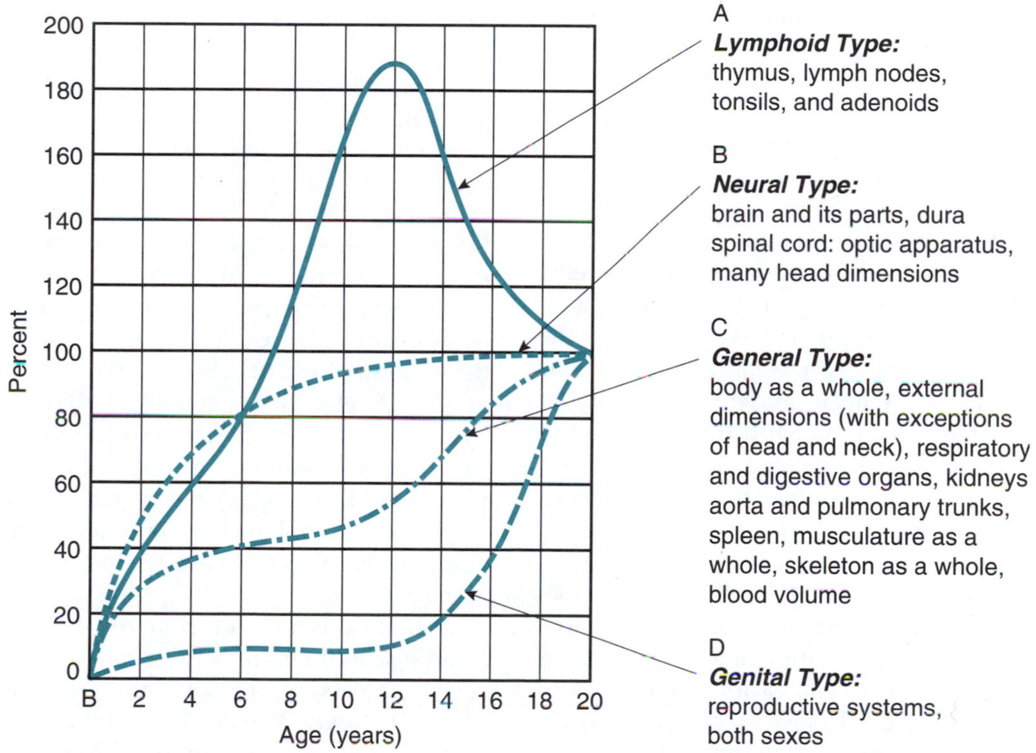

FIGURE 6.2 Curves of Organ Growth Drawn to a Common Scale by Computing Their Values at Successive Ages in Terms of Their Total (Average) Postnatal Increments

In general, the body systems increase in size and develop their unique functions at their own rate of speed.

Mental-Emotional Development and Growth

Like other areas of growth and development, mental-emotional traits are acquired in a progressive fashion. Preschool and early elementary school children desire immediate attention as they watch the world revolve around them. They are easily aroused emotionally and require frequent academic successes.

Cognitive development at this age involves the ever-increasing ability to infer and to build upon prior experience. By the end of middle years, children are quite adept at interpreting metaphors and analogies. They gradually learn to use inference to understand hidden meanings, double entendres, irony, and paradox.

By age five, most children have a basic vocabulary and basic skills in grammar and syntax. Between five years of age and adolescence, they learn that language is a powerful tool not only for academics but for social development, too. They learn figures of speech that equate two elements from different experiences. For example, very young elementary school students may take the comment, "Mr. Smith is a bear today" literally. Second grade elementary students are likely to know something is wrong with the sentence but may not know how to change it. By third and fourth grades, students understand the real meaning of the statement.

Storage and retrieval of information changes throughout the elementary and middle-school years, too. Both become more expedient as school demands greater interpretation of new experiences and development of critical learning skills. As students learn more, they also learn a series of ways to retain the new information (Levine et al., 1992).

While temper tantrums are somewhat acceptable in the toddler, this is not the case for a school-aged child. Children need to learn how to handle success and failure, and too much of either can lead to a problem. The emotional pitfalls of frustration, disappointment, and loss are challenges to most children. Teachers need to let them know what is appropriate emotional expression as well as teach recovery techniques. In progressing through the elementary years, students need to learn how to "save face" in a constructive fashion, a fashion that engenders self-esteem.

Of course self-esteem in the elementary and middle-school child may fluctuate from day to day, if not hour by hour. It is common for children at these ages to be in turmoil at least momentarily as they struggle to reevaluate themselves. It is healthy for them to test themselves. However, every teacher must be vigilant for those who shift into a downward spiral. While data are still being collected, it appears that positive self-esteem is crucial to both school performance and health status (e.g., avoidance of gateway drugs).

Social Development

During the first few years of life, a child's universe is home and family. Entry into preschool and school presents the need to develop several skills to facilitate socialization (Flavell & Ross, 1981). Socialization brings the child in tune with cultural influences, values, and models. Peers take on a new role as they explore autonomy and limits together. Relationships take on new meanings as they serve as sources of comparison for body image, style of dress, values toward school, and risk behaviors.

By late elementary school, students are keenly interested in what it means to be popular. Basic social skills are refined, and immediate desires are put on hold to engender long-term relationships. Students learn to balance competition and cooperation, to share, to offer praise, and to inhibit damaging actions.

While it is not unusual for elementary and middle-school children to sacrifice autonomy for social success, giving up free will should be watched closely. The need to learn refusal skills to prevent high-risk behaviors is important for all and a critical necessity for some students.

Also in the elementary and middle-school grades, new relationships with adults are forged. A favorite teacher, movie star, or a basketball player may become a student's "best" friend. The company of the best friend may be preferred over that of his or her parents on occasion. This is a normal part of development.

Moral Development

The moral development of children has come very much into the fore in the last few years, as increasing numbers of people think U.S. society is in deep moral trouble (Lickona, 1993). New texts such as *Moral, Character, and Civic Education in the Elementary School* (Benninga, 1991), and journals like the *Journal of Character Education* are gaining importance very quickly. This movement often cites health and education problems—poor school performance, early sexual activity, truancy, drug use, delinquency, and violence—as evidence of the need for moral education.

Morality refers to "right" and "wrong" behavior. Kohlberg (1963) recognized six stages of moral development, which correspond with the cognitive development of Piaget. A young child, in the first stage, bases moral choices on reward, punishment, and bowing to power. The "right" choice is "to stay out of trouble." Progressing into the second stage, children do what satisfies basic needs but with some reciprocity; that is, "You scratch my back and I'll scratch yours." In the third stage, children conform much more, engaging in behaviors that please others. They are nice approval-seekers. The fourth stage witnesses a "law-and-order" morality. During this time, children focus on authority and rules; they try to do their "duty." As they experience the fifth stage, values start to become relative, and laws might be changed, if agreed upon by everyone. The need for consensus is important at this stage. In the final stage, people develop a universal-ethical-principle orientation. That is, ethical principles are self-chosen based on abstract concepts, and morality is defined as decisions of conscience.

Progression through these stages is variable, and moral choices are made according to appropriate developmental levels. With practice, and as adulthood dawns, the general principle of concern for both self and others serves as the guide for real-life situations (Neutens, 1994).

SECTION I

Health Status, Deficits, and Learning

General Information

Problems of growth and development—physical, emotional, social, and moral—can confront any child. Depending on its nature, a problem may impede a child's learning ability. Although it is obvious that the child who has hearing or vision problems is likely to have difficulty, so too is the child who is not physically fit, lacks sleep, or is unable to relax. Listed below is some general information regarding growth, development, and personal health and fitness. (Specific symptoms of the problems presented later in this chapter.)

- Physical developmental disabilities range from mild growth-pattern lags to severe abnormalities.
- Children were more fit twenty years ago than they are today.
- Only about 36 percent of students in grades 1 through 12 participate in daily school physical education.
- Studies show that, in physical education, only 27 percent of class time is spent in actual physical activity.
- Dental caries is perhaps the most prevalent disease known, and, except in its early stages, it is irreversible and cumulative.

- Seventy percent of children ages 6 to 8 whose parents have less than high school education have dental caries; 92 percent of Native American/Alaska Native children in the same age group have caries; and 61 percent of African-American children in this age group have caries.
- At any given time, 5 to 7 percent of children have a 25 dB hearing loss, usually a self-limiting complication of otitis media with middle-ear effusion.
- Hearing impairment can often be prevented or delayed in onset.
- About 160,000 school-age children suffer eye injuries, and 100,000 of them are product-related eye injuries that occur in the home.
- About 2 to 5 percent of children have amblyopia (lazy eye), anisometropia (unequal refractive error), and strabismus (ocular misalignment), and these usually develop between infancy and ages 5 to 7.
- Nearly 20 percent of children have simple refractive errors by age 16.
- Slightly more than 9 percent of Americans are limited in their major activities (e.g., going to school, working, keeping house) due to chronic health conditions.
- Although early developmental screening allows for early intervention and remediation, this is not routinely occurring today.
- Nearly 6 million children under age 18 have some form of speech or language disorder.
- Communication disorders may be the earliest and most easily recognized symptom of other disabilities, mental retardation, cleft palate, autism, attention-deficit disorder, and cerebral palsy.
- Primary physicians and health care providers identify less than 5 percent of children with speech and language disorders.
- Postural habits established in childhood carry over to adulthood, with corresponding difficulty in spinal alignment.
- Common skin problems of children include acne, warts, sunburn, psoriasis, impetigo, pediculosis, ringworm, and scabies.
- Only 40 percent of children eligible for early periodic screening, diagnosis, and treatment (EPSDT) program services receive any screening.
- Relaxation is just as important for children as it is for adults, and should be incorporated into their lifestyle as early as possible to reduce stress.
- Most adults sleep eight or fewer hours a night, but elementary school children may require eight to ten hours of sleep.

SECTION II

Personal Health and Fitness Teaching Information

Lifestyle, Health Habits, and Taking Responsibility

The way you live and the habits you develop play a major role in determining your level of health. For example, how much sleep did you get last night? Did you start your day with a good breakfast? Did you exercise vigorously for at least 20 minutes today? Did you floss your teeth? Did you smoke or take other drugs? Each of these habits or ways of lifestyle impacts your health, and cumulatively, the impact can be very great.

The common thread interwoven throughout lifestyles and habits is that good health is often a choice, not chance. Every day children make choices about their health, and in so doing, establish early patterns of behavior that may place them at risk. The preschooler who doesn't wipe herself well after going to the bathroom develops a urethral or vaginal infection. The fourth grader who won't wear his glasses at school exacerbates his vision problem. The sixth grade student who doesn't wear a seatbelt is at greater risk of injury, as is the eighth grader who thinks it uncool to wear safety equipment when rollerblading.

Choice of lifestyle impacts those around us, too. The injured child incurs medical costs for his or her parents, and perhaps even time lost at work for the parents during recuperation. In contrast, children who learn to floss and brush teeth early are less likely to develop dental caries. This keeps health costs down and places the family in a preventive mode rather than a treatment mode. Children who eat healthy snacks and remain within defined weight limits are less likely to suffer the many health problems associated with being overweight. Obviously, prevention is the best strategy for a healthy future.

Children need to understand that in many ways they are responsible for their health status. It is essential that they also know this responsibility is easily carried out if they make healthful decisions, decisions that are generally good common sense. Table 6.2 provides examples of decisions that children can make regarding their own health.

Personal Appearance

One important aspect of development is the progressive realization that the body and its appearance influences other health dimensions. A student not reconciled with his or her personal appearance can become frustrated, socially isolated, and even physically ill (Levine et al., 1992; Jourard, 1974). Much experimentation occurs during these middle childhood years as children investigate who they are and how they compare to others in appearance, body build, and coordination.

The development of secondary sexual characteristics often increases curiosity and the desire for

Table 6.2 Health Issues and the Decisions Children Can Make for Themselves

Issue/Decision	Health Effects
Going to bed on time, especially on school nights	Being alert in school, or doing poorly and being cranky
Brushing and flossing teeth in the morning and before bedtime	Few or no dental cavities, or plenty of trips to the dentist
Eating cereals low in sugar	Fewer dental caries, less weight gain, and fewer behavioral effects from sugar, or the reverse
Selecting a snack to have at school	Good nutrition with energy for learning and play, or a short "fix" that lets you down later
Wearing warm clothing on cool days	Protecting your body, or leaving it exposed to the elements
Taking medicine when given by a parent or doctor	Trying to help yourself get better, or letting your sickness continue
Taking baths when needed rather than when wanted	Working with your parents to help your body and keep disease away, or leaving everything to chance.
Washing hands before meals	Avoiding getting sick or spreading your germs to other family members, or the reverse
Scheduling time for homework to reduce panic and stress later	Preventing high stress levels and worry, keeping blood pressure normal and your mind calm, versus a stress reaction

comparison. Curiosity may be shown if two youngsters unclothe (at least partially) and look each other over. Such exploration is common. In a sense, they are acquiring norms when they do this. Children may experiment with their own bodies, too.

At one time or another, children often believe they are the wrong size or shape, that their ears don't fit their head, and the like. This self-evaluation can be very critical and often is not shared with parents. Although most physical concerns can be taken in stride by children, teachers should be watchful for "hidden" expressions of somatic concern. These may include extreme modesty about undressing for physical education, withdrawal from activities that expose the body or are for body coordination, extraordinary measures to conceal blemishes, and the like.

Teachers, as well as parents, need to reassure children about both their uniqueness and similarities. But they must also respect a child's right to privacy, allowing them to take some measures to protect their personal appearance concerns.

Using the Senses

The senses are very important to health. They keep people in touch with the environment, both physical and emotional. While of course there are five senses—vision, hearing, touch, smell, and taste—this chapter addresses only vision and hearing since they most affect health status and academic performance.

Vision

Vision is the child's most precious sense. The preschooler's eyes allow him or her to explore and relate to the surrounding physical and social worlds. Upon entering school, the child discovers that he or she must begin to use vision as an instrument through which to learn. As the child progresses, the eyes convey to the mind the complexities of the larger world. Defective vision may account for slow scholastic achievement, impairment of normal psychosocial progress, and numerous emotional problems. The earlier visual defects are identified and corrected, the greater the child's chances for a normal life.

Some 80 percent of the work a child does in elementary school is built around visual acuity within arm's reach. Thus it is important that visual difficulties be corrected as early as possible in the primary grades. But 20 to 25 percent of school children have eye defects, and school surveys show that fewer than half of the children who need glasses have them.

Sensory input keeps us in touch with our environment, both physically and emotionally.

Normal vision involves both eye and brain development. Young children are normally farsighted, seeing large objects and print, and pictures fairly well. But the eyes and their muscles need to be trained to adjust to close work. Eye muscles, especially, need to mature in order for visual acuity to be considered normal.

The most common visual difficulties have to do with refraction errors. In an eye without a refractive error, light rays focus on the retina. Objects at a distance of 20 feet project rays that are so nearly parallel that they focus on the retina without any accommodation on the part of the eye. Because of this natural phenomenon, this distance has been accepted as a measure of normal vision acuity, or emmetropia. A child has 20/20 vision if he or she can see at 20 feet what other children with normal vision can see at 20 feet.

Four main vision defects occur among elementary school children: (1) nearsightedness, (2) farsightedness, (3) astigmatism, and (4) poor binocular or two-eyes vision such as double vision (strabismus).

General Symptoms of Eye Problems

No single physical symptom, behavior, or emotional disorder identifies the child with an eye or vision problem. Usually there is more than one telltale symptom when a child has a seeing or learning difficulty. And these usually occur as a syndrome of behaviors, (as described below). The following physical symptoms and behavioral conditions, occurring usually as syndromes, can help teachers in identifying children with eye and vision problems:

1. Appearance
   - *Lids:* Crusting, swollen, red; skin at outer corner cracked
   - *Eyes:* Sunken, protruding, crossed, bloodshot, presence of styes, watery, presence of discharge, swelling, irregular pupils
2. Behavior
   - Attempts to brush away blur
   - Blinks continually when reading
   - Cries frequently
   - Has frequent temper tantrums
   - Holds the book far away from the face when reading
   - Holds the page close to the face when reading
   - Holds the body tense when looking at distant objects
   - Reads for only a brief period before stopping
   - Reads when should be at play, as compensation
   - Rubs eyes frequently
   - Squints when reading
   - Screws up face when looking at distant objects
   - Shuts or covers one eye when reading
   - Thrusts head forward to see distant objects
   - Tilts head to one side when reading
   - Poor alignment in penmanship
   - Tends to look cross-eyed when reading
   - When reading, frequently moves book farther away and closer again
   - When reading, tends to lose place on the page
   - In reading and spelling, confuses *o* with *a*; *e* with *o*; *n* with *m*; *h*, *n*, and *r*; and/or *f* with *t*.
   - Makes guesses from a quick recognition of parts of a word in easy reading material
   - Prone to accidents; stumbles over objects in path or fails to appreciate height or steps, gets fingers caught in machines, and so forth
   - Frowns
   - Dislikes tasks requiring sustained visual concentration
   - Unusual fatigue after completing a visual task
   - Uses finger or marker to guide eyes
   - Says words aloud or lip-reads
   - Moves head rather than eyes while reading
   - Has difficulty in remembering what is read
   - Has poor hand-eye coordination, as when catching a ball or skipping rope
3. Typical complaints
   - Headaches
   - Nausea, dizziness
   - Burning, pain, itching of eyes
   - Blurring of vision at any time
   - Eyes sensitive to light
   - Cannot see well

Suggestions for Helping a Child with Vision Problems

1. Rearrange the seating plan to accommodate students with vision problems.
2. Rearrange pupils' and teacher's desks so pupils do not face the light.
3. Provide adjustable desk tops to ensure better light and no glare on work.
4. Permit a child to sit where necessary to obtain the best view.
5. Provide adequate lighting, replace burned-out lights in the classroom, and avoid glare and shadow.
6. Always provide clean chalkboards; use yellow chalk on gray-green or blue-green boards to avoid glare.
7. Provide clean, pastel-colored walls and white ceiling to avoid glare.
8. Select reading materials for clear type and pictures; adequate spacing between lines, words, and letters; adequate margins; and good-quality paper with a non-glossy finish.
9. Writing on chalkboard should be large and clear.
10. Amount of homework assigned should be appropriate for all children, and perhaps modified for those with severe visual loss.

Hearing

The ears are probably the second most important sense organs people have. We must not only learn by hearing, but learn to understand the sounds we hear. In addition, our sense of balance is in the inner ear. A child's hearing defect often leads to speech disorders, communication gaps, and emotional disturbances.

It is estimated that 1 out of 20 people in the United States has some degree of hearing loss, with about 0.6 percent of the school population having educationally significant losses. Hidden hearing damage threatens as many as 1 in 10 American youngsters, and some 400,000 children begin school each year handicapped by unrecognized hearing loss. The elementary classroom teacher can expect to find about two children in each classroom with a hearing problem in one or both ears. Most children with hearing loss acquire it gradually.

Hearing difficulties can be divided into two classes: (1) *conduction hearing losses,* which are associated with the conductive structures of the outer or middle ear; and (2) *sensorineural hearing losses,* which are associated with sensory receptors in the middle ear or fibers of the auditory nerve. Relatively few of the hearing problems found in children of school age are of the sensorineural type. Sometimes both conductive and sensorineural losses are present, in which case the impairment is termed *mixed.*

The most common cause of conductive impairment involving the outer ear is an accumulation of ear wax that blocks the canal. Conductive disorders of the middle ear are a more serious matter. Almost all middle-ear disease in childhood is due to malfunction of the eustachian tube. A watery fluid, or transudate, may fill the eustachian tube, resulting in pain and high fever. This condition is called *otitis media.*

Children with hearing losses may be described as either hard of hearing or deaf. The *hard of hearing* are those in whom the loss of hearing is educationally significant but whose residual hearing is functional for acquiring language, often with a hearing aid. The *deaf* are those whose sense of hearing is insufficient for understanding speech. Fortunately, most pupils are no more than hard of hearing.

Profound deafness is usually identified in early infancy. Any hearing impairment acquired before language has been mastered affects the entire child, not just the sense of hearing. Mild to moderate hearing loss is difficult for parents to detect. Often it is recognized only after several years of school. Meanwhile, it handicaps the growth of the child at the ages when speech, thought development, learning, and social relationships all depend on normal hearing. Because a hearing loss reduces or prevents normal acquisition of language, hearing-impaired pupils tend not only to score lower, as a group, on tests of intelligence, personality, adjustment, and social competence than those with normal hearing, but are also more likely to underachieve academically.

General Symptoms of Ear Problems

The teacher should be cognizant of any or all of the following conditions in a child:

1. Appearance
   - Discharge or odor from an ear
   - Strained facial expression
   - Cotton in an ear
   - Favoring one ear over the other
   - Appears mentally retarded
2. Behavior
   - Difficulty in talking and pronouncing
   - Inability to localize sound
   - Turning head to one side when spoken to
   - Persistently inattentive
   - Asks questions repeatedly
   - Fails to answer or answers incorrectly when called on
   - Watchful of the teacher
   - Slurs word endings
   - Speaks loudly
   - Turns volume up on radio or TV
   - Watches lips of other pupils as they speak
   - Learns slowly
   - Written work better than oral work
   - Looks at someone else's work before starting assignment
3. Typical complaints
   - Earache
   - Ringing or noise in the ear
   - Inability to hear
   - Asks people to speak louder
   - Asks the teacher to repeat the question

Suggestions for Helping a Hard-of-Hearing Child

1. Face the pupil as much as possible.
2. Move around the room as little as possible while carrying on a conversation.
3. Secure the child's attention before addressing him or her.
4. Talk slowly and enunciate clearly.
5. Ask the child to clarify or repeat what you said.
6. Prescribe advance reading on the subject to be discussed in class.
7. Appoint a "buddy" to help a hard-of-hearing child.
8. Foster understanding and awareness in the pupils in the classroom toward a hard-of-hearing child.
9. Place the child near the front of the room.

A neat appearance, alert responses, and a bright smile are all signs of a healthy child.

10. Avoid competing and distracting noises (e.g., air conditioners, fans) in the classroom.

Dental Health

Good, healthy teeth are essential to children for several reasons. They provide the hard chewing surfaces so necessary for the proper mastication and proper digestion of food. Teeth are also necessary for good pronunciation, and they mold the contour of the lower part of the face. Teeth help to project a child's appearance and personality. Good breath accompanies healthy teeth. Loss of several teeth, dental caries, poorly aligned teeth (malocclusion), and bad breath (halitosis) may interfere with a child's development and achievement in school.

Each of the curved rows of teeth makes up a dental arch. The upper arch is slightly larger than the lower one, so the upper teeth normally overlap the lower ones. Figure 6.3 illustrates the lower dental arch of primary or deciduous teeth. There are four incisors, two canines, and four molars, for a total of twenty teeth, ten on the top and ten on the bottom. Permanent, or adult, teeth begin to erupt around age 5 or 6. Figure 6.4 shows the lower dental arch of permanent or adult teeth. There are four incisors, two canines, four first premolars (bicuspids), and six molars (tricuspids) for a total of thirty-two teeth. The third molar is the so-called wisdom tooth.

Dental Caries

The most common defect of the teeth is decay. Dental cavities occur more frequently in school children than any other disorder or health problem. About 95 to 99 percent of all children suffer from such dental problems. The greatest incidence of caries is at ages 5 to 8 in the primary teeth and 12 to 18 in the permanent set.

The causes of dental decay include inherited susceptibility to caries, poor nutrition during the years that the teeth are calcifying, prevalence of acid-forming bacteria in the mouth, and eating too many sweets and starches. Decay is initiated by bacteria acting on carbohydrates. Harmful acid levels build up within fifteen minutes. The acids, produced by fermentation, combine with saliva in the mouth to cause erosion of tooth enamel. Calcified tissue is destroyed, and a small cavity, or hole, is started. When decay is limited to enamel and dentin, the tooth is sensitive to heat, cold, and sweets. When the pulp is involved, a toothache develops. But when the nerve is destroyed, pain ceases.

Malocclusion

Poorly aligned teeth may be caused by heredity, loss of a primary tooth and consequent drift of adjoining teeth toward the empty space, chronically breathing through the mouth, poor oral habits such as thumb- or finger-sucking, impacted teeth, or congenital problems such as cleft palate.

Malocclusion interferes with proper cleansing of teeth, disturbs chewing, increases the likelihood of injury to protruding teeth, and alters appearance. This condition may also cause unfortunate psychological and social effects. Often "buck teeth" become an emotional stigma for life.

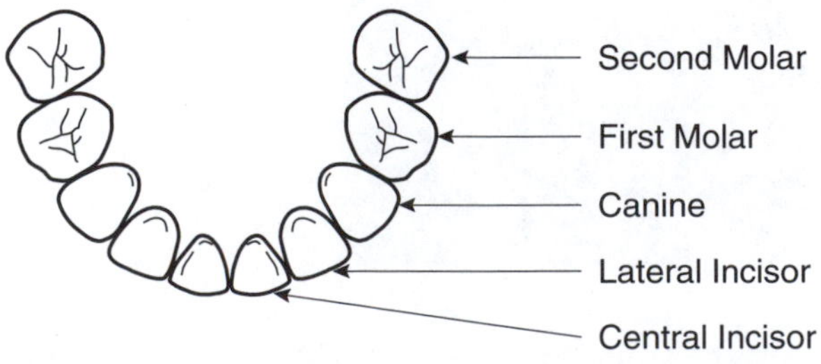

FIGURE 6.3 Primary or Deciduous Teeth

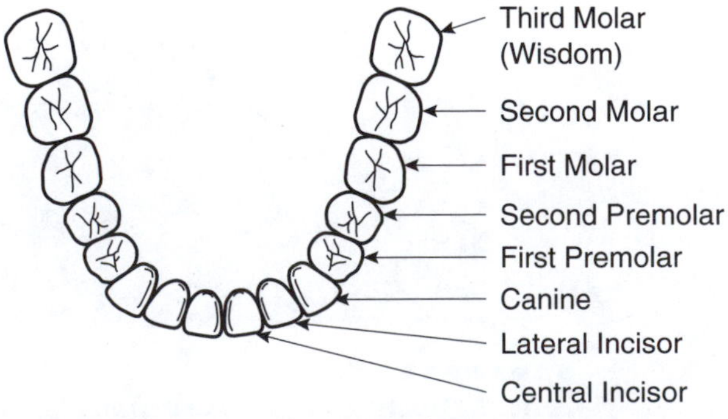

FIGURE 6.4 Secondary or Permanent Teeth

BOX 6.1 ■ ■ ■ ■ ■

EATING BETWEEN MEALS

Snacking between meals greatly increases your risk of dental caries.

Eating sugary foods and drinking soft drinks between meals are major contributors to dental caries. Sugary foods, such as chocolate bars, sugared cereals, cookies, candies, and soft drinks feed the bacteria in your mouth. Bacteria eat the sugar and excrete acids, which combine with saliva to form a very strong acid that dissolves the enamel of teeth.

Eating habits are important to slowing down tooth decay. First, don't snack on sweets. The less sugar you eat, the less food there is for bacteria. You are most likely to get cavities when you regularly eat sugar between meals.

Next, do not leave sugar acids on your teeth for long periods. Continually eating sweets increases exposure to sugar acids.

Do not eat sweets by themselves. If you are going to eat sugary foods, have them with meals rather than alone. The presence of other foods gets saliva flowing to help buffer and dilute any sugar acid.

Regardless of when you eat sweets, it is most important that you brush your teeth and mouth immediately afterward. Bacteria begin eating sugar immediately, and harmful acid levels build up within 15 minutes. By brushing immediately after eating, you reduce the amount of sugar available for bacteria.

After brushing for three minutes or longer, rinse your mouth with water to wash out loose food particles, sugar acid, and bacteria. If you cannot brush your teeth and mouth, refrain from eating sweets. Swishing with water lowers the risk of sugar acid forming in your mouth and hence lowers the risk of cavities.

You are at very high risk for dental caries if you are under age 25 and snack on sweets between meals.

When and how often you eat sweets affect your risk of dental caries. Eliminate sweet snacks immediately. If you must snack, then eat unsweetened foods, such as celery, cucumbers, cauliflower, and fresh fruits.

Gum Infections

Gingivitis is an inflammation of gum tissue. The gums appear red and swollen, feel tender, and tend to bleed if pressure is applied. The condition occurs most often when oral hygiene and dental care are neglected. Faulty brushing fails to remove bacteria and thus prevent plaque formation. Failure to remove plaque, a sticky bacterial deposit, from the teeth near the gum line in turn leads to the formation of calculus, or tartar. Removal of calculus by a dentist—cleaning the teeth—is important in avoiding gum trouble. Neglected gingival disease may result in a more advanced disease called *pyorrhea.*

General Symptoms of Tooth and Mouth Problems

1. Appearance
   - Cavities in mouth
   - Excessive tartar at the necks of teeth
   - Malocclusion
   - Irregular teeth
   - Bleeding or inflamed gums
   - Swollen jaw
   - Cracking of lips and corners of mouth
2. Behavior
   - Keeps mouth closed; refrains from smiling
   - Sensitive about missing teeth
   - Does not brush teeth regularly
   - Demonstrates a speech defect
   - Difficulty in mastication
   - Thumb-sucking
   - Rubs gums
   - Constantly picking teeth
3. Typical complaints
   - Toothache
   - Sensitivity to hot, cold, or sweets
   - Sore gums
   - Mouth feels sore
   - Others don't want to play with him or her

BOX 6.2 ■ ■ ■ ■ ■

EATING SWEETS

Eating sweets is a major risk factor for dental caries for all of us. Tooth decay is caused by sugar. Bacteria in the mouth feed on sugary foods and produce acids that dissolve the enamel of teeth. To reduce your chances of developing cavities, or dental caries, reduce the frequency of eating sweets and eating sweets by themselves. You are most likely to get cavities when you regularly eat sugar between meals and expose your teeth to sugar for long periods. Children, adolescents, and adults under the age of 25 have the highest risk of cavities, while those over 25 have a high risk of periodontal disease, such as gingivitis, in which plaque forms on the surface of the teeth next to the gums, causing irritation of the gums, or gingivae.

Some people think their teeth are safe from decay if they brush their teeth each time they eat sweets. This may not be entirely correct, as it is difficult to brush the teeth well enough to overcome all the effects of sugar. You would have to brush your teeth for three minutes within five minutes after eating sugary food. Since most persons find it inconvenient to brush teeth properly when they eat sugary foods, it is wise to limit sweets as much as possible. When you do eat sugary foods, have them with meals rather than alone. Other foods get saliva flowing to help buffer and dilute acids. It is always wise to brush as soon as you can after eating.

Sugar-rich foods are low in vitamins and minerals and are often high in fats. Such foods are called *empty calorie foods* because they are high in calories but low in essential nutrients. This is another reason not to eat too many sweets.

How much sugar is acceptable in your diet? The U.S. Dietary Goals suggest that refined sugars should make up no more than 10 percent of the total calories you eat each day. Your body does *not* need sugar! It needs complex carbohydrates for energy. Complex carbohydrates (from potatoes, rice, whole-grain pastas, and vegetables) provide more vitamins and minerals and longer-lasting energy than do sugary foods. Therefore, the official goal for sugar is actually too high. Think about displacing sugary foods with fresh fruits and vegetables.

How can you tell if a food has sugar in it? Most processed and refined foods have sugar, since sugar is both a sweetener and a preservative. The best thing to do when you are shopping is to read the label. If sugar, sucrose, dextrose, corn syrup, fructose, maltose, honey, molasses, turbinado, confectioner's sugar, monosaccharides, or disaccharides are one of the first few ingredients in the list on the package, assume that sugar is a major part of the food. If it is listed toward the end, it is present in smaller amounts. **ALWAYS READ THE LABEL!**

Suggestions for Helping the Child with Dental Problems

1. Provide time to brush teeth after snacks and lunches.
2. Have children who do not brush teeth in school rinse out mouth with water.
3. Discourage eating of sweets and drinking sugared soft drinks.
4. Discourage finger-sucking.
5. Demonstrate proper brushing technique.

Posture

Postural habits established in the early years carry over to adulthood, with corresponding effects on vertical alignment and body movement. But children with habitually poor posture have also been observed to be more susceptible to diseases, tire easily, be underweight, be self-conscious, have hearing defects, be restless, be timid, and have a greater incidence of asthma. Actually, 70 to 80 percent of all children and adults have varying degrees of postural malalignment.

BOX 6.3 ■ ■ ■ ■ ■

WAYS TO MAINTAIN ORAL HYGIENE

1. Brush your teeth properly for three or more minutes after each meal (or at least once a day).
2. Use a soft-bristle toothbrush.
3. Each day, floss the surfaces of teeth that brushing cannot clean.
4. Drink plenty of water and rinse your mouth out each time. Doing so reduces bacterial levels in the mouth.
5. Do not crack nuts or hard objects with your teeth.
6. Massage the gums each day with a toothbrush while brushing and with your fingers.
7. Have a dental checkup every six months.
8. Avoid drinking extremely hot or cold liquids.
9. Eat a balanced diet each day.
10. Avoid tobacco.
11. Drink fluoridated water.
12. Do not eat refined sugar (sucrose) products.
13. Assess your mouth for plaque once a month.
14. When playing contact sports that may injure your teeth, wear protective equipment.
15. See a dentist immediately if you injure your teeth or mouth.

Fortunately, most childhood postural problems may be corrected with a minimum of difficulty. When body mechanics improve in children with postural problems, there is almost always a corresponding improvement in health, physical efficiency, school work, and self-image.

Good standing posture may be defined as an imaginary straight line (plumb line) projected through (1) the earlobe, (2) the center of the shoulder, (3) the hip joint, (4) just behind the kneecap, and (5) through the ankle onto the floor. A child's posture may be subjectively appraised as either normal or deviating from the normal by observing where the plumb line falls relative to the child's five body landmarks.

In addition to posture as viewed from the side, a child's lateral body alignment should be assessed. The alignment of the head, neck, shoulder blades, spine, and hips should be balanced. Feet should naturally point straight ahead while standing and walking.

One observable posture defect is usually accompanied by one or more defects located in other parts of the human frame. For example, lordosis, an exaggerated curve in the lumbar region giving the appearance of a hollow back, is usually accompanied by such compensatory deviations as a forward-thrusting head, cervical lordosis, round shoulders, flat chest, knees bent backward, or flat feet.

General Symptoms of Posture Problems

1. Appearance
   - Head tilted forward, chin-in appearance
   - Exaggerated front-to-back spinal curves
   - Lateral spinal curves (scoliosis), one shoulder lower than the other
   - Flat-chestedness
   - Flat feet (no arch)
   - Cramped toes
   - Ptosis (protruding stomach, often associated with obesity)
   - Off balance
   - Hands and shoulder joints leaning in front of ears and hips
2. Behavior
   - Slouching forward
   - Lack of energy
   - Withdraws from strenuous activity
   - Clumsy and uncoordinated
   - Desires to go barefoot or take off shoes
   - Restless
   - Changes sitting positions often

3. Typical complaints
   - Sore feet
   - Sore back
   - Fatigue
   - Lack of sports skills

Suggestions for Helping the Child with Postural Defects

Encourage all children to

1. Sit and walk properly.
2. Keep feet flat on floor when sitting.
3. Keep the head up and chest out.
4. Use the backrests of chairs so that buttocks and back are resting against backrest.
5. Take advantage of many stretch periods interspersed with corrective exercises.
6. Practice coordination and graceful movements.

Exercise

Most experts concur that there is a youth fitness crisis today (Roberts, 1992; Centers for Disease Control, 1992). This crisis is evidenced in several ways: (1) about 40 percent of all children ages 5 to 8 display risk factors for heart disease, such as high cholesterol, hypertension, and obesity; (2) poor muscular strength and endurance, (3) 32 percent of fourth graders are "couch potato" TV watchers, accumulating six or more hours every day; (4) children are much fatter now than they were in the 1960s; and (5) in the average grade 5 physical education class, only 8.6 percent of activity 10.4 minutes per week is moderate to vigorous (Simons-Morton et al., 1993).

Lack of exercise affects more than the physical dimension of health. Page & Tucker (1994) found that adolescents who exercise infrequently experience more loneliness, shyness, and hopelessness than their peers who exercise. But to improve mental health and mood, exercise should be regular physical activity rather than cardiovascular-fitness exercises (Thirlaway & Benton, 1992). Generally, higher levels of activity produce better mood scores, unless, of course, the students are physically unfit. In other words, use common sense: start slow and progress gradually.

Exercising from an early age may reduce the incidence of chronic illnesses over time. It can reduce obesity, cholesterol level, and hypertension in children (Malina, 1990). When started in childhood, physical activity may become a part of one's overall lifestyle in later life.

Since children are usually involved in short-burst, high-energy play, they should be directed to take part in sustained activities that use large-muscle groups. Both aerobic and resistance training should be part of the exercise program. Of course the program should also be a positive and enjoyable experience for all participants. In addition to the obvious benefits, regular exercise improves motor skills, self-confidence, self-image, coordination, flexibility, balance, and posture. Teachers should work with parents to encourage exercise as a lifetime interest. Parental modeling, especially modeling the mother's behavior, plays an important role in whether a child will exercise on a regular basis (Stucky-Ropp & DiLorenzo, 1993).

Sleep

Sleep is important for good academic performance as well as for good health. Adequate sleep enhances motivation, concentration, mood, and attentiveness (Hobson, 1990). On the other hand, students who are deprived of sleep have an impaired ability to be productive, make good judgments, and even laugh at a good joke.

Unfortunately, many parents are poor models of good sleep habits since they "cheat" on their sleep in order to accomplish other tasks (Edlin & Golanty, 1992). Missing out on sixty to ninety minutes of sleep a night, rather than getting a complete night's rest of seven, eight, or even nine hours, is common.

Almost everyone has difficulty getting to sleep at one time or another. Being worried about an exam, an argument with a friend, being sick, or being very excited may cause sleep loss. Fortunately, most of us "get back on track" after a day or two.

The most common sleep disorders are insomnia (not enough sleep), excessive sleepiness, parasomnias (unusual experiences such as night terrors in small children, sleepwalking, difficulty in breathing, and kicking movements), and circadian-rhythm disorders (internal-clock malfunctions).

So many people are afflicted with sleep problems that they have become a medical subspecialty. Prior to visiting a specialist, however, the following might be tried first:

1. *Develop a regular sleep schedule. Children* should have a regularly scheduled bedtime. It should be part of their daily routine.
2. *Have some quiet time before going to bed.* This is very important for *children,* since hard play before bedtime augments mental and physical arousal.
3. *Sleep in a comfortable environment.* This varies a little from one person to another. For *children,* it is important to create a secure environment, which often means sleeping with a favorite toy, stuffed animal, or blanket.
4. *Snacks before bedtime should be small and compatible with sleep.* Eating a large meal before bedtime is counterproductive. So, too, is taking in large amounts of alcohol or caffeine. For *children,* a breakfast cereal should stop any hunger pangs and still allow sleep to occur. Children—and adults for that matter—should not drink too much fluid before bedtime or sleep will be interrupted by a distended bladder.

If all else fails, it would be beneficial to create and maintain a daily sleep log for awhile before seeing a physician. The log should contain the following information:

- Time you went to bed
- Time you fell asleep
- Number of times you woke up
- Feelings/thoughts at the time
- Time you woke up (for the day)
- Time you got up
- Feelings upon wakening
- Total time slept

Implications for Elementary and Middle-School Teachers

Summary Issues

1. Children develop in many ways: physically, emotionally, socially, and morally.
2. As children grow and develop on all fronts, they must complete certain developmental tasks.
3. Developmental tasks arise from (1) the physiological process of maturation, (2) social expectations, and (3) the child's personal values and aspirations.
4. Growth refers to quantitative changes—increases in size and structure. Development, by contrast, refers to changes that are qualitative in nature. Maturity marks the end of growth and development.
5. The growth and developmental processes of children follow basic patterns, which reflect the physical, emotional, social, intellectual, and behavioral traits of the whole child.
6. Growth in height and weight reflects general physical progress in the development of body systems and processes.
7. Mental-emotional traits are acquired in a progressive fashion.
8. Socialization brings the child in tune with cultural influences, values, and models.
9. Health and education problems—poor school performance, early sexual activity, truancy, drug use, delinquency, and violence—are often evidence of the need for moral education.
10. The way you live and the habits you develop play a major role in determining your level of health. Good health is often a choice, not chance.
11. One aspect of development is the progressive realization that the body and its appearance influence other health dimensions.
12. Vision is the child's most precious sense. Defective vision may account for slow scholastic achievement, impairment of

normal psychosocial progress, and numerous emotional problems.

13. A child's hearing defect can often lead to speech disorders, communication gaps, emotional disturbances, and in the case of an inner-ear problem, poor balance.
14. Good, healthy teeth are essential to the child for learning, good general health, appearance, and communication.
15. Postural habits established in the early years carry over to adulthood, as do any corresponding difficulties of vertical alignment and body movement.
16. Most experts concur that there is a youth-fitness crisis today. Promoting exercise at an early age may reduce the incidence of chronic illnesses over time.
17. Adequate sleep enhances motivation, concentration, mood, and attentiveness. Almost everyone has difficulty getting to sleep at one time or another.

Teacher Ramifications

In so far as growth, development, and personal health and fitness are concerned, a teacher should:

1. Monitor students for appropriate development and growth
2. Design lessons around the growth and developmental stages of their students
3. Encourage healthy experimentation that engenders self-confidence and skill development
4. Understand that their actions, lessons, and modeling affect all the components of student growth and development, including moral development
5. Teach students the role of self-responsibility regarding their health and health behavior
6. Support the school's role in helping the nation reach the objectives set forth in *Healthy Children 2000*. Specifically, the objectives related to school regarding this topic are:
   - #1.8. Increase to at least 50 percent the proportion of children and adolescents in grades 1 through 12 who participate in daily school physical education.
   - #1.9. Increase to at least 50 percent the proportion of school physical education class time that students spend being physically active, preferably engaging in lifetime physical activities.
   - #13.12. Increase to at least 90 percent the proportion of all children entering school programs for the first time who have already received an oral health screening, referral, and follow-up for necessary diagnostic, preventive, and treatment services.

SECTION III

Teaching Strategies for Growth, Development, and Personal Health and Fitness

The strategies in this section are divided into grades K–4, 5–6, and 7–8 levels. In addition to strategies that can be used in the classroom, some home activities are included. A home activity is designed for student-parent interaction. It is a way to engage the home in school-student learning, and parents can sign a slip of paper to confirm that an activity was completed. Evaluation of all strategies through use of the National Health Education Standards and performance indicators is indicated. Teachers may also write corresponding learning assessments.

K–4 Level

Strategy One

Objective: Students will understand that interests and abilities change as people grow older. Students may be introduced to the concept of setting goals.

Activity: Using a large chart, students will draw pictures or write words (depending on age level) to describe some things they enjoyed doing when they were younger; things they enjoy/are good at presently; and what they would like to be good at later. Discussion following completion can focus on how people's interests change and how setting goals can help you achieve what you would like to do.

Integration: Language Arts, Social Studies, Art

Related Health Content Area: Mental-emotional health

Health Education Standard and Performance Indicators: 1(1,2)

Strategy Two

Objective: Students will describe the ways in which people grow.

Activity: Ask students what it means to grow up. Elicit responses concerning physical growth, emotional growth, intellectual growth, and social growth. Discuss how we all grow from the time we are born until we die. Explain that growth means many different things.

Integration: Sciences, Language Arts, Math

Related Health Content Area: All

Health Education Standard and Performance Indicators: 1(1,2,5,7); 3(1,2,3); 4(1,4); 6(3)

5–6 Level

Strategy One

Objective: Students will realize that changes that take place at puberty begin at different ages. Students will be able to reduce personal anxiety regarding pubertal changes.

Activity: Previous to this lesson, students will ask their parents at what ages they began to walk and talk. The teacher will draw two continuums on the board, with ages ranging from 3 months to 4 years. On the first continuum, the students will enter the age at which they began to walk; on the second, they will enter the age at which they began to talk. (Note: The teacher should be prepared to accommodate those students who experienced growth and development problems.) Discuss various aspects of the age groupings. Ask the students if it matters today at which age they started to walk or talk. Show transparencies depicting age ranges for the onset/ending of puberty. Ask students why people go through puberty at different ages. Discuss various reasons—genetic, diet, general health, environment, and so forth. Discuss other stages of aging (getting old), emphasizing the lack of a specific starting age.

Integration: Math, Social Studies, Science, Home Economics

Related Health Content Areas: Human body, diseases, nutrition

Health Education Standard and Performance Indicators: 1(1,2,3,4,5)

Strategy Two

Objective: Students will recognize that a variety of changes take place at puberty.

Activity: Have students write the following across the top of a piece of paper (it may be helpful to turn it sideways):

Feelings Skin Friendships Body Parents

Ask students to write what things change as they get older in regard to the categories above (e.g., skin = acne, parents = let you do more things). Discuss what students have written and make a master list on the chalkboard.

Integration: Language Arts

Related Health Content Areas: Emotional well-being, family/relationships, human body

Health Education Standards and Performance Indicators: 1(1,2,3,8); 2(1,2); 4(4); 6(5)

7–8 Level

Strategy One

Objective: Students will demonstrate appropriate skills for coping with frustration and disappointment.

Activity: The following problem-based learning activity (see Chapter 4).

Shannon, an eighth grader, is one of the best soccer players in school and was always a starter. But recently, after the start of the season, a new student, Adrian, joined the team. Adrian and Shannon play the same position. Adrian, having come from a larger school, has played a lot more and is better than Shannon. The coach tells Shannon that Adrian is starting the match today against their rival, Robinson Middle School. Shannon tells the coach that she doesn't want to play at all if she can't start.

A. What is Shannon's problem in this vignette?
B. What options does she have?
C. What should she know about the whole situation? (What other information should she have?)
D. How does this information apply to her problem?
E. How do her options as what to do relate to her growth and development or mental health?
F. What is the best decision for her?
G. How can she evaluate her decision?

Integration: Physical education/fitness

Related Health Content Area: Mental-emotional health

Health Education Standards and Performance Indicators: 1(2,4); 5(1,2,3,4,5,7,8)

Strategy Two

Objective: Students will illustrate their individuality.

Activity: Have plenty of old magazines that contain a lot of pictures. Have students find pictures that they feel reflect a certain part of their personality. Make a collage of all the pictures. When they are complete, number them and put them on the bulletin board without the students' names showing. Have students try to guess which collage belongs to which student. (It would be a good idea for the teacher to put one up that depicts their personalities also.) A prize might be awarded to the student who gets the most correct answers.

Integration: Art, Social Studies

Related Health Content Areas: Emotional well-being, family and relationships

Health Education Standards and Performance Indicators: 1(2); 4(1,2,3,4)

Home Activities

Strategy One

Objective: Students will discover the differences and similarities in growth and development among family members.

Activity: Have the students compare family photos of adults from the time they were infants to the present. Compare and contrast the development of the adults and the student. Identify similar characteristics; compare growth rates at similar ages, and the like. Discuss growth rates, family characteristics, and so forth.

Integration: Science (genetics), Social studies (ethnic diversity)

Related Health Content Areas: Human body, mental-emotional health

Health Education Standard and Performance Indicators: 1(2,3,4,5)

Strategy Two

Objective: Students will recognize the similarities between their beliefs and their parents' beliefs.

Activity: Have the students imagine themselves as a married adult with a child of their own. The student is to write a letter to this child expressing his or her feelings about growing up, dating, relationships, and love. At the same time, the student's parent will write a letter to the student expressing his or her feelings about the same topics. Student and parent should then exchange letters and use them as a basis for discussion.

Integration: Social Studies, Language Arts

Related Health Content Areas: Emotional well-being, sexuality, families and relationships

Health Education Standards: 1,2,3,4,5,6

References

Benninga, J.S., ed. *Moral, Character, and Civic Education in the Elementary School.* Teachers College Press, New York, 1991.

Centers for Disease Control. Vigorous physical activity among high school students: United States, *Journal of the American Medical Association* 267(1992):1052.

Edlin, G., & Golanty, E. *Health and Wellness: A Holistic Approach.* Jones and Bartlett, Boston, 1992.

Flavell, J.H., & Ross, L., eds. *Social Cognitive Development.* Cambridge University Press, Cambridge, 1981.

Havighurst, R.J. *Developmental Tasks and Education.* Longman, Green, Arnold, New York, 1953.

Hobson, J.A. Sleep and dreaming, *Journal of Neurosciences* 10(1990):371–382.

Jourard, S.M. *Healthy Personality: An Approach from the Viewpoint of Humanistic Psychology.* Macmillan, New York, 1974.

Kohlberg, L. Development of children's orientation towards a moral order, I: Sequence in the development of moral thought, *Vita Humana* 6(1963):11.

Levine, M.D., Carey, W.B., & Crocker, A.C. *Developmental-Behavioral Pediatrics,* 2d ed. Saunders, Philadelphia, 1992.

Lickona, T. The return of character education, *Educational Leadership* 51,3(1993):6–11.

Malina, R.M. Growth, exercise, fitness, and later outcomes. In C. Bouchard, R.J. Shephard, T. Stephens, J.R. Sutton, & B.D. MacPherson, eds., *Exercise, Fitness, and Health.* Human Kinetics, Champaign, IL, 1990.

Neutens, J.J. *Discover: Healthy Sexual Development* (middle-school edition). American Guidance Service, Circle Pines, MN, 1994.

Page, R.M., & Tucker, L.A. Psychosocial discomfort and exercise frequency: An epidemiological study of adolescents, *Adolescence* 29,113(1994): 183–191.

Roberts, S.O. Child's play: Physical activity at an early age may help prevent chronic illnesses over a lifetime, *American Fitness* 10(1992):30.

Seaward, B.L. *Managing Stress: Principles and Strategies for Health and Well-being.* Jones and Bartlett, Boston, 1994.

Simons-Morton, B.G., Taylor, W.C., Snider, S.A., & Huang, I.W. The physical activity of fifth-grade students during physical education classes, *American Journal of Public Health* 83(1993):262.

Stucky-Ropp, R.C., & DiLorenzo, T.M. Determinants of exercise in children, *Preventive Medicine* 22, 6(1993):880–889.

Thirlaway, K., & Benton, D. Participation in physical activity and cardiovascular fitness have different effects on mental health and mood, *Journal of Psychosomatic Research* 36,7(1992):657–665.

7

Nutrition

Upon completion of this chapter, you should be able to:

- *Identify some of the major nutrition problems facing children and adolescents*
- *Synthesize and explain the relationship between lifestyle and nutrition*
- *List and critique the U.S. Dietary Guidelines*
- *Explain why dietary guidelines are difficult for a nation to adopt*
- *Identify and compare the sections of the Food Guide Pyramid, including examples of the food groups and suggested servings*
- *Explain the role of the six principal nutrients*
- *Provide suggestions for healthy eating habits for children*

SECTION I

Health Status, Deficits, and Learning

Eating is both a vital function and a cherished experience. However, the quantity and quality of foods that Americans consume vary to a great extent. Even though the United States is the leading food producer in the world, many Americans, rich and poor, still die of malnutrition or chronic diseases caused by poor nutrition; a few even die from lack of food. In too many cases, ignorance of the principles of nutrition prevents people from eating well. This is unnecessary in most cases, for the principles of nutrition are few and easily understood.

Food intake is essential to the building and repairing of body tissue. It also fuels energy production for warmth and strength. The challenge is to match our nutritional needs with the essential ingredients found in foods. This brings us to the key aspect of nutrition: balance. The well-fed person is not necessarily well nourished. Without the proper balance of vitamins, proteins, minerals, carbohydrates, essential fatty acids, fiber, and water, a person cannot be well nourished.

Listed below are some points about nutrition.

- Americans consume about 125 pounds of sweeteners per person per year, and while some provide energy, many provide little or no energy.
- Very few diseases are directly linked to excess sugar intake, and current amounts of sugar consumption are not a proven health risk.
- Research estimates show that 15 percent of adolescents ages 12 to 19 are overweight.
- The American Meat Institute reported that 1.5 billion pounds of red-meat hot dogs are made each year, which adds up to sixty hot dogs per year per person, most of them consumed between Memorial Day and Labor Day.
- About 16 percent of low-income children aged 5 and under experience growth retardation due to nutritional deficits.
- Growth retardation is especially evident in Asian and Pacific Islander children at ages 12 through 59 months, Hispanic children up to 2 years, and black infants through the first year.
- About 10 percent of children at 3 to 4 years show evidence of iron deficiency, with a higher prevalence among black children than whites and among low socioeconomic-status (SES) children compared to higher SES children.
- Insulin-dependent diabetes (Type I) begins in childhood and results from too little insulin produced by the pancreas, thereby causing an inability to regulate blood glucose.
- Atherosclerosis is a type of cardiovascular disease in which there is a build-up of fatty material on the artery walls.

- Plaque is the cholesterol-rich material associated with atherosclerosis, and it is made up of cholesterol, white blood cells, smooth muscle cells, and after time, calcium.
- Pellagra is a disease characterized by dermatitis, dementia, diarrhea, and eventually death; it is caused by a niacin deficiency.
- Dieters who consume less than 1200 kilocalories per day need supplements.
- Vitamin C may help protect the lungs from cigarette smoke.
- Heavy cigarette smokers need about 40 percent more vitamin C to maintain the same blood levels of vitamin C as do nonsmokers.
- Alcohol drinkers need extra amounts of niacin, vitamin B_6, thiamin, and folate because alcohol inhibits their absorption.
- Vitamin K production in the small intestine is inhibited by antibiotics.
- Vitamin D in the body can be lowered by some anticonvulsant medications.
- Scurvy is a disease caused by a vitamin C deficiency. The nickname *limeys* was given to British sailors in 1835, when they were first required to take lime or lemon juice as part of their rations.
- Women consume about 500 kilocalories more per day for the ten days prior to menses than at other times of their cycles.
- Young women involved in sports or dance (e.g., gymnastics or ballet) that requires lean bodies may be more predisposed to restrictive diets and subsequent eating disorders than their counterparts.
- Quick weight loss among wrestlers is common. Such diets can interfere with normal growth, and if done on a regular basis, can predispose the athlete to obesity and heart disease later in life.
- Foods appear to have little or no effect on teenage acne.
- Iron, calcium, and zinc needs increase during the growth spurt, yet more often than not, they are lacking from the adolescent diet.
- Children with hypertension should be monitored nutritionally for obesity, sodium intake, and perhaps potassium and calcium intake, as well as activity level and lifestyle.
- A child who has two obese parents stands an 80 percent chance of also being obese. This is in part due to heredity as well as nutrition.
- Bone is about 99 percent calcium and almost one-half of this is laid down during the adolescent growth spurt. Adolescents need calcium to the tune of 1200 mg per day to prevent osteoporosis in later life.

SECTION II

Nutrition Teaching Information

Lifestyle and Nutrition

What sounds simple presents a major problem for many people. The lifestyle most Americans lead is not conducive to sound nutritional habits or optimal well-being. Most people attempt to eat a variety of foods and hope their meals are balanced. They assume that they are getting the proper amounts of vitamins, minerals, and other essential nutrients. But this is not always true.

Americans consume many convenience and snack foods (e.g., french fries, potato chips, sweets, soft drinks). These kinds of foods are termed *empty calorie* foods because they are rich in sugar and/or salt but deficient in other nutrients. Eating such foods regularly not only develops poor eating habits and problems related to overweight, but can also lead to chronic-deficiency diseases.

Other aspects of lifestyle may contribute to vitamin and mineral deficiencies. Supermarkets abound in convenience foods which may contribute to selection by convenience rather than nutritional value. In order to retard spoilage and to lengthen shelf life, some foods are processed in a variety of ways that lead to loss of much of their nutrient value. For example, the high-speed milling of wheat into white flour removes vitamin E, bran, wheat germ, and most trace minerals. Although breads and cereals are often enriched, or fortified, by the addition of vitamins B_1, B_2, and niacin, twelve other essential B vitamins and most trace minerals are not returned.

Another habit that may contribute to nutritional deficiencies is eating in restaurants and cafeterias where food is kept warm in steam tables for many hours. Although such prolonged heating prevents the growth of germs, it also destroys a large portion of the vitamins B and C in most meats and vegetables. Yet most people assume that cooked and reheated food retains its original vitamins.

In addition, nutrients in the body are depleted when the liver makes enzymes to detoxify the more than 2000 possible chemicals that may find their way into our bodies. These chemicals include food preservatives, coloring agents, and sweeteners as well as insecticides, antibiotics, and so forth. Ingesting these chemicals adds to the detoxification load of the liver. In order to rid the body of these chemicals, the liver uses extra amounts of vitamins B_6, C, and E and minerals such as selenium to make its detoxicant enzymes. But if these micronutrients are not present in sufficient quantities, fatigue sets in and the body functions poorly. Such reactions often reflect nutrient deficiency.

Another burden on the liver arises from pollution. The body is continually exposed to pollutants in food, air, and water. Human metabolic processes eliminate these chemicals, but removal of ozone and nitrous oxide, for example, by the liver creates additional nutrient demands. Likewise, nutrient demands are raised in those who smoke; drink colas, coffee, and alcoholic beverages; and work under emotional stress.

In summary, significant losses of nutrients occur during the cooking, storage, transportation, and processing of foods. The lifestyles of many people further deplete vitamins and minerals in their bodies. Nutrient losses in foods and depletion in the body weaken natural resistance to stress, diseases, and other disorders. Many children, teenagers, and adults have nutrient deficiencies and do not know it. Consequently, their potential for optimal health is diminished; they function at a lowered level of well-being.

The prevention and treatment of heart disease, cancer, obesity, diabetes, arthritis, emotional disturbances, allergies, and other diseases may very well be found in nutrition; food provides everything the body synthesizes and uses. Without food, life cannot go on. A shortage of vitamins and minerals leads to a subsistence life, so to speak. Thus we should think of nutrition as helping us to attain optimal health. In general, we focus on counting calories and eating a balanced diet in terms of proteins, carbohydrates, and fats. Thus a person who eats the required number of calories each day is thought of as well fed. However, such a person may not be well nourished. Many persons eat a lot of calories but not enough vitamins and minerals.

The major consequence of poor eating is lowered immunity. Years ago, research throughout the world (Chandra, 1979; Chandra, 1986) pointed out that resistance is lowered when one does not eat properly. Malnourished persons have more frequent colds, respiratory infections, and diseases. Malnourished children are sick longer, more frequently, and more severely than well-fed children. Good nutrition during childhood is especially important, as good diet fortifies young bodies against many respiratory illnesses and helps to build natural immunity to such illnesses. A well-balanced diet is the child's best way to resist diseases and stay healthy.

Eating Habits

Good eating habits are best begun at an early age. In other words, the best way to maintain ideal weight and eat well throughout life is to learn how to eat and exercise early in life. Teachers should help parents teach their children proper exercising and eating. Of all the habits of living, the most important to good health is eating properly.

An Adequate Diet

At first glance, it may seem relatively simple to recommend an adequate diet to children or adults: simply follow the recommended guidelines. Unfortunately, things are much more complicated than this. Some of the confounding factors are (Farish, 1993):

1. *Individual differences.* This refers to both genetic and lifestyle differences. The "couch potato" has much different needs than does the athlete. No one standard meets the needs of everyone.
2. *Test-tube science versus the real world.* Research on food in the laboratory to discover nutrients may not produce the same results as when performed in the real world. Once that same food enters a real body different reactions may take place. For example, medications, alcohol intake, the combination with other nutrients, and so forth can lead to different absorption rates and nutritional status.
3. *Conflicting recommendations.* In the industrial world, each country has a different set of guidelines based upon the interpretation of data.
4. *Minimums and maximums.* Misinterpretation of the recommendations occurs, with some people thinking they are the "bare bones" minimums of what should be taken. Others believe the recommendations are the average, while still others believe they are the maximum amounts to be ingested. You can see why some people readily take supplements and others do not.

Dietary Goals and Guidelines

Federal dietary guidelines (USDA & USDHHS, 1990) are published to promote healthful diets for the general population. But as should be expected, individual variations due to disease conditions or other factors must modify the general guidelines. The guidelines are as follows:

- *Eat a variety of foods.* While this seems obvious, children can often get stuck in a rut when it comes to food. Diets should include milk, meat, fish, poultry, grains, cereals, fruits, vegetables, and dried beans.
- *Choose a diet low in unsaturated fat, saturated fat, and cholesterol.* If adults or children take in a lot of these, they have an increased likelihood of obesity, heart disease, and some cancers. Eat sparingly, if at all, fried foods, fatty meats, high-fat dairy products, and of course fats like butter and margarine. Be sure to eliminate foods (such as some nondairy creamers) that contain coconut, palm, or palm kernel oils. Since cholesterol is only found in animal products, including eggs, eat these in moderation.
- *Consume plenty of vegetables, fruits, and grain products.* These provide high amounts of minerals, vitamins, and carbohydrates while keeping fat low. In addition, the fiber content is high in fruits, vegetables, dried beans, and grains, which can help reduce cholesterol as well as reduce the risk of some forms of cancer.
- *Keep sugar intake moderate.* Sugar is low in needed vitamins and minerals and contributes to tooth decay. Candy, sodas, cookies, and table sugar consumption should be limited.
- *Salt and sodium should be used in moderation.* For many people, high-salt diets have been linked with high blood pressure. Reduce the amount of table salt used, as well as high-sodium foods like cheese, cured meats (ham and salami), potato chips, and similar snack foods.
- *Maintain a healthy weight.* Overweight people are at increased risk for heart disease, hypertension, diabetes, and some cancers. Change diet to fruits, vegetables, and whole grains rather than foods high in fat and sugar.
- *If you drink alcohol, do it in moderation.* Alcohol is high in k-calories but low in nutrients.

The Food Guide Pyramid

The Food Guide Pyramid shown in Figure 7.1 illustrates the five food groups and recommendations for a range of servings for each. It is helpful in planning diets that meet nutritional requirements without excess fat or energy (Smolin & Grosvenor, 1994). Since a variety of foods is necessary for good health, you should make daily selections from each group. The shape of the Pyramid emphasizes the relative importance of each group

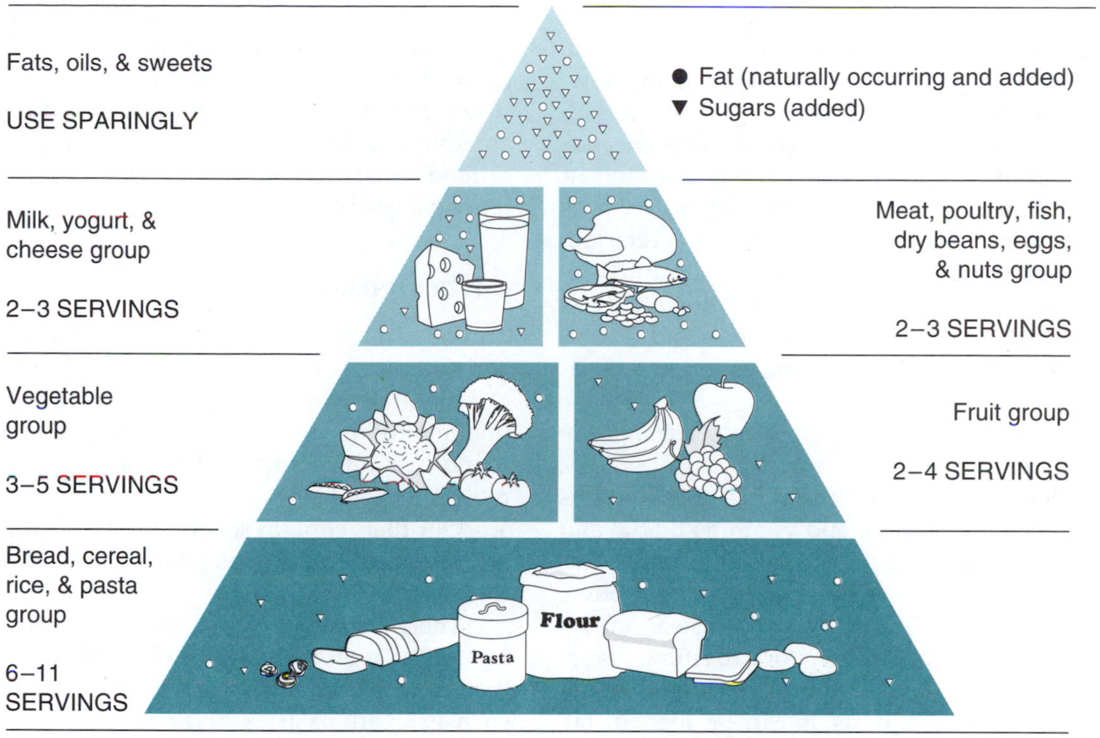

FIGURE 7.1 **USDA Recommended Diet: The Food Pyramid (*Source:* USDA, 1992).**

for your overall diet. Note that a sixth group, fats-oils-sweets, is recommended but, sparingly.

Starting at the base of the Pyramid, six to eleven servings of *bread, cereal, rice, and pasta* are recommended per day. These are rich in carbohydrates and are the foundation of a good diet. The nutrients provided include the B vitamins, iron, magnesium, zinc, and fiber. Examples of this food group are whole-grain breads, cereals, and brown rice. Examples of serving sizes are one slice of bread, one ounce of dry cereal, two cookies, one-half of a medium-sized donut.

The next level has two groups. First is the *vegetable group* with three to five servings per day. This group is important for proper intake of vitamins A and C, folate, iron, magnesium, and fiber. Some foods in this group are dark-green leafy vegetables (spinach), deep yellow vegetables (sweet potatoes, carrots), starchy vegetables (potatoes, corn), legumes (kidney beans), tomatoes, and green beans. Serving-size examples are one-half cup of cooked or raw vegetables, one cup of raw leafy vegetables, three-quarters of a cup of vegetable juice (about 6 oz.), and about ten french fries.

Second, on the same level, is the *fruit group*. Two-to-four servings a day are recommended, to supply vitamins A and C, potassium, and fiber. While fresh fruit may be best, it is not always possible, in which case, choose frozen fruit without sugar added. If canned fruit is selected, be sure it is in water rather than sugar syrup. If the latter has to be purchased, rinse the fruit in water before eating. To increase fiber, eat more whole fruits than juices. Remind children that only 100 percent fruit juice can be counted as fruit for this category. Examples of servings are three-quarters of a cup of fruit juice; one-half cup of chopped, cooked, or canned fruit; and one medium apple, orange, or banana.

Two groups are at the third level, also. The *milk, yogurt, and cheese group* is recommended at two to three servings per day. The ingredients in this group provide us with riboflavin, calcium, and protein. It is important to recommend low-fat milk for people over 2 years. The same advice holds true for yogurt. When consuming cheeses, low-fat kinds should be selected. Needless to say, when it comes to desserts, lower-fat frozen ones like ice milk and frozen yogurt are preferred. Serving examples for this group are one-and-one-half cups of ice cream, 2 cups of cottage cheese, 1 cup of milk or yogurt, one-and-one-half ounces of natural cheese, and 2 ounces of processed cheese.

Meat, poultry, fish, dried beans, eggs, and nuts are recommended at two to three servings per day. The minerals zinc and iron are obtained from this group, as well as protein and vitamins B_6, B_{12}, and niacin. Lean meat should be chosen, and skinless poultry. Fish and dry beans can be chosen often. All fat should be trimmed off, and instead of frying, try broiling, grilling, or roasting. High amounts of cholesterol are in egg yolks, so limit their intake. Nuts and seeds can be high in fat. Keep in mind that 3 ounces of meat is the size of an average hamburger. Examples of serving sizes: 2 to 3 ounces of cooked fish, poultry, or lean meat; two to three eggs; one-and-one-half cups cooked dry beans, and 1 cup of nuts.

At the top of the Pyramid is the smallest group, *fats, oils and sweets,* such as butter, mayonnaise, cream cheese, jam, jelly, sour cream, and salad dressing. While these may be high in energy, they are low in micronutrients and should be used sparingly. Obviously, low-fat spreads and dressings should be substituted for the regular ones whenever possible.

Digestion of Nutrients

Food both provides us with important chemicals needed by the body and supplies us with energy. Food is composed of six classes of nutrients: carbohydrates, proteins, water, minerals, vitamins, and lipids (fats). The *macronutrients* (*macro* because they are required in larger amounts than micronutrients) are carbohydrates, proteins, lipids, and water. Proteins, most carbohydrates, and most lipids cannot be used by the body until they are broken down into smaller chemical units. Vitamins and minerals, known as *micronutrients* (because they are needed in small amounts), are like water in that they need not be broken down; they are absorbed into the body as is. This breakdown of food substances and absorption of nutrients is termed *digestion*.

Carbohydrates

Carbohydrates are the principal source of the body's energy. There are two principal types of carbohydrates: *simple sugars,* which are found predominantly in fruit, and *complex carbohydrates,* found in grains, fruit, and the stems, leaves, and roots of vegetables.

Our diets contain several kinds of simple sugars. The most common is glucose. Others are fructose, sucrose, and lactose.

There are two major classes of complex carbohydrates: *starch* and *fiber.* Much of the starch in our diet comes from foods made from wheat flour, such as bread, pastries, and pastas.

The other major form of complex carbohydrate in our diet is cellulose, which is obtained from vegetable matter called *fiber* or *roughage.* Fiber has been greatly overlooked in the typical American diet of "meat, bread, and potatoes." Most American diets are deficient in fiber, and most Americans do not understand the role of fiber in the human body.

Fiber is mostly plant-cell wall that cannot be digested in the human gut. There are two kinds of fiber. The water-soluble kind, found *inside plant cells,* includes pectin in apples and beans, and gum in oat bran and vegetables. Water-insoluble fiber, found in plant *cell walls,* comprises cellulose in vegetables; hemicellulose in wheat bran, corn bran, the skin of potatoes, beans, and peanuts; and lignin in peas and whole grains. Overall, vegetable fibers make up 45 percent; cereal fiber, 35 percent; and fruit fibers, 29 percent of the typical American diet.

Most Americans need to double their intake of all kinds of fiber. All three fiber sources—vegetable, cereal, and fruit—need to be ingested regularly, each day. An average adult should eat 5 to 6 grams of crude fiber per day, or 100 mg of fiber per kilogram of body weight. Over the past

BOX 7.1 ■ ■ ■ ■ ■

FIBER: HOW MUCH OATMEAL CAN YOU EAT?

"Fiber" is one of those words that has a multiplicity of meanings and usages, leading to no end of confusion. Initially, the fiber content of foods was determined by subjecting various food items to harsh chemical treatment. The residue was known as "fiber," or more properly *crude fiber.* As a practical matter, it included most of the cellulose from plant cell walls, and little else.

In recent years, it has been recognized that there are several categories of macromolecules that resist digestion in humans, and therefore should be included as fiber. In addition to cellulose (particularly abundant in vegetables), there are other polysaccharides such as *pectin* (common in fruit), *hemicellulose* (abundant in grains), and *lignin* (which is not properly a carbohydrate at all, but is found in woody plants and is an important component of fiber). When all of these items are included as fiber, the term *dietary fiber* is used to distinguish it from crude fiber. Dietary fiber is generally three to four times more abundant than crude fiber, and in some foods may be ten times more abundant.

For purposes of examining the functions of fiber in the body, and as an aid in analyzing the various claims currently being made by cereal manufacturers and others, dietary fiber is best regarded as comprising two major types: *water-soluble fiber,* such as pectin, and *water-insoluble fiber,* such as cellulose.

Water-soluble fiber is important because it binds various substances, including bile salts and cholesterol, thereby reducing lipid uptake by the intestines. If no water-soluble fiber is present, the bile salts are reabsorbed by the small intestine. However, when bile salts are bound to water-soluble fiber, they are passed out in the feces, forcing the body to break down bodily cholesterol to form additional bile salts. Thus water-soluble fiber minimizes the absorption of cholesterol in the food, and reduces cholesterol produced by the body. Unfortunately, the trapped bile salts are converted by bacteria in the colon into substances that may promote cancer of the colon.

Water-insoluble fiber has a different set of functions:

1. It promotes peristalsis of the intestines and regular bowel activity because it is both indigestible and water-absorbent.
2. It promotes a feeling of satiety because of its effects on distending the digestive tract, a highly desirable outcome for anyone wishing to lose weight.
3. In large amounts, it correlates favorably with a reduced incidence of colon cancer, in part because it binds with the breakdown products of bile salts trapped by water-soluble fiber. A recent study also demonstrated that the consumption of high fiber cereals led to a sharp reduction in the production of abnormal cells in the colon of individuals with a history of colon cancer.

In short, a balance of water-soluble and water-insoluble fiber in the diet seems far better than excessive amounts of one, to the exclusion of the other. Thus, the oat bran (water-soluble fiber) now being touted as dietarily indispensable (at least by cereal manufacturers who sell oat bran) in the reduction of cholesterol levels should be balanced with wheat bran (water-insoluble), which seems to provide some protection from colon cancer.

Source: From D.J. Farish, *Human Biology.* ©1993. Boston: Jones and Bartlett, p. 145. Reprinted with permission.

fifteen years, persuasive evidence has linked increased fiber intake to the prevention and treatment of certain common Western diseases. Fiber may help to ameliorate or prevent diabetes, obesity, hyperlipidemia, hypertension, and cancer. Lack of fiber has been implicated in diverticulitis and constipation. Fiber affects large-bowel functions, increasing fecal bulk and stool frequency, shortening transit time, and altering microflora. Box 7.1 provides further information on fiber.

Proteins

Protein is essential to human life. The human body is approximately one-fifth protein, though the protein content constantly changes. The major functions of protein are growth, repair, and maintenance of the body. In a child, an absence of protein will terminate growth. More specifically, protein helps to control body-fluid balance and has a special role in detoxifying the body. That is, if protein intake is inadequate, the body's ability to detoxify foreign substances is impaired.

Water

Water accounts for 45 to 60 percent of the content of all living organisms. A person can live much longer without food than without water. The body uses water for digestion, absorption, circulation, transporting nutrients, excretion, building tissue, and maintaining body temperature. Since children tend to be more active than adults, they generally need more water. Six to twelve glasses daily are recommended, although much of this may be obtained from solid foods.

Minerals

Minerals serve two important functions in the body. They are structural components, such as the calcium in teeth and bones, and they regulate important body processes, such as digestion, metabolism, and muscle contraction. Since these body functions vary, minerals are needed in varying amounts. *Megaminerals*—calcium, phosphorus, magnesium, and potassium—are needed in amounts of 1 gram or more per day. *Trace minerals,* such as zinc and selenium, are needed in smaller amounts (milligrams). Mineral deficiencies cause malnutrition and lower immunity level. The richest sources of minerals are fish and fresh green vegetables, although the minerals available in the average diet seldom supply the FDA's recommended daily amounts.

Vitamins

Vitamins are organic compounds other than fats, carbohydrates, and proteins that are essential to human life. They help enzymes digest, absorb, and metabolize fats, carbohydrates, and proteins. They encourage chemical reactions but are not changed or incorporated into the products of the reaction themselves.

Water-soluble vitamins include B-complex and C vitamins. *Fat-soluble* vitamins—A, D, E and K—are found in butter, cream, vegetable oils, seeds, and the fats of meats and fish. Water-soluble vitamins are not stored in the body so they must be ingested daily. Fat-soluble vitamins are stored in body tissues, primarily the liver.

All vitamins can be destroyed by exposure to heat, light, oxygen, or radiation. Fat-soluble vitamins are more stable than water-soluble vitamins; they are less likely to be destroyed in the processing and cooking of foods.

Vitamins in ordinary foods are readily absorbed by the body but seldom at toxic levels. Excess water-soluble vitamins are usually excreted by the kidneys. Excess fat-soluble vitamins are stored in the liver. Toxicity from overdose of vitamins seldom occurs, although vitamin A toxicity is possible if 30,000 or more international units (IU) per day are ingested over two or more months. Children are especially susceptible to vitamin toxicity.

Eating a variety of foods and a balanced diet is the best way to provide the body with the vitamins it needs. The best source of vitamins is fresh, leafy, green vegetables. Legumes, nuts, and whole grains are also good sources of vitamins. Root vegetables and fruits have lesser amounts of vitamins. Lean meats are good sources of B-complex vitamins. A few vitamins (D, K, and several B-complex) are synthesized by bacteria in the large intestine.

In addition to choosing the right amounts from the basic food groups, nutritional habits are important to optimal well-being. Eating regularly contributes to good health. The body can adjust to almost any pattern of eating, whether three meals, or five or six. Also, eating a nutritious breakfast increases a person's efficiency throughout the day. Since the stomach empties every three to five hours, it is wise to get into a pattern of regular eating and getting a good start at breakfast.

Lipids

Lipids, or fats, are a group of diverse chemical substances that have the common property of being relatively insoluble in water. Perhaps the most familiar lipid is *triglyceride,* otherwise known as *body fat.* Excess calories, whether obtained from too much sugar or too much fat, are converted by the liver into triglycerides, which are stored in all-too-obvious places in the body.

Other lipids, such as cholesterol and lecithin, are essential constituents of cell membranes. The

BOX 7.2

CHOLESTEROL: UP CLOSE AND PERSONAL

Because the cholesterol-atherosclerosis connection figures so prominently in today's health-conscious society, let's examine the subject a little more fully. As usual, we will find that things are not nearly as simple as they first appear. First, we need to look at how cholesterol is transported in the blood.

When fatty acids and glycerol are absorbed by the cells of the intestinal lining, those cells recombine the fatty acids and glycerol to form fats (or, in nutritional terms, triglycerides) and then surround them with a protein coat before releasing them into the intercellular spaces where they are picked up by the lacteals. These tiny packages of protein and triglycerides are known as chylomicrons.

The chylomicrons are transported through the lymphatic system and are dumped into the general blood circulation. As they move through the body, they are removed by fat tissue and especially by the liver. The liver transforms them into very low density lipoproteins (VLDLs), which contain about 19 percent cholesterol by weight. As the VLDLs move back into the blood, the triglycerides are gradually removed by body cells, and the VLDLs are transformed into low density lipoproteins (LDLs), which are substantially richer in cholesterol (about 45 percent by weight). LDLs transport cholesterol through the blood for use by various body tissues—cholesterol being the forerunner of a variety of essential body chemicals, including vitamin D, various hormones, and bile salts, which are important in the digestion and absorption of lipids. Another group of lipoproteins, the high density lipoproteins (HDLs), transport cholesterol from the cells back to the liver for conversion into bile, much of which is ultimately lost in the feces. HDLs contain only about 15 percent cholesterol by weight.

A relatively high proportion of HDL is considered good because this is the group of lipoproteins that lowers blood cholesterol. Conversely, a relatively high proportion of LDL is troublesome because it carries much larger loads of cholesterol and, as we have seen, excess cholesterol in the blood leads to deposition of fatty deposits in the arteries.

To some extent, the ratio of LDL to HDL is genetically determined (which helps explain why some people can live seemingly forever on a high-fat diet without ever developing cardiovascular disease); to some extent, it is a function of dietary habits and exercise. (Exercising, especially running, raises the level of HDLs and lowers blood cholesterol levels. Excessive coffee consumption apparently raises and garlic apparently lowers blood cholesterol levels. However, no one has yet determined the net effect of garlic flavored coffee!)

Blood cholesterol readings below 200 mg per 100 ml of blood are considered good; levels between 200 and 240 mg per 100 ml of blood are considered problematic; and levels above 240 mg are grounds for intervention. However, what seems to be even more significant than total cholesterol readings as an indicator for possible cardiovascular problems in the future is the LDL/HDL ratio, which ideally should not exceed 4:1. As the American public becomes more sophisticated about such things, knowing one's LDL/HDL ratio will become more important than simply knowing one's total blood cholesterol reading—although whether either will ever become more essential as a conversation starter than knowing one's astrological sign remains uncertain at this point!

Source: Adapted from D. J. Farish, *Human Biology.* © 1993. Boston, Jones and Bartlett, p. 148. Reprinted with permission.

steroid hormones produced by the reproductive organs and adrenal glands are lipids; vitamins A, D, E, and K are lipids; and substances in liver bile that help digest fats, the bile acids, are lipids.

Dietary lipids come in three principal forms: cholesterol, saturated fat, and unsaturated fat. Saturated fat differs from unsaturated fat by having more hydrogen atom in each fat molecule. Saturated fats tend to be solid at room temperature, whereas unsaturated fats tend to be liquid.

The amounts of cholesterol, saturated fat, and unsaturated fat taken into the body depend on what kinds of foods are eaten. Some foods, such as egg yolk, contain large amounts of cholesterol, whereas others, such as vegetable oils, are high in unsaturated fat but contain no cholesterol. There is considerable controversy about the health effects of eating high amounts of certain kinds of fats, although the present consensus among nutritionists and medical researchers seems to be that diets containing more than 600 milligrams per day of cholesterol and 50 grams per day of saturated fat may contribute to heart and blood-vessel disease.

The body requires one type of unsaturated fat, *linoleic acid*. Not getting enough of it may lead to a deficiency disease characterized primarily by skin lesions. For this reason, you should not attempt to eliminate all lipids from your diet. Furthermore, fats provide energy. If you were to eliminate nearly all fat from your diet and not compensate with increased amounts of carbohydrate or protein, your body would break down its protein to supply energy.

Children and Nutrition

As children grow, their nutritional needs change. The information in this section addresses some of the important issues regarding children and nutrition. First and foremost, children do make choices. While their parents and caregivers may control

Eating a healthy meal together as a family doesn't just teach children good eating habits, it reinforces the value of close relationships and good communication skills.

what they are offered, the children themselves choose what they are going to eat. Just ask any parent who has tried to feed children something they don't want!

Modified Food Guide Pyramid

While children need the same variety of foods in the same pattern as adults, their serving amounts should be smaller (Smolin & Grosvenor, 1994). In the breads category, one slice of bread for those 4 years and up translates into one-half slice for those under 4 years. Adults may ingest one-half cup of cooked or raw vegetables, whereas 4- to 6-year-olds may eat one-third cup, and toddlers only 1 tablespoon for each year of age. For meat (or meat substitutes), the serving size for those 7 to 10 years may be the same as adults, while children between 1 and 3 years have serving sizes of 1 tablespoon per year of age. As for milk, it is recommended that children drink 2 cups of milk everyday, minimum.

Nutrients

Children should have a diet of complex *carbohydrates* from cereals, breads, and vegetables, and adequate fiber should be gained from these foods. It is not recommended to give children fiber supplements since they may then reduce the amount of food they eat, thereby limiting the essential nutrients gained. As far as *fat* is concerned, the need for it decreases markedly after the age of 2 years. The general rule of thumb is to limit fat intake to 30 percent of the total diet. Thus high-fat fast foods need to be balanced with more appropriate meals at home. As children get older, metabolism slows; however, the amount of energy expended in play activities is idiosyncratic. Some children are "couch potatoes" from early on, while others never stop moving. Consequently, *proteins and fluid* requirements vary from child to child. *Vitamin and mineral* supplements are generally unnecessary, but it is important to pay special attention to calcium and iron. The former is essential for bone density and the prevention of osteoporosis in later life. And iron-deficiency anemia is prevalent among children, particularly those between 1 and 4 years.

Healthy Eating Habits

As noted earlier, it is important to have children learn about nutrition and develop good nutritional habits as early as possible. Unhealthy habits may bring about immediate gratification, but a severe price could be paid in later life. Listed below are some basic suggestions regarding children's nutrition.

- Offer a balanced diet following the Food Guide Pyramid.
- Make eating a healthy, positive experience by setting an example for children, for instance, low-fat foods, not always eating in front of the TV, sharing meals rather than eating in isolation, not allowing meals to be "run-in, run-out" experiences, and so forth.
- Emphasize the importance of breakfast, since skipping breakfast can impede learning (Kruesi & Rapoport, 1986). If breakfast per se must be skipped, have children eat something nutritious on the way to school, or pack a healthy snack to eat in mid-morning rather than grabbing something from a vending machine.
- Fast food doesn't have to be ruled out altogether, but it should be eaten in moderation. Children can learn that low-fat fast food should be selected. For example, choosing a plain hamburger is much better than selecting one covered with sauce. Plain, grilled chicken is preferable to chicken dipped in batter and fried. Fast foods generally lack a lot of nutrients that must be made up in other meals.
- Temporary food fixations, called *food jags*, wherein a child just eats one kind of food, are common but usually do not last very long (Smolin & Grosvenor, 1994).
- When packing lunches for day camp, be sure they are nutritious, and be cautious about what is packed if no refrigeration is available.
- TV commercials advertising high-sugar cereals and other foods can be discussed before getting to the store.
- Since tooth decay is a major problem among children, sugary snacks should be eliminated or reduced. Remember, primary teeth guide the permanent teeth and therefore are just as important to keep clean.

Snacking

Snacking among children has been one of the most controversial topics in nutrition. It is well confirmed that excess snacking, especially close to mealtime, decreases appetite for meals. However, since children have small stomachs, they cannot eat much during regular meals even if they have not been snacking. Thus children may not be able to eat enough at meals, especially during rapid growth. In this case, snacks solve part of the problem. The teacher should help children become aware that some snacks are nutritious and others are not. Persistent nutrition education of children and their parents can mold children's snacking patterns in healthful ways.

Snacks loaded with sugar, salt, and fat but low in protein, fiber, vitamins, and minerals are bad. But if children snack on nutritious foods, especially any that are lacking from their regular meals, then snacking is a great idea. And a slice of cheese, a wheat cracker, or a banana at mid-morning or mid-afternoon can help keep children from tiring.

Special Considerations for the Teenager

In the late childhood or early teenage years, students generally experience puberty. The tremendous changes in their bodies include a decrease in body fat for males and an increase for females. By the time adolescents reach age 20, women have almost twice as much fat tissue and about two-thirds as much lean tissue as men. During adolescence, nutrient needs reach an all-time high for both genders, although the needs of boys are generally greater. Vitamin needs are high during adolescence because of all the cell division and growing. Teens should be especially cognizant of their folate and vitamin B_6 needs, since these are notoriously low in practice, especially in girls. While other vitamins are important during this

It is especially important for adolescents to eat a well-balanced diet. But, given the choice, young teens rarely choose the most nutritious snacks.

growth stage, they are usually met through regular meals.

As expected, the growth spurt at puberty requires a lot of calcium for bone growth and density. Iron deficiency is another concern. Boys initially require more iron, but as girls experience menses, their needs rise, too. Young athletes should be monitored for iron deficiency and supplements given as needed, especially to girls.

The primary nutritional danger in athletics is weight control. Football requires bulk, causing students to eat more than needed, whereas wrestling could cause students to get into a cycle of lose-gain-lose-gain according to weight class. Female students are not immune to such nutrition-roulette games. If they participate in dance (e.g., ballet) or gymnastics, dieting can assume a major role in their lives. This is especially true as they move through puberty and must address increases in adipose tissue.

Common Nutrition Problems in Children and Adolescents

Several problems may arise as a result of *malnutrition,* or poor nutritional status from too much or too little appropriate dietary intake. Too little, called *undernutrition,* results in retarded growth, weight loss, poor work or school performance, and in the case of starvation, eventual death. The eating disorder called *anorexia nervosa* is very common in adolescence and results in undernutrition. *Bulimia,* another eating disorder which consists of binging and purging, is often a precursor to anorexia nervosa. Box 7.3 explains these disorders in greater detail.

In the United States, the more common malnutrition problem is *overnutrition,* with about 15 percent of adolescents 12 to 19 years being overweight. This figure rises to 26 percent for those between the ages of 20 and 74. If a child becomes overweight, the condition may persist into adulthood and increase the risk for some chronic diseases in later life (USPHS, 1988). Obese children are likely to suffer emotional stress, too. While definitive data are lacking, it appears that adolescent obesity is increasing. If true, several factors no doubt play a role. Nonetheless, two obese parents have an 80 percent chance of having an obese child. The mix between heredity and environment is questionable; yet, no matter the degree of heredity involved, it is important for children to learn and practice sound nutrition.

Heart disease, including high cholesterol levels, is another problem children may face. Children living in the United States currently derive 37 percent of their energy from fat, and one goal of *Healthy Children 2000* is to reduce this to no more than 30 percent (USDHHS, 1992). Of course high cholesterol in children—a blood level greater than 170 mg per 100 ml—can lay the foundation for atherosclerosis. Atherosclerosis is the disease process in which fatty deposits called *plaque* adhere to the walls of arteries and impede blood flow. Children of parents who suffer coronary artery disease prior to age 55 or who have high levels of cholesterol should be monitored. *Hypertension* or high blood pressure can be a concern for children, too, since it often is carried into adulthood.

Two other areas of concern for adolescents are teenage pregnancy and alcohol consumption. It is obvious that nutritional needs change during pregnancy. Thus pregnant teenagers are often seen as high-risk patients and prenatal visits are a must. As for alcohol consumption, teens need to be aware that alcohol can reduce the body's amounts of vitamins A, D, and K.

Implications for Elementary and Middle-School Teachers

Summary Issues

1. The lifestyles of most Americans are not conducive to sound nutritional habits, especially their reliance on fast foods and convenience foods.
2. Significant losses of nutrients occur during cooking, storage, transportation, and processing of foods.
3. There is mounting evidence that health problems and diseases stem from vitamin and mineral deficiencies as well as from eating the incorrect foods.
4. One of the principal consequences of poor eating is lowered immune function.
5. There are four confounding factors regarding an adequate diet for everyone: individ-

BOX 7.3

EATING DISORDERS: ANOREXIA AND BULIMIA

Anorexia nervosa is a very serious eating disorder affecting approximately 0.5 percent of girls between the ages of 12 and 18. (Older women and males have much lower incidence.) It is manifested in the willful suppression of appetite, based on the perception (which may or may not be valid) by the individual that she is overweight or is inclined to become overweight. Sustained periods of near-starvation lead to shrinkage of the brain and reduced mental acuity, significant changes in endocrine function, and deficiencies in such minerals as iron, copper, and zinc, all of which tend to reinforce the behavioral manifestations of anorexia. In other words, anorectics tend to spiral downward, sometimes with fatal consequences (usually because of mineral imbalances leading to cardiac arrest).

The cause of the disorder is not well understood. Some authorities feel that it results from a problem with the area of the brain associated with eating, others conclude that it is a psychological disorder, often the result of a deteriorating mother-daughter relationship. Treatment includes psychotherapy; behavioral modification; use of appropriate medications; and hospital feedings. Recovery may take a year or more, and is not always successful—only 50 percent remain free of symptoms and another 25 percent have reduced symptoms. If untreated, about 5 percent of anorectics die.

Bulimia, or "binge-purge" behavior, is characterized by periodic eating binges followed by induced vomiting and extensive use of laxatives. Victims of this disorder are also usually young women, and although they are often of normal weight, their method of weight control can lead to serious problems such as loss of teeth enamel from the acidic vomit, mineral imbalance from laxative use and from vomiting, rectal bleeding, and liver, kidney, and heart damage. Some researchers think that this condition results from abnormalities in CCK production or reception; others feel that it is primarily psychological, resulting from attempts to obtain approval from unresponsive, perfectionist parents, and societal pressure to be thin.

The incidence of this condition in the United States is unknown, but as many as 20 percent of college women are estimated to have had some experience with bulimia. Bulimia is often more hidden than anorexia (since the victim is often within normal weight limits), and bulimics frequently suffer from the disease for six or seven years before seeking help. Antidepressant drugs, coupled with psychotherapy and behavioral therapy, are generally effective.

Source: D.J. Farish, *Human Biology.* ©1993. Boston: Jones and Bartlett, p. 166. Reprinted with permission.

ual differences, test-tube science versus reality, conflicting recommendations, and interpretation of minimums and maximums.

6. In the United States, there are seven dietary guidelines: eat a variety of foods; choose a diet low in unsaturated fat, saturated fat, and cholesterol; eat plenty of vegetables, fruits, and grains; keep sugar intake low; use salt and sodium in moderation; maintain a healthy weight; and drink alcohol only in moderation if at all.
7. The Food Guide Pyramid has five major food groups: bread, cereal, rice, and pasta; vegetable; fruit; milk, yogurt, and cheese; and meat, poultry, fish, dry beans, eggs, and nuts. Fats, oils, and sweets are separated into a sixth group and are to be used very sparingly.
8. Nutrients comprise carbohydrates, proteins, lipids (fats), minerals, vitamins, and water.
9. There are two major classes of complex carbohydrates: starch and fiber. Fiber is impor-

tant in the prevention and treatment of several common Western diseases, such as some cancers, high cholesterol, obesity, diabetes, and hypertension.

10. Proteins are essential; an absence in children can cause growth retardation.
11. Lipids are needed in only small amounts, but currently about 37 percent of children's energy comes from fat.
12. About 45 to 60 percent of all living organisms are made up of water.
13. Minerals are very important for children, especially calcium and iron.
14. The two major types of vitamins are water-soluble and fat-soluble. Given balanced diets, vitamin supplements are generally not required for children.
15. The Food Guide Pyramid should be modified for children in regard to serving size but remain the same as for adults in the balance of food groups.
16. Nutrient requirements for children and adolescents are different than for adults, and during adolescence, change for males and females.
17. Healthy eating habits must be established early.
18. Teenagers have special nutritional needs due to puberty, gender, and athletics.
19. Common nutrition problems in children and adolescents are malnutrition, anorexia nervosa, bulimia, heart disease, and hypertension.

Teacher Ramifications

In regard to nutrition and children, a teacher should:

1. Work with other health-team members to ascertain the nutritional status of students who are having difficulty learning
2. Serve as a role model in the school cafeteria and elsewhere by selecting nutritious meals and snacks
3. Cooperate with school food services to determine the nutrient content of school lunches compared to the *Dietary Guidelines for Americans*
4. Observe children during lunch and snack time and address any problems or myths concerning diet
5. Work with students and other health-team members to restrict or modify food vending machines in the schools
6. Support the school's role in helping the nation reach the following objectives set forth in *Healthy Children 2000:*
   - #2.3. Reduce overweight to a prevalence of no more than 20 percent among people aged 20 and older, and no more than 15 percent among adolescents aged 12 through 19.
   - #2.4. Reduce growth retardation among low-income children aged 5 and younger to less than 10 percent.
   - #2.5. Reduce dietary fat intake to an average of 30 percent of calories or less, and average saturated fat intake to less than 10 percent of calories among people aged 2 and older.
   - #2.7. Increase to at least 50 percent the proportion of overweight people aged 12 and older who have adopted sound dietary practices combined with regular physical activity to attain an appropriate body weight.
   - #2.10. Reduce iron deficiency to less than 3 percent among children aged 1 through 4 and among women of childbearing age.
   - #2.17. Increase to at least 90 percent the proportion of school lunch and breakfast services and child care food services with menus that are consistent with the nutrition principles in the *Dietary Guidelines for Americans.*
   - #2.19. Increase to at least 75 percent the proportion of the nation's schools that provide nutrition education from preschool through grade 12, preferably as a part of quality school health education.

SECTION III

Teaching Strategies for Nutrition

The strategies in this section are divided into grades K–4, 5–6, and 7–8 levels. In addition to strategies that can be used in the classroom, home activities are included. A home activity is designed for student-parent interaction. It is a way to engage the home in school-student learning, and parents can sign a slip of paper to confirm that an activity was completed. Evaluation of all strategies through use of the National Health Education Standards and performance indicators is indicated. Teachers may also write corresponding learning assessments.

K–4 Level

Strategy One

Objective: Students will match foods with the correct level of the Food Pyramid.

Activity: Have a diagram of the Food Pyramid for each student (or have students draw their own). Using a check sheet with common foods listed, students record what they ate the previous day. Students then match what they ate with the levels of the Food Pyramid, writing the name of the food either in the Pyramid itself or on lines next to the appropriate level. Discuss how the Food Pyramid can guide us in eating properly. Have each student analyze his or her own pyramid to see what needs to be decreased and increased.

Integration: Art, Language Arts

Related Health Content Areas: Growth and development, human body

Health Education Standards and Performance Indicators: 1(1); 2(2)

Strategy Two

Objective: Students will recognize the importance of a nutritious breakfast.

Activity: Survey students to see how many have had breakfast. Write on the board what types of foods were eaten. Discuss with students why it is important to have a balanced and nutritious breakfast as follows:

- A long period of time has passed since the last meal.
- It gives us energy to go to school or work.
- It gives us energy to think and learn.
- It gives us energy to play or participate in gym (or sports).

Integration: Science

Related Health Content Areas: Growth and development, fitness

Health Education Standards and Performance Indicators: 3(1); 6(2,4)

5–6 Level

Strategy One

Objective: Students will recognize that ethnic traditions and customs affect what we learn to eat.

Activity: Discuss variations in ethnic dietary habits (e.g., high rice intake and low cardiovascular disease among Orientals) and resulting health effects. Students may then bring in examples of traditional foods eaten in their families. These may be written, in the form of recipes, or actual dishes brought in for classmates to sample.

Integration: Social Studies, Home Economics

Related Health Content Areas: Growth and development, diseases, human body

Health Education Standards and Performance Indicators: 1(4,5); 4(1)

Strategy Two

Objective: Students will identify which foods are considered "good" and nutritious.

Activity: Have students write down several of their favorite foods. Ask for an example from a student. Discuss what types of nutrients this food provides for the student. Using the Food Pyramid as a guide, ask students if this is a food they should eat a lot of, or one they should have only once in awhile.

Integration: Science, Home Economics, Math

Related Health Content Areas: Growth and development, family, fitness

Health Education Standards and Performance Indicators: 2(3); 3(1)

Strategy Three

Objective: Students will apply the principles of the Food Pyramid to menus from the school cafeteria.

Activity: In conjunction with a food service representative (nutritionist), the students are to analyze the menus to determine whether they meet the recommendations in the Food Pyramid. This may be completed as a written exercise or class discussion.

Integration: Home Economics, Social Studies, Science

Related Health Content Areas: Consumer, growth and development, illness and disease

Health Education Standard and Performance Indicators: 2(1,2); 6(4)

7–8 Level

Strategy One

Objective: Students will recognize the effects of diet on diabetes.

Activity: Problem-based learning activity (See Chapter 4) as follows:

Donna is diabetic, but she's not very good at taking care of herself. Just before spring break, she took home her emergency diabetic kit. Usually she skips lunch because she is afraid of getting fat. Today, after physical education and skipping lunch again, Donna is acting funny. If you didn't know any better, you would think she'd had something alcoholic to drink. When you ask her about it, Donna says she's fine.

- What is the main and immediate problem in this vignette?
- What information should Donna and others have?
- How does this information apply to the immediate problem in the vignette?
- What is the best thing Donna could do regarding her overall health?
- How might she decide whether her decision was a good one?

Integration: Science

Related Health Content Areas: Diseases, growth and development, mental-emotional health

Health Education Standards and Performance Indicators: 2(2,6); 3(1); 6(3)

Strategy Two

Objective: Students will determine how their diets match the Food Pyramid recommendations.

Activity: Have students keep a log of their food intake (see Figure 7.2) for a few days prior to this lesson. (It may be helpful to allow a few minutes at the beginning or end of class on the days they are recording to ensure completion and accurate records.) Using the Food Pyramid guidelines, have students analyze their own dietary status and write up recommendations for improvement. Students should take into consideration any desires to lose or gain weight, involvement in strenuous physical activity (sports, dance, gymnastics, etc.), special dietary needs (e.g., for diabetes). The recommendations can be written in the form of a contract that includes the students' parents, and rewards can be given for achievement.

Day 1 ______________

Foods Eaten	Where They Fit in Food Pyramid
A.M.	
NOON	
P.M.	

FIGURE 7.2 Example of a Food Log

Integration: Home Economics, Physical Education, Science, Math, Language Arts

Related Health Content Areas: Fitness, growth and development, diseases, emotional well-being

Health Education Standards and Performance Indicators: 3(1); 6(2,4,5,6)

Home Activities

Strategy One

Objective: Students will be able to estimate amounts of fats, carbohydrates, sugar, and salt that are in their diet.

Activity: Using a variety of foods regularly used at home, have students, with their parents, analyze the food labels to identify amounts of the following:

- sugars (other names for sugar: sucrose, glucose, dextrose, lactose, fructose, maltose, honey, molasses, corn syrup, malt, maple syrup, corn sweetener, brown sugar, raw sugar, natural sweeteners)
- fats (other names for fats: butter, margarine, lard, shortening, hydrogenated oil, and corn, soy, palm, coconut, canola, vegetable oil)
- sodium (other names for sodium: baking powder, baking soda, MSG or monosodium glutamate, soy isolates, milk solids, sodium nitrites or nitrates)
- carbohydrates

Students should then calculate the total amounts in their daily diets and compare them to recommended daily amounts.

Integration: Science, Math

Related Health Content Areas: Disease, consumer health

Health Education Standards: 2; 3; 6

Strategy Two

Objective: Students will demonstrate the ability to develop and prepare a balanced meal.

Activity: Using any available references, have student develop a meal, analyze its nutritive content, modify it if necessary, and decide what items need to be purchased to prepare the meal. A parent should go with the student to the grocery store to purchase the items and analyze them for cost-effectiveness. Finally, allow the student to prepare the meal for the family. Make sure to give him or her positive feedback.

Integration: Home Economics, Physical Education, Science, Math

Related Health Content Areas: Growth and development, fitness, diseases

Health Education Standards: 3,6

References

Candra, R.K. Nutrition and immunity: Basic considerations; parts 1 & 2, *Contemporary Nutrition* 11, 12 (1986).

Chandra, R.K. Nutritional deficiency and susceptibility to infection, *Bulletin of the World Health Organization* 57,2 (1979):167–177.

Farish, D.J. *Human Biology.* Jones and Bartlett, Boston, 1993.

Kruesi, J.M.P., & Rapoport, J.L. Diet and human behavior: How much do they affect each other? *Annual Review of Nutrition* 6 (1986):113–130.

Smolin, L.A., & Grosvenor, M.B. *Nutrition: Science and Applications.* Saunders, Fort Worth, TX; 1994.

United States Department of Agriculture. *The Food Guide Pyramid* (Home and Gardens Bulletin No. 252. Human Nutrition Information Service, Hyattsville, MD, 1992).

United States Department of Agriculture. *Nutrition and Your Health: Dietary Guidelines for Americans* 3rd ed., (Home and Gardens Bulletin No. 232. U.S. Government Printing Office, Hyattsville, MD, 1990).

United States Department of Health and Human Services, Public Health Service. *Healthy Children 2000* (Jones and Bartlett, Boston, 1992).

United States Public Health Service. *Surgeon General's Report on Nutrition and Health* (Pub. No. 88–50210, 1988). U.S. Government Printing Office, Washington, DC.

8

Illness and Disease

At the conclusion of this chapter, you should be able to:

- *Explain the interplay of body, mind, and environment in regard to illness and disease*
- *Synthesize and explain the body's defense system, from the first line of defense to the final line of defense*
- *Recognize and explain autoimmune diseases as they apply to children*
- *Recognize the allergic reactions of asthma, anaphylactic shock, and contact dermatitis in children*
- *Know the variety of organisms causing infectious diseases*
- *Compare and explain the infectious-disease stages*
- *Identify and explain chronic diseases as they apply to children*
- *Comprehend lifestyle and prevention factors in common childhood diseases and apply this knowledge in the classroom*

SECTION I

Health Status, Deficits, and Learning

Complete freedom from disease and illness is a dream. However great the benefits of progress, improved sanitation, regular medical care, and a high standard of living have been, they do not ensure freedom from disease. Children are especially susceptible to infections and other ailments.

The common cold, influenza, measles, mumps, diphtheria, and strep throat are just a few of the common infections children contract. Children react emotionally to such infections as well as physiologically. Their social life is disrupted. They respond with fear and anxiety, which disrupts learning as well as overall development. Children need help in allaying such emotional stresses. And teachers should be aware that children need not only immunization against diseases, but also general information about illnesses and disease, how to care for oneself during illness, and how to keep from getting sick.

Listed below are some points about illness and absence.

- The common cold is very expensive, causing over 30 million days lost from school and work each year in the United States.
- Smallpox is an excellent example of how communicable diseases can be controlled.
- Children and even young babies can have high blood pressure.
- High blood pressure in children can be a sign of an underlying problem, such as kidney disease.
- Cancer is the chief cause of death by disease in children between the ages of 1 and 14 years.
- About one in three childhood deaths from cancer are from leukemia.
- Five-year survival rates for childhood cancers vary by site; for all sites, the rate is 68 percent. For bone cancer, it is 58 percent; neuroblastoma, 57 percent; brain and central nervous system, 60 percent; Wilms' tumor (kidney), 88 percent; Hodgkin's disease, 88 percent; and acute lymphocytic leukemia, 72 percent—Early detection is the key to survival.
- With about 3 million children under the age of 18 diagnosed with asthma, it is the leading cause of school absence due to illness.
- Children with chronic illnesses undergo several additional stressors, such as dealing with medications, being isolated from other children, worrying about being sick, watching parents argue over the best course of action, and so forth.

- Rheumatic heart disease and asthma are related to antigen-antibody reactions.
- Lyme disease, ankylosing spondylitis, and systemic lupus erythematosus are similar to juvenile rheumatoid arthritis in that all are classified as forms of childhood arthritis.
- There are two types of diabetes, with the children's form falling into the Type I, insulin-dependent, category.
- Hypoglycemia in diabetic children must be monitored to prevent possible death.
- Chicken pox, mumps, and rubella (German measles) are the three most common childhood diseases.
- Immunization for the major infectious diseases is a must to enter school.
- Children with infectious diseases can get behind in learning due to both absences from school and the inability to focus when present.

SECTION II

Illness and Disease Teaching Information

Illness and disease, like well-being, are cultural concepts and are interpreted through society's value system. For example, whether one takes a cold to bed or disregards it in his or her daily routine is directed by one's cultural perception of illness. Such cultural evaluation varies; and there is a great deal of confusion over what the concepts disease, infection, and disorder mean. The distinctions are discussed below.

For most people, life consists of extended periods of wellness punctuated by occasional illness. It would be foolish to pretend that you will never become sick or that diseases do not exist. Health is achieved not only by preventing illnesses but by having a good attitude during sickness and injury.

Attitudes toward illness are very important. Anger and frustration are common responses to sickness or injury. Some people get angry at their bodies for failing to function, or they become frustrated that they are unable to do all the things they want to do. But there are other, more positive ways to deal with illness. One way is to regard times of sickness as unavoidable parts of living. Another way is to recognize that sickness or injury can be your body's way of telling you that you need rest, that perhaps you have been pushing yourself too hard. Yet another is to use periods of illness to reexamine the stresses and habits that may contribute to susceptibility to sickness. As discussed more fully later in the chapter on emotional well-being (Chapter 10), we may "behave" ourselves into sickness by living in ways that are dispiriting. Viewed positively, however, many illnesses may become more tolerable. And by reducing anger, frustration, and worry, you can speed the healing process.

Distinguishing between Illness and Disease

There are a number of important distinctions between illness and disease. Illness is felt, whereas disease is diagnosed by a physician. A person may "feel ill" without a disease in evidence; a person may have a disease without any illness or suffering. For example, millions of Americans have the disease of high blood pressure, which may be symptomless until a heart attack occurs.

The onset and severity of any illness can be affected by the ways in which a person deals with it. If you become angry or depressed at being sick or excessively concerned about the outcome of the illness, you can interfere with the body's ability to heal. Disturbed emotions may lower resistance to disease by reducing the immunological responsiveness of the body. Stress and worry can also produce physiological changes that interfere with the natural healing mechanisms of the body, and contribute to illness and disease. As Thomas (1979) suggests,

> Far from being ineptly put together, [people] are amazingly tough, durable organisms, full of health, ready for most contingencies. The new danger to our well-being . . . is in becoming a nation of healthy hypochondriacs, living gingerly, worrying ourselves half to death.

Thus optimism can reduce the severity of illness and disease, as well as one's susceptibility to becoming sick.

Causes of Disease

Traditionally, medical practitioners refer to diseases as resulting from specific causes. The cause of a disease is known as its *etiology.* For example, specific bacteria are said to cause pneumonia or gonorrhea; certain viruses are said to cause measles, mumps, and hepatitis; a broken leg may have been caused by a fall.

Few diseases have a single cause though. Whether a person gets sick depends on a wide range of modifying factors (see Figure 8.1). Dubos (1968) points out that:

> All manifestations of human disease are the consequence of the interplay between body, mind, and environment. This situation creates a difficult dilemma for physicians and medical scientists. They recognize that the analytic breakdown of the problems of disease into their component parts never results in a true picture; yet they know from practical experience that the artificial reduction of these problems into their constituent parts, or their conversion into simpler models, is an absolute necessity for scientific progress.

The common cold, one of the most widespread human diseases, involves infection of the upper respiratory tract (nose and throat) by any one of hundreds of different cold viruses (see Box 8.1) yet the presence of a virus does not always cause a cold. In experiments with volunteer subjects in which suspensions of a cold virus were sprayed into the nose and throat, not everyone in the study developed symptoms. For a variety of reasons, some persons were more resistant to the virus than others.

Similarly, the cause of tuberculosis is not simply the presence of the infecting organism, *Mycobacterium tuberculosis.* Tuberculosis (TB) was one of the leading causes of death in the United States at the turn of the century, but today few deaths are attributed to it even though the bacterium has not disappeared from the environment. Robert Koch, a famous microbiologist of the nineteenth century, called TB "the disease of poverty" because it tended to be associated with squalor, overcrowding, poor nutrition, and poor sanitation. Many persons today have small tubercular lesions in their lungs, yet they never have any symptoms of illness because their lives do not match the other criteria.

FIGURE 8.1 Internal and External Factors Determine Whether Disease Results from Infectious Agents.

BOX 8.1 ■ ■ ■ ■ ■

THE COMMON COLD

Virtually everybody catches a cold sometime or other. Schoolchildren may contract as many as a dozen colds a year. It is estimated that 100 million serious colds occur each year in the U.S., causing 30 million days lost at school and work. Sales of over-the-counter cold remedies (which do not cure colds but may relieve symptoms) amount to about $1 billion annually. The common cold is clearly something that everyone prefers not to catch or to suffer from.

In 1914 a German scientist, W. Von Kause, first proposed that colds are caused by viruses. However, an actual cold virus (adenovirus R-167) wasn't isolated until 1953. Finally, in 1985, a detailed three-dimensional picture of a cold virus was obtained by using high-energy X-rays. Despite these major advances in cold virus research, a cure for the common cold is still not in sight. Even the development of a vaccine that would prevent colds is doubtful because of the large number of different viruses that can cause colds and the ease with which cold viruses change their antigenic properties.

Six major classes of cold viruses—rhinoviruses, coronaviruses, adenoviruses, myxoviruses, paramyxoviruses, and coxsackieviruses—have been identified. Within the rhinovirus class alone more than 120 different types have been observed. To prevent infection by all 120, many vaccines would have to be developed and administered. Scientists hope to find some common feature shared by most of the cold viruses so that a single vaccine could prevent most colds. However, this prospect is quite remote and may not be possible.

New evidence shows that most colds are not transmitted through the air by sneezing or coughing but by hand-to-hand contact. Infected persons have viruses on their hands and transfer viruses to others by hand-to-hand contact. The second person becomes infected by touching his or her nose with a hand or contaminated object. Frequent washing of hands when around people with colds may reduce chances of catching a cold.

The idea that cold, damp weather or drafts predispose people to catching cold has been disproved in numerous experiments. Volunteers who are deliberately infected with cold viruses and then placed in a cold damp room for two to three hours did not catch cold more easily than a control group. Recent experiments show that a nasal spray containing alpha-interferon can reduce the chances of catching a cold if the nasal spray is used just prior to exposure. The problem with interferon is that it is a potent drug and its safety has not been demonstrated, especially in children, and for the drug to be effective, you would have to spray interferon into your nose daily; since you never know when or where you may become exposed to cold viruses.

The unfortunate conclusion is that a cure for the common cold is uncertain, certainly years in the future.

Thus discussing a disease in terms of a single cause is mostly a matter of convenience; many factors contribute to the initiation and course of a disease. It is possible, however, to classify diseases according to the *principal* factor causing them. The principal factors accounting for nearly all diseases are (1) heredity, (2) infectious organisms, (3) lifestyle and personal habits, (4) accidents, and (5) poisons and toxic chemicals.

Keep in mind that, with rare exceptions, anyone can influence the development of a disease for better or worse. Disease disrupts a person's balance of body, mind, spirit, and interactions with other people. So whatever can be done to restore harmony can ameliorate or help cure most diseases and improve or reestablish health.

Staying Healthy: The Body's Defenses

Most people feel well most of the time. This is because the body contains a remarkable array of defense mechanisms that help keep noxious substances and disease-causing organisms out of the body and help eliminate any diseased cells and infectious organisms found in the body.

Your body provides habitat for a variety of viruses, bacteria, and other pathogens. These microorganisms are always present, yet they rarely make you sick or cause disease. Every day you ingest harmful organisms and toxic substances in the food you eat, the air you breathe, and the water you drink. Yet your body rarely falls prey to these harmful substances. If you become sick, it is probably because you have had excessive or prolonged exposure to a harmful substance, or because you have become more susceptible to it.

Most of the responses of the body's defense systems, as well as the detoxification of chemicals in the liver and the repair of damage to cells and tissues, are physiological processes regulated automatically by the body itself. But these defense mechanisms can be hampered by poor nutrition, stressful environment, emotional upset, and negative attitude. Understanding how the body's defense mechanisms protect you from disease will also help you to understand how physical and mental well-being and harmonious interactions with the environment can keep the body's defenses functioning optimally.

The First Line of Defense: Keeping Harmful Substances Out

The best way to prevent disease caused by foreign substances, whether pathogens or poisons, is to exclude them from the body. The skin keeps out most microorganisms and harmful substances (see Figure 8.2). In addition, the mildly acidic surface of the skin provides a poor habitat for most harmful bacteria, while allowing certain beneficial bacteria to colonize the skin.

The *mucous membranes* provide another vital barrier to disease-causing substances. Our eyes, nose, throat, and breathing passages are protected by membranes that continuously produce secretions that flush away harmful particles. These membranes also secrete enzymes that degrade foreign substances. The mouth, gastrointestinal tract (digestive system), and excretory organs are similarly encased and protected by membranes that guard the body's internal cells and organs.

Tears keep the surface of the eye moist and wash foreign particles out. Earwax protects the

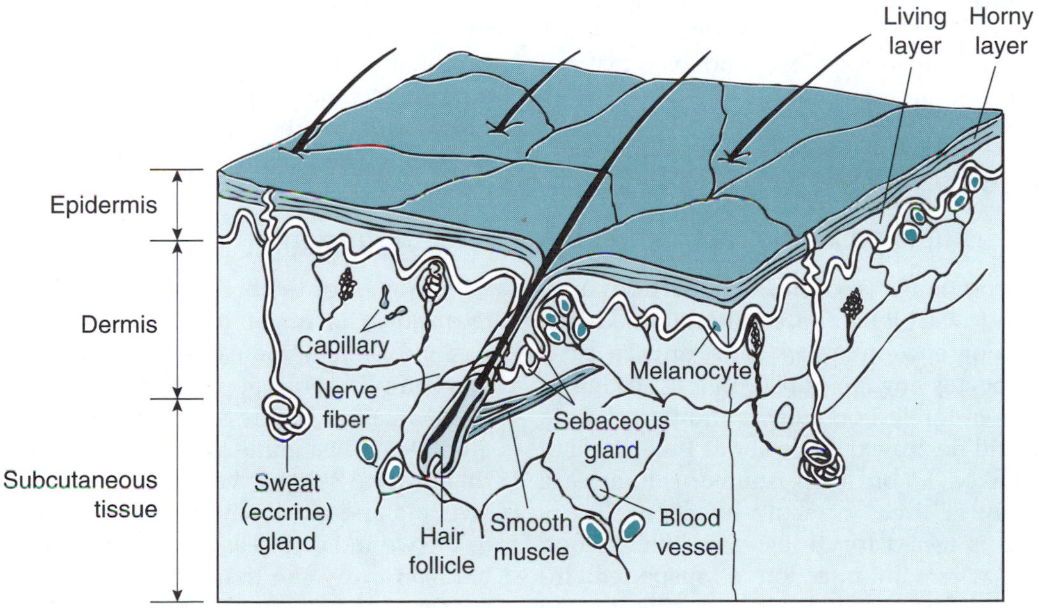

FIGURE 8.2 **Skin Provides the First Line of Defense. It Is a Complex Organ of Several Layers of Specialized Organelles.**

delicate hearing apparatus. The mucous coating of the respiratory tract is sticky, providing a trap for irritating particles and organisms; and microscopic, hairlike fibers called *cilia* keep the mucus of the respiratory tract moving out of the bronchial tubes so that eventually you are able to cough or spit out the irritating substances. Sneezing and blowing the nose eliminate irritating particles that are inhaled.

Enzymes and substances in the blood form a clot that rapidly seals any break in the skin and prevents entry of harmful substances and organisms. Other enzymes and special cells in the blood attack and kill any microorganisms that enter the body through the wound before it is sealed.

If a toxic chemical or pathogen should enter the bloodstream or gastrointestinal tract, other defenses are called into action. In the stomach, strong acid secretions and special enzymes help destroy pathogens. For toxic chemicals, the body has a vast array of enzymes, especially those synthesized in the liver, that *biotransform,* or detoxify, most harmful chemicals. One form of detoxification carried out by liver enzymes is the biotransformation of alcohol, a highly toxic substance that, if allowed to accumulate in the body, may cause serious disease and even death. But enzymes convert alcohol into carbon dioxide and water. The unpleasant symptoms of alcohol intoxication are felt when the body's enzymes cannot biotransform ingested alcohol fast enough.

Internal Defenses

White Blood Cells and Macrophages

If microorganisms or foreign particles find their way into the blood or accumulate in body tissue, they soon encounter *leukocytes,* or *white blood cells.* Leukocytes engage in *phagocytosis* (eating of cells) wherein foreign organisms and particles are engulfed and destroyed. Only about 1 blood cell in 700 is a leukocyte, but their number can increase dramatically in times of acute infection. This is why blood is tested for an elevated white blood cell count when an infection is suspected: increased production of white blood cells by the bone marrow is the body's response to infectious organisms proliferating in the body.

Other specialized phagocytic cells, *macrophages* ("big eaters"), are associated with specific organs and tissues and are vital to the body's defense mechanisms.

Both leukocytes and macrophages have a relatively brief life span, usually a few weeks or months, after which they themselves are destroyed and replaced by new leukocytes and macrophages. Your health depends on the continuous monitoring and removal of foreign material and cellular debris from all regions of the body by phagocytic cells.

The ways in which the body regulates the production of essential white blood cells are not well understood. Occasionally, production of white blood cells goes out of control and too many white blood cells crowd out other blood substances. The result is *leukemia,* a form of cancer. Leukemia can be either acute or chronic. The acute form is characterized by rapid cell proliferation. Chronic leukemia, the more easily manageable form of the disease, generally cycles through periods of normal and abnormal production of white blood cells. The disease is said to be *in remission* when the white cell level is normal.

Remember, you may be able to influence the course of infectious diseases, possibly even cancer, by stimulating or retarding the production of white blood cells. Even though the physiological mechanisms by which the mind may affect the production of white blood cells are not yet known, a person can help healing by using relaxation and visualization techniques to influence the body's physiology and cellular defenses.

Inflammation

Another of the body's internal defenses is *inflammation,* a reaction of tissue to injury or the invasion of microorganisms. Inflammation consists of a complex series of events in a wounded or diseased area (see Figure 8.3). The damaged cells usually release histamine and related substances that dilate local blood vessels. This often causes swelling and pain. White blood cells are attracted to the wound or diseased region in large numbers to clean away the tissue debris and any foreign matter that has entered the body. A mixture of white blood cells and debris from damaged cells makes up pus, which sometimes accumulates in wounds and infected areas. The presence of pus

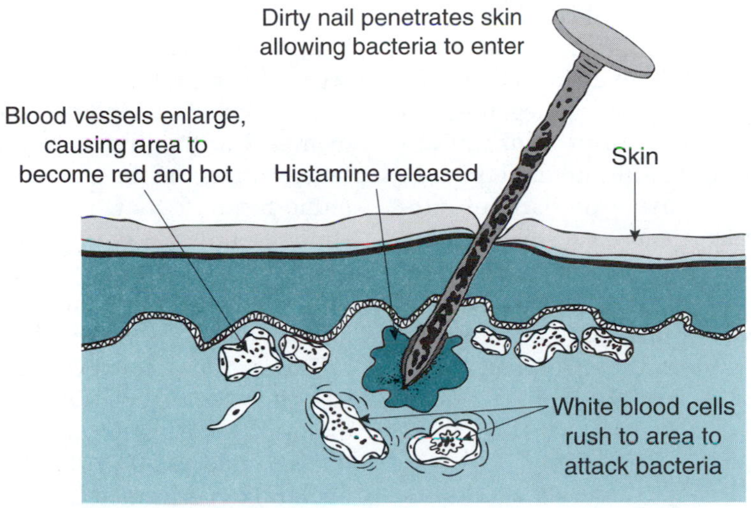

FIGURE 8.3 Penetration of the Skin by an Unsterile Object Often Produces Inflammation.

tells you that your body's defenses are working and that healing is taking place.

Interferon

Humans and animals have a special internal defense mechanism that protects them from virus infections. Viruses are particles of genetic material (RNA or DNA) encapsulated in a protein shell. They can only grow and reproduce in cells they infect. Infection of even one cell in the body by a single virus can result in the rapid production of hundreds or thousands of identical new viruses by that cell. The new viruses, released from that cell, attack other cells. That is why viral infections spread so quickly through the body and why viral diseases can make you extremely sick in a short time. To combat virus infections, T cells and virally infected cells produce *interferon*, which increases the resistance of uninfected cells. "In essence, the infected cell is committing cellular suicide, . . . but since the viruses within the infected cell are also destroyed, the infected cell is acting for the greater good of the body as a whole" (Farish, 1993, p. 202).

Each animal makes its own special kinds of interferon, which can vary from one tissue to another. Nobody knows exactly how interferon inhibits viruses, but it is clear that viruses do not multiply in cells containing interferon. Even more intriguing is that once interferon production in a cell has been stimulated by viral infection, that cell and others in its neighborhood become resistant to many other kinds of viruses.

Although the use of pure interferon to treat certain viral diseases was predicted soon after its discovery in 1957, until recently it was difficult to obtain enough to conduct clinical studies of its efficacy. Now, however, genetically engineered organisms produce large amounts of interferon, and soon more information about its potential usefulness in treating viral diseases such as herpes infections (cold sores) and the common cold will be at hand. There is also some hope that interferon will treat certain kinds of cancer.

The Final Defense: Immune Responses

When foreign substances, such as bacteria, viruses, pollen, cells and molecules from other organisms, and many industrial chemicals, enter the body, a complex series of reactions called *immune responses* take place. The outcome is the production of protein molecules, called *antibodies*, and certain kinds of blood cells, called lymphocytes, that attach to the foreign substances and begin to eliminate them from the body. Antibodies and lymphocytes inactivate the foreign material so that it can be digested and removed by phagocytic cells in the blood. Any substance that stimulates immune responses is called an *antigen* (*anti*body *gen*erator).

The immune responses provide the body's last defense against disease, and are responsible for the immunity that may follow an infection. The other defenses mentioned can be regarded as outer defenses that the body uses until the immune system can produce sufficient antibodies to neutralize invading organisms or harmful substances. Typically it takes the body a week or more to develop an immune response to a substance. This is why other, faster-acting defense mechanisms are also needed. For healing to be complete, the body's immune system must respond to infecting organisms and destroy them all.

The Lymphatic System

The cells responsible for the recognition of antigens and the production of antibodies originate mainly in bone marrow and are transported to all parts of the body through the *lymphatic system* (see color plates). The lymphatic vessels contain a circulating fluid called *lymph.* At intervals along the lymphatic vessels are masses of specialized tissue called *lymph nodes,* which filter out bacteria and other foreign particles from the lymph. They also manufacture antibody-producing cells (lymphocytes). "Swollen glands" are enlarged lymph nodes engaged in the removal of invading organisms from the body.

The tonsils, adenoids, spleen, and thymus are members of the immune system. They carry out several functions in maintaining an effective immune response as well as produce lymphocytes. Until recently, it was a frequent practice to remove tonsils (tonsillectomy) or adenoids (adenoidectomy) if they became inflamed, on the theory that if the organs were removed they could not become inflamed. Today, however, the importance of these tissues to the defenses of the body is widely recognized, and most health care practitioners agree that no child or adult should have either of these operations performed unless there is compelling medical reason to do so.

The lymphatic cells are called *B lymphocytes* and *T lymphocytes.* B lymphocytes produce specific antibodies (the protein molecules that attach to particular antigens), whereas T lymphocytes attack any foreign substances at once (see Figure 8.4).

It is thought that T lymphocytes play a crucial role in the detection of cancer cells and other abnormal cells. Most scientists believe that the human organism produces cancer cells throughout

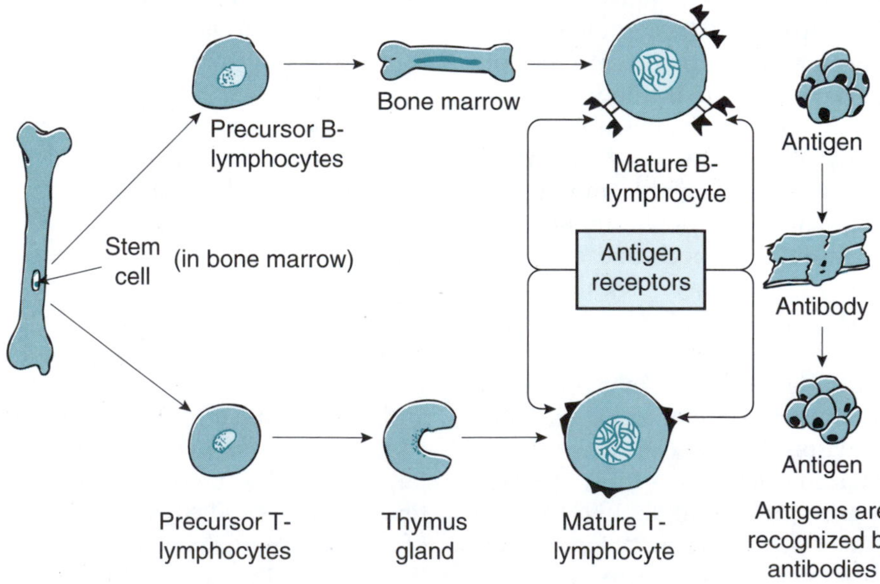

FIGURE 8.4 The Synthesis of Immune System Cells Begins in Bone Marrow. Precursor Cells Are Processed in Various Parts of the Body and Acquire Their Specialized Functions. Mature T Lymphocytes Attack and Destroy Invading Microoganisms Directly. Mature B Lymphocytes Manufacture Antibody Proteins That Bind to Antigens and Inactivate Foreign Organisms and Toxins.

its life, but that their number is small and that when they do develop, they are destroyed by vigilant T lymphocytes. If this hypothesis is correct, then life-long health is highly dependent on the activeness of the immune responses.

Recognition of "Self"

So far we have described the ability of the immune system to recognize and destroy virtually any substance or organism that is foreign to the body. What prevents the immune system from turning on your own tissues and cells? By mechanisms yet to be discovered, the immune system is able to distinguish between "self" and all other substances, which are "not self." It is thought that during embryonic development, as tissues are being formed, the antibody-producing cells directed against the body's normal cellular components are destroyed or inactivated, although scientists do not yet know how.

During fetal development, before a child's own immunological system is functional, he or she re-

BOX 8.2 ■ ■ ■ ■ ■

ACNE

Acne—pimples, whiteheads, blackheads, or "zits"—on the face and occasionally on the shoulders, chest, and back—afflicts millions of people. Acne is so common among adolescents that many consider it normal for that stage of life. Few of those afflicted with acne agree, however; they spend millions of dollars on acne medications each year.

Acne comes from the blocking of oil-producing glands (sebaceous glands) in the skin. Normally these tiny glands produce an oily substance, sebum, which drains onto the skin through a pore. For reasons that are not understood, sometimes a pore becomes plugged by dead cells, bacteria, and sebum, preventing sebum from getting out. When this material builds up within the gland, along with skin pigment particles (causing the blackhead) and white blood cells, a pus-filled pimple forms.

No one knows what causes the plugging of sebaceous glands in acne. Acne is not caused by overconsumption of chocolate, cola drinks, or greasy foods. Neither is it a bacterial infection of the skin, though it may worsen because of the degradative action of certain bacteria on sebum. Some acne may result from physically covering the pores of sebaceous glands. Athletes and hikers can develop acne in skin areas pressed by their gear. Wearing a hat can lead to acne on the forehead. Even resting your hands on your face while studying can sometimes produce a localized bout of acne. Virtually all cosmetics, especially the pancake type, are likely to worsen acne.

Acne can be affected by hormones. Sebum production increases in response to the sex hormone testosterone. In some women, pregnancy or birth control pills makes acne worse, whereas in others, pregnancy or oral contraceptives may clear up acne. Some women have minor flare-ups of acne near the beginning of menstruation.

Because the cause of acne is unknown, there is no known single way to clear it up; neither is there a simple preventive measure. Most dermatologists recommend a combination of cleanliness and certain types of medications to control acne. They especially suggest proper washing that removes surface oils and dirt but that does not irritate the skin. Medicines containing benzoyl peroxide are often useful. Antibiotics, especially tetracycline, may not be the best course of treatment except in severe cases. Disfiguring acne can be treated with a new drug, 13-cisretinoic acid (trade name: Acutane). Although this drug is very effective, it produces a number of side effects including elevated cholesterol in the blood. This drug should only be used under close medical supervision.

For many, acne is worst in times of emotional turmoil. Some experts in psychosomatic medicine suggest that acne is a response to the anger engendered by the belief that one's sense of independence or individuality is being threatened. More than one person has had acne clear up as soon as he or she moved away from home to go to college. As with many other conditions, the role of the mind in prevention and treatment of acne cannot be ignored.

ceives antibodies from the mother's blood. In this way, a newborn is protected from infections and other foreign substances for several months after birth. Antibodies are also passed to the child in the mother's milk, which is one reason that breast-feeding is so beneficial. Eventually the child's own immune system becomes capable of producing antibodies.

One of the principal causes of diseases in infants and young children is malnutrition or starvation, either of which interferes with the immune system. This explains why malnutrition increases the chances of contracting infectious diseases as well as their severity.

Autoimmune Diseases

Hypersensitivity can be a problem when it comes to the immune system. Autoimmunity (as well as allergy and rejection of tissue transplant) is an example of a hypersensitive immune system. As you would expect, the immune system must function with precision to distinguish "self" from "nonself." Any mistake that results in antibodies attacking the body's own cells could result in serious disease or death. Such *autoimmune diseases* do exist. Some genetic disorders, fortunately quite rare, result in either loss of immune responsiveness or a breakdown in the mechanisms responsible for "self" recognition. Other autoimmune disorders may (or may not) have a genetic basis but still cause serious diseases and even death.

Juvenile diabetes results from an autoimmune attack. The attack is on the insulin-producing cells of the pancreas.

Rheumatic fever may come after a streptococcal infection. Although proteins are released from the streptococci to stimulate antibody formation, these same antibodies attack body tissues also. The reasons for this are as yet unclear.

Lupus erythematosus is a very severe autoimmune disorder that mainly affects women of 18 to 35 years. In this disease, for reasons still unknown, autoantibodies are synthesized and directed against the person's own DNA and cell nuclei. Many organs of the body may be affected simultaneously, causing extensive damage. The symptoms—rashes, pain, and anemia—usually flare up and fade away again throughout life.

Another serious disease caused partly by an autoimmune response—one that affects millions of people—is *rheumatoid arthritis.* In this disease, autoantibodies are directed primarily against the body's joints, producing inflammation, pain, and suffering. There is also evidence that, in some people, the symptoms of arthritis can be arrested or reversed by nutritional changes or changes in mental state. However, no single nutritional or mental change—or medical treatment—has been scientifically demonstrated to lead to a cure or permanent remission of this disease.

An autoimmune disease that affects the central nervous system is *multiple sclerosis* (MS). Recent research suggests that MS may be initiated by a viral infection that triggers the immune system to produce antibodies directed against myelin, which sheathes and insulates nerve fibers in the brain and spinal cord. Interferon is one of the drugs being tested in patients with MS to see whether it can reduce or eliminate attacks and symptoms.

Some rare, genetic immune-deficiency disorders, such as *agammaglobulinemia,* result in inability to produce any antibodies. In this case, when a mother's antibodies begin to disappear from her newborn's blood, it suffers from recurrent infections. These children's survival depends on antibiotic therapy, injections of antibodies, and, for a few such children, living in an isolated, germ-free environment. The most famous case of agammaglobulinemia is David, the "bubble-boy," who was delivered under sterile conditions and kept in a germ-free environment for twelve years in a Texas hospital. David was born without a thymus gland, lymph nodes, or tonsils, and he lacked the ability to make antibodies. Shortly before his twelfth birthday, David's physicians, along with David and his family, decided to attempt a bone-marrow transplant from his sister in order to provide him with cells capable of producing antibodies. But the transplanted tissue was rejected, and David died in 1984.

Blood Transfusions and Rh Factors

Today people are concerned about blood transfusions because of possible contamination with AIDS. In the early part of this century, a blood transfusion often led to death because the patient's immune system recognized the donor blood as "foreign" and attacked with phagocytic cells and antibodies. The antibodies cause clumps of blood cells to form in the veins and arteries, impeding the flow of blood, oxygen, and waste products. If oxygen and

Table 8.1 How Blood Transfusions Are Determined According to ABO Blood Groups

Blood Group	Genotype	Antigens on Red Blood Cells	Transfusions Cannot Be Accepted from	Transfusions Are Accepted from
O (universal donor)	OO	None	A, B, AB	O
A	AA, AO	A	B, AB	A, O
B	BB, BO	B	A, AB	B, O
AB (universal recipient)	AB	A, B	None	A, B, AB, O

nutrients are prevented from reaching essential tissues, such as the heart or brain, death may occur.

Red blood cells have many potential antigens on their cell surfaces, each of which can evoke an antibody response. However, you do not make antibodies against your own antigens. The two most important groups of human red blood cell antigens are the ABO and Rh-positive/Rh-negative groups. There are many other groups of antigens on red blood cells, but these are by far the most important ones in terms of immune responses that can endanger health. Table 8.1 shows the pattern of donor-recipient ABO blood types that must be matched for a successful transfusion.

People with type O blood have neither A nor B antigens on their red blood cells. Their immune system makes A and B antibodies early in life because these antigens are prevalent in bacteria and food plants. People with type O blood are *universal donors;* their blood cells do not stimulate an antibody response in the recipient, no matter what his or her blood type. People with type A blood have both antigens present on their red blood cells and do not synthesize A or B antibodies because these antigens are recognized as "self" and those antibody-producing cells are destroyed in the embryo. People with type AB blood are *universal recipients;* they can accept blood from any of the four groups.

The Rh-positive antigen and the antibody that reacts against it cause problems primarily in pregnancy (see Figure 8.5). A woman is termed

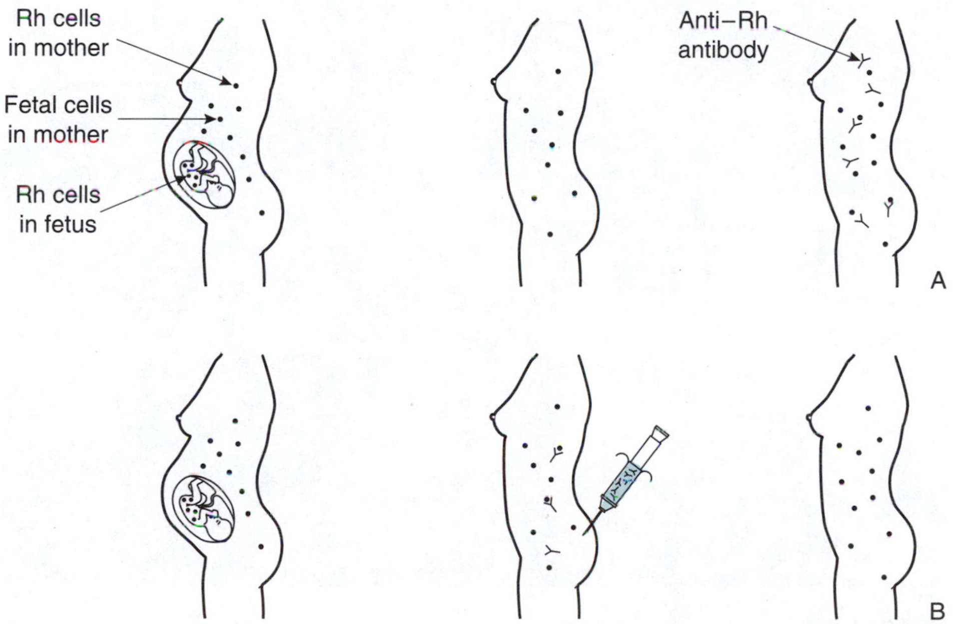

FIGURE 8.5 Rh Incompatibility, A. during the First Pregnancy; B. during the Second Pregnancy (*Source:* D.J. Farish, *Human Biology.* © 1993. Boston: Jones and Bartlett, p. 219. Reprinted with permission.)

Rh-negative if her red blood cells do not contain any of this antigen. If the red blood cells of a developing fetus have the Rh-positive antigen (inherited from the father), and if any of the fetus's red blood cells enter the mother's blood supply, production of anti-Rh antibodies can result. This usually does not cause any difficulty during the first pregnancy and might even go unnoticed until the woman becomes pregnant again.

If a second fetus is also Rh-positive, the Rh-positive antibodies synthesized in the mother's blood during the first pregnancy attack the developing infant's red blood cells, resulting in anemia, brain damage, or even death. Fortunately, doctors can manage this problem. Right after the first child is delivered, the mother is given an injection of anti-Rh antibodies that destroy any fetal blood cells in her blood. Her immune system is prevented from responding to the fetal antigen and producing Rh-positive antibodies that might endanger a fetus during a subsequent pregnancy.

Vaccination: Priming the Immune System

One of the greatest achievements of modern medical science is the development of vaccinations against serious bacterial and viral diseases, including smallpox, whooping cough, poliomyelitis, measles, diphtheria, and tetanus. Vaccination is the administration of substances called *vaccines*, usually by injection, that stimulate the immune response to specific infecting organisms if subsequently encountered.

Vaccinations come in three forms (Farish, 1993):

1. *Dead organisms:* Vaccinations for diphtheria, whooping cough (pertussis), and typhoid fever use dead organisms. Even though the organisms are dead, they stimulate the formation of antibodies.
2. *Attenuated organisms:* Viral vaccinations for polio, smallpox, measles, and yellow fever employ attenuated organisms. Although

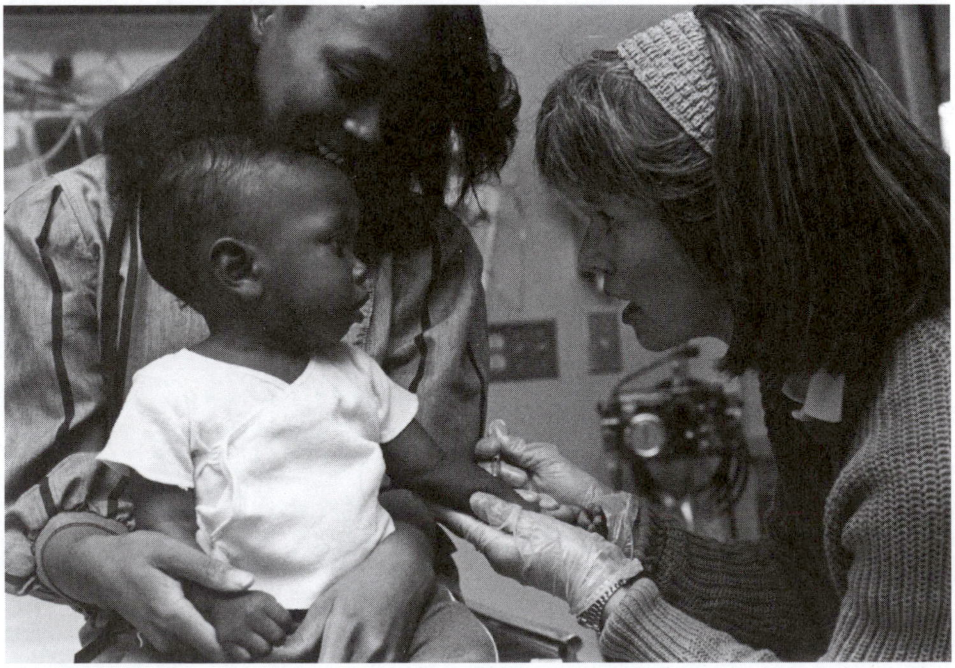

Widespread vaccination of infants and children has significantly lowered the incidence of life-threatening bacterial and viral diseases.

alive, the organisms have been altered to reduce their potency.

3. *Toxins:* In some diseases, the waste products of an organism bring about the disease, rather than the organism itself. Botulism and tetanus are examples. These waste products are called *toxins.* For vaccination purposes, the toxins are rendered harmless.

When a person is vaccinated, specific antigens—from inactivated viruses, bacteria, or toxins—are injected into the body. The immune system responds with lymphocytes and antibodies directed against those antigens. This is called *active immunity* because it results from exposure to the vaccine. Active immunity occurs with exposure to the disease naturally, too. If the body later encounters the natural disease-causing agents, it already has immunity and is protected. For example, the polio vaccine currently in use in this country, developed by Albert Sabin, uses genetically inactivated strains of polio virus that cannot cause the disease but can stimulate long-lasting immunity. Genetic inactivation produces a strain of virus that is incapable of causing disease but that has antigens similar to those of the original virus. The antibody made in response is effective against the naturally occurring virus.

In general, vaccination is safe and effective for disease prevention and has resulted in vastly improved human health. The reason that a single (or at most, several) inoculation produces long-term immunity is that the immune system, once stimulated by a particular antigen, maintains special white blood cells that "remember" that particular antigen. If the body is again challenged by that antigen, even after many years, those "memory cells" proliferate rapidly and produce sufficient antibodies to combat the disease.

Serious diseases for which vaccines are available are listed in Table 8.2. Vaccination for diseases such as influenza is controversial, since it is not clear that the benefits outweigh the risks for all people. Some people may respond adversely to any vaccination because of emotional anxiety or allergic reactions, or may contract the disease because of some unforeseen complication in their own biochemical processes. Most healthy people recover quickly from a bout of flu and thus probably don't need flu shots. Smallpox immunizations are no longer necessary or recommended; the risks of adverse reaction from the shot far outweigh the risk of contracting smallpox, since no cases have been reported for a number of years.

One of the most recent additions to the list of immunizations is *hepatitis B* vaccine. According to the American School Health Association (1995, p. 4),

> Each year 300,000 Americans contract hepatitis B, a very contagious virus, and each year 5000 of these Americans die from hepatitis B–related liver disease and cirrhosis. . . . Because 75 percent of all hepatitis B cases reportedly occur among persons between the ages of 15 and 39, the American School Health Association [recommends] that all youth be vaccinated against hepatitis B and [urges] school health professionals to initiate hepatitis B prevention programs.

Hepatitis B vaccination is also recommended for particular groups at high risk—health care workers, who are exposed to the disease, heroin addicts, male homosexuals, and sexually promiscuous persons.

Passive immunity occurs when we are injected with preformed antibodies (rather than forming our own for active immunity). While preformed antibodies fight disease, they are short-lived. Also, since no memory cells are made and no antibodies are developed, passive immunity is ineffective in the long run.

Of course another way to fight disease, well-known to teachers and students alike, is antibiotics. These drugs are used to treat bacterial diseases.

Allergies

Like autoimmune disease, allergies are considered to be a problem of overactivity within the immune system. Allergies are responses of the immune system to foreign substances called *allergens.* Pollens, grasses, grains, molds, dust, animal hair, foods, and drugs contain allergy-causing antigens. In fact, almost any foreign substance can be an allergen.

The allergic response to the allergen (antigen) is an increase in a class of *immunoglobulins* (a group of circulating blood proteins that act as an

Table 8.2 Immunizations Available in the United States

Type of Immunization	Effectiveness of Immunization and Frequency of Booster Doses
Cholera	Only partial immunity; recommended renewal every 6 months for duration of exposure
Diphtheria	Highly effective; recommended renewal every 10 years
Influenza	Renew every year (because viral strains change easily)
Mumps	Believed to confer lifetime immunity
Bubonic plague	Incomplete protection; boosters necessary every 3 to 6 months
Polio	Long-lasting immunity; no booster necessary unless exposure anticipated
Rabies	A vaccination each day for 14 to 21 days beginning soon after the bite (before symptoms appear)
German measles	Highly effective; need for boosters not established
Measles	Highly effective; usually produces lifelong immunity
Smallpox	Immunization no longer required
Spotted fever	Effectiveness not established
Tetanus	Very effective; renew every 10 years or when treated for a contaminated wound if more than 5 years have elapsed since last booster
Tuberculosis	Highly effective
Typhoid fever	About 80 percent effective
Typhus	Renew every year (if exposed)
Whooping cough	Highly effective
Yellow fever	Highly effective; provides long-lasting immunity
Hepatitis B	Effective; only for individuals at risk

antibody) called *IgE.* This in turn brings about the release of large quantities of *histamine,* which causes localized swelling of tissues, particularly in the mucus membranes. This reaction is excellent in fighting parasitic worm infections but is of no value as an allergic reaction.

Some common allergic reactions are:

Hay fever: This is a reaction to pollens from various plants; grasses and ragweed are examples. Swollen, red eyes and nasal passages testify to the discomfort. *Antihistamines* can be taken to alleviate it.

Asthma: This is a much more serious condition than hay fever because the reaction takes place in the bronchioles of the lungs. The victim experiences muscle spasms in the bronchiole walls, making breathing very difficult. Unfortunately, antihistamines are of little or no value.

Anaphylactic shock: This is the most serious reaction because the entire body can be affected. Examples are bee stings or penicillin, with the allergen being injected directly into the blood. Now you know why your doctor has you stay in the office for a few minutes after a penicillin shot. When anaphylactic shock occurs, histamine is released into the bloodstream, causing dilation of peripheral blood vessels and subsequent rapid drop in blood pressure, putting the person into shock. Noradrenalin can be administered to counteract these effects. (Anaphylactic shock is discussed under emergency care, too.)

BOX 8.3 ■ ■ ■ ■ ■

THE CONQUEST OF SMALLPOX

Smallpox is an ancient disease. The earliest direct evidence of it is found on the mummy of Pharoah Ramses V, who died around 1160 B.C. Written records from China and India indicate that smallpox was known earlier. Apparently a form of vaccination was practiced by the Chinese and Indians thousands of years ago: the inhalation of dried material from pox sores. The drying probably killed the virus without destroying its capacity to stimulate the body's production of antibodies, which provided immunity.

However, in Europe it was not until the eighteenth century that vaccination against smallpox became widespread. You may have heard the expression "a complexion as clear as a milkmaid's." Edward Jenner, an English physician, noticed that milkmaids almost never contracted smallpox. He reasoned that they escaped smallpox because most of them had been infected with the similar, but much milder, disease cowpox, which somehow made them resistant to the more serious smallpox. In 1796, Jenner exposed an 8-year-old boy, James Phipps, to cowpox and subsequently to smallpox. The boy survived. Within a few years vaccination became widespread.

Despite massive vaccination programs, in 1967 smallpox was still endemic in 33 countries, and there were 10 million to 15 million cases worldwide. Three facts led the World Health Organization to attempt total eradication of the disease: (1) There are no animal carriers, (2) There is no human chronic carrier state, (3) There exists a safe, effective vaccine. In October 1977, what is hoped to be the last naturally occurring case of smallpox in the world was found in Somalia. No cases have been reported since then.

Contact dermatitis: This includes poison ivy and the like. The hypersensitivity in these cases usually reaches a peak forty-eight hours after contact, much longer than the others discussed so far. The delay occurs because the antigen is not the poison oak or ivy. Rather, it is a substance formed after penetrating the skin and binding with body proteins.

Infectious Diseases

A remarkable variety of organisms, ranging from viruses to worms, can infect the human body and, under certain conditions, cause *infectious diseases.* An organism that can produce a disease in an animal, including humans is a *pathogen.* The major kinds of pathogens, illustrated in Figure 8.6, are:

Bacteria: Single-cell organisms causing diseases such as diphtheria, TB, staphylococcus and streptococcus infections.

Viruses: The smallest organisms, which can cause the common cold, viral hepatitis, human immunodeficiency syndrome (HIV), and acquired immunodeficiency syndrome (AIDS).

Protozoa: These single-cell pathogens are responsible for malaria, African sleeping sickness, and one of the most common sexually transmitted diseases in the United States, trichomoniasis.

Fungi: Examples of infectious disease from fungi include jock itch, ringworm, athlete's foot, and the vaginal yeast infection candidiasis.

Parasitic worms: These are sometimes called *helminths.* As pathogens, they cause havoc in at least one-third of the world. They can range in size from microscopic (pinworm) to several feet (tapeworm). Parasitic worms are generally subdivided into two groups: roundworms and flatworms. The former cause a variety of mild infections. Flatworms, however, can be deadly in large numbers.

Most pathogens can be transmitted from person to person and so cause *communicable diseases.* Colds, measles, mumps, and gonorrhea are com-

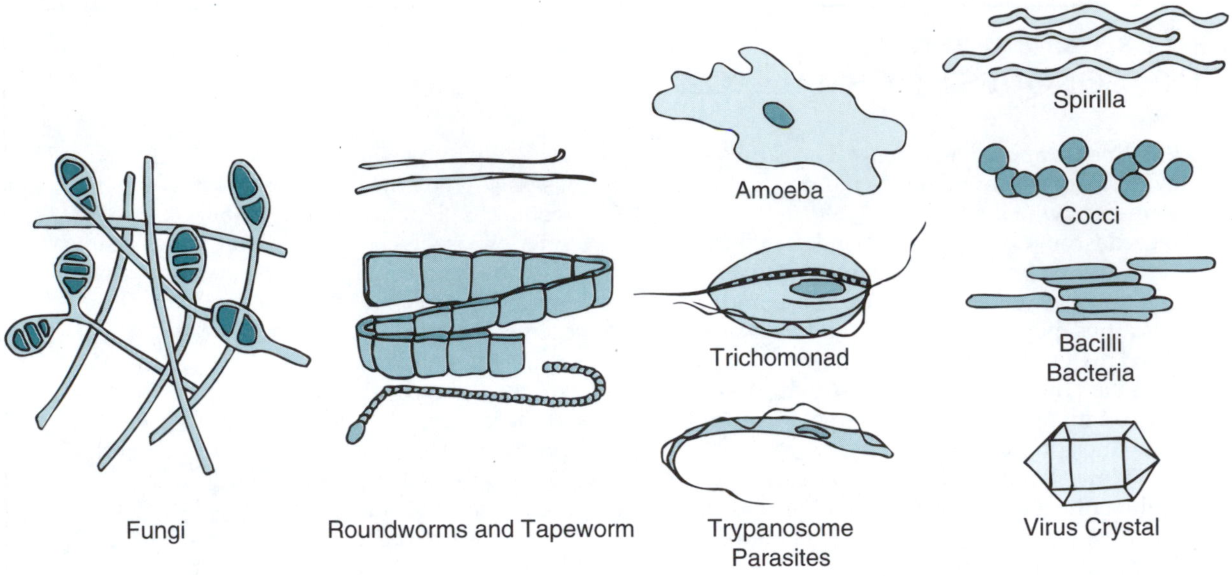

FIGURE 8.6 Different Kinds of Infectious Disease–Causing Organisms

municable diseases. Pathogenic organisms may be transferred to people from animals via a *vector*, or a carrier of the disease. For example, malaria is caused by parasitic protozoa. These microscopic organisms are transmitted to people by infected mosquitoes; the mosquito is the vector. Rabies is caused by a virus that can be transmitted through the bite of an infected dog, bat, or other animal. The animal is the vector for rabies in people. Some types of viruses remain in the body for life (see Table 8.3).

Infectious Disease Stages

All of us know of situations where several children have been exposed to a specific pathogen yet only one or two contract the disease. This may be due to *predisposing factors*, conditions that make some people more susceptible to getting the disease than others. For example, the children who became infected may have been more vulnerable due to fatigue, inadequate nutrition, a preexisting health problem, or poor living conditions.

Once a pathogen infects us, however, a disease follows a predictable course. That course is divided into the following five stages:

1. *Incubation stage:* This is the length of time from when a person first becomes infected until when symptoms of an infection appear. The incubation period varies from pathogen to pathogen. In some cases, it may be a few hours (common cold), whereas for others it may be several years (AIDS). If the body can fight off the infection during this stage, you may never become ill. You can spread the disease during this stage.
2. *Prodromal stage:* This stage follows the incubation period and is generally short in duration. The body begins to react to the pathogen and a general feeling of malaise begins—for example, headache, runny nose, slight fever, fatigue, which can sometimes occur with the flu. The pathogen increases in number and you remain contagious.
3. *Illness stage:* You (and maybe everyone around you) know that you are ill. All the signs and symptoms are evident. It is best to stay away from people, since you are most likely to transmit the infection to others during this stage. Medical help may be needed to help the body's defenses.

Table 8.3 Some of the Viruses that Remain in the Body for Life Once a Person Has Been Infected

Type	Symptoms	Spread by	Remains in
Herpes Simplex I	Cold sores on lips or mouth	Direct contact; most infectious when lesions are present	Nerve cells
Herpes Simplex II	Painful blisters on genital organs	Direct contact; oral-genital sex can transmit Type I or II to mouth or genitals	Nerve cells
Cytomegalovirus (CMV)	No symptoms in most children or adults; can cause stillbirth and mental retardation in fetuses	Body fluids: blood, urine, saliva	White blood cells
Varicella-Zoster virus	Chicken pox in children; shingles in adults	Close contact	Nerve cells
Epstein-Barr virus (EBV)	Mononucleosis: fatigue, malaise, headache, nausea, sore throat, fever	Saliva (kissing)	Lymph glands
Human papillomavirus (HPV)	Warts in, on, and around the genital area	Direct contact, usually through sexual intercourse	Skin cells (at infected site)
Human immunodeficiency virus (HIV)	Symptomless for many years; thereafter, unexplained weight loss, persistent fatigue, chronic diarrhea	Body fluids: blood, urine, saliva	Multiple tissue cell

4. *Convalescence stage:* During this stage, the signs and symptoms gradually dissipate. You are not well, but the worst is over.
5. *Recuperation stage:* This is sometimes called the *recovery period*. Your body regains strength as you move to your pre-illness state of health. Depending upon the disease, you may recuperate fully or suffer a relapse. Full recuperation may include immunity, depending upon the disease and the host. In other instances, you may recuperate but be a carrier for the disease.

Table 8.4 illustrates the symptoms, incubation period, transmission and communicability, and home-care treatment for several common infectious diseases.

Human Immunodeficiency Virus: A Worldwide Problem

The human immunodeficiency virus (HIV) can attack the immune system, especially T-lymphocytes, causing acquired immunodeficiency syndrome (AIDS). The spread of this disease is worldwide, costing vast amounts in terms of human life, misery, medical care, and of course economics. From 1991 to 1995, the number of infected people living in Thailand alone tripled (Charles, 1995). Alarms have gone off in India, where the city of Bombay contains almost one-third of the 1 million AIDS cases in that nation (CDC 1995). In Russia, concern about AIDS led to a law that all foreigners who plan to visit for longer than three months must show recent evidence that they are HIV-negative or undergo HIV testing upon arrival (*Lancet*, 1995). In the United States, the rising rate of HIV infection has been linked to several risk factors, including TB. A CDC study found that more than one-third of young adult TB patients were treated for HIV infection or AIDS, too. This coinfection greatly increases morbidity and cost (*AIDS Alert*, 1995). AIDS has become a leading killer in the United States, with 1 in 250 Americans infected with HIV. In short, HIV infection and AIDS is a serious health and social problem.

HIV infection and AIDS present problems to children and adolescents as well as adults. Today's children confront drug and sexual issues that place them at risk for contracting HIV. But the epidemic has spread its effects to children not only

Table 8.4 Communicable Diseases

Disease	Symptoms and Incubation Period	Transmission and Communicability	Treatment and Home Care
Chickenpox (varicella)	Acute viral disease; onset is sudden with high fever; maculopapular rash and vesicular scabs in multiple stages of healing. Incubation is 10 to 21 days.	Spread by droplet or airborne secretions; scabs not infectious. Communicable: 1 day before rash to 5-6 days after eruption.	Isolate. Treat symptomatically: fluids for fever, Tylenol. Prevent scratching. Observe for signs of complications—notify physician.
Mumps	Acute viral disease, characterized by fever, swelling, and tenderness of one or more salivary glands. Potential complications, including meningoencephalitis.	Spread by droplet and direct and indirect contact with saliva of infected person. Communicable: 5 days before to 9 days after swelling appears. Most infectious 48 hours prior to swelling.	Prevent by vaccination. Isolate. Treat symptomatically: ice pack and encourage fluids, Tylenol. Watch for symptoms of neurological involvement: fever, headache, vomiting, stiff neck.
Measles (rubeola)	Acute viral disease, characterized by conjunctivitis, bronchitis, Koplik's spots on buccal mucosa. Dusky red and splotchy rash 3 to 4 days. Usually photophobia. Complications can be severe in respiratory tract, eye, ear, and nervous system. Incubation is 10 to 12 days.	Spread by droplet or direct contact. Communicable: 5th day of incubation to first few days of rash (5–7 days).	Treat symptomatically: bedrest until cough and fever subside; force fluids, dim lights in room; tepid baths and lotion to relieve itching. Observe for signs of neurological complications.
German measles (rubella)	Viral infection. Slight fever, mild coryza and headache. Discrete pink-red maculopapules that last about 3 days. Incubation is 14 to 21 days.	Spread by direct and indirect contact with droplets. Fetus may contract measles in utero if mother has the disease. Check rubella titer in women who may become pregnant. Communicable: 7 days before rash to 5 days after rash appears.	Basically a benign disease. Treat symptomatically: bedrest until fever subsides. Encourage fluids and give Tylenol.

Table 8.4 Communicable Diseases–*continued*

Disease	Symptoms and Incubation Period	Transmission and Communicability	Treatment and Home Care
Diphtheria	Local and systemic manifestations. Malaise, fever, cough with stridor. Toxin has affinity for renal, nervous, and cardiac tissue. Incubation 2 to 6 days or longer.	Spread by droplets from respiratory tract or carrier. Communicable: 2–4 weeks if untreated; 1–2 days with antibiotic treatment.	Antitoxin must be given early; give antibiotic therapy to kill toxin. Strict bedrest; prevent exertion. Liquid or soft diet. Observe for respiratory complications. Hospitalization may be required for suctioning and oxygen; emergency tracheotomy may be necessary.
Whooping cough (pertussis)	Dry cough occurring in paroxysms. Dyspnea and fever may be present. Lymphocytosis. Incubation is 5 to 21 days.	Direct contact or droplet from infected person. Communicable: 7 days after exposure to 3 weeks after onset.	Treat symptomatically: rest, warm, humid air. Maintain nutritional status. Protect from secondary infections.

Source: From S. Smith & C.M. Smith, *Personal Health Choices*. © 1990. Boston: Jones and Bartlett. Reprinted with permission.

through actual infection but also through the loss of parents to AIDS. As mothers and fathers die, their children become the orphans of this epidemic. These children will be in many classrooms throughout the country.

Box 8.4 provides information about HIV infection and AIDS. Of course, not all HIV-infected persons contract AIDS. The reasons for this are still under investigation, which, it is hoped, will provide answers to some puzzling questions.

Treatment regimens for those who contract AIDS are being tested on several fronts. Present treatment slows the progression of the disease but fails to stop it. Medical treatment combined with responsible behavior and health practices have increased life expectancy for many AIDS victims. Vaccines are being investigated but appear to be several years away from being available to the public.

Other Sexually Transmitted Diseases

There are several diseases in addition to HIV/AIDS that can be transmitted through sexual activity, specifically sexual intercourse. The most common STDs are chlamydia, gonorrhea, genital warts, herpes, syphilis, urinary and vaginal infections, and hepatitis B. There has been an increase in the spread of STDs in recent years. Table 8.5 shows the symptoms and long-term complications of selected STDs.

A few points of note about STDs are the following:

- There are an estimated 1 million new infections of gonorrhea in the United States each year.
- Women are far more likely to suffer serious short- and long-term effects from gonorrhea and most other STDs.
- Among sexually active young persons, genital herpes accounts for about 50 to 70 percent of genital ulcer disease, and primary syphilis for about another 10 to 20 percent.
- Human papillomavirus (genital warts) has increased fivefold between 1966 and 1990 and is still rising.

BOX 8.4 ■ ■ ■ ■ ■

HIV/AIDS FACT SHEET

Cause: Human immunodeficiency virus that attacks the immune system, particularly the T-lymphocytes, making the person more susceptible to other diseases. When the immune system is no longer functioning effectively, the person has AIDS (acquired immunodeficiency syndrome).

Specific conditions/diseases related to AIDS: Some of the serious conditions that occur due to a weakened immune system are: *Pneumocystis carinii* pneumonia, Kaposi's sarcoma, a form of cancer, and tuberculosis. These diseases are opportunistic since they only take advantage of compromised immune systems.

Incubation period and symptoms of HIV infection: The incubation period may be 5 to 10 years, and early symptoms are difficult to spot. The initial symptoms may mimic minor illnesses and may disappear only to reappear. The usual things to look for are:

- Recurring fever or night sweats
- Unexplained weight loss more than 10 pounds
- Unusual sores or white spots on tongue or mouth
- Persistent, unexplained cough
- Chronic diarrhea
- Chronic unexplained tiredness
- Swollen lymph glands
- Persistent yeast infections

These symptoms warrant an HIV test.

HIV testing: Two separate blood tests (ELISA and Western blot) have almost 100% accuracy. These tests check for the presence of HIV-antibodies, which show up about 3 months after being infected (could be up to 6 months). Recommend two tests 6 months apart. New tests are on the horizon. Negative results do not mean you cannot get it in the future.

Spread of HIV infection and AIDS: HIV is in the blood, semen, or vaginal secretions of an infected person. Two principal modes of transmission are sexual intercourse (vaginal or anal) and contaminated needles used to inject drugs. Other modes include:

- Oral sex can spread HIV
- Passed on through pregnancy (1 in 4 infants born to HIV mothers contract it)
- Cleaning up spilled blood without wearing gloves
- Breastfeeding by an infected mother
- Presence of another sexually transmitted disease
- Indiscriminate sexual behavior
- Needle-sharing for tattoos, drugs, piercing ears, steroid injections
- Multiple sex partners

How HIV Is NOT spread:

- Bitten by mosquitoes or animals
- Sharing telephones, clothes, toilets
- Touching, hugging an infected person
- Attending or going to places where HIV people may go (malls)
- By dentists or other health care professionals
- Artificial insemination at a qualified, controlled facility
- Eating food handled by an HIV-infected person
- Sharing eating utensils or drinking glasses
- From saliva, such as kissing
- Playing sports (if injury occurs, just avoid the blood)
- Donating or receiving blood transfusions
- Organ or tissue transplants

Assessing risk: The following questions can be asked:

- Have you ever had unprotected sex (vaginal, oral, anal) with a man or woman who you know was HIV-infected or injects drugs and shares needles with someone who is infected?
- Have you now or in the past had multiple sex partners?
- Have you had sex with someone you normally wouldn't and who could be infected?
- Have you used needles or syringes that were used by someone before you?
- Did you or any of your partners get treatment for hemophilia or have a blood transfusion or organ transplant between 1978 and 1985?

Answering "yes" to any of the above does not mean you have HIV. You may want to go to a clinic or doctor to talk about your situation, get information, and then decide if you need testing or counseling. Early diagnosis is important, especially in light of new advances in treatment.

Source: From A.C. Novello, Surgeon General's report to the American public on HIV infection and AIDS (Atlanta: CDC National AIDS Clearinghouse, 1993).

Table 8.5 Selected Sexually Transmitted Diseases

STD	Symptoms	Long-Term Complications
AIDS	Flulike symptoms followed by any of a number of diseases characteristic of immunodeficiency	Results in a chronic, progressive disease. Associated with a mononucleosislike syndrome or aseptic meningitis. Eventually leads to secondary cancers or neurologic diseases. Mortality rate is presumed to be 100%.
Chlamydia	Usually within 3 weeks; infected men have a discharge from the penis and painful urination; women may have a vaginal discharge but often are asymptomatic.	In males, it can spread to the prostate. In females, it can cause Pelvic Inflammatory Disease (PID) and sterility. In both sexes, it can cause aching joints, arthritis, conjunctivitis in the eyes if spread via the hands
Gardnerella	Yellow-green vaginal discharge with an unpleasant odor; painful urination; vaginal itching	In females, upper genital-tract pelvic infection. In males, upper genital-tract infection
Genital warts	Usually within 1 to 3 months: small, dry growths on the genitals, anus, cervix, and possibly mouth	In females, can cause cervical intraepithelial neoplasia, invasive cancer, as well as other female genital cancers
Gonorrhea	Usually within 2 weeks: discharge from the penis, vagina, or anus; pain on urination or defecation or during sexual intercourse; pain and swelling in the pelvic region; genital and oral infections may be asymptomatic	For males, can become infertile. For females, inflammation and pain in the reproductive system, along with infertility. In both sexes, can spread through the bloodstream to joints (arthritis) and brain (meningitis)
Hepatitis	Low-grade fever, fatigue, headaches, loss of appetite, nausea, dark urine, jaundice	In both sexes, become a chronic carrier of hepatitis, development of hepatocellular carcinoma or cirrhosis of the liver
Herpes genitalis	Usually within 2 weeks: painful blisters appear on site(s) of infection: genitals, anus, cervix, occasionally itching, painful urination, and fever	In females, can pass to an infant during delivery if the doctor is not informed
Pubic lice	Usually within 5 weeks: intense itching in the genital region; lice may be visible in pubic hair; small white eggs may be visible on pubic hair	In both sexes, reoccurrence of the disease.
Syphilis	Usually within 3 weeks: a chancre (painless sore) appears on the genitals, anus, or mouth; secondary stage—skin rash—appears if left untreated; tertiary stage includes diseases of several body organs	In both sexes, third stage syphilis (2 to 20 years after infection) can result in painful skin ulcers, bone pain, heart damage, rupture of major blood vessels, madness and death
Trichomoniasis	Yellowish green vaginal discharge with an unpleasant odor; vaginal itching; occasionally painful intercourse	In both sexes, reoccurrence of the disease.

BOX 8.5 ■ ■ ■ ■ ■

NEWLY EMERGING INFECTIOUS DISEASES

In the 1960s, it was thought that infectious diseases had been conquered or were well on the way to being obliterated. Medicine and health education turned their energies toward chronic diseases, forgetting that most infectious organisms were waiting in the wings, looking for opportunities. The human population continued to grow at an almost alarming rate and new technology furthered our belief that we could escape the limits of our ecosystem. However, more and more scientists urged us to understand that we still remain part of the food chain, to eat and to be eaten. According to McNeill (Garrett, 1994, p. 6), "It is worth keeping in mind that the more we win, the more we drive infections to the margins of human experience, the more we clear a path for possible catastrophic infection." HIV/AIDS is seen by many as a warning sign or the first step in the process of reducing the number of human inhabitants. In the words of Preston (1994, p. 407, ". . . It could also be said that the extreme amplification of the human race . . . has suddenly produced a very large quantity of meat, which is sitting everywhere in the biosphere and may not be able to defend itself against a life form that might want to consume it."

The germs that once succumbed to antibiotics have managed to toughen their walls to an almost impermeable state and patiently wait for favorable conditions. In the United States and elsewhere, this has been evident in *Staphylococcus aureus* outbreaks, *Streptococcus* resistance (Jim Henson, inventor of the Muppets, died from this supposedly curable bacteria), *Pneumococcus* infections (resistant strains are causing increased otitis media infections and hearing loss in children), *N. gonorrhoeae* strains (now withstand penicillin and tetracycline), *Shigella dysenteriae* (in Ontario, Canada, one half of all infections in 1990 were caused by strains resistant to four or more antibiotics), and other bacteria. Today's newspapers steadily reveal regional outbreaks of TB, hepatitis A, and other infectious diseases.

As rainforests are cleared, new (at least to most of us) viruses emerge. HIV is of course now well known, and one of the most important lessons learned from it is that in a very short time this microbe spread worldwide. Other viruses to watch for are Lassa, dengue, hantaviruses, Marburg, Ebola Sudan, Ebola Zaire, and Ebola Reston. In the U.S., Ebola Reston (Reston, VA) frightened most public health and medical officials with its ability to destroy quickly and efficiently. Fortunately, it was harmless to human beings. But the question is, will it be the next time?

Ebola Zaire, however, is not harmless to humans, and makes HIV/AIDS pale by comparison as to swiftness of death and disability. In his book about Ebola, Preston (1994, pp. 106–107) describes it this way: "Ebola kills a great deal of tissue while the host is still alive. It triggers a creeping, spotty necrosis that spreads though all internal organs. The liver bulges up. . . begins to liquefy . . . then cracks apart. The kidneys become jammed . . . the blood becomes toxic with urine . . . the lining of the gut sloughs off . . . and is defecated with large amounts of blood. . . . Testicles bloat up and turn black and blue . . . and the nipples may bleed . . . labia turn blue . . . and there may be massive vaginal bleeding. The eyeballs may fill with blood. Droplets of blood stand out on the eyelid. The tongue turns brilliant red . . . sloughs off, and is swallowed or spat out." In short, the victim crashes and bleeds out.

The point is, infectious diseases are coming back—and they are doing so with a vengeance.

- The incidence of primary and secondary syphilis has increased, as has the incidence of congenital syphilis.

Data regarding sexual behavior are covered in detail in Chapter 12, but it should be understood here that grade 7 appears to be a pivotal year. That is, just as with many other high-risk behaviors, such as drug abuse, it appears that many students make major decisions about how they will behave during the seventh grade. The decision pathway regarding the spread of disease allows for several intervention points. The first, of course, is the decision to engage in sexual relations. The second decision is to use protection from STDs and/or conception. The third decision is to seek treatment if problems are recognized. The fourth decision is to discontinue behavior that results in the likelihood of disease transmission.

Of course prevention is the preferred choice, with abstinence from sexual relations being the least risky option to attain it. If this fails, the alternative is to use a latex condom. Latex condoms are the only kind acceptable for STD prevention. Sexual activity should not be an isolated part of a relationship. While there may be much to gain in the eyes of the couple, there is much to lose also. Given the rise in STDs and HIV in young adults, it is important for young couples to discuss their sexual activity with each other. Leaving it to chance, or passion, is irresponsible.

Noninfectious and Chronic Diseases

Chronic diseases are those that begin slowly and develop over a long period of time. Unlike some infectious diseases that take a long time to develop, such as TB, the noninfectious, chronic diseases are not "caught" or transmitted as are infectious diseases.

The majority of chronic diseases that afflict Americans today, such as diabetes, cardiovascular diseases, ulcers, colitis, and even cancer, have no single, principal environmental or genetic cause and are increasingly regarded as *diseases of lifestyle.* This means that factors in our daily lives contribute to the development and progression of a disease. These factors include stress, poor nutrition, weakened immunological defenses, destructive habits such as smoking cigarettes or drinking alcohol, being overweight, and probably many more. This is not to rule out genetic predisposition or physiological defect, but rather to show that, more often than not, such diseases are preventable with appropriate health behavior. Medical science is increasingly aware of the multifactorial nature of many diseases and increasingly encourages responsible behavior.

Cardiovascular Disease

Each year in the United States, more deaths result from cardiovascular diseases than from all other causes combined. The American Heart Association (1995) lists five forms of *cardiovascular disease,* or disease of the heart and blood vessels. They are coronary artery disease, high blood pressure, rheumatic heart disease, stroke, and congenital heart disease. This section addresses cardiovascular diseases as they apply to children.

Coronary Artery Disease

The coronary arteries (see color plates) supply blood to the heart muscle. Over years, fatty deposits called *plaque* build up on the inner walls of these arteries. This is called *coronary atherosclerosis.* Eventually, the fatty build up reduces blood flow to the heart muscle, resulting in chest pain, or *angina pectoris.* Continued build-up may cause a complete blockage of blood—usually from a fatty clot—to certain areas of the heart, bringing about a *myocardial infarction,* or heart attack.

Hyperlipidemia or high blood cholesterol plays a role in the development of coronary heart disease. It is recommended that cholesterol levels not exceed 200 mg/dL blood, even though about one-half of American adults over 20 have levels somewhat higher. Very high cholesterol is considered to be a level of 240 mg/dL or more.

In regard to children, the American Heart Association (1995) notes:

- Atherosclerosis has its beginnings in young people.
- Both eating patterns and genetics affect blood cholesterol levels.
- Lowering cholesterol levels in children and adolescents may be beneficial.

While a change in diet may help some children and adults, for others, diet modification may have little or no effect. This is probably due to a genetic predisposition.

High Blood Pressure

Blood pressure (BP) is the amount of force or pressure exerted by the heart to pump blood. Each time the heart contracts *(systolic pressure)*, the blood pressure in the arteries rises. As expected, when the heart relaxes *(diastolic pressure)*, blood pressure goes down. When you get your blood pressure taken you are given both figures—an upper and a lower, which is the systolic over the diastolic. Hypertension, or high blood pressure, means that the heart must exert an abnormally great amount of pressure to pump blood.

Children can and do have high blood pressure. The threshold for significant hypertension in children is (AHA, 1995):

Age	*BP*
3–5	>116/76
6–9	>122/78
10–12	>126/82
13–15	>136/86
16–18	>142/92

More often than not, the cause of high blood pressure is unknown. However, in children it can be caused by other diseases such as kidney or heart disease. This is called *secondary hypertension*. Successful treatment of the other disease generally results in normal blood pressure. A small number of children have *primary* or *essential hypertension*, which means there is no known cause.

High blood pressure is more common among African Americans than among Caucasian Americans. Also, it is higher in overweight children. Children with a modest elevation in blood pressure do not necessarily carry their hypertension into adulthood. However, children with repeated high blood-pressure measures (especially diastolic), continued overweight, and/or a family history of hypertension may be at higher risk of being primary hypertensive adults.

If a child is hypertensive, the following recommendations may be applicable (AHA, 1981):

- Blood pressure should be checked on a periodic basis.
- An overweight child should be placed on a diet to gradually bring weight to a normal level.
- Parents or guardians should be supportive of weight loss approaches by purchasing appropriate foods and preparing them in appealing, nutritious ways.
- Generally, exercise can be continued but it should be discussed with the child's physician.
- The home should be free from cigarette smoke, and of course the child should not smoke.
- Meals and snacks should be planned to reduce salt intake.
- Parents and, when necessary, teachers should encourage compliance with prescribed medications.
- The child should not be treated like a "sick" child by being sheltered or kept out of school or extracurricular activities.

Rheumatic Heart Disease

Rheumatic fever follows strep throat infections caused by the streptococcal bacteria. To fight the infection, the body develops antibodies (antigen-antibody response), but in some cases, the antibodies attack the heart valves (see color plates). This is *rheumatic heart disease*. Sometimes a rash also develops (scarlet fever). Fortunately, rheumatic fever does not follow all strep throats. When it does, the length of time between the streptococcal throat infection and rheumatic fever is two to four weeks.

Appropriate medical treatment of strep throat is the best prevention for rheumatic fever. Therefore, look for a sudden onset of sore throat, painful swallowing, tender and swollen glands under the jaw angle, and fever. In some cases, the symptoms may be very mild. The only way to know for certain is by having a doctor or nurse do a throat-culture laboratory test.

Some pertinent information about rheumatic fever is as follows (AHA, 1988):

- Strep throat is communicable, but rheumatic fever is not.
- Children between 5 and 15 years are most likely to experience rheumatic fever.
- Rheumatic fever can be contracted repeatedly. If it recurs, the child increases susceptibility to subsequent attacks and may need to be put on continuous medication.
- There is no magic cure for rheumatic fever. Although it usually goes away in a few weeks or months, any heart damage that occurs is permanent.
- Rheumatic fever is not inherited, but a familial tendency can exist.
- Activities do not need to be restricted after the illness subsides; however, this should be discussed with a doctor if any question arises.
- The child who has rheumatic heart disease is at risk of developing an infection at the heart valve called *bacterial endocarditis.* To prevent infection, teeth must be cleaned regularly and cavities filled promptly. Before seeing a dentist, these children are usually prescribed protective antibiotics to reduce the possibility of infection from bacteria entering the bloodstream.

Innocent Heart Murmurs

Childhood heart murmurs are often concerns to teachers and parents alike. Most are classified as *"innocent" heart murmurs,* and come from the sounds made by blood moving through the valves and chambers of the heart or the blood vessels near the heart. Another name is *functional murmurs.* These murmurs become louder as heart rate increases (e.g., due to physical education, excitement, or fear). Such murmurs are common in childhood and should not be a cause for alarm.

During a medical check-up further tests could be ordered to rule out any other problem. If it is an innocent heart murmur, then the child can be treated as any other child in regard to physical activity and diet.

Lifestyle and Cardiovascular Disease Risks

While a genetic predisposition to cardiovascular disease (CVD) cannot be changed, lifestyle changes can reduce the risk of developing one as follows:

1. Don't smoke.
2. Keep blood pressure under control.
3. Modify diet to reduce cholesterol and lose weight.
4. Be tested for "adult" diabetes and keep it under control.
5. Exercise regularly to give your heart a workout.

Cancer

Although cancer in children is rare, it the chief cause of death *by disease* for children between 1 and 14 years. Approximately one-third of these cancer deaths are from leukemia. The most common sites of childhood cancers are the blood and bone marrow, bone, lymph nodes, brain, nervous system, and soft tissues. As for adults, the overall cancer mortality rate has risen over the past several years. However, the reason for the rise is lung cancer. If that site were excluded from calculations, the overall cancer mortality would have declined 14 percent between 1950 and 1990 (American Cancer Society, 1994).

Cancer is the term for a group of diseases, each characterized by uncontrolled growth of abnormal cells. These cells form a mass called a *tumor.* Noncancerous, or *benign,* tumors do not spread to other parts of the body. Cancerous, or *malignant,* tumors spread to and destroy surrounding tissues. The cancerous cells move to other parts of the body—this is called *metastasis*—via the blood stream or lymph system. As to be expected, once a cancer has spread it is much more difficult to treat.

Early detection is the key. In children, however, cancer can be difficult to detect. Regular check-ups at the doctor's office are a must. Also, parents and teachers should be watchful of unusual symptoms that persist. The signs to watch for in children are:

- An unusual mass or swelling
- Unexplained paleness and loss of energy
- Sudden tendency to bruise easily
- A persistent, localized pain or limping
- Prolonged, unexplained fever
- Frequent headaches, especially accompanied by vomiting
- Sudden eye or vision changes
- Excessive, rapid weight loss

The American Cancer Society (1994) lists seven signs of cancer for people of all ages. They are:

1. Change in bowel or bladder habits
2. *A* sore that does not heal
3. *U*nusual bleeding or discharge
4. *T*hickening or lump in the breast or elsewhere
5. *I*ndigestion or difficulty in swallowing
6. *O*bvious change in a wart or mole
7. *N*agging cough or hoarseness

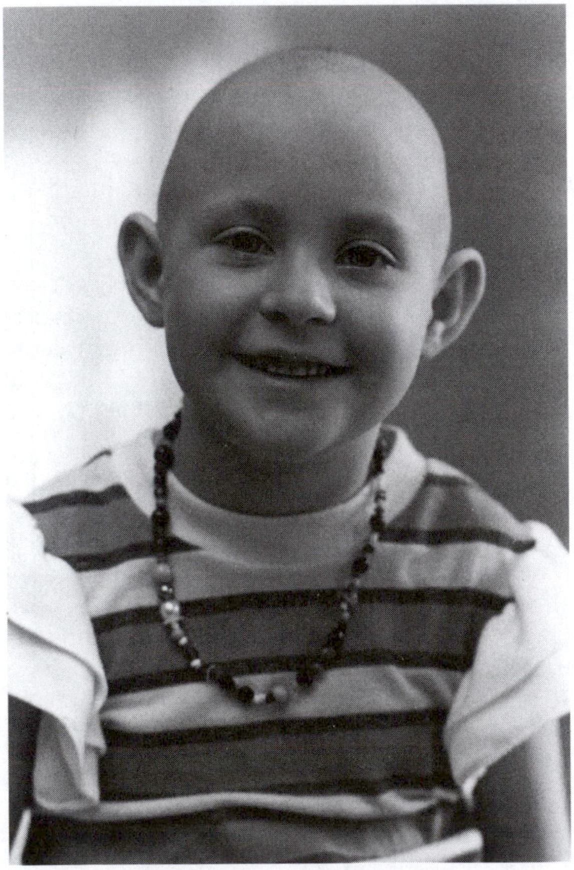

Leukemia is the leading cause of death from disease for children between the ages of 1 and 14. Since the mid-1960s, however, survival rates have increased from 4 percent to 72 percent.

Causes of Cancer

Carcinogens is the name given to cancer-causing agents. Research shows that cancer can be caused by both internal factors (genes, hormones, immune conditions) and external (chemical, radiation, viruses) ones. These factors may act together, or perhaps in sequence, to bring about cancer. In other words, there is probably no one cause of cancer.

In regard to external carcinogenic factors, you have no doubt heard that tar in tobacco smoke, ultraviolet radiation from the sun, and some industrial chemicals are carcinogenic. Viruses, despite some controversy, have been added to the list of external factors. One example is the human papillomavirus (HPV) that causes genital warts. There are a number of variants of this virus, many of which appear to be precursors to cervical cancer in women. Similarly, certain forms of childhood leukemia are associated with the retrovirus HTLV-1 (human T-cell leukemia/lymphoma virus I). Non-Hodgkin's lymphoma is linked to human immunodeficiency virus (HIV) and HTLV-1. In Africa, Burkitt's lymphoma is partly caused by the Epstein-Barr herpes virus (EBV).

Of course the most talked-about internal carcinogenic factor is genetics. Research has shown that oncogenes, which play a role in normal cell growth, can mutate, allowing runaway growth of cells. Suppressor genes can also mutate to allow abnormal growth. Breast cancer has a very strong familial link. Nonetheless, the exact interplay of genetics and other carcinogenic agents is unknown. Immune conditions can be conducive to cancer development, as is evidenced by Kaposi's sarcoma in AIDS patients.

Cancer Treatment and Survival

The best method of cancer treatment depends upon the nature of the cancer. The usual methods are surgery, radiation therapy, chemotherapy, hormones, or immunotherapy. The areas under greatest investigation today are immunotherapy (ways to help the body use its own defenses), gene therapy (including genetic engineering), a combination of approaches (chemotherapy plus surgery or radiation), and vaccines. The goal of all therapies is to eliminate the cancer cells.

Cancer survival rate is measured in blocks of five years, and it varies considerably depending on the site of the cancer. Definite strides have been made over the last few decades. For example, from the 1960s to mid-1980s, the survival rate for childhood leukemia improved from 4 to 72 percent (ACS, 1994).

Lifestyle and Cancer Risk

There is no doubt that, in many instances, cancer can be prevented by living a healthy lifestyle. It is generally believed that 90 percent of skin cancers could be prevented by protection from the sun's rays. Obviously all cancers related to cigarette smoking and heavy alcohol use could be prevented with changes in lifestyle. Dietary changes—eating a variety of foods, staying at a desirable weight, avoiding fatty foods, eating foods with adequate starch and fiber as well as high in vitamins A and C, and drinking alcohol only in moderation—could prevent cancer in many people.

Early detection is another important factor. This requires self-examination and physician screening on a regular basis. These techniques can detect cancers of the breast, tongue, mouth, colon, rectum, prostate, testis, cervix, and melanoma at an early stage. Earlier treatment means a greater likelihood of survival. While there is presently a 68 percent survival rate for all cancers, with early detection and treatment this could rise to 90 percent.

Respiratory Diseases

Although there are several respiratory diseases, one stands out among children—*asthma*. It is the most common chronic childhood condition, and the leading cause of school absence for illness. Slightly more than 6 percent of children (more than 3 million) have asthma. In other words, two children out of a class of thirty are likely to suffer from asthma (National Institutes of Health, 1993).

As mentioned above, asthma is a very severe allergic reaction that takes place in the bronchioles of the lungs. The bronchiole walls spasm, making breathing very difficult. Characteristically, the asthmatic child also experiences symptoms such as coughing, wheezing, chest tightness, and shortness of breath. Common asthma triggers include allergens (pollen, molds, dust mites, and animal dander), irritants (strong odors, cold air, cigarette smoke, weather changes), upper respiratory infections (cold or flu), and physical exercise (especially in cold weather). Emotional situations can induce an asthma attack too. This is not to say that such students are "more emotional" than others. Rather, it is important for all students and teachers to know that asthmatic students deal with all the same problems others do, in addition to suffering from a chronic illness. Walsh & Ryan-Wenger (1992) found that the most frequent stressor of children with asthma was "feeling sick," followed by being left out of a group and not being good enough for sports.

Lifestyle and Asthma

Some suggestions for school personnel in dealing with asthma are listed below (U.S. Department of Health and Human Services, U.S. Department of Education, 1991).

- Know the early warning signs of an asthma episode.
- Develop an asthma-management program, including policies and procedures for administering medication and specific actions for staff members.
- Realize that a student with asthma may feel tired, anxious about access to medication, embarrassed about disruptions and absences as well as the illness itself.
- Assist the student in dealing with these feelings.
- Keep confidentiality.
- Encourage students with asthma to modify their own stressors.
- Remind children with asthma to medicate themselves prior to events known to exacerbate it.
- Know the side effects of asthma medications.
- Reduce or eliminate known asthma triggers in the school.

- Treat the child with asthma as normally as possible, allowing participation in physical activities and keeping academic expectancies on par with the student's abilities.
- Allow a student with asthma to do a quiet activity during recovery from an acute episode.

Since almost all classrooms in the United States are likely to have a student with asthma, the teacher should integrate asthma lessons into the curriculum. Two publications may be of benefit: *Asthma Awareness: Curriculum for the Elementary Classroom*, by the National Institutes of Health and National Heart, Lung, and Blood Institute (1993; specifically for elementary school), and *Managing Asthma*, by the U.S. Department of Health and Human Services in conjunction with the U.S. Department of Education (1991).

Chronic Digestive Illnesses

In addition to a student with asthma, teachers are likely to have a student in class who has diabetes. *Diabetes* is a chronic disease that impairs the body's ability to use food properly. More specifically, it is a problem with the way the body uses glucose and insulin. There are two types of diabetes. Type I diabetes, also called *insulin-dependent diabetes*, can occur at any age but usually happens in childhood or young adulthood. The problem for the student with insulin-dependent diabetes is that the pancreas does not produce enough insulin to convert sugar, or glucose, to energy for the cells. The glucose remains in the blood but cannot be used when the body needs it.

Students with Type I diabetes are always juggling three elements to keep their blood glucose levels (diabetes) under control: food, exercise, and insulin. If the balance is not kept, two emergencies await the student (and the teacher). *Hypoglycemia*, or low blood sugar, can induce *insulin shock*. The other condition results from high blood sugar, or *hyperglycemia*, which is not as serious as hypoglycemia. Low blood sugar can result from eating too little food or not eating soon enough, too much exercise without eating, or too much insulin. (Chapter 9 explains how to handle diabetic emergencies.)

The causes of Type I diabetes are unknown. However, the following are linked to this type: a history of Type I in the family, and/or viruses that have injured the pancreas, and/or a problem with the immune system.

Type II diabetes is mainly a disease of people over 40 years who are overweight. In this group of people, enough insulin is made but the body is unable to use it appropriately. Type II diabetics are generally required to lose weight, exercise regularly, and if necessary, take medication. Causation for Type II is tenuous also. However, in addition to being more likely to occur in overweight people over 40, it is more likely in those who have a family history of diabetes; have delivered a baby weighing more than nine pounds; have high blood pressure; and/or are Native American, African American, or Hispanic American. Risk increases with multiple factors. Both types of diabetes are very likely a result of complex environmental and hereditary interactions.

Lifestyle and Diabetes

Some points of consideration for teachers who have diabetic students are:

- Treat the student with diabetes like any other student.
- Let the student follow his or her routine—extra snacks, testing blood sugar—inconspicuously.
- Be alert for low blood sugar levels and know what to do in case of an emergency; keep sugar readily available.
- Don't require physical activity immediately before a meal, when the student may need food to keep the food-insulin-exercise balance.
- Participation in sports is fine, but a snack before strenuous exercise may be appropriate.

Inherited (Genetic) Diseases

About 5 percent of human beings are born with hereditary defects that result in anatomical or physiological abnormalities. These inherited abnormalities are called *genetic diseases*. They result from anomalies in the physical structure of a person's chromosomes, the microscopic structures that contain all the hereditary material (DNA).

Changes in the genetic material result from *mutations;* and many environmental substances, such as chemicals, X-rays, and atomic radiation, can increase the probability of mutations.

Altogether, about 3000 human genetic diseases resulting from single-gene defects have been identified. Most, fortunately, are quite rare. Serious genetic defects often do not permit the fetus to survive to birth and are the cause of as many as half of all spontaneous abortions (miscarriages).

In order to assign a disease or defect to genetic causes, at least one of three criteria must be met: (1) the disease must show a pattern of inheritance from generation to generation according to the laws of Mendel, (2) the chromosomes of cells in affected individuals must show some observable abnormality, or (3) a basic biochemical defect, such as absence of an essential enzyme, must be demonstrated in cells of the affected individual.

Sometimes a particular disease is said to "run in the family." This means that there is a higher frequency of that disease among closely related persons than in the general population. This is called a *familial pattern*. However, such diseases are not necessarily due to genetic anomalies; they may instead be due to some factor in the family's environment. This is an exceedingly important point. People who are told that a disease is "familial" often believe that it is inherited and believe they are doomed to get it even though they have no symptoms. Believing a disease is genetic can lead to unnecessary feelings of hopelessness and worry that can undermine one's health.

Many common diseases are regarded in our society as hereditary or as having a strong genetic basis even though the disease does not follow any of the rules for inheritance. Examples of diseases with familial patterns are allergies, alcoholism, schizophrenia, diabetes, rheumatoid arthritis, hypertension, and even some rare forms of cancer, but it is incorrect to regard these as genetic diseases. They are caused by complex interactions of genes with a particular environment, and they can be started and affected by nutrition, stress, and emotions, hormones, drugs, and other environmental factors. From the standpoint of personal health, it is advisable not to accept a genetic explanation for a disease unless the scientific evidence is unambiguous.

Doctors and other medical scientists sometimes refer to a person's *genetic susceptibility*, meaning that someone's overall genetic make-up may make him or her prone to a particular disease. The term can lead to confusion if the person believes a genetic disease is involved. Many people think of diseases in absolute terms: either one's genes *or* the environment is at fault. However, the expression of genes is always influenced to some degree by both internal and external environments.

For example, not everyone who smokes two to three packs of cigarettes a day for many years dies of lung cancer. From this fact, some people (especially those who are employed by tobacco companies) argue that cigarette smoking is a relatively harmless habit and that those who do contract lung cancer were genetically susceptible in the first place. A similarly deceptive argument has been used to support the notion that exposure to radiation is safer for some people than for others because people vary genetically in their ability to repair radiation-damaged cells. To push this kind of argument to absurdity, one could argue that people over seven feet tall are genetically defective and prone to head injury since they are more likely to hit their heads on doorways and low-hanging objects.

The point is that the environmental factor in question is hazardous, whether it is cigarette smoke, radiation, or low doorways. The fact that people respond differently to these items does not mean that they are genetically handicapped in any way. Each of us can choose and change our environment; we cannot choose or change our genes.

Implications for Elementary and Middle-School Teachers

Summary Issues

1. Health is achieved by not only preventing illness but having a good attitude during sickness and injury.
2. Illness can be used positively to examine our lifestyle, fitness level, mental attitude, sources of stress, and future susceptibility.

3. Few diseases have a single cause; more often than not, disease results from an interplay of body, mind, and environment—or in epidemiological terms, host, agent, and environment.
4. The first lines of defense against disease are the skin, mucous membranes, tears, earwax, cilia, and special enzymes.
5. White blood cells are important for defense, with leukocytes carrying out phagocytosis (eating of cells) with other specialized cells called *macrophages* (big eaters) of foreign organisms and particles.
6. Inflammation is one of the body's internal defenses.
7. Interferon is produced by T cells and virally infected cells to combat viruses.
8. Immune responses are the lines of final defense, with antigens acting as the stimuli for the immune response. Antigens are "antibody generators."
9. The lymphatic system plays a major role in our body's defense system. B lymphocytes produce specific antibodies, whereas T lymphocytes attack any foreign substances at once.
10. Autoimmune diseases generally involve a hypersensitivity in which antibodies attack the body's own cells or tissues. This is the mechanism of juvenile diabetes, rheumatic fever, and rheumatoid arthritis.
11. Rh factor is especially important in pregnant women.
12. Vaccinations are one of three types: dead organisms, attenuated organisms, or toxins.
13. There are two types of immunity: passive and active.
14. Allergies are a problem of overactivity of the immune system; asthma, anaphylactic shock, and hay fever are examples.
15. The five types of organisms involved in infectious disease are bacteria, viruses, protozoa, fungi, and parasitic worms.
16. The five stages of disease are incubation, prodromal, illness, convalescence, and recuperation or recovery.
17. HIV attacks the immune system, especially T-lymphocytes, and causes AIDS.
18. Chronic diseases are not "caught"; they develop over a long period of time and are frequently associated with lifestyle.
19. The cardiovascular diseases associated with children are high blood cholesterol, hypertension, rheumatic heart disease, and innocent heart murmurs.
20. Cancer is the chief cause of death by disease for children between 1 and 14 years.
21. Cancer can be caused by both internal factors (genes, hormones, immune conditions) and external factors (chemical, radiation, viruses).
22. The leading cause of school absence for illness is asthma, which is a severe allergic reaction.
23. Insulin-dependent diabetes usually occurs in childhood and young adulthood and requires a balancing act among food, exercise, and insulin. An imbalance can cause insulin shock, which must be treated immediately or death can ensue.
24. Some diseases are inherited, and in many cases, we may inherit a genetic susceptibility to a particular disease.

Teacher Ramifications

In regard to illness and disease, a teacher should:

1. Identify those children who have special conditions such as diabetes, asthma, rheumatic heart disease, and so forth. Prepare for possible emergencies and know how to integrate the children and any unique medical treatments into the everyday classroom.
2. Be alert to any discrimination of these students by others in the class who do not suffer from these chronic conditions.
3. Be active in establishing management and emergency plans for students with special health needs.
4. Understand and teach how many chronic conditions are affected by lifestyle and how a healthy lifestyle can ameliorate such conditions.

5. Support the school's role in helping the nation reach the objectives set forth in *Healthy Children 2000* and *Healthy Youth 2000:*
   - #15.5. Increase to at least 90 percent the proportion of people with high blood pressure who are taking action to lower it.
   - #15.6. Reduce the mean serum cholesterol level among adults to no more than 200 mg/dL.
   - #16.9. Increase to at least 60 percent the proportion of people of all ages who limit sun exposure, use sunscreens and protective clothing when exposed to sunlight, and avoid artificial sources of ultraviolet light (e.g., sun lamps, tanning booths).
   - #17.2. Reduce to no more than 8 percent the proportion of people who experience a limitation in major activity due to chronic conditions (special target populations: low-income people, Native Americans, Alaska Natives, and African Americans).
   - #17.4. Reduce to no more than 10 percent the proportion of people with asthma who require limitations on activity.
   - #17.20. Increase to 50 the number of states that have service systems for children with or at risk of chronic and disabling conditions, as required by Public Law 101–239.
   - #18.1. Confine annual incidence of diagnosed AIDS cases to no more than 98,000.
   - #18.4. Increase to at least 50 percent the proportion of sexually active, unmarried people who used a condom at last sexual intercourse (special target populations: young men and women 15 to 19 years and intravenous drug users).
   - #20.1. Reduce indigenous cases of vaccine-preventable diseases as listed in Table 8.6.
   - #21.2. Increase to at least 50 percent the proportion of people who have received, as a minimum and within the appropriate interval, all the screening and immunization services and at least one of the counseling services appropriate for their age and gender as recommended by the U.S. Preventive Services Task Force.

Table 8.6 Some Vaccine-Preventable Diseases

Disease	1988 (Baseline)	2000 (Target)
Diphtheria in people 25 and younger	1	0
Tetanus in people 25 and younger	3	0
Polio (wild-type virus)	0	0
Measles	3058	0
Rubella	225	0
Congenital rubella syndrome	6	0
Mumps	4866	500
Pertussis	3450	1000

SECTION III

Teaching Strategies for Illness and Disease

The strategies in this section are divided into grade K–4, 5–6, and 7–8 levels. In addition to strategies that can be used in the classroom, home activities are included. A home activity is designed for student-parent interaction. It is a way to engage the home in school-student learning, and parents can sign a slip of paper to confirm that an activity was completed. Evaluation of all strategies through use of the National Health Education Standards and performance indicators is indicated. Teachers may also choose to write corresponding learning assessments.

K–4 Level

Strategy One

Objective: Students will be able to state methods to avoid transmitting or catching colds.

Activity: Using a cartoon character draw several pictures of situations depicting good and bad health habits. If a flannel board is used, students may place the cartoon figure in the situations depicting how to prevent colds. Some of the good health habits to be included are:

- Using tissues when coughing/sneezing
- Eating a balanced diet
- Getting the proper amount of sleep
- Drinking plenty of fluids
- Wearing proper clothing for the weather
- Washing hands several times a day
- Keeping feet dry
- Getting plenty of exercise
- Not playing with someone who is sick
- Not using the same glass, fork, etc.
- Disposing of used tissues properly

Integration: Science, Social Studies

Related Health Content Areas: Nutrition, consumerism, substance use and abuse, physical fitness

Health Education Standards and Performance Indicators: 1(1,5,6,8); 3(1,2,3,4)

Strategy Two

Objective: Students will identify communicable diseases that can be prevented by vaccinations.

Activity: Write the names of several common communicable diseases on the board (measles, diphtheria, polio, tuberculosis, colds, flu, hepatitis, whooping cough, etc.). Ask students if they know which ones can be prevented. Direct student discussion toward use of vaccinations for prevention. Discuss importance of getting all vaccinations on time.

Integration: Science, Social Studies

Related Health Content Areas: Growth and development, consumerism, families

Health Education Standards and Performance Indicators: 1(1,6,8); 2(2)

5–6 Level

Strategy One

Objective: Students will be able to identify ways in which disease is spread.

Activity: Diseases are spread in the following ways: through the air; through personal, direct contact; by insects; in food; in water; and by animals and pets. In this exercise, students are to simulate ways in which microbes are spread as follows:

1. Place cocoa or flour in palm of hand and cough. The action of the flour can be compared to that of an airborne microbe.
2. Place red lipstick on palm of hand or a clean glass. Have another student touch palm or glass. Look for transfer of lipstick.
3. Attach transparent sticky tape to the feet of a large model of a fly. Land the fly on flour and dust, and then on a piece of white or black paper. Look for flour and dust on the paper.
4. Set up culture plates of several foods and observe for bacterial growth.
5. Set up culture plates of different samples of water (pond, river, lake, tap) and observe for bacterial growth.

Integration: Science, Social Studies

Related Health Content Areas: Environment, growth and development

Health Education Standards and Performance Indicators: 1(1,6,8); 3(1,4)

Strategy Two

Objective: Students will examine personal beliefs and opinions regarding persons infected with HIV (human immunodeficiency virus).

Activity: Have students write a short story about a student infected with HIV who goes to a new school. (Note: Be aware that students may already have personal experience with this disease.) Instruct students to be sure to include the new student's beliefs about HIV and AIDS. Ask for volunteers to read their stories to the class. (The teacher may wish to read them over first.) Discuss the various beliefs expressed in the stories, affirming those that are accurate and correcting those that are myths or misconceptions.

Integration: Science, Social Studies, Language Arts

Related Health Content Areas: Families and relationships, sexuality, growth and development

Health Education Standards and Performance Indicators: 4(4); 7(2)

7–8 Level

Strategy One

Objective: Students will determine how communicable diseases can be passed through casual contact.

Activity: Purchase some fluorescent powder (usually found at variety or costume stores). Have students lightly dust their hands with the powder and then go about their normal activities. If students can be gathered together again at the end of the school day, continue until then; if not, continue until the end of the class period. Acquire a few black lights and have students shine these around the room (or the school) to find where the powder has been left. Discuss with students how viruses and bacteria can do the same thing, and that this is one way in which diseases can be transmitted.

Integration: Science, Social Studies

Related Health Content Area: Diseases

Health Education Standard and Performance Indicators: 1(1,6,8)

Strategy Two

Objective: (1) To recognize the symptoms of disease, and (2) to demonstrate how to get help

Activity: Problem-based learning activity (see Chapter 4) as follows:

Alyssia has been feeling really tired for the past four or five weeks. She thinks she might have had a fever, but she doesn't seem to have one now. She also had white patches on the back of her throat, but they're not as bad as they were. She thought about telling her parents. She didn't, though, because whatever it is seems to be going away.

- What is Alyssia's problem in this vignette?
- What options does she have?
- What other information would be useful?
- What is the best decision for her?
- How can she evaluate her decision?

Integration: Science, Social Studies

Related Health Content Areas: Mental-emotional health, family life

Health Education Standards and Performance Indicators: 2(2); 3(1)

Strategy Three

Objective: Students will investigate a sample epidemic, constructing a "chain of infection" (see Figure 8.7) to describe the components of the epidemic.

Activity: Provide students with some basic information about an epidemic acquired from the local health department. Include who was ill, where they were when they became ill, and the like. Also give students access to resource materials that contain information on the disease. Then, using the chain of infection as the basis for their discussions, students should try to match information on this specific disease to the links in the chain of infection. After completing their research, students should try to hypothesize how the epidemic occurred.

Integration: Science, Social Studies

Related Health Content Areas: Environment, human body

Health Education Standard and Performance Indicators: 1(8,9)

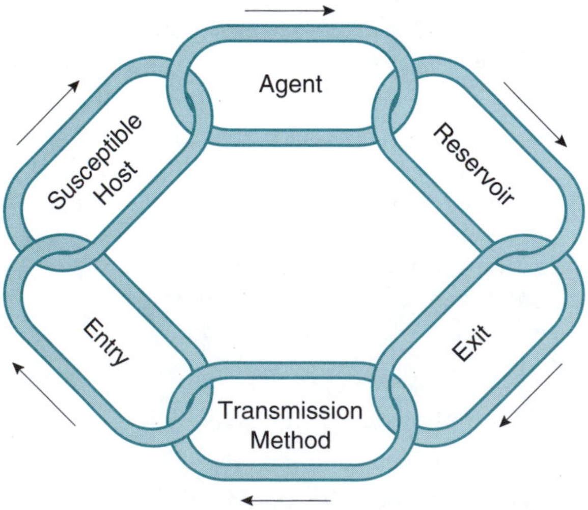

FIGURE 8.7 Chain of Infection

Home Activities

Strategy One

Objective: Students will identify how heredity plays a role in disease risk.

Activity: Students are to draw a family tree (see Figure 8.8) listing at least three generations. They are then to identify any diseases or chronic conditions that afflict any of the persons included in the tree. Students can color-code diseases so that it is easier to see how they might afflict different generations. Discussions can center on how heredity is a factor in disease risk. Students can analyze the diseases and conditions in the tree and determine if they are at increased risk for any of them.

Integration: Science, Social Studies, Art

Related Health Content Area: Growth and development

Health Education Standards: 1,2,3,

Strategy Two

Objective: Students will discuss with their parents their beliefs regarding death and dying.

Activity: Parents and students may wish to use a Living Will kit, which can be purchased at most office supply stores. Parents and stu-

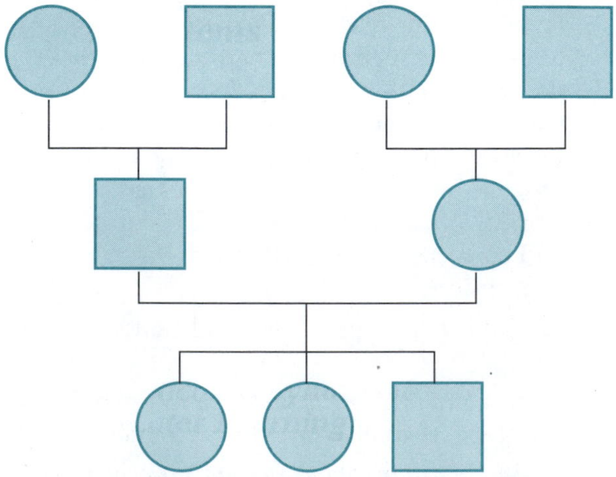

FIGURE 8.8 Family Tree

dents are to discuss their views on death and dying, particularly in terms of extraordinary measures, terminal illness, machine-assisted living, organ donation, burial versus cremation, and so forth. Make sure students realize that the discussion is strictly for the purpose of becoming informed and understanding what their parents believe.

Integration: Science

Related Health Content Areas: Illness and disease, growth and development

Health Education Standards: 5,6,7

References

American Cancer Society. *Cancer Facts and Figures 1994*. ACS, Atlanta, 1994.

American Heart Association. *You, Your Child, and Rheumatic Fever* pamphlet AHA, Dallas, TX, 1988.

American Heart Association. *AHA Scientific/Medical Position: Cholesterol in Children*. AHA, Dallas, TX, 1995.

American Heart Association. *AHA Scientific/Medical Position: Hyperlipidemia in Children*. AHA, Dallas, TX, 1995.

American Heart Association. *About High Blood Pressure in Children* (pamphlet). AHA, Dallas, TX, 1981.

American Heart Association. *AHA Scientific/Medical Position: High Blood Pressure in Children*. AHA, Dallas, TX, 1995.

American Medical Association. *Healthy Youth 2000*. Department of Adolescent Health, AMA, Chicago, 1990.

American School Health Association. *Pulse*, January-February, 1995.

Charles, D. Rapidly rising HIV rate causes serious concern. Centers for Disease Control and Prevention National AIDS Clearinghouse, Atlanta, 1995.

Centers for Disease Control. Health expert says India lax over fighting AIDS. CDC National AIDS Clearinghouse, Atlanta, 1995.

Dubos, R. *Man, Medicine, and Environment*. Praeger, New York, 1968.

Farish, D.J. *Human Biology*. Jones and Bartlett, Boston, 1993.

Garrett, L. *The Coming Plague*. Penguin Books, New York, 1994.

National Institutes of Health, and National Heart, Lung, and Blood Institute. *Asthma Awareness: Curriculum for the Elementary Classroom* (NIH Publication No. 93–2894). Washington, DC, 1993).

Novello, A.C. *Surgeon General's Report to the American Public on HIV Infection and AIDS*. CDC National AIDS Clearinghouse, Atlanta, 1993.

Preston, R. *The Hot Zone*. Doubleday, New York, 1994.

Smith, S.F. & Smith, C.M. *Personal Health Choices*. Jones and Bartlett, Boston, 1990.

Thomas, L. *The Medusa and the Snail*. Viking-Penguin, New York, 1979.

Russia's HIV law passed, *Lancet* 345, 8949 (1995):644.

U.S. Department of Health and Human Services and U.S. Department of Education. *Managing Asthma: A Guide for Schools* (NIH Publication No. 91–2650). Bethesda, MD, 1991.

U.S. Department of Health and Human Services. *Healthy Children 2000*. Jones and Bartlett, Boston, 1992.

U.S. paying high price for HIV and TB epidemics. *AIDS Alert* 10, 3 (1995):43.

Walsh, M. & Ryan-Wenger, N.M. Sources of stress in children with asthma, *Journal of School Health* 62, 10 (1992):459–463.

9

Safety, Injury Prevention, and Emergency Care

At the conclusion of this chapter, you should be able to:

- *Explain the seriousness of accidents among the school-age population*
- *Know the major accidents that cause death and disability in the school-age population*
- *Discuss safety measures in the home, playground, and school*
- *Explain how to prevent three types of poisoning*
- *Discuss and present information about obtaining help from Emergency Medical Services*
- *Know the ABCs of cardiopulmonary resuscitation and emergency care*
- *Explain basic emergency-care steps for selected common problems experienced by children*
- *Know the universal steps for avoiding spread of bloodborne pathogens*
- *Comprehend the responsibility and liability of a teacher regarding injury prevention and emergency care*

SECTION I

Health Status, Deficits, and Learning

The safety area of health education has traditionally covered two domains. First, and most obvious, is accident prevention—stopping unplanned and potentially damaging events. Second is the task of reducing the damage caused by accidents that do occur; this is termed *accident mitigation.* In fire safety, for example, the first domain would entail such activities as storing the gasoline for the lawnmower outside to prevent a fire. Accident mitigation would be the installation of smoke detectors in case a fire did break out.

Education in both these domains is very much a necessity. Although the 1980s heralded a decrease in the number of accidental deaths, in 1993 the number increased for the first time in five years (National Safety Council, 1995). Some other facts about accidents:

- Unintentional injuries are the leading cause of death for those between the ages of 1 and 24 years.
- Children and adolescents between the ages of 1 and 24 years have motor vehicle accidents as the leading cause of unintentional-injury deaths, followed by drowning, fires, and burns.
- Males are injured at school twice as often as females (about 71% to 29%), and almost one half (47%) of incidents are to children between 10 and 14 years.
- Forty-one percent of school injuries occur in recreational areas, and many school injuries result in surgery or hospitalization.
- Accidents in the home accounted for over 22,000 deaths in 1993, reflecting a 7 percent rise from 1992.
- Five-gallon bucket drownings are all too common, with 130 emergency room visits and 50 deaths attributed to them each year.
- The highest rate of firework-related injuries is suffered by children 10 to 14 years.
- The greatest odds for dying of poisoning during the first twenty years of life are in the first year of life and late teens.
- Between the ages of 5 and 14 years, death from a firearm wound is preceded only by motor vehicle accidents, drowning, and fires.
- Unintentional deaths from flying in commercial or private planes are declining.

- Sports injuries can be fatal, including high school football (3 deaths in 1993 due to head injuries, 8 by systemic failure).
- Storms can be killers, with most deaths stemming from flash floods, snow/blizzards, lightning, and tornadoes.
- The ABCs of emergency care are *a*irway open, *b*reathing, and *c*irculation at the carotid pulse.
- Body sizes vary and for emergency care an infant is anyone under one year of age, a child is anyone between one and eight years of age, and children more than eight years old are classified as adults.
- Cardiopulmonary resuscitation (CPR) is a combination of rescue breathing (mouth-to-mouth) and external chest compression, and is different for adults and children.
- Children with diabetes can experience two types of emergencies—diabetic coma and insulin shock—and the two are at opposite ends of the blood-sugar continuum.
- The cost of unintentional injuries is $407.5 billion per year, which is equivalent to 80 cents of every dollar paid in 1993 federal personal income taxes.
- Fifty-five percent of all injury deaths in 1991 were from motor vehicle– and firearm-related injuries.
- In 1991 firearm deaths, 49 percent were suicides, 47 percent homicides, and 4 percent accidents. Males are much more likely to be involved in all types of firearm-related deaths, and accidents are highest in the 15 to 24 age group.
- The National Safety Council monitors information on sick-building syndrome, which occurs in some modern office buildings. Workers most often exhibit headache, dizziness, and disorientation symptoms.

SECTION II

Safety, Injury Prevention, and Emergency Care Teaching Information

The need for safety and efforts to provide it have been part of people's lives since the beginning of human existence, when survival and safety were much the same thing. Although the hazards have changed over the millennia, the fundamental problem is the same. Ever since early humans sought shelter and developed weapons to protect themselves, the anticipation of danger and the ability to overcome it have been major keys to safety and survival.

Accidents don't just happen. They result from violations of rules, regulations, procedures, and courtesies that have evolved over many years. Accidents are always a symptom of disorder or failure to adapt. The disorder may be in the habits of an individual, the customs of the community, or the breakdown of a machine. An accident or near-accident, no matter what the degree of severity, is a signal that something or someone is not functioning as it should.

Approximately 15 percent of accidents are caused by hazardous conditions in our environment. The remaining 85 percent have human causes. Among elementary school children, the human element responsible for contributing to accidents is fourfold: (1) lack of knowledge of and experience with cause and effect; (2) lack of skill in such activities as swimming, using playground equipment, and crossing busy highways; (3) improper attitudes and personal traits—foolhardiness and taking unnecessary chances; and (4) poor emotional health, which results in an accident-prone frame of mind.

This last factor should be of special interest to elementary school teachers. Children lacking phys-

The foundations for safety begin at home but must be reinforced in the school and the community.

ical skills may develop emotional problems that create an accident habit or behavioral pattern as an adjustment compensation. Such careless children have more emotional outbursts, lack self-control, and are likely to be more impulsive and act more hastily than others. Thus accident prevention in the school involves fostering a safe physical and social environment, promoting emotional and mental well-being, and providing opportunities for children to practice safety precautions.

Participation in a variety of activities, familiar or unfamiliar, always presents possibilities of accidents. Many accidents are caused neither by carelessness nor poor mental attitudes. Curiosity leads children to explore, and since their curiosity is not checked by fear, they do not perceive the dangers of new objects and situations. With experience and increased insight, they gradually learn to be more cautious. Accidents are the leading cause of death among school-age children. Approximately two thirds of childhood accidents occur before the child is 9 years old, with 2 and 3 years being the most vulnerable. At these ages, children are exploring the environment for themselves.

Certain environments are hazardous. Of every five school accidents, two occur in unorganized activities and three in organized activities. The classroom, the gymnasium, and the street are the most common sites for accidents. Elementary school teachers must assume responsibility for providing a safe environment and direct safety instruction.

Safety is, first, a cultural concept. It can also be thought of as a series of habits that should be inculcated during children's formative years. When integrated with the other essential skills of living, the skills of safety become the basis for a sensible and rational lifestyle. Although the foundation for safety is laid in the home by parents, it must be reinforced in the school and the community. Today's children must be able to solve problems so as to have safe but nonetheless exciting and challenging adventures.

The elementary school teacher's responsibility is to instill in pupils attitudes that encourage them to act in the interest of their own safety, that of their families, and that of society. Safety education is not only training in conservation of life and the prevention of accidents, but also instruction in how to be a good citizen. Other responsibilities of the teacher are to guide students in molding sound values, direct their thinking and decision-making, and help them regulate their behavior. Education for the elementary school child is an on-going process of living, and safety education is a continuous process of conserving children's lives and well-being.

Concern for safety in the classroom, and in life, should not stifle initiative, adventure, and discovery. Indeed, such concern should lead to opportunities for a more abundant and richer style of living. Freedom from accidents and injuries is part of optimal well-being; and children should develop as many dimensions of themselves as possible. In doing so, they acquire the capacity to function more fully. Safety education provides insurance for children to develop in this direction, and should be generated by teachers both through the school environment and in classroom instruction.

Safety at Home

Young people are sometimes the victims of a fire in the home. Because of the high incidence of home fires, it is important that children understand how fires start and how to prevent them. It takes three things to start a fire: oxygen, heat, and combustible material. Since oxygen is part of the environment, the only things that can be controlled are the sources of heat and the combustible material.

Sources of Heat

Several kinds of heat may be found in the home. *Matches* are present in most homes, and one of the most common admonitions children hear is, "Don't play with matches." Safety matches cannot be ignited without the striker strip provided. Other matches will strike on any surface.

Lighters can be unpredictable. Even when used properly, they may flare up when ignited. Using a lighter should be left to adults, and the lighter should always be pointed away from faces and clothing when put into use.

The *pilot light* on a stove or heater may not seem dangerous, but it can ignite flammable vapors in the air.

Space heaters, fireplaces, and kitchen stoves produce heat or fire that can spread if combustible material is allowed to come too close to them.

Combustible Materials

Flammable liquids such as gasoline, kerosene, lighter fluid, alcohol-based nail polish remover, and rubber cement are frequent fuels for home fires, so too are natural and synthetic materials, especially lightweight varieties used in clothing; and upholstered furniture, mattresses, and bedding.

Preventing Fires

Here are some basic safety habits that children should learn and share with their families and friends:

1. Don't play with matches.
2. Keep matches away from younger brothers and sisters.
3. If lighter fluid, or any flammable liquid, spills on you or your clothes, wash it off immediately.
4. Don't get too close to a space heater, fireplace, kitchen stove, or oven.
5. Caution any smokers in your family not to smoke while sitting in upholstered furniture or in bed, especially when sleepy, on medication, or on alcohol.
6. Keep clothing, especially sleeves and shirt hems, away from stoves, open flames, heaters, and any other source of heat.
7. Never light a fire in a fireplace or wood-burning stove. Always allow parents to do this.
8. Never lean over a fireplace or put hands inside for warmth.
9. Remind parents to inspect working fireplaces and chimneys frequently and keep them in good condition.

Additional Safety Precautions

Smoke detectors are a good idea for homes; installed and maintained correctly, they can save lives. Students should encourage parents to test smoke detectors once a month to be sure they are in working condition.

Home fire drills are also a good idea. The family should plan escape routes and practice what to do in case the smoke detector goes off. There should be alternative exits planned, as the first choice may be blocked by smoke and/or fire. A meeting place outside the house should be selected, where everyone can go to be sure all family members were able to leave the house. In the event of a fire, it may be necessary to pass through smoke-filled halls. Since smoke rises, safe passage requires keeping close to the floor, perhaps even crawling. If it is necessary to open a door to escape, it should be felt to see if it is hot to the touch. If it is, fire may be just outside, so escape should be made by an alternative route.

Reporting Fires

There are some important things teachers and children should know about helping to reduce the seriousness of burns until professional help can be obtained:

1. If clothing catches fire, do not run. Stop! Drop to the ground and roll back and forth to smother the flames.
2. If skin is burned, hold the burn under cool running water.
3. Never put grease or butter on a burn, or try to clean it.
4. Never pull clothing over a burn or try to remove pieces of clothing sticking to it.
5. Never break burn blisters.
6. A burn should be covered with a clean, dry sheet to protect it.
7. Get the patient to a doctor.

Safety on the Playground

The playground is vital to a child's development. Play is natural to children and it is there that they learn many lessons. Some of these are how to interact with others, to take turns, to share, and to cooperate. Children can make a playground anywhere: at school, at home, or at a friend's house. It is important that they learn what is safe and unsafe behavior at a playground.

The Consumer Product Safety Commission estimated 266,869 emergency room–treated cases associated with playground equipment (National Safety Council, 1994). The causes of the accidents vary, but seven out of ten injuries are caused by falls. Of course most such injuries are sustained on *climbing apparatus* such as monkey bars and chinning bars. Most often, the victims fall when they slip, lose their grip, or lose their balance. Another location of falls is related to *swings and swing sets,* specifically, over the side, from the platform, and from the ladder. Other playground injuries result from striking protruding bolts, the side rim, or edge; or slipping on the ladder and striking the steps. *Merry-go-rounds* and *seesaw* injuries, for the most part, result from falls too. It is natural for children to roughhouse, and this often leads to accidents. It is important to teach safety without dampening imaginative play. Children need to be encouraged with positively presented safety concepts.

Preventing Playground Accidents

Safety on swings: Sit in the center of the swing. Never stand or kneel. Hold on with both hands. Stop the swing before getting off. Don't walk too close to a moving swing. Have only one person in one swing at a time. Never swing empty swings or twist swing chains. Never put head and feet through exercise rings on swing sets.

Safety on slides: Hold on with both hands while going up the steps. Take one step at a time. Never go up the sliding surface or the frame. Slide down feet first, sitting up, one at a time. Be sure no one is in front of the slide before sliding down. Be patient and wait for a turn. Leave the front of the slide after taking a turn. Don't use a metal slide that has been in the sun.

Safety on climbing apparatus: Use the correct grip. Use fingers and thumbs for climbing and holding. Use both hands. Watch carefully when climbing down and avoid those climbing up. Avoid having too many people on the equipment at once. Everyone should start at the same end of the equipment and move in the same direction.

Stay well behind the person in front and avoid swinging feet. Never use equipment when it is wet. Avoid speed contests and trying to cover too large a distance in one move. Drop from the bars with knees slightly bent and land on both feet.

Safety on seesaws: Sit facing one another; do not lean back. Keep a firm hold with both hands. Never stand or run on the board. Keep feet from under the board as it goes down. Tell partner before getting off. Never jolt the other person by hitting the ground hard with either end of the board.

Safety with Bicycles, Roller Skates, and Skateboards

Bicycle Safety

The Consumer Product Commission estimated 600,649 emergency room–treated cases associated with bicycles and accessories (National Safety Council, 1994). As to be expected, the vast majority of these injuries involved children under 15 years. Bicycles are a major form of transportation for children. Thus it is important for children to understand how bicycle accidents happen and how they can be prevented.

There are four major ways to get hurt on a bicycle. The first is *collision,* either with a car or another bicycle. Collisions happen in one of several ways:

1. *Driveway rideout* occurs when a child rides out of a driveway and is hit by a car. This type accounts for about 8 percent of all collisions between a car and a bike.
2. *Running a stop sign.* Most of those who get hit riding through stop signs knew they were supposed to stop. They just didn't understand why, didn't feel like stopping, or got distracted. About 10 percent of car-with-bike crashes occur this way.

Children are natural risk-takers. These skateboarders are clearly more interested in adventure than safety.

3. *Turning without warning* occurs when a rider makes a left turn without looking behind for traffic or signaling his or her intention. This type accounts for another 10 percent of all crashes between bikes and cars.
4. *Nighttime riding* is a risk factor. Certain types of accidents occur most often after dark. A car may come up behind a rider to overtake and instead hit the bicycle and rider. Such collisions can be very serious. They account for about 25 percent of fatal car-with-bike collisions. Although most of these accidents involve older riders, children riding bicycles at night should learn to be cautious.
5. *Following the leader* is a dangerous game. Many collisions between cars and bikes occur when children are following each other. The leader may run a stop sign and get through, but the second one gets hit. This practice is very difficult to counter; children should be urged to watch out for their own safety and everyone else's when riding in groups.

Loss of control is the second major cause of bicycling injuries. Faulty brakes; riding too large a bicycle; riding double (e.g., on a banana seat, rear fender, handlebars, or the horizontal bar on a boy's bike); stunting; hitting a hole, bump, or other obstacle have all been implicated. Another cause of loss of control is when the rider's foot slips from one or both pedals.

Getting feet, hands, or clothing caught in the bicycle is the third major cause of these injuries.

The fourth major cause of injuries during bike-riding stems from *mechanical and structural problems*. These include brake failure, wobbling or disengagement of the wheel or steering mechanism, difficulty in shifting gears, chain slippage, pedals falling off, and frame breakage.

To prevent bicycle-related injuries, children need to learn and obey traffic laws. They also need to be taught how to select, maintain, and store a bike.

Here are some tips for bicycle safety:

- *Know and obey traffic laws and signals*. The laws that govern automobiles also apply to bicyclists. Bike riders must show the same courtesy they hope drivers will show them. Always yield the right of way to cars and pedestrians. Be alert for people stepping out from between parked cars. Be prepared to use the bell or horn as a warning, but always be ready to yield. Always stop at stop signs and traffic lights. Know and use hand signals. Always check behind when making a left turn. Walk the bicycle when crossing busy streets. Look carefully in all directions when riding out of driveways.
- Don't ride a bike it is not in *good working condition.*
- *Ride near the curb, in the same direction as traffic. Always ride single file*. Don't travel on routes with high-speed or *heavy traffic*. Look for safer, less-traveled routes.
- *Don't stunt or clown* on a bicycle. This can result in serious injury. Bikes are fun, but safety is serious business.
- Avoid playing *follow the leader* on your bike.
- Never *carry a passenger.*
- Use a *basket or carrier* for packages.
- Be alert to the *condition of riding surfaces* and what's happening around you. Watch for sewer grates, potholes, rocks, and other bad surface conditions, which can easily throw the best riders. Ride slowly enough to avoid unexpected obstacles, such as car doors opening suddenly or cars backing out of driveways or parking lots.
- Avoid *riding in wet weather.* It's hard for cars to see bicyclists in the rain. Wet tires can skid, and wet hand brakes may not stop a bike.
- Be cautious when *riding at night.* If it's necessary to ride at dusk or in darkness, make sure lights and reflectors are in good working order. Wear white or light-colored clothing, and ride slowly. Reflector tape on clothing also improves visibility.
- *Avoid skidding*. Slow down on rough or slippery roads and when riding downhill. Watch for loose sand and gravel.
- *Helmets save lives*. About 75 percent of bicycle fatalities result from head injuries. Many other

people are disabled as a result of hitting their heads. The cost of a helmet is small when compared with that of a head injury. Hardshell helmets are recommended.

- *Choose the proper-sized bicycle.* The rider should be able to straddle the seat with both feet flat on the ground, and with no less than a one-inch clearance between the frame's top tube (on a boy's bike) and the rider's crotch. The rule is to buy a bicycle that fits today. Some bikes were manufactured and sold before current guidelines went into effect. Students should watch for these older bikes and the following hazards: sharp edges; a bent or broken frame; protrusions above the top frame or between the seat and the handlebars; faulty brakes; a nonderailleur bike without a chain guard; a bike without reflectors or lights; and tires with thin tread and cracked surfaces or sidewalls.
- *Maintaining the bike* is essential to safety. While most children don't have the skills to repair their own bicycles, they should be aware when something needs repair and alert their parents. It is recommended that bicycles have a tune-up and safety check at least once a year.
- *Bicycles should be stored indoors* to prevent rust and to keep all parts in order. Keeping a bicycle inside also helps prevent its theft.

Roller Skate Safety

Roller skating is very popular with children, but they can fall hard while learning to skate. Following are some of the major causes of roller-skating accidents:

1. *Poor or uneven surfaces.* Cracked or uneven cement sidewalks or streets, rocks, tree branches, and other debris can cause tripping or skidding.
2. *Structural problems* in the skates, for example, a loose axle or wheel
3. The *human factor* can play a major role. This includes skating too close to other skaters, inexperience with the skates or doing trick skating, horseplay and pushing, lack of attention, misusing the skates (e.g., going up and down stairs with skates on).
4. Roller skating in *traffic.*

To prevent skating accidents, it is important to learn to select skates properly and to use them properly. Always buy or rent skates that fit well. Buy them for the size the child is now, not to grow into. Check for sharp points and edges that can cut in the event of a fall.

In using roller skates, these points should be kept in mind:

1. Learn to perform basic skating maneuvers well before attempting more complicated ones.
2. Check the skating surface carefully before and while skating. Avoid uneven or broken pavement and branches or rocks in the skating path.
3. Don't roller skate in the streets unless they are closed to traffic to allow skating.
4. Don't hitch a ride on a bicycle or car while roller skating.
5. Wear safety equipment, such as protective knee and elbow pads, when roller skating. This can help prevent serious injuries. Other recommended equipment includes wrist braces, helmet, and mouth guard, which may prevent knocked-out or broken teeth.
6. Learn how to fall in case of lost balance. Try to roll onto fleshy parts of the body, such as buttocks, upper legs, and shoulders. Try to relax rather than going stiff.

Keep roller skates in good condition. Make sure the wheels and straps are in good condition. Keep skates dry and clean. Lubricate them when needed. Keep skates in a dry place away from moisture, which can rust them.

Skateboard Safety

Skateboards can be a lot of fun, but skateboarding is dangerous unless precautions are taken. The U.S. Consumer Product Safety Commission estimated 56,435 emergency room–treated cases related to skateboards in 1991 (National Safety

Council, 1994). Selecting a proper skateboard is important. Skateboards come in many shapes, sizes, and colors. There is no rule about which is best. Before buying one, gather as much information as possible. Visit stores where skateboards are sold and look at several kinds. Go to a library and read magazines or books on skateboarding.

There are several points to keep in mind when riding a skateboard:

1. Use protective equipment. Closed-toe, nonslip shoes as well as helmets, gloves, and padding can reduce the number and severity of injuries.
2. Check the riding surface for holes, bumps, rocks, and other obstacles.
3. Avoid riding in the street.
4. Never hitch a ride from a car or bicycle.
5. Allow only one person on a skateboard at a time.
6. Learn how to fall. (See roller skating safety, above, for details.) This reduces the chances of being severely injured.

As with all recreational equipment, proper maintenance is important to help make skateboarding safe. Make sure all parts of the skateboard are in good condition and that nothing is broken, bent, or cracked. Keep the skateboard in a dry place to prevent rust and warping.

Poison Prevention

Most poisonings involve preschool children, but there are many hazards to older children as well. It is important for children to understand the sources of poisonous substances in their environments and know how to avoid accidental poisoning.

There are three types of poisoning: drug poisoning, usually from an accidental over-dose; household chemical poisoning; and vapor poisoning.

Preventing Drug Poisoning

Overdoses, especially of aspirin, tranquilizers, and iron tablets, kill more children than any other drugs. It is important to teach children the proper attitudes toward drugs. They should be taught that medicine is not food or drink. They should understand that pills are not candy, and that cough syrups are not syrup for pancakes or waffles even though they look and flow like these substances. No one should use or give another person someone else's medicine. Medicine should always be taken and administered in a lighted room, and all instructions should be carefully followed.

Preventing Household-Chemical Poisoning

In the home, poisonous substances are stored mainly in the bathroom, kitchen, garage, basement, and storage areas. Children should understand that the substances kept in these storage areas are for special purposes and not for human consumption. A good rule is "always ask first" before eating or drinking anything.

Preventing Vapor Poisoning

Children and adults are often victims of poisoning from vapors in the air. When sprays are being used around the house, keep other people out of the area. Examples include flea sprays for pets, bug sprays, and household cleaners. Sprays should never be allowed into the eyes or the lungs.

Emergency Care*

Teachers need to remember that injuries are the leading cause of death and disability in children. The emotional impact is tremendous when you consider family members and friends. Emergency care and first aid training are a must for anyone who works or lives with children. Such training may mean the difference between life and death, rapid or long-term recovery, and temporary or permanent disability.

*This section is largely based on information from the National Safety Council, *First Aid and CPR* 2nd ed. (Boston: Jones and Bartlett Publishers, 1993).

Calling Emergency Medical Services for Help

Contacting Emergency Medical Services (EMS) for assistance is easy in communities with a 911 service. However, in communities that do not have this service, children should be shown the EMS numbers on the inside cover of the telephone book. To expedite calls for help, a list of phone numbers should also be placed near your telephone. These numbers may include:

1. *Rescue squad/fire department.* The rescue squad is often part of the fire department. It is made up of specially trained paramedics.
2. *Police.* While they may not be able to respond medically, they can assist in getting someone to a hospital quickly.
3. *Ambulance service.* Check to see if the local ambulance service has trained paramedics or if it is simply a means of transport.
4. *Your doctor.* Although your doctor may not be immediately available, he or she can be alerted.
5. *Poison control center.* These centers function differently from city to city. You need to call them before an emergency to see if they will give you information or if they just provide it to doctors.

The following pointers are for using a 911 service:

1. *When to call.* If you feel that you need assistance in any way, call. In emergency situations, you have little time to deliberate, so it is better to call than not to call.

2. *Instructions to children.* Children need to be educated about 911 services. Let them know that they dial "9-1-1." Do not tell them to dial "nine-eleven."

3. *What happens next.* After dialing the number, children need to know what will happen. First, the phone will be answered by a trained professional dispatcher—a person who is trained to handle emergencies over the telephone. Since the amount of training varies from locale to locale, it may be wise to find out how much training is received and exactly what can be expected from the dispatcher.

4. *Talking with the dispatcher.* Be sure to speak slowly and clearly. Don't shout! If the 9 1 1 system does not automatically log your telephone number and address, be certain to have your child provide that information first. The child should expect a series of key questions so that the dispatcher knows the nature of the emergency and level of response required, that is, medical, fire, or police assistance. Be prepared to answer a lot of questions. If you are not asked about something that you believe is important, pass the information along to the dispatcher. If someone is injured, the dispatcher may ask if you can help, such as by doing CPR. Many dispatchers are trained to talk you through the help you need to give, and they may stay on the line until help arrives. These prearrival instructions can save lives. The instructions vary depending on the situation. You may be asked to get to a safe environment.

5. *Key information.* If the situation is a medical one, the following information should be given to the dispatcher so that it can be relayed to the medical team en route to your location:

A. Medical or patient problem (what happened)
B. Gender and approximate age of the patient
C. Is the patient breathing?
D. Is the patient conscious?

6. *Hanging up the phone.* Always be the last to hang up in case the dispatcher needs more information. You may want to wait and have the dispatcher tell you when it is OK to hang up.

ABCs of Emergency Care and CPR

When a medical emergency arises, the following steps can be used. These steps are delineated below and illustrated in Figure 9.1.

1. *Victim assessment.* Is the person responsive; can the person hear you when you say, "Are you OK?" If he or she responds, say who you are, ask permission to help, and monitor ABCs (below). If the person is not responsive,

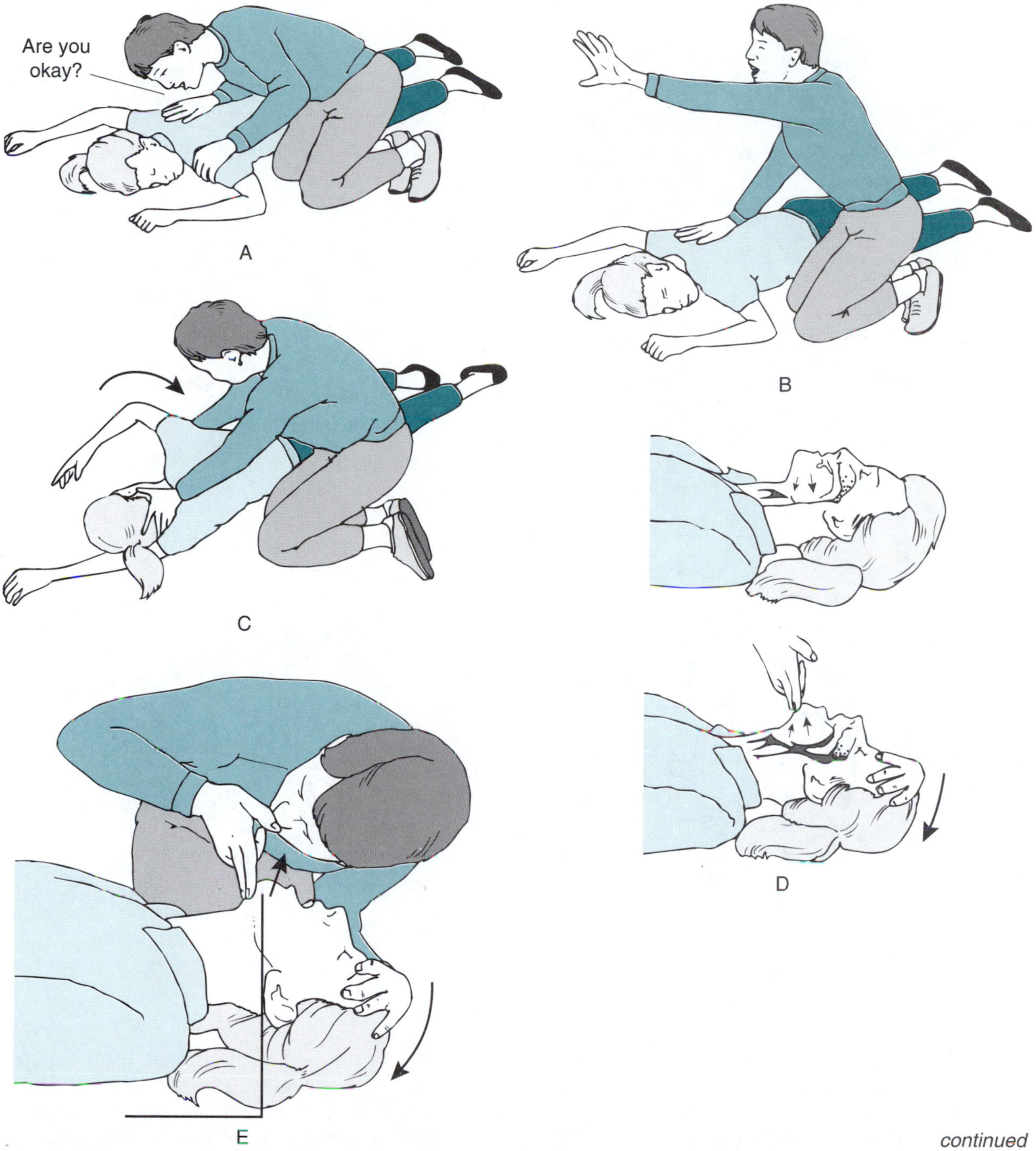

continued

FIGURE 9.1 Cardiopulmonary Resuscitation. *A.* Determining Responsiveness; *B.* Calling for Help; *C.* Positioning the Victim; *D.* Opening the Airway by Tilting the Head and Lifting the Chin; *E.* Determining Breathlessness; *F.* Mouth-to-Mouth Rescue Breathing; *G.* Determining Pulselessness; *H.* External Chest Compression (*Source:* From National Safety Council, *First Aid and CPR* Second Edition. © 1993. Boston: Jones and Bartlett, p. 46. Reprinted with permission.)

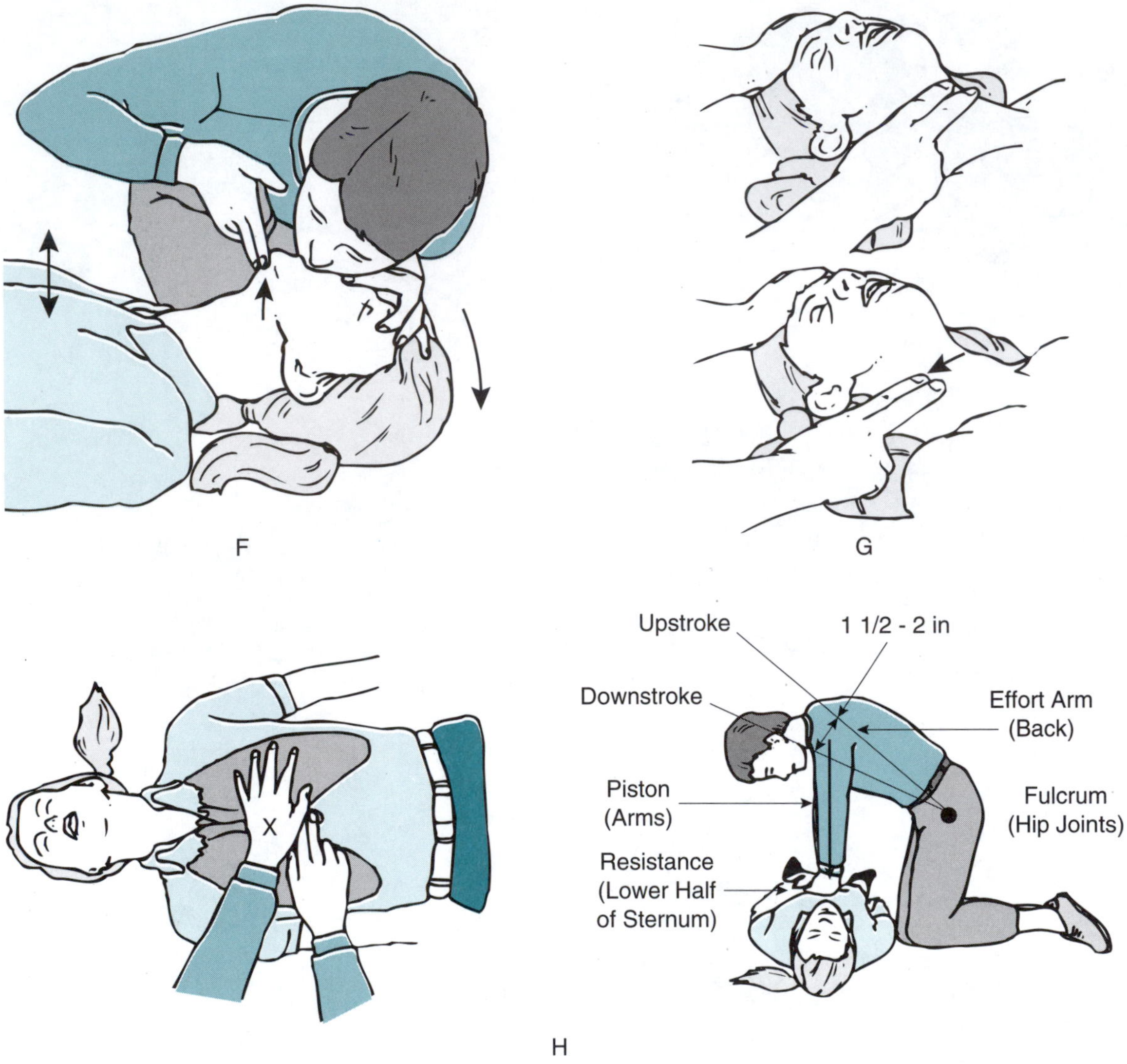

FIGURE 9.1—***continued***

you should call for EMS assistance and then monitor the ABCs.

2. *ABCs.*
   A. Airway. Is the airway open?
   B. Breathing. Is the person breathing?
   C. Circulation. Is there a carotid pulse?
3. If the *airway is not open,* use the head-tilt/chin-lift method to clear it if possible. The obstruction may be caused by the tongue, vomit, a foreign body, swelling, or a spasm.
4. *Watch for the chest to rise and fall,* listen for air exchange, and feel for expulsion of air onto your cheek (this should not take longer than 3 to 5 seconds). If the victim is *not* breathing, give two quick breaths.
5. *Check for a pulse* in the carotid artery in the neck. If there is a pulse, give rescue breaths every 5 or 6 seconds until breathing resumes, or until help arrives. Be sure to check the carotid pulse every minute to be certain there is still a pulse.

Table 9.1 CPR Review for Children and Adults

Item	Child (1–8 Years)	Adult (>8 Years)
How to open airway	Head-tilt/chin-lift	Head-tilt/chin-lift
How to check breathing	Look at chest and listen and feel for air (3–5 seconds)	Look at chest and listen and feel for air (3–5 seconds)
What kinds of breaths	Slow, make chest rise and fall	Slow, make chest rise and fall
Where to check pulse	Carotid artery (5–10 seconds)	Carotid artery (5–10 seconds)
Hand position for chest compressions	1 finger's width above tip of sternum	1 finger's width above tip of sternum
Compress with	Heel of 1 hand	Heels of 2 hands, one hand on top of the other
Compression depth	1 to $1\frac{1}{2}$ inches	$1\frac{1}{2}$ inches to 2 inches
Compression rate	100 per minute	80–100 per minute
Compression-breath ratio	5:1	15:2
How to count for compression rate	1 and 2 and 3 and 4 and 5 and breathe	1 and 2 and 3 and 4 and 5 and 6 and . . . 15 and breathe, breathe
How often to reassess	Every few minutes	Every few minutes
After reassessment, resume CPR with	Compressions	Compressions
How often to give only breaths during rescue breathing	Every 3 seconds	Every 5 seconds

Source: Adapted from National Safety Council, *First Aid and CPR* 2nd ed. (Boston: Jones and Bartlett, 1993), p. 46.

If the airway is open and the victim is able to breathe but lacks a pulse, you would begin *cardiopulmonary resuscitation* (CPR), also shown in Figure 9.1.

CPR combines rescue breathing and external chest compressions. Knowledge of this technique is important, especially for drowning, suffocation, drug overdose, electrocution, and heart attack victims. Once you start CPR, you should continue until (a) pulse and breathing are regained, (b) someone can replace you, (c) the situation becomes too unsafe, (d) you are too exhausted to continue, or (e) a physician tells you to stop.

CPR works through chest compression, which causes blood to move through the heart and circulatory system. When done effectively, CPR provides one-fourth to one-third normal blood flow. Effective rescue breaths (mouth-to-mouth) provides about 16 percent oxygen—enough to live. Table 9.1 provides an overview of CPR information for children and adults.

Emergency Care for Common Childhood Problems

Myriad emergency problems can arise when working with children. Table 9.2 briefly outlines common problems and what you can do for each. They are presented in alphabetical order. Figure 9.2 illustrates the Heimlich Maneuver, and Figure 9.3 shows the technique for controlling a nosebleed.

Emergency Care and Bloodborne Pathogens

As pointed out in Table 9.2, emergency care requiring exposure to blood can place the teacher at risk for bloodborne pathogens. The most significant ones are the hepatitis B virus (HBV) and the human immunodeficiency virus (HIV).

HBV is very infectious. It attacks the liver and can bring about a flulike illness that can last for

Text continued on page 208

Table 9.2 Emergency Care for Common Childhood Problems

Common Problem	Emergency Care
Anaphylactic shock (e.g., from wasp sting): A severe allergic reaction which can occur within minutes or seconds and can cause death. About 60–80% of these deaths are caused by an inability to breathe because of swollen air passages.	For a sensitive person, seek medical attention as quickly as possible. Help administer medication (epinephrine injection kit may be carried by the victim). CPR may be required in some instances.
Animal bite Sixty to 90% of animal bites are by dogs. One in 10 need stitches; all need cleaning. Some bacteria from a bite can be deadly, i.e., rabies.	If bleeding heavily (rare), treat for bleeding. If little bleeding, wash with soap and water for 5–10 minutes with no scrubbing; allow some blood flow to get bacteria out. Rinse with running water. Cover with dressing but do not seal wound. Seek medical help. If rabies suspected, try to locate animal's owner; do not kill the animal.
Bleeding Rapid bleeding can lead to shock and death. A loss of one pint of blood puts a child in extreme danger. Bleeding can be arterial, venous, or capillary.	Place a sterile gauze over the wound (or a towel or whatever is available). Protect yourself with latex gloves or plastic wrap if possible. Apply direct pressure over the wound. Do not remove first dressing if blood-soaked. Elevate body part above victim's heart and continue direct pressure. Use brachial or femoral pressure points, if necessary, and continue direct pressure. Do not remove an impaled object.
Broken Bone(s) A fracture is a crack or break in the bone. It is called *open* when the skin is broken and *closed* when it isn't. Look for: swelling, deformity, pain and tenderness, inability to use that part of the body. In a severe accident, expect fractures.	Broken bones usually not life threatening. Treat for shock. Do not move injured area unless necessary; check for symptoms. Do not try to put bones back together beneath the skin. Compare area to noninjured area (e.g., other arm). Make comfortable until help arrives.
Choking Most common cause is from trying to swallow a large piece of food. Other causes include eating too fast, eating while talking or laughing, walking or running with objects in the mouth.	Shout for help to someone who can get medical assistance. Perform the Heimlich maneuver (Figure 9.2): Stand behind victim, wrap your arms around the victim's waist. Make a fist with one hand and place the thumb-side just above the victim's navel, well below the tip of the sternum; grasp your fist with your other hand. Press fist into victim's abdomen with quick upward thrust. Give up to 5 thrusts and check your technique. Repeat cycles of 5 until object is coughed up, or victim breathes or coughs forcefully, or becomes unconscious, or you are relieved by EMS.

Table 9.2 Emergency Care for Common Childhood Problems—*continued*

Common Problem	Emergency Care
Diabetes: Diabetic Coma Sometimes called *ketoacidosis.* Opposite of insulin shock. Herein blood sugar becomes too high because of too little insulin. Symptoms: gradual onset, drowsiness, very thirsty, frequent urination, skin flushed, sweet breath, breathing is heavy, vomiting, eventual stupor or unconsciousness.	Child should go to the hospital or receive immediate medical help. Teacher can make the victim feel as comfortable as possible and offer verbal encouragement.
Diabetes: Insulin Shock Too much insulin and too little sugar in the blood. Symptoms: sudden onset, staggering or poor coordination, anger or bad temper, pale color, disorientation, sudden hunger, sweating, eventual stupor or unconsciousness.	Provide sugar if the person can swallow without choking: soft drinks, juice, candy (no diet drinks). If the child fails to respond in 10 minutes or so, take child to the hospital. Think diabetes and remember this condition could be fatal.
Epileptic Seizures These can be convulsive or nonconvulsive. Convulsive ones are usually associated with epilepsy. In the generalized tonic-clonic (grand mal) seizure, symptoms may be: fall, rigidity followed by muscle jerks, shallow breathing, bluish skin, possible loss of bladder or bowel control, usually lasts 3–5 minutes. When normal breathing restarts, child may be confused and/or tired. Full consciousness returns fairly quickly.	Look for medical ID. Protect from furniture and other objects. Loosen collar. Turn on side to keep airway clear. Be reassuring when consciousness returns. If lasts less than 5 minutes, may want hospital or clinic evaluation (know parents' wishes). If there are multiple seizures or one lasts longer than 5 minutes, call for EMS assistance. If child is diabetic or injured, get aid immediately.
Fainting The least serious type of shock; when the brain's blood flow is interrupted. Symptoms: dizziness, nausea, paleness, sweating.	Prevent from falling, if possible. Have person lie down, and elevate legs 8–12 inches. Wipe forehead with cool, wet cloth. Do not use smelling salts, do not slap the victim, and do not give fluids or food.
Knocked-Out Tooth About 2 million teeth are accidently knocked out yearly but 90% can be saved with good first aid.	Rinse dirty tooth in gentle, running water; do not scrub or remove tissue fragments. Gently insert tooth and hold in socket on way to dentist. If not possible, place tooth in cup of cold, whole milk (avoid low-fat, powdered, or yogurt). If child gets to dentist in 30 minutes, tooth is likely to be saved. (Bring the tooth!)
Nosebleed For children this may be more frightening than dangerous. 90% of nosebleeds are through the nostril(s), with 10% into the throat.	Provide reassurance, keep victim calm. Keep in sitting position to reduce blood pressure. Keep head tilted slightly forward. Do not probe for foreign object (if suspected). Use thumb and forefinger to apply steady pressure to both nostrils for 5 minutes (tell child to breathe through mouth), then release (Figure 9.3). May apply ice over the nose. If bleeding persists, gently blow nose to remove clots and apply pressure for another 5 minutes.

Table 9.2 Emergency Care for Common Childhood Problems–*continued*

Common Problem	Emergency Care
Open Wounds This could be a simple scrape (abrasion), cut (incision), tearing (laceration), stab (puncture), or tissue torn from the body and left as hanging flap (avulsion). Ears, fingers, and hands are subject to avulsions. Open wounds break the skin and could become infected.	For severe wounds, a physician should be seen. In the meantime, control for bleeding; do not wash the wound. In less severe wounds, remove clothing covering the wound, protecting yourself with latex gloves, plastic materials, or extra coverings (gauze). Control bleeding as described above. With punctures, do not remove an impaled object. Cleanse the wound gently with clean cloth soaked with soap and water; wash edges of wound. Hydrogen peroxide (3%) can be used to remove old clots (not to disinfect). Flush with water and apply sterile gauze dressing and bandage. If dressing becomes wet, change it to prevent infection. If bleeding continues, leave dressing on and see a doctor.
Shock Refers to a circulatory system failure. Symptoms: rapid breathing and pulse, pale or bluish skin, cool and wet (clammy) skin, heavy sweating, nausea, and in severe cases, loss of consciousness.	As a general rule, keep victim on his or her back. Keep victim calm; loosen tight clothing. Elevate legs 8–12 inches to allow blood to drain back to the heart more readily (but don't do this if it will cause more harm to injured areas). Do not give food or drink. Cover with warm blankets but do not overheat.
Swallowed Poison Deaths from swallowed poison have decreased for children under 5. Yet, for every death, 80,000–90,000 nonfatal cases are seen in emergency rooms. Signs and symptoms: abdominal pain and cramping, nausea or vomiting, burns around the mouth, drowsiness or unconsciousness, poison containers nearby.	Determine: Who—age and size of victim What—type of poison How much—bottle, taste How—circumstances surrounding event When—the poison was taken Contact poison control center or hospital (more than 70% of poisonings can be treated over the phone). Check pulse and repirations often. Unless advised, do not give fluids to dilute unless caustics (acids and alkalis) have been swallowed. Do not induce vomiting unless advised.

several months. In some people, HBV may have no symptoms yet leave the victim as a chronic carrier, passing it along to others. In severe cases, it can cause cirrhosis of the liver, liver cancer, and death.

HIV causes AIDS (acquired immunodeficiency syndrome) by attacking the immune system, making us susceptible to infections that eventually prove fatal. Although there

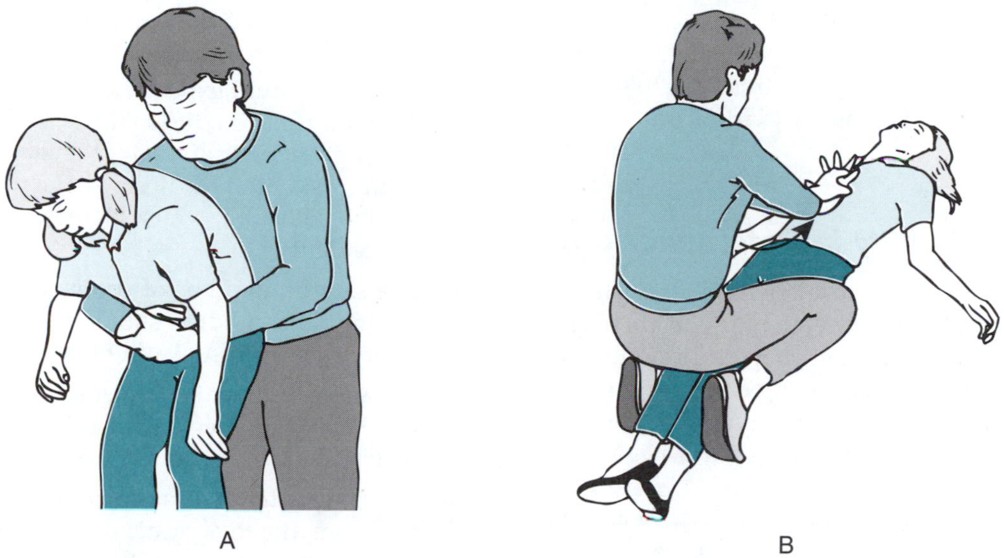

FIGURE 9.2 Heimlich Maneuver, *A.* with Child Standing; *B.* with Child Lying

is a vaccine for hepatitis B, this is not the case for HIV.

The universal precautions to prevent infection from bloodborne infections are as follows (National Safety Council, 1993):

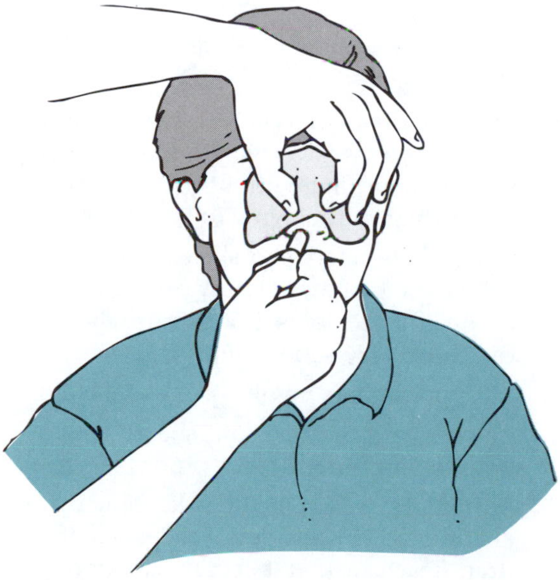

FIGURE 9.3 Controlling Nosebleed with Pressure and Sterile Cotton Packing

1. Keep open wounds covered with dressings to prevent contact with blood.
2. Use latex gloves in every situation involving blood or other body fluids.
3. If latex gloves are not available, use the most waterproof material available, or extra gauze dressings to form a barrier.
4. Whenever possible, use a mouth-to-barrier device for protection when doing rescue breathing. There may be blood in the mouth.

After a person is exposed to blood or other body fluids:

1. Wash the exposed area immediately with soap and running water. Scrub vigorously with lots of lather.
2. Report the incident promptly, according to your workplace policy.
3. Get medical help, treatment, and counseling. If your workplace is covered by OSHA's Bloodborne Standards, your employer must keep medical records confidential.

4. Ask about HBV globulin (HBIG) if you haven't had the HBV vaccine. It can provide short-term protection. It is followed by vaccination against HBV.

Teacher Liability in Emergency Care

As a teacher, you are responsible for the children under your charge. Consequently, you are likely to be found *liable* (negligent) if you do not act as a reasonable and/or prudent person in an emergency situation. You have a duty to act. Remember that failure to act can be deemed as negligent as doing the wrong thing.

Teachers should be fully aware of school policies in regard to administering first aid and emergency care. They should be cognizant of students who have conditions that may require such care—those with diabetes, asthma, or the like. With this knowledge, the teacher can actually prepare for possible emergency situations such as diabetic coma.

Of course "an ounce of prevention is worth a pound of cure." Teachers need the foresight to plan and implement activities that are the least likely to cause injury. Supervision on the playground and in the classroom is essential. Elementary and middle-school parents want to know what steps the school has taken, and in particular what the teacher can do, to prevent and, when necessary, treat accidents. Liability insurance coverage should be in effect for all teachers to protect them from the economic drain of lawsuits. This type of protection can often be gained from membership in professional organizations if not through the school itself.

Implications for Elementary and Middle-School Teachers

Summary Issues

1. Accidents result from a violation of rules, regulations, procedures, and courtesies and may be a symptom of disorder or failure to adapt.
2. Approximately 85 percent of accidents can be attributed to human causes.
3. Teachers should expect accidents when dealing with children due to (a) lack of knowledge, (b) lack of skill, (c) if they take unnecessary risks, and (d) if they have poor emotional health, which increases their risk of accidents.
4. Fire safety should be of special concern to parents, and children should be taught basic safety rules for preventing fires.
5. Smoke detectors are a must for homes and should be checked once a month. Fire drills should be conducted regularly.
6. Over a quarter of a million emergency room visits are due to accidents on playgrounds, with most injuries resulting from falls.
7. Young children need to be taught safety on swings, slides, climbing apparatus, and seesaws to reduce accidents.
8. More than half a million accidents bringing people to emergency rooms are related to bicycles, so children (as well as adults) should know the four major ways they can get injured on a bicycle: collision, loss of control, getting limbs caught, and mechanical or structural problems with the bike.
9. The majority of bicycle collisions occur in the following ways: driveway rideout, running a stop sign, turning without warning, nighttime riding, and playing follow the leader.
10. Roller skate safety and skateboard safety need to be taught, not only due to the high number of accidents, but because the falls can cause very serious injury.
11. Most poisonings involve preschool children.
12. The three types of poisoning are: drug, household chemical, and vapor.
13. Poison prevention includes keeping drugs and toxic chemicals out of the reach of children. Teach "ask first" before eating or drinking anything.
14. Injuries are the leading cause of death and disability in children.

15. Children in preschool and kindergarten should know how to dial 9 1 1 EMS. All children should know that a professional dispatcher answers and will ask questions. Children should remain calm, speak slowly and clearly, and not hang up until told to do so.
16. The ABCs of emergency care are: Airway open? Breathing? Circulation (pulse)?
17. Cardiopulmonary resuscitation (CPR) is different for children under 8 years from those over 8 years in regard to the way you compress, the compression rate, the compression-breath ratio, and how often to give only breaths during rescue breathing.
18. Universal precautions should be taken to avoid bloodborne pathogens when dealing with accidents involving blood. The two major pathogens are hepatitis B virus and human immunodeficiency virus.
19. Teachers have a responsibility to administer emergency care to those children under their charge.
20. Teachers should have liability insurance coverage and know the school policy in regard to emergency care.

Teacher Ramifications

In regard to safety, injury prevention, and emergency care, a teacher should:

1. Acquire basic knowledge and skills in emergency care.
2. Teach and model safe behavior in all childhood settings, including home and school.
3. Have input into the school safety and emergency care policy.
4. Know the preexisting conditions (e.g., diabetes) of each of his or her students that pose potential emergency problems.
5. Support the school's role in helping the nation reach the objectives set forth in *Healthy Children 2000* (1992) and *Healthy Youth 2000* (1990). Specifically, the objectives related to schools regarding unintentional injury are:

#9.3a. Reduce deaths among children aged 14 and younger caused by motor vehicle crashes to no more than 5.5 per 100,000 people.

#9.3b. Reduce deaths among youth aged 15 through 24 caused by motor vehicle crashes to no more than 33 per 100,000 people.

#9.5. Reduce drowning deaths to no more than 1.3 per 100,000 people. (Highest drowning rates are among children 4 years and younger and men 15 through 34 years.)

#9.6. Reduce residential fire deaths to no more than 1.2 per 100,000 people. (The baseline rate for children 4 years and under is 4.4 per 100,000.)

#9.8. Reduce nonfatal poisoning to no more than 88 emergency-department treatments per 100,000 people. (The baseline rate for children 4 years and younger is 650 per 100,000—we need a big drop in numbers!)

#9.12. Increase the use of occupant-protection systems, such as safety belts, inflatable safety restraints, and child safety seats, to at least 85 percent of motor vehicle occupants. The target for those 4 years and under is 95 percent.

#9.13. Increase the use of helmets to at least 80 percent of motorcyclists and at least 50 percent of bicyclists. (The baseline for bicyclists is 8 percent.)

#9.17. Increase the presence of functional smoke detectors to at least one on each habitable floor of all inhabited residential dwellings.

#9.18. Provide academic instruction on injury prevention and control, preferably as part of quality school health education, in at least 50 percent of public school systems for grades K through 12.

SECTION III

Teaching Strategies for Safety and Injury Prevention

The strategies in this section are divided into grades K–4, 5–6, and 7–8 levels. In addition to strategies that can be used in the classroom, home activities are included. A home activity is designed for student-parent interaction. It is a way to engage the home in school-student learning, and parents can sign a slip of paper to confirm that an activity was completed. Evaluation of all strategies through the use of the National Health Education Standards and performance indicators is indicated. Teachers may also choose to write corresponding learning assessments.

K–4 Level

Strategy One

Objective: Students will be able to demonstrate how to cross the street safely.

Activity: Layout a street intersection in the classroom using masking tape. Have students simulate crossing under different traffic conditions: no cars present, cars present, cars turning, traffic lights, and patrol person (see Figure 9.4). Explain briefly how to cross a street safely while students demonstrate.

Integration: Social Studies

Related Health Content Area: Growth and development

Health Education Standards and Performance Indicators: 1(8); 3(3,5)

Strategy Two

Objective: Students will demonstrate proper behavior while getting on and off, and riding in a school bus.

Activity: Have a school bus brought to a safe area of the parking lot. (You may wish to have a police officer or other safety person present.) Have students practice the proper way to get on and off the bus, for instance, crossing the street after disembarking. You may wish to have the safety expert give the students situations and have them demonstrate the proper procedures. You may also wish to involve a bus driver.

Integration: Social Studies

Related Health Content Area: Growth and development

Health Education Standards and Performance Indicators: 1(6,8); 3(1,3,5)

Strategy Three

Objective: Students will demonstrate appropriate water safety techniques.

Activity: Arrange for time at a local pool, or at the school pool if one is available. Invite physical fitness teachers, local lifeguards, and/or police and fire personnel to participate in this activity. Have the proper techniques for water safety demonstrated and then practiced by the entire class.

Integration: Science, Physical Fitness

Related Health Content Areas: Consumer, environmental

Health Education Standard and Performance Indicators: 1(8); 3(1,3,5)

(a) Crossing street by yourself

(b) Crossing street with others

(c) Crossing street with patrol boy

(d) Crossing street with signal lights

(e) Crossing street with traffic

FIGURE 9.4 Steps for Practice Session for Safety in Crossing Streets

5–6 Level

Strategy One

Objective: Students will be able to state the rules for safe bicycle riding.

Activity: Using pictures and/or drawings or simulations, have students analyze different situations to determine what the bicycle rider is doing correctly or incorrectly. The basic bicycle rules of the road to be included are:

- Always ride with traffic
- Ride on the right side of the road
- Never hitch a ride
- Walk your bike across busy intersections
- Ride single file
- Don't carry riders
- Yield right of way to pedestrians
- Do not carry anything in your hands
- Keep both hands on the handlebars
- Give proper arm signals
- Look before changing direction or lane
- Obey all traffic signals
- Have bicycle inspected for safety twice a year
- Adjust speed to road conditions, weather, traffic, and experience as a rider
- Select the safest route to your destination, avoiding busy streets and intersections.

The quiz in Figure 9.5 may be administered after the above demonstrations. (The correct answers to the questions are printed in bold.)

Integration: Social Studies

Related Health Content Area: Growth and development

Health Education Standards and Performance Indicators: 1(1,6,7); 3(1,5); 6(1,3)

Strategy Two

Objective: Students will demonstrate proficiency in basic techniques of bandaging and splinting.

Activity: Place students into groups of four or five. Have prepared ahead of time several notebooks each one containing a different set of instructions and diagrams of basic bandaging and splinting techniques using readily available materials (e.g., tree limbs, pillows, blankets, newspaper, etc.) Each group is to work on one notebook for a class period. Then each day the groups are to complete a different notebook, making sure everyone in the group is proficient.

Integration: Science

Related Health Content Areas: Violence, growth and development

Health Education Standards and Performance Indicators: 2(2,6); 3(5)

7–8 Level

Strategy One

Objective: Students will acknowledge the difficulty of distinguishing between medicines and candies. This activity is especially important for those students who babysit or are responsible for younger siblings at home.

Activity: Have matched pairs of plastic bags, with candy/gum in one bag and medicine in the other (e.g., pseudoephedrine and Red Hots candy). Number each bag. (It is a good idea, for safety, to also staple the bags closed.) Place them on a table, making sure labels are face down. Students are to identify each sample only by sight; they may not touch, move, or smell any of the samples. After students identify as many as possible, discuss the problem that can arise for young children who are unable to read.

This lesson can be modified by having some other unlabelled medicines that students must identify by using a Physician's Desk Reference (PDR). A variety of questions can be asked of the students regarding the medications.

Integration: Science

1. A bicycle is considered a vehicle and should be ridden on the right-hand side of the street. **T** F
2. Bicycle riders should observe and obey all traffic signs, stop signs, signals, and other traffic control devices. **T** F
3. Bike riders should try to crowd ahead between cars at a stop light so they can be in front when the light changes. T **F**
4. Pedestrians do not have the right of way over bicycles on sidewalks or crosswalks. T **F**
5. The signal for a right turn is extending the right arm straight out. T **F**
6. Night riding without a white headlight or red taillight or reflector is unsafe. **T** F
7. Bicycle riders hitching a ride on another vehicle can easily have an accident. **T** F
8. It is safe and proper for a bike rider to carry a passenger. T **F**
9. A bike in poor mechanical condition is safe if the rider is skilled. T **F**
10. It is safe to ride bikes three abreast when riding in a group. T **F**
11. The roadway is a safe place to park your bike. T **F**
12. Bikes should be inspected twice a year by a reliable service person. **T** F
13. The headlight of a bicycle should be seen from at least 500 ft. **T** F
14. Riding single file is the sensible thing to do. **T** F
15. The proper way to make a left turn is to cut the corner. T **F**
16. It is safe to enter the street from the sidewalk without first seeing whether a car is coming. T **F**
17. When passing a slow-moving car going in the same direction, you should pass to the left. **T** F
18. Bicyclists should keep to the right while riding in the street. **T** F
19. Bike riders should give hand signals when stopping or turning. **T** F
20. Hitching a ride on another vehicle is safe if the rider is careful. T **F**
21. An icy or slippery street is a dangerous place to ride a bike. **T** F
22. A bike rider should look only straight ahead when crossing an intersection. T **F**
23. It is safe for two people to be on a bike if one is on the handlebars. T **F**
24. Cyclists should ride at least three feet away from parked cars. **T** F
25. On country roads cyclists should keep to the left, same as pedestrians. T **F**
26. Broken or loose spokes should be replaced immediately. **T** F
27. Pedals should not be worn or broken. **T** F
28. A broken coaster brake can be easily fixed at home. T **F**
29. Handlebars should be loose so you can change riding positions. T **F**
30. Your chain should be loose enough to slip off easily. T **F**
31. The whole bicycle should be cleaned and oiled occasionally. **T** F
32. Saddle and handlebars should be adjusted to your height. **T** F
33. Riding bikes off curbs doesn't damage them. T **F**
34. It is permissible to ride with small children in baskets. T **F**
35. Persons riding bikes are subject to the same traffic laws that govern automobile drivers. **T** F
36. Blue is a good color to wear when biking after dark T **F**
37. It is not neccessary to stop at intersections if there is no traffic. T **F**
38. You can drive a bike, but not a car, in either direction on a one-way street. T **F**
39. There is danger of skidding on curves even if the road is not wet. **T** F
40. If you live in the country, you can ride on either side of the road. T **F**
41. Even a skilled bike rider should walk his or her bike through heavy traffic. **T** F
42. If you don't ride on busy streets, you don't need a horn or bell. T **F**
43. Cyclists have the right of way over pedestrians. T **F**
44. The faster you ride, the safer it is. T **F**
45. A warped wheel rim can cause an accident. **T** F
46. When riding at night, ride to the left so you can see approaching headlights. T **F**
47. A good bicycle never really needs greasing and oiling. T **F**
48. A loose saddle is a potential danger to a cyclist. **T** F
49. It is a bad idea to wax the metal finish of your bike. T **F**
50. When cycling, you should pay strict attention to what you're doing. **T** F

FIGURE 9.5 Bike Riding Quiz

Related Health Content Areas: Diseases, consumer, substance use/abuse

Health Education Standards and Performance Indicators: 1(1,7); 3(1,4)

Strategy Two

Objective: Students will be able to differentiate between a safe bicycle and an unsafe one.

Activity: Have a local cycling enthusiast or someone from a cycling shop present a program on safety. Students may bring their bicycles to class to use in demonstrations on ways of keeping a bicycle in good working order:

1. Handlebars
   A. Keep tightened
   B. Adjust to appropriate level
2. Saddle
   A. Tilt upward in front
   B. Adjust to body height
   C. Tighten all nuts
3. Wheels
   A. Run freely
   B. Spokes straight
   C. Replace any broken spokes
   D. No wobble
   E. Oil bearings
4. Reflectors
   A. Front, rear, and side
   B. Visible for 300 feet
5. Brake
   A. Quick
   B. Even
6. Chain
   A. Fits snugly
   B. Links in good condition
   C. Cleaned and oiled frequently
7. Pedals
   A. Treads in good condition
   B. Lubricate and tighten pedal bearings and spindle
8. Tires
   A. Inflate to correct air pressure
   B. Remove foreign objects
9. Light: visible for 500 feet
10. Warning device: horn or bell in working order

Integration: Science

Related Health Content Area: Growth and development

Health Education Standards and Performance Indicators: 1(1); 2(2); 3(1)

Home Activities

Strategy One

Objective: Students will determine effective escape routes from their residences.

Activity: Students are to draw a floor plan of their home or apartment (graph paper is very helpful in this exercise). Demonstrate for them how to identify doors, windows, stairs, and so forth. Then have students determine and map on their diagrams the following:

- A fire escape route if a fire occurs in the kitchen during daylight hours
- A fire escape route for all family members if they are sleeping in their bedrooms when a fire breaks out

Students should also determine a safe meeting place outside the home. They may receive extra credit for staging and monitoring a fire drill with all their family members.

Integration: Math, Science, Social Studies

Related Health Content Areas: Family life, consumer health

Health Education Standards: 1,3 (Performance indicators vary by grade level.)

Strategy Two

Objective: Students will assess their homes for safety problems and safeguards.

Activity: Using a checklist provided by the local fire department or local Red Cross, students will assess the home for safety problems. Students will also note safeguards that are already in place. Parents and students are then to develop a plan to correct any problem areas.

Integration: Science

Related Health Content Area: Family

Health Education Standards: 3,7

References

American Medical Association. *Healthy Youth 2000.* Department of Adolescent Health, Chicago, AMA, 1990.

Healthy Children 2000. Jones and Barlett, Boston, 1992.

National Safety Council. *Accident Facts.* NSC, Itasca, IL, 1994.

National Safety Council. *First Aid and CPR* 2nd ed. Jones and Bartlett, Boston, 1993.

10

Emotional Well-Being and Stress Reduction

At the conclusion of the chapter, you should be able to:

- *Define the meanings of mental health and emotional well-being*
- *Explain the complexities of mental health in the classroom*
- *Distinguish among the components in self-structure and positive self-concept*
- *Synthesize the mental health needs and tasks confronting children and youth*
- *Illustrate inspiriting and dispiriting events*
- *Explain the dimensions of stress and stress reduction*
- *Elaborate upon the role of the teacher in establishing emotional well-being for students*

SECTION I

Health Status, Deficits, and Learning

Lack of emotional well-being in children is not a new phenomenon. Over twenty years ago, it was estimated that in any class of thirty elementary students, ". . . two pupils will spend some time in an institution for the treatment of a psychosis, five will need psychiatric care, eight or more will have disappointing or disastrous marriages, and twenty who go to medical hospitals will actually be there for a mental illness (Bernard, 1970). Given the complexity of today's world, these figures may very well hold true for current students.

Listed below are some basic points about mental health.

- Between 15 and 30 percent of elementary school children have significant mental health needs (Goodwin et al., 1988; Irigon et al., 1981; Schulman et al., 1973).
- It is estimated that 12 percent of youth under 18 years suffer from mental disorders (*Healthy Children 2000*).
- Suicide is one of the leading causes of death among adolescents.
- Homicide is a leading cause of death for children (1–14 years) and adolescents (15–24 years).
- Approximately 7 million school children cope daily with parents who are alcoholics (Knight et al., 1992).
- In the United States, living with an alcoholic parent may be the most widespread cause of severe distress for school-aged children (Brenner, 1984).
- Children with recurrent abdominal pain (RAP) tend to have higher mean stress scores than children who do not (Sharrer et al., 1991).
- Substance-abusing adolescents are twenty-five times more likely to feel extremely hopeless than those who do not abuse substances (Page et al., 1993).
- Loneliness is another factor indicative of hopelessness. Lonely students who get drunk are almost sixteen times more likely to feel extremely hopeless than other students (Page et al., 1993).
- Poor decision-making, low self-image, low self-confidence, and lack of conflict resolution skills appear to be the hallmark of one-fifth of elementary school students (Goodwin et al., 1988).
- Middle-school children are in pivotal years, making decisions about school and health that can affect them for the rest of their lives.
- The transition from elementary school to middle-school or junior high can be a major source of stress (Atkins, 1992).

- Children with chronic health problems, such as diabetes, experience a greater number of stressors than children without such health problems.
- Being left out of the group and not being able to take part in sports are two serious stressors for asthmatic children (Walsh & Ryan-Wenger, 1992).
- Children exposed to drugs prenatally or environmentally may manifest disruptive classroom behavior as early as grades K–3 (Kne et al., 1994).
- Low-birthweight children are more likely to experience behavioral and learning problems in elementary school than normal-birthweight children (Klebanov et al., 1994).
- Anywhere from 20 to 60 percent of high school students have occasional suicidal thoughts (Smith et al., 1986).
- Psychosocial distress, problems with drug involvement, and disrupted family relations are key factors in suicidal thoughts among potential high school dropouts (Thompson et al., 1994).
- About one-fifth of elementary school students have communication apprehension requiring intervention (Holbrook, 1987; Harris, 1980).
- Students with special health care needs can create unique demands on classroom structure, environment, and hygiene, as well as teacher-student schedules and curricular plans.
- Fostering peer acceptance of disabled students can be a significant challenge to teachers.
- Student-discipline policies are idiosyncratic and impact the mental health of the teacher, the students, and the classroom as a whole.
- Obese children do not necessarily have lower self-esteem than do non-obese children (Brown University, 1993).
- People with low self-esteem tend to get into relationships that perpetuate their negative self-views (*Psychology Today*, 1992).
- Signs of stress overload are evident in preschoolers as well as school-age children.
- Slightly more than one half of children diagnosed with emotional problems do not receive counseling, medication, or even referral from their pediatricians (Binns et al., 1993).

SECTION II

Emotional Well-Being and Stress Reduction Teaching Information

The Concept of Emotional Well-Being

Emotional well-being can be likened to the quality of life itself. Our whole approach to life is dependent on our emotional well-being. Some of us lead happy, wholesome, well-adjusted lives. Others approach each day as sheer drudgery and find life a chore. All too often, these unhappy individuals spend a lifetime in misery. Their coping behavior becomes negative, and they enter a downward spiral that may lead to mental disturbance or suicide.

Meeting life's demands is no easy task. One has to work at good mental health, since life is a series of minor and major developmental tasks. When we fulfill these tasks, our self-esteem receives a boost, and we move closer to full functioning. When we fail, our course—for better or worse—becomes altered.

Emotional well-being is a complex, multifaceted portion of total well-being. The National Association for Mental Health (1965) has attempted to clarify the concept by stating that the emotionally healthy person (1) feels good about the self, (2) feels right about others, and (3) is able to meet the demands of life. In more detailed terms, Jourard (1974) stated that emotionally healthy people:

1. Are competent at satisfying their basic needs
2. Have a firm grasp on reality
3. Have achieved a healthy self-structure and self-esteem
4. Have secure and authentic relationships with others
5. Have the capacity to experience a broad range of emotion and to control its expression

The remainder of this section addresses each of these five characteristics.

Needs and Emotional Well-Being

Needs and wants are oftentimes confused. Close inspection, however, shows that wants change frequently and are great in number. Listen to a five year old as he or she watches commercials on TV, and you will hear a long list of wants. The youngster may want the $50 toy, but probably doesn't need it for survival. However, wanting an expensive computer game may be perceived as a need to achieve status among peers, which is essential to some people. In other words, on occasion wants may be construed as needs to achieve emotional well-being. Generally, needs are what we require to sustain life and to foster growth.

Much of our behavior is motivated by the desire to fulfill certain basic needs, of which there are two general kinds: *maintenance needs,* or those for physical survival; and *growth needs,* sometimes called needs for self-actualization, emotional stimulation, and spiritual growth. This theory of needs, advanced by Maslow (1970), states that these needs function in an hierarchical sequence. That is, basic needs, the lowest level, must be met before we can address those at higher levels. The hierarchy (see Figure 10.1) starts with *physical needs* (food, water), then *safety needs* (shelter, protection, sense of security), *belonging and love needs* (affection, accepting relationships with others), and *esteem needs* (respect by self and others, status, success). Having met these needs—or at least coping with them well—we can move toward *self-actualization.* Self-actualization "cannot be sought as a goal in its own right. . . . Rather, it is a by-product of active commitment of one's own talents to causes outside of the self, such as the quest for beauty, truth, or justice" (Jourard, 1974, p. 24).

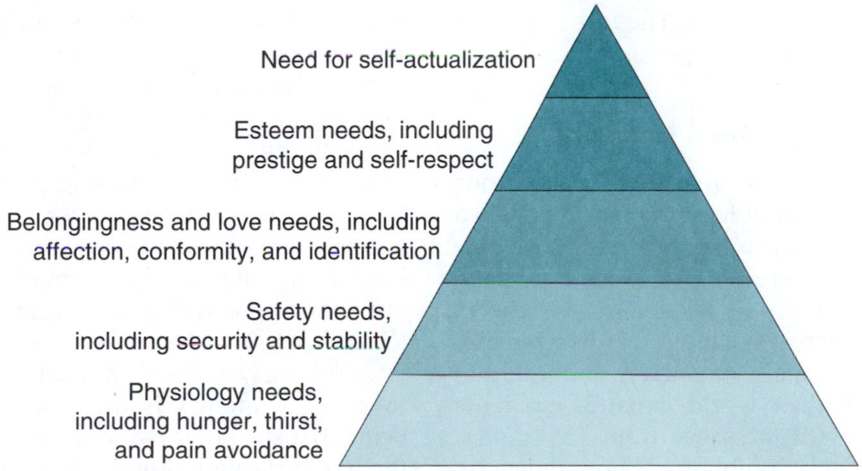

FIGURE 10.1 Maslow's Hierarchy of Human Needs

Although the basic needs are intrinsic to all humans, the ways in which people satisfy them are not. Everyone may need to eat, but not everyone obtains food in the same way. Neither does everyone eat the same kind of food. Similarly, people engage in a great variety of living arrangements, jobs, and recreation to find the best way to fulfill their needs for love, security, and self-esteem. The many different ways in which people fulfill their basic needs are remarkable examples of human creativity.

From childhood on, people develop and refine strategies for meeting their basic needs. In infants, the repertoire of need-fulfilling abilities is very limited. A baby can cry for food or attention, and smile to encourage touching and play, which fulfill needs for love and stimulation. As people grow up, they acquire more tools to fulfill their needs. Among them are a set of values, beliefs, attitudes, and behaviors that they expect will help them by producing harmonious interactions with the environment—especially with people with whom they exchange love and trust. When individuals fulfill their needs, they experience joy, happiness, and contentment. When individuals are not successful, however they experience emotional distress. We get hungry when we need food and thirsty when we need water. Hunger and thirst are basic discomforts that motivate us to fulfill those maintenance needs. If we confront an obstacle that prevents us from satisfying a certain need, we can become frustrated and angry. If our security is threatened, we can become fearful or anxious. The loss of love or self-esteem can bring about depression.

Reality and Emotional Well-Being

Our actions and thoughts are often based on our feelings and needs—or at least the perceptions we have of our needs. But to be certain that our perceptions and beliefs are on target, we must take steps to verify them; we need a reality check. While this holds true for all ages, it is especially important during the elementary and middle-school years. As their world expands, students are bombarded with messages from TV, comics, movies, friends, and family as to "how things really are." At times these messages are subtle, while on other occasions they are very blatant.

Peer pressure is one example of how a child can be led to perceive the world in a particular way. If the friend is very influential—has status—the weaker child succumbs to accepting the friend's perspective. It is for this reason (among others) that parents are so concerned about their children's friends.

Reality testing is an examination of perceptions and beliefs. Children can be taught this at a very early age by learning the following steps:

1. State your belief or perception in a sentence (be sure it is stated clearly).
2. Ask yourself, "What proof do I have to support this perception or belief?"
3. Now ask yourself, "Is there any other way of explaining this evidence or proof?"
4. Compare this perception or belief with other perceptions or beliefs that you know to be valid, and ask yourself, "Is this perception consistent with other perceptions?"

Here is an example. Several years ago, a young man complained that he tried very hard to win the love of his parents when he was growing up. However, he lamented, no matter how hard he tried, they always liked his older brother better. Since then, he has continually felt in second place. The proof of this, he recalled, was that his parents let his brother do almost everything, while he had to stand back and watch. He didn't think there was any other way of explaining this evidence. He never addressed the issue with his brother to get his perceptions. However, after some encouragement, he spoke with his brother and discovered a totally different picture. His brother claimed to be the "fall guy," having to take all the responsibility to get things done, including protecting his little brother so life could be easier for him. What the younger brother saw as favoring, the older one saw as exploitation. This provided a whole new outlook for the young man, changing his picture to one with a greater reality base.

Obviously keeping in touch with reality leads to positive mental health and emotional well-being. It also allows us to expand from perceiving the world through our needs to experiencing aesthetic sensing, that is, contemplating reality for its own sake.

Self-Structure, Self-Esteem, and Emotional Well-Being

Self-structure implies that the "self" is made up of several facets. One aspect is the *real self*—what really makes us tick, so to speak. Another facet is how we see ourselves, our *self-concept*. A third aspect of our self-structure is how we picture ourselves at our best, our *self-ideal* or *ideal self*. A fourth facet is our *public selves*—how we want others to see us. *Self-esteem* refers to how we value our self.

The self-concept is made up of our beliefs about ourself. It is important to understand that self-concept is open to influence by others. This can be an asset or a liability. If we get positive feedback, self-concept is likely to be positive. However, the old tune of "sticks and stones may break my bones, but words will never hurt me" doesn't hold true for most children (or for that matter, most adults). If the feedback we get from others is negative, our self-concept is likely to be damaged. Another point about self-concept is that it is not a fixed entity. Rather, it consists of beliefs that can be changed. We can grow and become. We must be careful to recognize that self-concept is a description rather than a prescription.

The ideal self serves as a measure of our actions. In other words, it can be our conscience. The key for a self-ideal is that it be realistic and provide emotionally healthy goals. Consequently, reevaluation of the ideal self is important. The "oughts" and "shoulds" of our lives must be reexamined on a continual basis. As we grow, our values change and so might the standards against which we measure ourselves. The greater the discrepancy between self-concept and ideal self, the less likely is emotional well-being. For example, if your ideal self believes that you should have integrity and yet you deceive your best friend or intimate partner, the distance between how you see yourself and the way you ought to be gets larger. The greater this distance becomes—in this case, the more or longer that you continue the deception—the greater the likelihood of emotional upset.

BOX 10.1 ■ ■ ■ ■ ■

HOW TO BE SOMEBODY

Yetta Bernhard, a therapist and educator, offered some sage advice in her book entitled *How to Be Somebody*. Since it is out of print, the following shares some of her thoughts:

To be a SOMEBODY, it is your job to:

- Risk being authentic.
- Act "as if" you were worth an investment of work (even if you don't think so).
- Have the courage to include yourself when you feel left out.
- Say that you are unavailable at this time.
- Accept your right to goof, and to dedicate yourself to utilizing your goofs as learning processes.
- Risk decision-making.
- Accommodate at times as an act of self-expansion (accomodation can help us grow if we are open to it.)
- Allow expressions of pride in yourself (don't be your own worst enemy).
- Be open about what has nurturing meaning to you.
- Look at the many ways you tie yourself up in knots and find ways to free yourself from self-imposed restrictions, limitations, and sabotages (those "oughts" and "shoulds").
- Judge only to change, not to deprecate.
- Risk engaging in self-validating behavior.
- Dare to be all you can.
- Take responsibility for self-care.
- Say, "I count."

Source: Adapted from Yetta Bernhard, *How to Be Somebody* (Berkeley, CA: Ten Speed Press, 1975).

A feeling of belonging, balanced with a unique sense of self, is important to self-esteem at any age.

Think about your public selves. You are a student; you are a friend; and you are a son or daughter. We all engage in several roles, primarily for expedience. The image we wish to portray in each role is both expressed and shaped by our conversation and behavior. Feedback from those around us lets us know how we are doing in sculpting our particular image. Once in awhile, we may let an image slip, revealing our real self. This is fine as long as our public selves are in concert with the real self. In fact, one of the best measures of emotional well-being is the degree of similarity from one facet of our self-structure to another. The common thread throughout self-structure to assure mental health must be the real self. Emotional problems arise when we alienate our real self from the images we portray.

How you feel about yourself—your self-esteem—is influenced by others and your self-concept and self-ideal. Some children are told at a very young age that they are unworthy—"You are a bad child," "You're no good, just like your father." While the exact words may be forgotten, the message is not. When we fail to meet goals set forth in the self-ideal, we may develop a low opinion of ourselves. More often than not, the problem is an unattainable goal or unrealistic standards (shoulds and oughts) rather than something really being wrong with us.

Self-esteem can range from high to low. High self-esteem people respect themselves, consider themselves worthy, recognize their limitations, and expect to grow. In contrast, those with low self-esteem grow very little, if at all. They may enter a downward spiral, meeting with frustration, anger, depression, loneliness, and even suicide. Low self-esteem has been linked with a history of sexually transmitted diseases (Orr et al., 1989), substance abuse, alcohol and tobacco use, and poor school achievement. In fact, almost all negative health behavior has been linked to low self-esteem. Most of these linkages are derived from empirical evidence. From a research perspective, the body of evidence is inconclusive.

Bean (1992) believes that four characteristics are necessary for self-esteem to prosper at any age. These are:

1. *Connectedness:* A feeling that you are linked to someone or to others; feeling like you belong
2. *Uniqueness:* The feeling that you have special qualities, making you different from yet respected by others
3. *Power:* The sense that you can impact others, as well as having inner resources
4. *Models:* People you see as reference points for goals, values, ideals, and personal standards to be followed throughout life.

Lacking any one of these characteristics puts self-esteem in jeopardy. This, in turn, can make us vulnerable to stress.

Following are some suggestions to work toward or maintain positive self-esteem:

- Don't stay around friends or situations that drain you and make you feel inadequate. You may have the wrong "friends."

- Don't take criticism so personally that it is defeating. Disappointment is to be expected, but then plan for improvement.
- Enjoy some "alone time."
- A religious path might be a good route to explore.
- Pay attention to people who respect you; learn from what they see.
- Employ the power of positive thinking when you start out on a project; believe in what you do.
- Understand your uniqueness and relish it.
- Seek professional help when it is appropriate to do so (Smith, 1990).

Relationships and Emotional Well-Being

Emotionally healthy relationships provide security and authenticity to all involved. Although this exists in many families, there are many others that are devoid of these characteristics. Witness the number of abuse cases, the divorce rates, and the relationships in which members are simply strangers playing a role. As a teacher, you will see parents who prevent growth in their children by robbing them of decision-making, either through ignorance or because their own self-esteem is placed in jeopardy if their children grow. They may want their children to remain children, fostering dependence rather than independence.

In contrast, the emotionally healthy family engenders growth. Each person feels secure enough to communicate openly and honestly—no games are played. Demands on family members are fair and reasonable. Everyone respects and protects the freedom of the others. Needless to say, these characteristics are at differing levels as the family grows together and greater independence is achieved by the children. Interestingly, these same characteristics apply to couple relationships.

In intimate relationships, depth of *self-disclosure* increases as the relationship grows. That is, each person reveals more and more of his or her personal thoughts and feelings to the partner as time goes on. This exchange of vulnerability (vulnerable because you are taking risks by sharing) proceeds to the same levels for both people, and it is called *mutual self-disclosure.* Unlike formal relationships, the partners willingly make their worlds known to each other. In the course of friendship, much is shared. However, for true intimacy to develop, the sharing of hopes, fears, joys, sorrows, future plans, and the like is both broader and of greater depth. The self-disclosure is authentic. Impasses are brought into the open and resolved in a manner that enhances the relationship.

Emotional Expression and Emotional Well-Being

Emotional experiences provide meaning to life. They can vary tremendously, from the depths of sorrow to the heights of joy. No doubt we have all weathered boredom, depression, anxiety, fear, anger, and guilt from time to time. But we have also enjoyed pleasure, bouts of laughter, the feeling of freedom, and the closeness of affection and tenderness. Although these appear to be at opposite ends of a continuum, they are interconnected by the fact that they are all emotions and, as such, usher forth very similar (if not identical) physiological responses.

Dealing with emotions can be a difficult task for many. Years ago, a student requested that she be made not to feel any emotions. She explained that she was embarrassed many times in class and outside of class because she "wore her emotions on her sleeve." What she failed to realize is that due to the interconnectedness, stopping one emotion (e.g., sorrow) can severely inhibit the experience of the others.

In regard to the expression of emotions, we can (1) express them immediately in an uncontrolled fashion, (2) suppress them, or (3) repress them. In young children, the immediate, uncontrolled expression of emotion is expected. However, as we mature, our nervous system develops and we can increasingly control our emotional responses. While immediate, uncontrolled release can reduce tension, it is inappropriate for most adults because it (1) goes against societal norms and (2) often leaves the person out of touch with reality. Imagine what would happen if you had a temper tantrum in your professor's or principal's office. Several years ago, a male student described how he had gotten into an argument with his girlfriend, and in the midst of screaming at her, picked up his stereo receiver and threw it on the floor. He came back to reality rather quickly, and as you would guess, it was a real shock. Getting out of touch with reality is even more serious if abuse is directed toward others. Think about the father who unleashes his rage by hitting an innocent bystander, his four-year-old son. At the time, he is totally out of control and does not realize what he is doing. But no matter how remorseful he may be later, the damage is done.

Emotional suppression can be either unhealthy or healthy. The former is the case when the suppression is prolonged or chronic. In some families, children learn quickly to suppress their emotions because they may upset a parent; they "walk on egg shells" during this critical part of their lives. Physical harm in the form of ulcers, elevated blood pressure, colitis, headaches, and repeated abdominal pain can result. In school, these children display an inability to concentrate, impaired relationships, poor work habits, and even impaired reality contact.

Healthy emotional suppression means that a person *chooses* suppression over expression. You may choose to suppress a spontaneous outburst of laughter because you are in the middle of a church service or an examination. Suppression is a wise choice if an important value would be jeopardized by immediate release of emotion.

Another way to handle emotions is to repress them. In this case, a person takes active steps to avoid or deny emotional experiences. Repression is both automatic and unconscious. As expected, anyone who follows this pathway will not know true feelings. This is important not only to the repressor but also to the other persons around him or her because authentic communication is impossible. Sometimes pent-up emotions may explode in small ways. For example, a wife who has irritated her husband for a long time may end up in a huge fight over some "trivial annoyance"—squeezing the toothpaste tube at the top, say. Similarly, a husband might find his wife shouting about the toilet seat being up. In these instances, the issues are not nearly as important as are the underlying feelings. If the couple had been authentic from the beginning, rather than repressing their feelings, arguments of this nature would likely not occur.

Emotional Distress

We all feel emotional distress. Occasionally feeling angry, anxious, blue, lonely, or depressed is normal. Most of us would prefer always to feel happy, content, and secure, but that is not possible—or desirable. If nothing ever changed, we might escape emotional distress, but such an existence would be boring.

Humans need certain kinds of stimulation; they do not tolerate isolation very well. People are creative, curious, interactive beings who induce change in their lives simply by living. Situations that require adjustment arise all the time. Very often the message that it is time for an adjustment in one's thoughts, attitudes, or behavior is communicated by emotional distress, and failure to heed such messages may bring about stress-related illness. Negative emotions signal that something is not right with life, and they motivate individuals to seek ways to feel better. Viewed in this way, emotional distress can be seen as a stimulus for personal growth and self-improvement.

The discussion below considers the dynamics of emotional distress and the ways in which negative feelings can be used to accomplish personal growth. Please remember that the unpleasant feelings, the fears, frustrations, and sadness of everyday life are quite different from the severe emotional distress associated with prolonged periods of abnormal thought that seriously disrupt some lives for months or even years. Unfortunately, many conditions that involve feeling bad are often labeled mental illness and carry with them the stigma of being "crazy." This is not the case in some parts of the world, where social customs and even employment practices recognize that everyone has occasional blue days and antisocial periods. In this book, differentiate between the emotional distress that accompanies problems of living, and the abnormal thoughts, feelings, and behavior that are often the result of severe abnormalities in brain physiology and biochemistry or brain injury.

BOX 10.2 ■ ■ ■ ■ ■
DEALING WITH ANGER

Anger is one of the most common expressions of emotional distress. At all stages of life from infancy to old age, people get angry if their needs are not met. They get angry if they are cheated, lied to, hurt, punished, betrayed, or prevented from realizing their desires. People get angry when others whom they care for are hurt. They sometimes get angry at others—as a form of self-defense—when they feel disappointed with themselves or guilty about something they did (or did not) do.

For many people, anger is difficult to deal with, usually because it is difficult to express. When it is directed toward an authority figure, anger can be difficult to express for fear of retaliation. Anger at a loved one is sometimes hard to express because of the risk that the other person may become angry in turn and withdraw his or her love. Some people are confused by their anger at loved ones. They see it as inconsistent with love and hence become unable to express it, even if they feel justified in doing so. Another reason anger is hard to deal with is that it is often associated with the desire to inflict physical harm.

Psychologists say that anger is the result of frustration, which is the feeling that comes when you are prevented from attaining a particular goal. Therefore, one good way to handle anger is to assess the merits of the goal you cannot attain and the strategy you have been employing to attain it. We often get angry with other people because we ask them for things they cannot give, or because they are not providing the help we expect from them. Often, however, we haven't told them what the goal is, or how we expect them to help. So it's no wonder they don't perform the way we want them to.

Before you get angry at someone or something, ask yourself if your goal is attainable. Have you expected too much of yourself? Have you expected too much of someone else? Have you tried to get what you want in the best possible way? If you have set an unattainable goal for yourself, or your strategy for attaining a goal is not well thought out, then you have no one (or nothing) to blame for your anger but yourself—and this realization usually makes angry feelings evaporate. Remember, most of the time other people don't make you angry. *You* make yourself angry. Being honest with yourself and direct with others is one way to prevent anger, and a reassessment of your goals and strategies is one way to difuse an anger-provoking situation.

There are times, of course, when feeling anger and expressing it are appropriate. For example, anger is justified when someone knowingly physically or psychologically abuses you or someone or something you care for. Anger is also appropriate if the person abuses himself or herself. Another time is when someone breaks a promise. It's always wise to be very clear about promises. There would be a lot less anger and frustration if people promised to do only things that they knew they could follow through on.

What about dealing with someone who is angry at you? Receiving anger makes you want to protect yourself from physical or psychological harm resulting from hostility. One way to protect yourself is to get angry in return. However, this is rarely a good situation. It is better to realize that the angry person is frustrated, disappointed, and emotionally upset. If the angry person were wounded and bleeding, you would try to help. Think of anger as an emotional wound. Be patient with the angry person, and try to offer support. This will help remove the pain of frustration, and eventually the anger will subside.

Dealing with Emotional Distress

Such is the condition of human life that people never reach complete satisfaction. Even if all your maintenance needs were met, and even if you lived in wonderfully harmonious family relationships and worked at a fulfilling job, you would still face frustration and conflict because you would continue to seek new and enriching experiences. There are times, of course, when everything seems to be going really well, and reasonably long periods of great joy are possible. One of the principal goals of holistic health is to maximize the time you are joyous and happy, and to minimize emotional distress.

The various ways people devise to solve their life problems are *coping strategies*. Coping is a form of self-initiated problem-solving. There are three general ways people can cope: (1) they can try to change the situation that is causing the emotional distress, (2) they can try to alter their interpretation of the significance of the situation so it has less importance and therefore is not so distressing, or (3) they can try to alter the negative feeling without trying to change the situation or how they think about it.

There are many ways of changing a situation that is causing emotional distress. One is to make a rational appraisal of the situation and attack the problem directly by removing or surmounting the obstacle. Another is to withdraw from the situation, by either avoiding it altogether or deciding to be patient in the belief that circumstances will ultimately change. Still another way to change the situation is to adapt oneself to it. This can be done by changing habitual ways of thinking, feeling, and behaving, by modifying unrealistic assumptions about how people are supposed to act, and by increasing self-knowledge and insight.

Attempts to alter the significance or interpretation of a distressing situation are probably used the most often. One way people do this is to make positive comparisons, which are represented by sayings like "count your blessings," "we're all in the same boat," or "things are bound to get better." Another way is to focus on the good in a situation and minimize or ignore the bad. Almost everyone can see the flaws in another person, but how often do we notice a person's good qualities?

It is also impossible to devalue a goal that might have been important and to replace it with another. For example, one might come to believe that taking time for meditation and physical relaxation each day is preferable to a day full of tension-producing work. Another way to alter the significance of a situation is to turn awareness for a time to the inner, private, perhaps mystical nature of being rather than on external experience and pressures. This can be done by increasing both body and mental awareness through any number of methods, such as exercise, yoga, dance, and various forms of meditation. Those who take time to expand self-awareness often claim increased self-knowledge and greater mastery over their feelings; they say that they have found a way to personal and emotional peace. In response to the charge that they are simply escaping from their problems, they answer that there is much to gain by "turning off the world" for a brief period each day. It's still there when you turn it on again, but it usually looks a lot different . . . and better.

People can also cope with a distressing situation by trying to alter their negative feelings about it. Some people release their emotions in ways other than confronting the distressing situation. For example, they can express anger at a boss or a family member by taking part in competitive sports or by hitting a punching bag. Some people adjust by accepting the bad feelings that accompany difficulties, thinking that perhaps it was "meant to be" or that "you have to take the bad with the good." And some people are like the Biblical Job: they endure their distress in the belief that such behavior is a virtue that will be rewarded in the hereafter. People also try to cope by escaping into books, films, or television, or by ingesting alcohol or drugs. Although trying to change how you feel can help reduce the intensity of a negative emotional state, it does not change the situation causing the problem, and in some cases may actually delay permanent solution.

Depression and Suicide

We can feel sad at any given time in our lives. However, depression is different from sadness. Sadness, unlike depression, is usually of short duration, tied to a specific cause such as loss of self-esteem or a relationship, and does not take over the entire personality, jading perceptions, thoughts, and behaviors.

Depression is characterized by pain that threads throughout your entire being, robbing you of life energy. You do not feel pleasure in anything, and often feel unworthy, isolated, unwanted, and unloved. At one time, it was believed that only adults could experience such feelings. However, recent evidence shows that both children and adolescents endure depressive episodes (Brent, 1993). The underlying causes of depression can be a chemical imbalance, stress, emotional problems, or unknown reasons.

As a teacher, you should look for any of the following signs:

- Loss of interest
- Trouble sleeping and waking up unrested
- Difficulty concentrating
- Low self-esteem
- Unexplained moodiness
- Irritable (more than usual)
- No appetite and no enjoyment from eating
- Weight loss
- Feelings of hopelessness
- Physical complaints: stomachaches, constipation

Many children today live in conditions that are *dispiriting* rather than *inspiriting*. That is, they live in ways that make them feel worthless, hopeless, isolated, frustrated, and low in self-esteem. Dispiriting events foster illness and reduce effectiveness in living. For example, lonely adolescents who abuse drugs are twenty-five times more likely to feel extremely hopeless than students who are not lonely and do not use drugs (Page et al., 1993). The same investigation showed that lonely students who got drunk were almost sixteen times more likely to feel extremely hopeless. Recurrent abdominal pain (RAP) has been shown to be a psychosomatic response in children to environmental stressors (Sharrer et al., 1991). RAP is frequently reported at ages 5 to 6, with girls peaking around age 9 and boys at age 14. Teachers have also reported unhappiness, depression, low self-confidence, and negative self-image as mental health problems in elementary school children (Goodwin et al., 1988).

The link between depression and suicide has been known for quite some time, especially in adults. In recent years, however, the connection has been recognized in children and adolescents, too (Kelly, 1991; Thompson et al., 1994; Jacobsen et al., 1994.). Today, as well as in the past, many childhood suicides are called "accidents." But investigation into the hanging deaths of children aged 2 1/2 to 13 in two counties revealed three unequivocal suicides, five accidental deaths, and four questionable deaths (Clark et al., 1993). Suicide among children is now considered a serious public health problem (Brent, 1993).

Teachers must know the signs of dispiritedness as well as depression. Since suicide is not an impulsive act, school personnel should be alert for such dispiriting conditions as a previous history of problems, a death, the end of a meaningful relationship, a family with much discord (e.g., one or both parents being alcoholic, or domestic violence) and child or sexual abuse (van Egmond et al., 1993), drug involvement in conjunction with other signs, poor adaptation to a chronic illness (Goldston et al., 1994), high-risk youth who may drop out of school (Thompson et al., 1994), physically and mentally challenged students (Guetzloe, 1991), and selected demographics. In regard to demographics, Razin et al. (1991) discovered that suicidal behavior is disproportionately frequent among inner-city Hispanic adolescent girls. The phenomenon is generally related to poverty and poor family relationships.

In addition to signs of depression and dispiriting events, more immediate warning signs of suicide include: (1) extreme behavioral changes, (2) having a sibling who made a suicide attempt (Wagner & Cohen, 1994), (3) previous suicide attempts, (4) a suicidal threat or statement.

Anytime you believe someone is displaying these signals, intervene promptly. Listed below are some suggestions to help you with the intervention:

1. Be nonjudgmental.
2. Treat the precipitating problem or depression seriously.
3. Communicate your concern and support.

4. Ask directly, "Have you been thinking of killing yourself?" You are not likely to be putting ideas into someone's head; usually he or she is glad you brought it up so it can be discussed.
5. Evaluate the seriousness of the risk by asking the person if he or she has a plan to commit suicide. If they tell you a plan, see if the person has the means at hand (e.g., a rope for hanging, pills, gun, etc.).
6. Do not promise secrecy or confidentiality.
7. Contact someone who will be able to help, such as a mental health worker, counselor, psychologist, or in the case of a child, a parent.
8. Do not leave the person alone if risk is imminent or if he or she will not seek help.
9. If the person is a friend (versus a student or someone left in your charge), it may be appropriate to negotiate a "no-suicide" agreement. If he or she refuses to do this or modifies the agreement, the risk goes up and you need professional help. If your friend agrees to the no-suicide pact, still go for professional advice. Remember, you may be saving a life.

As a teacher, you need to work closely with mental health professionals during suicide follow-up as well as any treatment plan. Data show that most suicides happen within three months of the beginning of improvement, when energy levels are back up and original plans can be carried out.

The best avenue, of course, is to develop a prevention program in the school (Thompson et al., 1994). This should comprise a broad screening protocol to look at the multiple facets of adolescent behavior (depression, stress, family discord, school performance, self-esteem, drug involvement, sibling history related to suicide, sexual abuse). Initial screening may be general in nature, with more in-depth information collected secondarily.

The next part of such a program is the intervention component. The focus should be on underlying causes, not just on suicidal behavior. This means that the school and community must work in concert to address high-risk-youth problems. In addition to the obvious problems, life skills programs must be implemented to train students in decision-making, communication, conflict resolution, refusal, and problem-solving skills. A third component of a prevention program is to systematically evaluate the outcomes as well as the processes.

While teachers cannot accomplish everything, a good program should be able to reach vulnerable children and adolescents to stem the rising tide of suicide.

Stress and Stress Reduction

As humans, we experience *stress.* In many instances, it is good stress and called *eustress.* Falling in love, meeting a professional athlete, seeing a rock star, all could be examples of eustress. For children, eustress may result from being invited to a birthday party or seeing their favorite teacher in the grocery store. Most of us, however, conjure up negative thoughts when we hear the word *stress.* We think about the type of stress called *distress,* which can be either acute or chronic. Acute stress appears quickly, is intense, and dissipates rapidly. In contrast, chronic stress may be less intense but lingers for long periods of time (Seaward, 1994).

Adults need to recognize that children suffer from distress too. On a personal level, it may be over appearance, peer pressure, disagreements with parents, and fear from many stressors—real or imagined. Chronic stressors may be in the form of living in a violent neighborhood, abusive parents, or lack of adequate nourishment or appropriate housing. Suffering from a chronic illness or disabling condition can be a long-term stressor too. For example, three major stressors of children with asthma are "feeling sick," feelings of being left out of the group, and the inability to be good at sports (Walsh et al., 1992). Chronic illnesses also place additional stressors on the family, often keeping things at home very tense as arguments ensue about the cause, treatment, and prognosis of the condition. Unfortunately, teachers are usually ill equipped to handle the problems of chronically ill and/or mainstreamed mentally disabled students (Everett et al., 1994).

Pressure from teachers and parents to achieve academically can serve as a stressor for many chil-

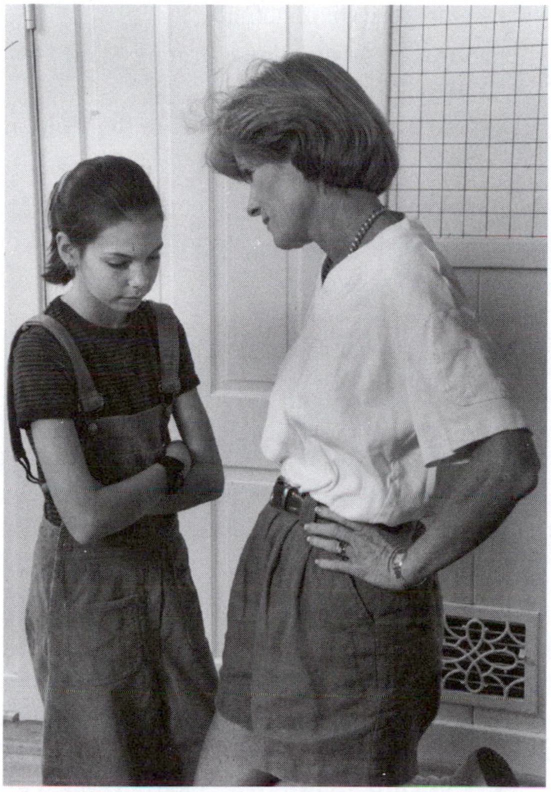

Arguments with parents can be a significant source of stress for young teens, just as close communication with parents can help put stressful situations in perspective.

dren. For most students, school stressors are acute—taking an exam, reading in front of the entire class, being called upon by the teacher, or taking a shower after physical education class. However, for other students, school may be a constant source of distress. It can start with the transition into kindergarten, but the most difficult transition is the shift into middle or junior high school. The buildings are generally larger, the curriculum different, and shuffling from room to room for classes can be confusing. All of this goes on while students are dealing with hormonal and physical changes.

For students who struggle academically, grades and report cards are constant reminders of unmet goals and expectations. Many times children make unrealistic demands on themselves, even with the simplest of assignments. Of course this can be compounded by the biggest stressor of all for many students—pleasing their parents. Peer pressure and the need to belong can make school a very unfriendly place too.

On the home front, children often face life "in the fast lane." Working parents may assuage guilt by enrolling children in as many extracurricular activities as possible to make up for the time they cannot spend with them during the week. As a result, many children are overscheduled, running from swimming practice, to Girl Scouts, to soccer, to choir practice, to music lessons. While some children can handle this pace, many others feel stressed out and pressured. There is no time for just sitting around.

Some signs of stress are as follows (Larigne et al., 1993):

Preschool

- Agitation
- Unusual whining
- Unusual clinginess
- Constant need for reassurance
- Inability to be playful, humorous
- Difficulty decompressing
- Worrisome behavior persisting more than two weeks

School-age

- Aggressive behavior
- Bed-wetting
- Sleeping problems
- Separation problems
- Withdrawn
- Resistance to participation
- Diarrhea or constipation
- Physical ailments on Sundays or Mondays

The relationship among eustress, distress, health, and performance is illustrated in Figure 10.2. Notice that too little or too much stimulation causes distress, with accompanying poor health and poor performance. The child who is bored in school may suffer as much distress as the child who finds school to be too challenging. However,

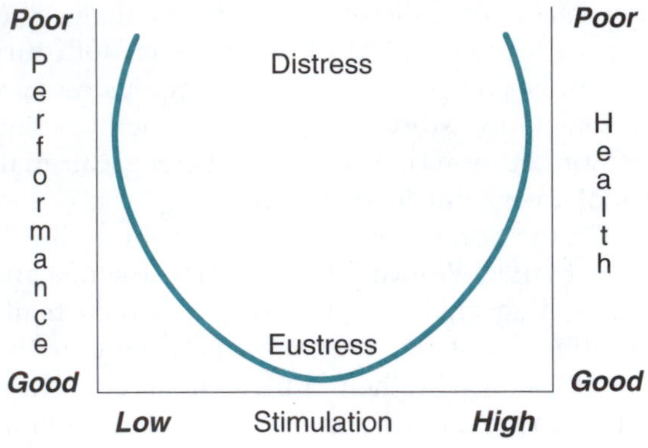

FIGURE 10.2 Stimulation, Stress, Health, and Performance

when work demands are appropriate—that is, stimulation level is suitable for the student—eustress results, with concomitant high performance and positive health.

The figure implies that a stress-reduction program should contain two facets. First, each of us needs to find out where our optimal level of stress is and use it to our advantage. Second, we must learn how to use coping skills and relaxation techniques to keep us out of the danger zone. Since both points are idiosyncratic, it is a challenge for a teacher to help each student individually as well as collectively.

To help prevent or reduce stress in children, the following are offered as suggestions (Lavigne et al., 1993; Atkins, 1992):

- Have an open-door policy, letting children know they can come to you anytime for help, support, or just a listening ear.
- Arrange a balance of quiet and active activities.
- Allow children time to be "bored."
- Give children free time to be creative and learn how to handle free time.
- Do not overschedule, and speak with parents who fall into this trap.
- Encourage parents to do more with their children by doing less.
- Talk with children about their activities, curricular and extracurricular, to understand their perspective on their lives.
- Endorse periodic inactivity.
- Encourage some daydreaming and some solitude.
- Do not dismiss anxiety; reassure the child and help him or her work through it.

The Teacher and the Emotionally Healthy Classroom

Several studies (Epstein & Cullinan, 1986; Korup, 1985; Frick, 1985) have shown that children do indeed experience mental health problems. In one study, school personnel listed the following as the top twelve mental health problems faced by elementary school children, meaning that at least one-fifth of the children exhibited these characteristics (Goodwin et al., 1988):

1. Poor decision-making and/or problem-solving skills
2. Poor self-image and negative self-statements
3. Low self-confidence
4. Difficulty in resolving interpersonal conflicts
5. Unhappy and depressed
6. Poor refusal skills and overly influenced by peers
7. Manipulative and controlling
8. Poor study habits and planning skills
9. Little motivation
10. Unable to concentrate, inattentive
11. Disobedient, disrespectful, and stubborn
12. Argumentative and verbally abusive

In the same study, school personnel believed that 80 percent of the causes for the twelve problems were home-related, while school-related causes accounted for only 5 percent of the problems. Although the causes of the problems may be argued, the fact still remains that students in a typical classroom enter with unique and varied backgrounds.

The school system comprises many people, but none are as important as the teacher in regard to establishing an emotionally healthy classroom. There is no doubt that some teachers bring about negative effects—intensifying low self-esteem, raising anxiety levels, inducing stress, and increasing self-defeating behaviors. In contrast, other teachers produce conditions that are inspiriting, thereby mobilizing children toward positive academic performance and health.

A teacher's personality is very important to the emotional climate of the classroom. A warm, friendly teacher generally brings higher achievement than the achievement-oriented teacher, whose students may plan well but at the expense of group relations. Supportive teachers find less test anxiety among their students. If you visit the classrooms of two different instructors, the effects of different personalities can be immediately apparent. The irritable, dominating, or careless teacher has students who show signs of strain and worry. In another classroom, students are confident, energetic, industrious, and cooperative. Their teacher is likely to be a poised, happy individual. In short, teacher personality is contagious. First and second graders are well aware of this fact—just listen to them talk among themselves.

The teacher's responsibility for the emotional climate of the classroom goes well beyond the contagiousness of a healthy personality. When the kindergarten students play school, teacher's mannerisms, voice, tone, and statements are all imitated. Their make-believe teacher is very similar to the real one. Teachers must understand that when they are imitated, they are likely to have a very strong influence on those children. In other words, they become a model for their students. And remember, it is not a matter of choice to be a model or not. Therefore, you should demonstrate the markings of emotional well-being so that you are a model worthy of emulation.

Here are twenty ways to foster mental-emotional well-being in your classroom:

- Realize that the causes of behavior are generally multiple and complex rather than single and simple.
- All persons have problems in adjusting (indecision, tension), and they should be considered serious only if prolonged.
- Know the growth patterns of children and be able to discern what is typical in order to understand what is atypical.
- Do not confuse what is normal with what is desirable.
- Teach in a way that facilitates the children's decision-making abilities.
- Accept the teacher's responsibility for affective teaching.
- Take time for yourself, including working out any hang-ups.
- Look at the other person's viewpoint and possess the flexibility to accept alternatives.
- Understand that younger children are just learning a sense of control.
- Be able to tolerate ambiguity.
- Deal with each child as a unique individual.
- Develop the skill to be an effective listener.
- Be consistent with all children regarding expectations and guidelines.
- Earn respect from your students rather than demanding it, and respect them in turn.
- Provide activities that are inspiriting.
- Be a skilled observer and know your limitations in helping a student suffering emotional distress.
- Demonstrate a sense of humor.
- Express your emotions through "I" statements.
- Work with parents to counteract negative home influences.
- Use a lot of common sense.

Implications for Elementary and Middle-school Teachers

Summary Issues

1. Emotional well-being permeates our total being and makes life worth living.
2. Emotionally healthy people are competent at satisfying their needs, have a firm grasp on reality, possess a healthy self-structure, are usually high in self-esteem, secure authentic relationships, and experience a wide range of emotions.
3. Our needs, from lowest to highest, are: physical, safety, belonging and love, esteem, and self-actualization.
4. Everyone satisfies their needs in different ways.

5. Reality checks are important for children in order to counteract messages from commercials, TV, music videos, and peers.
6. Self-structure comprises the real self, the self-concept, the ideal self, and the public selves. The real self should be interwoven throughout the structure, including all of our public selves.
7. The yardstick by which people measure their behavior can sometimes be wrong, rather than the behavior itself. Living by "shoulds and oughts" can be unhealthy.
8. Self-esteem is important for school performance and health. Low self-esteem is linked to stress and greater vulnerability to illness and suicide.
9. Self-esteem involves connectedness, uniqueness, power, and models. We all have a need to be somebody.
10. One of the ways an emotionally healthy family engenders growth is through open and honest communication in a secure environment. Self-disclosure is a necessity for intimacy.
11. Emotions bring meaning to life, and we have a choice whether to express them immediately, suppress them, or repress them. Uncontrolled expression is the hallmark of young children but not healthy adults. The latter learn to suppress their emotions in healthy ways—choosing when to suppress and express.
12. Emotional distress is common to all of us, and we can cope by changing the situation, altering our perception of the situation, or altering our negative feelings about the situation.
13. Depression may be due to a chemical imbalance, stress, emotional problems or unrecognized causes.
14. Depression can be as severe for children as it is for adults and similarly is an indicator for potential suicide.
15. Inspiriting events are those that mobilize the forces of wellness and emotional well-being, whereas dispiriting events foster illness and reduce the effectiveness in living.
16. Suicide is a social-health problem for children as well as for adolescents.
17. Signs imminent of suicide include extreme behavioral changes, previous suicide attempts, and a suicidal threat or statement.
18. Children experience several stressors, including adjustment to school, which is particularly difficult as they enter middle or junior high school.
19. Life "in the fast lane" exists for children as well as adults. Oftentimes, though, children have no choice about it.
20. Too much or too little stimulation can cause distress, with accompanying poor health and performance.
21. Elementary and middle-school children experience mental health problems requiring intervention by the teacher.
22. The teacher bears a responsibility to create an emotionally healthy environment for all students. The teacher's personality can play a major role in creating a positive classroom environment.

Teacher Ramifications

In regard to emotional well-being, a teacher should:

1. Recognize the signs and symptoms of poor mental health, and monitor each student regularly throughout the school year.
2. Know the school policies regarding psychosocial referrals and suicide intervention.
3. Employ a curriculum and teaching strategies that bolster self-esteem, address anxiety issues, reduce stress, and allow students to learn about the self.
4. Comprehend the needs of special-needs students as they apply to emotional well-being, and take steps to ensure that these needs are met.
5. Be able to explain the interrelationship of emotional well-being to all other dimensions of health and to the traditional health content areas.

SECTION III

Teaching Strategies for Emotional Well-Being

The strategies in this section are divided into grade K–4, 5–6, and 7–8 levels. In addition to strategies that can be used in the classroom, home activities are included. A home activity is designed for student-parent interaction. It is a way to engage the home in school-student learning, and parents can sign a slip of paper to confirm that an activity was completed. Evaluation of all strategies through the use of the National Health Education Standards and performance indicators is indicated. Teachers may also choose to write corresponding learning assessments.

K–4 Level

Strategy One

Objective: Students will be able to recognize some qualities of a good friend.

Activity: Divide students up into pairs or threes. Give each group one of the characteristics of a good friend below. Each group is to think of a situation they can role-play that illustrates the characteristic.

- honest
- helpful
- cooperative
- cheerful
- fun to be with
- good companion
- able to bring out the best in others
- kind and considerate
- thoughtful and polite
- clean and neat
- interested in you
- responsible and dependable
- good listener

Integration: Social Studies

Related Health Content Areas: Growth and development, families and relationships

Health Education Standards and Performance Indicators: 1(1); 5(2)

Strategy Two

Objective: Students will understand new situations, how they can be depressive, and how to cope.

Activity: Problem-based learning activity (see Chapter 4) as follows: Kirsten's best friend, Ashley, moved away five months ago. Kirsten is terribly lonely. She doesn't play with any of her other friends, she doesn't want to go out any where, she doesn't even really care how she looks at school. Her friends have given up trying to get her to talk with them. Kirsten's teacher and parents are very concerned.

- What is wrong with Kirsten?
- Do her parents and teacher have a reason to be concerned?
- Can Kirsten's other friends help her? How?
- What can Kirsten do to make herself feel better?

Integration: Social Studies

Related Health Content Areas: Families and relationships, growth and development

Health Education Standards and Performance Indicators: 5(2,3,4); 7(4)

5–6 Level

Strategy One

Objective: Students will be able to describe effective ways to deal with problem situations.

Activity: The teacher prepares a worksheet on three problem situations (see below), reads each to the students, and then discusses their suggestions for solving each problem.

The following questions are suggested as a follow-up for stimulating and guiding the discussion of each problem:

- Is there a problem?
- Who has it?
- Is it a recurring problem?
- How would you solve it?
- Is there a good immediate solution?
- Is this the best solution for later on?
- Do you agree with ____ and his/her solution?
- How would you solve it differently?
- Does anyone have a different solution?

Situation 1: Getting Along with Others

Shara and Elisha are team captains. Today they are playing softball against each other. Shara says, "Out" on one play and Elisha disagrees. They begin to argue and Shara hits Elisha. What should Elisha do?

Possible Alternatives

1. Hit Shara back.
2. Tell the teacher Shara hit her.
3. Ask Shara if that made her feel better and suggest doing the play over.
4. Call Shara a name.
5. Run away from Shara.

Situation 2: Homework

Jason has just started working on his homework. Aaron calls Jason and asks if he can come out after supper. What should Jason do?

Possible Alternatives

1. Close his book, forget about his homework, and go out.
2. Plan on copying Peter's homework in the morning, and go over to Aaron's house.
3. Tell Aaron he has to finish his homework, but if it's not too late he'll be over later.
4. Tell Aaron he's busy and will come over tomorrow after school.
5. Go to Aaron's house and stay up late to do the homework.

Situation 3: Lying

Alex and some other boys are on the playground throwing rocks. Alex's rock hits a classroom window and breaks it. The classroom is empty; no one saw Alex throw the rock. What should Alex do when the teacher asks the class about the broken window?

Possible Alternatives

1. Admit he broke the window
2. Say he saw nothing
3. Blame it on someone else
4. Say nothing at school, but that evening tell his parents that he broke a window at school

Integration: Social Studies

Related Health Content Areas: Growth and development, families and relationships

Health Education Standards and Performance Indicators: 1(4); 5(3,7,8)

Strategy Two

Objective: Students will give examples of characteristics of good emotional well-being.

Activity: The teacher may wish to post a list of the characteristics of good emotional well-being (see below). In a large-group format, ask students to give examples of situations that depict the various characteristics. The teacher may also wish to have pictures and/or drawings that depict the characteristics.

- Be cheerful
- Be calm about things you do
- Think before you do things
- Be dependable
- Be patient
- Practice self-control
- Respect the rights of others
- Plan what you do
- Be fair

- Do your share
- Do unto others as you would have them do unto you
- Do something for others without any strings attached
- Believe in yourself
- Develop good skills in school
- Develop good social skills

Integration: Social Studies, Art

Related Health Content Areas: Growth and development, families and relationships

Health Education Standards and Performance Indicators: 1(2,4); 5(5)

7–8 Level

Strategy One

Objective: Students will expand their understanding of the range of emotions and practice interpreting body language.

Activity: Use a poster, pictures, or drawings of a wide variety of facial expressions depicting different emotions such as the one in Figure 10.3. (If labeled, cover the wording.) In either large or small groups, have students try to identify the emotions shown. Near the end of class, identify each expression, allowing students to fill in blanks on their papers.

FIGURE 10.3 Facial Expressions Depicting a Variety of Emotions

Students can then write out definitions of the ten emotions with which they are least familiar.

Integration: Art, Language Arts

Related Health Content Areas: Human body, growth and development, family life and relationships

Health Education Standard and Performance Indicators: 5(1,5)

Strategy Two

Objective: Students will identify typical situations in which they feel angry.

Activity: Have students brainstorm typical things that happen at school or at home that cause them to feel angry. Discuss the fact that although the specifics of a situation may differ from person to person, very often the overall issues are very similar among people their age.

Next, have students discuss how they react when they feel angry. (It may be helpful to list these on the board but do not identify them with any particular student. Then have the class discuss the various responses and facilitate a discussion on positive and negative ways of dealing with feelings.

Integration: Social Studies, Home Economics/Family Living

Related Health Content Areas: Violence, family

Health Education Standard and Performance Indicators: 5(1,3,5,6,7,8)

Strategy Three

Objective: Students will develop situations that are common stressors for young teenagers and then role-play positive coping strategies.

Activity: Have students work in groups to develop common situations arising among young teenagers that create stress and conflict. Students should develop these to include possible dialogue. After discussing the situations the students devise, have each group develop a role-play of positive coping strategies. Discuss how positive coping strategies are beneficial to everyone involved; and have students determine why this is true.

Integration: Social Studies

Related Health Content Areas: Violence, growth and development, family relations

Health Education Standard and Performance Indicators: 5(5,6,7,8)

Home Activities

Strategy One

Objective: Students will identify and analyze coping strategies.

Activity: Using actual situations that have occurred between each student and friends, siblings, or parents, have the students identify the various coping strategies that were used by participants—denial, identification, compensation, rationalization, projection, daydreaming, displacement, reaction formation, regression, and/or sublimation. Discuss how some can cause more trouble than others. Discuss more effective means of dealing with the situations.

Integration: Social Studies

Related Health Content Areas: Growth and development, family life and relationships

Health Education Standard: 5

Strategy Two

Objective: Students will demonstrate skills for coping with conflict.

Activity: Problem-based activity as follows:

Yeepay had only attended Washington Middle School for one year. She had made many friends, but some kids made fun of her. Yesterday in art class, Marion had intentionally broken part of her clay sculpture. Mr. Harrison had written Marion up and sent her to the vice principal, but that didn't help Yeepay. She was very angry; she had worked for over a week on the sculpture.

- What is the main problem in this vignette?
- Does being a relatively new student make any difference in this case?
- What could the teacher, Mr. Harrison, do to reduce the conflict?
- What can Marion do to reduce her anger?
- What can Yeepay do now?
- What can Marion do now?

Integration: Art

Related Health Content Areas: Violence, growth and development, family and relationships

Health Education Standards: 5,6

References

Atkins, A. School stress: Expert advice on helping your kids handle the pressure, *Better Homes and Gardens* 70 (1992):37–39.

Bean, R. *The Four Conditions of Self-Esteem: A New Approach for Elementary and Middle Schools.* ETR Associates, Santa Cruz, CA, 1992.

Bernard, H.W. *Mental Health in the Classroom* McGraw Hill, New York, 1970.

Binns, J., Christoffel, K.K., Rosenbaum, D., Arend, R., Smith, K., Hayford, J.R., & McGuire, P.A. Behavioral and Emotional Problems among Preschool Children in Pediatric Primary Care: Prevalence and Pediatrician's Recognition, *Pediatrics* 7 (1993):649.

Brenner, A. *Helping Children Cope with Stress.* D.C. Heath, Lexington, MA, 1984, pp. 151–164.

Brent, D.A. Depression and suicide in children and adolescents, *Pediatrics in Review* 14, 10 (1993): 380–388.

Brown University. Preventing weight loss and body image problems in your children, *Brown University Child and Adolescent Behavior Letter* 9(1993):3.

Brown University. Sibling care lowers children's self-esteem, *Brown University Child and Adolescent Behavior Letter* 8(1992):4.

Clark, M.A., Feczko, J.D., Hawley, D.A., Pless, J.E., Tate, L.R., & Fardal, P.M. Asphyxial deaths due to hanging in children, *Journal of Forensic Sciences* 38, 2(1993):344–352.

Editors. Mired in misery, *Psychology Today* 25(1992):16.

Epstein, M.H., & Cullinan, D. Depression in children, *Journal of School Health* 56, 1(1986):10–12.

Everett, S.A., Price, J.H., Tellojohann, S.K. Secondary health educators' perceived self-efficacy in teaching mainstreamed mentally disabled students, *Journal of School Health* 64, 6(1994):261–265.

Frick, S.B. Diagnosing boredom, confusion, and adaptation in school children, *Journal of School Health* 55,7(1985):254–257.

Goldston, D.B., Kovacs, M., Ho, V.Y., Parrone, P.L., & Stiffler, L. Suicidal ideation and suicide attempts among youth with insulin-dependent diabetes mellitus, *Journal of the American Academy of Child and Adolescent Psychiatry* 33,2(1994):240–246.

Goodwin, L.D., Goodwin, W.L., & Cantrill, J.L. The mental health needs of elementary school children, *Journal of School Health* 58, 7(1988):282–287.

Guetzloe, E.C. Suicide and the exceptional child, *ERIC Digest* (#E508). Educational Resources Information Center Clearinghouse on Handicapped and Gifted Children, Reston, VA, 1991.

Harris, K.R. The sustained effects of cognitive modification and informed teachers on children's communication apprehension, *Communication Quarterly* 28 (1988):47–56.

Holbrook, H.T. Communication apprehension: The quiet student in your classroom, *ERIC Digest* (#ED284315). Educational Resources Information Center Clearinghouse on Reading and Communication Skills, Urbana, IL, 1987.

Irigon, F.F., Sarno, M., Sera, J., & Westgard, R. Child Development Centers program: An effective school-based mental health service, *Child Welfare* 60(1981):569–577.

Jacobsen, T., Huss, M., & Ziegenhain, U. Prepubertal suicide attempts (letter), *Journal of the American Academy of Child and Adolescent Psychiatry* 33, 6(1994):908–909.

Jourard, S.M. *Healthy Personalilty.* Macmillan, New York, 1974.

Kelly, G.L. Childhood depression and suicide, *Nursing Clinics of North America* 26, 3(1991):545–558.

Klebanov, P.K., Brooks-Gunn, J., & McCormick, M.C. Classroom behavior of very low-birthweight elementary school children, *Pediatrics* 94(1994): 700–709.

Kne, T., Shaw, M.W., Garfield, E.F., & Hicks, J. A program to address the special needs of drug-exposed children, *Journal of School Health* 64, 6(1994):251–253.

Knight, S.M., Vail-Smith, K., & Barnes, A.M. Children in the classroom: A survey of teacher perceptions and training needs, *Journal of School Health* 62, 8(1992):367–371.

Korup, U.L. Parent and teacher perceptions of depression in children, *Journal of School Health* 55, 9(1985):367–369.

Lavigne, J.V., Binns, H.J., Christoffel, K.K., Rosenbaum, D., Arend, R., Smith, K., Hayford, J., & McGuire, P.A. Behavioral and emotional problems among preschool children in pediatric primary care: Prevalence and pediatricians' recognition, *Pediatrics* 91(1993):649–656.

Maslow, A.H. *Motivation and Personality* 2d ed. Harper and Row, New York, 1970.

National Association for Mental Health. *Mental Health*. NAMH, New York, 1965.

Newacheck, P., Jameson, W.J., & Halfon, N. Health status and income: The impact of poverty on child health, *Journal of School Health* 64, 6(1994):229–233.

Orr, D.P., Wilbrandt, J.L., Brack, C.J., et al. Reported sexual behaviors and self-esteem among young adolescents, *Am J Dis Child* 143(1989):86–90.

Page, R.M., Allen, O., Moore, L., & Hewitt, C. Co-occurrence of substance use and loneliness as a risk factor for adolescent hopelessness, *Journal of School Health* 63, 2(1993):106–110.

Piaget, J. *The Development of Thought: Equilibration of Cognitive Structure*. Viking Press, New York, 1977.

Razin, A.M., O'Dowd, M.A., Nathan, A., Rodriguez, I., et al. Suicidal behavior among inner-city Hispanic adolescent females, *General Hospital Psychiatry* 13, 1(1991):45–58.

Schulman, J.L., Ford, R.C., Busk, P.L., & Kaspar, J.C. Mental health in the schools, *Elementary School Journal* 74(1973):48–56.

Sharrer, V.W., & Ryan-Wenger, N.M. Measurements of stress and coping among school-aged children with and without recurrent abdominal pain, *Journal of School Health* 61, 2(1991):86–91.

Smith, K., & Crawford, S. Suicidal behavior among "normal" high school students, *Suicide: Life-Threatening Behavior* 16(1986):313–325.

Smith, S.F., & Smith, C.M. *Personal Health Choices*. Jones and Bartlett, Boston, 1990.

Thompson, E.A., Moody, K.A., & Eggert, L.L. Discriminating suicide ideation among high-risk youth, *Journal of School Health* 64, 9(1994):361–367.

van Egmond, M., Garnefski, N., Jonker, D., & Kerkhof, A. The relationship between sexual abuse and female suicidal behavior, *Crisis* 14, 3(1993):129–139.

Wagner, B.M., & Cohen, P. Adolescent sibling differences in suicidal symptoms: The role of parent-child relationships, *Journal of Abnormal Child Psychology* 22, 3(1994):321–327.

Walsh, M., & Ryan-Wenger, N.M. Sources of stress in children with asthma, *Journal of School Health* 62, 10(1992):459–463.

11

Alcohol, Tobacco, and Other Drugs

Upon completion of this chapter, you should be able to:

- *Explain the scope of substance use and abuse in the student population*
- *Define selected terms as they apply to substance use and abuse*
- *Identify symptoms of users*
- *Explain trade names, slang terms, dependence, tolerance, modes of administration, possible effects, and withdrawal syndromes for the most commonly abused drugs*
- *Employ several teaching strategies at different educational levels*

SECTION I

Health Status, Deficits, and Learning

Perhaps no other health issue today commands more public attention than drug use and abuse. Nearly every school system has a formal drug-education program to address the dilemma. This is not too surprising given the fact that drug use by children inhibits, perhaps even blocks, learning. As witnessed by scores of teachers, drug abuse robs many children of a secure, enjoyable youth and too often robs them of life itself.

General Highlights

- Drug addiction is an "equal-opportunity" affliction; it is found in all social classes, religions, and races, and both genders.
- All drugs with abuse potential alter brain activity.
- Most heavy users of drugs use more than one psychoactive substance simultaneously.
- Most drug use is learned from others.
- Biological factors may contribute to drug abuse.
- No single theory explains why people use and/or abuse drugs.
- When drug use becomes consistent and habitual, it usually occurs in the peer group setting with people the user likes.
- The same dose of a drug does not have the same effect on everyone.
- The form in which a drug is taken can influence its effect.
- Most drugs cross the placental barrier from a mother to a fetus.
- The liver is the primary organ that metabolizes drugs.
- Tolerance to one drug can often cause tolerance to other drugs.
- Physical dependence is characterized by withdrawal symptoms when usage is stopped.
- Psychological dependence on a drug often leads to drug abuse.
- Hereditary factors may predispose some children to become psychologically dependent on drugs with abuse potential.

Incidence and Prevalence

A national survey on drug use was conducted on students in grades 8, 10, and 12 as well as on young adults from 1975 to 1993 (Johnston et al., 1994). Overall, survey results revealed an upward trend in drug abuse. This was a complete change

Much of the material in this chapter is from W. Witters, P. Venturelli, & G. Hanson, *Drugs and Society* 3d ed. (Boston: Jones and Bartlett, 1992).

Kids least likely to become involved in drugs are independent thinkers with many interests and an open line of communication with parents.

from the late 1960s, which evidenced a downward trend in drug use among students. This fact should cause alarms to go off. The data below (on grade 8 except where overall trends are noted) outline the problem in more detail:

- Data revealed a "softening" of attitude toward drug use among students, that is, beliefs that it probably is not harmful.
- Eighth graders were exhibiting a significant increase in drug use.
- Rises in the use of "gateway" drugs—alcohol, tobacco, inhalants, marijuana—showed that a large number of eighth graders were already at risk of proceeding further to such drugs as LSD, cocaine, amphetamines, and heroin.
- Initiation of daily smoking most often occurred in grades 6 through 9 with a clear cohort effect. (Early, high rate of smoking usually remains so throughout the life cycle.)
- Cigarettes were tried by nearly one half of eighth graders (45%), and 17 percent, or one in seven, smoked in the prior month. Only 52 percent thought there was great risk associated with being a pack-a-day smoker.
- Smokeless tobacco was tried by 30 percent of the male eighth graders; it is used currently by 11 percent of them; and used daily by 2.9 percent.
- By the eighth grade, 67 percent of youngsters reported having tried alcohol, and more than a quarter said they have already been drunk at least once.
- Among eighth graders, almost one in five (19%) had used inhalants; 11 percent had used them in the last twelve months; and 5 percent had used them in last month. This is the only class of drugs for which use is substantially higher in grade 8 than in grades 10 or 12, which makes inhalants the most widely used class of *illicitly* used drugs among eighth graders.
- Marijuana was tried by one in every eight eighth graders (13%), and had been used in the prior month by 5.1 percent.
- Prescription-type stimulants (stay-awake pills, diet pills, look-alikes) were tried by 12 percent, with 3.6 percent using them in the prior thirty days.
- Data revealed at least some experience with other illicit drugs: tranquilizers (4.4%), LSD

(3.5%), other hallucinogens (1.7%), crack (1.7%), other cocaine (2.4%), heroin (1.4%), and steroids (1.6% overall; 2.5% among males).

- Hispanics had the highest rates of use for nearly all drugs in grade 8 but not in grade 12, which suggested a considerably higher school dropout rate.
- African American students had consistently lower usage rates on most drugs than Caucasian students.
- There is little male-female difference in grade-8 drug use.

The points from the same study below reflect the incidence of use as reported by eighth graders when they were in grade 6:

- Eleven percent reported use of inhalants by grade 6.
- Thirty-seven percent noted alcohol use by the end of grade 6.
- The peak ages for initiation of cigarette smoking appeared to be in grades 6 and 7 (22%), with a considerable number starting even earlier.
- Nine percent of eighth graders reported having been drunk by the end of grade 6, and seniors' data showed the peak ages of initiation being grades 7 through 9.
- Seven percent of eighth graders had already tried inhalants prior to grade 6.
- The highest initiation rates for marijuana were reported to be grades 9 through 11.

From the data, it is clear that legal drugs are most likely to be initiated at an early age, with inhalants and marijuana likely to come next. This is consistent with the so-called gateway and progression models of drug use.

Assessment Criteria

Some of the symptoms of possible drug use and abuse are listed below (L.A.W., 1985). Realize that more than one symptom should be displayed before suspecting use, and that a physical impairment or disorder may cause some of these same symptoms. In other words, move with "deliberate speed" before identifying a child with a drug use or abuse problem.

- Abrupt changes in behavior
- Diminished drive or ambition
- Moodiness
- Shortened attention span
- Impaired communication such as slurred speech or jumbled thinking
- Significant change in the quality of school work
- Deteriorating judgment and loss of short-term memory
- Distinct lessening of family closeness and warmth
- Sudden carelessness of appearance (the word *sudden* is important since children and adolescents don't always dress the way we think they ought to)
- Inappropriate overreaction to even mild criticism (out of character for the particular student)
- Secretiveness regarding whereabouts and personal possessions
- Friends who avoid introduction or appearance in the child's home
- Use of words that have odd, underworld connotations
- Desperation for and/or secretiveness about money
- Rapid appetite or weight loss
- "Drifting off" beyond normal daydreaming
- Extreme behavioral changes, such as hallucinations, violence, unconsciousness, and the like (could indicate a dangerous situation is close at hand, needing fast medical attention)
- Unprescribed or unidentifiable pills
- Strange "contraptions" or hidden articles
- Articles missing from the house (child could be stealing to get money to pay for drugs)

In regard to some specific drugs, the following symptoms may be apparent (Witters et al., 1992):

Depressants

- May seem intoxicated but with no odor of alcohol on the breath

- Movements may include stumbling or staggering
- Loss of interest in activities that were interesting previously
- Falling asleep in class even when interested

Volatile Substances

- An odor of the substance on breath and/or clothes
- Mouth irritations or ulcerations
- Runny nose and/or watery eyes
- Loss in muscle coordination or increased drowsiness

Marijuana

- Clothes have odor of burned marijuana
- Eyes, especially the whites of the eyes, may appear irritated
- May behave more quietly or subdued than in the past

Stimulants

- Pupils of the eyes may be more dilated
- Complaints of a dry mouth, dry lips, dry nose, or bad breath
- Long periods of anorexia (not eating)
- Needle tracks on the body if shooting up

Hallucinogens

- Appearance of daydreaming or being in a trance
- Looking at everyday objects carefully and for a long period of time
- Distortion of body image, senses, perhaps even leading to panic

Narcotics

- Needle marks if shooting up, or raw, red nostrils if sniffing
- Generally lethargic, even to the point of drowsiness
- (As with many other drugs) purposive in getting money

In contrast, the child who is least likely to use drugs may display the following (L.A.W., 1985):

- Comes from a strong family
- Family has clear rules against drug use
- Child has strong religious convictions
- Child is an independent thinker, not easily swayed by peer pressure
- Parents know the child's friends and the friends' parents
- Child often invites friends into the home, and their behavior is open rather than secretive
- Child is busy, productive, and pursues many interests
- Child has good self-confidence, good secure feeling of self
- Parents are comfortable with their own use of alcohol, drugs, and pills; set a good example in using these; and are comfortable in discussing their use
- Parents set a good example in handling crisis situations

SECTION II

Alcohol, Tobacco, and Other Drugs Teaching Information

Drug use and abuse is a very old problem. Historical records document drug use as far back as 2240 B.C., when the Babylonian king and lawgiver, Hammaurabi, wrote about alcohol-related problems. The problems today, however, are of greater magnitude because: (1) drugs are commonplace and involve nearly every social group, (2) drugs are more potent than they were years ago, (3) the possibility of serious accidents from drug use is more likely, and (4) "gateway" drugs are being used by younger children, which in turn are associated with multiple drug use and other high-risk behaviors, including delinquency, truancy, and poor school performance.

Drugs and Drug Terminology

Generally speaking, "a drug is any substance that modifies biological, psychological, or social behavior" (Witters et al., 1992, p. 4). Since it is impossible to categorize drugs into single chemical categories, they are classified in several other ways. One way is by usage. This typology consists of medications—both prescription and over-the-counter (OTC) drugs—and psychoactive recreational drugs. Medications, of course, are to be taken for illness. Those requiring a physician's approval are prescription drugs (e.g., antibiotics, drugs to lower blood pressure, etc.). Those that can be bought without a prescription (e.g., headache and cold remedies, vaginal yeast infection preparations, etc.) are OTC drugs. More and more drugs are being placed on the OTC market.

Psychoactive recreational drugs are usually illegal substances such as marijuana, LSD, and cocaine. However, they also include legal substances such as alcohol, tobacco, and caffeine, and legal prescription drugs like tranquilizers and amphetamines. More than one quarter of legal drugs and virtually all illegal drugs are psychoactive; that is, they alter thoughts, feelings, perceptions, and moods. The commonly abused psychoactive drugs are:

1. *Organic solvents:* Inhalants such as airplane glue, paint thinner, gasoline, as well as some foods, herbs, and vitamins
2. *Depressants:* Alcohol, barbiturates, methaqualone, and other sedatives
3. *Cannabis:* Marijuana and hashish
4. *Stimulants:* Amphetamines, cocaine, and caffeine as well as coffee, tea, and tobacco (although tobacco may have a calming effect at times and a stimulating effect at others)
5. *Hallucinogens:* Lysergic acid diethylamide (LSD), peyote, mescaline, and phencyclidine (PCP)
6. *Narcotics:* Codeine, heroin, morphine, and opium

Table 11.1 provides details on each of these commonly abused drugs. Specifically, it explains medical usage, trade names, slang terms, physical and psychological dependence, tolerance, modes of administration, possible effects, effects of overdose, and withdrawal syndromes.

Gateway drugs are those that often lead to the use of more powerful addictive drugs. For example, alcohol, tobacco, and marijuana are known gateway drugs for children and adolescents.

Drug or substance abuse is the willful misuse of legal or illegal drugs for convenience or recreation. Misuse, in contrast, is the inappropriate use of OTC or prescribed drugs, such as excessive use, mixing drugs with alcohol, giving prescription drugs to others without medical consent, and the like.

Reasons for Psychoactive Drug Use

While drug use and abuse may occur at any time in a student's life, middle-school youth are considered to be most vulnerable. According to the Carnegie Foundation's report (1989), students in the middle-school years are at a "turning point" in their lives, toward either a productive life or a diminished future. Figure 11.1 shows that many students begin drug use at this time.

As presented in Chapter 1, children who experience several risk factors are more likely to use and abuse drugs than those with few or none. According to Hawkins et al. (1985), the risk factors for drug use include:

- Social and economic deprivation
- Neighborhood disorganization and low neighborhood attachment
- Poor family structure and lack of clear policies on drug use
- Parental use of drugs, including tobacco and alcohol, or a family history of alcoholism
- Living in a community favorable to drug use and abuse

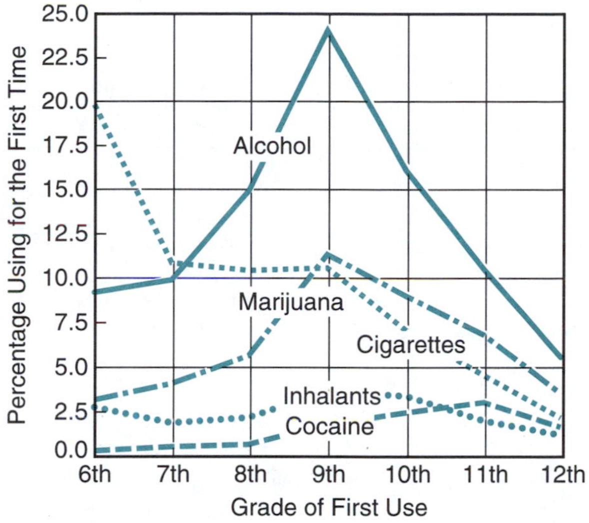

FIGURE 11.1 Grade of First Use of Drugs in Percentages as Reported by High School Seniors (*Source:* National Commission on Drug-Free Schools, *Toward a Drug Free Generation: A Nation's Responsibility.* Washington, DC, 1990)

- Low parental expectations for childhood success
- Availability of drugs—alcohol, tobacco, and others
- No clear school policies on tobacco use
- Poor school performance, little commitment to school, lack of involvement in school activities, and changing schools often
- Influential peers who use drugs
- Cultures that promote drug use (e.g., some Southeast Asian families give cigarettes as party favors at weddings)

The major influences are the following:

1. *Peer pressure:* This is particularly strong for young people, and for some it is a rite of passage. Four types of groups of adolescents may be important in distinguishing among peer groups. The first group conform with parental values and conventional society and never use drugs. The second group generally conform but are influenced by, other role models—music, videos, and so forth—promoting different lifestyles. This group may use drugs intermittently. The third group go through a much greater turbulent period, finding themselves in conflict with parents, teachers, and society. Close attachments with family members and the opposite sex are almost nonexistent. These students seek out same-gender friends who are in similar circumstances. Gateway drugs tend to escalate to other types of drugs. The fourth group comprises alienated adolescents who are in continual conflict with authority figures. They frequently perform poorly in school, steal, and even deal drugs.

2. *Self-esteem:* Young people who see themselves in a poor light are susceptible to peer pressure. They may use drugs as a way to cope too.

3. *Curiosity:* The younger years are a time for experimentation in many aspects of life, including drugs.

4. *Media and modeling:* The media offer many roles to children, as do adults. Family members and teachers are especially important role models. Athletes play an important role too, as seen in alcohol and smokeless tobacco commercials.

5. *Alienation:* As noted above, some children and adolescents are very alienated from those around them. They believe that life is a matter of luck or fate, rendering them helpless to control the events around them (Sykes & Matza, 1975).

Whatever the reasons for drug use, they are usually complex and present a challenge to the educator.

How Drugs Work

The effects of drugs on the body vary with several factors—administration, distribution, dosage, frequency, tolerance, and expectation. The manner in which a drug is taken influences the rate of passage into the bloodstream, subsequent distribution to the site of action, and ultimately, how much will exert an effect. Modes of administration include oral ingestion, inhalation, injection, implantation, and suppositories.

Regardless of the nature of administration, most drugs are distributed throughout the body in the blood. Once in the blood, a drug is rapidly diluted and carried to organs and other body struc-

Table 11.1 Drugs of Use and Abuse

Drugs/CSA Schedules		Medical Uses	Trade or Other Names	Slang Names
		Narcotics		
Opium	II III V	Analgesic, antidiarrheal	Dover's Powder, Paregoric, Parepectolin	Opium
Morphine	II III	Analgesic, antitussive	Morphine, MS-Contin, Roxanol, Roxanol-SR	M, Morpho, Morph, Tab, White, Stuff, Miss, Emma, Monkey
Codeine	II III V	Analgesic, antitussive	Tylenol w/Codeine, Empirin w/Codeine, Robitussin A-C, Fiorinal w/Codeine	School Boy
Heroin	I	None	Diacetylmorphine	Horse, Smack, II, Stuff, Junk
Hydromorphone	II	Analgesic	Dilaudid	Little D, Lords
Meperidine (Pethidine)	II	Analgesic	Demerol, Mepergan	Isonipecaine, Dolantol
Methadone	II	Analgesic	Dolophine, Methadone, Methadose	Dollies, Dolls, Amidone
Other Narcotics	I II III IV V	Analgesic, antidiarrheal, antitussive	Numorphan, Percodan, Percocet, Tylox, Tussionex, Fentanyl, Darvon, Lomotil, Talwin[1]	T. and Blue's, Designer Drugs, (Fentanyl Derivatives), China White
		Depressants		
Chloral Hydrate	IV	Hypnotic	Noctec	—
Barbiturates	II III IV	Anesthetic, anticonvulsant, sedative, hypnotic, veterinary euthanasia agent	Amytal, Butisol, Fiorinal, Lotusate, Nembutal, Seconal, Tuinal, Phenobarbital	Yellows, Yellow Jackets, Barbs, Reds, Redbirds, Tooies, Phennies
Benzodiazepines	IV	Antianxiety, anticonvulsant, sedative, hypnotic	Ativan, Dalmane, Diazepam, Librium, Xanax, Serax, Valium, Tranxene, Verstran, Versed, Halcion, Paxipam, Restoril	Downers, Goof Balls, Sleeping Pills, Candy
Methaqualone	I	Sedative, hypnotic	Quaalude	Lude, Quay, Quad, Mandrex
Glutethimide	III	Sedative, hypnotic	Doriden	—
Other Depressants	III IV	Antianxiety, sedative, hypnotic	Equanil, Miltown, Noludar, Placidyl, Valmid	Tranquilizers, Muscle Relaxants, Sleeping Pills

Source: From W. Witters, P. Venturelli, & G. Hanson, *Drugs and Society* Third Edition. © 1992. Boston: Jones and Bartlett; adapted from U.S. Department of Justice/Drug Enforcement Administration, *Drugs of Abuse* 1989 edition (Washington, DC: Government Printing Office, 1989); Reprinted with permission.

Dependence Physical	Dependence Psychological	Tolerance	Duration (hours)	Administration Methods	Possible Effects	Effects of Overdose	Withdrawal Syndrome
				Narcotics			
High	High	Yes	3–6	Oral, smoked	Euphoria, drowsiness, respiratory depression, constricted pupils, nausea	Slow and shallow breathing, clammy skin, convulsions, coma, possible death	Watery eyes, runny nose, yawning, loss of appetite, irritability, tremors, panic, cramps, nausea, chills and sweating
High	High	Yes	3–6	Oral, smoked, injected			
Moderate	Moderate	Yes	3–6	Oral, injected			
High	High	Yes	3–6	Injected, sniffed smoked			
High	High	Yes	3–6	Oral, injected			
High	High	Yes	3–6	Oral, injected			
High	High-Low	Yes	12–24	Oral, injected			
High-Low	High-Low	Yes	Variable	Oral, injected			
				Depressants			
Moderate	Moderate	Yes	5–8	Oral	Slurred speech, disorientation, drunken behavior without odor of alcohol	Shallow respiration, clammy skin, dilated pupils, weak and rapid pulse, coma, possible death	Anxiety, insomnia, tremors, delirium, convulsions, possible death
High-Mod.	High-Mod.	Yes	1–16	Oral			
Low	Low	Yes	4–8	Oral			
High	High	Yes	4–8	Oral			
High	Moderate	Yes	4–8	Oral			
Moderate	Moderate	Yes	4–8	Oral			

continued

Table 11.1 Drugs of Use and Abuse–*Continued*

Drugs/CSA Schedules		Medical Uses	Trade or Other Names	Slang Names
		Stimulants		
Cocaine[1]	II	Local anesthetic		Bump, Toot, C, Coke, Flake, Snow, Candy, Crack
Amphetamines	II	Attention deficit disorders, narcolepsy, weight control	Biphetamine, Desoxyn, Dexedrine	Pep Pills, Bennies, Uppers, Truck Drivers, Dexies, Black Beauties, Speed
Phenmetrazine	II	Weight control	Preludin	Uppers, Peaches, Hearts
Methylphenidate	II	Attention deficit disorders, narcolepsy	Ritalin	Speed, Meth, Crystal, Crank, Go Fast
Other Stimulants	III IV	Weight control	Adipex, Cylert, Didrex, Ionamin, Melfiat, Plegine, Sanorex, Tenuate, Tepanil, Prelu-2	—
		Hallucinogens		
LSD	I	None		Acid, Microdot, Cubes
Mescaline and Peyote	I	None		Mesc Buttons, Cactus
Amphetamine Variants	I	None	2,5-DMA, PMA, STP, MDA, MDMA, TMA, DOM, DOA	Ecstasy, Designer Drugs
Phencyclidine	II	None	PCP	PCP, Angel Dust, Hog, Peace Pill
Phencyclidine Analogues	I	None	PCE, PCPy, TCP	—
Other Hallucinogens	I	None	Bufotenine, Ibogaine, DMT, DET, Psilocybin, Psilocyn	Sacred Mushrooms, Magic Mushrooms, Mushrooms
		Cannabis		
Marijuana	I	None		Pot, Grass, Reefer, Roach, Maui Wowie, Joint, Weed, Loco Weed, Mary Jane
Tetrahydrocannabinol	I II	Cancer chemotherapy antinauseant	TWC, Marinol	THC
Hashish	I	None		Hash
Hashish Oil	I	None		Hash Oil
		Inhalants		
		None	Gasoline, Airplane Glue, Veg. Spray, Hairspray, Deodorants, Spray Paint, Liquid Paper, Paint Thinner, Rubber Cement	Sniffing, Glue Sniffing, Snorting

Dependence Physical—	Psychological	Tolerance	Duration (hours)	Administration Methods	Possible Effects	Effects of Overdose	Withdrawal Syndrome
				Stimulants			
Possible	High	Yes	1–2	Sniffed, smoked, injected	Increased alertness, excitation, euphoria, increased pulse rate & blood pressure, insomnia, loss of appetite	Agitation, increase in body temperature, hallucinations, convulsions, possible death	Apathy, long periods of sleep, irritability, depression, disorientation
Possible	High	Yes	2–4	Oral, injected			
Possible	High	Yes	2–4	Oral, injected			
Possible	Moderate	Yes	2–4	Oral, injected			
Possible	High	Yes	2–4	Oral, injected			
				Hallucinogens			
None	Unknown	Yes	8–12	Oral	Illusions and hallucinations, poor perception of time and distance	Longer, more intense "trip" episodes, psychosis, possible death	Withdrawal syndrome not reported
None	Unknown	Yes	8–12	Oral			
Unknown	Unknown	Yes	Variable	Oral, injected			
Unknown	High	Yes	Days	Smoked, oral, injected			
Unknown	High	Yes	Days	Smoked, oral, injected			
None	Unknown	Possible	Variable	Smoked, oral, injected, sniffed			
				Cannabis			
Unknown	Moderate	Yes	2–4	Smoked, oral	Euphoria, relaxed inhibitions, increased appetite, disoriented behavior	Fatigue, paranoia, possible psychosis	Insomnia, hyperactivity, and decreased appetite occasionally reported
Unknown	Moderate	Yes	2–4	Smoked, oral			
Unknown	Moderate	Yes	2–4	Smoked, oral			
Unknown	Moderate	Yes	2–4	Smoked, oral			
				Inhalants			
None	Unknown	Yes	30 min.	Sniffed	Euphoria, headaches, nausea, fainting, stupor, rapid heartbeat	Damage to lungs, liver, kidneys, bone marrow, suffocation, choking, anemia, possible stroke, sudden death	Insomnia, Increased appetite, depression, irritability, headache

tures. It only takes about one minute for drugs to circulate completely throughout the body.

Needless to say, drug effects are related to the amount taken. A small amount of a drug may have one effect, while a larger amount may have either a greater effect or perhaps a totally different effect.

One of the most important modifying factors in drug effects is tolerance, which brings about a decreased response to the same dosage over time. Keep in mind that the development of tolerance for one drug may cause tolerance for a related drug—alcohol and barbiturates are examples of such a cross-tolerance.

The time of day that a drug is taken is a modifying variable too. For example, a drink "for the road" taken at the end of a late-night party produces a longer-lasting rise in blood-alcohol level than an identical drink taken earlier in the evening. This is because of the decreased rate of metabolism due to earlier drinks.

Other modifying factors are the user's expectation of the drug effect as well as the setting in which the drug is taken. These are evidenced when a placebo—an inert substance—is taken.

Gateway Drugs

Tobacco: Smoking and Smokeless

The use of tobacco in our culture probably originated in sixteenth-century Europe through Spanish sailors returning from voyages to the New World. Apparently the sailors learned about pipe smoking from Native Americans. The smoking habit spread quickly in Europe. However, by the nineteenth century, changing social customs had largely replaced smoking with tobacco chewing and the even more popular habit of sniffing it in the form of snuff. It wasn't until the 1880s, when the cigarette machine was invented in the United States, that cigarette smoking became popular.

In 1964, the first Surgeon General's report on smoking and health noted that smoking was related to several diseases, including lung cancer. In 1966, warning labels became required on cigarette packages. More recently, C. Everett Koop, the former Surgeon General, stated that "Cigarette smoking is associated with more deaths and illness than drugs, alcohol, accidents, and AIDS combined" (1991). This is not surprising, since by the early 1990s there were about 1200 deaths per day—fifty each hour—related to cigarette smoking (Matza & Loya, 1994). Ask your class to look at their vacant seats when they are leaving the room and to imagine that all of them smoked and all of them died—all within that hour.

The Smoking Pathway

The most familiar chemical constituent of tobacco is nicotine, but when tobacco is burned, approximately 4000 other chemical substances are released and carried in the smoke. Besides all these chemical compounds, tobacco smoke contains countless microscopic particles that contribute to the yellowish-brown residue of tobacco smoke known as *tar*.

Most of the physiological effects of tobacco are attributable to nicotine. A student who smokes a typical filter cigarette containing 1 to 2 milligrams (mg) of nicotine takes in about 90 percent of this amount. Cigars contain about 120 mg of nicotine—enough to kill a person who inhales, as with a cigarette. The nicotine is carried by the blood to the heart and from there throughout the body. It reaches the brain in seven seconds, which is twice as fast as from intravenous administration of a drug in the arm (Witters et al., 1992).

Nicotine first stimulates and then depresses the nervous system. It increases respiration rate at low-dose levels and stimulates the cardiovascular system, causing increases in coronary blood flow, heart rate, and blood pressure. It increases the oxygen requirements of the heart muscle but not the oxygen supply, a lethal combination of events for people susceptible to heart attacks.

The chemicals responsible for hunger contractions are inhibited by nicotine, and perhaps other chemicals too. This effect decreases feelings of hunger because blood sugar levels rise slightly and the taste buds are deadened. This may explain why many smokers gain weight when they quit. Of course, this is in conjunction with a decreased heart rate and metabolic rate when a person stops smoking; the less-stressed body probably converts more food to fat.

In addition to dying at an earlier age than nonsmokers, smokers are more prone to emphysema, cardiovascular disease, bronchopulmonary disease, and of course cancer.

If a woman smokes during pregnancy, there are harmful effects on the fetus. There is a greater likelihood of spontaneous abortion, impaired fetal growth, stillbirth, premature birth, and neonatal death. Babies born to mothers who smoke are very likely to have a low birthweight, which can lead to a series of other problems. If a pregnant woman refrains from smoking during an entire pregnancy, the baby will probably be born at normal size and strength.

Sudden infant death syndrome (SIDS) is associated with infants born to mothers who smoked during their pregnancy too. Even when just the father smokes, the fetus may be affected by second-hand smoke, also called *environmental tobacco smoke* (ETS). There is a much higher mortality rate for newborn infants whose fathers smoke more than ten cigarettes a day. And babies fathered by heavy smokers have twice the expected incidence of severe birth defects.

Environmental Tobacco Smoke

Studies of second-hand smoke, exhaled smoke from burning tobacco that pollutes the air and is breathed by smokers and nonsmokers alike, has been shown to be very detrimental to health. Likewise, sidestream smoke, smoke released into the air directly from the lighted tip of a cigarette, is dangerous. Thousands of deaths have been attributed to environmental exposure to tobacco smoke (Glantz & Parmley, 1991). Imagine yourself at work, sitting in a smoke-filled room for eight hours every day. Just by being in the room, this is equivalent to smoking one cigarette every one of those eight hours. This is the major reason why smoking in public places has been banned.

Children are definitely affected by environmental tobacco smoke. Children who are subjected to smoke from their parents have up to 300,000 lower-respiratory infections such as pneumonia and bronchitis each year, up to one million asthma attacks, and up to 15,000 hospitalizations. There are increases in middle-ear infections and reduced lung functioning also (Glantz, 1992; Koop, 1989; USDHHS, 1986; USEPA, 1992).

Smokeless Tobacco

Chewing tobacco and snuff are the two products classified as smokeless tobacco. Snuff is powdered or finely cut tobacco leaves that are not chewed but instead placed between the lip or cheek and gum. This method is called *dipping*. Chewing tobacco is sold as either loose-leaf or a plug.

Increasing use of smokeless tobacco is found in young males, with an estimated 25 to 35 percent using the products in some areas of the country. In Alaska, investigation revealed that 17 percent of five-year-old girls and 10 percent of five-year-old boys used smokeless tobacco (Wolfe, 1987).

While advertising claims often imply that smokeless tobacco is a safe alternative to smoking, research shows otherwise. The health problems associated with smokeless tobacco are (McDermott & Marty, 1986; Advisory Committee to the Surgeon General, 1986):

- Excessive tooth abrasions
- Association with cancers of the pharynx, esophagus, urinary bladder, and pancreas
- Increase in heart rate and blood pressure (as with cigarettes)
- Association with gum disease
- Darkened teeth and bad breath
- Increase in dental caries
- Reduced ability to fight disease due to suppressed immunological responses

Conclusions about Tobacco

More and more evidence is accumulating that tobacco is a more serious gateway drug than previously thought. In a study of high school seniors, cigarette smokers were ten times more likely to use cocaine regularly than seniors who did not smoke (NIDA, 1990). Furthermore, a study by Coambs (1988) revealed that "die-hard" smokers started at younger ages. These facts are particularly important when it is realized that the tobacco companies target younger audiences, despite their protestations to the contrary. Recall the well-publicized study in which children played a game involving twenty-two product logos, and that some children recognized Joe Camel, the Camel cigarette character, more readily than Walt Disney's Mickey Mouse (Fischer & Schwartz, 1991).

Alcohol

Except during Prohibition, alcoholic beverages have enjoyed widespread and immense popularity with the American public. In fact, alcohol is the most widely used drug in our society today. Because it is so readily available and widely accepted, many children and adults consider alcohol to be a social substance rather than a drug. Consequently, alcohol abuse is one of the most significant health-related problems in the United States (and many other countries).

For school-age populations, alcohol is an illegal drug. Nonetheless, it appears to be the drug of choice among students. Students as young as three years have used alcohol (and tobacco), often being exposed through peers, older siblings, and even parents (National Commission on Drug-Free Schools, 1990).

The Alcohol Pathway

Although *alcohol* refers to a whole class of chemical agents, in everyday usage it generally means ethanol (ethyl alcohol, grain alcohol). Other kinds of alcohol include methyl (wood) alcohol and isopropyl (rubbing) alcohol, which are not for internal consumption. The amount of ethyl alcohol in any commercial product is listed on the label. The amount of alcohol in beer and wine is given as the percentage of the total volume (e.g., beer is generally 4 percent alcohol). The amount of alcohol in distilled liquors (scotch, vodka, rum, etc.) is given in so-called proof, a number that represents twice the percentage of alcohol in the product. Thus 80-proof whiskey is 40 percent alcohol.

As illustrated in Figure 11.2, alcohol is ingested orally. It enters the bloodstream quickly and directly from the stomach, and even more rapidly through the walls of the small intestine. Once in the blood, alcohol is carried to all the body's tissues and organs. Although not strictly a food, alcohol does contain calories—in fact, almost twice as many calories per gram as sugar.

Several factors affect the rate at which alcohol is absorbed into the tissues. For example, food in the stomach, especially fatty foods or proteins, slows its absorption. Nonalcoholic substances in beer, wine, and cocktails also slow absorption of alcohol. But carbon dioxide in beverages such as champagne, sparkling wines, beer, and carbonated mixed drinks increases the rate of alcohol absorption.

The concentration of alcohol in the blood is called the *blood alcohol content* (BAC). A simple way to estimate BAC is to assume that ingesting one standard drink per hour (one beer, one glass of wine, one mixed drink), which contains about half an ounce of ethyl alcohol, gives a BAC of 0.02 in a 150-pound man. Thus the BAC of an average-sized man who drinks five beers during the first hour at a party will be 0.10; this is the level of alcohol in the blood that violates the drinking-and-driving law in most states. Needless to say, this shorthand method of determining BAC changes with body size, composition, and gender. According to Jones and Jones (1976), women tend to have a higher BAC from the same number of drinks as men because they generally weigh less than men, have proportionately more body fat (which does not absorb alcohol as readily as muscle and other tissue), and have sex hormones that tend to increase alcohol absorption and decrease its elimination.

Alcohol is eliminated from the body in two ways. Approximately 10 percent is excreted, unchanged, through sweat, urine, and breath (hence breath analyzers). Alcohol that is not excreted is broken down, primarily by the liver, winding up as carbon dioxide and water. The liver detoxifies alcohol at a rate of about half an ounce per hour, and there is no way to speed up the process. Drinking a lot of coffee and taking a cold shower simply produces a wet, wide-awake person who has drunk alcohol.

Fetal Alcohol Syndrome and Later Learning

Drinking during pregnancy can bring about several adverse effects. Generally, women who

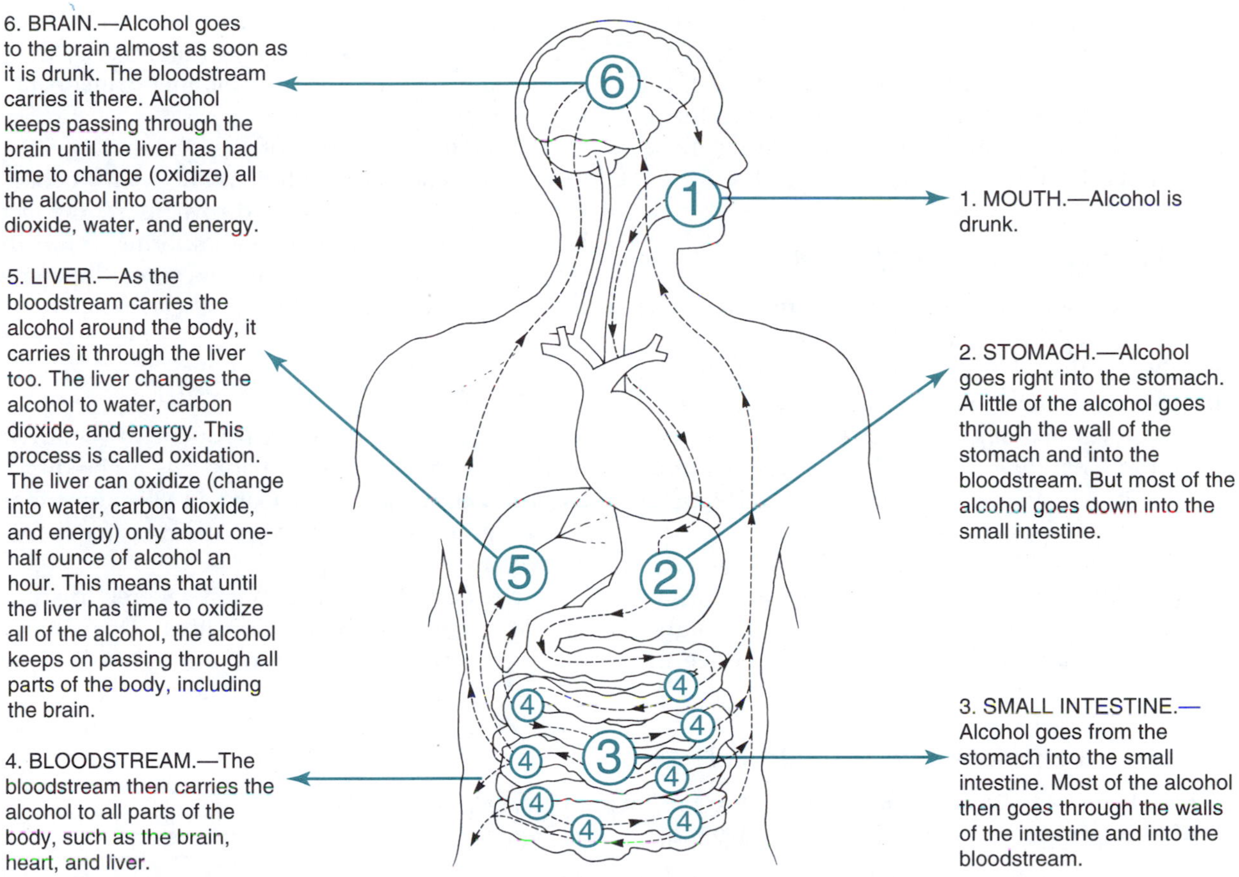

FIGURE 11.2 Alcohol Absorption Pathway (*Source:* National Institute on Alcohol Abuse and Alcoholism, *Alcohol Health and Research World* (Washington, DC: U.S. Department of Health and Human Services, 1988)

drink heavily have a higher rate of spontaneous abortion. Infants born to drinking mothers have a high probability of being afflicted with fetal alcohol syndrome (FAS). These children may experience facial deformities, growth deficiency, and mental retardation. Thus even a couple of drinks during pregnancy can endanger normal fetal development.

As for the school-aged child, the effect of prenatal exposure on growth is still significant at 6 years (Day & Richardson, 1994). The effect on growth appears to be proportional to the amount of alcohol consumed. Intellectual development is affected even with small amounts of prenatal exposure to alcohol. One study found that seven-year-old children who had been exposed to more than 1 ounce of alcohol a day during pregnancy had a decrement of 7 IQ points compared to children exposed to less than 1 ounce per day (Streissguth et al., 1991). Other problems were fluctuating attentional states, problems with spatial learning and complex problem-solving tasks, and poor experiential learning in short-term recall of complex problems. According to Coles et al. (1991), school achievement scores are related to prenatal alcohol exposure too.

Teachers may find that behavioral problems, including attention deficits and impulsiveness, may be linked to prenatal exposure to alcohol (Brown et al., 1991). And such problems may be evident in children who were exposed to alcohol but do not demonstrate other symptoms of FAS

(Streissguth et al., 1991). A German study, testing FAS children over a period of fourteen years, found that 63 percent suffered from at least one psychiatric syndrome, most often hyperkinetic, emotional, speech, and eating disorders (Brown University, 1994).

Behavioral Effects of Alcohol

As shown in Table 11.2, the behavioral effects of alcohol depend on the BAC. A key point to remember is that the reduction of inhibitions and impaired judgment may encourage youth to engage in additional high-risk behaviors. And as discussed in Chapter 1, alcohol is related to lowered academic achievement, delinquency, early pregnancy, and dropping out of school.

Both physical and psychological tolerance to alcohol can be acquired through regular use. The nervous system adapts over time so that higher and higher amounts are required to produce the same effects. While most adults understand that behavioral effects are strongly influenced by their mental and emotional states, younger drinkers fail to grasp this concept.

Alcoholism is a state of physical and psychological addiction to alcohol. While many people picture the alcoholic as a skid-row figure, the fact is that the majority of those suffering from alcoholism are employed, family-centered people leading relatively normal lives otherwise.

Alcoholism and the Family

Alcoholism occurs more frequently in children of alcoholics, and thus probably has a hereditary basis (Cotton, 1979; McCord, 1988). In other words, teachers should recognize this as a risk factor when working with students.

As expected, alcoholism can severely disrupt marriage and family relationships. One family member's drinking problem can cause all the

Table 11.2 **Behavioral Effects of Alcohol**

Number of Drinks	Ounces of Alcohol	BAC (g/100 ml)	Approximate Time for Removal	Effects
1 beer, glass of wine, or mixed drink	½	0.02	1 hour	Feeling relaxed or loosened up
2½ beers, glasses of wine, or mixed drinks	1¼	0.05	2½ hours	Feeling high; decrease in inhibitions; increase in confidence; judgment impaired
5 beers, glasses of wine, or mixed drinks	2½	0.10	5 hours	Memory impaired; muscular coordination reduced; slurred speech; euphoric or sad feelings
10 beers, glasses of wine, or mixed drinks	5	0.20	10 hours	Slowed reflexes; erratic changes in feelings
15 beers, glasses of wine, or mixed drinks	7½	0.30	15–16 hours	Stuporous, complete loss of coordination; little sensation
20 beers, glasses of wine, or mixed drinks	10	0.40	20 hours	May become comatose; breathing may cease
25–30 beers, glasses of wine, or mixed drinks	15–20	0.50	26 hours	Fatal amount for most people

other family members mental and emotional suffering, and sometimes financial hardship. Family members try to cope with the problem in many ways. Unfortunately, the children of alcoholics typically feel shame, because they either believe they are the cause of the problem or that they should be able to get their parent to stop drinking. Again, living in such a family serves as a health risk factor even when the student does not drink.

Family members of alcoholics may attend Alanon, an organization that helps spouses, families, and friends of alcoholics. Alateen is a similar organization that helps children of alcoholics. When necessary, help should be sought.

Conclusions about Alcohol

Like tobacco, alcohol is a gateway drug for young students. With two-thirds of youngsters reporting having tried alcohol by grade 8 and more than a quarter stating they have been drunk at least once, the need for prevention and early intervention is obvious. Teachers need to know the risk factors and recognize the symptoms of alcohol use and abuse so that appropriate interventions may be carried out.

Volatile Drugs: Inhalants

This is the only category of drugs of which use is substantially higher in grade 8 than in grades 10 or 12 (Johnston et al., 1994). Most if not all of these chemicals are not regulated like other drugs of abuse, so they are readily available to children. There is no regulation because inhalants—glue, paint thinner, aerosols from paints, some solvents, nail polish remover, cookware coating agents, lighter and cleaning fluids, and gasoline—are generally never intended for human consumption.

Volatile drugs enter the body through the lungs. Initially nausea, coughing, and sneezing result. Continued use, however, can produce an anesthetic effect. Low dosages often bring about mild stimulation, followed by disorientation, dizziness, and hallucinations. Loss of control and

Chemical inhalants are the most widely used class of illicit drugs among eighth graders. The main factors contributing to their popularity include availability and peer pressure.

lack of coordination are common too. Violent behavior may occur at higher doses, and eventually the user may lose consciousness.

The principal cause of death from inhalant exposure is heart arrhythmia (Jaffe, 1990). If a child breathes in the vapors from a plastic bag to get maximum effect, hypoxia may occur, causing brain damage or death. Other toxic consequences include damage to the kidneys, brain, heart muscle, and peripheral nerves.

In the field of medicine, the only forms of inhalants with abuse potential are the anesthetics. The most readily available, and therefore the most abused, anesthetic gas is nitrous oxide. It is used for minor outpatient procedures by both dentists and physicians.

Marijuana

Marijuana has been the object of research and controversy for many years. In 1753, it was classified as *Cannabis sativa* by Carolus Linnaeus, a Swedish botanist. *Cannabis* comes from the Greek word for hemp and it applies to marijuana because the woody fibers of the stem produce a fiber that can be made into cloth and rope.

The primary mind-altering ingredient in marijuana is delta-9-tetrahydrocannabinol, or THC. This psychoactive substance is largely located in the flowering tops and upper leaves of the female plant. More specifically, THC is found in the resin, and the potency of the resin varies according to which part of the plant is consumed. Lower leaves and stems have less resin (and therefore THC) than the upper leaves and flowers.

One of the most potent types of marijuana is called *sinsemilla,* meaning without seeds. It is produced when male plants are eradicated from the growing field so that they cannot pollinate the female plants. As a result, the potency of the female plants increases dramatically. Cannabis native to the United States generally has a lower concentration of THC than that grown in Jamaica, Colombia, and Mexico.

Hashish is a cannabis derivative containing the purest form of resin. This form is used primarily outside the United States. Another form, ganja, comes from the dried tops of female plants and is used in India.

The Marijuana Pathway

When taken into the lungs, THC quickly leaves the blood to enter the tissues. It can remain in the body fat for long periods of time. For example, five days after a single injection, 20 percent of the THC remains stored and 20 percent of THC metabolites remain in the blood. Complete elimination of a single dose can take up to 30 days, thereby making it detectable via a blood test for days or even weeks after the last marijuana cigarette.

Smoking marijuana makes it much more potent than either intravenous injection or oral ingestion. By smoking, the THC can reach the brain in about fourteen seconds. The effects of smoking vary according to user expectations, the social setting, and prior experience (Jaffe, 1990). In addition to mood alteration, coordination, memory, and self-perception may be affected. High exposure may cause hallucinations, delusions, and paranoia.

Cannabis can increase heart rate, the degree of which is correlated to the amount of THC consumed. It may cause reddening of the eyes too. On occasion, marijuana may act like an aphrodisiac by lowering inhibitions. High doses over time, however, are linked to decreased sex drive, possibly due to lowered levels of testosterone. Although data on carcinogenic effects are mixed, evidence suggests that many twenty-year-old smokers of both hashish and tobacco have lung damage comparable to that of heavy tobacco smokers over forty years (Jones, 1980; Hollister, 1986). Some studies (e.g. Jones, 1980), but not all, have found that the immune system is compromised by smoking marijuana. Specifically, marijuana may interfere with T-lymphocyte function.

Tolerance to some effects builds over time so that larger doses are needed to bring about the same effects. Mild physical dependence occurs in some people, as evidenced by withdrawal symptoms—sleep disturbances, irritability, anorexia, weight loss, sweating, and gastrointestinal upset. Psychological dependence is seen in heavy users (Hollister, 1986).

Behavioral Effects of Marijuana

Low to moderate doses bring on a state of relaxation and mild euphoria for most users. This feeling lasts two to three hours if one "joint" is smoked. Altered perception of time and space may occur, as well as impaired memory of recent events and impaired physical coordination. Overall, little danger is encountered unless the user is in an unfamiliar environment or attempts an activity requiring quick judgment, reflexes, and coordination—driving a car, operating machinery, and similar operations.

Large doses can cause paranoia, and extreme reactions can take place if marijuana has been treated with other drugs such as LSD, PCP, and the like. In regard to chronic effects, there is very little reliable evidence. Nonetheless, the amotivational syndrome has been linked with chronic usage. In other words, people who are high or stoned lack the desire to perform hard work. Students who are chronic users tend to have lower grades, a higher number of absences, and a higher dropout rate. Some of this may be the influence of the peer group too.

Nonprescription Drugs

Nonprescription or over-the-counter (OTC) drugs are substances that may be purchased and used without supervision of a physician. It is important to understand what they can and cannot do if misuse and harm are to be prevented. While these products are generally administered by parents to their children, it is important for children to comprehend the inherent dangers if they are abused. Listed below are some facts:

- Excessive use of some OTC medications (e.g., nasal sprays) can cause physical dependence, tolerance, and withdrawal symptoms.
- OTC cold medications do not alter the course of the common cold but may relieve symptoms such as nasal congestion and coughing.
- OTC diet aids have little value.
- Frequent use of OTC antacids can be habit-forming.

Many children do not believe that recreational drug use is harmful. Teaching them about the actual effects of their bodies may help students to make wise decisions regrading the role of drugs in their own lives.

- Some external analgesics for muscle aches smell like candy and may be mistaken for such by small children.
- OTC drugs can interact with prescription drugs in a dangerous, sometimes lethal, manner.
- Antihistamines reduce congestion caused by allergies but are ineffective for virus-induced colds.
- Frequent use of decongestant nasal sprays can cause rebound congestion due to tissue dependence. That is, nasal passages become even more congested than usual when the product is discontinued.
- In general, stay-awake or energy-promoting OTC stimulants contain high doses of caffeine, which can lead to a false sense of alertness, which in turn may bring about vehicle accidents or dependence among students who use them regularly.

To reduce problems with OTC drugs, some rules for use are:

1. Know what you are taking. What is the principal ingredient?
2. Know the effects. What is the desired effect and possible undesired effects?
3. Read and follow the warnings to protect yourself and/or others.
4. Do not use any product for more than a week or two. Consult a health professional if symptoms persist.
5. Be very, very careful if you are taking a prescription product at the same time. You may want to consult a health professional.
6. Ask your pharmacist if you need help.
7. Only take something if you really need it. OTCs are drugs.

Progressive Drugs: Beyond the Gateway

Elementary and middle-school students are more likely to be involved with gateway drugs than with those that follow. Consequently, these "other" drugs are addressed only briefly. (See again Table 11.1 for further information on these drugs.)

Depressants

Depressants are a diverse group of drugs that reduce central nervous system (CNS) activity and diminish alertness. Classification often comes from the degree of effect. Drugs causing a mild depression of the CNS are called *sedatives*. They are used to relieve anxiety, fear, and apprehension. Those that produce sleep are called *hypnotics*.

Tolerance develops when using depressant drugs. In fact, tolerance to one kind of depressant drug can cause tolerance to other kinds of depressants. As mentioned above, this effect is termed *cross-tolerance*. While physical dependence can occur, it is a relatively slow process.

Stimulants

Stimulants are frequently divided into major and minor categories. The major stimulants cause increased alertness, excitation, and euphoria. These so-called *uppers* include amphetamines, cocaine, and crack cocaine. Ritalin is a type of amphetamine used to treat children with attention deficit disorder (ADD). Though a stimulant, it has a paradoxical calming effect on children with hyperkinesis. Tolerance can develop for the major stimulants, as can psychological dependence. The jury is still out in regard to physical dependence, but it appears likely with long-term use.

Minor stimulants are used widely in the United States because of the mild lift in mood they give the user. The most popular ones are the caffeinelike drugs (xanthines). Many beverages contain caffeine (from highest to lowest amounts): brewed coffee, instant coffee, decaffeinated coffee, tea, cocoa, Coca-Cola, Pepsi-Cola, and a chocolate bar (Witter et al., 1992). A tolerance can develop to the xanthines so that increased consumption is required to maintain effects. As to be expected, the severity of psychological dependence on caffeine is relatively minor compared to that of the major stimulants. Physical dependence on caffeine, if it occurs, is less than that from the major stimulants.

Crack Cocaine and Later Learning

Crack is a special type of free-based cocaine. It is quite inexpensive and therefore available to the younger population. The low cost, combined with the fact that it is much less dangerous to smoke than typical free-basing, has increased use among adolescents. Powdered cocaine hydrochloride, sodium bicarbonate, and water are mixed together to form a paste. The dried substance is hard, hence the street name *rocks,* and can be 90 percent pure cocaine. It is generally smoked in a glass water pipe, with the fumes being absorbed into the lungs. An intense rush can occur in as little as ten seconds, and the high lasts about three to five minutes. This is followed by depression, which may have ten- to forty-minute duration. Crack cocaine has great potential for addiction—at least as great as free-based cocaine.

Infants can be exposed to crack cocaine either prenatally or neonatally through passive inhalation of second-hand smoke (Randall, 1992; Batlle and Wilcox, 1993). Whether the effects of such exposure are lasting is debatable. Currently, there is no scientific evidence to support any particular stance. The primary finding thus far is that early intervention with "crack kids" may produce excellent benefits and that the usual gloomy prognosis may be inaccurate.

Hallucinogens

Hallucinogens are drugs that can bring about psychedelic effects. That is, they are a group of substances that alter perception, thought, and feeling in a fashion that does not normally occur. Synthetic products, such as lysergic acid diethylamide (LSD), are hallucinogenic, as are naturally occuring plants, such as the *Psilocybe mexicana* mushroom and the peyote cactus.

While this group of drugs does not appear to bring about physical dependence, there are some definite hazards to them. The user may experience loss of control, paranoia, and loss of identity and personal boundaries. A "bad trip" can have a profound influence on the user. Bad trips are most likely to occur when a user takes the drug in a threatening, hostile environment rather than a warm, comfortable one. And flashbacks can occur with LSD usage so that, without warning, the user may experience unexpected visual and time distortions that last a few minutes to several hours. Flashbacks can happen months to years after use of LSD.

Narcotics

Narcotic analgesics are one of the most commonly prescribed pain relievers today. While these products are excellent at reducing pain, there is risk in their usage. There is great potential for abuse, tolerance, and physical dependence. Opioid narcotic analgesics are derivatives of the opium plant and include heroin, morphine, and codeine.

Morphine is about ten times as strong as opium and is used therapeutically in medicine. Codeine is frequently combined with acetaminophen (e.g., Tylenol with Codeine) to reduce pain. Codeine is also used in cough preparations to suppress the cough reflex.

Heroin is not approved for any medical use and is the most likely opioid narcotic to be abused. It is more addictive than the other narcotics because of the rapid intense feeling of euphoria it produces. Although heroin may be sniffed, smoked, and injected just under the skin or into a muscle, addicts usually "mainline" the drug. In this way, the drug goes directly into the bloodstream, bypassing all body-protection devices. Needle-sharing is common among addicts and has contributed to the incidence of HIV infection.

Withdrawal symptoms from heroin can be devastating if the individual has been a long-time user. The severity depends on the purity and strength of the heroin, too, as well as the personality of the user.

Designer Drugs: The Imitators

According to Henderson (1988), designer drugs are:

- Exclusively drugs of abuse
- Synthesized from common chemicals
- Initially exempt from control by the Drug Enforcement Administration because of their novel chemical structures

- Marketed on the street with attractive, exotic names

Designer drugs are also called *lookalikes*. Designer amphetamines have been quite common over the years, with some of them causing a hallucinogenic effect too. Methylenedioxymethamphetamine (MMDA or ecstasy) and methylendioxyamphetamine (MDA) are examples of designer drugs having both amphetamine and hallucinogenic properties. Although designer drugs were banned in 1986, many still circulate among youth. These drugs can be very dangerous, even cause death, as "street chemists" do not worry about contamination.

Implications for Elementary and Middle-School Teachers

Summary Issues

The principal issues in this chapter are:

1. During the past few years, more and more young students are of the belief that drug use is probably not all that harmful. However, drug use is associated with early sexual behavior, lowered academic performance, truancy, delinquency, teen pregnancy, and conduct disorders.
2. Evidence shows that drug use among grade 8 students is on the rise.
3. Use of gateway drugs—tobacco, alcohol, inhalants—is common among eighth graders and is often initiated by the end of grade 6.
4. In grades K–8, there are no apparent gender differences in drug use and abuse.
5. Certain telltale signs can be used by teachers to identify students who may be experiencing drug problems.
6. The two general classifications of drugs are prescription and over-the-counter drugs.
7. Commonly abused psychoactive drugs include organic solvents, depressants, Cannabis, stimulants, hallucinogens, and narcotics.
8. There are several environmental and personal factors that place students at greater than usual risk of using drugs. Some of the major influences are peer pressure, including friends, TV, and music videos; self-esteem; curiosity; media and modeling; and alienation from peers, family, teachers, and/or society in general.
9. The effect of drugs on the body varies with administration, distribution, dosage, frequency, tolerance, and expectation.
10. The most familiar chemical constituents of tobacco are nicotine and tar. Nicotine first acts like a stimulant and then a depressant.
11. SIDS and other health problems in infants are related to mothers (or fathers) who smoked during pregnancy. Drinking during pregnancy can produce the fetal alcohol syndrome. It is best not to use any drugs when pregnant.
12. Environmental tobacco smoke has many detrimental effects on children, increasing incidence of lower-respiratory infections, middle-ear infections, and hospitalizations.
13. Smokeless tobacco is not a safe alternative to smoking tobacco as there are several health problems associated with this product.
14. Alcohol, overall, appears to be the drug of choice for many students. Wood (methyl) and rubbing (isopropyl) alcohol are not intended for internal consumption.
15. Blood alcohol content (BAC) varies with gender, body size, and body composition. Behavioral effects depend on the BAC. Physical and psychological tolerance and dependence to alcohol occurs over time. Alcoholism is an addiction to ethanol.
16. Children living in the home of an alcoholic(s) may require intervention.
17. Inhalants are used by more students in the eighth grade than in any other grade K–12.
18. The primary psychoactive substance in marijuana is THC. The amount of THC consumed depends upon the part of the plant used and the mode of administration.
19. Adverse physical and behavioral effects from marijuana are uncommon. Nonetheless, more research is required.
20. Elementary and middle-school students involved with gateway drugs are more likely

to move onto depressants, stimulants, hallucinogens, and the like.

Teacher Ramifications

In regard to drug use and abuse, a teacher should:

1. Monitor students for possible drug use by using already-established profiles
2. Serve as a role model to students concerning drug usage
3. Comprehend the need for drug education to deter the rising trend in drug use among students
4. Provide educational opportunities to students that develop cognitive, affective, and practice skills in regard to drug use
5. Support the schools' role in helping the nation reach the objectives set forth in *Healthy Children 2000.* Specifically, the objectives related to schools regarding drugs are:
   - #3.10. Establish tobacco-free environments and include tobacco-use prevention in the curricula of all elementary, middle, and secondary schools, preferably as part of quality school health education.
   - #4.13. Provide to children in all school districts and private schools primary and secondary school educational programs on alcohol and other drugs, preferably as part of quality school health education.
   - #3.11. Increase to at least 75 percent the proportion of worksites (i.e., schools) with a formal smoking policy that prohibits or severely restricts smoking at the site.
   - #4.14. Extend adoption of alcohol and drug policies for the work environment to at least 60 percent of worksites with fifty or more employees.
   - #8.9. Increase to at least 75 percent the proportion of people aged ten and older who have discussed issues related to nutrition, physical activity, sexual behavior, tobacco, alcohol, other drugs, or safety with family members on at least one occasion during the preceding month.

SECTION III

Teaching Strategies for Alcohol, Tobacco, and Other Drugs

The strategies in this section are divided into grade K–4, 5–6, and 7–8 levels. In addition to strategies that can be used in the classroom, home activities are included. A home activity is designed for student-parent interaction. It is a way to engage the home in school-student learning, and parents can sign a slip of paper to confirm that an activity was completed. Evaluation of all strategies through the use of the National Health Education Standards and performance indicators is indicated. Teachers may also choose to write corresponding learning assessments.

K–4 Level

Strategy One

Objective: Students will recognize the dangers of riding in a vehicle with a drunk driver.

Activity: Collect newspaper articles about motor vehicle accidents involving drivers under the influence of alcohol or drugs. (Note: Be aware that some students may be acquainted with or related to victims of drunk drivers.) Discuss how alcohol and drugs affect a driver's ability. Have students brainstorm ways they can avoid riding with a driver under the influence of alcohol or other drugs.

Integration: Social Studies, Science

Related Health Content Areas: Family life, growth and development, mental-emotional health, diseases

Health Education Standards and Performance Indicators: 3(3,6); 5(2,3,4,6)

Strategy Two

Objective: Students will be able to identify substances that are considered drugs.

Activity: Have students work cooperatively in pairs or threes to brainstorm different items that they think are drugs. This should include such things as medicines, tobacco, alcohol, some herbs, and so forth.

In a discussion format, ask students to give their ideas. The teacher should write the ideas on the board in two groups: those that are considered helpful and those that are considered not helpful. Discuss the importance of using only the drugs that are considered helpful, and then only as directed.

Integration: Science, Math

Related Health Content Areas: Growth and development, human body, emotional well-being

Health Education Standards and Performance Indicators: 3(1,3); 5(6)

5–6 Level

Strategy One

Objective: Students will be able to describe the different ways drugs affect the body.

Activity: In a group, have students discuss the effects of depressant drugs, that is, ways in which certain drugs can slow down or depress the body's systems:

- Destroy vitamins A, B_6, C, and E, making you feel depressed and tired
- Make nerves sluggish
- Cause you to lose your balance
- Impair ability to see or hear clearly
- Slow down heart rate
- Slow down breathing
- Lower blood pressure
- Make you feel sleepy

Then have students discuss the effects of stimulant drugs as they did with depressant drugs. Students may also complete the crossword puzzle in Figure 11.3 to help learn some of the symptoms of drug use.

Integration: Science, Language Arts

Related Health Content Areas: Growth and development, human body, emotional well-being

Health Education Standard and Performance Indicators: 1(1,2,3)

Strategy Two

Objective: Students will be able to describe how chemicals from cigarettes may accumulate in lung tissue.

Activity: Students and the teacher are to construct and use a "smoking machine" (see directions below). Have students take turns pumping the machine. (Note: Make sure students are not asthmatic or allergic to cigarette smoke prior to the demonstration.) Ask students what they observe as more and more smoke is pumped. What is happening to the water? Ask students what they think this would do to a person's lungs. Discuss the meaning of the words *second-hand* or *side stream smoke.* Ask students to describe how they have felt when they have been around heavy smokers.

Directions

Numerous smoking machines are sold commercially. The two most popular ones are Nicotina and Smoking Sam. The kind of smoking machine used should be relevant to the purpose of the demonstration or experiment. Nicotina is excellent for demonstrating that tar is part of cigarette smoke and that it is inhaled. Smoking Sam does much the same thing,

A. ***Depressants—ACROSS***

1. Mixed up
2. When one slides one's words together, one talks with slurred __________.
3. Sleepiness
4. Walks crookedly
5. Unable to concentrate
6. Too much alcohol will make one __________.
7. Unable to stand without swaying (two words; first word is a contraction)

B. ***Stimulants—DOWN***

8. Usually when one gets "butterflies" in one's stomach, it is because one is __________.
9. Craving a drink of water
10. Uneasy
11. Perspire
12. Talky
13. When the dots in the middle of the eyes get big, one has ________. (two words)

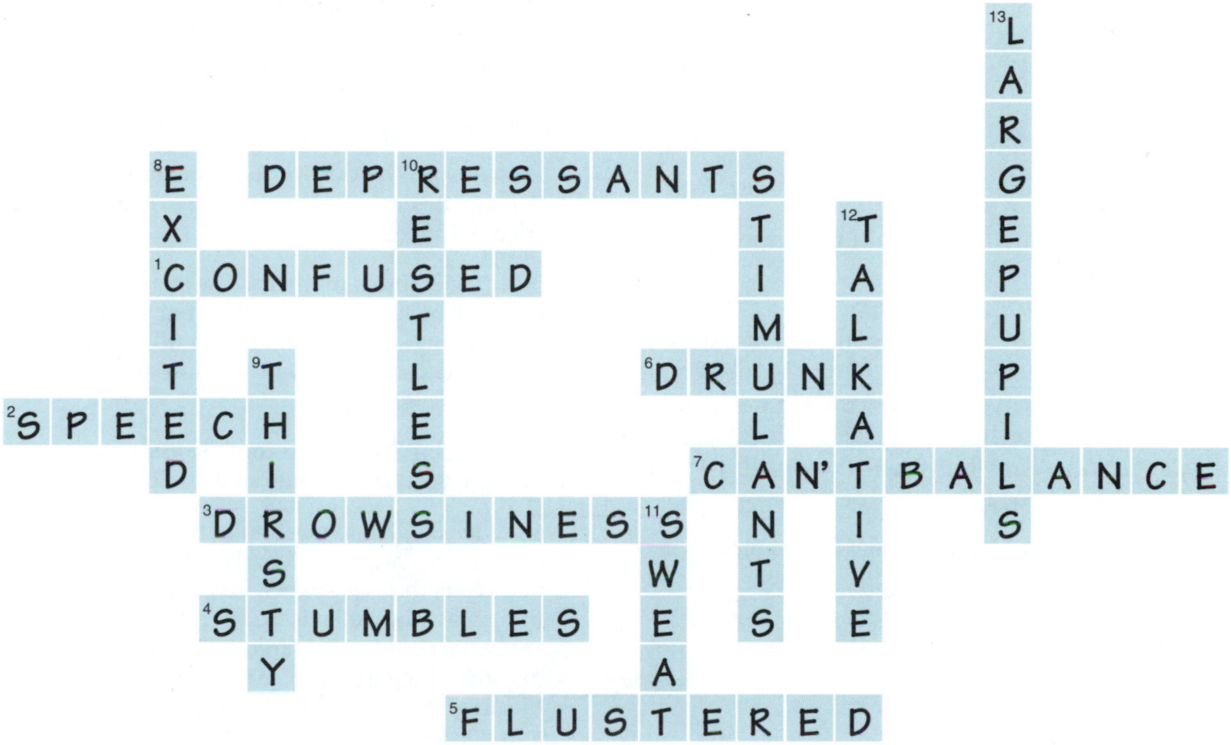

FIGURE 11.3 Crossword Puzzle about Substance Abuse

except that the two glass jars, filled with white angel hair, simulate human lungs. When these commercial machines are not available, the amount of tar in one or more cigarettes may be demonstrated by collecting tar on cotton pellets, angel hair, or filter paper placed in the tubing of a teacher-made machine. Tar can also be observed as a residue on the tubing and containers and as a discoloration of water through which cigarette smoke has been filtered. Smoking machines may be adapted to a variety of demonstrations. The following machine may be constructed for classroom demonstrations and experiments.

Equipment: A large gallon jar with a two-hole stopper, cigarettes, delivery tubes (glass), cigarette holder, vacuum pump.

Procedure: Assemble cigarette tar–separating apparatus as shown in Figure 11.4. Fill the gallon jar half full of water. Place a cigarette in intake and light. Pump vacuum pump so as to draw

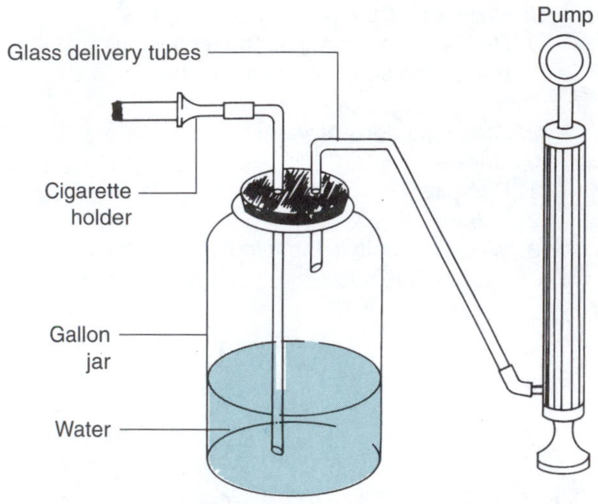

FIGURE 11.4 How to Design a Classroom Smoking Machine

smoke from cigarette into gallon jar and water, and continue until the cigarette is burned completely. Replace with additional cigarettes until tars can be seen in the water. Examine the color of the water; smell and taste the liquid.

Integration: Science

Related Health Content Areas: Emotional well-being, human body

Health Education Standards and Performance Indicators: 1(3,7); 3(3)

Strategy Three

Objective: Students will be able to illustrate the organs affected by various drugs using a diagram.

Activity: Provide students with diagrams of the human body. Each student is to use information previously acquired in class to diagram how selected drugs move through the body. Color-coding may be used to denote the organs that are affected. Students should then explain how each drug affects those organ systems.

Integration: Science

Related Health Content Areas: Human body, emotional well-being

Health Education Standard and Performance Indicators: 1(1); 6(3)

7–8 Level

Strategy One

Objective: Students will be able to state why people often take up smoking.

Activity: Give students the following situations and ask them to role-play them:

Situation 1: Three students are standing in a corner talking. A fourth student is off by him- or herself, but decides to join the others. When the student walks over to the group, he or she sees that they are smoking, and decides to join them.

Discussion: Why do you think the fourth student decided to smoke? Do you have to smoke if your friends smoke?

Situation 2: Jose's mother is furious with him because he never obeys her. He is fed up with hearing her nag and scream at him all the time. He goes off where she won't see him and smokes a couple of cigarettes.

Discussion: Why do you think Jose was smoking? What else could Jose have done to release his anger?

Situation 3: Dad comes home from work and sits down in his favorite chair. He takes off his shoes and reads the newspaper. His daughter sits near him, watching television. While reading, Dad smokes a couple of cigarettes. Then he gets up to get something to drink, leaving another cigarette burning in the ashtray. His daughter goes over and takes a few drags from it.

Discussion: Why was the father smoking? Why might the daughter have sneaked a few puffs? Does smoking mean that you are grown up?

Integration: Science

Related Health Content Areas: Emotional well-being, growth and development, families and relationships

Health Education Standards and Performance Indicators: 1(3,7); 3(3)

Strategy Two

Objective: Students will be able to identify drinks that contain alcohol and identify behaviors common to people who have had too much to drink.

Activity: Have students work with one or two partners to come up with a list of different drinks that they know have alcohol in them. Have each small group provide an example, and write it on the board. Discuss how alcohol can be drunk straight or added to any number of other drinks. You may also discuss the myth that some alcoholic drinks (e.g., whiskey, vodka, gin, etc.) are stronger than others (beer, wine).

After completion of the above, have students again work with their partners to think of some examples of how they believe drunk people act. (Be aware that some students may be speaking from personal experience or experience with family members.) Have students volunteer to write examples on the board. Discuss how alcohol can affect the way our bodies function.

Integration: Science, Social Studies, Language Arts

Related Health Content Areas: Violence, safety, families and relationships, emotional well-being

Health Education Standards and Performance Indicators: 1(3,4,6); 3(1,3)

Home Activities

Strategy One

Objective: Students will identify and assess drugs that are in the home.

Activity: Have students and their parents make a list of the drugs in the home. Next to each drug, they are to indicate its use and expiration date. Be sure to have students look in medicine cabinets. The more obvious drugs, such as tobacco and alcohol, should be included. Students can discuss the use of the drugs with their parents and, in particular, share their feelings about these drugs.

Integration: Science, Social Studies

Related Health Content Areas: Family life

Health Education Standards and Performance Indicators: 3,7 (Performance indicators vary by grade level.)

Strategy Two

Objective: Students will demonstrate how to handle an alcohol-related emergency.

Activity: Problem-based learning activity (see Chapter 4) as follows: Keisha is to go over to her neighbor's house after school. Her mother will pick her up there after she returns from a dental appointment. When Keisha gets to Mrs. Bowman's house, she finds her passed out in front of the television with a liquor bottle sitting on the table next to her chair.

- What is Keisha's problem in this vignette?
- What options does she have?
- Is there other information that she could use to help her make a decision?
- What is the best decision for Keisha?
- How can she evaluate her decision?
- How does the decision Keisha makes relate to her maturity?

Integration: Social Studies, Science

Related Health Content Areas: Emotional well-being, safety, families and relationships

Health Education Standards: 2,7

References

Advisory Committee to the Surgeon General. *Health Consequences of Using Smokeless Tobacco.* U.S. Department of Health and Human Services, Bethesda, MD, 1986.

Batlle, M.A., & Wilcox, W.D. Pulmonary edema in an infant following passive inhalation of free-based "crack" cocaine, *Clinical Pediatrics* 32(1993): 105–106.

Brown, R., Smith, I., Platzman, K., Erickson, S., & Falek, A. Effects of prenatal alcohol exposure at school age, II: Attention and behavior, *Neurotoxicology and Teratology* 13(1991):369–376.

Brown University. Fetal alcohol syndrome portends grim future for affected children, *Brown University Child and Adolescent Behavior Letter* 10(1995):8.

Carnegie Foundation Council on Adolescent Development. *Turning Points: Preparing American Youth for the 21st Century.* Washington, DC, 1989.

Coles, C., Brown, R., Smith, I., Platzman, K., Siverstein, J., Erickson, S., & Falek, A. Effects of prenatal alcohol exposure at school age, I: Physical and cognitive development, *Neurotoxicology and Teratology* 13(1991):357–367.

Cotton, N.S. The familial evidence of alcoholism: A review, *Journal of Studies on Alcohol* 40(1979):89–116.

Day, N.L., & Richardson, G.A. Comparative teratogenicity of alcohol and other drugs: Prenatal exposure to alcohol or other drugs can impair physical, intellectual, and behavioral development, *Alcohol Health and Research World* (Special issue) 18(1994):42–49.

Fischer, P.M., & Schwartz, M.P. Brand logo recognition by children aged 3 to 6 years, *Journal of the American Medical Association* 266(1991):3145–3148.

Glantz, S. *Tobacco, Biology, and Politics.* Health EDCO, Waco, TX, 1992.

Glantz, S., & Parmley, W. Passive smoking and heart disease: Epidemiology, physiology, and biochemistry, *Circulation* (1991)83:1–12.

Hawkins, J.D., Lishner, D.M., & Catalano, R.F. Childhood predictors of adolescent substance abuse. In C.L. Jones and R.J. Battjes, eds., *Etiology of Drug Abuse: Implications for Prevention,* U.S. Department of Health and Human Services, Washington, DC, 1985.

Henderson, G. Designer drugs: Past history and future prospects, *Journal of Forensic Sciences* 33(1988): 569–575.

Hollister, L.E. Health aspects of Cannabis, *Pharmacological Reviews* 38(1986):39–42.

Jaffe, J.H. Drug addiction and drug abuse. In A. Gilman, T. Rall, A. Nies, & P. Taylor, eds., *Pharmacological Basis of Therapeutics* 8th ed. Pergamon Press, New York, 1990.

Jones, B.M., & Jones M.K. Women and alcohol: Intoxication, metabolism, and the menstrual cycle. In M. Greenblatt and M.A. Schuckit, eds., *Alcoholism Problems in Women and Children. Grune & Stratton, New York, 1976.*

Jones R.T. Human effects: An overview, *Marijuana Research Findings* (NIDA Research Monograph No. 31), NIDA, Washington, DC, 1980.

Johnston, L.D., O'Malley, P.M., & Bachman, J. *Monitoring the Future Study, 1975–1993* (USDHHS, NIH Publication No. 94-3809), National Institute on Drug Abuse, Washington, DC, 1994.

Koop, C.E. Smoking: Everything you and your family need to know (video). Home Box Office Productions, Atlanta, 1989.

Koop, C.E. *Memoirs of America's Family Doctor.* Random House, New York, 1991.

L.A.W. Publications. *Let's All Work to Fight Drug Abuse.* C & L Publishing, Addison, TX, 1985.

Matza, N., & Loya, R. Tobacco-use prevention. In P. Cortese and K. Middleton, eds., *The Comprehensive School Health Challenge.* ETR Associates, Santa Cruz, CA, 1994.

McDermott, R.J., & Marty, P.J. Dipping and chewing behavior among university students: Prevalence and patterns of use, *Journal of School Health* 46(1986):175–179.

McCord, J. Identifying developmental paradigms leading to alcoholism, *Journal of Studies on Alcohol* 49(1988):357–362.

National Commission on Drug-Free Schools.*Toward a Drug-Free-Generation: A Nation's Responsibility.* Washington, DC, 1990.

National Institute on Drug Abuse. *Monitoring the Future Study.* Institute for Social Research, Ann Arbor, MI, 1990.

Randall, T. Infants, children test positive for cocaine after exposure to second-hand crack smoke, *Journal of the American Medical Association* 267(1992): 1044–1046.

Streissguth, A., Barr, H., & Sampson, P. Moderate prenatal alcohol exposure: Effects on child IQ and learning problems age 7 1/2 years, *Alcoholism: Clinical and Experimental Research* 14(1990): 662–669.

Streissguth, A., Aase J.J., Clarren, S., Randels, S., LaDue, R., & Smith, D. Fetal alcohol syndrome in adolescents and adults, *Journal of the American Medical Association* 265(1991):1961–1967.

Surgeon General of the United States. *Report on Smoking and Health.* U.S. Government Printing Office, Washington, DC, 1964.

Sykes, G.M., & Matza, D. Techniques of neutralization, *American Sociological Review* 22(1975): 664–670.

U.S. Department of Health and Human Services. The health consequences of involuntary smoking: A report of the Surgeon General (Pub. no. (CDC) 87–8398), Washington, DC, 1986.

U.S. Environmental Protection Agency. Respiratory health effects of passive smoking: Lung cancer and other disorders (EPA/600/6–90/006F) Washington, DC, 1992.

Witters, W., Venturelli, P., & Hanson, P. *Drugs and Society.* Jones and Bartlett, Boston, 1992.

Wolfe, R. Smokeless tobacco: The fatal pitch, *Multinational Monitor* (1987):20–21.

12

Family, Relationships, and Sexuality

At the conclusion of this chapter, you should be able to:

- *Explain the role of the family*
- *Compare and contrast the different family structures found in the United States*
- *Distinguish among ways in which parents can encourage healthy child development*
- *Identify characteristics of a healthy relationship*
- *Demonstrate or explain how to communicate in a relationship, including using refusal skills*
- *Synthesize issues surrounding sexual relations*
- *Describe the processes of conception, pregnancy, and childbirth*
- *Discuss the relationship between gender identity and sex roles*
- *Explain the role of homosexuality in a health curriculum*

SECTION I

Health Status, Deficits, and Learning

The family is the central unit of our society. It is also the place where we first learn about relationships and sexuality. All three of these life aspects—family, relationships, and sexuality—tend to impact our ability to perform in the world, including academic performance.

Listed below are some points about family, relationships, and sexuality:

- About 15 percent of families today are headed by women, many of whom are poverty-stricken, thereby placing themselves and their children in high-risk situations. Single-motherhood is often the result of divorce.
- Recent studies indicate that children who live with one parent are at greater risk for twenty problems, ranging from suicide to premature sexual activity, drug use, and school absenteeism, than children from two-parent families.
- A recent survey shows that sexual difficulties rank fourth (after rapid social change, child and spouse abuse, and money) as a major problem facing families.
- A teen sex line sponsored by Planned Parenthood of Toronto finds the most common requests to be for information, counseling, referrals about pregnancy, birth control, relationships, STDs, HIV/AIDS, and normalcy of sexual growth and behavior.
- Research evidence indicates that adolescent pregnancy and child-rearing usually retard an adolescent's achievement and economic independence.
- The greater frequency of poor health outcomes among adolescents who give birth stems from socioeconomic and behavioral factors—low income, low level of education, poor nutrition—rather than inherent medical risks.
- Teens account for almost one-third of all unintended pregnancies, with 75 percent of all teenage pregnancies happening to those who fail to use contraception.
- Most youngsters believe their parents are the most important source of sexuality information, followed by their friends, school coursework, and TV.
- Family support, guidance, and structure have a significant impact on adolescent sexual activity. Adolescents residing with both parents are less permissive about nonmarital sex, followed by those who live with one remarried parent.

- Parental involvement with their adolescent (school, athletics, music, dance) doubles the odds of the adolescent practicing abstinence, compared to those whose parents are not involved.
- U.S. teenagers initiate sexual intercourse at about the same age as do teens in western Europe and Canada; however, U.S. teens are much more likely to become pregnant.

SECTION II

Family, Relationships, and Sexuality Teaching Information

Family Life

Family life in the United States has changed considerably over the years. In the early 1800s, the average size was about six, ten if extended family members were counted. Today we find families to average slightly greater than three in number. Another major change is the tremendous decrease in nuclear families with a corresponding increase in single-parent families. Women head approximately 15 percent of today's families. And more mothers are working outside the home now than in the past. Violence, drugs, and other social-health issues stretch families and family coping skills to the maximum.

Despite these dramatic changes, the family still serves as the basic social unit in our society. Families continue to play a major role in the socialization of children. From the time an infant enters the family, he or she learns social rules, right from wrong, and family values. Through the family, cultural traditions are kept intact. For some, apple pie and the Fourth of July hold great meaning. For others, the celebration of Cinco de Mayo (May 5th) is the highlight of family memories, while the Martin Luther King holiday has great significance for still other families.

Family members, especially during the growing years, are dependent upon one another. That is, family members have a great impact on one another. This impact can be healthy and positive, or dysfunctional and negative. In healthy families, each member has, and accepts, an important role. Parents are to be providers of shelter, food, a safe environment, and love. They are the first teachers each of their children meet and thus have a tremendous responsibility to model and educate in a fashion that engenders healthy growth. They should exemplify sharing, communication, problem-solving, decision-making, and similar skills. Parents have this responsibility 24 hours a day, 7 days a week, 365 days a year. The fact that they go to work, have a multitude of community commitments, and have no time for themselves makes no difference. The younger members of the family count on them. At a very young age, children bear little responsibility. However, as they become older, their responsibility increases proportionately—at least in a healthy family. For example, in the O'Connell family, the mother expects Elizabeth, a third grader, to watch over her younger sister, Emily, when they are outside playing. While Elizabeth may not cherish this task, it is part of her responsibility as a family member.

These same responsibilities take place in many different family structures. The traditional view of the family is a married couple living with their children—the *nuclear family*. But a family structure that is popular today is a married couple without children. And another family form is the *blended family*, in which a father or mother remarries after divorce (or widowhood) and the children from both families live together. *Single-parent families* are common also. They can result from divorce, separation, death of a spouse, or a never-married parent. In some cases of divorce, children end up with two families when a judge awards joint custody. In this case, children may share two homes and two family lives. The *extended family* consists of the nuclear family plus grandparents, uncles, aunts, or other relatives. Although common in the past, this occurs much less today. For some children, homes are temporary because they live in a *foster family,* in which a couple agree to take care of the children for a period of time. Foster children may come from broken homes or homes in which they were abused. Each one of these family structures can be healthy given the right conditions. However, some structures call for more responsibility to be taken by the children than do others.

Family Problems, Coping, and Strong Families

As families evolve, they are likely to experience problems from time to time. The addition of a new baby or an elderly family member can be a mixed blessing for the parents and/or the children. Tragedies such as injury, illness, and of course death can place great stress on family members. The loss of a job by one or both parents creates hardships and may force a family to change their style of living drastically. Almost one half of children living in the United States today live at or below the national poverty level (Center for the Study of Social Policy, 1993). Family problems also arise when children engage in unhealthful behavior such as using drugs or other high-risk behaviors.

One of the principal challenges to families is divorce. With only 40 percent of today's children residing with their birth parents, it should not be surprising that many children worry about their family status (Center for the Study of Social Policy, 1993). Divorce separates parents from children both physically and emotionally, the latter starting when a parent becomes absorbed in the floundering marriage. Children's stress is frequently compounded by their belief that they are not loved or that they caused the divorce. Teachers should watch for feelings of anger, fear, insecurity and depression as well as guilt in such students. All can impede the natural learning process.

More often than not, the mother becomes the custodial parent after divorce. Less than one third of departing fathers make significant monetary contributions to support their families, so most single-parent mothers must work. Most lose out economically. Many must move to more modest housing and give up "luxuries" such as a car. The physical and emotional stresses of working, balancing a budget, running the house, functioning as both father and mother, and being solely in charge can exhaust even the best-organized and most emotionally stable women. Many of them work long hours and become socially isolated as

Pets are often considered important family members. They contribute unconditional friendship and are a good way to teach children to take responsibility for others' needs.

well. Again, teachers need to have an understanding of these conditions so that their demands on such students and their parent do not contribute to an already overstressed family. Some children require help from a school counselor or psychologist. As time goes on, however, single-parenting may become easier as adjustments are made.

There are several things divorcing and divorced parents can do to help tensions subside and bring children back to a sense of well-being:

- Assure each child that the break-up was not his or her fault.
- Assure each child that he or she is still loved.
- Talk with each child about anger, fear, guilt, and depression.
- Be honest about your own feelings.
- Be honest about the financial situation.
- Do not tear down the reputation of the absent parent.
- Hide any quarrels with the absent parent.
- Encourage frequent contact with the absent parent (if he or she is emotionally well adjusted enough).
- Discourage fantasies and hopes for reconciliation (unless feasible).
- Discuss and reach agreement with the absent parent on rules of child-rearing and discipline, and keep them consistently.
- Keep consistent schedules for meals, school, bedtime, and the like.
- Look to others (parents, siblings, friends, a competent housekeeper) for support when stressed.
- Seek professional counseling or therapy for self or children if stressed.

Within five years, most children whose parents break up have to learn to adjust to a stepparent (Einstein, 1979). It is hard to make generalizations about how children react to a new adult in the home since each situation is different. However, some jealousy and resentment are common. Blending new families is easier if the stepparent does not try to replace the biological parent, but rather becomes a third (or fourth) parent. Relationships develop slowly and should not be rushed. The stepparent and biological parent should agree on child-rearing and discipline and be consistent, supporting each other when necessary. Although it is normal for one child to warm up to a stepparent before others, showing favoritism should be studiously avoided.

Stepfathers are usually more acceptable to children than are stepmothers, and younger children accept stepparents more easily than do older children (Stapleton & MacCormack, 1981). Initially children may have more behavioral problems in the reconstituted family than in the single-parent family, but over an extended period, remarriage can mitigate the negative effects of the divorce and single-parent experience if the new partner is supportive, caring, and willing to work at becoming a parent. Designing workable relationships between children and stepparents can seem overwhelmingly difficult at times. Teachers need to remember that these can be very stressful times for some children. In addition to getting a "new" parent, "new" grandparents may be in the scene too. While visiting arrangements can be complicated at any time, the holiday season can be especially distressing as a child is passed about from home to home. All family members must work as a team to effectively bring about a positive family atmosphere.

Sometimes families become dysfunctional. In a *dysfunctional* family, patterns of interaction are disjointed or destroyed so that the needs of family members are not met. In such families, the rights of children are frequently ignored as evidenced by physical abuse, sexual abuse, neglect, and other unhealthy behaviors. As a teacher, you should expect to see the effects of child abuse sometime in your career, since more than two million cases of child abuse are reported to local and state authorities each year (*Healthy Children 2000,* 1992). (Chapter 13 discusses this and related abuse matters in greater detail.)

Stressful events take their toll even in strong families. However, these families usually meet the challenges in healthy ways. Each member is committed to supporting the family and respecting individual members. This is not to say there are never any family arguments; of course there are. The difference is that strong families develop sound conflict-resolution skills. The following characteristics describe a strong family with good coping abilities (Stinnet & DeFrain, 1985; Neutens, 1994a):

- *Commitment:* To the family and each member
- *Appreciation:* By all members for all family members
- *Communication:* The family has good communication skills and younger members are taught these skills
- *Time:* Much quality time is spent together as a family (and this does not mean watching TV)
- *Spiritual wellness:* Families that cope well or are strong families have a sense of a greater power in life that helps them through good times and bad times; it need not be formal religion per se
- *Coping ability:* In simplistic terms, strong families see "challenges" rather than "problems," and use these challenges as a means for family growth
- *Sharing feelings and concerns:* This is an important part of communication and involves emotional expression
- *Privacy:* Time is given to all family members to do things alone, and when doors are closed, knocking is more appropriate than barging in (unless a parent is worried about a very young child)
- *Decision-making:* As children grow older, parents encourage their involvement in making family decisions. Children learn negotiation skills by working through issues like curfews, dating, and after-school activities.

Communication in Families

Communication among family members, particularly between parents and their children, is of utmost importance for a strong family. This is the forum in which young children learn to communicate outside the family too. As children shift from the early elementary school years to middle and junior high school, they frequently see communication with their parents as a problem. The list following shows how some students perceive their parents regarding communication:

- Don't care
- Don't understand me, my problems, or my friends
- Think my problems are just "kid stuff" and nothing to worry about
- Are good at talking but poor at listening
- Use sarcasm to communicate
- Just give advice based on their own experiences
- Won't talk at all
- Embarrassed about talking when it comes to some things (e.g., sexuality, drugs).

There is no doubt that their perceptions may be right on target in some instances. However, children need to learn that they may have to accept responsibility for initiating communication. Part of their responsibility is to establish a good background or setting for communication. This could include all or any of the following (Neutens, 1994a):

- Every so often, if not daily, ask parents how their day went or how they are feeling. Let them know you would like to learn a little bit about their daily lives.
- Ask for advice, even on some "minor" issues, just to get parents involved and to get them used to working with you. (Of course, early elementary school children must learn not to abuse this tactic by becoming "pests.")
- Spend time with parents, preferably time that enhances communication. Even if it is in front of the TV, talk during the commercials.
- Of course being honest is more than a common courtesy. It is basic to good communication, and children need to learn to communicate honestly. If they fear repercussions, they can express this to their parents prior to disclosure of a fact or feeling.

If the suggestions above are already being carried out but communication still wanes, children can simply tell their parents that they want to talk with them about "talking." Of course the reverse holds true too; that is, parents can talk with their children about talking or communicating with one another. In this type of discussion, the following points may be of value (Neutens, 1994a):

1. Parents should be "askable," in the sense that they appear open to questions and comments.
2. Parents should not be expected to have all the answers, but they should be willing to look them up with their children.
3. Parents and children should understand that questioning values is a way to explore and to understand, not necessarily a means of rejection.
4. Questioning or talking about something does not mean that a child is doing it (e.g., drugs, alcohol, tobacco, sexual behavior).
5. Disagreement on an issue should not engender disrespect.
6. Information from parents to children or vice versa does not mean consent to do something.
7. Some rules can be helpful to ward off "pushy" peers, and a child's input into these rules is critical since they can be used as reasons why they can or cannot do something.
8. Mistakes on both sides will be made, and each side should be forgiving.
9. As children grow and mature, freedom to make their own decisions should be increased.
10. Common sense should prevail.

Family Support in School Transition

The shift from elementary school to middle school or junior high can be a scary time for many students. They no longer have one teacher who knows them well; instead they have many teachers. The personal care and praise for effort received in elementary school might be replaced by performance-based expectations. Their every minute is no longer monitored; they are expected to work more on their own. The sixth grader leaves behind the "big kid" status to become a "little kid" again. From a mental-health standpoint, this is a time when self-esteem can falter as feelings of alienation and vulnerability rise. Of course mental-health issues can be compounded by changes in physical status such as puberty.

Families can provide much-needed support at this time. Steinberg and Levine (1990) suggest that parents should

- Prepare a child by talking about the changes well ahead of time
- Get involved with the school through parent-teacher conferences, committee work, or PTA
- Help the child work independently at home before the transition
- Support the friendships that will carry over from elementary school, keeping contact over the summer months or carpooling together
- Suggest extracurricular activities involving competition only among equal-level peers rather than with students who are a year or two older
- Talk to children about drugs, sexuality, peer groups, and refusal skills so that they will not be caught unprepared when such topics arise
- Roll with some mood changes and fluctuation in grades, at least for awhile.

Of course students should be encouraged to talk with their parents about any problems or fears as well.

Relationships

In the early elementary school years, children generally play with whoever is available. They may happily tell you they have many "best" friends. However, over time cliques develop, and friendships are founded on reasons very dissimilar to those originally used. During the middle and late elementary-school years, students become cognizant that several different groups, cliques, or classifications of students and friends exist—"jocks," "brains," "troublemakers," and so on. Selection of friends is an important issue, to children and to their parents. Teachers can play a significant role in friendship by teaching about it as well as taking it into account in seating arrangements and group assignments.

Finding good friends becomes more complicated as children grow older and make more of an emotional investment in their friendships.

Children need to understand that friendships involve responsibility. Some of the responsibilities to be borne by both people are:

- Respect for the other person
- A willingness to work at the friendship
- Giving a friend the freedom to be him- or herself
- Voluntarily expressing hopes, fears, joys, and sorrows (within limits)
- The desire to be a good listener
- Revealing as much of yourself as a friend has revealed to you; that is, friends stay at about the same level of sharing with one another
- Keeping information confidential
- Trust.

Popularity, Peer Pressure, and High-Risk Behaviors

These issues impact even young children as they watch how to dress, what to say, and of course how to act. The need to fit in is critical during the middle school and junior high years. A child quickly learns he or she is a "somebody" or a "nobody." However, fitting in at all costs can be expensive. While that is obvious to parents, who spend the money on designer clothes, it should be just as obvious in terms of high-risk behaviors. *High-risk behaviors* are those that place a child in greater than usual danger. For example, failure to wear a helmet when riding a bicycle places a child at greater risk of injury than wearing one. Smoking, using drugs, engaging in sexual relations outside of a committed, marital relationship (especially unprotected sexual intercourse) are examples of other high-risk behaviors.

Children need to know that rejection is an unfortunate but inevitable part of life. It can be very disappointing but should not be devastating. In fact, if exclusion from a group occurs because a child will not engage in a high-risk behavior, he or she is actually saying, "My health is more important than belonging to a group that practices high-risk behaviors." Such children need to be shown that their decision, although a painful one, is best for both the short term and the long term.

During the early years, and especially in middle school, students must acquire knowledge and the ability to set limits, communicate effectively, and employ refusal skills. These basic skills are a necessity to help students deal with daily pressures. Remember that peer pressure is not always a negative influence. The point is what kind of peer pressure a child faces. Pressure to behave in a health-enhancing fashion can go a long way in helping a child. Another plus is that parents and peers are not always opposing forces; peers do not always lead children astray. Parents who take an active role in their children's lives are less likely to have their children succumb to pressure that conflicts with family values.

Communication Skills

As with parent-child relationships, friend-friend relationships (including intimate ones) demand strong communication skills. Real communication involves *self-disclosure* in which both people reveal the real self rather than playing a role. Now, we all play roles—student, teacher, parent, friend—but our real self should be central to all these roles. In communicating with friends, dialogue should be open, honest, and continuous (versus sporadic). The depth of self-disclosure between people varies with the degree of friendship. Some "friendships" involve only knowing one another's name. Deeper friendships require that each person reveal more and more of him- or herself. Assuming that this equal sharing is not abused by the friend, we develop trust in him or her, which further deepens the friendship. The by-product of this broad and deep self-disclosure and consequent trust is true intimacy. The latter involves great depths in sharing, although in all relationships there is usually a part of the self that is not shared with others. Eventually, the sharing may be physical in nature as well as verbal.

For sound communication, the speaker's responsibility is to get a message across in a plain, understandable fashion. The active listener's task is to receive the message and to interpret it in the way intended by the speaker. Boxes 12.1 and 12.2 provide lists of "Do's" and "Don'ts" of effective communication.

As communication between friends increases, thoughts of love often emerge. This is especially true during the middle and junior high school years, when pubertal changes are taking place. One of the most frequently asked questions at this time is, "How do I know if I'm in love?" At this age, students have little for comparison—primarily love within the family, perhaps for a neighbor or teacher. To ascertain whether a feeling is love or infatuation, the student should look for the following signs of infatuation:

1. Is the student able to think about only the other person and nothing else?
2. Does the student's happiness or sadness depend on how the other person reacts?
3. Does the student feel unable to be spontaneous at almost everything because of worry about how the other person will react?
4. Does the student exaggerate the other's good qualities and ignore some of the real facts?
5. Is the student possessive about the other person?

If the answer to these questions is yes, it is infatuation.

Setting Limits and Using Refusal Skills

Establishing behavioral limits within relationships is very important for personal integrity and is the foundation for refusal skills. You protect your real self and your values when you set limits. When you know what you are willing to do and not willing to do, you know when to say no. Suppose two students, Michael and Ramona, are faced with two different problems. Michael is being pressured by his friends to smoke cigarettes. Ramona is being pushed by her boyfriend to engage in unwanted sexual behavior.

Four steps are involved in the "saying no" process:

Step 1: Choose behaviors that are acceptable to you. This should be done in advance to the

BOX 12.1 ■ ■ ■ ■ ■ ■

DO'S OF COMMUNICATION

1. *Do use "I statements" to express yourself.* Many times people use "you" statements such as, "You always wait so long to call me. You are so selfish." This type of statement will cause the other person to become defensive and angry right from the start. Instead, take the responsibility to use an "I statement"—a statement that expresses the way you feel in terms of you. An "I statement" to replace the "You statement" above might be, "I feel hurt when I don't hear from you."
2. *Do be specific.* You may have vague feelings that are difficult to explain, but try to state your feelings as specifically as possible, especially when making a request for a behavior change. If you are not specific, then the other person may misinterpret your request. For example, it's not ideal to tell a parent, "I'll be home early tonight." It would be better to say, "I'll be home by 10:30 tonight." This leaves no room for varying interpretations. By the same token, you should ask for specific messages from your parents: "You can leave for the day if you clean your room" is preferable to "You can leave for the day if you help a little around the house."
3. *Do show respect, warmth, and caring.* Remember, self-disclosure makes you and your partner vulnerable, so be respectful. Be reassuring.
4. *Do be genuine.* Like you, most people respond well to honesty and genuineness rather than deception and superficiality.
5. *Do be an active listener.* Get involved as a listener by nodding your head, changing facial expressions, making brief comments, or asking questions. Do not interrupt. These practices show you are really listening and that you care. The speaker should not be the only player on the conversational team.
6. *Do maintain eye contact.* This is vital for good communication. Think about how you feel when the person you are talking with looks around the room, gazes out the window, or glances at a watch or clock.
7. *Do give feedback.* Restate what you think you heard the speaker say. This restatement does not have to be word for word; in fact it's better if you summarize what has been said by using your own words. Feedback like this lets both of you know that the message sent was indeed the message received.
8. *Do support your friend's or partner's efforts to disclose.* It takes courage to speak out, especially regarding a personal problem. Let your friend know you are glad he or she cares enough about your relationship to raise the issue. Say something that conveys, "Thank you for sharing that with me. I know it was difficult and I'm glad you care enough to trust me."
9. *Do consider compromise.* Your viewpoint counts; but so does your friend's viewpoint. You need to show that you respect his or her viewpoint and feelings, even if you may disagree with him or her about a particular issue.
10. *Do confront.* You need to represent yourself in your relationships. This means that you should confront your friend, dating partner, or parents openly and honestly to let him or her know how you feel. Your friend or parents should not be expected to read your mind or pry thoughts out of you.

Source: From J. Neutens, *Discover: Healthy Sexuality* (Circle Pines, MN: American Guidance Service, 1993), p. 59.

situation arising, if possible. For example, Michael could read some information about the effects of cigarette smoking and Ramona could talk with her friends, parents, or others about what is acceptable behavior for someone her age. This information can be gathered and considered, and then a decision made in order to set limits in a nonpressured

BOX 12.2

DON'TS OF COMMUNICATION

1. *Don't be sarcastic.* Throwing out verbal barbs, jabs, or mean-spirited jokes can make your partner or friend feel hurt, angry, and resentful. Such behavior can even close down communication. Sarcastic remarks usually result if you have not taken enough responsibility to express your feelings previously. Anger, frustration, or jealousy you keep hidden may come out in this negative way.
2. *Don't assume you know what your partner or friend is thinking.* Assuming you know what your partner is thinking can be very destructive. Like your friend, you are not a mind reader. If you want or need to know what he or she is thinking, it is your responsibility to ask.
3. *Don't use "yes/no" questions.* You will not discover much about your friend or partner through questions that require only a yes or no answer. Ask open-ended questions. For example, instead of saying, "Did you like the party?" you might try, "What went through your mind at the party last night?" This technique will be especially helpful if your partner is having difficulty disclosing information or feelings.
4. *Don't play games or manipulate.* This behavior shows that you and your partner have poor, limited communication. A relationship that relies on this type of behavior will eventually dissolve. Playing games and using manipulation tells your partner or friend that you really do not respect or care for him or her.
5. *Don't use labels or name-calling.* This is especially necessary to keep in mind during moments of anger. Negative labels usually add fuel to the fire during an argument. Remember, too, that once something is said, it cannot be taken back.
6. *Don't act disinterested or be impatient.* If you seem disinterested or appear not to take what your partner says seriously, you are telling your partner that you do not care.
7. *Don't bring up old issues.* Old, unrelated issues should not be brought up while discussing a current issue. Many times in an argument someone will raise old issues or hurts as ammunition for his or her side. Stick to the here and now. If old issues are still upsetting you, bring them up separately, at a different time.
8. *Don't overload your partner with complaints.* While you may have many things you would like to discuss with your friend, partner, or parents, do not give a long list of complaints. Deal with them one at a time. Otherwise working out the relationship may appear hopeless.
9. *Don't sabotage yourself.* This is related to Number 9 on the "Do's" list. Do not make yourself invisible or remain unheard. It is your responsibility to keep people from walking all over you. You must sometimes remind others that you count, that you are a somebody who deserves respect.

Source: From J. Neutens, *Discover: Healthy Sexuality* (Circle Pines, MN: American Guidance Service, 1993), p. 60.

way. In our illustrations, Michael wants to retain his friendships but does not want to smoke. Similarly, Ramona decides to set a limit at hugging.

Step 2: Let your friend(s) know how you feel by communicating to them in an honest, genuine manner. By doing so, you are showing respect for yourself; you are saying, "I count," or "I am important," or "My health is important to me." You are letting people know that you are the "captain of your own ship" rather than allowing others to run it. Michael could tell his friends that he is happy to be part of the group and wants to participate in activities that will help his health rather than hurt it. Ramona can tell her boyfriend that she is glad he is attracted to her, but . . . .

Step 3: The "no" in the message should be loud and clear so that there is no misunderstanding. Unfortunately, many adults and children hedge or try to drop hints, which confuses the situation. Remember that the message that is sent is not always received the way it is intended. Therefore, "no" may have to be said more than once to make certain that it is understood. Mixed messages do not work.

Step 4: At this final step, an alternative behavior might be offered. Ramona can suggest that while kissing is out for her, she would like a lot of hugs. Michael may not have an appropriate alternative behavior to suggest, but he would communicate that he wants to remain a member of the group as a nonsmoker.

This four-step approach to setting limits and saying no requires assertiveness. You are asserting your right to a healthy life. You are letting your friends know that you are not rejecting them but are simply saying no to their suggested activity. You can still like them, and they should be able to still like you and respect you for your decision.

Conflict and Conflict Resolution

Conflict with peers, friends, and family is an expected part of life. Nonetheless, few people have the skills necessary to resolve the friction. When someone is criticized, it is easy to become defensive and then move into an attack mode. This approach usually escalates the conflict. As pointed out in Box 12.1, the use of "I" statements, which is best in any communication, is essential in conflict situations. The examples below show how "you-messages" inflame a situation, whereas "I-messages" help diffuse it:

Situation: Parent to child: The child does not wear his bicycle helmet

You-message: You're foolish not to wear that helmet.

I-message: When you don't wear your helmet, I worry [feelings] that you will get hurt [effect of not wearing the helmet].

Situation: Student to student: Response to pressure to try drinking beer

You-message: You think you're a cool dude because you sip beer.

I-message: When you drink beer, I wonder [feelings] how it will change you [effect of drinking the beer]. I like myself [feelings] just the way I am and don't want that stuff in my body.

Situation: Student to student: Response to pressure to engage in unwanted sexual behavior

You-message: You only think about what you want and don't care about my feelings.

I-message: When you want to go further than I do, I get upset [feelings] because I think that you don't love me for me, but rather just for what you think you can do with me [effect].

Remember that the goal of conflict resolution is a "win-win" situation, rather than one person winning and the other losing. Box 12.3 outlines the basic steps for resolving conflicts. This approach brings conflict into the realms of appropriate communication, thoughtfulness, logic, and most importantly, allows each person to retain self-respect while giving respect to the other person. While the steps may seem too structured, you are encouraged to use them in the order given until you *and the person you have the conflict with* are able to modify them to fit your resolution style.

Sexuality

The word *sexuality* ushers forth a kaleidoscope of interpretations (Neutens, 1994b). That is, your definition of sexuality may vary from those around you, friends, parents, and partner alike. A working definition is as follows: "Sexuality is a natural and personal biopsychosocial expression that begins at birth and ends at death" (Neutens, 1994a, p. 3). A breakdown of the terms is as follows:

Natural. Sexual functioning is as inherent to us as is swallowing in that it is a normal biologic function. Only when it is altered from its natural expression do problems arise. To use the swallowing analogy, most of us are not

BOX 12.3

STEPS IN CONFLICT RESOLUTION

1. Invite the other person to talk with you about the problem you are having in the relationship. If he or she can't talk right now, then agree upon a time and place to discuss it later.
2. When you do get together, state your complaint specifically. Use "I statements" and stick to one issue. Assert yourself and let your feelings be known.
3. To be sure the complaint has been understood, ask your friend (parent, sibling, partner) to paraphrase your complaint. In other words, have him or her give you feedback. If necessary, clarify what you meant to correct any misunderstandings.
4. Request a reasonable behavior change that serves both your needs and solves the problem. Remember that the other person is important too.
5 Once again, ask for feedback—this time to make certain that your requested behavioral change was understood.
6. Give the other person a minute or so to think about your request.
7. Allow the other person to express feelings regarding your complaint or request. If he or she is reluctant to disclose feelings, you may need to ask for them.
8. Now you give feedback. Let the person know what message you received about his or her feelings. Keep the next step in mind.
9. Take as much time as you need to think or calm down *before* replying. You don't want to speak out of anger. Also, the process of resolving conflict should not be rushed if you want to reach an agreement that will be kept.
10. Allow your friend (parent, sibling, partner) to (a) accept your request with no conditions, or (b) accept your request under certain conditions. For example, you may request that your friend not smoke cigarettes. This request might be accepted under the condition that he or she does not smoke in your presence. Any counterdemand or condition should be discussed fully. In this case, you may or may not agree with the counterdemand of simply not smoking in your presence.
11. If the two of you cannot reach agreement, it may be best to address the problem again at a later time. It is best if the two of you agree upon another date and time so that the problem won't just get swept under the rug. Depending upon the problem, you both may have to live with the knowledge that you disagree on the issue. However, sometimes the lack of conflict resolution may indicate that relationship between friends is so strained that it may have to be ended.
12. When you reach an agreement through negotiation, celebrate with a verbal commitment to act, or even with a physical sign such as a handshake.

Source: Adapted from J. Neutens, *Discover: Healthy Sexual Development* high school ed. (Circle Pines, MN: American Guidance Service, 1993), p. 63.

concerned with swallowing unless we have a sore throat or a condition that draws it to our attention. Similarly, if our sexuality is in a healthy state, we tend not to worry about it.

Personal. Our sexuality is unique to us, as is our sexual expression.

Biopsychosocial

Bio-. The "bio" portion of the word refers to the biological dimension of sexuality. Specifically, it has to do with our body and how it functions—the anatomy and physiology.

Psycho-. This is the psychological dimension of sexuality, dealing with feelings, beliefs, and personal values. It is how we think and feel about our sexuality.

Social-. This dimension includes cultural background, educational level, religion, and all those events around us.

Birth to death. Sexuality begins at birth (if not before) and continues throughout our lifetimes. Very shortly after birth, boys obtain erections and girls usually experience vaginal lubrication. At the other end of life, aging modifies some modes of sexual expression but does not necessarily end it. Sexual functioning, such as the act of sexual intercourse, may be impeded (i.e., taken from its natural context) in many ways throughout this time frame, due to biological (illness), psychological (negative views), or sociological (religious restrictions) factors.

One of the key points about this working definition is the term *biopsychosocial.* It should be understood that these three dimensions work together, and that a change in one can affect the two others. For example, you can look in a mirror at your body (biological dimension) and feel that you look good, bad, or sexy (psychological dimension) based upon what society says is good, bad, or sexy (sociological dimension). If you get a large pimple on your nose (bio), you might develop a poor body image (psycho) because you know people will definitely comment on it, or at least look at you strangely (socio). From a sexual-functioning standpoint, if a partner tells you that you are a lousy lover, you may develop a low self-esteem in regard to sexuality, which in turn could inhibit appropriate biological functioning (e.g., erections for males and vaginal lubrication for females).

Puberty: Sexual Changes during Adolescence

While all three dimensions of sexuality change during puberty, the biological dimension is most notable. The initial major physical change in the shift from childhood to adolescence is the *growth spurt.* This is the obvious rapid growth in height and weight beginning around twelve years in girls and fourteen years in boys. The range in girls can be from as early as eight years to as late as seventeen, and in boys it can be as early as eleven or as late as eighteen. Individual differences mean that no two people change at the same rate, nor in the same way. And since not all body parts grow at the same rate, awkwardness is to be expected.

Puberty refers to the changes in the body that make the former child physically capable of reproduction. Both the growth spurt and puberty are triggered by a small area in the brain called the *hypothalamus,* which in turn affects the pituitary gland (sometimes called the *master gland*), which releases hormones to influence many other glands. *Hormones* are chemical messengers and simulators of body glands. Two of the hormones secreted by the pituitary gland, called *gonadotropins* (gonad-stimulating substances), are follicle-stimulating hormone (FSH) and luteinizing hormone (LH). These stimulate the development of sex hormones in ovaries and testicles, and prepare the body for reproduction by creating numerous physical changes (Figure 12.1). Box 12.4 provides a brief dis-

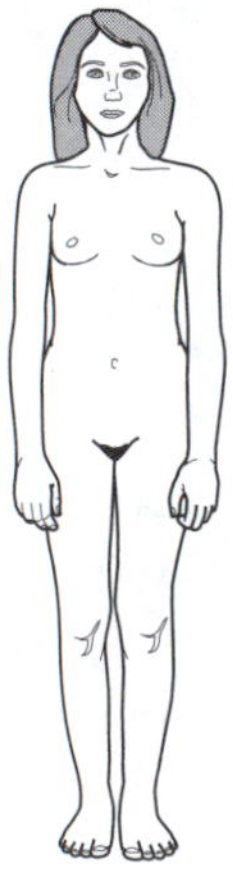

Female

- Growth of breasts
- Development of fat deposits
- Enlargement and preparation of uterus for pregnancy
- Growth of hair on armpits and pubis
- Enlargement of vagina, labia, and clitoris
- Onset of menstruation
- Beginning of secretion of vaginal fluids

Male

- Recession of scalp hair, growth of facial hair
- Growth of larynx and vocal cords (voice pitch deepens)
- Development of muscles and bones
- Growth of hair on chest, abdomen, armpits, and pubis
- Enlargement of penis, testes, and scrotum
- Development of ducts and glands that transport and nurture sperm
- Beginning of ejaculation

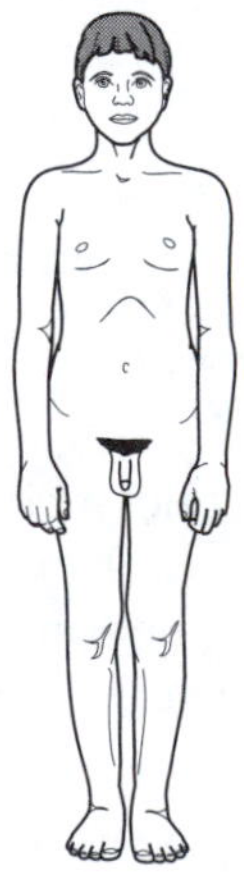

FIGURE 12.1 Female and Male Changes of Puberty

BOX 12.4 ■ ■ ■ ■ ■
PHYSICAL CHANGES DURING PUBERTY

- *Skin:* When hormones begin to circulate in the bloodstream, they may cause acne pimples on the face, neck, chest, or back in both girls and boys. This is a temporary condition, and you cannot do much about it except continue good hygiene and maybe use some over-the-counter preparations to dry the pimples out.
- *Sweat glands:* Puberty stimulates changes in the sweat glands, especially under the arms. As a youngster, you did not have to worry about perspiration or body odor. But as you shift into adulthood, deodorant products take on a new importance.
- *Breast development:* For girls this is a very reliable indicator of puberty, which happens before menstruation. For some girls, it may occur by age eight or nine, while for others it may be age thirteen. This age range is quite normal. Also remember that the breasts do not grow at the same rate so one may be larger than the other. This, too, is normal. Perhaps it is most important to understand that breast size or shape has no bearing on nursing a baby or on sexual response. Some boys may experience a slight increase in breast size. This is normal and often goes away within a year.
- *Body hair:* Pubic hair is generally the second sign of puberty for girls. It generally grows before underarm or leg hair. The amount of body hair is determined by your genetic background, as can be seen by differences among ethnic groups. For boys, puberty brings forth pubic hair, underarm hair, and facial hair. Some boys grow a lot of hair on their chest, arms, legs, and backs, while others grow only small amounts of hair in those places. These individual differences are normal and vary by ethnic background. One other change in males is that the hairline on the forehead may start to recede.
- *Voice:* In boys the voice box, called the *larnyx,* gets bigger, causing the voice to deepen. It is very common for a young man's voice "to crack" or go back and forth in mid-sentence. Girls do not go through this experience.
- *Sexual desire:* Release of the sexual hormones allows both boys and girls to respond to sexual stimuli—a movie, a picture, a person, or almost anything. You may respond with a faster heart beat, quicker breathing, an exciting feeling, clammy hands, and, in the male, an erection (hardening of the penis) and, in the female, a wet feeling in the vagina. These are normal responses and occur naturally. While you may not have control over how you respond to some stimuli, you do have control over what you do about them. In short, you are in charge of and responsible for your behavior.

Source: Adapted from J. Neutens, *Discover: Healthy Sexual Development* high school ed. (Circle Pines, MN: American Guidance Service, 1993), p. 18.

cussion of the bodily changes in language that can be understood by adolescents.

In women, the ovaries secrete *estrogens,* hormones that are feminizing in their effects, and *progesterone,* a hormone that prepares the uterus for pregnancy. Women produce small amounts of androgens in their ovaries and adrenal cortices, but it is the estrogens that cause most of the *secondary sex characteristics* that develop at puberty. These include enlargement of the breasts, uterus, and vagina; broadening of the hips; development of fat deposits on the breasts and buttocks; an increase in vaginal secretions; and the onset of menstruation (*menarche*), which is at a mean age of 12.6 in the United States. Girls also begin to grow hair in their pubic area and armpits, a change triggered chiefly by androgens.

The *menstrual cycle* comprises five physiological events and lasts about twenty-eight days in a physically mature woman, though the normal cycle ranges from twenty-four days to forty-five days. The five events, depicted in Figure 12.2, in chronological order, are:

1. *Menstruation.* This phase begins the menstrual cycle and is recognized by the sloughing off of the endometrium and unfertilized egg from the uterus through the vagina. It is sometimes called *menses.*
2. *Preovulatory phase.* As the name implies, this part of the cycle occurs prior to ovulation and is sometimes called the *proliferative phase.* This is the time when an egg begins to mature and the endometrium starts to build up in preparation for implantation of a fertilized egg. Estrogen causes the endometrial build-up.
3. *Ovulation.* This phase refers to the release of the egg from the ovary.
4. *Postovulatory phase.* Taking place after ovulation, this phase involves the hormone progesterone, which is secreted by the corpus luteum in the ovary to thicken and retain the endometrial lining of the uterus for possible implantation. Other names for this phase are the *secretory* or *luteal* phase.
5. *Premenstrual phase.* Also called *premenses,* this phase occurs if there is no fertilization. The thickened endometrium starts to break down in preparation to be expelled during menses.

In men, large amounts of androgens, principally testosterone, and a small amount of estrogens are secreted by the testes; more androgens and perhaps estrogens are secreted by the adrenal cortices. The androgens create the male secondary sex characteristics. These include growth of muscles and pubic and underarm hair, the beginning of a beard, enlargement of the penis and scrotum, deepening of the voice, maturation of internal sexual organs, and thickening of skin-gland secretions (which may lead to acne). Ejaculation is now possible, and may happen spontaneously as wet dreams (nocturnal emissions). Ejaculations during sleep may be associated with erotic dreams, or simply occur as a release of sexual tensions built up during sleep.

Both sexes may experience emotional turbulence as their hormonal patterns shift and become temporarily imbalanced.

The changes of puberty may be a source of embarrassment or fear to those who do not know that the new things their bodies are doing have a natural, expected biological basis. In the past, girls who were not taught about menstruation feared that they were bleeding to death. Because they had learned to regard their genital area as taboo, they were afraid to tell anybody and instead secretly suffered, worried, and tried to hide the blood. Today girls still find the onset of menstruation a significant milestone in their lives, for various reasons: being like (or different from) their friends; seeing it as a badge of maturity or womanhood; being bothered by the inconvenience and messiness of menstrual flow; or feeling new physical discomfort, emotional changes, or restrictions on their activities. The potential for becoming pregnant, although not usually regarded as significant since ovulation occurs on an erratic basis during the first year of menstruation does exist.

Responsibility and High-Risk Sexual Behaviors

Sexual responsibility means deciding what is right and what is wrong regarding sexual matters. It implies that you make decisions that show respect for yourself and those around you. It also signifies that you are willing and able to accept the consequences of your sexual actions. The list below shows some of the areas of responsibility facing elementary, middle-school, and junior-high students:

- Personal hygiene; taking care of your body by being clean
- Saying no to unwanted touch
- Staying away from relatives and friends who make you feel bad
- Reporting unwanted touch or other intimate behaviors by family members, family friends, older students, acquaintances, and strangers
- Letting your friends know what you like and dislike
- Making well-thought-out decisions rather than "sex-drive" decisions
- Knowing that abstinence is the best way to avoid pregnancy and STDs

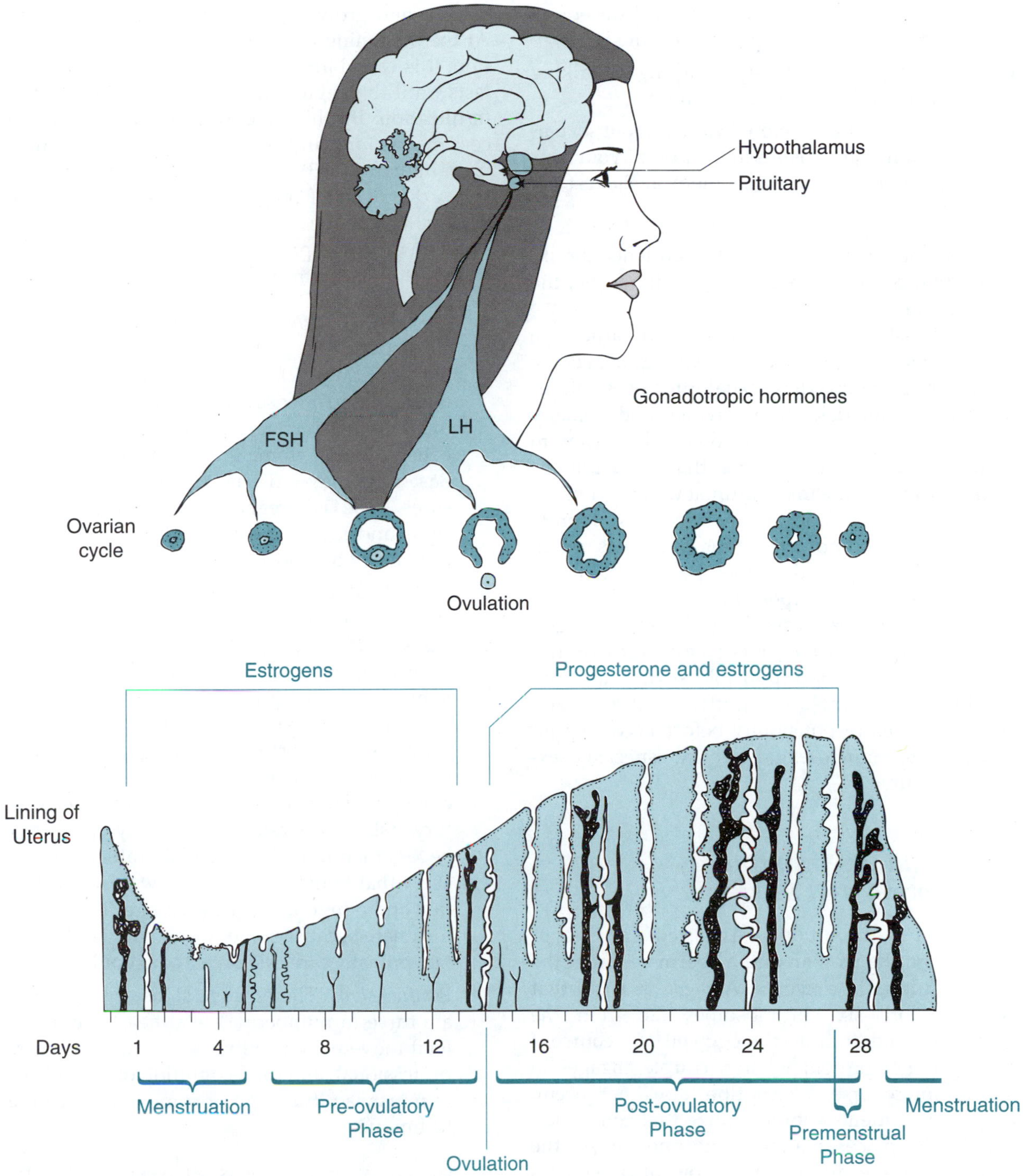

FIGURE 12.2 Hormonal Control of the Menstrual Cycle

- Understanding that any form of contraception still presents a risk of pregnancy and STDs
- Knowledge of sexuality—reading or talking with an adult to gain information
- Examining your personal values about sexuality and not just dismissing those of your parents without first giving them an honest examination.

This is not an exhaustive list. Students should know that once they become sexually active, the list becomes longer.

High-risk behaviors, as discussed earlier, are actions that place students in greater than average danger. It is obvious that sexual intercourse places them at greater risk for pregnancy and sexually transmitted diseases. Even some adults, not to mention adolescents, believe that sexual intercourse is a quick means to intimacy. This is not the case, however. In addition to the risks of pregnancy, STDs, and no true intimacy, there is risk in exposing the body—the other person might not like it. Emotions are exposed too.

Needless to say, especially at younger ages, the decision to *abstain,* or not have sexual intercourse, is a sign of responsible sexual decision-making. Adolescents, like adults, must learn and practice sexual responsibility before becoming involved in too much sexual activity, especially sexual intercourse.

The Road to Parenthood: Conception and Pregnancy

Conception is the union of two cells, an egg or ovum from the woman and a sperm cell from the man, resulting in a zygote. A *zygote* is a cell that contains forty-six chromosomes (26 from the sperm cell and 26 from the egg cell). Of course if an egg is not present when a couple engages in sexual intercourse, conception does not occur. However, students should realize that conception could take place at almost anytime during the menstrual cycle due to physiological differences from cycle to cycle. The usual site for *fertilization* (conception) is in a fallopian tube. The zygote then travels for about three days to the uterus before being implanted in the endometrial lining. There it divides and grows, going through several stages. At the beginning of the third week after fertilization, it is called an *embryo.* The embryonic period lasts until the beginning of the eighth week after fertilization. By this time, the embryo is nearly 4 centimeters long and is now called a *fetus* (Gant & Cunningham, 1993).

A diagnosis of pregnancy is usually very important to both the woman and the man involved. The signs and symptoms of pregnancy are divided into the following three categories:

- *Presumptive signs.* These signs are primarily subjective. They include (1) nausea and possible vomiting, (2) frequent urination, (3) fatigue, (4) no menses, (5) increased skin pigmentation, (6) changes in the breasts, and (7) a belief by the woman that she is pregnant. Based on these criteria, a woman may "presume" she is pregnant. Nonetheless, these signs and symptoms alone do not warrant a pregnancy diagnosis.
- *Probable signs.* These are evidenced by (1) enlargement of the abdomen, (2) changes in the shape and size of the uterus, (3) changes in the cervix, and (4) endocrine tests. The presence of human chorionic gonadotropin (hCG) in the mother's blood and its excretion in the urine provides an opportunity for an endocrine pregnancy test. Home pregnancy tests employ principles similar to those used for clinical laboratory tests. However, their accuracy appears to be less than tests done in a laboratory. Studies show that home tests have a low false-positive rate and a high false-negative rate. That is unfortunate because some women may fail to obtain prenatal care as soon as they should.
- *Positive signs.* The positive signs of pregnancy are three in number: (1) fetal heart action, (2) fetal movement as witnessed by a health care professional, and (3) recognition of an embryo or fetus via ultrasound or some other imaging technique.

Generally pregnancy is 40 weeks in length; this is also called 40 weeks of gestation. However, an infant born at from 37 weeks to 42 weeks of gestation is referred to as a *term baby.* A *preterm* or *premature baby* is one born before 37 weeks. Because of today's obstetrical skill and neonatal care in technologically advanced hospitals, many infants born at 25 or 26 weeks can turn out to be healthy, lively youngsters.

The Road to Parenthood: Childbirth

Few human events are as dramatic as childbirth. We can only surmise what a new baby feels during the hours-long journey from the uterus to the outside world. Whether painful, frightening, or exhilarating, it must be intense.

The release of intense emotions during childbirth is heightened by the inherent risk of danger to mother and baby. In a small percentage of births, certain life-threatening complications do arise. The mother can bleed extensively, infection may occur, or the baby's oxygen supply can be cut off as it makes the transition from the amniotic fluid to air. If the air supply is cut off too long, brain damage and even death can result. The goals of childbirth are to make the experience as rewarding as possible and as safe as possible.

Not many years ago, many expectant mothers and their families feared childbirth. They knew it was painful, that the baby could be stillborn, that the mother could die. The high risks led to the development of a specialized type of medical practice—obstetrics and later perinatology (the subspecialty of high-risk pregnancies)—dedicated to controlling the complications of pregnancy and childbirth. With the advent of anesthesia, antibiotic therapy, identification of high-risk mothers, fetal monitoring, and trained birth attendants, the incidences of maternal and infant mortality and maternal and infant illness have plummeted. The perinatal death rate (sum of stillbirths plus neonatal deaths) has fallen nearly 50 percent in just the last twenty-five years. In the last fifty years, maternal mortality rate has dropped remarkably too; it is now at 7.8 deaths per 100,000 live births (Gant & Cunningham, 1993).

Several programs and organizations teach families how to prepare for childbirth. One of these is the Lamaze course, named after a French doctor who developed a popular program. Almost all childbirth-preparation courses teach the biology of pregnancy and childbirth as well as breathing and relaxation exercises to help the delivery proceed smoothly. While attending the six- to eight-week courses, parents-to-be meet other expectant couples with whom they can share anxieties and experiences. In class, couples learn of the many choices they have about childbirth and how to find the setting and professional help they prefer.

Women typically begin labor (see Figure 12.3) with uterine contractions that are fifteen to twenty minutes apart and that gradually increase in strength and frequency. During this *first stage* of labor, the lengthwise muscles of the cervix are working to enlarge *(dilate)* and thin *(efface)* the opening of the cervix.

During this stage, which may last from two hours to a day or more, the health care practitioner monitors the baby's life signs. When the baby's head begins to move through the dilated cervix into the birth canal, most women feel a tremendous urge to push, or bear down, with all their strength. This period is the *second stage* of labor. It is usually much shorter than the first stage, and most women become more actively involved during this phase of the birth. Muscular, breathing, and relaxation exercises, and/or anesthesiology (such as an epidural) can help women cope with the intensity of second stage of labor. Many birth settings accommodate the individual needs of the laboring woman. Depending on the progress of labor and comfort of the woman, various positions may be used throughout labor and delivery. The woman may spend the early part of the second stage in a semiupright position and then, as the bearing down becomes more intense, be more comfortable lying on her side for delivery so that the baby exerts less pressure on her spine.

The second stage of labor ends when the baby is delivered and the umbilical cord is severed. During the *third stage* of labor, the placenta separates from the uterine wall. Uterine contractions continue until the placenta is expelled through the vagina, thus ending labor.

During the second stage of labor, the doctor may perform an episiotomy to allow the baby to pass through without tearing the perineum. This procedure is sometimes necessary even though the incision that results may cause discomfort after delivery. If the baby has difficulty coming out, the doctor may decide to use *forceps*, a metal tong-

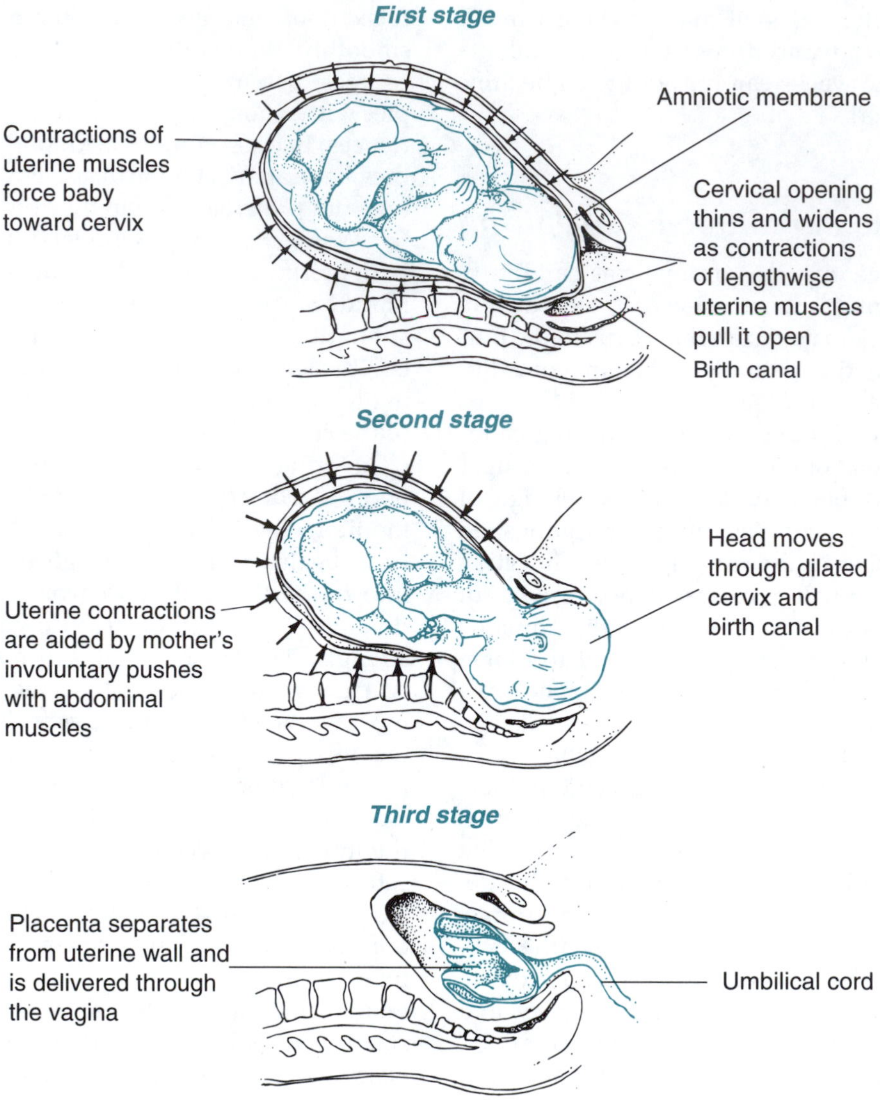

FIGURE 12.3 The Three Stages of Labor

like device used to pull the baby from the birth canal. This procedure should only be performed by a trained obstetrician. In recent years, some doctors have switched to a suction-cup device—*vacuum forceps*—applied to the baby's head. If neither of these methods is judged adequate for a vaginal delivery and if monitoring devices indicate that the baby's life signs are slowing, the doctor may elect to deliver the baby by *cesarean section,* that is, an incision in the mother's abdomen and uterus.

Doctors elect cesarean section (C-section) for four major reasons. One is that the labor is not progressing or the birth canal is too small. A second is breech presentation, in which the fetus has its feet instead of its head nearest the cervical canal. A third is fetal distress as determined by electronic monitoring or stethoscope. Finally, if a woman has previously had a caesarean-section birth, some doctors prefer to repeat it so that the "weakened" uterus does not rupture during labor. This fourth reason is not used much today; most obstetricians

BOX 12.5 ■ ■ ■ ■ ■

METHODS OF FERTILITY CONTROL

Nonprescription Methods

- *Withdrawal:* Also known as coitus interruptus; almost useless as a technique
- *Douching:* Flushing of the vagina; very ineffective as a contraceptive
- *Condom:* A thin sheath that fits over the penis to protect against both pregnancy and STDs. It can be effective if used properly. A female condom designed to completely line the vagina is available.
- *Vaginal spermicides:* Come as foams, creams, suppositories, and contraceptive sponges. They can be effective if used in the correct manner.
- *Natural family planning:* Includes the calendar method and the sympto-thermal method, both of which attempt to identify the time of ovulation and thereby predict when not to have sexual intercourse. This method is effective only for couples who are diligent in its usage.

Prescription Methods

- *Diaphragm and spermicide:* The diaphragm is a round, soft latex dome inserted through the vagina to fit over the cervix; should be used with a spermicide.
- *Cervical cap:* Similar to the diaphragm except smaller; may not be as effective.
- *Intrauterine devices:* Small flexible objects that are fitted into the uterus; generally used by women who have already delivered at least one baby.
- *Progestin implant:* A set of six hollow capsules containing progestin,which are inserted under the skin (frequently in the upper arm); can work as long as five years.
- *Oral contraceptives:* "The pill"; several are available on the market, each with a different hormonal content, arrangement, or distribution.

Surgical Methods

- *Vasectomy:* A male sterilization procedure that effectively creates a block in the vas deferens so that sperm are not present in the ejaculate.
- *Tubal ligation:* A female sterilization procedure in which the fallopian tubes are cut or tied off, preventing the union of egg and sperm.

perform a VBAC—vaginal delivery after a previous C-section.

Gender Identity and Sex Role

The awareness of being male or female is called *gender identity,* and gender-specific behavior is referred to as the *sex role.* Having been sex-typed at birth, the infant is thereafter treated by adults as they think appropriate for that gender, and eventually the infant incorporates into its self-image awareness of being male or female. By about two years, a child's gender identity may be fixed for life. How the child acts on the knowledge depends on a variety of factors. Children learn attitudes and behavior by modeling after parents, teachers, celebrities, and fictional characters, and they are also trained by reward and punishment. Whatever the sources of information and influence, children learn early in life which attitudes and behavior are appropriate for boys and which are appropriate for girls. By the age of three years, children are capable of citing a long list of items of behavior that are characteristic of one gender or the other.

Exactly which attitudes and behaviors are deemed appropriate for both sexes depends on the culture. In some societies, sex roles are strictly defined, and little deviance from the stereotype is allowed. Our culture possesses a set of stereotypes that includes economic role; dominance or submissiveness in social relationships; responsibilities for home and child care; and mode of dress, personal appearance, and expression of emotions.

There is little evidence that our culture's stereotypes were ever the predominant behavioral pattern, except perhaps on television shows and in romantic fiction. Today the American sex-role stereotypes are myths: approximately 50 percent of the labor force consists of women; couples in increasing numbers are sharing the responsibilities of family care; women are becoming more assertive about their needs and wants; and men are becoming freer to express their feelings.

Sexual Orientation

Another aspect of our culture is the overall belief that people should be sexual only with members of the opposite sex, and that same-sex (homosexual) relationships are wrong, illegal, immoral, or indicative of psychological disorientation. In some other cultures, homosexuality is to some degree condoned. While the origins of sexual orientation are still being investigated, it is believed that it is well established before the age of five years (Bidwell, 1988). For most children and adolescents, our cultural expectations may not present a problem; however, this is not the case for youngsters who experience strong same-gender attractions (Blumenfeld, 1994).

These students can become very intimidated and frightened by what they hear and see in regard to gays. Worse yet, many can develop low self-esteem, social isolation, and feelings of self-hatred. All of this can lead to lowered academic performance, chronic truancy, even dropping out. While some others bury themselves in school work, earning stellar grades, their emotional lives can become wastelands, placing them at greater health risks. One study found that 58 percent of young gay males suffered from a substance-abuse disorder (Remafedi, 1985). Unlike other minorities (African American, Latino), these students generally lack parental or religious support. These same

Some researchers believe that sexual orientation is well established by the age of five. But teaching the acceptance of same-sex families and sexual partnering is still controversial in many elementary and middle-school systems.

derogatory attitudes and behaviors can push heterosexual students into early, unwanted sexual activity just to prove their heterosexuality.

It is widely recognized that most curricula fail to address the issue of gayness. This is particularly so in the elementary, middle, and junior high school years. The usual major roadblocks are teachers—those who do not think it should be in the curriculum or those who do but do not have the necessary experience to teach about it; administrators—principals, school board officials, and others—who may automatically reject any attempts to teach about so-called LesBiGay issues; students; parents; and other community people. Blumenfeld (1994) offers several strategies for dealing with these groups of people. From a curricular standpoint, he suggests that content at the elementary and middle-school level should do the following:

- Counteract gender- and sexuality-based stereotypes
- Identify and discuss stereotypes in student literature and behavior
- Reflect on real-life situations to show the diversity of relationships and family structures
- Identify vocabulary that is sexist
- Acknowledge and support self-identified lesbian/gay families in the community
- Present LesBiGay culture in the context of literature, art, and family life rather than just in terms of sexuality.

In addition to the instructional component, gay students and their families should have resources available, including (1) access to school and nonschool counselors, (2) written and video materials, and (3) support groups and systems. Schools can establish written policies regarding the consequences of homophobic harassment, just as they do for sexual harassment.

In many communities, the actions suggested above could cause quite a stir. According to Skonie-Hardin (1994), it may be wise to postpone the teaching of some controversial material until program credibility is established. First, a committee should be formed to receive community input and establish objectives for a program. And while it would be good to include all topics of human sexuality, program excellence should not be based on content alone.

Implications for Elementary and Middle-School Teachers

Summary Issues

1. The average family size today is slightly greater than three in number.
2. Nuclear families are decreasing in number, whereas single-parent families are increasing.
3. Women head approximately 15 percent of today's families.
4. Family structure may consist of any of the following: nuclear, blended, single-parent, extended, and foster.
5. One of the principal challenges to families consisting of married parents today is divorce.
6. In most divorce situations, the mother becomes the custodial parent yet loses out economically, often putting herself and her children in poverty.
7. Divorced parents can work together to reduce tensions and bring their children back to a sense of well-being.
8. Stepfamilies are very workable but require great efforts by all members, especially at the outset.
9. Characteristics of a strong family include: commitment, appreciation, communication, time spent together, spiritual wellness, coping ability, shared feelings and concerns, privacy, and appropriate decision-making.
10. Communication between parents (guardians) and children is essential, and children can learn to initiate communication if it is lacking within the family.
11. Families should be actively supportive when a child shifts from elementary school to middle school or junior high.
12. Strong friendships require responsible behavior and commitment.
13. High-risk behaviors are those that place us in greater than average danger. Negative

peer pressure can induce us to engage in high-risk behaviors.

14. Real communication involves self-disclosure in which you reveal the real self rather than playing a role. The breadth and depth of self-disclosure increase to bring about close friendships. As trust develops, intimacy becomes a by-product of the self-disclosure. We usually do not reveal all of ourselves to other people, however; some parts of us are too private.
15. We should use "I statements" and do certain other things to promote effective communication. There are a series of things we should not do also.
16. Setting limits and using refusal skills is a four-step process: choosing behaviors acceptable to you, communicating this to other people, making the "no" in the message clear, and suggesting an alternative behavior, if appropriate.
17. Conflict resolution is a skill that can be learned and practiced early in life.
18. Sexuality can be defined as a natural and personal biopsychosocial expression beginning in the womb and ending in the tomb.
19. Puberty ushers forth changes in size, weight, skin, sweat glands, breast development, body hair, voice, and sexual desire.
20. The menstrual cycle is comprised of five physiological events: menses, preovulation, ovulation, postovulation, and premenses.
21. No matter what our age, all of us have sexual responsibilities.
22. The signs and symptoms of pregnancy include the three categories of presumptive, probable, and positive. Pregnancy tests fall into the probable category.
23. The gestation period averages 40 weeks, with anywhere from 37 to 42 weeks falling into the normal range.
24. There are three stages of labor.
25. The awareness of being male or female is called *gender identity,* and gender-specific behavior is referred to as the *sex role.*
26. Sexual orientation may be in the form of heterosexuality, bisexuality, or homosexuality, with the latter including gays and lesbians.
27. The school can take several steps to reduce or eliminate homophobic harassment.

Teacher Ramifications

In regard to family life, relationships, and sexuality, a teacher should:

1. Show students how to identify high-risk behaviors
2. Provide students with opportunities to practice setting limits, making decisions, and using refusal skills
3. Teach and demonstrate effective communication techniques with students' parents, siblings, friends, and others as well as provide occasions for practice
4. Use a curriculum that allows students to analyze the influence of culture, media, and technology on family life, relationships, and sexuality
5. Use lesson plans that involve skill development so that students can be cooperative in and advocate for strong families
6. Support the school's role in helping the nation reach the following objectives set forth in *Healthy Children 2000:*
   - #5.1. Reduce pregnancies among girls aged seventeen and younger to no more than 50 per 1000 adolescents
   - #5.2. Reduce to no more than 30 percent the proportion of all pregnancies that are unintended
   - #5.4. Reduce the proportion of adolescents who have engaged in sexual intercourse to no more than 15 percent by age fifteen and no more than 40 percent by age seventeen
   - #5.5. Increase to at least 40 percent the proportion of ever-sexually-active adolescents aged seventeen and younger who have abstained from sexual activity for the previous three months
   - #5.6. Increase to at least 90 percent the proportion of sexually active, unmarried people aged nineteen and younger who use contraception, especially combined-method contraception, that both effec-

tively prevents pregnancy and provides barrier protection against disease

#5.8. Increase to at least 85 percent the proportion of people aged ten through eighteen who have discussed human sexuality, including values surrounding sexuality, with their parents and/or have received information through another parentally endorsed source, such as youth, school, or religious programs.

SECTION III

Teaching Strategies for Family, Relationships, and Sexuality

The strategies in this section are divided into grade K–4, 5–6, and 7–8 levels. In addition to strategies that can be used in the classroom, home activities are included. A home activity is designed for student-parent interaction. It is a way to engage the home in school-student learning, and parents can sign a slip of paper to confirm that an activity was completed. Evaluation of all strategies through the use of the National Health Education Standards and performance indicators is indicated. Teachers may also choose to write corresponding learning assessments.

K–4 Level

Strategy One

Objective: Students will recognize birth as a natural process for a variety of species.

Activity: Students and teachers are to raise guppies, chicks, or gerbils to observe birth and development.

A. *Demonstration:* Incubate some chicken eggs.
Subobjective: Students will explain what happens inside a chicken egg as it incubates.
Procedure: If electricity is available in your classroom, a simple incubator can be made at a very low cost (Figure 12.4). Obtain two cardboard boxes, one large and one small. Cut one end from the small box and cut a six-inch-square window in a side of the large box. Next, cut a slit in the top of the smaller box and suspend an electric lamp in it. There should be a long cord attached to the lamp.

Place the small box inside the large box, and pack crumpled newspaper between the boxes on all sides. Be sure the open end of the small box fits against the side of the large box in which the window was cut. Fit a glass plate over the window, and place a thermometer in the box so that you can read it through the window.

Now you are ready to begin the experiment. It is necessary to have a constant temperature of 103°F (40°C) night and day for 21 days. By trying out different bulbs and changing the amount of newspaper, after a few days you will be able to regulate your incubator to this temperature. A small dish of water should be placed in the incubator.

Now obtain a dozen fertile eggs. Place the eggs in the incubator and leave them. At the end of three days, remove one of the eggs and carefully crack it into a shallow saucer. A three-day embryo will usually show the heart already beating, which may continue for half an hour. Remove an egg every three days, and observe the development of the embryo. Some of the eggs can be left for the full 21 days to see if any of them will hatch.

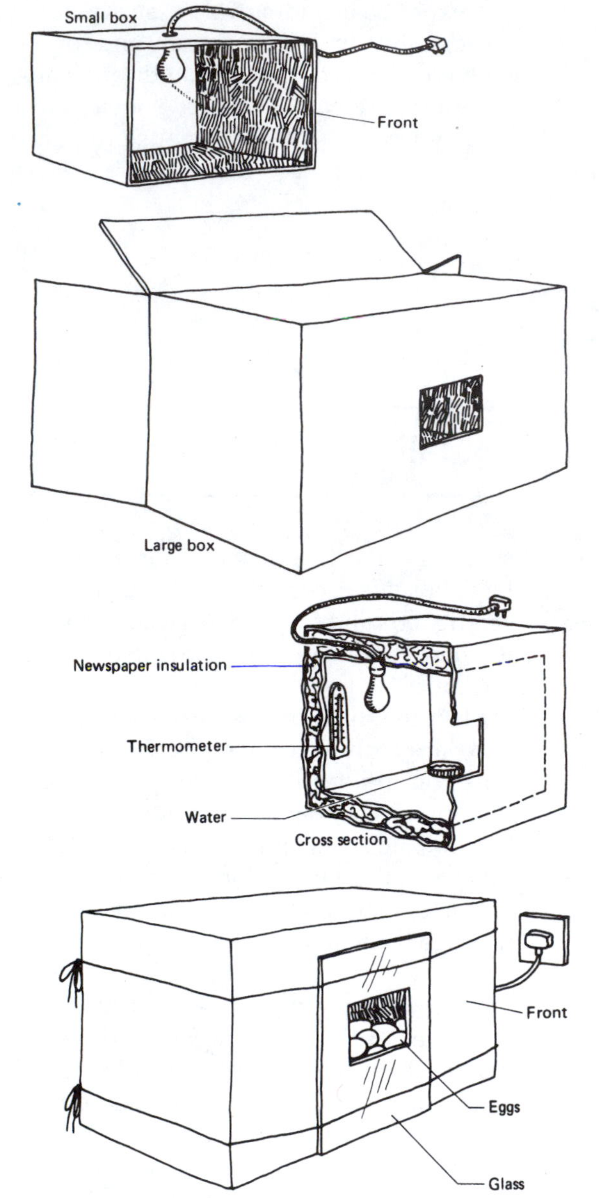

FIGURE 12.4 Plans for a Classroom Egg Incubator

B. *Demonstration:* Raise gerbils
Subobjective: Students will explain reproduction in mammals using gerbils.
Procedure: Purchase a pair of gerbils nine to twelve weeks prior to beginning of this unit (sexual maturity occurs between eleven and twelve weeks). This gives the gerbils time to get used to each other. Gerbils will mate by fourteen weeks; the gestation period is twenty-four to thirty days. Since a pregnant gerbil gains very little weight, it is often difficult to tell whether it is pregnant.

Both mother and father are affectionate toward the babies, so there is no reason to separate the parents. A hamster cage may be used. Use hamster litter or cedar shavings as a floor cover in the cage. Gerbils are very clean, hence odorless, but the cage needs to be cleaned about every two weeks. They nibble on sunflower seeds and corn. Carrots, celery, and lettuce may also be included in the diet. Keep the diet high in protein and low in fat. Add a little evaporated milk to the diet during pregnancy and nursing. Gerbils drink very little water, but it should be provided in a trough so that they can drink standing upright.

Do not handle gerbils after a litter is born or attempt to clean the cage, as they are very sensitive at this time.

For more information on raising gerbils, chicks, or guppies, visit a local pet shop or library.

C. *Demonstration:* Raise guppies
Subobjective: Students will answer key questions about the birth process using guppies as examples.
Procedure: The following key questions are broken into three sequences so that they can be used to guide student observation and help children discover for themselves:
1. Two weeks before birth:
   a. Which is the mother guppy?
   b. What part of her body is the largest?
   c. Is the mother guppy the same color as the father guppy?
   d. Can you see through the mother's stomach?
2. A day or two before birth:
   a. Is the mother's body bigger now than before?
   b. Can you still see through the mother's body?
   c. What can you see?

   d. Can you see any dark spots?
   e. Where are these black spots?
3. After the babies are born:
   a. Is the mother's body as big as it was several days ago?
   b. What color is the mother's stomach?
   c. Where did the dark spots in the mother's stomach go?
   d. How many baby guppies are there?
   e. Where do babies come from?

Similar questions may be developed for chicks.

Integration: Science, Math

Related Health Content Areas: Nutrition, growth and development, emotional well-being

Health Education Standard and Performance Indicator: 1(3)

Strategy Two

Objective: Students will be able to identify some adults who can help them.

Activity: Have students name at least two adults that they could talk to if they needed help. Lists may include parents, teachers, clergy, public safety personnel, firefighters, neighbors, and so forth. Discuss with students that not all adults can be trusted. Have students brainstorm characteristics of those adults who can be trusted and those who cannot be trusted.

Integration: Social Studies, Language Arts

Related Health Content Areas: Safety, violence prevention

Health Education Standards and Performance Indicators: 2(2); 6(2); 7(3)

5–6 Level

Strategy One

Objective: Students will recognize that all people have something to offer others.

Activity: Have students list all members of their family (including stepparents, grandparents, etc.) in a column down the left-hand side of a piece of paper. Next to each name, making a second column down the right, have the student list two good things about that person and the way he or she acts toward others, especially the student. Then, in large or small groups, have students give examples of what they have written. Facilitate discussion toward our reliance and interdependence on members of our families. Discuss what the students do for the people in their families.

Integration: Social Studies

Related Health Content Areas: Emotional well-being, growth and development

Health Education Standards and Performance Indicators: 1(2,4); 5(2,3)

Strategy Two

Objective: Students will explore the process of human fetal development and birth.

Activity: Prepare a question box in advance, and give each student an index card. Explain that while they watch a short video they should write down on the cards any questions they may have. They will have time to do this after the video finishes also. Show the video (suggestion: Fetal Development, 15 min, AIMS Media, 6901 Woodley Ave, Van Nuys, CA 91406-4878).

After the video is complete, have all students put their cards in the box. If time allows, you may begin to answer them immediately. If not, you may wish to set aside the next class period to do so. Often, answering the questions will spark more and more discussion.

Integration: Science, Math

Related Health Content Areas: Human body, nutrition, substance use/abuse, growth and development

Health Education Standards and Performance Indicators: 1(1,2,3); 3(1)

7–8 Level

Strategy One

Objective: Students will discover a variety of factual information concerning pregnancy.

Activity: Prior to class, set up stations to include at least the following:

1. Models of the stages of fetal development (sometimes available from a local health dept.)
2. Diagrams of the stages of labor and birth
3. Large "coffee-table" books with photographs of the developing fetus or videos (suggested: *The Incredible Machine,* National Geographic Society)
4. Dictionaries or medical encyclopedias (suggested: *AMA Home Medical Encyclopedia,* Pleasantville, NY: Readers Digest, 1989)
5. Computer (if available) with appropriate software on conception, fetal development, and birth
6. "Catch-up" station with fact sheet as follows:

FETAL DEVELOPMENT FACT SHEET

After the embryo implants itself in the lining of the uterus, special cells from the embryo and the uterus begin to develop into a structure known as the *PLACENTA.* This mass of tissue, attached to the wall of the uterus, will, for the next nine months, absorb nutrients from the mother's bloodstream and pass them to the blood of the *FETUS.* The developing fetus is contained in the *AMNIOTIC SAC,* which is filled with a clear liquid called *amniotic fluid* that helps to protect the fetus.

Stages of Development during Pregnancy

By 3rd week: Heart and blood vessels developing

First Month

4th week: Nervous system and digestive system developing

5th week: Fingers begin to form; lungs, larynx, trachea developing

6th week: Kidneys developing (will start to function in approximately 2 weeks)

7th week: Reproductive system begins to develop

Second Month

8th week: Bone substance begins to grow (will continue until the end of puberty); brain has grown rapidly and is now one half the length of the entire body (weight: 5 gms, or ⅕ oz)

8 to 12 weeks: Body length increases rapidly; arms and legs form

Third Month

12 weeks: Heartbeat is audible (you can hear it); genitals show sex of child; can kick legs, close fingers, and turn head

Fourth Month

13 to 16 weeks: Grows rapidly; at 16 weeks, weight is 6.5 oz. Head is erect and off chest; skeleton would show on X-rays.

Fifth Month

17 to 20 weeks: Eyes and ears almost fully developed; fingernails and fingerprints form; eyebrows and head hair visible

Sixth Month

21 to 25 weeks: Weight about 2 pounds; body proportions improve; skin is wrinkled and pinkish-blue

Seventh Month

26 to 29 weeks: Eyes open
As the time of birth approaches, the fetus turns so that the head is down. The head is heavier, and this position allows more movement of the fetus's arms and legs.

Eighth Month

30 weeks: Weight is about 3 pounds, 8 oz

Ninth Month

30 to 38 weeks: *Finishing period.* Fetus gains a lot of weight and loses its wrinkled appearance; subcutaneous fat (layer of fat just below the skin) develops

Near the time of birth: Amniotic sac tears, allowing the fluid inside to drain out through the vagina (when the "water breaks"); labor begins with the muscles of the uterus contracting at regular intervals

Next, give each student a handout with ten questions (see Figure 12.5) to be completed by moving through the stations. Assign students to small groups equal to the number of stations that are set up. Students are to work cooperatively within their groups to find out which questions must be answered at which station, and to ensure that everyone in the group finds the correct answer.

Integration: Science, Computer Skills, Language Arts

Related Health Content Areas: Growth and development, human body

Health Education Standards and Performance Indicators: 1(3); 3(1)

Strategy Two

Objective: Students will recognize that parenting is a difficult and time-consuming job. Students will recognize that parents are sometimes unsure about what is best.

Activity: Give each student a copy of the Parental Interview (Figure 12.6). Ask that it be completed by the next class period for use in a group discussion. The interview must be completed in the student's handwriting for credit. (Note: If there have been divorces, remarriages, or adoptions among the students' families, use whatever set of circumstances applied to a child *first* entering a parent's or guardian's life.) Parents not wishing to participate should indicate such by signing in the appropriate place.

Integration: Language Arts

Related Health Content Areas: Growth and development, emotional well-being

Health Education Standards and Performance Indicators: 1(4); 6(2)

Based on today's lesson, answer the following questions. Be aware that not all of the answers will be found at the same station.

1. What happens to a woman's urinary bladder during the birth process?
2. At what stage of development does the fetus get its nervous system?
3. Just before a normal birth, in which direction is the head of the fetus?
4. What are the last two months of the pregnancy called? Why?
5. What is the placenta? What is its function?
6. Identify the photographs on pages ______ and ______ of the ____________ book.
7. Define amniotic sac.
8. Explain what a cesarean section (C-section) is.
9. At what age do the bones of the body begin to grow? At what age do they usually stop growing?
10. At what stage of pregnancy are you most likely to:
    a. Hear a heart rate? ____________________
    b. Have fingernails? ____________________
    c. Have the skeleton show up on X-rays? ____________________
    d. Have heart development? ____________________
    e. Have kidney function? ____________________

FIGURE 12.5 Fetal Development Questions

Dear Parents or Guardians: We will soon be discussing the responsibilities involved in being a parent. To help prepare for this discussion, your son or daughter is to interview you using the questions below. The questions are not meant to make anyone uncomfortable, but rather to help your son or daughter understand parenthood.

To Students: You are to interview your parent or guardian using the following questions:

1. What were the biggest changes that occurred in your lifestyle after your first child arrived?

   ____

   ____

   ____

2. What change was the most unexpected?

   ____

   ____

   ____

3. Is it difficult being a parent? ________ Why?

   ____

   ____

   ____

4. If you were giving someone advice on having children, what would be the most important things that you would tell the person?

   ____

   ____

   ____

   ____

____
Signature of interviewer

____
Signature of parent/guardian who participated

____
Signature of parent/guardian who wished not to complete interview

FIGURE 12.6 Parental Interview

Strategy Three

Objective: Students will project into the future, setting long-term goals for what they wish to accomplish and then determining the impact of an unplanned pregnancy on those goals.

Activity: Using the time-line model in Figure 12.7, students are to attempt to plan their futures. Upon completion, students are to compare this lifestyle with what would occur if they had an unplanned pregnancy before graduating from high school. They will need information on the number of years of schooling necessary for certain professions or other occupations after high school. Students will also need access to salary information for various occupations. (Salary may also include allowances, and housing means where the student lives and with whom—parents, roommate, alone, etc.)

Integration: Social Studies

Related Health Content Area: Growth and development

Health Education Standard and Performance Indicators: 6(3,4)

Home Activities

Strategy One

Objective: Students will practice decision-making skills.

Activity: Problem-based activity as follows:

Amelia, 14, has always believed that you should not have sex before marriage. She has been "going with" Felipe since sixth grade. They love each other. Felipe says it's okay to have sex if you are really sure you love someone. Tonight Amelia will be alone with Felipe at his house watching television. She is afraid of what might happen.

1. What is Amelia afraid of?
2. What is the best thing she can do to reduce her fears?
3. What is Felipe's role in addressing the problem?

Integration: Social Studies

Related Health Content Areas: Growth and development, mental

Health Education Standards: 5,6

Strategy Two

Objective: Students will recognize the importance of rules and policies for children.

Activity: The students' parents are to have their children write down the rules they think they should have to follow regarding homework, curfew, clothing, household chores, music/television, computer games, grades, and the like. Parents may wish to make their own list as well, or simply respond to and

	Age/Current Date	Age/5 years	Age/10 years	Age/15 years
Education				
Employment				
Salary				
Housing				
Marital Status				
# Children				

FIGURE 12.7 Time-Line Model

discuss the student's list. Issues that are in contention should be discussed calmly, with the parent giving the rationale for his or her rule. It is not necessary for the parent and student to agree on all rules, but all should be discussed and explained.

Integration: Social Studies

Related Health Content Areas: Safety, growth and development, emotional well-being

Health Education Standards: 5,6

References

AIMS Media. *Fetal Development.* Van Nuys, CA, 91406–4878.

American Medical Association. *American Medical Association Home Medical Encyclopedia.* Reader's Digest, Pleasantville, NY, 1989.

Bidwell, R.J. The gay and lesbian teen: A case of denied adolescence, *Journal of Pediatric Health Care* 2, 1(1988):3–8.

Blumenfeld, W.J. Gay, lesbian, bisexual, and questioning youth. In J. Drolet and K. Clark, eds., *The Sexuality Education Challenge.* ETR Associates, Santa Cruz, CA, 1994, ch. 19.

Center for the Study of Social Policy. *Kids Count Data Book.* Annie E. Casey Foundation, Washington, DC, 1993.

Einstein, E. Stepfamily lives. *Human Behavior* (1979): 63–68.

Gant, N.F., Cunningham, F.G. *Basic Gynecology and Obstetrics.* Appleton and Lange, East Norwalk, CT, 1993.

National Geographic Society. *The Incredible Machine.* Washington, DC, 20036–4688.

Neutens, J. *Discover: Healthy Sexual Development* high school ed. American Guidance Service, Circle Pines, MN, 1993.

Neutens, J. *Discover: Healthy Sexual Development* middle school/junior high school ed. American Guidance Service, Circle Pines, MN, 1994a.

Neutens, J. Sexuality education: A kaleidoscope of interpretations. In J. Drolet and K. Clark, eds., *The Sexuality Education Challenge.* ETR Associates, Santa Cruz, CA, 1994b.

Remafedi, G. *Male homosexuality: The adolescent's perspective.* Adolescent Health Program, University of Minnesota, Minneapolis, 1985.

Skonie-Hardin, S. Sexuality education in the middle and junior high school classroom. In J. Drolet and K. Clark, eds., *The Sexuality Education Challenge.* ETR Associates, Santa Cruz, CA, 1994.

Stapleton, C., MacCormack, N. When Parents Divorce (DHHS Publication No. 81–1120). U.S. Government Printing Office, Washington, DC, 1981.

Steinberg, L., Levine, A. *You and Your Adolescent.* Harper Perennial, New York, 1990.

Stinnett, N., DeFrain, J. *Secrets of Strong Families.* Little, Brown, Boston, 1985.

U.S. Department of Health and Human Services. *Healthy Children 2000.* Jones and Bartlett, Boston, 1992.

13

Violence Prevention

At the conclusion of this chapter, you should be able to:

- *Identify the various types of violence for which young people are especially at risk*
- *Discuss possible influences the media have on violence in society and individuals*
- *Define domestic violence and sexual assault*
- *Provide students with an understanding of what violence means*
- *Explain bullying and its effects*
- *Provide students with nonviolent alternatives for dealing with conflict*
- *Explain the kinds of interventions that are possible*

SECTION I

Health Status, Deficits, and Learning

The inclusion of a chapter on violence prevention in a health-teaching-methods textbook is a recent development, necessitated by the tremendous increase in violent injury and death among our youth. Some facts about violence are:

- One out of eight children who die before the age of twenty-one die from gunshot wounds.
- On average, six children and teens die each day in gun homicides.
- It is more likely for a teenage boy to die from being shot than from any natural cause.
- Unintentional shootings between children are the fifth leading cause of accidental death for those 0 to 14 years.
- An average of every six hours, an American teenager commits suicide with a handgun.
- An estimated 25 million American households contain handguns. Half of handgun owners report that they keep their handguns loaded and unlocked at home.
- According to media reports, nearly 40 percent of the children who are accidentally shot by other children were shot with guns left loaded and unlocked in the homes of friends or relatives.
- Nearly one-fourth of students nationwide have carried a weapon, including a gun, knife, or club, to school.
- It is estimated that the annual number of cases of domestic violence in the United States is 1.5 million.
- Fifty-three percent of men who abuse their partners are also reported to abuse their children.
- The annual incidence of sexual assault is 73 out of 100,000 females, accounting for 6 percent of all violent crimes.
- It has been reported that as many as 44 percent of women have been victims of actual or attempted sexual assault at some time in their lives, and that as many as 50 percent of these have been victims on more than one occasion.

SECTION II

Violence Prevention Teaching Information

Violence and Society

Seldom does a day pass that the news is not filled with reports of murders, rapes, and assaults. In 1992, 25,000 U.S. citizens were murdered. Even more distressing is the increasing involvement of younger and younger adolescents and children (see Figure 13.1). Thirty-five of every 100,000 homicides in 1991 were fifteen to nineteen-year-old males.

Violence as the answer to our conflicts has become all too common. After any of the more sensational incidents, violence and its effects are uniformly condemned. But seldom does the outcry last. We have become complacent and frustrated by our perceived lack of control.

More pervasive, though, than the newsworthy events are the everyday, sometimes indirect, subtle exposures to violence in schools, in entertainment media (movies, television, magazines, books, music), and on our streets and homes. Children report a surprisingly high incidence of violent occurrences while en route to or from, or at school. According to a recent study, 1 in 5 eighth

Despite the growing violence and prevalence of guns in schools, toy guns and war play are still an integral part of most boys' childhoods.

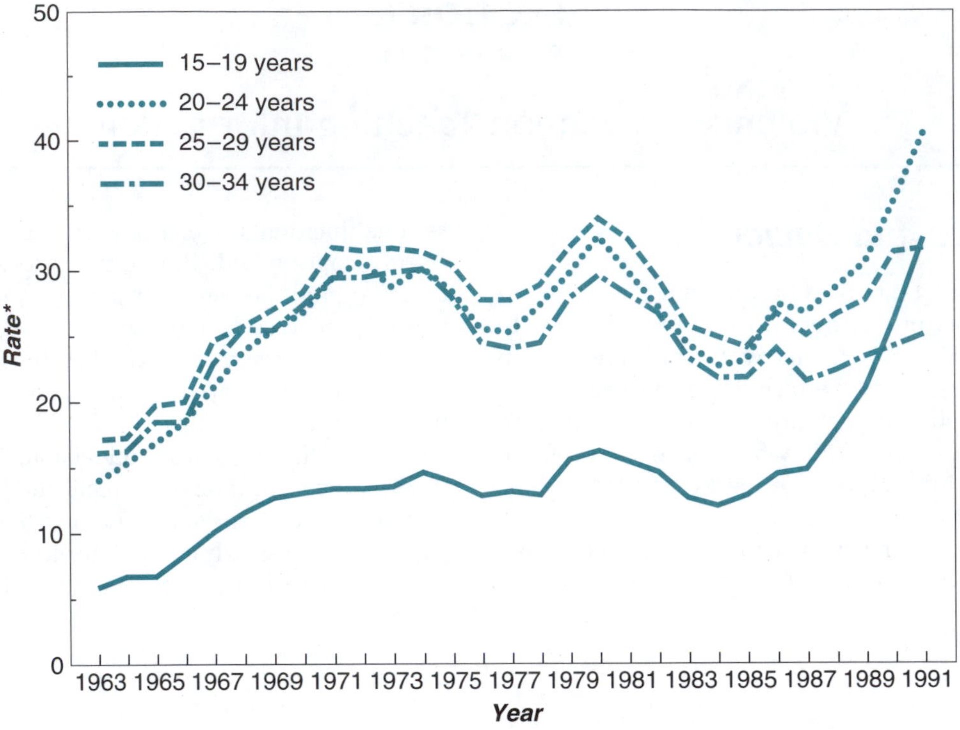

* Per 100,000 population

FIGURE 13.1 Age-Specific Rate of Homicide for Males 15–34 years by Age Group and Year, 1963–1991 (*Source:* From Homicides among 15–19-year-old males–U.S., 1963–1991, *Morbidity and Mortality Report* 43, 40 (1994): 726)

graders report having been threatened with a weapon in school. Approximately 1 in 10 eighth graders have been injured by a weapon in school, and almost 50 percent have had property stolen (Kann et al., 1994).

The entertainment media bring us realistic dramatizations of murders, rapes, beatings, and even torture. Video games, a significant pastime for many children and adolescents, often center on violent themes and characters. Lyrics of popular songs and their video depictions illustrate a disregard for other human beings, seemingly condoning mistreatment of others, especially women and girls.

Driving a car, being a spectator at a sporting event or a concert, or going to work—all place us at risk for involvement in a violent episode. This constant exposure to violence seems to have dulled our abhorrence of the behavior. Oftentimes, we appear to view it as an appropriate response to the frustrations of unemployment, marital difficulties, racism, and the stresses of daily life. Much of our attitude is deeply ingrained, carried over from centuries past when being brave, honorable, and strong was demonstrated by the ability to be violent whenever necessary.

Contributing Factors

Three decades of research suggest a causal link between exposure of children to violent images on television and subsequent violent behavior (Sege & Dietz, 1994). It would be simplistic, however, to blame all the violence in society on television, or the other media. Numerous other factors contribute to what has been termed an epidemic. These include domestic violence, socioeconomic factors, the presence of readily available firearms, and poor educational achievement.

Television and Other Media

Many American children spend more time watching television than they do working on school work. The television set has become a central feature of the modern household. Because of this, it has the tremendous potential to be a powerful educational medium.

Yet violence on television is frequent, inconsequential, effective, and rewarded (Sege & Dietz, 1994). Violence ends confrontations quickly and without the need for patience, negotiation, and compromise. On television, heroes as well as villains use violence to effectively solve problems and resolve conflicts. Very rarely does it cause pain or suffering; often instead perpetrators receive positive affirmation for their deeds.

Children learn from what they see. Thus it should surprise no one that the violence on television provokes violent or aggressive behavior in children. More specifically:

- The absence of consequences of violence children see, and the rapidity with which difficulties are resolved by its use, increase the likelihood that violence will be among the first strategies a child selects rather than the last.
- The rewards heroes receive for their violent behavior legitimize and tacitly endorse violence as a means of solving problems.
- The frequency with which children view violence and the lack of long-term consequences for the victims desensitize children, leading them to passively accept violence as a fact of life (Sege & Dietz, 1994).

By portraying violence as the normal means of conflict resolution, the media give youth the message that violence is socially acceptable and the best way to resolve problems (Elders, 1994). In his testimony before Congress, Slaby (1992) identified four harmful effects televised violence have on viewers:

1. An "aggressor effect," defined as an increased tendency for people who watch large amounts of television to behave violently towards others
2. Increased fearfulness of becoming a victim of violence
3. A "bystander" effect, characterized as callousness and desensitization towards actual violence
4. A cycle wherein aggressive children who watch a lot of violence on television identify with violent characters, act like those characters, and seek out more and more violent programming.

Violent behavior shares the following characteristics with other high-risk behaviors among youths: early initiation of delinquent behavior, lack of parental support and guidance, school failure, and inability to resist peer influences (Page et al., 1992). Violent children and adolescents are typically outside the mainstream and fail to form attachments to prosocial peers and institutions of society. These children often exhibit academic skill deficits and difficulties, and are rejected by those adults and peers who act in prosocial ways (Page et al., 1992).

Perhaps even more important than the violence children view on television, though, is the violence they see in their own homes and communities.

Domestic Violence

Violent children usually come from violent families, where children observe parents resolve conflict by violent means, and learn to handle personal conflicts and stress in a similar manner (Page et al., 1992). Violence is a learned response that the child has modeled as a problem-solving strategy. The children who live in violent households do not learn empathetic behavior, nor do they learn adequate cognitive strategies for dealing with anger. It is no surprise that they are not prepared to deal with various stressors once they enter school.

Lack of appropriate parenting is also a significant variable in the development of violent behavior (Page et al., 1992). Lack of, as well as excessive, parental monitoring and discipline; poor supervision; inconsistent rule application; and adversarial interactions are more likely to be present among children exhibiting violent behavior than among those who do not (Loeber, 1982; Wodarski & Hedrick, 1987).

The American Medical Association has made diagnosis and prevention of family violence one of its top public health priorities for 1995. This includes child physical abuse, child sexual abuse, domestic violence or spousal abuse, and elder abuse (McAfee, 1995). The long-term effects of such violence include trauma-related disorders (including post-traumatic stress disorder, especially among rape victims); personality disorders; addictive disorders; and even physical disorders (Elders, 1994).

Definitions for the various types of abuse vary widely. The National Center on Child Abuse and Neglect (NCCAN) (1992) offers the following definitions:

- Physical abuse: Physical acts that caused or could have caused physical injury to a child
- Sexual abuse: Involvement of a child in sexual activity to provide sexual gratification or financial benefit for the perpetrator, including contacts for sexual purposes, prostitution, pornography, or other sexually exploitative activities
- Psychological or emotional abuse: Acts or omissions that caused or could have caused conduct, cognitive, affective, or other mental disorders
- Neglect: Failure to provide needed, age-appropriate care.

Definitions which further specify the types of acts considered abusive vary from study to study and state to state. The Council on Scientific Affairs, American Medical Association (1993), provides the following as examples: sexual abuse may include fondling of nongenital body parts, molestations with genital contact, and heterosexual and homosexual acts. Physical abuse may include punching, beating, kicking, biting, burning, or otherwise harming a person. It is not necessary that the person intend to hurt the other person; the injury may occur during an argument or punishment of a child.

A major factor in domestic violence is the presence of firearms in the home. It is estimated that 1.2 million elementary-age children have access to guns in their homes (Elders, 1994). A gun purchased for self-protection is forty-three times more likely to be used for purposes other than to protect the home. If there is a gun in the home, (1) the occupants are eight times more likely to be killed by, or to kill, a family member or intimate acquaintances; (2) occupants are three times more likely to be killed by, or to kill, a stranger in the home; and (3) occupants are five times more likely to commit suicide (Elders, 1994).

Recommendations from the 1994 National Conference on Family Violence: Health and Justice stress the importance of primary prevention through education and attitudinal changes (McAfee 1995). How children interpret experiences, how they act with others, and how they view themselves serve as the foundation upon which they gradually build behaviors. In order for children to mature and move to higher-order thinking skills, as well as other prosocial behaviors, interventions must begin early.

Socioeconomics and Ethnicity

Low-income people, more than those with higher incomes, are victims of violent crimes. Poverty appears to be a major factor associated with a higher risk for murder of acquaintances and family members, as well as robbery-motivated killings of strangers (U.S. Department of Health and Human Services, 1994). Young males in the lowest socioeconomic levels are the most likely to be perpetrators, as well as victims, of violent behavior (Page et al., 1992). Homicide is the number-one cause of death among black youth. The homicide rate for young black men increased by 40 percent between 1984 and 1987 to nearly 86 per 100,000, more than seven times the rate for young white men (U.S. Department of Health and Human Services, 1994). Race, however, appears not to be as important a risk factor for violent death as socioeconomic status. Racial differences in homicide rates are significantly reduced when socioeconomic factors are taken into account.

Sexual Assault

Sexual assault may be defined as any sexual act performed by one person on another without that person's consent. The use of threats or force may render the victim unable to appropriately respond. In 1992, almost 4 percent of all violent crimes were incidents of sexual assault (U.S. Department of Justice, 1993).

Society has held many misconceptions about victims of sexual assault. These include the beliefs that women who are assaulted encourage the assault by their behavior or dress, that they do not offer sufficient resistance to the assault, and that they are promiscuous (ACOG, 1992).

Sexual assault may occur to people across all age, ethnic, and socioeconomic groups. Most often the perpetrator is someone who is known to the victim. Date rape is a sexual assault committed against a friend, acquaintance, or "date"; statutory rape is sexual assault committed against a person under the legal age for sexual intercourse.

People who are sexually assaulted lose control over their lives for the period of the assault. Since their lives may be threatened, they may experience intense anxiety and fear for a prolonged period of time. Counseling may be necessary in order for the victims to regain a sense of control over their bodies and lives in general.

Violence and the Schools

The professionals who work in schools are charged with preserving an environment into which families can send their children to receive training and preparation to participate and contribute to society. But children's sense of safety is repeatedly undermined as they see—in the home, school, community and media—that the world is a violent and dangerous place, and that people regularly hurt each other and use fighting to solve their problems (Levin, 1994). As parents and teachers, we often feel powerless to protect our children from this violence.

While the amount and severity of the violence to which children are exposed and the degree to which they are affected varies across society, few children are exempt. Figure 13.2 illustrates the range of children's exposure to violence. The lowest level, entertainment violence, touches most children's lives; the highest level, chronic and direct exposure, touches far fewer children, but in a much profounder manner.

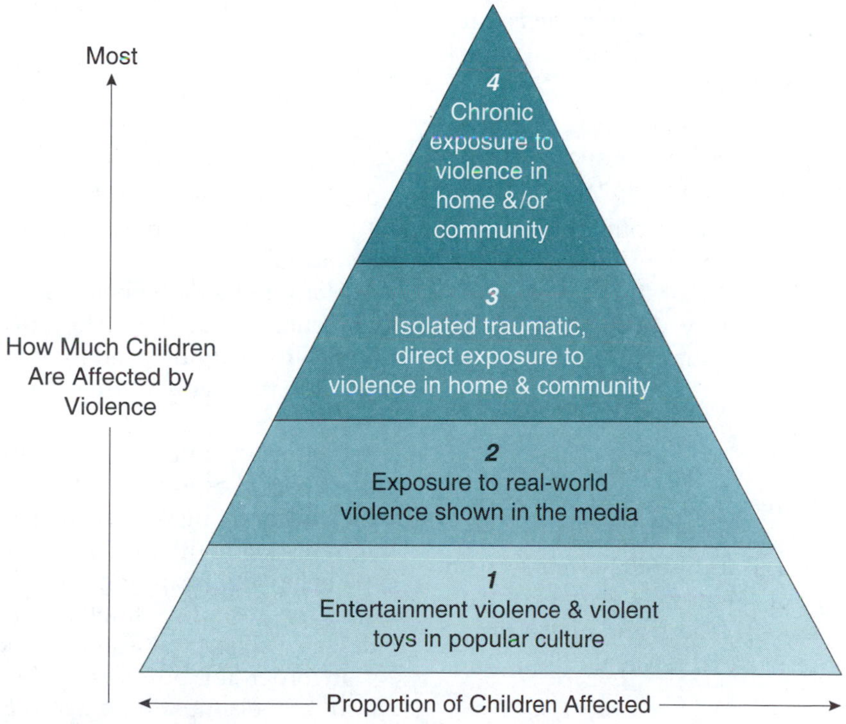

FIGURE 13.2 The Continuum of Violence in Children's Lives (*Source:* Reprinted with permission from *Teaching Young Children in Violent Times: Building a Peaceable Classroom,* by Diane E. Levin, Educators for Social Responsibility, Cambridge, MA, 1994)

The meaning that children give to this violence depends largely on their individual characteristics, level of development, family background, and prior experiences. Adults can help children work through their experiences with violence, counteracting the negative effects that exposure can have on children's thoughts, feelings, and future development.

Prevalence

In a national school-based survey conducted by the Centers for Disease Control and state and local education agencies, the following results were reported for 1993 (Kann et al., 1994):

- Nearly one-fourth (22%) of students nationwide had carried a weapon, including a gun, knife, or club, during the thirty days preceding the survey.
- Nationwide, 7.9 percent of students had carried a gun during the thirty days preceding the survey.
- 4.4 percent of students had missed at least one day of school during the thirty days preceding the survey because they felt unsafe at school or traveling to and from school.
- Nationwide, 16.2 percent of students had been in a physical fight on school property during the twelve months preceding the survey.
- Nationwide, approximately one-third of students (32.7%) had property such as a car, clothing, or books stolen or deliberately damaged on school property during the twelve months preceding the survey.

The boys most at risk for antisocial behavior as teenagers and adults were rated as overactive as early as kindergarten. That is, research has shown that hyperactivity increases the risk of later antisocial behavior. Males who are most likely to be troublemakers as teenagers and adults were seen in kindergarten as impulsive, low in anxiety or caution, low in desire to help others, and unconcerned about angering others (Tremblay et al., 1994).

Bullies

At the elementary and middle-school levels, one of the most common causes of trouble between students is bullying. *Bullying* is defined as a form of aggression in which one or more students physically and/or psychologically (and more recently, sexually) harass another student repeatedly over a period of time (Batsche & Knoff, 1994). Very often, the action is unprovoked, and the bully is seen as stronger than the victim by their peers. During their years at school, 15 to 20 percent of all students will experience some form of bullying, and 90 percent of those students bullied state that they experienced a drop in grades (Batsche & Knoff, 1994).

Bullies intimidate those they believe cannot, or will not, retaliate or those with whom they have been successful in the past. The bullies themselves believe they pick on their victim(s) because they are provoked or because they do not like the victim(s). Many bullies come from family environments where they have been successful in bullying adults, or where they have received positive feedback for such actions.

Batsche & Knoff (1994) reported that bullying is intergenerational; that is, a bully at school is a victim at home. Bullies come from homes where parents: (1) prefer physical means of discipline (authoritarian), (2) are sometimes hostile and rejecting, (3) are described as both hostile and permissive (inconsistent parenting/little supervision), (4) have poor problem-solving skills, and (5) teach their children to strike back at the least provocation.

Many bullies like being a bully and perceive their actions as justified. They are characterized by impulsivity, a strong need to dominate others, and little empathy with victims. Bullying is all about control.

Victims of bullying might exhibit fearfulness and anxiety, especially in the environment in which the bullying has taken place. These students might respond with avoidance, withdrawal, or escape behaviors (skipping school, avoiding certain classes or areas in school, running away, or suicide), as well as poor academic performance.

In order for bullying to be reduced significantly, schools must send a strong message to students and staff that it is unacceptable. Batsche & Knoff (1994) recommend the following strategies and components necessary to construct a comprehensive plan to control and prevent bullying:

1. Promote facts, not myths, about bullying.
2. Dispel beliefs about aggressive behavior.
3. Conduct a school-wide assessment of bullying.
4. Develop a student code of conduct.
5. Provide counseling services for bullies and victims.
6. Involve parents in the intervention process.
7. Implement intervention strategies specific to aggressive children.
8. Inform students and teachers of the effects of the plan.

Strategies and Interventions

You can't reciprocate hate and violence with hate and violence. . . .

An eye for an eye will make the whole world blind.
—Sonia, age 19 (Goodwillie, 1993)

As a society, we need to concentrate less on fixing the results of violence, and more on preventing it. Violence, though, is a complex problem, not amenable to simple solutions.

Violence prevention, from a public health perspective, means two things: reducing our children's risk of facing violence in the future, and preventing the immediate threat of violence to our adolescents and young children (Elders, 1994). We must deal not only with the individual child, but also with the family, the social environment, and the community with a coordinated long-term program.

As a teacher, you should recognize that there are behaviors and strategies that can help you safeguard yourself and the students in your classroom, thereby decreasing the chances of becoming a victim of violence. Canter & Garrison (1994) have identified some characteristics of teachers whose classrooms are relatively violence-free. These teachers:

- Develop positive relationships with students, not only inside the classroom but in the school and community
- Take preventive action by creating a classroom environment where the teacher is clearly in control
- Know how to defuse a confrontation
- Insist on backup support.

Children's conflicts are complex social interactions, as are adults' conflicts. If parents and teachers learn to understand children's conflicts, they will be in a better position to help young children break the current cycle of widespread violence. Conflicts among children are a natural occurrence, although traditionally, they have been viewed as undesirable. Wheeler (1994) reports the recent theory suggesting that peer conflicts contribute to a child's development and represent an important form of social interaction. Thus the focus, for

Learning itself is a form of violence prevention. Parents of academically successful students are more likely to play an active role in their child's homework and study habits.

teachers and other adults, should be on helping children develop conflict-resolution strategies that are independent of adult intervention. More specifically, Wheeler (1994) has identified the following implications for teachers from research on children's conflicts:

- Teachers need to be aware of children's intentions in their disputes. Is this an issue that the children are truly trying to resolve, or is it verbal play? Help children make clear their own understanding of a conflict.
- Teachers should be conscious of individual and cultural differences in the way children conduct their conflicts.
- Children's ability to resolve conflicts increases as their verbal competence and ability to take other perspective grows. If the children involved in a dispute are verbal and empathetic, let them try to work things out for themselves.
- By observing the issues involved in children's conflicts, teachers may decide whether to intervene. Possession issues and name-calling generate less discussion than issues about facts or play decisions.
- Children who explain their actions to each other are likely to create their own solutions. In conflicts characterized by physical strategies and simple verbal opposition, teachers should help children find more words to use.
- Teachers should ask whether the children were playing together before the conflict. Prior interaction and friendship motivate children to resolve disputes on their own.
- Teachers can reduce the frustration of constant conflict by making play spaces accessible and providing ample materials for sharing.
- Children often rely on adults, who are frequently happy to supply a "fair" solution. Instead, teachers should try to give children time and space to develop their own resolutions, allow them the choice of negotiating, changing the activity, dropping the issue, or creating new rules that seem fair to them.
- Conflicts do not often involve aggression, and children are frequently capable of resolving their disputes. Teachers should provide appropriate guidance, yet allow children to manage their own conflicts and resolutions.

Every person in school must help establish an environment that says to students: We respect each other and we respect the sanctity of our school. Teachers should strive to expand the children's understanding of positive ways people can treat each other even when conflicts arise.

Finally, learning itself is a form of violence prevention. The cognitive skills children develop during their school years help them to reason their way through stressful and dangerous situations. Their capacity to think can help them see beyond the prevailing assumption that one has no choice but to fight (Prothrow-Stith, 1991).

Children who succeed in school are at less risk for violence than their unsuccessful peers. And this correlation between violence and school failure holds true for all groups of young people in our society (Prothrow-Stith, 1991).

Clark (in Prothrow-Stith, 1991) found that the parents of the academically successful young people he studied, all of whom were poor, shared certain traits. They believed that education could make the lives of their children better, and they shared this belief with their children. They helped prepare their young children for school by talking to them, reading to them, and playing word and math games with them. They trained their small children to do homework by setting aside a time and place for them to work every day. They supervised their children's leisure time, limiting their access to risky peers and activities, and they encouraged their children's efforts with love and support.

Teaching Conflict Resolution

Although staying in school is, in and of itself, one pathway to successfully avoiding violence, the addition of conflict-avoidance/resolution skills decreases the risk even further. There are many programs throughout the country that endeavor to teach children how to manage their anger and any subsequent conflicts. All of these programs share the ideas that:

- Conflict is a normal part of human interaction.
- When people take the time to explore their prejudices, they can learn how to get along with (and enjoy) people whose backgrounds are different.

- Most disputes do not have to have a winner and loser. Win-win is the ideal way to resolve most disputes.
- Children (and adults) who learn how to assert themselves nonviolently can avoid becoming bullies or victims.
- The self-esteem of children is enhanced if they learn to build nonviolent, nonhostile relationships with their peers (Prothrow-Stith 1991).

Some school systems have implemented peer mediation programs. These systems believe that keeping weapons out—as desirable as that may be—does not necessarily keep out violence. A mediation program, in order to be successful, must have carefully trained peer mediators; outreach to students, school staff, and parents; confidentiality and trust; the full support of the staff and administration; and an emergency system capable of quick action (Merina, 1995).

For most conflict-resolution programs, the rules of mediation are carefully followed: Listen carefully to what the other person is saying, restate the problem in your own words, do not interrupt, and agree to solve the problem.

We must teach children how to resolve conflicts peacefully, especially those at high risk. While they are still open to positive influences, we can impart knowledge and modify behaviors for addressing conflicts of any magnitude.

Children who feel mistrustful and unsafe devote a great proportion of their energy, thoughts, and feelings into avoiding danger, thereby undermining the course of development and learning. To break the intergenerational cycle of violence, we must begin early in a child's life. Research has shown that comprehensive school health education is effective in influencing youth's behaviors and establishing a pattern of healthy behavior in the future (Elders, 1994).

Implications for Elementary and Middle-School Teachers

Summary Issues

1. Violence has become epidemic in our society.
2. Younger and younger children and adolescents are involved in violent acts.
3. Media portrayals of violence are one factor contributing to the increase in violent behavior.
4. Children spend more time watching television than they do doing their school work.
5. Violence on television seldom has negative consequences.
6. People have become desensitized to the tremendous amount of violence.
7. Four harmful effects of violence have been identified: the aggressor effect, increased fearfulness, the bystander effect, and the intergenerational cycle of violence.
8. Violent behavior has common characteristics with other high-risk behaviors.
9. Violent children often come from violent families.
10. Children in violent families do not learn other strategies to cope with problems.
11. Lack of appropriate parenting is another factor contributing to violence in children.
12. Domestic violence includes child physical abuse, sexual abuse, spousal abuse, and elder abuse.
13. Widespread access to firearms in the home contributes to increased violent behavior.
14. Poverty, not ethnicity, is a predisposing factor for violent behavior.
15. Sexual assaults account for 4 percent of all violent crimes.
16. Society holds many misconceptions about sexual assault.
17. All children are exposed to violence to varying degrees.
18. A child's response to violence is dependent on his or her socialization and family circumstances.
19. Boys at risk for antisocial behavior may be identified as early as kindergarten.
20. Bullying is the most common form of violent behavior in elementary and middle schools.
21. Bullying is physically or psychologically harassing another person.
22. Bullies believe their behavior is justified.
23. Victims of bullying may exhibit negative psychological and academic effects.

24. Teachers may create a classroom atmosphere that helps reduce violent behavior.
25. Allow children to resolve their own conflicts whenever possible.
26. Children who succeed in school are less violence-prone.
27. Health education is effective in influencing children's behaviors.

Teacher Ramifications

In regard to violence prevention in the schools, teachers should:

1. Remain current in regard to the literature and research findings about factors contributing to violence
2. Teach about conflict and conflict-resolution skills
3. Know their state guidelines and policies for teachers pertaining to child abuse, including physical abuse, sexual abuse, psychological abuse, and neglect
4. Teach about behaviors that reduce high-risk situations for violence
5. Employ strategies to reduce and eliminate bullying
6. Adapt or adopt teacher characteristics that are associated with violence-free classrooms
7. Support the school's role in helping the nation reach the following objectives set forth in *Healthy Children 2000* (1994):
   - #7.3. Reduce weapon-related violent deaths from major causes to no more than 12.6 per 100,000 people.
   - #7.4. Reverse to less than 25.2 per 1,000 children the rising incidence of maltreatment of children younger than eighteen years.
   - #7.6. Reduce assault injuries among people aged twelve and older to no more than 10 per 1,000 people.
   - #7.7. Reduce rape and attempted rape of women aged twelve and older to no more than 108 per 100,000 women.
   - #7.8. Reduce by 15 percent the incidence of injurious suicide attempts among adolescents aged fourteen through seventeen.
   - #7.9. Reduce by 20 percent the incidence of physical fighting among adolescents aged fourteen through seventeen.
   - #7.10. Reduce by 20 percent the incidence of weapon-carrying by adolescents aged fourteen through seventeen.

SECTION III

Teaching Strategies for Violence Prevention

The strategies in this section are divided into grades K–4, 5–6, and 7–8 levels. In addition to strategies that can be used in the classroom, home activities are included. A home activity is designed for student-parent interaction. It is a way to engage the home in school-student learning, and parents can sign a slip of paper to confirm that an activity was completed. Evaluation of all strategies through the use of the National Health Education Standards and performance indicators is indicated. Teachers may also choose to write corresponding learning assessments.

K–4 Level

Strategy One

Objective: Students will be able to identify violent situations in the television shows they watch.

Activity: In a large-group discussion, the teacher is to have students give examples of the various television shows they watch. Names of the shows are to be written on the board. The teacher then asks the students to think about different things they have seen on the shows (this may be done in small groups). Students are, specifically, to try to remember shows where someone was hurt by violence. In a large group, the teacher is to facilitate a discussion on alternative ways the show's characters could have dealt with their problem.

Integration: Social Studies

Related Health Content Areas: Growth and development, growth and injury prevention

Health Education Standards and Performance Indicators: 3(1); 4(3); 6(1,3)

Strategy Two

Objective: Students will be able to tell the difference between toys and adult weapons.

Activity: Using catalogs, magazines, advertising, and the like, have students cut out pictures of adult weapons and children's toys. They should keep the pictures in two separate groups. Ask the students to hold up examples of "safe" toys. Then ask them to hold up examples of adult weapons. See whether all of the students are classifying the pictures correctly.

Integration: Social Studies, Language Arts

Related Health Content Areas: Safety

Health Education Standards and Performance Indicators: 3(1,6); 4(3)

5–6 Level

Strategy One

Objective: Students will recognize how body language can convey different messages.

Activity: Have all the students stand where they can move freely, possibly in a circle. Ask them to strike poses that show various emotions. Examples: winning a race; falling down and missing a game-winning catch; winning the geography bee over one hundred other students; having your best friend move away; and arguing with their teacher. After the students have become familiar with winning and losing poses, give several students "secret" poses to do. Have the other students try to guess whether it is a "winning" pose or a "losing" pose. Discuss how body language sends strong messages on how we feel.

Integration: Science, Social Studies

Related Health Content Areas: Growth and development, emotional well-being

Health Education Standards and Performance Indicators: 5 (1,2,7,8); 7(1)

Strategy Two

Objective: Students will understand the harmful results of playing with guns.

Activity: Have several students volunteer to role-play situations using the following rules:

- Do not touch a gun; get away.
- If a friend brings a gun to show you, tell your friend that you do not want to be around guns because someone could get hurt or killed.
- Tell a trusted adult about the gun.

Have students come up with their own scenarios to role-play. (You may wish to give them the assignment the day before.)

Integration: Social Studies, Language Arts

Related Health Content Areas: Safety

Health Education Standards and Performance Indicators: 1(6,7); 3(1,5,6)

Strategy Three

Objective: Students will demonstrate positive means of awareness and safety while walking with friends.

Activity: Have students develop situations that could be hazardous to children walking with their friends. (The teacher may wish to include some of his or her own along with these.) These situations might include topics such as strangers lurking, other people in fights, drunken drivers, and gang activity. Discuss the situations, and have students demonstrate what they would do to maintain their safety. Focus on awareness of surroundings being a key to prevention.

Integration: Social Studies

Related Health Content Areas: Alcohol, tobacco, and other drugs, safety

Health Education Standard and Performance Indicator: 3(6)

7–8 Level

Strategy One

Objective: Students will be able to define what violence means to them. Students will be able to identify criteria for violent acts.

Activity: Have students brainstorm definitions of the terms *personal safety* and *violence prevention*. Write all responses on the board. Facilitate discussion, possibly using the following questions:

- What does it mean to be safe?
- Does safety concern only adults? children? How is it different for different age groups?
- Can violence be verbal or emotional as well as physical?

Discuss the fact that most violence occurs between people who know each other, and that this is the opposite of what many people believe. Use current events to demonstrate this (have local newspapers or articles related to this topic).

Then discuss prevention as the best way to avoid being harmed. Explain that once you are in a situation, your options are severely limited; you may not be in total control of what happens to you. (Connect this with discussions regarding pregnancy, STD transmission, rape prevention, suicide, etc.)

Integration: Social Studies

Related Health Content Areas: Safety; family, relationships, and sexuality; emotional well-being

Health Education Standards and Performance Indicators: 3(6); 5(7)

Strategy Two

Objective: Students will be able to demonstrate nonviolent techniques to solve tense or angry situations.

Activity: Give students a handout with the following headings:

I get angry when . . .

When I'm angry, . . .

Instruct students to think about things that make them angry. After listing several of these in the first column, students should then write what they do or how they behave when they get angry. Have students compare their list with that of someone else in class. How many are similar? different? Then have volunteers from the class give examples and list them on the board. Ask students to identify which responses seem likely to lead to nonviolent solutions and which are most likely to end in some type of violence.

Next discuss the fight-or-flight response, covering what happens physically to the body when someone gets angry or upset. Since anger is a physical as well as mental response, physical activity can often help to reduce the strong feelings being experienced. (This is one reason why physical fighting is an option for some people; they do not know what else to do with their strong physical feelings.)

Have students think of different positive ways to deal with anger—both the physical and mental parts of it. Pair students off, and have them choose three "angry" situations and develop a method to deal with them in a nonviolent, positive manner.

Integration: Science, Social Studies

Related Health Content Areas: Emotional well-being, safety and injury prevention

Health Education Standards and Performance Indicators: 5(7,8); 6(3)

Home Activities

Strategy One

Objective: Students will explore various types of violent behavior.

Activity: Using the local newspaper and/or magazines (e.g., *Time, People, U.S. News and World Report*), have students locate articles dealing with violence. They should read the articles (or have them summarized for them) and be prepared to explain what happened. Discuss with students why certain situations occur, and how other people cope with them differently. Emphasize the option of finding nonviolent means to resolve conflicts.

Integration: Social Studies, Language Arts

Related Health Content Areas: Emotional well-being; family, relationships, and sexuality; growth and development

Health Education Standards: 1,5

Strategy Two

Objective: Students will view demonstrations of appropriate ways to handle firearms.

Activity: Utilizing the expertise of either a parent/guardian or a member of a local hunter-safety group, arrange a demonstration on firearms. This should include how to handle one properly, how to tell if a gun is loaded, what to do in different types of situations (e.g., a young child with a gun, a friend who wants to show off a gun, etc.).

Integration: Social Studies, Math, Science

Related Health Content Areas: Safety

Health Education Standard: 3

References

American College of Obstetricians-Gynecologists. *The Battered Woman* (pub. no. 124). ACOG, Washington, DC, 1989.

American College of Obstetricians-Gynecologists. *Sexual Assault* (pub. no. 172). ACOG, Washington, DC, 1992.

Batsche, G.M., & Knoff, H. Bullies and their victims: Understanding a pervasive problem in the schools, *School Psychology Review* 23, 2(1994): 165–173.

Canter, L., & Garrison R. (1994). *Scared or Prepared: How to Prevent Violence and Create a Safer School Environment* (video). Canter & Associates, P.O. Box 2113, Santa Monica, CA 90407-2113.

Center for the Prevention of Handgun Violence. *Straight Talk about Risks.* Washington, DC, 1992.

Council on Scientific Affairs, American Medical Association. Adolescents as victims of family violence, *Journal of American Medical Association*, 270,15(1993):1850–1856.

Elders, J. Violence as a public health issue for children, *Childhood Education* 70, 5(1994):260–262.

Goodwillie, S., ed. *Voices from the Future: Children Speak Out about Violence in America.* Crown, New York, 1993.

James, B. School violence and the law: The search for suitable tools, *School Psychology Review* 23, 2(1994):190–203.

Kann, L., Warren, C., Harris, W., Collins, J., Douglas, K., Collins, M., Williams, B., Ross, J., & Kolbe, L. Youth risk-behavior surveillance: United States, 1993, *Journal of School Health* 65, 5(1994): 163–170.

Levin, D. Building a peaceable classroom, *Childhood Education* 70, 5(1994):267–270.

Loeber R. The stability of antisocial and delinquent child behavior: A review, *Child Development* 53(1983):1431–1436.

McAfee, R. Physicians and domestic violence: Can we make a difference? *Journal of the American Medical Association* 273, 22(1995):1790–1791.

Merina, A. Can we talk? How peer mediation reduces school violence, *NEA Today* (1995)10–11.

MMWR. Homicides among 15- to 19-year-old males, U.S., 1963–1991, *Morbidity & Mortality Weekly Report* 43, 40(1994):726.

National Center on Child Abuse and Neglect. *National Child Abuse and Neglect Data System: 1990 Summary Data Component* (pub. no. ACF 92-30361). U.S. Department of Health and Human Services, Washington, DC, 1992.

Page, R.M., Kitchin-Becker, S., Solovan, D., Golec, T., & Herbert, D.L. Interpersonal violence: A priority issue for health education, *Journal of Health Education* 23, 5(1992):286–292.

Prothrow-Stith, D. *Deadly Consequences.* Harper Perennial, New York, 1991.

Sege, R., & Dietz, W. Television viewing and violence in children: The pediatrician as agent for change, *Pediatrics* 94, 4(1994):600–607.

Slaby, R. Television violence: Effects and remedies. Testimony before U.S. House of Representatives Judiciary Subcommittee on Crime and Criminal Justice, Dec. 12, 1992.

Television Violence: Effects and Remedies. U.S. House of Representatives Judiciary Subcommittee on Crime and Criminal Justice, 1992.

Tremblay, R., Pihl, R., Vitaro, F., & Dobkin, P. Predicting early onset of male antisocial behavior from preschool behavior, *Archives of General Psychiatry* 51(1994):732–739.

U.S. Department of Health and Human Services. *Healthy People 2000*. Washington, DC, 1994.

U.S. Department of Justice. *Bureau of Justice Statistics: Sourcebook of Criminal Justice Statistics* (No. 0-16-045627-4, NCJ-148211). U.S. Government Printing Office, Washington, DC, 1993.

Wheeler, E.J. Peer conflicts in the classroom: Drawing implications from research, *Childhood Education* 70, 5(1994):296–299.

Wodarski, J.S., & Hedrick, M. Violent children: A practice paradigm, *Social Work in Education* 1987:28–42.

14

Consumer Health

Upon completion of this chapter, you should be able to:

- *Describe the role of a wise consumer*
- *Distinguish among the different health care professionals in the medical field*
- *Determine when to seek help*
- *Explain how to select a health care facility*
- *Identify the similarities and differences in the changing health care–insurance system*
- *List and explain the role of various government organizations in consumer health*

SECTION I

Health Status, Deficits, and Learning

You live with consumer health every day, assuming that you wash, eat, and use any other products that affect your physical, social, mental-emotional, or spiritual well-being. But you may select products either judiciously or almost at random. Following are some examples:

- Almost all packaged foods come with FDA-required nutrition facts labels. Do you know how to read them?
- Do you evaluate health ads on TV, radio, and in magazines?
- What is the best shampoo for your hair—full body, dry hair, oily hair? And is there a significant difference in these shampoos?
- Which of the following fast foods has the least fat content: Wendy's Light Roast Beef Deluxe sandwich, or McDonald's McGrilled Chicken Classic? How can you find out?
- Do food preservatives cause hyperactivity or other problems in children?
- What is the best over-the-counter cold remedy you can buy, and why do you say it is the best?
- How should parents pick a doctor for their child?
- If you were to select a different doctor, how would you go about it, and would you select a primary-care doctor or a specialist?
- What do ads mean when they say, "Four out of five doctors recommend . . ."?
- What is the difference between a sunscreen rated SPF2 and one rated SPF15?
- Is a salicylate product better than ibuprofen or acetaminophen products for headaches?
- Would you recommend Tylenol to a friend who has arthritis and wants to reduce his or her inflammation?
- What is the principal ingredient in Alka-Seltzer Extra Strength to give you "fast, fast relief"?
- If your doctor prescribes a generic drug, is it as good as a brand name one?
- Are cosmetics regulated by the FDA?
- If you or a friend wanted to lose weight, what program would you recommend?
- What type of health insurance are you on now? Does it cover HIV/AIDS, pregnancy, or a hospital stay over seven days?
- How much is "too much" to pay for health insurance?

SECTION II

Consumer Health Teaching Information

Often this content area of health education is a "forgotten" area. Many people believe that, of all the areas of our lives, consumer health has the least significant role. This is unfortunate because just the opposite is true. Being a health consumer affects every aspect of our health. The products you purchase, whether to clear your skin, take away your headache, or something else, affect your physical, mental-emotional, social, and spiritual well-being. How you choose your doctor will have a significant impact on your health as he or she treats you over the years. Electing to take a course on first aid or prevention of illness definitely impacts your health, and can have an impact on others too. The foods you ingest play a major role in weight gain or loss as well as nutritional status. In short, consumer health is a reality that you live with on a daily basis. Whether choosing a soap to wash with or an exercise class to join, you are making consumer health decisions. Obviously, you can maximize your health if you are a wise consumer.

Becoming a Wise Health Consumer

One of the first steps in becoming a wiser health consumer is to know how your beliefs affect your buying decisions. Do you believe that vitamin C cures a cold? How much have your beliefs about illness prevention and cure been shaped by family, friends, the media, and health care professionals? Wise health consumers base decisions on facts, not on personal motivation (e.g., buying a low-protection sunscreen to get tan fast).

Evaluating Advertisements for Health Products or Services

From a very young age, we are bombarded with advertisements telling us what is good for us or otherwise seducing us into purchases. The myriad cereal commercials on Saturday morning cartoon shows may offer different toys, but the theme of being "good or healthy for you" is common to all. While children may not have the money to purchase the products (as advertisers know), they can apply tremendous pressure on their parents to buy cereals that are high in sugar and low in nutrition.

Children need to learn that most commercials contain very little information but a lot of persuasion. The ability to distinguish between the two is very important if they are to become wise health consumers. Some of the advertising approaches used to entice are:

- *Testimonials and authority figures.* This is one of the oldest forms of advertising. A celebrity or expert assures you that the product is an excellent one and that you should use it too. For many this can be appealing. Advertisers have used the "real-people" approach in testimonials also. In this case, they try to persuade you that "ordinary" people find their product appealing and that you should buy it. Either way, children and adults need to raise the following questions:
    1. How truthful is the person in the ad?
    2. Is the amount of money paid to the person biasing his or her viewpoint so that he or she says the product is better than it really is?
    3. Do you really think it is a product you need, and if so, why?
- *Bandwagon appeal.* This approach tells you that "everyone" is using the product—everyone but you. You need to "jump on the bandwagon" and purchase this "leading product." But is the product really the nation's leading product? Who is likely to use this product? Is the product very different from what you are currently using?
- *Scientific approach.* This is the "four out of five doctors recommend" approach. Another com-

mon phrase is "hospital-tested." Frequently this tactic has an actor dressed in a laboratory coat to look official. Unfortunately, these phrases have little meaning. They simply try to appeal to the consumer who believes that if a study was done or a "scientific" person supports the product, it has to be good. Children should ask: What does "hospital-tested" mean, and what were the results? What information is given about the "study"? Why does this approach appeal to you, and how does it affect your other buying habits?

- *Fear approach.* If people cannot be seduced into or told to buy something, perhaps they can be made so anxiety-ridden that they will buy the product. You could be pregnant, so why wait for a visit to the doctor? Get a home pregnancy test. "One in five Americans experience . . .," so you had better buy this product now! Questions you may ask are:
  1. How often does this disease, illness, or disability really occur in the American population versus what the ad claims?
  2. Why did this fear technique grab you; should you see a physician or other health care professional?
  3. Is this really the best brand based upon its ingredients?
- *Miracle-cure approach.* This is a very fraudulent approach wherein ads attempt to sell products to people with incurable disorders or diseases. Generally, these products have not been tested yet their claims of success are ridiculously high. The diseases especially targeted are arthritis, AIDS, and certain kinds of cancers. But any disease for which there is no medical cure is seen as a sales opportunity by some companies, with little or no regard for the people involved. Some questions to ask here are:
  1. Does the ad claim to cure an incurable disease, or at least imply cure?
  2. Is the ad more emotional than factual?
  3. Does the product cost more than similar products on the market, or is the cost portrayed as being "high, but you are worth it"?
- *Infomercial.* This is unlike a regular TV commercial because it usually lasts for 30 minutes or more. Because it can be confused for a TV show, you may watch a few minutes of the program before realizing you are about to be seduced, enticed, flattered, or frightened into purchasing the product. Infomercials function like news shows in many ways, but the news is not always accurate. In these cases, raise the following questions:
  1. Is the health problem addressed really important enough to require 30 to 60 minutes of information (e.g., hair loss) compared to other health problems (e.g., cancer)?
  2. Who is sponsoring this show?
  3. How accurate is the information presented?
- *Superiority.* The suggestion in this approach is that only superior people embrace and use this product. Of course you could be superior if you used the product too. Children (and many adults) need to remember that a Mercedes Benz or a feast in an expensive restaurant does not come with the purchased product. Ask yourself:
  1. How realistic is this picture?
  2. Why do you want to be like those depicted, and would purchasing the product make you similar to them?
  3. Should the word *superior* be replaced by *snobby,* and what does that mean to you?
- *Advertorials.* These are most often seen in glossy magazines and are a combination of an advertisement and an editorial. They consist of several pages and mimic the look of an editorial. Unless you notice the word *advertisement* in fine print, you may be lulled into believing everything you read. The obvious approach here is that consumers are more likely to believe something written in an editorial than they are an ad. Some of the more common products advertised this way are fitness products, grooming aids, and other health-related products. Questions to be raised include:
  1. Is the word *advertisement* written anywhere on these pages? Look for fine print.
  2. Is there anything mentioned in the table of contents of the publication about these pages?
  3. Is an editor's or author's name given for these pages?
  4. If this form of ad is appealing to you, why?

All of us are drawn in by different ads (or why would there be so many different ones?). The difference is the degree to which we are influenced by the ads. If we feel good about ourselves, our knowledge, and our skills, we are less likely to be influenced by external sources. Even so, health-product marketers work every day to win you over; billions of dollars are involved. This fact alone makes it difficult for organizations such as the American Cancer Society to battle Madison Avenue. This being the case, it is a must that we learn to evaluate advertisements early in life.

Evaluation of Health and Health-Related Products

One of the best ways to evaluate products is to read the label. The Food and Drug Administration (FDA) requires that packaged foods, cosmetics, grooming products, and drugs show a list of contents on the label.

Food Labels

The easiest labels to read are food labels. The ingredients are listed in order from the greatest to the least amount present. Exceptions are food products produced by small businesses or sold in packages too small to fit the labeling information, which are exempt from the federal labeling law. Restaurants and foods prepared on site (e.g., baked goods, deli food) are exempt also. Grocery stores have been asked to voluntarily provide the consumer with information about raw fruits, vegetables, and fish.

In addition to listing contents, a label entitled "Nutrition Facts" was required beginning in 1993. Figure 14.1 illustrates a nutrient label for a can of pork and beans. Below the title is the serving size, based upon a standard list of serving sizes, followed by the number of servings within the container. The standardized serving size simplifies comparison of nutrient content in like products and is expressed in common household or metric terms. Following this section, the label must show the total number of calories, the number of calories from fat, total fat, saturated fat, cholesterol, sodium, total carbohydrate, dietary fiber, sugars, and protein. The "% Daily Value" shows how this food fits into the overall daily diet based on a 2000 calorie diet.

Comparing the nutritional labels of name-brand foods against store brands to make informed decisions is a good way to combat the effects of costly and persuasive advertising campaigns.

The amount of vitamins and minerals (e.g., calcium, iron) is provided as a percent of daily value (if present at all in the product). These are the mandatory listings; the manufacturer may offer more information about potassium, soluble and insoluble fiber, and so forth.

Over-the-Counter Medications

OTC medications are often seen as the answer to many health problems. Some of the most popular ones include pain relievers, vitamins, skin products, antacids, laxatives, eye medications, cold remedies, antihistamines, and cough suppressants. While

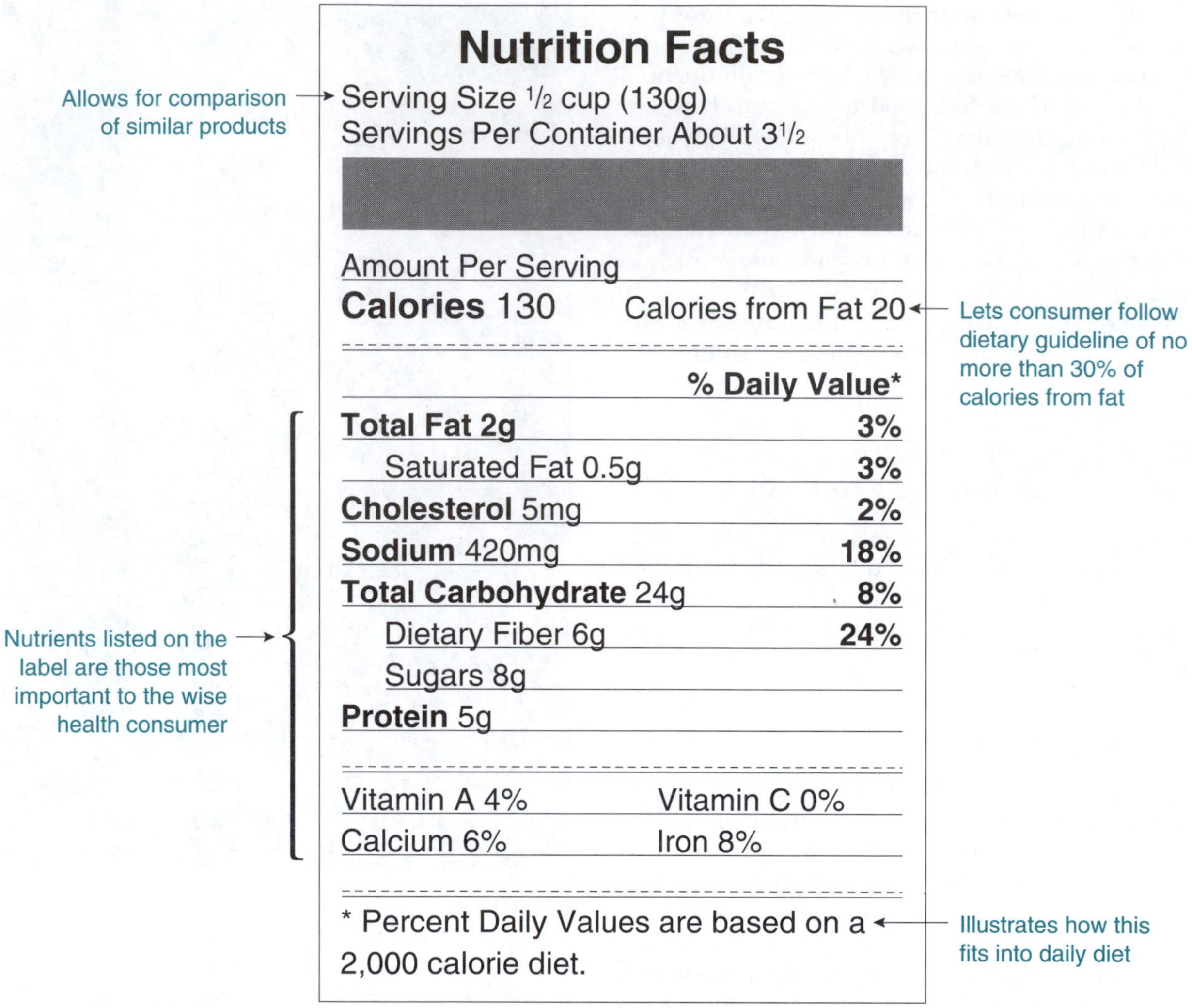

FIGURE 14.1 Example of a Nutrition Label

word-of-mouth may be how these are bought, it is important to know how to read the labels.

The FDA requires specific information on an OTC product. Labels must include: (1) approved uses of the product, (2) instructions on safe usage, and (3) warnings to users at greatest risk (Gilbertson, 1990). Unfortunately, many health consumers read only the product name. It is vital that children learn how to read these labels, especially given the fact that so many OTC medications are available in unlocked medicine cabinets. They need to know that some OTC products, such as some antacids, can be addictive and produce withdrawal consequences (Hanson & Venturelli, 1995).

Hanson and Venturelli (1995, p. 397) recommend the following rules to reduce problems when taking OTC medications:

1. *Always know what you are taking.* Read and know the active ingredients.
2. *Know the effects.* Understand both the positive and negative effects.
3. *Read and heed the warnings and cautions.* Remember, the warnings are there to protect you.
4. *Do not use anything for more than one or two weeks.* Otherwise, consult a physician.

5. *Be particularly cautious if also taking prescription drugs.* Drug interactions can have serious side effects.
6. *If you have questions, ask a pharmacist.*
7. *If you do not need it, don't use it!*

Grooming Aids

Think about the grooming products you have used in the last few days—toothpaste, shampoo, hair conditioner, skin lotions, shaving creams or lotions, hair gels, eye liner or shadow, lipstick, and so on. The common messages behind ads for these products are that (1) you will look good if you use it, and (2) you will become popular. Of course the ads also hint that you will be sexier. Wise consumers realize that no matter how much of something they use, they will always be themselves rather than an idealized advertising image.

When purchasing these products, it is best to look at the list of ingredients. Even if you do not understand all of them, use them for comparison purposes. This is especially useful when comparing high priced brands to lower priced ones. More often than not, the ingredients are almost identical. A few things to keep in mind when using these products: (1) be certain to read the directions on the package or package insert, (2) never share or use other people's cosmetics, (3) use only clean tap water, not saliva, to dilute face make-up and skin care products, and (4) replace cosmetics every three to six months.

Consumerism in the Health-Care Industry

Health care in the United States has become a big industry. Demands to control cost, achieve universal access, and promote generalism over specialization have ushered forth some major changes in recent years. Almost from the beginning of medicine, physicians and patients worked together for both healing and payment. However, the current shift is away from the traditional fee-for-service medicine to managed care (see Box 14.1). "In 1988, indemnity insurance accounted for 72.6 percent of the private health-insurance mar-

BOX 14.1 ■ ■ ■ ■ ■
ABOUT MANAGED-CARE ORGANIZATIONS

The changing health care market has given rise to several acronyms and terms within managed care. This list illustrates some of the more common definitions.

Managed care: A system that combines delivery and financing of medical care by means of any of the following four features: (1) contracts with chosen physicians and hospitals to give health-care services to enrolled members, who usually pay a monthly premium, (2) the doctors assume some financial risk, (3) quality and utilization controls by the organization that providing doctors must accept, and (4) patients have financial incentives to use only doctors who are in the plan.

HMO (health maintenance organization): A business that gets a fixed amount of money from the government or an employer for each person enrolled in the HMO plan. A specified set of services is available, and members are not reimbursed for care provided or authorized by the HMO.

PPO (preferred provider organization): A business that contracts with employers to provide health care at a lower cost than that given to the community at large. Therefore, members must use the "preferred providers" or pay more.

EPO (exclusive provider organization): Similar to the PPO in that the benefits are greater when exclusive providers are used, but dissimilar to the PPO in that benefits are reduced dramatically or perhaps eliminated if some other provider is used.

Group practice model: A group of physicians who have an office with centralized billing, benefits, and expectations. Ownership is held by the partners in the group. Productivity may play a strong role in such a group, depending upon the organizational arrangements.

ket; by 1993, it had shrunk to 33.3 percent" (Weiss, 1995, p. 10). This trend is much more than economic; the conventional physician-patient relationship has been altered too. As the marketplace demanded lower costs, managed-care organizations, through hospitals or other means, brought physicians on as employees. The days of independence came to an end for many physicians. The lack of independence is reflected not only in business arrangement, but also in what medicines can be prescribed and what surgeries can be performed. In other words, the managed-care organization often tells the physicians which drugs can be used to treat particular diseases or illnesses, no longer leaving the decision-making to the physician. The managed-care organizations and government place great emphasis on primary care, too.

Selection of a Health-Care Provider

In the fee-for-service model, patients could choose almost anyone they desired to be their physicians. However, with the switch to managed care, patients have to select a physician who is a member of the managed-care organization connected with their place of work. When this first came about, in the mid-1990s, many people had to select another physician as they moved into managed care.

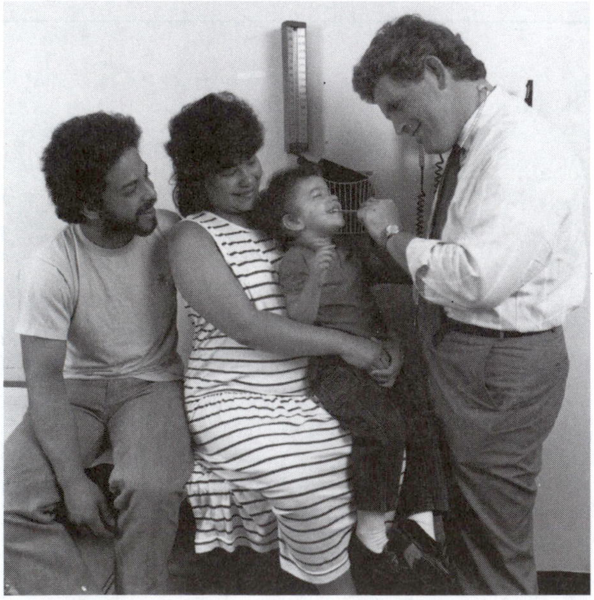

It is wise to shop around for health-care providers. Find someone you trust and respect, and make sure you both outline your expectations and concerns up front.

The emphasis on primary care today means that you are likely to visit a *primary-care physician* before seeing anyone else. Primary-care physicians are those who practice family medicine, internal medicine, pediatrics, or gynecology. These physicians are trained for screening as well as diagnosis and treatment, and generally have greater orientation toward prevention than some of the specialties. Primary-care physicians refer to *specialists* such as cardiologists, pediatric surgeons, and oncologists. Box 14.2 shows several types of physicians and their areas of specialization.

As for training, there are two types of medical degrees available in the United States—the MD, or doctor of medicine, familiar to most people; and the DO, or doctor of osteopathy, received from colleges of osteopathy. Today the training programs for both degrees are very similar. Since about 90 percent of physicians are MDs, more detail about their training is provided here. Four years of college is generally required, followed by four years of medical school. The MD degree is awarded upon completion of medical school. However, in order to practice medicine, a minimum of one year of internship is also required. Most interns continue on through a residency program to specialize in a particular medical area—family practice, internal medicine, pediatrics, obstetrics and gynecology, cardiology, surgery, and so on. The lengths of the residency programs vary according to specialty. For example, family medicine and internal medicine are usually two years beyond the internship year, whereas obstetrics-gynecology is three years and surgery is four years. MDs become board-certified after successful completion of the residency and examinations. Some *subspecialists* continue their education in fellowships to specialize even further. For example, a gynecologic oncologist completes an additional three years after the residency in obstetrics and gynecology.

BOX 14.2

PHYSICIANS: PRIMARY-CARE AND SPECIALISTS

Physician providers have been generally divided into two groups: primary-care providers (often called *gatekeepers*) and specialty providers.

Gatekeepers: Primary-care physicians (family practitioners, internists, pediatricians, obstetrician-gynecologists, and osteopaths). In managed-care organizations, a patient must consult a primary-care physician to get a referral to a specialist if deemed appropriate. Gatekeepers authorize all medical services, including non-emergency hospitalizations and diagnostic workups.

Family practitioners: Have a wide range of medical knowledge and administer health care to people of all ages. Generally have a background or knowledge in health promotion and community health.

Internists: Graduates of an internal medicine residency program who administer health care to the adult population. Some internists have a special interest in the geriatric population.

Pediatricians: Have special training in the medical problems and treatment of infants, children, and adolescents

Obstetrician-gynecologists: Graduate from a four-year program with emphasis on obstetrics (pregnancy and delivery of babies) and gynecology (health and disease in women, including surgery)

Osteopaths: Graduates of an osteopathic medicine program; may function similarly to family practitioners

Specialists: Physicians who specialize in a particular area of medicine. In the examples below, all receive the MD degree except for dentists, who generally earn the DDS degree.

Allergists: All types of allergies such as asthma in children

Anesthesiologists: Administer medication (anesthetics) during surgery

Cardiologists: Diseases of the heart

Dentists: Mouth, tooth, and jaw care

Endocrinologists: The endocrine system

Oncologists: Cancer. Subspecialist could be a gynecologic oncologist, who specializes in cancer of the female reproductive system.

Orthopedists: The skeletal system

Psychiatrists: Mental illness

It is best to choose a provider when you are healthy. The following can be kept in mind:

- Does the health-care provider have good knowledge and experience regarding your particular medical condition (e.g., diabetes)?
- Are good credentials—readily available, recognized schools, board-certified in the specialty and perhaps a subspecialty, association with a teaching hospital—evident?
- Does the provider have a manner that is compatible with yours?
- What hospital(s) does the provider have admitting privileges with?
- How are emergencies and off-hour situations handled?
- What is the payment plan? What if your insurance does not handle it? Is payment needed up-front for any procedures?
- How open is the primary care provider to making a referral if you request it?

Box 14.3 lists alternative health-care providers, that is, providers who administer health care in a manner different from traditional physician providers.

When to Seek Professional Help

Obviously, professional help should be sought in medical emergencies. This can often be done by dialing 911. However, if a situation is serious but

BOX 14.3 ■ ■ ■ ■ ■
ALTERNATIVE HEALTH-CARE PROVIDERS

Allopathic medicine is what all medical doctors practice. It is traditional medicine in the United States and Canada.

Acupuncture originated in about 2500 B.C. in China to relieve pain and treat disease. The theory is that energy flows along certain lines, or meridians, in the body and if it is blocked then illness results. Sharp needles are inserted through the skin along the meridian lines to allow energy to flow, restoring the balance between yin and yang. In the United States, some medical doctors use acupuncture during surgery as the only anesthetic to block pain.

Chiropractic medicine was promoted in the United States by Daniel David Palmer on the belief that all diseases are caused by subluxed (misaligned) vertebrae around the spinal cord. Treatment consists of spinal adjustments and manipulations to allow the body to heal itself. Some chiropractors have more holistic approach than others.

Herbal medicine uses different plant materials to treat disease. This approach has been around for a long time, and several drugs used in allopathic medicine are derived from plants.

Homeopathic medicine is based on the theory by Dr. Samuel Hahnemann that tiny doses of various substances (drugs—herbal or chemical) can produce diseaselike symptoms. These substances, when administered appropriately, stimulate natural defenses to promote healing. It allows for the release of vital forces.

Naturopathic medicine consists of numerous strategies such as herbalism, acupuncture, color therapy, water therapy, nutrition therapy, and massage. It is believed that all diseases are caused by the accumulation of toxic substances in the body, that a disease is actually the body's expression of trying to remove the toxins, and that given time, the body can heal itself.

not acute, you may want to seek advice from your health-care provider. Examples might be:

- Any unusual bleeding (stool, urine)
- Sharp pain in the abdomen or elsewhere
- One of the seven signs of cancer
- A minor illness that lingers for more than a week
- A depressed feeling that lasts for more than a day or two or thoughts of suicide

It is your responsibility to help the health-care provider find out more about your problem. One of the best ways is to communicate clearly and concisely. If need be, prepare notes about symptoms (when, how long, how severe); your current medical status and any relevant family history; and questions you want to ask (cause, treatment options, medications, diet, physical exercise, possibility of recurrence).

The Road Back to Full Health

Just as you need to cooperate with your health-care provider to diagnose a problem, it is your responsibility to participate in your recovery. Depending upon your illness and treatment plan, you may do any or all of the following:

- Take your medication as prescribed and until it is all gone.
- Obtain bedrest or remain home for a few days, if recommended.
- Modify your diet or nutritional intake.
- Change your lifestyle to one that is health-enhancing.
- Engage in regular exercise.
- Stop smoking or abusing alcohol.

Once you are in good health, your responsibility does not end. You should keep a set of personal records about your health status. This is especially true for parents of young children. These records can include:

- Immunization schedule (see Box 14.4)
- Notable illnesses (e.g., chronic ear infections, nosebleeds, etc.), date, duration, and treatment
- Allergic reactions to medicines, foods, plants (poison ivy), or bee stings
- Present medications, including prescription glasses
- Anything in your family history that may have a bearing on your health

Gathering Health Information

Whether as a consumer or as a teacher, the acquisition of information about health and illness is essential. The key, of course, is to gather data that are recent, accurate, and usable. One avenue to do this is to read newspapers and magazine columns written by recognized health-care providers. Another is to watch TV shows devoted to good health, or listen to radio programs. Of course renting or purchasing videotapes is yet another option.

Children can be taught to look for all of these sources in the home with help from their parents. It is an excellent means to make health a "family matter." It is recommended that each home have

BOX 14.4 ■ ■ ■ ■ ■

CHILDHOOD EXAMINATION AND IMMUNIZATION SCHEDULE

This is a typical recommended schedule. It may vary by physician or physician group. The infant schedule is shown as a reference point. Developmental questionnaires are often used, too.

When	*What*
1 month	Hepatitis B vaccine 2
2 months	Diphtheria-pertussis-tetanus (DPT); Haemophilis influenza B vaccine (HIB 1), Oral polio vaccine (OPV 1)
3 months	Prescreening, urinalysis
4 months	DPT, HIB 2, OPV 2
6 months	DPT, HIB 3, OPV 3
9 months	Hematrocrit-blood screen for anemia (HCT),
12 months	HBV 3, TB test
15 months	DPT, HIB 4, measles-mumps-rubella (MMR)
2 years	Wellness check
3 years	Eye examination (Snellen), blood pressure (BP)
4 years	BP, cholesterol screen
5 years	DPT, OPV 4, TB skin test, hearing, visual screening, HCT, urinalysis, developmental questionnaire, school-readiness screening
6 years	Eye exam (Snellen), HBV
8 years	Eye exam (Snellen), BP, urinalysis
10 years	MMR booster, eye exam (Snellen), cholesterol screening, BP, scoliosis screening, urinalysis
12 years	Adult diphtheria-tetanus booster, HCT in girls, scoliosis screening, urinalysis, eye exam (Snellen)
14 years	Eye exam (Snellen), HCT in girls, scoliosis screening, urinalysis

at least one up-to-date reference book on health and disease, as well as one on first aid. Students can go with their parents to a local library to seek information on specific topics. Reference librarians at school or in a public library can be of great assistance to students, parents, and teachers.

Some of the more popular medical journals, such as the *New England Journal of Medicine* or the *Journal of the American Medical Association*, can be reviewed by teachers and parents. Of course health-education journals published by professional organizations are superb sources too. The *Journal of School Health*, published by the American School Health Association, deals with health issues specifically involving children. The *Journal of Health Education*, published by the American Association for the Advancement of Health, addresses health issues for all ages. Several other journals and resources are listed in Appendix B.

For the computer-literate (or those learning to be computer-literate), software packages can be purchased to learn about body systems, drug effects, and so on (see Appendix C). As CD-ROM has entered the computer scene, more and more information about health has become available. Entire encyclopedia sets are on one CD-ROM, just waiting to be sought out. The more adventurous students and teachers can enter cyberspace via the Internet to cruise the "information superhighway." The opportunities on the Internet and Worldwide Web (WWW) are almost limitless. Data from libraries throughout the world can be retrieved, as well as current information from government documents and clearinghouses. The findings from these sources can be downloaded and printed, or in some cases, faxed.

If your computer skills are in need of help, an alternative would be to contact a voluntary health agency or city/county public health department. Examples of the former include:

American Arthritis Foundation

American Cancer Society

American Diabetes Association

American Heart Association

American Kidney Foundation

American Lung Association

American Red Cross

March of Dimes

Muscular Dystrophy Association

National Society to Prevent Blindness

Several of these agencies have free pamphlets, and many have developed ready-made curricula to be used in schools. Teachers may use their services for guest speakers, videos, and the like also. These are also listed in Appendix B.

Other sources are the various hotlines. The following are examples:

CDC National AIDS Hotline 1–800–342–AIDS

CDC Spanish AIDS Hotline 1–800–344–7432 (SIDA)

National Indian AIDS Hotline 1–800–283–2437

Center for Substance Abuse Prevention (CSAP) 1–800–729–6686

National Institute for Drug Abuse 1–800–662–4357 (English); 1–800–662–9832 (Spanish)

Children of the Night (all ages) 1–800–551–1300

Classroom Calls, CDC National AIDS Hotline 1–800–342–AIDS

Crisis Intervention Center 1–800–999–9999

National Runaway Switchboard 1–800–621–4000

Rape, Abuse, and Incest National Network 1–800–656–HOPE

Consumer Protection Agencies

While it is important to gather your own information and take responsibility for your own health, you cannot solve all problems. Several government agencies exist to help you with this formidable task.

Centers for Disease Control (CDC): Major responsibility is collecting data and preventing the spread of diseases

Consumer Product Safety Commission (CPSC): Enforces laws for safe products, including toys

CDC Division of Adolescent and School Health (DASH): Provides funding to state and local agencies, national organizations, and universities to develop, implement, and evaluate programs

Environmental Protection Agency (EPA): Enforces laws and sets policy regarding pollution

Food and Drug Administration (FDA): Regulates food and drug products, including labeling and enforcement of laws

Federal Trade Commission (FTC): Monitors and regulates the use of the media, advertising, and all other forms of mass communication for selling

National Institutes of Health (NIH): In addition to in-house research, distributes grants for other studies on health and disease

Implications for Elementary and Middle-School Teachers

Summary Issues

1. Some of the "red flags" to watch for in advertisements are testimonials and authority figures, bandwagon appeals, scientific approaches with no depth, fear approaches, miracle cures, infomercials, superiority appeals, and advertorials.
2. It is important to learn what advertisements are most enticing to us and then analyze why they are so appealing to us.
3. Food labels are of great significance not only to determine the nutritional value of an item but also to compare similar products.
4. Certain information is required on the labels of over-the-counter medications; these should be read prior to purchase or usage.
5. Grooming aids often have exotic names or their packages make exaggerated claims, requiring wise consumers to read the content labels.
6. The health-care industry has been undergoing some major changes in recent years, with managed-care organizations coming to the forefront.
7. The traditional physician-patient relationship and fee-for-service approach has been altered significantly.
8. Primary-care physicians (gatekeepers) are the mainstay in managed-care organizations, and must be seen for all nonemergency care and referrals to specialists. Family practitioners, internists, pediatric physicians, obstetrician-gynecologists, and sometimes osteopaths are generally seen as primary-care physicians.
9. Most MDs (medical doctors) receive an undergraduate degree, followed by four years in medical school, and then a residency in a specialty.
10. There are several types of alternative health-care providers whose functions are different from medical doctors. Examples include chiropractic, homeopathic, and naturopathic providers.
11. Knowing when to seek medical help is important in terms of saving money, resource utilization, and responsible behavior.
12. All patients have the responsibility to communicate accurately and honestly with their health-care provider. Taking a list of symptoms and questions with you is appropriate.
13. There are several ways that health information can be accessed—newspapers, magazines, TV, radio, videotapes, medical journals, health education journals, computer software, the Internet and Worldwide Web, voluntary health organizations, professional hotlines, and of course government agencies such as public health departments.
14. To help us carry out our responsibility to become wise consumers, several federal and state government agencies operate on our behalf.

Teacher Ramifications

In regard to consumer health, teachers should:

1. Teach how to identify characteristics of valid health information and the ability to analyze ads, products, and services
2. Be able to locate resources in the home, school, and community that provide valid health information

3. Explain how the media influence the selection of health information and products
4. Demonstrate how to locate health resources and products
5. Demonstrate how to compare costs and ingredients in health products and food items
6. Describe when to seek professional help and explain the characteristics of a good health-care professional
7. Explain how the health care market is changing and how it affects students and their families.

SECTION III

Teaching Strategies for Consumer Health

The strategies in this section are divided into grades K–4, 5–6, and 7–8 levels. In addition to strategies that can be used in the classroom, home activities are included. A home activity is designed for student-parent interaction. It is a way to engage the home in school-student learning, and parents can sign a slip of paper to confirm that an activity was completed. Evaluation of all strategies through the use of the National Health Education Standards and performance indicators is indicated. Teachers may also choose to write corresponding learning assessments.

K–4 Level

Strategy One

Objective: Students will explain how the media influence the selection of products.

Activity: Take a poll of the students (or have the students conduct their own polls) asking what type of breakfast cereal they eat and why they chose that particular type (e.g., a parent chose it, they like the flavor, they like the character associated with it, etc.). Discuss how advertising is used to affect the way we purchase items. This influence is strong enough that we buy foods not because they are good for us but rather because of advertising. Discuss whether ads can be believed to be true.

Integration: Language Arts

Related Health Content Area: Nutrition

Health Education Standards and Performance Indicators: 1(4); 2(3); 4(2,4)

Strategy Two

Objective: Students will recognize how advertising attempts to get people to purchase products.

Activity: Using several samples of magazine ads, local billboards, popular television commercials, or the like, have students work in pairs to determine how the advertiser is trying to sell the product (use of beautiful models or scenery, exciting activities, etc.). Discuss how the people and places in the ads compare to real, everyday people.

Integration: Social Studies, Art, Music

Related Health Content Areas: Fitness, emotional well-being, growth and development

Health Education Standards and Performance Indicators: 2(1,3); 4(1,2,4)

5–6 Level

Strategy One

Objective: Students will become proficient at locating various health services in the local telephone book.

Activity: Using the telephone book, have students find the name, address, and telephone number of the following:

Family physician
Family dentist
Family ophthalmologist/optometrist
Local hospital
Pharmacy
Poison control center (phone number only)
Local mental health agency
Crisis hotline (phone number only)
Minister/priest
Emergency personnel (ambulance, fire, police)

Integration: Language Arts, Social Studies

Related Health Content Areas: Safety, diseases

Health Education Standard and Performance Indicators: 2(2,4)

Strategy Two

Objective: Students will determine that name-brand items are not always the best buy.

Activity: Problem-based learning activity (see Chapter 4) as follows:

Jonathan's parents bought him a new pair of shoes for school. They were not the name brand Jonathan wanted (the name brand everyone in school had), but they were very, very similar in looks. Even Jonathan had to admit that you couldn't really tell the difference. They actually were made much better and were more comfortable than the popular name brand. But Jonathan refused to wear them because they didn't have the right label. Jonathan's parents told him to wear the ones they bought or he could just wear last year's shoes. Jonathan was upset.

- What is Jonathan's problem in this vignette?
- What options does he have?
- What other information would be helpful to Jonathan?
- How does Jonathan's decision reflect his maturity level?
- What is the best decision for Jonathan?
- How can he evaluate his decision?

Integration: Social Studies

Related Health Content Areas: Growth and development, emotional well-being

Health Education Standards and Performance Indicators: 1(4); 2(3); 4(2,4)

7–8 Level

Strategy One

Objective: Students will recognize the reality of trying to live within a budget.

Activity: Give students a description of a minimum-wage job that they are to pretend to hold for a period of one month. Then have them find an affordable apartment and car in the newspaper classified advertisements. They may secure a personal loan for the car payments, but it cannot exceed $2500. Next have the students estimate expenses for all utilities, food, medical/dental care, and so forth. Parents can be used as resources. Finally, students must then prepare a balance sheet, showing how much they expended. (Note: This activity can easily be integrated with caring for a baby and used in conjunction with the family life unit.)

Integration: Math

Related Health Content Areas: Family life, nutrition, growth and development, diseases, emotional well-being

Health Education Standards and Performance Indicators: 2(2,5); 3(1); 6(2,3)

Strategy Two

Objective: Students will evaluate various advertisements for evidence of quackery.

Activity: Collect a variety of advertising that depicts possible quackery. In small groups, have students analyze the ads for signs of quackery (e.g., false promises, miracles, fast cures). Discuss the methods people use to prey on others, especially the undereducated elderly.

Integration: Social Studies, Science, Language Arts

Related Health Content Areas: Illness and disease, nutrition

Health Education Standards and Performance Indicators: 2(1,3,5); 4(2)

Strategy Three

Objective: Students will be able to summarize and compare traditional and nontraditional types of health care.

Activity: Have students research various types of health care such as Oriental herbal medicine, naturopathy, acupuncture, massage therapy, and the like, as well as traditional Western medicine. Students should then compare and contrast the various methods and summarize each one. This may be done as a group exercise.

Integration: Social Studies

Related Health Content Areas: Illness and disease

Health Education Standard and Performance Indicators: 7(1,2)

Home Activities

Strategy One

Objective: Students will analyze the costs of purchasing nutritious foods.

Activity: Have students compare the costs associated with purchasing unprepared foods and bulk items versus convenience foods. In conjunction with teaching about a balanced daily diet, have them also compare cost and nutritive value of various foods.

Integration: Math

Related Health Content Areas: Nutrition

Health Education Standards: 2,3

Strategy Two

Objective: Students will observe parents' shopping choices.

Activity: Students are to accompany a parent on shopping trip to (preferably) the grocery or drug store. While purchasing various items, parents should explain the reasons behind buying one brand instead of another. Students should also be given the opportunity to deduce why certain choices were made by looking at such factors as cost, quantity, and so forth.

Integration: Social Studies, Math, Science, Language Arts

Related Health Content Areas: Nutrition, diseases and illness, family life

Health Education Standards: 2,3

References

Gilbertson, W. The FDA's OTC drug review. In T. Covington, ed., *Handbook of Nonprescription Drugs* 10th ed. American Pharmaceutical Association, Washington, DC, 1990, pp. 21–37.

Hanson, G., & Venturelli, P.J. *Drugs and Society.* Jones and Bartlett, Boston, 1995.

Joint Committee on National Health Education Standards. *National Health Education Standards: Achieving Literacy.* American Cancer Society, Atlanta, GA, 1995.

Weiss, B. Managed care: There's no stopping it now, *Medical Economics,* Obstetrics/gynecology ed. 14, 4(1995):10–29.

15

Environmental Conservation

Upon completion of this chapter, you should be able to:

- *Explain interdependence within the ecosystem*
- *Compare and contrast the causes of air, water, land, radiation, and noise pollution*
- *List and explain methods of environmental conservation*

SECTION I

Health Status, Deficits, and Learning

Where progress and pollution are concerned, we are on the horns of a dilemma. On the one hand, humans have been tremendously successful in overcoming the restraints that their environment and competing organisms have imposed on them throughout history. Modern technological advances have turned science fiction into reality. On the other hand, the by-products of technology have the unique capacity for creating ecological mires that may be instrumental in human destruction.

It is difficult to comprehend why people continue to abuse the ecosystem—the interrelationship among air, water, land, plants, animals, and all other living creatures. Perhaps the answer lies in the fact that humans have never really been anything but polluters. At no time have men and women ever learned to deal with their overzealous needs and waste materials.

This makes sense when you consider that early humans were somewhat kept in check by nature's own selection process. The environment was able to assimilate humans and to accept their thoughtless acts because they were few in number. As time passed and humans became more effective in overcoming the many restraints imposed by the environment, the population increased rapidly. It follows that as the population increased, so did demands on the environment. These unchecked demands have taken their toll and are now at an intolerable level. Even to the most naive, it should be obvious that the environment can no longer continue to meet human needs if present practices are continued.

The following list highlights some points about the environment:

- A major environmental problem for children one to five years is lead poisoning, with 1.7 million children having elevated blood levels during testing from 1988 to 1991.
- Listening to loud music (96 dB or more) while exercising for twenty minutes increases the potential for permanent hearing loss.
- Swimming at polluted beaches (not necessarily visible pollution) increases the likelihood of respiratory, ear, and eye symptoms.
- Drinking fountains in some U.S. schools contain significant amounts of lead and copper.
- Allergies, especially asthma and hay fever, are becoming more common, along with the indication that air pollution is a contributing factor.
- Sulphur dioxide causes nasal congestion in children and an increase in lymphocytes.
- Ozone exposure results in nasal congestion and increased levels of histamine.
- Asthma in black children from low-income families may be exacerbated following periods of high ozone-pollution levels.
- Our livestock produce twenty times more excrement than the entire U.S. human population.
- It takes about 2500 gallons of water to produce one pound of meat.
- America's trash, in 1988, consisted of 71.6 million tons of paper, 31.6 million tons of yard trimmings, 13.2 million tons of food scraps, 12.5 million tons of plastics, 12.5 million tons of glass, 15.3 million tons of metals, and almost 21 million tons of other substances. That's a lot of trash!

It is important to teach young children the importance of preserving the environment. These first graders are raising the American flag during an Earth Day celebration.

SECTION II

Environmental Conservation Teaching Information

Pollution can best be described as any human-caused change in the ecosystem that renders the environment less desirable for sustaining life. Beyond a shadow of a doubt, countless ecological atrocities are the cause of the major pollutants we know today. These pollutants inhibit the natural functions of the highly interdependent ecosystem. Once one aspect is set askew, one or more other phases are also affected. In essence, nature's system of checks and balances has been usurped.

The answer sounds simple: People must quickly learn to live within the natural limitations of the environment. To accomplish this goal requires that each person realize and accept the fact that the environment does *not* belong to humans, but rather that they belong to the environment. The human organism is simply not *independent* of the environment, but in the truest sense of the word, is *interdependent* with all other forms of life on our planet. Like all organisms, a person is the product of both heredity and environment and needs to be aware that all organisms and environments are continually changing. Indeed, the social and physical environments in the last hundred years have changed dramatically. In trying to cope with many rapid changes, people have been progressively degrading their environment. Unfortunately, the world has not fully committed itself to fostering a sensible program of global environmental conservation. The consequences will be catastrophic unless there is productive action in the near future. Education at an early age is one approach that answers this urgent call for conservation.

The basic goal of environmental education should be to make everyone aware that everyone is absolutely dependent on the environment, and that everyone affects it. At the primary-school level, the emphasis should be on the environment in the school and neighborhood. In the intermediate grades, the teacher should progress to the community and region. He or she should guide the children to discover problems by forcing them to examine their interactions with the environment. How do we use the environment to satisfy our needs? These and other questions should be answered during the discovery process. In lieu of these learning experiences, there should be a twofold program in the elementary schools. The indirect approach is for the teacher to plan and facilitate a physical environment in the classroom, and in the school generally, that is conducive to positive learning and sound personality development. It would reinforce the second, or direct, approach.

Environmental Hazards to Health

The environment includes everything to which we are exposed, both internally and externally. The term *environment* in this chapter refers to all external factors, natural and man-made, that affect health and well-being. In order to survive, all animals, including humans, have certain basic biological needs that must be met, including adequate air, water, food, and shelter. To the extent that individuals are deprived of any of these factors, or that the factors are impure or toxic, health is adversely affected. Anyone who has had difficulty breathing or persistent eye irritation from smoggy, dusty, or pollen-laden air realizes that health is diminished by poor air quality. Anyone who has become sick from inhaling chemical fumes, drinking contaminated water, or eating spoiled food knows how important to health is the quality of air, water, and food.

Optimizing health means keeping the quality of the environment high. But magazine and newspaper headlines tell us almost daily that the environment is becoming increasingly polluted and unhealthy, and that people's lives are becoming increasingly affected by this pollution. The effects are widespread, and some damage may be long-lasting or even irreversible. It may be many more years before our society realizes the extent of air, water, and land pollution, and perhaps longer before we are prepared to pay the price, both in money and lifestyle changes, that will be required to clean up and maintain a healthy environment.

Environmental health hazards stem from many causes, which is the reason why solutions to environmental problems are not easily found. Many factors have to be considered in assessing pollution and deciding what to do about the problems.

We cannot expect the government—or any organization, for that matter—to solve this country's pollution and health problems. As the character Pogo declared a number of years ago in a comic strip of the same name created by Walt Kelly, "We have met the enemy and he is us!" Each of us must assume responsibility for living in a manner that brings the greatest personal health and satisfaction while at the same time causing the least damage to the environment that we share with all living organisms.

Therein lies the dilemma. How can each one of us achieve a healthy lifestyle and at the same time live in ways that pollute the environment and create health hazards for everyone? Solutions to environmental problems will require major changes in the values of our society.

Air Pollution

Every person breathes about 35 pounds of air a day, more than 6 tons over the course of a year. Pure, unpolluted air is essential for all body functions and for health. Fresh, clean air consists of about 21 percent oxygen, 78 percent nitrogen, and trace amounts of seven other gases. It is the oxygen in air that is essential to human life.

Air pollution reduces the quality of the air we breathe, both limiting the availability of oxygen and forcing us to breathe substances that are harmful to the lungs, blood, and tissues.

In addition to causing breathing problems and serious illness, air pollution can damage vegetation; diminish the growth of vegetables, grains, and flowers; and even reduce milk and egg production. It can also corrode metals, erode stone, and cause paper, leather, and rubber products to disintegrate.

In many U.S. cities, smog results from the action of sunlight on various airborne chemicals and particles and gases in the air emitted by automobiles, electricity-generating plants, blast furnaces, oil refineries, and many other sources. The major kinds of "aerial garbage" are described in Figure 15.1.

Smoggy, polluted air not only is irritating to the eyes and lungs but also contributes to more serious health problems, such as allergies, lung infections, and heart disease. Carbon monoxide, one of the components of smog, interferes with the binding of oxygen to the hemoglobin in red blood cells. If the air contains 80 parts per million (ppm) of carbon monoxide, the body's supply of oxygen is reduced by about 15 percent. In heavily congested traffic, the levels of carbon monoxide may reach 400 ppm, and people are frequently stuck in traffic jams for hours at a time. It is no surprise that many commuters in large cities arrive home with headaches. Car mechanics and parking lot attendants are also often exposed to high levels of carbon monoxide for extended periods and may develop health problems as a consequence.

Sulfur oxides are produced when coal or oil containing sulfur is burned. If the air is damp, sulfuric acid, a very corrosive substance, is formed. Damp air laden with sulfur oxides can pit metals and erode stone buildings as well as damage lung tissue.

Acid rain is produced in air containing sulfur oxides and can damage crops and forests far from the original site of the air pollution. Most scientists and environmentalists who are familiar with the facts concerning the dispute over acid rain agree

Carbon Monoxide
A poisonous gas from car exhaust that drives out oxygen in the bloodstream. Large amounts can kill; small amounts can cause dizziness, headaches, and fatigue. Often exists in tunnels, garages, and heavy traffic. Especially dangerous for people with heart disease, asthma, anemia, and so on.

Hydrocarbons
Unburned chemicals in combustion, such as car exhaust, which react in air to produce smog. Hydrocarbons have produced cancer in animals.

Sulfur Oxides
Poisonous gases that come from factories and power plants burning coal or oil-containing sulfur. Forms sulfur dioxide, a poison that irritates the eyes, nose, and throat, damages the lungs, kills plants, rusts metals, and reduces visibility.

Particulates
Solid and liquid matter in air such as smoke, fly ash, dust, and fumes. They may settle to the ground or stay suspended. They soil clothes, dirty window sills, scatter light, and carry poisonous gases to lungs. They come from autos, fuels, smelters, building materials, fertilizers, and so on.

Nitrogen Oxides
A result of burning fuels that convert the nitrogen and oxygen in the air to nitrogen dioxide. Can cause a stinking brown haze that irritates the eyes and nose, shuts out sunlight, and destroys the view.

Photochemical Smog
A mixture of gases and particles oxidized by the sun from products of gasoline and other burning fuels. They irritate the eyes, nose, and throat, make breathing difficult, and damage crops.

FIGURE 15.1 Components of Smog (*Source:* Data from U.S. Environmental Protection Agency.)

that forests, lakes, and rivers are damaged by it. Many kinds of fish are finding it more and more difficult to survive and reproduce in water that is increasingly acidic.

Acid rain consists of about 70 percent sulfur dioxide; the remaining 30 percent is derived from nitrogen oxides. The sulfur and nitrogen oxides released into the atmosphere react with water to produce sulfuric and nitric acids that fall into lakes and rivers, raising their acidity. Acid rain is a global problem.

Solutions to the acid rain problem involve difficult economic and political decisions, and require the cooperation of many countries. Acid rain can fall thousands of miles from the source of the sulfur dioxide emissions, which explains why it is so difficult to assign blame. Meanwhile, forests continue to be damaged and many forms of animal life will suffer and die because of acid rain.

Nitrogen oxides, which are produced mostly by automobile exhausts, interfere with the oxygen-carrying capacity of the lungs and blood cells. Photochemical smog containing nitrogen oxide is formed over large cities such as Los Angeles by the action of sunlight on the various nitrogen compounds in the polluted air. This gives the air a hazy, brownish appearance, limits visibility, and irritates eyes and lungs.

In regard to children specifically, the effects of summer air pollution have been linked to coughing symptoms and lower respiratory tract symptoms (Schwartz et al., 1994; Koltai, 1994). These same negative effects are seen across the world. A Canadian study of ten rural communities found that exposure to ozone and sulfate is detrimental to childhood respiratory health (Stern et al., 1994). Studies in Finland and Japan demonstrate negative effects on childhood health too (Rusznak et al., 1994). Asthma may be particularly exacerbated in children exposed to ozone pollution (White et al., 1994).

In addition to widespread outdoor pollution, the lungs are assaulted by indoor pollutants. Not only is cigarette smoking harmful to the person who smokes, but second-hand smoke often creates indoor air pollution that is more harmful than all but the worst forms of outdoor smog. Carbon monoxide indoors may be increased by cigarette smoking to levels that are regarded as hazardous to workers in industry and so are prohibited by law. For example, factories are not allowed to exceed carbon monoxide levels of 50 ppm, and the Federal Air Quality Standard Act sets the allowable level in outdoor air at 9 ppm. Yet the air in bars, conference rooms, and other places where many people are smoking may contain levels of carbon monoxide as high as 50 ppm (Table 15.1).

Table 15.1 Symptoms of Carbon Monoxide Poisoning

Percentage of CO in Hemoglobin	Symptoms
0–2	No symptoms
2–5	No symptoms in most people, but sensitive tests reveal slight impairment of arithmetic and other cognitive abilities. Levels of 2 to 5 percent are found in light or moderate smokers.
5–10	Slight breathlessness on severe exertion. Levels of 5 to 10 percent are found in smokers who inhale one or more packs of cigarettes per day.
10–20	Mild headache, breathlessness on moderate exertion. These levels are sometimes seen in smokers who are exposed to additional CO from other sources.
20–30	Throbbing headache, irritability, impaired judgment, defective memory, rapid fatigue
30–40	Severe headache, weakness, nausea, dimness of vision, confusion
40–50	Confusion, hallucinations, ataxia, hyperventilation, and collapse
50–60	Deep coma with possible convulsions
Above 60	Usually results in death

Water Pollution

After air, water is the body's most immediate requirement. We can survive without air for only a few minutes and without water perhaps several days. The human body is about 60 percent water, which is essential to every function carried out by the organs and tissues, including digestion, blood circulation, and excretion.

Agriculture and industry in this country are enormous consumers of water. Several hundred gallons of water are necessary to produce a pound of flour; brewing a barrel of beer consumes a thousand gallons; a ton of newspaper takes about a quarter of a million gallons; a ton of steel requires more than half a million gallons; and irrigating an acre of orange trees requires a million gallons of water a year. Plentiful water is vital to the maintenance of our lifestyles, as it is to the body's health.

Water is continuously recycled in the environment by evaporation and rain. However, as more and more water becomes polluted from pesticides, chemicals, oil spills, and sewage, less and less of it is suitable for human consumption and agricultural use. Of special concern is the chemical contamination of rivers, lakes, and underground water supplies, which provide most of our water needs.

Waterborne diseases such as cholera, typhoid fever, and dysentery have been virtually eliminated in North America through sanitation and water treatment. In many communities, the water supplied to homes is purified by sedimentation filtration and/or chlorination, although adding chlorine to water to kill dangerous bacteria may create other health hazards. The interaction of chlorine with other chemicals in the water produces toxic substances such as chloroform and chloramines, which are carcinogens. The widespread use of detergents, herbicides, pesticides, fertilizers, and other chemicals has also contributed to water pollution.

Analysis of drinking water from communities across the United States has shown that much of it is unsafe and unhealthful (Box 15.1). Studies in Wisconsin (Goldring et al., 1994), and Arizona and California (MMWR, 1994) have shown water supplies to be contaminated with arsenic and lead, respectively. Surface water in many communities is very dangerous to children's health because of the presence of various pathogens (Gutteridge & Haworth, 1994), 2,4-D, atrazine, and metolachlor (Hall et al., 1993). In a New Jersey study, the water from school fountains at fifty schools was analyzed at varying points during the day. The early-morning levels of lead and copper decreased significantly after ten minutes of flushing, but increased significantly by lunchtime after normal fountain use. It is no wonder that many people today are forced to drink bottled, distilled, or spring water to protect their health.

Land Pollution

Until recently, little public attention has been given to the disposal of solid wastes. Each year in the United States we junk millions of autos; millions of tons of trash and garbage; and billions of cans, bottles, and jars. In short, every day we dispose of almost a billion pounds of solid wastes. While each household plays a role, it is minor in comparison to agriculture, mining, and other industries.

One of the major problems is how to dispose of the waste. Today, the following ways are used:

Sanitary landfills. This has long been the most common way to get rid of our trash. Landfills are designated, supervised pits in which waste is dumped and then covered with a layer of soil to reduce odor and assist decomposition. But one problem is that materials can seep into the ground, causing soil and water pollution. Another problem is that we are quickly running out of space to put the landfills.

Incineration or combustion. This approach is becoming popular in a number of communities. Waste is burned at very high temperatures and the residual products are placed in sanitary landfills. This greatly reduces the need for sanitary landfills; however, it does contribute somewhat to air pollution.

Open dumping. This technique has been used by both households and industries. It is simply dumping wastes at a dump site. Open dumping is discouraged in many parts of the

BOX 15.1 ■ ■ ■ ■ ■

WIDESPREAD CONTAMINATION OF DRINKING WATER EXISTS IN THE UNITED STATES

Over one hundred chemicals potentially hazardous to health have been introduced into drinking water supplies across the country as a result of environmental pollution from various sources. The Environmental Protection Agency (EPA), which is responsible for monitoring our drinking water and for setting standards, has established safe levels for about 20 of the more common pollutants in drinking water.

In many areas other compounds have seeped into underground water supplies from nearby industrial complexes or toxic waste dumps. Other hazardous substances found in drinking water are benzene, carbon tetrachloride, dioxin, ethylene dibromide (EDB), polychlorinated biphenyls (PCBs), and vinyl chloride. All of these chemicals are carcinogens. Children are usually more vulnerable to ingestion of toxic substances than adults because of their smaller size and because they are still growing.

Many kinds of home water purifiers are now on the market, but many of them are not very efficient at filtering out hazardous substances despite manufacturers' claims. Safe drinking water is going to be increasingly hard to find in the future.

Pollutant	Maximum level (mg/l)	Pollutant	Maximum level (mg/l)
	Inorganic Chemicals		
Arsenic	0.05	Lead	0.025
Barium	1.0	Manganese	0.05
Cadmium	0.01	Mercury	0.002
Chromium	0.05	Nitrites and nitrates	10.0
Copper	10.0	Selenium	0.045
Detergents	0.5	Silver	0.05
Fluoride	1.4	Sulfate	250.0
Iron	0.3	Total dissolved solids	500.0
Organic Chemicals		*Radioactive Substances*	
Endrin	0.0002	Radium 226 and 228	5 pCi/l
Lindane	0.004	Gross alpha particle activity	15 pCi/l
Methoxychlor	0.1		
Toxaphene	0.005		
Total trihalomethanes (THM)	0.1*		

*EPA has slated a future goal of 0.01–0.025 mg/l for THM.

United States and is now illegal in a number of communities.

Ocean dumping. Some communities have been involved in placing their trash on large barges and dumping it at sea. As you would expect, marine biologists are concerned about harm to plants and fish.

While disposing of wastes in general is a dilemma, it is especially so when the wastes are hazardous. Since 1980, 40,000 uncontrolled hazardous waste sites have been identified, and in 1995 about 1300 were on the Superfund priority list for clean-up (USDHNS, 1995). Hazardous waste consists of materials that are flammable, corrosive, toxic, or chemically reactive. Because most of these toxic substances are not readily broken down or inactivated in the environment, the health problems resulting from such wastes may increase in the years ahead. For example, in Oak Ridge, Tennessee, the Department of Energy has several "hot" ponds containing radioactive wastes from as far back as the Manhattan Project (the development of the first nuclear bomb that was used in World War II). Disposal of nuclear waste is a major problem for this and other communities (Lee, 1994; Clifford, 1994).

Pesticides and Related Chemicals

Soil and water in the United States have become increasingly polluted by chemicals used to control weeds, insects, and plant diseases. Any substance capable of killing or limiting the growth of living organisms is called a *pesticide.* Chemicals that are specific for certain classes of organisms are called *insecticides, rodenticides, fungicides, herbicides,* and so on. Pesticide use has been beneficial to agriculture, but it has also created serious environmental and health problems, which are not easily resolved (Hall et al., 1993). DDT, probably the most widely disseminated pesticide in the world, has now been banned from use in the United States.

The principal danger from continued widespread use of pesticides is that most are carcinogens and teratogens (i.e., cause damage to developing embryos). Pesticides are found in farmland and forest soils, and because they are washed out of the soil by rain and irrigation, they are also found in rivers, lakes, and oceans. Their harmful effects are enhanced by accumulation over time in animal and human tissues. And the chemicals become more and more concentrated in organisms as they move up the food chain.

The fish, fowl, and beef that people eat nowadays may contain high levels of pesticides, which become part of human body tissues. Several agencies of the federal government monitor pesticide contamination in various foods, and the government must determine what levels should be regarded as dangerous to health. It is easy to understand how government decisions can provoke heated controversy between consumers, concerned with health, and producers of food, who are concerned with productivity.

No pesticide is safe, and most can cause short- or long-term health problems. Evidence is also beginning to show that common pesticides used around the home and garden can cause headaches, allergies, and flulike symptoms. Everyone needs to be aware that pesticides are dangerous, so if they must be used, all precautions against exposure should be observed.

Heavy-Metal Pollution

Many heavy metals are toxic to living organisms when they are in the body in more than minute amounts. These metals include beryllium, cadmium, nickel, arsenic, manganese, and especially lead and mercury. Because these heavy metals are vital to many manufacturing processes and industries, the amounts entering the environment have increased sharply in recent years. Heavy metals affect health in a variety of ways—all of them detrimental. They inhibit many essential enzyme reactions in body cells. They damage blood cells, producing symptoms of anemia. And they damage cells of the nervous system, causing headaches, loss of coordination, drowsiness, mental retardation, and even death.

Lead

Lead is a cumulative cellular poison which presents the most serious health hazard because of the enormous amounts used and because it contaminates air, food, and water. Early symptoms of *plumbism* (lead poisoning) are loss of appetite, weakness, and anemia. Because such general symptoms can result from many causes, a diagnosis of plumbism often is not made until more serious symptoms develop (Table 15.2). One of the greatest tragedies of lead poisoning is that children are the chief victims.

In addition to airborne lead-pollution poisoning, small children become poisoned because of a condition known as *pica,* an appetite for unusual substances or abnormal kinds of food. Many older paints contain lead and are sweet to the taste. As paint flakes off walls in old buildings, children

Table 15.2 The Effect of Lead Accumulation in People

Amount of Lead in Blood (micrograms/100 ml)	Observable Effects
10	Enzyme inhibition, learning disabilities
15–40	Red blood cells affected
40–50	Anemia
50–60	Central nervous system affected, cognitive disabilities
60–100	Permanent brain damage

Source: Data from *Air Quality Criteria for Lead*, 600/8-77-017. Environmental Protection Agency, pp. 13–25.

crawling around are apt to eat the paint flakes. Mothers do not usually notice any unusual symptoms until the lead poisoning has advanced to a stage where brain damage has already occurred. Studies of children with learning disabilities suspected to have been caused by lead poisoning have shown them to have more than five times the normal amount of lead in their bodies.

Radiation

There are two principal types of radiation. *Ionizing radiation* causes electrically charged particles, called *ions,* to be produced in the molecules it strikes. Examples are rays from the sun and universe (cosmic rays), X-rays, and radioactivity. The second type is *nonionizing radiation,* which comes from sources such as microwaves. As implied, no ions are produced. While health concerns exist for exposure to either type, overexposure to ionizing radiation is of greatest concern because it can cause cancer and birth defects, and injure the immune system.

Exposure to Ionizing Radiation

Sources of ionizing radiation are both natural and human-made. Radiation from the sun, from rocks and soil with radioactive deposits, and radon gas expose us to radiation. Exposure usually goes unnoticed at the time. But think about all the people who have gotten sunburned.

Radon gas is a result of the natural decay of uranium in some soils, granite, shale, phosphate, and pitchblende. Soils contaminated with uranium or phosphate by-products release radon gas too. When the gas is released outdoors it is diluted and presents no problem. However, indoors (home or office) concentrations can become high. Depending upon concentration and length of exposure, lung cancer may result (Lubin et al., 1995). The levels commonly found in U.S. dwellings show that the risk of developing cancer is low (Alavanja et al., 1994; Chaffey, 1994).

Technologies developed in recent years have produced a marked increase in overall exposure to radiation, especially for certain occupational groups such as X-ray technicians and nuclear-industry workers; power plants, weapons, and nuclear medicine are examples.

Radiation hazards tend to remain more localized than those stemming from chemical pollution of air and water. A medical X-ray exposes the patient and persons in the immediate vicinity, such as the doctor or technician. Exposure to radioactivity is usually limited to persons who live or work near radioactive materials, such as those produced in nuclear power plants and those found in uranium mines or places where radioisotopes are used. However, radioactive materials can be spread over large areas as fallout from atomic explosions (Chernobyl) and uranium mining. There has been concern that the higher incidence of leukemia reported among children in southern Utah might be due to atomic test explosions carried out in neighboring Nevada in the 1950s. In 1984, a federal judge ruled in a suit filed by leukemia patients that the federal government was liable for damages when the evidence appeared convincing that the leukemia was caused by radioactive fallout. In addition, at least seven states in the southwest have large areas polluted with millions of tons of radioactive debris resulting from uranium mining. The radioactive materials are spread further by wind and rain, which wash them into the rivers.

Exposure to Nonionizing Radiation

Like ionizing radiation, exposure to nonionizing radiation can come from both natural and human-made sources. Ultraviolet light from the sun is a natural form and can cause skin cancer. The thinning of the ozone layer by air pollution allows more and more ultraviolet light to attack our skin, which appears to be increasing skin cancers already (Gloster, 1996; Madronich, 1994). Significant skin exposure to the sun may cause immunologic changes that alter host resistance to infectious diseases, too (Kripke, 1994). On the other hand, one epidemiologic study found that sunlight may be a protective factor for ovarian cancer mortality (Lefkowitz, 1994). In short, the health effects can be beneficial or detrimental depending upon the form and amount of ultraviolet light, as well as the skin type of the individual exposed (Ohnaka, 1993).

Another form of nonionizing radiation, called *electromagnetic (EM) radiation*, such as that from radio, television, radar, microwaves, and computer display terminals, is widespread in the environment. In the medical world, magnetic resonance imaging (MRI) and ultrasound equipment gives off EM. Virtually all forms of electronic communication and other aspects of our technological society depend on using low-level EM radiation. Over the years, various concerns have been raised regarding possible deleterious biological effects of long-term exposure to this kind of radiation. Despite considerable research into the biological consequences of such exposure, no harmful effects have been consistently observed or documented (Moulder, 1995).

Noise Pollution

Have you ever been kept awake during the night by a dripping faucet? Do fire and ambulance sirens put you on edge? Does the persistent pounding of rock music affect you? Have you ever found yourself thinking, "If that noise doesn't stop. I'm going to scream"?

Most of us are disturbed almost every day by some kind of noise. We usually dismiss our annoyance, accepting noise as an inevitable part of the environment. Yet noise interferes with sleep and causes fatigue, irritability, anger, tension, and anxiety. High levels of noise, such as exposure to high-intensity rock music, jet planes, and jackhammers, can cause permanent hearing loss as well as physiological changes that are detrimental to health. An investigation of people who exercise for twenty minutes at a time and listen to music at 96 dB at the same time has shown increased potential for permanent hearing loss (Vittilow et al., 1994). Background noise, however, has been shown to have little effect on working-memory capacity for speech-reading performance (Lisle and Ronnberg, 1993).

Sound activates the nervous system, and in so doing, affects functions of the endocrine, cardiovascular, and reproductive systems (Raloff, 1984). In other words, noise is a stressor. It can increase blood pressure, alter hormone levels, constrict blood vessels—in short, contribute to the development of disease, just as do other kinds of stress. Many people live and work amidst the din of urban environments, tending to forget how necessary to health and how comforting silence can be to one's state of mind. Only if people have the good fortune to spend time in the woods or mountains are we able to become aware of the quiet. The human need for stillness was expressed most eloquently in 1854 by Chief Seattle (after whom the modern city is named):

> There is no quiet place in the white man's cities. No place to hear the unfurling of leaves in spring or the rustle of insect's wings. But perhaps it is because I am savage and do not understand. The clatter only seems to insult the ears. And what is there to life if a man cannot hear the lonely cry of the whippoorwill or the arguments of the frogs around a pond at night? I am a red man and do not understand. The Indian prefers the soft sound of the wind darting over the face of a pond, and the smell of the wind itself, cleansed by a midday rain or scented with the pinion pine.

Environmental Protection

Steps to protect the environment must be made at both global and individual levels.

Children can participate in recycling activities at the store and at home, by searching for labels to see if a manufacturer has used recycled materials in its packaging and by sorting empty containers according to their recycling codes.

Global Prevention

Environmental problems compete with a host of other problems for public attention. While many in the United States and other countries decry pollution, issues of unemployment, inflation, and trade take precedence. Interestingly, environmental quality is seen as a more serious problem in developing nations than in industrialized countries (Dunlap et al., 1993). But awareness of problems must still be brought to the forefront. The nations of the world must understand their interdependence, not only economic but environmental.

In the United States, the federal government created the Environmental Protection Agency (EPA) in 1970. This agency, in conjunction with others, has been partly responsible for improvement in environmental conservation. In 1995, the EPA established a five-year strategic plan with the following core principles:

- Ecosystem protection
- Environmental justice
- Pollution prevention
- Strong science and data
- Partnerships
- Reinventing EPA management
- Environmental accountability

While the EPA embraces these formidable tasks, related organizations, industry, and local governments must accept responsibility for their action or inaction.

Individual and State Prevention

As they accumulate around us, we are realizing that finding new places for both common trash and hazardous waste is increasingly difficult. Instead of constantly searching for new sites, though, it is better to reduce the amount of trash generated to begin with—the less trash, the less need for waste management. In short, one basic solution is *source reduction*, or waste prevention, which includes all activities to reduce the overall amount or toxicity of waste created (USEPA, 1994). Source reduction conserves resources and cuts waste disposal costs by reducing the need for recycling, composting, incinerating, and landfilling.

The EPA has suggested "the 4 *R*s" of environmental conservation:

Reduce the amount of trash discarded (source reduction)

Reuse products and containers

Recycle materials, and compost

Respond by being less wasteful and talking about environmental conservation

First, source reduction involves a reduction in the amount of packaging and adoption of practices to reduce waste toxicity. Some examples are (USEPA, 1994):

- When comparing two similar products, purchase the one with less packaging.
- Support stores that use little or no packaging for most products.
- Buy items in bulk whenever available.
- Use products you already have rather than discarding them and buying new ones.
- Use a plunger rather than a drain cleaner.
- Mix 1 tablespoon of vinegar or lemon juice in 1 quart of water instead of buying a glass cleaner. Spray on and wipe off with a newspaper.
- Deodorize rugs by sprinkling baking soda and vacuuming after 15 minutes.
- Put brewer's yeast or garlic in your pet's food, and sprinkle fennel, rue, rosemary, or eucalyptus seeds/leaves where it sleeps rather than buying flea and tick products.
- Use nonhazardous, or less hazardous, substances to accomplish tasks—plant marigolds rather than using pesticides to get rid of some pests.
- Go to the library or buy books about household products that can be used in place of hazardous products.
- When using hazardous products, follow the directions closely and be certain to keep them out of the hands of children.
- When disposing of hazardous waste, follow community regulations.

Second, in order to reuse products and containers, consider:

- Carrying your mug or reusable container with you for drinks
- Using utensils, dishes, cloth napkins, and other reusable tableware
- Purchasing products that are refillable
- Repairing things rather than discarding them and buying new ones
- Renting tools and other items, or borrowing from a neighbor
- Selling items in garage sales or donating to organizations rather than discarding them

The third *R* is recycling. In this case you can:

- Look for and choose recyclable products and containers, and carry through on recycling them
- Buy items made from recyclable materials
- Compost food scraps and yard trimmings, and then use the compost to enrich lawns and gardens or as potting soil for plants
- Give compostable materials to a neighbor or community organization to compost if you are unable to do it

The fourth *R*, respond, should be easy for all of us. We can do many of the things already mentioned and we can all talk about environmental conservation. You can also do the following:

- Let store managers, community leaders, and politicians know your preferences.
- Share information about how you carry out the 4 *R*s with neighbors, family, friends, and others.
- Telephone or write to companies about the positive as well as negative steps they take concerning conservation.
- Encourage schools to teach about environmental conservation, including the 4 *R*s.
- Participate in communitywide environmental programs such as recycling.

Implications for Elementary and Middle-School Teachers

Summary Issues

1. The ecosystem is a complex interaction of all living things with the air, water, and land around them.
2. The environment can no longer meet human needs if we continue our current practices.
3. Pollution is human-caused change in the ecosystem that renders the environment less able to sustain life.
4. The environment includes everything to which we are exposed, both internally and externally.
5. Environmental health hazards stem from many causes, which is one reason why solutions to environmental problems are not easily found.
6. The major kinds of airborne garbage are carbon monoxide, sulfur and nitrogen oxides, hydrocarbons, particulates, and photochemical smog.
7. Respiratory problems and asthma in children are linked to air pollution, in particular to sulfates, particulates, and ozone.
8. Indoor air pollution is common and can be more harmful than outdoor smog.
9. Much of the water in the United States is unsafe or unhealthful, including that pumped into schools.
10. The two primary ways to dispose of waste in the United States are sanitary landfills and incineration.
11. Pesticides can be very toxic; they must be used with caution, if at all.
12. Lead poisoning is the most common form of heavy-metal pollution among children.
13. Ionizing radiation is generally of greater concern than nonionizing radiation, and sources of the former are both natural and human-made.
14. Radon gas is classified as ionizing radiation but appears to confer low risk for developing cancer, dependent upon length and intensity of exposure. The risk may increase greatly if combined with cigarette smoke (including second-hand).
15. Ultraviolet light is a form of nonionizing radiation, as is electromagnetic radiation from computer display terminals.
16. Noise pollution has distinct impacts on our nervous, endocrine, cardiovascular, and reproductive systems.
17. Environmental conservation needs to occur at both global and individual levels.
18. The EPA's strategy is seven-fold: ecosytem protection, environmental justice, pollution prevention, strong science and data, partnerships, reinventing EPA management, and environmental accountability.
19. The 4 *R*s of conservation are Reduce, Reuse, Recycle, and Respond.
20. Each person has to accept responsibility for the environment.

Teacher Ramifications

In regard to environmental conservation, a teacher should:

1. Be aware of the environmental problems facing the school and community, and be able to relate them to students
2. Serve as a role model by practicing the 4 *R*s of environmental conservation
3. Emphasize source reduction, including ways that children can participate
4. Support the school's role in helping the nation reach the following objectives set forth in *Healthy Children 2000* and *Healthy Youth 2000:*
   - #11.1. Reduce asthma morbidity, as measured by a reduction in asthma hospitalizations to no more than 160 per 100,000 people. In children, the target is no more than 225 per 100,000. (The baseline was 284 children per 100,000 measured in 1987.)
   - #11.4. Reduce the prevalence of blood lead levels exceeding 15 μg/dL among children six months through five years to no more than 500,000 and zero respectively. The target for inner-city, low-income black children is 75,000 and zero respectively.

#11.6. Increase to at least 40 percent the proportion of homes in which homeowners/occupants have tested for radon concentrations and that have either been found to pose minimal risk or have been modified to reduce risks to health.

#11.11. Perform tests for lead-based paint in at least 50 percent of homes built before 1950.

SECTION III

Teaching Strategies for Environmental Conservation

The strategies in this section are divided into grade K–4, 5–6, and 7–8 levels. In addition to strategies that can be used in the classroom, home activities are included. A home activity is designed for student-parent interaction. It is a way to engage the home in school-student learning, and parents can sign a slip of paper to confirm that an activity was completed. Evaluation of all strategies through the use of the National Health Education Standards and performance indicators is indicated. Teachers may also choose to write corresponding learning assessments.

K–4 Level

Strategy One

Objective: Students will recognize that it is not necessary to use all of the disposable items we currently use. Students will discuss how using fewer disposable items will positively affect landfills.

Activity: Have students brainstorm a list of items we use on a daily basis that are disposable. This may be done as a class, with the teacher writing the ideas on the board, or in small groups. Next see if students can identify some comparable items that were used in the past that were not disposable. Examples: fountain pens versus throwaway pens; refillable glass milk bottles versus disposable plastic milk bottles.

Discuss with students how in this era of convenience, we have come to depend on items that are disposable, that the cost of this is increased use of landfill space, and so forth.

Integration: Science, Social Studies

Related Health Content Areas: Consumerism, nutrition

Health Education Standards and Performance Indicators: 1(5); 7(2,3,4)

Strategy Two

Objective: Students will plan and carry out a recycling program at school.

Activity: Have students meet with people from the local recycling agency, if possible, to learn which things are recyclable and which are not.

Have students decide what items could be recycled at school. (Coordination will be needed to have items picked up or taken to the recycling site in the community.) Then have students decorate large boxes to be used to collect the recyclables, and label them properly.

Integration: Science, Social Studies, Language Arts

Related Health Content Areas: Family, safety

Health Education Standards and Performance Indicators: 1(5); 7(2,3,4)

5–6 Level

Strategy One

Objective: Students will be able to identify sources of noise pollution.

Activity: Have students record different sound sources in the community and simultaneously monitor the noise levels with a noise meter. Discuss the various sounds and their noise levels. Develop a histogram depicting the extent of noise pollution from each recorded source. Some sources are autos, airplanes, industrial machines, trains, crowds, home appliances, physical education class, and the cafeteria.

Integration: Science, Technology, Music, Math

Related Health Content Areas: Growth and development, safety

Health Education Standards and Performance Indicators: 1(5); 4(3)

A Poor Place to Live

Abuse of land, air, and water create problems that turn appealing areas into ghettos of ugliness and decay. The accompanying illustration tells the story of a watershed area where users of resources have sacrificed their environment for the quick profit—the short-term gain. Follow the keys below to condition depicted by related keys in the illustration.

1. Lack of Water Control. A rampant stream destroys valuable land, fails to recharge ground water supplies, and jeopardizes lives. Usually it goes through periodic low-water cycles that make it an unreliable source of supply for cities. Not all streams should be dammed, of course, but some must be.
2. Ruinous Forestry Practices. Here, cut-and-get-out logging operations, inadequate fire protection, and other short-sighted actions have led to watershed soil erosion, downstream flooding, and loss of habitat for wildlife. Recreation opportunities are destroyed.
3. Poor Farming Methods. Overuse of land and repeated planting of the same crops have exhausted the soil's fertility. The absence of contour farming leads to rapid runoff and results in erosion by wind and water.
4. Uncontrolled Growth of Suburbs. Lack of effective zoning and building regulations speeds decay. Open green space is chopped up into inadequate patches. "Bedroom" suburbs like this produce monotony, blight, and high crime rates.
5. Upstream Industrial Pollution. Industries that disregard downstream and downwind pollution degrade the entire watershed. Rural areas often encourage industrial parks without requiring adequate pollution controls.
6. Pollution from Mines. Mining companies abandon underground working without a thought that eventually they will cave in and create surface pockets or feed deadly acid water into streams. Others strip off valuable topsoil and leave ugly scars which add to stream pollution and deterioration of the area.

7. & 9. Faulty Industrial Zoning. Unregulated placing of industry pollutes city's air and water and downgrades value of adjacent property.

8. Improper Waste Disposal. Sewage treatment and waste disposal facilities lag behind population growth, hastening the poisonous suicide of the city.
10. The Polluted River. Pollution the full length of the river has made it an open sewer. Fish cannot live in it, people dislike drinking it even after costly purification. Swimming is impossible and boating unpleasant.
11. Poorly Managed Traffic. A source of air pollution, frustration, and sudden death, poorly planned traffic facilities—added to substandard mass transportation—strangle the central city.
12. Trapped by Towers. As the population grows and open space is lost to monstrous high-rise apartments, city dwellers become imprisoned by their own "progress." They live elbow-to-elbow. The more fortunate breathe filtered air at home and at work. Others sneeze and sniffle through smog-filled days and nights.

continued

FIGURE 15.2
Which America Do You Choose? a. A poor place to live–why? b. A good place to live–why? (*Source:* From *Conservation Chart: Which America Do You Choose?* U.S. Department of the Interior, Washington, DC)

Strategy Two

Objective: Students will describe how ecology is a way of keeping nature in balance.

Activity: Using Figure 15.2, have pupils identify what people have done right and wrong in regard to their environment.

Integration: Science, Social Studies, Math

A Good Place to Live

The balance of Nature and the quality of man's environment can be maintained in an increasingly popular watershed if sound conservation practices are followed. Some of the benefits are listed below and are keyed to the right half of the illustration.

1. Proper Forestry and Mining. Good forest management means selective cutting, fire protection, and planting new trees. Such practices promote continuing yields of forest products. Stripmined areas have been re-covered with topsoil. Planting holds the soil in place and keeps streams silt-free.
2. Space to Roam. Wilderness areas are protected, providing assured wildlife habitat, a healthy forest base for the watershed, and outdoor recreation for all.
3. Multipurpose Reservoir. Flood control, power generation, municipal and industrial water supply source, and outdoor recreation facilities are some of the benefits of this reservoir.
4. Farm Land Management. Rotation of crops and grasslands, contour strip planting, wildlife hedgerows, all make this farm flourish while protecting the health and quality of the land.
5. Irrigation. Water provided by a diversion dam and a high-line canal turns normally non-productive land into fertile farms.
6. Industrial Parks. Planning and zoning provide attractive and efficient clustering of industry, to the benefit of both industry and city. Sources of industrial water and air pollution are controlled within the regulated industrial park complex.
7. Fish Hatchery. Hatcheries provide fish to supplement stocks in reservoirs, streams, and lakes.
8. Satelite Communities. Self-contained communities like this offer the services and advantages of close-in suburban living. The beauty of the natural terrain and setting is carefully preserved.
9. Waste Disposal. Efficient sewage plants treat effluents from city systems, keeping the river clean. Refuse is burned to generate power in plants equipped with air pollution abatement devices.
10. The Beautiful City. Careful planning and development provide a beautiful, livable Central City environment. Area-wide master plans control the city's growth, provide a smooth traffic flow, and promote work and living patterns oriented not to technology but to people.

11. & 13. Highways and Rapid Transit. Recessed and underground superhighways, combined with a rapid transit system that extends to the suburban satellite communities, provide efficient movement of people and goods to and from the Central City. With home-to-work rapid transit, private car use is reduced. Combining highway and rapid transit operations uses less open space and requires fewer river crossings.

12. City Park and Recreation Areas. Planned parks like this provide the Central City with large wedges of open space and afford many forms of recreation and cultural facilities for the city dweller.
14. Footpaths and Bicycle Trails. Trails follow the natural terrain of the river banks from city to headwaters.
15. Green Spaces. Through proper planning and zoning, abundant open space in and around the city is preserved. This green space provides a natural source of beauty and recreation opportunities.
16. The Clean River. Pollution control and good watershed management keep the river clean, making it a recreational delight.
17. Scenic Easements. Scenic easements along river banks protect the natural beauty of the river. Pollution control is made easier and bank erosion prevented. Outdoor recreation opportunities abound in the natural areas preserved.

FIGURE 15.2–*continued*

Related Health Content Areas: Families, safety, consumerism, disease

Health Education Standards and Performance Indicators: 1(5); 4(3)

7–8 Level

Strategy One

Objective: Students will be able to describe how pollution results when ecosystems are disturbed.

Activity: The Bass Ecosystem Game in Figure 15.3. Have pupils duplicate the original board and make enough organisms—exchange pieces—and pollution-result cards so that everyone can participate. Pupils can also make their own dice. For best results, have four or five players per card plus a banker, or a card for each pupil plus a banker.

Rules of the Game

1. High throw of the die determines the starting player.
2. All players place a token in the *Start* space on the board.
3. Each player throws the die to determine the number of spaces to move ahead on the board.
4. Each player interprets the consequence of his or her move:
   a. A player who lands on an *Organism* space (sunfish, rotifers, algae, bass, weeds, bacteria, minnows, worms, and copepods) takes an organism of the designated species and places it in his or her lake.
   b. A player who lands on an *Organism exchange* space may exchange extra pieces in his or her possession for others that are equal to or higher than his or her original organism in the food chain. Or the player may exchange his or her one piece for an organism from the banker.
   c. A player who lands on a *Pollution* space then throws the die again to determine the source of the pollution and suffers the consequences outlined on the *Pollution-Result* card (teacher can draft cards if this is preferred to students doing so).
5. Overpopulation occurs when a player gains more than the number provided for in the lake. For example, there are three minnows in the lake, so although a player may keep more than three minnows, he or she may not make an exchange for any more than three. If the lake becomes overpopulated overall, a player must return all the extras of that species and pay a penalty (a series of consequences of overpopulation, which the teacher can draft).
6. A player wins by covering each organism in his or her lake with an organism exchange card, that is, constructing an ecosystem.

Integration: Art, Science

Related Health Content Areas: Safety, growth and development

Health Education Standards and Performance Indicators: 1(5); 4(3)

Strategy Two

Objective: Students will take an active interest in their environment and the community.

Activity: Have ready in advance a list of several government officials, including local congresspersons and appropriate state-agency heads. Have students write a letter to one of them expressing concern over an environmental issue of their choice.

Integration: Language Arts, Social Studies, Science

Related Health Content Areas: Family, safety, diseases

Health Education Standards and Performance Indicators: 3(1); 7(1,2,4)

Strategy Three

Objective: Students will debate the pros and cons of landfills.

Activity: Have students research the topic of landfills as a means of waste disposal. This may include a visit to a site and/or a guest speaker from landfill management or envi-

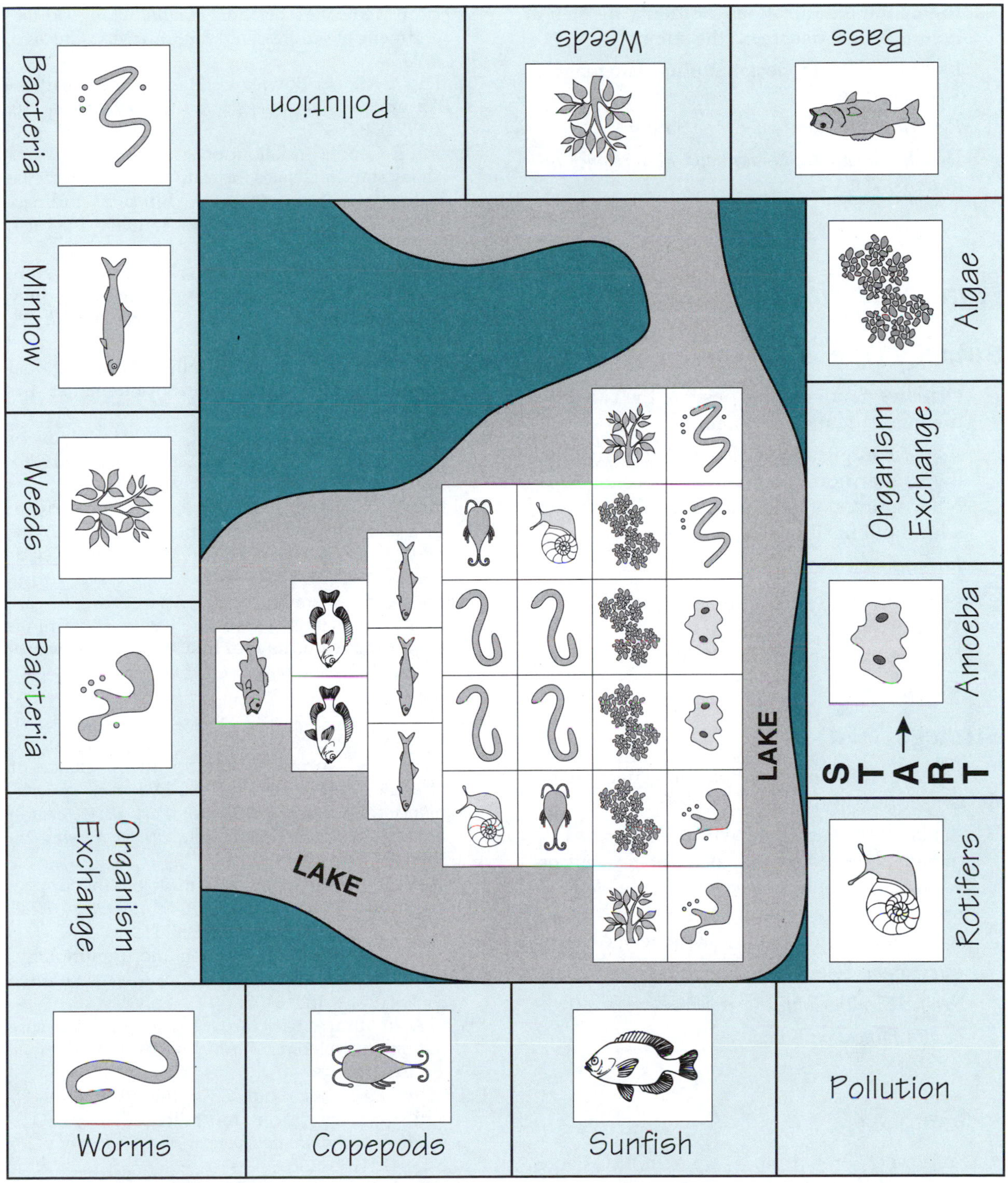

FIGURE 15.3 Bass Ecosystem Game

ronmental organizations. Students are then to hold a formal debate on the subject.

Integration: Math, Social Studies, Language Arts, Science

Related Health Content Areas: Safety

Health Education Standard and Performance Indicators: 7(1,2,4,5)

Home Activities

Strategy One

Objective: Students will observe the balance of life in an aquatic ecosystem.

Activity: Pupils are to plan and construct their own aquariums at home. References and other sources of help are readily available at a local public library or pet store.

Integration: Science

Related Health Content Areas: Growth and development

Health Education Standards: 1,7

Strategy Two

Objective: Students will take an active role in conserving in their communities.

Activity: Students, along with other family members, are to take part in one of the many organized river or lake clean-ups, road-side clean-ups, or park clean-ups. If none is planned in a community, students may organize one.

Integration: Science, Social Studies

Related Health Content Areas: Safety, family

Health Education Standards: 1,7

References

Alavanja, M.C., Brownson, R.C., Lubin, J.H., Berger, E., Chang, J., & Boice, J.D. Residential radon exposure and lung cancer among nonsmoking women, *Journal of the National Cancer Institute* 86, 24(1994):1829–1837.

American Medical Association. *Healthy Youth 2000*. Department of Adolescent Health, AMA, Chicago, 1990.

Chaffey, C.M., & Bowie, C. Radon and health—An update, *Journal of Public Health Medicine*, 16, 4(1994):465–470.

Clifford, F. Caught in fallout of waste war: The Ward Valley standoff leaves the state's nuclear-medicine industry with no place to dump its radioactive trash, *Los Angeles Times*, January 14, 1994, p. A1.

Corbett, S.J., Rubin, G.L., Curry, G.K., & Kleinbaum, D.G. The health effects of swimming at Sydney beaches, *American Journal of Public Health* 83, 12(1993):1701–1706.

Dunlap, R.E., Gallup, G.H., & Gallup, A.M. Of global concern: Results of the health-of-the-planet survey, *Environment* 35 (1993):6–23.

Gloster, H.M., & Brodland, D.G. Epidemiology of skin cancer, *Dermatologic Surgery* 22, 3(1996): 217–226.

Goldring, J., Haupert, T., & Stoll, R. Arsenic in private drinking well-water in Outagamie and Winnebago counties, Wisconsin, *Wisconsin Medical Journal* 93, 8(1994):441–443.

Gutteridge, W., & Haworth, E.A. An outbreak of gastrointestinal illness associated with contamination of the mains supply by river water, *Communicable Diseases Report: CDR Review* 4, 4(1994): R50–R51.

Hall, J.C., Van deynze, T.D., Struger, J., & Chan, C.H. Enzyme immunoassay-based survey of precipitation and surface water for the presence of atrazine, metolachlor, and 2,4-D, *Journal of Environmental Science and Health Part B: Pesticides, Food Contaminants, and Agricultural Wastes* 28, 5(1993):577–598.

Koltai, P.G. Effects of air pollution on the upper-respiratory-tract of children, *Otolaryngology: Head and Neck Surgery* 111, 1(1994):9–11.

Kripke, M.L. Ultraviolet radiation and immunology: Something new under the sun, *Cancer Research* 54, 23(1994):6102–6105.

Lee, G.A. In dump's backyard, nuclear waste is wearing out its welcome, *Washington Post*, November 29, 1994, p. A3.

Lefkowitz, E.S., & Garland, C.F. Sunlight, vitamin D, and ovarian cancer mortality rates in U.S. women, *International Journal of Epidemiology* 23, 6(1994):1133–1136.

Lisle, B., & Ronnberg, J. The effects of background noise and working-memory capacity on speech-reading performance, *Scandinavian Audiology* 22, 2(1993):67–70.

Lubin, J.H., Boice, J.D., Edling, C., Hornung, R.W., Howe, G.R., Kunz, E., Kusiak, R.A., Morrison, H.I., Radford, E.P., & Samet, J.M. Lung cancer in radon-exposed miners and estimation from indoor exposure, *Journal of the National Cancer Institute* 87, 11(1995):817–827.

Madronich, S., & de Gruijl, F.R. Stratospheric ozone depletion between 1979 and 1992: Implications for biologically active ultraviolet-B radiation and nonmelanoma skin cancer incidence, *Photochemistry and Photobiology* 59, 5(1994):541–546.

MMWR. Lead-contaminated drinking water in bulk water-storage tanks: Arizona and California, *Morbidity & Mortality Weekly Report* 43, 41(1994):751.

Moulder, J.E., & Foster, K.R. Biological effects of power-frequency fields as they relate to carcinogens, *Proceedings of Society of Experimental Biology in Medicine* 209, 4(1995):309–324.

Murphy, E.A. Effectiveness of flushing on reducing lead and copper levels in school drinking water, *Environmental Health Perspectives* 101, 3(1993): 240–241.

Ohnaka, T. Health effects of ultraviolet radiation, *Annals of Physiological Anthropology* 12, 1(1993):1–10.

Raloff, J. Agent orange: What isn't settled, *Science News* (1984):314–317.

Rusznak, C., Devalia, J.L., & Davies, R.J. The impact of pollution on allergic disease, *Allergy* 49, 18 suppl.(1994):21–27.

Schwartz, J., Dockery, D.W., Neas, L.M., Wypij, D., et al. Acute effects of summer air pollution on respiratory symptom–reporting in children, *American Journal of Respiratory & Critical Care Medicine* 150, 5(part 1) (1994):1234–1242.

Stern, B.R., Raizenne, M.E., Burnett, R.T., Jones, L., Kearney, J., & Franklin, C.A. Air pollution and childhood respiratory health: Exposure to sulfate and ozone in ten Canadian rural communities, *Environmental Research* 66, 2(1994):125–142.

U.S. Department of Health and Human Services. *Healthy Children 2000*. Jones and Bartlett, Boston, 1992.

U.S. Environmental Protection Agency. *Consumer's Handbook for Reducing Solid Waste* (no. EPA530–K–92–003). Washington, DC, 1994.

Vittilow, M., Windmill, I.M., Yates, J.W., & Cunningham, D.R. Effect of simultaneous exercise and noise exposure (music) on hearing, *Journal of the American Academy of Audiology* 5, 5(1994):343–348.

White, M.C., Etzel, R.A., Wilcox, W.D., & Lloyd, C. Exacerbations of childhood asthma and ozone pollution in Atlanta, *Environmental Research* 65, 1(1994):56–68.

16

The Human Body

Upon completion of this chapter, you should be able to:

- *List the ten body systems and their organs*
- *Explain the structures and functions involved in all the body systems*
- *Discuss the role of each body system in relation to health*
- *Discuss the interrelationship among the systems*
- *List and explain the role of the organs that make up the various body systems*
- *Apply your knowledge to related chapters such as effects of drugs on the body and food intake.*

SECTION I

Health Status, Deficits, and Learning

Your body carries out a variety of functions twenty-four hours a day, every day, with very few breakdowns. Every facet of your life affects your body in some way. What you eat, how much you exercise, your hygienic behavior, the risks you take, the consumer products you use, your drug habits, even where you live impact your body, for better or worse. Concerns about your body may range from your appearance to severe illness and the threat of death. Regardless, there is no doubt that learning may be hampered when something—or even the fear of something—is wrong with our body.

The following list provides some basic points about the human body:

- Although each body system is unique, they are all interrelated.
- A tearing of ligaments or tendons surrounding a joint is called a *sprain,* and most often occurs in the knee, wrist, or ankle. A strain is similar but with no rupture of tissue.
- Dislocations are most likely to occur in the knee or shoulder joints.
- If muscle is not used, it will atrophy (waste away)—to be replaced by fibrous and fatty tissue.
- *Muscle tone* refers to the fact that skeletal muscles are always in a state of partial (about 10%) sustained contraction. Muscle tone is important for posture.
- The nerve cell, or neuron, in the nervous system either responds or fails to respond. There is no such thing as a partial response.
- A decision to do something, like ice skating, comes from the cerebrum. However, the cerebellum sends out the message to the necessary muscles.
- In the autonomic nervous system, the sympathetic division dilates the pupil of the eye, whereas the parasympathetic division constricts it. Similarly, it is the sympathetic system that increases the rate and force of heart contractions, while the parasympathetic division reverses those effects.
- An abnormality in the pituitary gland affecting the growth hormone could cause dwarfism or giantism, or acromegaly.
- The body's natural pain relievers are hormones called *endorphins* because they imitate morphine and heroin.
- When someone has a higher-than-usual number of lymphocytes and a higher number of them are immature or abnormal, they might have infectious mononucleosis.
- Heart murmurs may be mild, resulting from a growth spurt in puberty, or they may be se-

vere and organic, as a result of rheumatic fever or a birth defect.

- The lymphatic system is an accessory to the circulatory system.
- A car running in a closed garage is dangerous because the carbon monoxide given off can prevent oxygen exchange, eventually causing death.
- Pneumonia is an infectious disease resulting in fluid collection in the alveoli of the lungs.
- Spasms in the respiratory diaphragm cause a sudden burst of air to the larynx, with subsequent closing of the glottis and result in a hiccup.
- The common cold is an upper-respiratory infection and may be caused by any of more than one hundred related viruses.
- The abdominal cavity is at greater pressure than the chest cavity, and on occasion, contents of the stomach may be pushed back up into the esophagus. Acidic stomach contents irritate the tissue, bringing about heartburn.
- In our part of the world, diarrhea is a nuisance associated with flu or infection, whereas in other parts of the world it may be a deadly disease stemming from a cholera outbreak.
- The urinary system is less prone to disease than many of the other systems; however, excess uric acid could cause kidney stones or gout.
- About 17 percent of a woman's total body weight must be in the form of fat if she is to experience her first period (menses).
- Diseases gained through sexual activity can be devastating to the body and, if untreated, may prevent the reproductive system from carrying out the goal of reproduction.

SECTION II

The Human Body Teaching Information

The human body is a marvel of nature consisting of ten systems and their organs. The skeletal system gives us appearance and protection; the muscular system allows for locomotion; the nervous system facilitates communication; the endocrine system regulates body functions and provides a stress-defense mechanism; the cardiovascular system transports blood and other substances; the digestive system processes fuel; the excretory system removes wastes; the respiratory system allows for gaseous exchange; the lymphatic system protects the body; and the reproductive system procreates the species. Collectively, these systems make the human body a complex living "machine." Its different parts act on and react to one another in ways quite impossible for any other machine. This machine requires a balanced blending of nutrition, exercise, rest, sleep, affection, spiritual purpose, and social interaction to function optimally.

Skeletal System

It is common to hear children ask the question, How many bones are there in the body? The correct answer is generally accepted to be 206 bones. However, that number applies to the adult skeleton; we do not start out with 206. Babies have about 350 soft bones, but many of these fuse together by 20 to 25 years into 206 hard, permanent bones of differing shapes and sizes. Men's bones are usually larger and heavier than women's bones.

From an organizational standpoint, the skeletal system has two main parts (see Plates 1 and 2). The *axial skeleton* (central part of the body) consists of the skull, spine, ribs, and sternum for a total of eighty bones. The *appendicular skeleton* (the parts dealing with the limbs) consists of the shoulders and pelvis and their attached limb bones, for a total of 126 in all.

When teaching about the body systems it is helpful to demonstrate how each system is at work in everyday activities that children recognize.

The skeleton is more than a moveable frame. It has five principal functions:

1. *Protection:* The hard, bony tissue provides internal soft tissues with a defense against trauma. The skull protects the brain; the vertebral column protects the spinal cord. The rib cage and the bones of the pelvis protect the organs in the thorax and the lower part of the abdomen.
2. *Support:* Most of the body's structures are soft, pliable, and delicate. The skeleton's rigid framework provides a means of suspension for body systems.
3. *Muscle attachment and movement:* Muscles are attached to bone by tendons. The rigidity of bone, combined with the elasticity and contractility of muscle, makes the arms and legs strong levers, tools, or weapons.
4. *Reservoir for minerals:* The *osseous* (bony) tissues of all parts of the skeletal system provide the body with a vast depot of mineral salts, such as calcium and phosphates.
5. *Blood-cell formation:* During late fetal life, and continuing in some bones throughout adult life, the red marrow of long bones, the ribs, the sternum, and the pelvic bones produce blood cells, a process called *hematopoiesis*.

It is important to remember that the skeleton is composed of living tissues. Its materials are constantly being dissolved, passed into the bloodstream, and replenished by other tissues and from food. Tooth enamel, by comparison, is a dead substance.

Types of Bones

Each bone is a distinct structural unit. Its pattern varies according to its functions, which are represented by the five basic types of bones:

1. *Long bones:* Long bones are the largest in the body. Included in this group are the

Children should understand that no body system stands alone. Something as common as a broken arm has implications for more than the skeletal system as the body learns to compensate for and repair the injured limb.

prominent bones of the arms and legs. Each has a shaft and two ends. The general function of long bones is to act as levers. Examples are the femur of the leg and the humerus of the upper arm.

2. *Short bones:* These differ from long bones in that they are smaller and have less prominent ends. They are cuboid and are composed of cancellated bone enclosed in a thin shell of compact bone. Their principal function is to provide strength. Examples are the carpals of the wrist and the tarsals of the ankle.
3. *Flat bones:* These are platelike and usually have two broad surfaces (tables) and narrow edges by which one flat bone articulates with another. Each flat bone is thin and made up of two plates of compact bone that enclose a layer of cancellated bone. The general function of these bones is protection. Examples are the ribs, the scapula at the back of the shoulder, and the cranium.
4. *Irregular bones:* These are so named because of their shapes. Several surfaces may articulate with several other bones. Some of the bones of the skull are irregular, as are the vertebrae and hip bones. The thinner parts of irregular bones consist of two thin plates of compact bone with cancellous bone between them. The general function of irregular bone is articulation.
5. *Sesamoid bones.* These are small, rounded bones that enter into the formation of joints or are associated with cartilage, ligaments, or another bone. An example is the patella (kneecap), the largest of the sesamoid bones.

The Axial Skeleton

Skull

The skull, often bringing images of a pirate's skull and crossbones to children, consists of twenty-two bones: eight cranial bones and fourteen facial bones (Plate 5). The principal bones are described as follows:

1. The *cranium* encloses and protects the brain. The frontal, parietal, occipital, and temporal bones are part of the cranium.

2. The *frontal bone* forms the forehead, roofs of the eyes, and the nasal cavity. The *occipital bone* is the base and back of the cranium. The *parietal bones* form the sides and roof of the cranium. The *temporal bones* comprise the sides and base of the cranium.
3. The *facial bones* are united except for the *mandible,* or lower jaw. The *maxillary bones* form the upper jaw.

Vertebrae

The functions of the *vertebral column* are to protect the spinal cord and to bear body weight. There are *seven cervical vertebrae, twelve thoracic vertebrae, five lumbar vertebrae,* and *five sacral vertebrae* fused into the *sacrum,* and *three to five coccygeal vertebrae* fused into the *coccyx* or tailbone (Plate 2). The fused sacrum provides support for the hips. The vertebrae are separated by intervertebral disks, which function as friction pads and shock absorbers.

Sternum and Ribs

You have twelve pairs of ribs. Seven pairs (1–7) are *true ribs,* and three pairs (8–10) are *false ribs.* The remaining two pairs (11 and 12) are called *floating ribs.* All twelve pairs articulate (connect by movable joints) with the thoracic vertebrae in your back. However, only the first ten pair are joined to the sternum in your front. Pairs 10 and 11 end in the muscle at the sides of your body, and that is why they are called floating ribs. Pairs 8 through 10 articulate indirectly with the sternum through a fusion of cartilage, thereby earning the name false ribs.

The breast bone or *sternum* has three parts: the upper *manubrium;* the *body,* which is the principal part; and the *xiphoid process.*

This rib cage protects our lungs and is a place of attachment for our breathing muscles.

Pelvic Girdle

The *pelvic girdle* (hip) consists of bones that are fused with the sacrum in your back and they are joined together by cartilage in the front. The functions of the pelvic girdle are to protect the abdominal and pelvic organs and to transfer the weight of the trunk to the lower limbs.

Pelvic measurements in size and shape show considerable variation. This is true not only between men and women, but also among women. Generally, about one half of women have a true female pelvis (a *gynecoid*), which is wider in all diameters than a man's pelvis (an *android*). As you would expect, the wider pelvic girdle in a woman is important for childbearing and delivery.

Pectoral Girdle

The rodlike bones that join your sternum to the bones at the back are called the *clavicles,* or collar bones. You can feel them easily with your fingers. The bones they connect to at the back are your shoulder blades, or *scapula.* In other words, the clavicles connect your scapula to your sternum. When you compare your pectoral girdle to your pelvic girdle, the most noticeable difference is that your shoulder girdle is much more flexible. This is because your scapula are held in place by muscles that allow your arms greater mobility than your legs. Try moving your foot through 360° the same way you can move your hand.

Lower Limbs and Feet

Anatomically, the lower limb between your pelvic girdle and your knee is called the *thigh.* The thigh bone, or *femur,* is the longest, strongest, and heaviest bone in your skeleton. The leg is that portion of the lower limb between your knee and ankle containing the medial (toward the middle) *tibia* and lateral (toward the outer part) *fibula.* The weight of the body is transmitted from the femur to the foot by way of the tibia. In contrast, the slenderest bone in the body is the fibula, the purpose of which is to increase the available area for muscle attachments in the leg.

The *ankle and foot* are comprised of twenty-six bones arranged into three sets. The seven *tarsal bones* resemble the carpals of the wrist but are larger. Five *metatarsal bones,* similar to the metacarpals of the hand, form the sole of the foot as well as the longitudinal arch. The fourteen *phalanges* of the toes are like the phalanges of the fingers.

Upper Limbs and Hands

The bones in our upper limbs are those in the arm, forearm, and hand. The *humerus* is the single bone of the arm. On the medial side of the forearm is the *ulna;* the *radius* is on the lateral (thumb) side. Eight irregular *carpal bones,* arranged in two rows of four bones each, make up the wrist. The *hand* (metacarpus) consists of five *metacarpal* bones. The finger bones are called *phalanges,* with a single bone called a *phalanx.*

Muscular System

Muscle tissue, which constitutes about 40 to 50 percent of the body weight, predominantly consists of contractile cells called *muscle fibers.* Through contraction, muscle cells produce movement and do work. In addition to the function of movement, muscles are important for body support, maintenance of posture, and production of heat for normal body temperature. (Plates 3 and 4 illustrate muscular system.)

Types of Muscles

There are three types of muscles, as described below:

1. *Skeletal muscle* is striated, voluntary, and attached to the skeleton. Contractions of skeletal muscles are usually rapid and forceful. The obvious example is the biceps muscle, which may contain 260,000 fibers.
2. *Smooth muscle* is nonstriated and involuntary. Contractions are strong and slow. Smooth muscles are found in the walls of respiratory, digestive, reproductive, urinary, and circulatory systems (all tubes), as well as in the uterus and bladder (hollow organs).
3. *Cardiac muscle,* as the name implies, is found only in the heart. It is striated, involuntary, and has strong, rhythmic contractions. Unlike the other muscles, the cardiac muscle is myogenic; that is, nerve stimulation to the heart muscle is not necessary since it initiates its own action.

Skeletal Muscles

When you want action, it is the skeletal muscles that you call on. Their principal function is to produce movement by contracting (they cannot push). To accomplish this, they must have two attachments (see Figure 16.1a): one to the bone that is fixed, called the *origin* of the muscle; the other to the bone to be moved, called the *insertion* of the muscle. Muscles are attached to bones by tendons, which are cords or bands of white, fibrous connective tissue. This does not mean that muscles attach only to bones; some attach to other muscles as well. The skeletal muscles comprise about 23 percent of the woman's body and 40 percent of man's body.

If you have looked at Plates 3 and 4, you may have found the names of the muscles confusing. Nonetheless, there is logic in muscle names. They are named for various traits as follows:

- *Location:* Intercostal (between the ribs), brachii (arm), occipitalis (head)
- *Action:* Adductor, flexor, extensor
- *Shape or size:* Trapezius (trapezoid), maximus (largest), minimus (smallest), longus (long), brevis (short)
- *Direction of fibers:* Rectus (straight), transversus (across)
- *Number of heads of origin:* Biceps (two heads), triceps (three heads), quadriceps (four heads)
- *Points of attachment:* Sternocleidomastoid (sternum, clavicle, and mastoid process of the temporal bone)

The motions produced by muscle contraction are described with reference to the standard anatomical position of the body—standing erect, with arms straight down and palms directed forward (see Figure 16.1b). Movements parallel to the longitudinal axis are flexion, or folding together—as in "flexing your biceps." Extension is an unfolding movement in the opposite direction. Abduction refers to movement away from the axis of the body; adduction means toward the axis.

Muscles that produce movement in directions opposite to one another are *antagonists.* Muscles that work together to accomplish a particular movement are *synergists.* Two muscles that bend

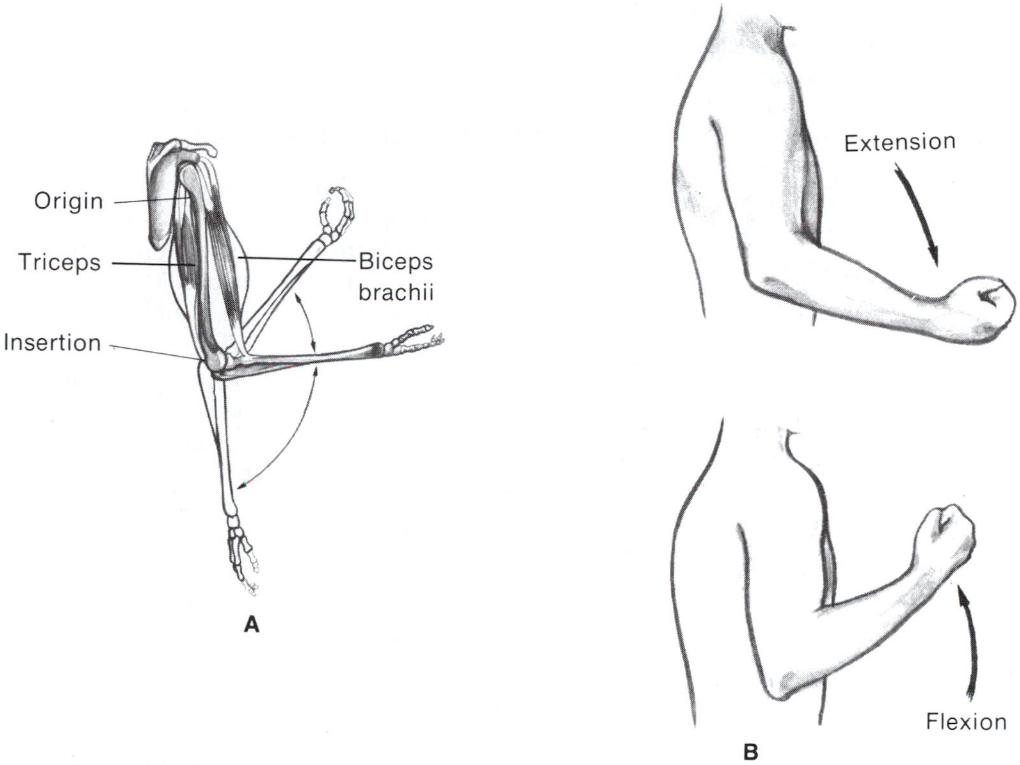

FIGURE 16.1 a, Skeletal Muscle Attachments. The origin is attached to the less movable bone, whereas the insertion is attached to the more movable bone. b, Two examples of muscle action.

an arm at the elbow are synergists with one another (e.g., the biceps and brachialis flex the lower arm), but both are antagonistic to a muscle that straightens the arm (e.g., the triceps extends the lower arm).

Health Problems in the Skeletal-Muscular Systems

Since these two body systems are so interdependent, they are discussed together here. There are several health problems that may arise in the skeletal and muscular systems. In children, they usually revolve around injuries such as fractures or sprains. Another problem, involving the joints, is arthritis, particularly rheumatoid arthritis, which afflicts almost 75,000 children under the age of 18 years. Approximately six times as many girls suffer from this disease as do boys (Farish, 1993). The newest form of arthritis is Lyme disease. Osteoporosis is involved in most hip fractures in older persons, especially older women. The older person who suffers a hip fracture is immobile for weeks, even months, whereas the younger person who experiences a fracture is up and running around in a very short period of time.

Nervous System

The skeletal-muscular body systems, among other things, are important for movement. For example, if someone throws a snowball at you, you want to duck or run out of harm's way as soon as possible. To do this, you need feedback from your eyes and messages sent to your muscles as well as coordination of senses and movement. All of this must be done instantaneously or you will be snow-covered. You can thank your nervous system for getting you out of trouble. It is the nervous system that ensures that the organs and systems operate in smooth coordination (Plate 11). Conditions within and outside the body are constantly changing, and one purpose of the nervous system is to respond to these internal and external changes so that the body may adapt itself.

The nervous system is divided into two parts: the *central nervous system* (CNS) and the *peripheral nervous system* (PNS). The CNS consists of the *brain* and the *spinal cord,* which runs up inside the vertebral column and expands into the brain. Communicating centers within the CNS and various nerve tracts make possible the appropriate response to sensory stimuli. The PNS is a network of nerves and sense organs that gathers information from the rest of the body and feeds it into the brain. For convenience, peripheral efferent nerve fibers distributed to smooth muscle, cardiac muscle, and glands are referred to as the *autonomic nervous system* (ANS).

The Neuron

The basic unit of nervous tissue is the nerve cell, or *neuron* (see Figure 16.2). Neurons are composed of a cell body containing a large nucleus with one or more nucleoli, mitochondria, Golgi apparatus, Nissl bodies (associated with the conduction of a nerve impulse), and numerous ribosomes. Extending from this cell body are two types of threadlike projections of cytoplasm, the *nerve fibers: dendrites,* which conduct impulses to the cell body, and *axons,* which conduct impulses away from the cell body.

Types of Neurons

Neurons are classified according to their function as follows:

1. *Motor neurons:* These pass messages from centers in the brain and spinal cord to effector organs such as muscles and glands.
2. *Association (interneuron) neurons:* Also called *internuncial* or *intercalated neurons,* these relay messages between the neurons within the brain and spinal cord.
3. *Sensory neurons:* These receive messages from the environment and pass them to centers in the brain and spinal cord.

The Nerve Impulse

Communication in the nervous system is carried out through an electrical impulse, which travels from one neuron to the next (or perhaps to a muscle end plate) via a synapse. More specifically, in a resting neuron, the cell membrane is electrically charged, or *polarized.* When the nerve fiber is sufficiently stimulated, this resting potential (polarization) is changed to an action potential—*depolarized.* This change in states is an all-or-none response; that is, the neuron responds completely or not at all. At the outset of the discussion of the nervous system, it was noted that as a system it responds instantaneously. This means that the action potential lasts only about one thousandth of a second.

The action potential goes the length of the nerve fiber and is transmitted from neuron to neuron by means of a synapse. A *synapse* is a small "gap" or region between the end of one axon and the beginning of another axon or perhaps the end plate of a muscle (see Figure 16.3). It is at the synapse where transference of the electrical impulse occurs. However, transference across the synapse is usually chemical in nature. A neurotransmitter (chemical) is released to diffuse across the synapse to receptors. As you would expect, synapses are highly susceptible to changing physiological conditions, including any drugs that may increase or decrease the effectiveness of the neurotransmitters. As a result, our nervous system may respond more quickly or more slowly, which may or may not be appropriate at the time.

The Central Nervous System

The central nervous system (CNS) consists of the brain and the spinal cord.

Divisions of the Brain

From a developmental standpoint, the brain (Plate 11) can be divided into three large areas: the forebrain, the midbrain, and the hindbrain. These areas can be further subdivided as shown in the following outline:

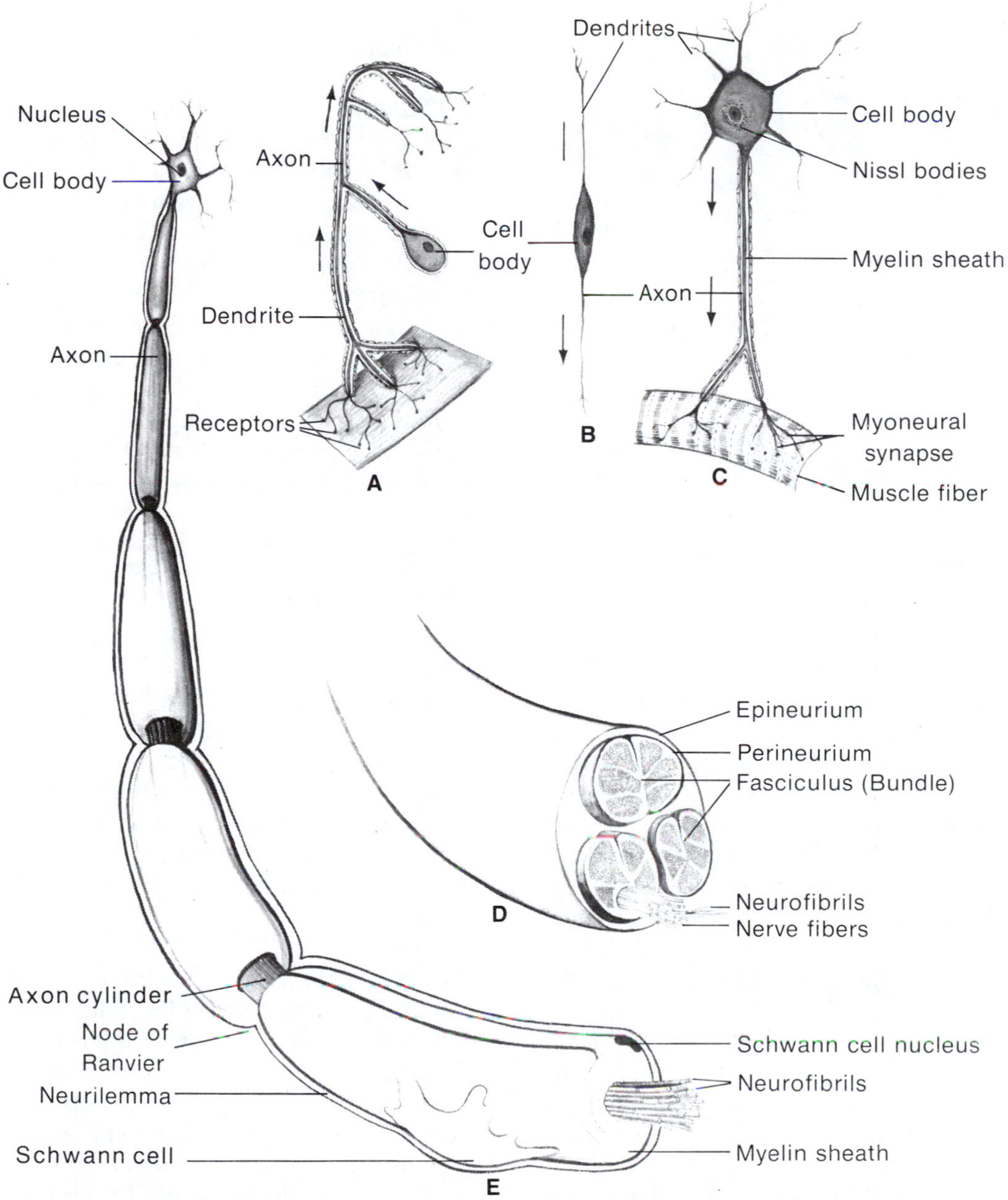

FIGURE 16.2 **The Structure of the Neuron. a. Monopolar sensory neuron. b. Bipolar retinal neuron in the eye. c. Multipolar motor neuron, showing a muscle-nerve synapse. d. Structure of a typical nerve. e. An enlarged extension of an axon, showing its protective myelin sheath and neurilemma.**

I. Forebrain (prosencephalon)
   A. Telencephalon (cerebrum)
      1. Cerebral cortex (gray matter)
      2. White matter (core)
   B. Diencephalon
      1. Thalamus
      2. Hypothalamus

II. Midbrain (mesencephalon)
   A. Corpora quadrigemina
   B. Cerebrum

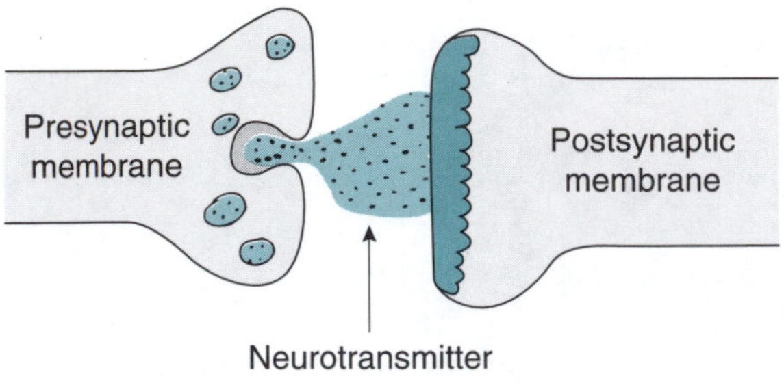

FIGURE 16.3 Chemical synapse with neurotransmitters

III. Hindbrain (rhombencephalon)
   A. Pons
   B. Medulla
   C. Cerebellum

The largest part of the brain is the cerebrum, which is divided into the right and left cerebral hemispheres. The brain stem is the lower stemlike portion of the brain connecting the cerebral hemispheres with the spinal cord. It consists of, from the top down, the diencephalon, midbrain, pons, and medulla. The midbrain contains a massive number of cerebral nerve fibers. Below, it is connected with the pons, which is connected with the medulla. Finally, the medulla connects with the spinal cord through a large opening in the base of the skull (see Figure 16.4).

Next in size to the cerebral hemisphere is the cerebellum, which is behind the brain stem. It is connected with the pons, medulla, and midbrain by the three *cerebellar peduncles.* Collectively, the cerebellum, pons, and medulla make up the major parts of the hindbrain.

The Cerebrum The cerebrum, the largest part of the human brain, accounts for up to four fifths of the brain's total mass and weight (Figure 16.4 and Plate 11). It fills the entire upper portion of the cranial cavity and contains billions of neurons and synapses. These form a network of pathways. The outer nerve tissue of the cerebral hemispheres is gray matter and called the *cerebral cortex.* This gray matter is arranged in folds or convolutions *(gyri),* separated by depressions *(sulci)* or deep grooves called *fissures.* The cerebral hemispheres are largely white matter with a few areas of gray matter.

Thalamus The thalamus is a large oval structure of gray matter; it bounds the third ventricle. (The third ventricle is one of four ventricles, or small cavities, of the brain filled with cerebrospinal fluid. There are two lateral, the third and the fourth ventricles.) The thalamus receives all sensory impulses, either directly or indirectly, from all parts of the body. Some of the impulses are associated, some are sorted out, and others are relayed to specific areas of the cerebral cortex. The thalamus is a sensory-integrating center where malaise, crude touch, pain, and temperature are interpreted. For this reason, it is believed to be a center for primitive, crude sensation. In addition, the thalamus is connected with the motor system and can expedite or inhibit motor impulses from the cerebral cortex.

Hypothalamus The hypothalamus is the principal center integrating the autonomic or peripheral functions. It is directly below the thalamus, forming the floor of the third ventricle.

The hypothalamus is part of an extensive system that regulates food and water intake. Research on animals shows that the hypothalamus's drinking center is lateral, and its appetite center is medial.

Cerebellum The cerebellum occupies the lower and posterior part of the skull cavity. It lies below the posterior portion of the cerebrum and behind the pons and upper part of the medulla. The cerebellum is oval and constricted in the center. When cut in two, it resembles a tree and thus sometimes has been called the *arbor vitae,* tree of life. Like the cerebrum, it has a cortex of gray matter and an interior of gray and white matter.

The cerebellum is made up mainly of masses of nerve tissue called *peduncles.* These are pathways between the cerebellum and the rest of the central nervous system. The cerebellum is a reflex center through which coordination and refinement of muscular movement are brought about. Coordination of impulses from sensory organs and muscle contractions facilitates equi-

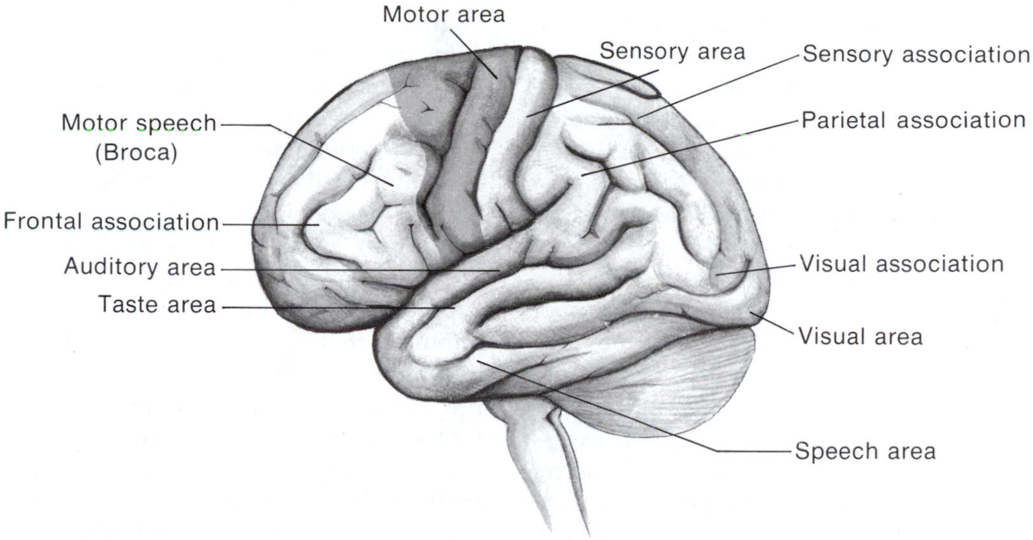

FIGURE 16.4 **Left Side of the Brain Showing the Cerebrum, Cerebellum, Pons, Medulla, and Spinal Cord**

librium. It is believed that motion sickness is partly due to a disorganization of the part of the cerebellum that coordinates posture and balance through the medulla. Damage to the cerebellum leads to jerkiness of voluntary movements and poor balance.

Medulla The medulla is continuous with the spinal cord and, together with the pons, is a major component of the reticular formation of nerves that constitutes the upper part of the extrapyramidal pathway.

Reflex activities such as sneezing, coughing, vomiting, and alimentary-tract movements, as well as the major system reflex controls, make the medulla the vital reflex center of the body.

Spinal Cord

The cord of nervous tissue enclosed within the vertebral column that extends from the medulla of the brain stem to the level of the first lumbar vertebra is the spinal cord. The spinal cord controls many of the *reflex activities* of the body. It also transmits impulses to and from the brain via ascending and descending tracts.

The Peripheral Nervous System

The peripheral nervous system (PNS) is made up of all the nervous tissue outside the CNS (brain and spinal cord). This includes *cranial nerves* from the brain, *spinal nerves* from the spinal cord, and associated sensory inputs. The PNS transmits signals between the CNS and other parts of the body. The fibers of these nerves may have afferent or efferent neurons.

The *afferent division* of neurons carries information from their endings (may be sensory input) to the CNS. In contrast, neurons in the *efferent division* carry messages from the CNS to muscles or glands. The efferent division is composed of the somatic nervous system and the autonomic nervous system. The *somatic nervous system* is made up of all the peripheral fibers going from the CNS to skeletal muscles. All other tissues—heart, glands, intestines, and all smooth muscle such as blood vessels—are innervated by *autonomic nervous system.*

The Autonomic Nervous System (ANS)

Examination of our internal organs, which are under the influence of the ANS, shows that they are innervated by two sets of neurons. One set increases the activity of the organ (except for the heart) and is called the *parasympathetic system.* The other set decreases the organ's activity and is called the *sympathetic system.* The sympathetic and parasympathetic nervous system are *antagonistic.* This means that the nerves from the two divisions can produce opposite effects. However, they also provide a correlated adjustment to meet any physiological demand. Generally, the effects of parasympathetic stimulation are most obvious during calm and rest. For example, fibers in the oculomotor nerve stimulate the smooth circular muscle of the iris, protecting the eye from excess light; fibers in the facial nerve stimulate the secretion of saliva, aiding digestion. Digestion is most suitably carried out during rest, and it is aided further by the vagus parasympathetic fibers, which stimulate secretion of digestive juices and increase the activity of the smooth muscle of the digestive tract. Other vagus nerve fibers decrease the rate and force of the heartbeat during rest—a reasonable adjustment in as much as the skeletal muscles are inactive and the body's requirement for blood is lower at that time.

In summary, the functions of the *parasympathetic* division are conservative. Narrowing the pupil to protect the eye from excessive light; promoting the digestive processes in a restful environment; slowing the heartbeat to allow the heart muscle and the skeletal muscles to recover their tone; and emptying the bowel and bladder to remove the body's waste materials—these are a few of the many ways the parasympathetic division contributes to the maintenance of a constant internal environment.

The *sympathetic* division is greatly influenced by changes in the environment. It acts to prepare the body for stressful situations and has effects mainly opposite to those of the parasympathetic division. These are commonly referred to as the *fight or flight response.* Fear, pain, anger, and other emotions have a strong influence on the sympathetic system. This effect is made even more general because sympathetic preganglionic fibers innervate the adrenal gland, which secretes the hormone epinephrine into the circulation. Epinephrine and norepinephrine have a stimulating effect. For this reason, the sympathetic division might be called the *emergency system,* since it prepares us to remain and fight, or to take flight.

To prepare the body for stress, the sympathetic division produces effects primarily opposite to those described for the parasympathetic chain. Sympathetic fibers innervate the smooth muscles of the eye that contract and increase the size of the pupil, thus increasing its sensitivity in dim light. Muscular exertions require an increased blood supply, and this is accomplished by sympathetic impulses that stimulate the smooth muscles of tiny blood vessels within the digestive tract, cutting down the flow of blood to the stomach and intestine and increasing the flow to skeletal muscle. This augmented blood supply is also aided by cervical sympathetic impulses that cause an increase in the rate and force of the heartbeat.

Whether you are standing, sitting, sleeping, eating, digesting food, or eliminating wastes, your nervous system activates the organs required for the activity. Suppose you have just finished eating and are doing nothing more than sitting on the beach watching the surf crash. Messages flow along parasympathetic nerves, stimulating into action all body parts that function in digestion. At this time, sympathetic nerves of the digestive system are relatively inactive. Blood vessels supplying your digestive tract are wide open, but those supplying limb muscles and kidney tissue are constricted. But suppose you decide to go swimming before giving your system enough time to digest the food. The strong stimulus triggers chemical messages that race through your body, inhibit parasympathetic nerves, and excite sympathetic nerves. Digestion stops; your skeletal muscles quiver with the excitement of fresh forced blood; and you race into the water. As you exert your skeletal muscles while swimming, the smooth muscles lining your digestive tract remain inactive, allowing the partially digested food to remain stationary, causing cramps. Only when you stop swimming and begin resting again do the antagonistic pathways shift priorities so that digestion resumes and the cramp goes away.

The ANS is under the influence of the CNS at all times, especially certain higher centers of the cerebral cortex, thalamus, hypothalamus, medulla, and spinal cord. Afferent impulses keep these centers informed as to the physiological state of the body and its parts, and efferent impulses are sent from them to the autonomic system to make adjustments as required to maintain the homeostatic state.

Sensory Mechanisms

A *sense organ*, or receptor, is a specialized nervous tissue situated at the peripheral endings of the dendrites of afferent neurons. The receptor's primary function is to provide the body with information, both conscious and unconscious, about degrees of change in the organism's external and internal environment.

Classification of Sense Organs

Many have tried to classify the senses into groups, but no one has been entirely successful. Traditionally, the special senses are smell, vision, hearing, equilibrium, and taste; the cutaneous senses are those associated with receptors in the skin; and the visceral senses perceive the body's internal condition (Plate 16).

Different sensations are evoked by stimulation of various specialized sensory receptors. Some of these may be grouped according to the nature of the stimulus:

- *Chemoreceptors:* Sensitive to chemical stimuli (necessary for taste and smell)
- *Pressoreceptors:* Sensitive to mechanical stimuli (necessary for touch, pain, temperature, pressure, sound, and motion)
- *Photoreceptors:* Sensitive to visible light (necessary for sight)

Another classification of the receptors categorizes them according to their somatic or visceral locations:

- *Teleceptors:* Detect environmental changes occurring some distance from the body (e.g., light rays, sound waves, and odors are detected by teleceptors of the eye, ear, and nose)
- *Exteroceptors:* Detect the environmental changes that directly affect the skin (temperature, touch, pressure, or pain)
- *Proprioceptors:* Provide the body with information about its position in space (muscles, tendons, joints)
- *Interoceptors:* Maintain the environment within the organs (smooth-muscle contraction, peristalsis, visceral contractions)

Health Problems of the Nervous System

Sometimes children (and adults) may develop meningitis wherein the membranes covering the brain can swell. There is less reason for alarm if this condition is caused by a virus rather than bacteria. Middle-ear infections in children should be watched closely since, on occasion, these bacteria cross the blood-brain barrier to gain access. Cerebral palsy generally results from an injury prior to or after birth in which parts of motor centers of the cerebrum are destroyed. Epilepsy involves an excess of activity in a portion of the brain causing a seizure.

Endocrine System

The endocrine system is one of the body's two major communication systems (the other being the nervous system). Rather than nerve impulses, however, the endocrine system has chemical messengers called *hormones*. Hormones are produced by specific tissues and delivered by the blood to target organs (cells). Hormonal responses of the body generally are slower, of longer duration, and of wider distribution than the immediate response of muscles and glands to nervous system stimuli. In other words, the endocrine system won't do you much good when dodging snowballs.

Glands of the endocrine system (Plate 9) include the following:

1. Pituitary gland (anterior and posterior)
2. Thyroid gland
3. Four parathyroid glands
4. Two adrenal glands
5. Pancreas
6. Two ovaries
7. Two testes
8. Pineal gland (not pictured)
9. Thymus gland (in a child)

The endocrine glands have ducts, and all except the parathyroid glands secrete more than one hormone. Keep in mind that hormone levels in the bloodstream are very low compared to substances like cholesterol or glucose. Some of the regulatory and coordinating functions of these glands are (Sloane, 1994):

1. Reproduction and lactation
2. Immune system processes
3. Acid-base balance
4. Fluid intake, intracellular and extracellular fluid-volume balance
5. Carbohydrate, protein, lipid, and nucleic acid metabolism
6. Digestion, absorption, and nutrient distribution
7. Blood pressure
8. Stress resistance
9. Adaptation to environmental changes

Pituitary Gland

The pituitary gland, about the size of a pea, is made up of an *anterior lobe* and a *posterior lobe.*

The Anterior Lobe

The anterior lobe secretes several hormones, one of which is the *growth hormone* (GH), which controls all body cells capable of growth with special emphasis on bones and skeletal muscles.

If GH secretion is abnormal, the result may be:

1. Dwarfism from a *hyposecretion* (deficiency) of GH during childhood.
2. Giantism from a *hypersecretion* (excess secretion) of GH during adolescence and prior to the closing of the epiphyseal plates, resulting in excessive growth of the long bones (pituitary giantism).
3. Acromegaly, which occurs with hypersecretion of GH after the closing of epiphyseal plates, causing a disproportionate enlargement of soft tissues, growth in thickness of flat bones of the face, and increase in hand and foot size. It is relatively uncommon.

Thyroid-stimulating hormone (TSH) comes from the anterior lobe of the pituitary gland too. Its target organ is the thyroid gland, increasing growth and development of the thyroid as well as the rate of metabolism. Another hormone is *adrenocorticotropic hormone* (ACTH), also known as *corticotropin.* The target organ herein is the adrenal cortex. Hormones related to ACTH are *endorphins.* They are often called *endogenous opiates* because they mimic the effect of morphine by providing natural pain relief (analgesia) in response to stress or exercise.

Other hormones secreted from the anterior lobe include the gonadotropic hormones *follicle stimulating hormone* (FSH) and *luteinizing hormone* (LH) with the target organs being the reproductive system. These hormones are discussed further in the reproductive-system section of this chapter. Finally, *prolactin* (PRL) is secreted during pregnancy and breastfeeding.

The Posterior Lobe

Two hormones are associated with the posterior lobe, ADH and oxytocin. *ADH,* also called *vasopressin,* promotes water retention and can help elevate blood pressure. *Oxytocin* brings about milk ejection in nursing mothers and causes uterine contraction during sexual intercourse or labor and delivery of a baby. This hormone appears to have no function in males.

Thyroid Gland

The thyroid gland secretes two hormones. *Thyroxine,* or *tetraiodothyronine* (T_4), comprises 90 percent of thyroid gland secretion, whereas *triiodothyronine* (T_3) is secreted in small amounts. The thyroid hormones increase metabolic rate and influence the normal growth and maturation of bone, teeth, and nervous and connective tissues. When too little is secreted, termed *hypothyroidism,* depressed metabolic activity can result in increased fat deposition, sluggishness, and constipation. In a young child, hypothyroidism may cause a condition called *cretinism,* with attendant physical and mental retardation. In contrast, *hyperthyroidism* increases metabolic activity, possibly leading to weight loss, nervousness, diarrhea, and elevated heart rate. A severe condition results in goiter, or Grave's disease.

Parathyroid Glands

Two small brownish-yellow parathyroid glands lie on the capsule of the posterior aspect of each thyroid lobe. The four minute glands consist of densely packed secretory cells held in close association with capillaries by a fibrous meshwork. These glands are essential to life, for they regulate the supply, distribution, and metabolism of calcium and phosphorus in the body.

Adrenal Glands

The two adrenal, or suprarenal, glands lie one on each side, just above the kidneys, and are usually covered by perirenal fat. Each appears to be a single compact unit but is actually composed of two endocrine glands. The outer part, the *cortex*, secretes several *steroid* hormones synthesized from cholesterol; the core of the gland, the *medulla*, has an entirely separate function, the secretion of epinephrine and norepinephrine.

Adrenal Cortex

The adrenal cortex secretes so many hormones that the classic experiment of removing the glands from animals led to a bewildering series of results. In general, however, the animals showed poor performance and low tolerance to infection, temperature changes, or any form of stress. They also suffered profound water and electrolyte disturbances. These animals usually died after a few weeks, but their life could be extended for a short time by giving them unlimited access to salt and water.

Histologically, the cortex is subdivided into three zones. The outermost zone, or *zone glomerulosa*, is responsible for the secretion of *mineralocorticoids*, principally aldosterone. The middle zone, or *zone fasciculata*, is the widest of the three zones and secretes the *glucocorticoids*. The inner zone synthesizes sex hormones.

Adrenal Medulla

The adrenal medulla makes up the pulpy center of the gland in which groups of irregular cells are located amidst veins that collect blood from the sinusoids. This gland produces two very similar hormones, *epinephrine* (80%) and *norepinephrine* (20%), also known as *adrenaline* and *noradrenaline* respectively. They are sometimes referred to as *catecholamines*. Both hormones elevate blood pressure; epinephrine accelerates the heart rate, and norepinephrine acts as a vasoconstrictor. The two hormones together promote glycogenolysis (glucogenesis), the breakdown of liver glycogen to glucose, causing an increase in blood-sugar concentration. Of the two, epinephrine functions most closely as the emergency hormone for the body. Its functions of increasing the blood glucose level (by glycogenolysis) and the blood flow to the skeletal muscles (vasodilation of arterioles), heart, and viscera serve to shunt or direct the circulation of blood where necessary during exertion or stress.

The adrenal medulla, unlike the thyroid and other endocrine glands, is not essential for life. It can be removed surgically without causing untreatable damage.

Adrenal Hormones and Stress

When an individual is under severe emotional stress, such as rage or fear, a marked excess of epinephrine is poured into the blood, enabling the person to perform feats of muscular exertion of which he or she would not ordinarily be capable. As mentioned earlier, this has been called the emergency functions of the adrenals, or the *fight or flight response*.

Pancreas

The pancreas lies close to the posterior abdominal wall behind the stomach. It functions as both an exocrine and endocrine gland. Its exocrine functions involve the secretion of digestive enzymes into the small intestine (discussed later in this chapter). The endocrine function of the pancreas is carried on by groups of special tissue scattered throughout the pancreatic tissue called the *islets of Langerhans*. The number of cells in these islets varies from several hundred thousand to a few million. Each islet consists of several types of cells; those designated as *alpha* and *beta* predominate. The hormone *insulin* is secreted by the beta cells, and another hormone, *glucagon*, by the alpha cells. Both are polypeptides and can be synthesized commercially.

The earliest studies on the impact of insulin on carbohydrate metabolism showed four basic effects:

1. Increases rate of glucose metabolism
2. Regulates blood-glucose concentration
3. Increases glycogen storage in the tissues
4. Promotes a positive nitrogen balance

Other Endocrine Glands

The *pineal gland* is a cone-shaped gland in the roof of the third ventricle of the brain. It is very small (5 mm long and 9 mm wide). Covered by a capsule of pia mater (the innermost membrane covering the brain and spinal cord), it consists of parenchymal and glial cells. Although the exact function of the gland is still in doubt, some investigators believe it secretes melatonin, a polypeptide hormone that inhibits the secretion of ovarian hormones. It is functional in early childhood and is largely fibrous connective tissue in the adult. Other hormones reportedly secreted by the pineal gland are adrenoglomerulotropin, which stimulates the adrenal cortex to secrete aldosterone, and serotonin, which is a neurotransmitter. The exact nature and function of the pineal gland is still to be determined.

The *thymus gland*, like the pineal gland, is functional before and during puberty. After puberty, the lymphocytic thymic tissue atrophies and is replaced by connective tissue. The thymus gland plays an essential role in the immune response of the body. It produces a polypeptide called *thymosin*, which plays an important part in the maturation of T-lymphocytes.

Health Problems of the Endocrine System

One of the most common diseases associated with the endocrine system, and in particular the pancreas, is juvenile-onset diabetes (Type I). Unlike Type II diabetes, which has onset in adulthood, Type I commences in infancy or childhood. It is the most common cause of hyperglycemia (high blood-sugar levels). Addison's disease is a deficiency failure of the adrenal cortex. The severity of this disease can range from relatively minor to death. Former President John F. Kennedy suffered from a mild case of this disease.

Cardiovascular System

The cardiovascular system consists of the (1) heart, (2) arteries, (3) capillaries, (4) veins, and (5) blood (Plates 6, 7, and 8). The importance of this system to our health is underscored by the fact that heart disease, stroke, hardening of the arteries, and high blood pressure rank in the top fifteen killers in the United States.

The Heart

The heart is a hollow, muscular organ that can be thought of as two separate pumps operating in parallel. The right heart receives blood from the tissues and pumps it through the pulmonary arteries to the lungs. There it passes through capillaries, where it is oxygenated and its carbon dioxide removed. The pulmonary veins return the blood to the left heart, which pumps it out again through the aorta to supply the tissues of the body.

Structure

Heart muscle, or *myocardium*, resembles voluntary skeletal muscle in that its fibers are striated. However, in voluntary muscle, the fibers are separate; in heart muscle, which is involuntary, they are joined by side branches, and each fiber has one central nucleus.

The inner lining of the heart is called the *endocardium*. It covers all the heart's projections and irregularities and is modified to form the cardiac valves. The endocardial lining of the heart is continuous with the endothelium that lines all of the arteries, veins, and capillaries of the body. An inflammation of this lining is called *endocarditis*. This may involve the cardiac valves that have been destroyed by rheumatic fever or congenital malfunctions.

Cavities of the Heart

The right and left sides of the heart are separated by a muscular partition, the *septum.* Each half is divided into an upper compartment, the *atrium,* and a lower compartment, the *ventricle.* Before birth, there is an opening in the partition between the two atria. Soon after birth, this closes so that there is no longer any communication between the right and left sides of the heart. The partition between the atria is called the *interatrial septum;* that between the ventricles is the *interventricular septum.* Each atrium communicates with the ventricle below it on the same side by the atrioventricular orifice of the right and left atrioventricular valves.

The left ventricle ejects blood into the systemic circulatory system under higher pressure than is required of the right ventricle for ejecting blood into the pulmonary (lungs) circulation, which offers less resistance. The thicker muscle is on the left side, where it is needed for this stronger pumping action. The right and left sides of the heart contract and relax almost simultaneously.

Valves of the Heart

On the right, the atrioventricular (AV) valve is composed of three irregularly shaped flaps or cusps and is called the *tricuspid valve* (Plate 8). The left AV valve, which bears two flaps or cusps, is called the *bicuspid* or *mitral valve.* It is much stronger and thicker than the tricuspid valve. The object of both valves is to allow blood to flow freely from the atria to the ventricles but to prevent its flow in the other direction.

Cardiac Cycle

The task of the heart is to propel blood to all parts of the body. In doing so, it pumps in definite strokes or beats. In the healthy adult, these occur on average about seventy-two times per minute. That is 4,320 beats per hour, for a total of 103,680 beats a day!

Heartbeats may be felt by placing the hand over the region of the apex of the heart, the area just under the left breast about 3.5 inches from the sternum. The sensation felt is one of bumping or thrusting, each thrust corresponding to a contraction of the heart.

The series of actions the heart performs is spoken of as its cycle. Starting with any one of the separate actions or movements of the heart, the sequence of events that follows until the original action repeats itself constitutes a complete *cardiac cycle.* The contraction of the heart is called *systole;* its relaxation is called *diastole.*

For convenience, we can consider the events of the heartbeat starting from diastole, when the heart is relaxed and relatively flaccid. Venous blood from the superior and inferior venae cavae enters the right atrium; at the same time, oxygenated blood from the pulmonary veins returns to the left atrium. Meanwhile, the valves between the atria and the ventricles on each side are open so that the blood can flow through the atria and into the ventricles. The combination of the mild muscular contraction of the atria and the increased pressure of the full atrial chambers ultimately drains the atrial blood into the ventricles.

Shortly thereafter, the ventricles contract. The rising pressure closes the AV valves (Plate 8). As the pressure rises, it forces the pulmonary and aortic valves to open, so that the blood is driven out into the circulation. When contraction is completed, the ventricles relax. The blood in the aorta and pulmonary artery attempts to reflux or flow back into the ventricles. But the semilunar valves of the aorta and pulmonary artery close and prevent this reverse flow. During ventricular contraction, the atria once more relax and venous blood starts to fill them. When the ventricles are completely relaxed, the tricuspid and mitral valves open again, blood flows into the ventricles, and the next cycle begins.

Heart Sounds

A great deal of information is obtained by carefully listening to the heart with a stethoscope. The first heart sound is associated with the initiation of ventricular systole and the closing of the mitral and tricuspid valves. This first sound is low-pitched and longer than the second sound. Both sounds can be heard over the entire area of the heart, but the first sound, "lubb," is heard most clearly in the region of the apex.

The second sound, "dupp," is sharper, shorter, and lower pitched. It is heard best over the second right rib, since here the aorta is nearest to the chest surface. The second sound is caused mainly by the closing of the semilunar valves during ventricular diastole. The momentum of the moving blood closes the valve cusps, preventing a backflow into the heart. The faint third sound sometimes may be heard following the second in early ventricular diastole. The fourth sound occurs during atrial contraction and immediately precedes the first heart sound.

Defects in the valves can cause excessive turbulence or regurgitation of the blood, resulting in abnormal sounds. Abnormal sounds are called *murmurs.*

The sounds emanating from a heart in utero are much different. The heartbeat of a fetus is more like a "swishing" sound rather than the usual "lubb-dupp."

General Circulation

The general circulation is shown diagrammatically in Plate 7. The heart is a muscular organ that can be thought of as two parallel pumps. The right heart receives blood from the veins draining the tissues and pumps it through the pulmonary arteries to the lungs. Here it passes through capillaries in which it is oxygenated and its carbon dioxide removed. The pulmonary veins return the blood to the left heart, which pumps it out again through the aorta, from which arise the various systemic arteries that distribute blood to the other tissues.

Thus there are two parallel circulations: the pulmonary circulation, for gas exchange in the lungs; and the systemic circulation, for maintaining a constant internal environment in the other tissues. Note that all blood goes through first one system and then the other.

Blood Vessels

Arteries carry blood away from the heart to the tissues; *veins* return blood from the tissues to the heart. The large arteries nearest the heart divide into smaller vessels. These divide into still smaller ones, and so on. The smallest arteries are called *arterioles.* These lead into vessels of narrow caliber, the *capillaries.* The capillaries branch and form a network where the exchange of materials between blood and tissue fluid takes place. After passing through the capillary network, the blood is collected into the smallest veins, the *venules.* The venules unite to form small veins; these combine to make ever-larger vessels until eventually the great veins that enter the heart are reached.

The distention of the arteries during systole extends to the periphery and can be detected as a throbbing sensation, known as the *pulse,* in several arteries near the skin.

Capillaries

The walls of the capillaries consist of one layer of endothelial cells continuous with the layer that lines the arteries, veins, and heart. The capillaries form an interlacing network of variable size.

As noted, it is in the capillary beds that the main work of blood is done—the exchange of materials between cells and blood. A molecule diffuses through the capillary wall into the tissue fluid and from the tissue fluid into the cell, or in the reverse direction. In addition to diffusion, some of the fluid part of the blood filtrates through the capillary walls, especially at the arterioles, where the blood pressure is high, so that the blood continually contributes to the tissue fluid.

Blood

Functions of the Blood

Everything required by the tissues for energy or synthesis is carried in the blood, and all waste products derived from the tissues are removed by the blood. Following are some of the more important functions of blood:

1. Supplies the cells and tissues with oxygen and nutrients for growth, repair, and other life activities
2. Transports the waste products of cellular metabolism, including carbon dioxide, to the excretory organs for elimination

3. White blood cells, antibodies, and other protective substances provide an important defense against damage from injury and disease
4. Helps regulate and equalize body temperature by distributing heat to the body parts
5. Transports hormones, the secretions of the endocrine glands, to the cells and tissues
6. Plays an important role in maintaining the acid or alkaline balance of the tissues
7. Can help to maintain its own volume and composition by forming a clot, reducing bleeding, and preventing the escape of body fluids
8. Bathes the various body cells and tissues in fluid, regulating the water and salt content of all tissues. At the same time, it maintains the osmotic concentrations throughout the body.

Characteristics of Blood

Blood is bright red (indicating that it is well oxygenated) in the arteries, and dark red (less oxygenated) in the veins. Water flows four to five times faster than blood because blood is four to five times thicker (a property called *viscosity*). Blood's specific gravity (density compared to water) varies between 1.045 and 1.065 (water is 1.0), and its temperature and pH are 38° C (100.4° F) and about 7.38 respectively. The volume of blood in the body has been measured in many ways but can be expected to vary with the size of the body. A useful estimate is that its weight is 8 percent of the body's weight. The blood volume of a man of average size is approximately 6 liters.

Seen with the naked eye, blood appears to be opaque and homogenous, but microscopic examination reveals that it consists of cell fragments and an intracellular fluid, plasma.

When blood is obtained from a person's vein (by venipuncture) and transferred to a test tube, and clotting is prevented by adding certain chemicals called *anticoagulants,* it separates into two distinct layers. The upper layer, yellow and transparent, contains most of the chemical components of the blood in solution; this is the plasma. Plasma constitutes about 55 percent of the blood's volume. The lower portion of the blood sample consists of the formed elements: the red blood cells (erythrocytes), the white blood cells (leukocytes), and the platelets (thrombocytes). These are often called *corpuscles,* meaning "little bodies." The percentage of total blood volume contributed by these formed elements is called the *hematocrit.*

Leukocytes

The white blood cells, or leukocytes, are concerned primarily with the body's defense against infection. Leukocytes vary in size and shape. They are less numerous than erythrocytes, but are larger than the red cells. White blood cells are extremely active and move under their own power by ameboid motion, often against the flow of the bloodstream. Unlike erythrocytes, white blood cells pass out of the bloodstream and into the intracellular spaces to consume foreign materials (such as bacteria) found between the cells.

Platelets (Thrombocytes)

The platelet or thrombocyte is not a cell in the strictest sense, but a cell fragment. It is made in the bone marrow by the largest cells there. Platelets play a role in blood clotting and repair of ruptured blood vessels. After leaving the bone marrow, a platelet survives for about ten days and then is cleared by the spleen.

Blood platelets are vital to life. They adhere to other platelets and to the inner surfaces of small blood vessels. When a blood vessel is torn or severed, platelets begin to pile up immediately, adhering to the torn surface of the vessel and to other platelets, forming a plug to slow the loss of blood. As they adhere, they release chemicals of *coagulation* and a clot begins to form behind the platelet plug. The clot ultimately enmeshes more platelets, red cells, and some white cells. A special spiral protein in the platelets contracts much like the proteins in the muscles. When the clot is big enough, the protein contracts and the clot becomes firm. This process is called *clot retraction.* The firm clot forms a bridge over which healing takes place.

Cardiovascular Response to Activity

The heart is one of the most fascinating organs of the body. One of the strongest muscles of the body, it pumps blood through the arteries to all parts of the body. Exercise and stress make the heart beat faster, increasing blood volume per minute by as much as ten times in trained athletes. During a night's sleep, the heart does work equivalent to carrying a thirty-pound pack almost to the top of the Empire State Building—not bad for an organ the size of a clenched fist.

The five quarts of blood in an average adult are replaced once a month. It takes about twenty-three seconds for the blood to round the circulatory system. During this time, the blood holds enough oxygen for about five minutes during rest; the same amount is used in a fraction of a minute during strenuous exercise. Yet when 10 percent of the blood is lost over a short period, the body goes into shock. Death results when 40 percent is lost.

The average adult male has 100,000 miles or more of blood vessels. It is the smallest vessels, the capillaries, in which the exchange of substances takes place between the blood and the rest of the body. Although vessels are elastic, arteries lose their elasticity if the body is not exercised regularly and if the diet is rich in fats. No wonder physiologists say that you are as old as your blood vessels.

Health Problems of the Cardiovascular System

High blood pressure is one of the most common disorders, as is an elevated cholesterol level. Generally, high blood pressure means greater than 140 mm Hg systolic and 90 mm Hg diastolic. When fatty plaques develop on the inside walls of the arteries, they eventually calcify, causing atherosclerosis. From a drug standpoint, the "innocuous" medication called *aspirin* inhibits platelet action, reducing spontaneous clotting. Of course hemophilia is a problem with blood clotting too.

Although not a health problem per se (although it may be a problem nonetheless), blushing is evidence that our nervous system is working in tandem with our cardiovascular system. Our ANS interacts with our arterioles to cause a blush. Fainting is a more severe interaction. When the sympathetic system is strongly suppressed, our blood vessels expand, causing a rapid drop in blood pressure, which leaves the brain momentarily deficient of blood and leads to fainting.

Lymphatic System

Closely related to the cardiovascular system is the lymphatic system (Plate 10), which is important to the body's defense mechanisms. This system consists of organs that produce and store lymphocytes, lymph, and lymphatic vessels that return the lymph to the circulation. *Lymph* is a clear fluid containing a low count of granular leukocytes and a varying number of lymphocytes.

Functions of the Lymphatic System

Most of the tissues of the body, with the notable exception of the central nervous system, are drained by the lymphatic system. It is this system that gathers and drains filtered fluid and cellular constituents that accumulate in the spaces between the cells. The larger lymphatic vessels drain into veins, which return the lymph to the blood. Specifically, lymph and the lymphatic system serve the following functions:

1. *Defense mechanism:* Lymphocyte production phagocytizes (ingests) pathogenic organisms.
2. *Immunity:* Production of antibodies aids in combating disease and infection.
3. *Tissue drainage:* Networks of vessels drain the spaces between the tissue cells and return the metabolites to the system, where they can be reused.
4. *Excretion:* The lymphatic system removes impurities such as carbon particles, waste products, and dead blood cells.
5. *Digestion:* Intestinal lacteals (intestinal lymphatics) absorb end products of fat digestion and distribute them via the circulatory system.

(The defense role of lymphatic system in disease is discussed more fully in Chapter 8.)

Lymphatic Tissues

The following organs containing lymphoid tissue perform somewhat different functions, particularly with respect to the substances that they filter.

Tonsils

These masses are found just beneath the epithelium of the mouth and throat, and include the *palatine tonsils* (at each side of the soft palate), the pharyngeal tonsils (behind the nose on the back wall of the upper pharynx, sometimes called the *adenoids*); and the *lingual tonsils* (at the back of the tongue). Any or all of these tonsils may become so infected with bacteria that their surgical removal is indicated.

Thymus

The thymus gland, usually comprised of two lobes, plays a key role in the formation of antibodies in the first few weeks of life, and the development of immunity. It is located at the base of the neck and manufactures lymphocytes. Removal of the thymus causes a decrease in lymphocyte production throughout the body and a decrease in size of the spleen and lymph nodes. The thymus is most active during early life; after puberty it undergoes degenerative changes and is replaced by adipose tissue.

Spleen

The spleen is situated in the left abdomen next to the stomach. It is designed to filter blood and produce lymphocytes that carry on phagocytosis. The spleen has many functions concerned with lymphatic and blood circulation. Prominent structures inside the spleen are round masses of lymphoid tissue, and these justify its classification as a lymphatic organ.

Lymph Nodes

Lymphatic tissue filters and removes bacteria. Along the course of the lymphatic vessels are small bodies of lymphatic tissue called *lymph nodes* (Plate 10). These usually are oval and are commonly referred to as *microkidneys.*

Research indicates that lymph nodes may afford some protection against infection and disease. Lymphocytes (leukocytes) of the lymph nodes and spleen destroy bacteria and antigens that are introduced into the body. Lymph nodes commonly become swollen and inflamed during severe bacterial infections.

All lymphatic vessels form networks and, at certain points, carry lymph into the regional lymph nodes. Groups of large nodes are in the neck (cervical), under the arm (axillary), at the elbow (cubital), and in the groin (inguinal).

Health Problems of the Lymphatic System

The lymphatic system plays a very important role in our immune response. (This is discussed more fully in Chapter 8.) Leukemia, the uncontrolled replication of white blood cells, is one problem faced by children and adults alike. When the lymphatic system allows abnormally high levels of interstitial fluid to collect, edema may result. Elephantiasis is such a condition brought on by the presence of a parasitic worm. In pictures or news stories about starvation, it is common to see children with pencil-thin limbs and a bloated abdomen. In this disease, called *kwashiorkor,* the muscles atrophy and interstitial fluid accumulates rather than returning to the circulatory system (Farish, 1993).

Digestive System

"The digestive system is one of the most interesting yet most abused of the body's systems" (Farish, 1993, p. 123). Think about what you eat or drink and the effect it might have on your digestive system. Think about a kindergarten child who eats playground soil at recess, with little or no repercussions. If that same dirt had entered through a cut in the skin, infection could result. There is no doubt that the digestive system is used and abused; fortunately, it is also resilient. Plate 14 illustrates the digestive system, and Figure 16.5

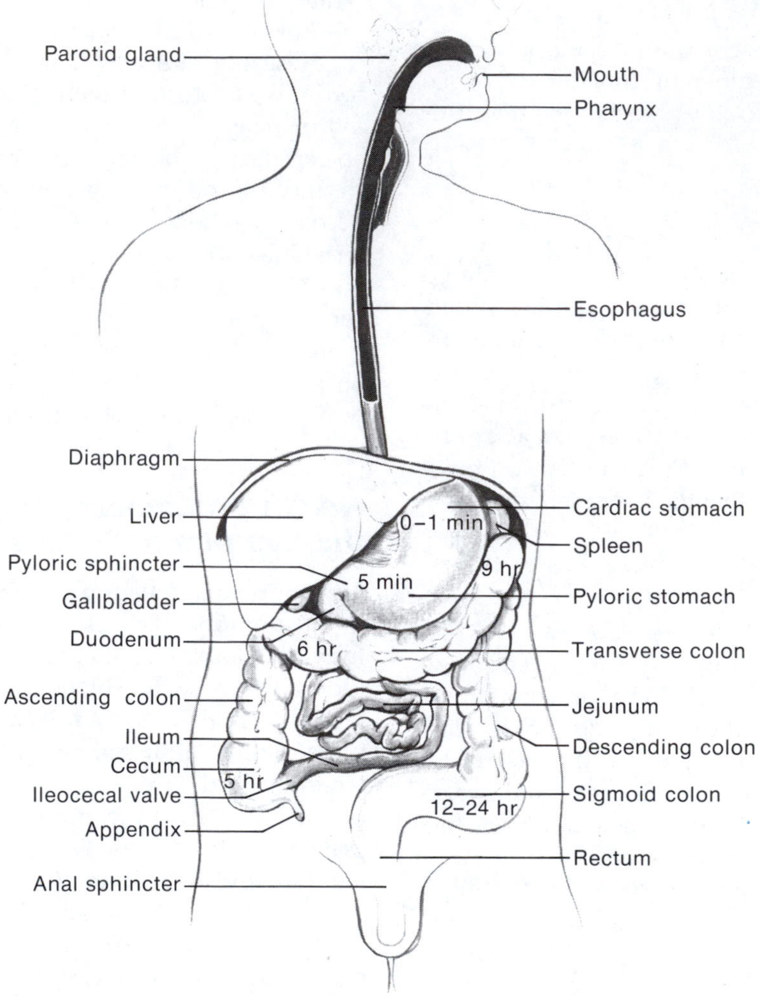

FIGURE 16.5 **The Digestive Tract. Times indicated along the tract represent how long it takes food to pass through each area during digestion.**

shows the digestive tract in conjunction with the length of time it takes for food to pass through each area during digestion.

Before food can be absorbed, it must undergo a number of changes. Some of these are purely mechanical; others are highly complex chemical reactions. Most foodstuffs are constructed of molecules too large to pass through the walls of the intestine, and the purpose of digestion is to convert these into smaller molecules.

All of this action begins in the mouth and eventually moves through the alimentary canal, which extends from the mouth to the anus. During digestion, hydrolysis occurs. That is, complex molecules are broken down by digestive enzymes known collectively as the *hydrolases.* These enzymes are present in the secretions of the several digestive glands of the alimentary tract: the salivary glands, the gastric glands, the pancreas, and the intestinal glands.

Mouth

When food is taken into the mouth, it is cut and ground by the teeth, mixed with saliva, and finally molded into a semidigestible mass called a *bolus*. Saliva contains a large amount of water, the enzyme salivary amylase (ptyalin), and mucus, which helps to hold the food together and lubricate it for passage down the esophagus. The mechanical breakdown of food (*mastication*) is carried out by the *teeth*.

Stomach

The irregularly shaped stomach lies slightly to the left side in the upper portion of the abdomen, just beneath the ribs and just below the diaphragm, which separates the abdominal and thoracic cavities. The stomach has two functions. First, it receives the bolus of swallowed food from the esophagus and begins the digestion of proteins. Second, the stomach delivers food to the intestine.

Small Intestine

The food leaves the stomach through the pyloric sphincter and enters the small intestine, in which most digestion and absorption take place. The first section of the small intestine is the *duodenum*. The duodenum leads into the middle portion, the *jejunum*, and the small intestine terminates in the *ileum*. The entire small intestine of an adult male is about 7.5 meters (23 feet) long and 2.5 cm (1 inch) in diameter.

Partially digested food from the stomach passes into the duodenum, where the acidity of the food stimulates the intestine to secrete hormones. These in turn stimulate the pancreas to secrete pancreatic juices and the liver to secrete bile.

Bile salts are produced by the liver and stored in concentrated form in the gallbladder when the intestine is empty. When the chyme, or food, reaches the intestine from the stomach, the bile salts digest and absorb fats. Bile salts emulsify the fats into minute particles, providing a larger surface for the action of pancreatic lipase.

Since the small intestine is where absorption of the end products of digestion occurs, special structural adaptations increase the absorptive surface area. The innermost lining of the small intestine is not smooth, but has numerous fingerlike projections called *villi*, which greatly increase the absorptive surface.

Gallbladder

The gallbladder, or *cholecyst*, is a pear-shaped sac lying on the underside of the liver. *Bile* passes from the liver, where it is produced, by way of the hepatic duct into the common bile duct and the gallbladder. The gallbladder stores bile as bile salts until needed for digestion, at which time they are released into the small intestine.

Pancreas

The *pancreas* is the most active and versatile of the digestive organs (Plate 9). In the absence of other digestive secretions, its enzymes alone are capable of almost completing the digestion of food. Pancreatic secretions into the duodenum contain all the enzymes needed to break down foodstuffs.

Large Intestine

In humans, the junction between the small intestine and the large intestine (colon or large bowel) is usually in the lower right portion of the abdominal cavity. A blind sac, the *cecum*, projects from the large intestine near the point of puncture, the *ileocecal (ileocolic) valve*. Here a small, fingerlike process, the *appendix*, projects from the cecum. The appendix frequently becomes infected and sometimes must be removed surgically (appendectomy).

The cecum and appendix serve no known purpose except as storage centers for microorganisms that aid digestion. Humans cannot digest the complex cellulose found in plant cells without assistance; the stored microbes digest this cellulose for them, but most of the nutritional value of the material is lost. The duodenum, not the cecum, is the principal site of digestion.

The large intestine is about 2 meters (5–6 feet) long, and its secretions are named according to the directions they travel and the shapes they assume.

The cecum leads into the *ascending colon*, which is followed by the *transverse colon*, *descending colon*, *sigmoid colon* (shaped like the letter "S"), *rectum*, and *anus*.

The major function of the large intestine is the reabsorption of water into the body. If all the water in which enzymes are secreted into the digestive tract were lost in the waste material (feces), dehydration would occur.

A second function of the large intestine is the removal of the waste products of digestion by *defecation*. The large bowel is also where excess salts, such as those of calcium and iron, are excreted when their concentration in the blood is higher than normal. The last portion of the large intestine, the rectum, stores the waste materials until defecation occurs. The feces are expelled through the anus.

Occasionally, the colon becomes irritated, and peristalsis moves the material through it faster than normal. As a result, not enough water is reabsorbed, and a watery waste material, *diarrhea*, persists until the cause of the irritation is remedied. Conversely, if material moves too slowly, too much water is reabsorbed, and constipation results. Diarrhea may be the result of a bacillary dysentery or many other causes. *Constipation*, on the other hand, results from an overstimulation of the intestinal muscle, narrowing the canal and preventing passage of fecal material. Nervous tension, excessive amounts of bulky foods in the diet, and use of laxatives contribute to constipation.

Liver

The liver, the largest of the glandular organs of the body, is situated in the upper right quadrant of the abdominal cavity. It lies to a large extent under the shelter of the lower ribs, its upper surface conforming to the lower surface of the diaphragm.

The liver can be thought of as a chemical factory. Besides storing fat-soluble vitamins and maintaining about a twelve-hour supply of sugar, the liver synthesizes bile for the small intestine. Perhaps the liver's most important function is to detoxify poisons and complex body chemicals. When these chemicals are broken down into simpler substances, they can be excreted by the kidneys. Many poisons and drugs, such as alcohol, caffeine, and nicotine, are detoxified by the liver. The liver is also capable of making antibiotics, as when it converts the chemical prontosil into sulfanilamide in the fight against bacteria and viruses.

The liver has numerous functions:

1. Production
   a. Blood plasma proteins
   b. Antibodies to fight off diseases
   c. Heparin, a substance that prevents blood clotting
   d. Bile pigments from red blood cells in the form of bilirubin and biliverdin
2. Storage
   a. Vitamins and minerals
   b. Glucose in the form of glycogen
3. Conversion and use
   a. Fats (desaturation)
   b. Carbohydrates (glycogenesis)
   c. Proteins (deamination)
4. Removal
   a. Old blood cells and toxins by phagocytosis (Kupffer cells)
   b. Waste products (urea and ammonia) from amino acids

Health Problems of the Digestive System

Tooth decay (dental caries) is a problem with the digestive system requiring frequent brushing and flossing. Stomach ulcers (gastric ulcers) occur for some people when the lining of the stomach is attacked by pepsin and hydrochloride. For others, the same process takes place at the beginning of the small intestine and they have duodenal ulcers. This disorder can cause bleeding as the lining is eaten away, and the person may even develop a perforated ulcer if a hole is formed. Heartburn is a common problem of the digestive system too. In this case, the sphincter closing off the esophagus from the stomach fails to function properly, allowing some of the stomach contents to be regurgitated back into the esophagus. This highly acid material irritates the tissues, causing heartburn. Although not related, a similar action takes place with vomiting, when the sphincter opens and allows food to be expelled. This mechanism is very important in removing tainted food and the like.

Of course, it is possible to have too much of a good thing, because excessive vomiting causes a loss of bodily fluids and upsets the natural pH balance.

Respiratory System

Nature designed the body so that the cardiovascular system is complemented by the respiratory system (Plate 13). Oxygen is necessary for life. The lungs, where exchange of gases takes place, contain 700 million to 800 million air sacs, or alveoli. The inner surface of the lungs in an adult is equivalent to the size of a tennis court. Lungs help us to breathe about 12,000 liters of air each day.

The respiratory system consists of:

1. nostrils (nose)
2. trachea
3. bronchus and bronchioles
4. lungs (air sacs)

The trachea divides into two *bronchi* that enter the right and left lung. The right bronchus is shorter, wider, and more vertical than the left. Within the lungs, the bronchi subdivide into smaller branches, the bronchial tubes, and finally into bronchioles (see Figure 16.6). Each bronchiole terminates in an elongated sac called the *atrium;* these are lined with numerous pouches, *alveoli* or air cells. Alveolar walls are very thin, highly vas-

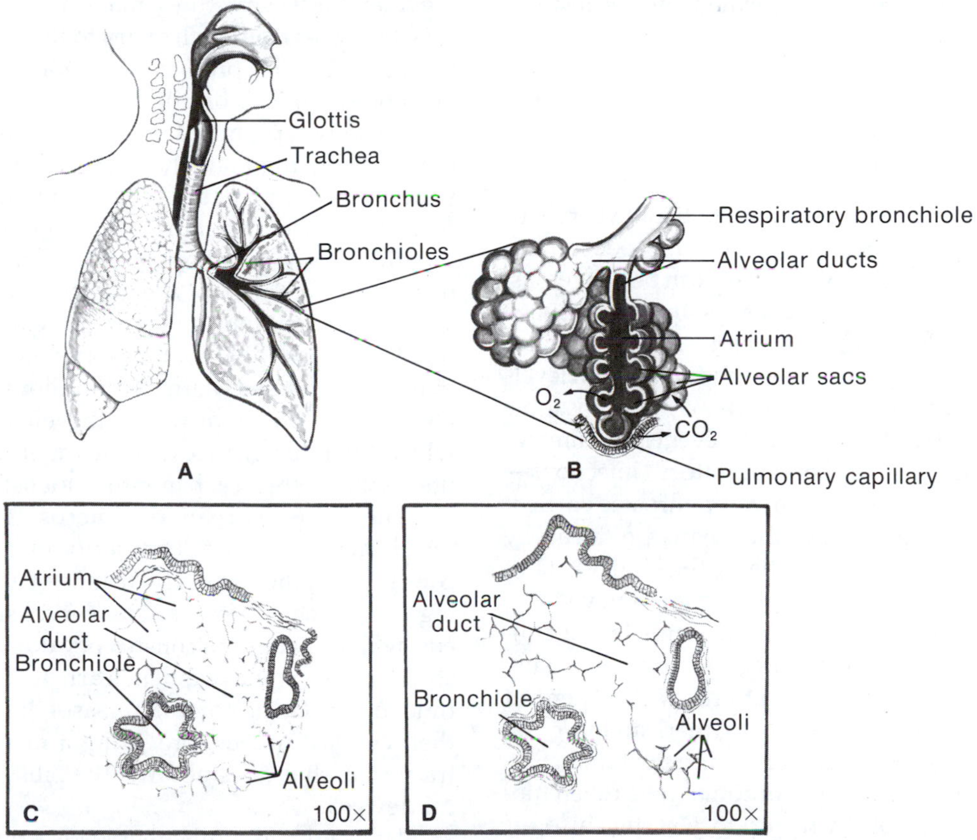

FIGURE 16.6 **Internal Structure of the Lungs. a, Relationship of the lungs to the head and neck. b, External and internal appearance of a lung lobule, showing the atrium and alveolar sacs. c, Section of a lung, magnified 100 times. d, Section of a similar lung with emphysema. Note the decreased number of alveolar sacs and consequent diminishing in the gas-exchange area of lung tissue.**

cular, and lined with squamous epithelium. An exchange of gases between the blood and the air occurs through the walls of the capillaries in the alveoli. The term *intrapulmonary* refers to the spaces within the alveolar sacs.

The two lungs vary in shape and size. The right lung is the larger and has three lobes. It is wider than the left lung but a little shorter. The left lung is divided into two lobes and is somewhat narrower and longer than the right.

The movement of air into and out of the lungs depends on the rhythmical contraction and relaxation of the diaphragm, the intercostal muscles, and other respiratory muscles. Because muscles contract in response to volleys of impulses over the nerves serving them, there must be a control center. This control is performed by the respiratory center in the brain.

Health Problems of the Respiratory System

Some children play a game where they hyperventilate to make themselves dizzy or bring about an "altered state of consciousness." This can be dangerous, since one potential consequence is unconsciousness. The same holds true for athletes who hyperventilate before their event in hopes of building oxygen levels (which incidentally doesn't work). While this is futile in any event, it can be deadly if the event is swimming.

In childhood, upper-respiratory infections—colds and flu—are common. Strep throat is particularly threatening because the toxins produced by the invading bacteria can inflame the kidneys, damage heart valves, or precipitate rheumatic fever.

One of the major health problems facing children is asthma. It is estimated that twice as many children as adults develop asthma, with 90 percent of the cases allergic reactions (American Lung Association 1994; U.S. Dept. of Health & Human Services, 1992). Hiccups, pneumonia, and tuberculosis are problems of the respiratory system also.

Reproductive Systems

All the body systems discussed thus far are very similar for males and females. However, no other system shows such great dissimilarities between men and women than do the reproductive systems (Plate 15). From a purely biological perspective, the other systems keep us in a "maintenance" position until we are ready to reproduce. Another difference is that other body systems start functioning at conception or birth, whereas the reproductive system begins functioning a decade or so later.

Female Reproductive System

A woman's internal sexual organs consist of two *ovaries,* which lie on either side of the abdominal cavity, the *fallopian tubes,* the *uterus,* and the *vagina;* together these structures make up a specialized tube that goes from each ovary to the outside of the body. The ovaries produce fertilizable ova and sex hormones, which control the development of the female body type, maintain normal sexual physiology, and help maintain the course of a normal pregnancy. The fallopian tubes gather and transport ova that are released from the ovaries (about one each month). The two fallopian tubes connect to the uterus, an organ about the size of a woman's fist, situated just behind the pelvic bone and the bladder. The uterus is part of the passageway for sperm that move from the vagina to the fallopian tubes; after fertilization, it provides the environment in which the fetus grows. It is the inner lining of the uterus that is shed each month in menstruation.

The lower part of the uterus is the *cervix,* which means "neck." The cavity of the uterus is connected to the vagina by means of a small opening called the *cervical os.* The cervix secretes mucus, which changes in consistency during the menstrual cycle. Some women learn to estimate the time of *ovulation* (ovum release) by examining their cervical mucus, providing a method of contraception that does not involve pills or mechanical devices.

The vagina is a tube that leads from the cervix to the outside of the body. Normally, the vagina is narrow, but it can readily widen to accommodate the penis during intercourse, a tampon during menstruation, the passage of a baby during childbirth, or a pelvic examination. The vagina possesses a unique physiology that is maintained by the secretions of the vaginal walls. These secretions help control the growth of microorganisms that normally inhabit the vagina and help to cleanse it. Because the vagina is self-cleansing, it is usually unnecessary to employ any external cleansing measures such as douching. Very often, douching merely upsets the natural chemical balance of the vagina and increases the risk of vaginal infections, or *vaginitis*.

A woman's external genitals (Plate 15) consist of two pairs of fleshy folds that surround the opening of the vagina, and the *clitoris*. The smaller, inner pair of folds are called the *labia minora*, and the larger, outer pair are called the *labia majora*. The clitoris, a highly sensitive sexual organ, is situated above the vaginal opening (see Figure 16.7).

The opening of the *urethra*, the exit tube for urine, is located in the vaginal region just below the clitoris. The fact that the urethra is only about one half inch long and so close to the vagina makes it susceptible to irritation and infection, called *urethritis*, which is characterized by a burning sensation during urination and usually the frequent urge to urinate. Occasionally, bacteria introduced into the urethra migrate to the bladder and produce an infection called *cystitis*. The symptoms of cystitis are similar to those of urethritis.

If a woman develops a mild case of urethritis or cystitis, she can often eliminate the irritating bacteria by drinking a lot of fluids to wash the bacteria from the urinary tract, and by making the urine more acidic, either by taking high doses of vitamin C or drinking acidic fruit juices. It is not advisable to drink alcohol or ingest caffeine or spices at this time, for these substances may irritate an already inflamed urinary tract. If pain is severe or there is blood in the urine, a physician should be consulted.

A woman's secondary sex characteristics include the breasts, a network of milk glands and milk ducts embedded in fatty tissue. Breast size among women varies with the amount of fatty tissue in the breasts. There is little variation among women in the amount of milk-producing tissue; thus, a woman's ability to breastfeed is unrelated to the size of her breasts.

The breasts are supplied with nerve endings that are important in the delivery of milk to a nursing baby. These nerves also make the breast highly sensitive to touch, and many women find certain forms of tactile stimulation to be sexually pleasurable. Sexual arousal, tactile stimulation, and cold temperatures can cause small muscles in the nipples to contract, resulting in erection.

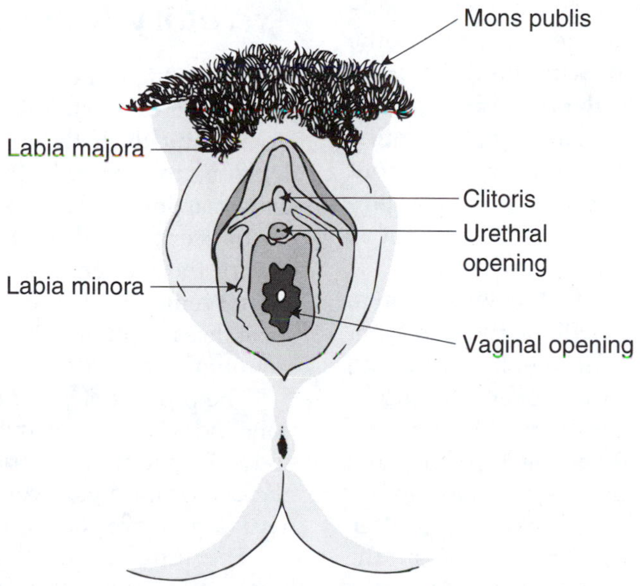

FIGURE 16.7 External Female Genitalia

Male Reproductive System

The principal role of male sexual organs is to make viable sperm cells and deliver them into the female reproductive tract during sexual intercourse. The male reproductive system consists of two *testes* (singular: testis), the sites of sperm and sex hormone production; a series of sperm ducts that originate at the testes, course through the pelvis, and terminate at the urethra of the penis; glands that produce seminal fluid; and the *penis,* the organ of copulation (Plate 15).

The testes are in a flesh-covered sac, the *scrotum,* that hangs outside the man's body. In the embryo, the testes develop inside the body, but just before birth they descend into the scrotum. Inside the scrotum, the testes are kept a few degrees cooler than the internal body temperature, a condition that is apparently necessary for the production of fertile sperm. One testis is usually a little higher than the other.

Sperm are deposited in the female reproductive system during sexual intercourse. At that time, the male and female reproductive tracts form an uninterrupted passageway from the testes to the fallopian tubes, where fertilization of the ovum takes place. When a man ejaculates, sperm are propelled through the sperm ducts and out of the penis by contractions of the smooth muscles of the pelvis. As they make their way out of the male body, the sperm mix with fluid from the seminal vesicles, prostate gland, and Cowper's glands to form semen. Semen, a gelatinous, milky fluid that is emitted at ejaculation, contains about 300 million sperm cells and about 3 to 6 ml of seminal fluid. Seminal fluid contributes 95 percent or more of the volume of semen.

Normally the penis is soft, but when a man becomes sexually aroused, it fills with blood, enlarges, and becomes erect. All men are born with a fold of skin, the *foreskin,* that covers the end of the penis. For centuries, Jewish and Muslim families have surgically removed the foreskin from male children for religious reasons. Nowadays, *circumcision,* as this procedure is called, is often carried out routinely on newborn boys in the United States, regardless of religion. Although there is no clear medical indication that circumcision is beneficial, removal of the foreskin does eliminate the build-up of *smegma,* a white, cheesy substance that can accumulate under the foreskin. Some scientists have suggested that smegma may contribute to penile and cervical cancer in a few individuals. However, empirical evidence does not support this. The belief that circumcision leads to an increase in sexual arousal because it exposes the glans, and the related belief that circumcision produces inability to delay ejaculation, have been shown to be incorrect. For most men, circumcision has no effect on sexual arousal or sexual activity.

Health Problems of the Reproductive System

The most common problems of the reproductive systems are sexually transmitted diseases. Included in this category of problems is HIV (human immunodeficiency virus) infection and AIDS (acquired immunodeficiency syndrome). The repercussions of sexually transmitted diseases may range from inconvenience, to infertility, to death.

Excretory System

The active life of every cell is accompanied by the production of waste materials. These must be removed quickly if the activities of the tissues are not to be impaired. In the chemistry of the body, some reactions produce starting materials for others, but certain end products may accumulate and disturb the sequence of essential reactions if they are not removed. These materials are the excretory substances, and they are produced in different amounts by all cells.

The process of *excretion* consists of the separation and removal of substances harmful to the body. Excretion is carried out by the salivary glands, skin, lungs, liver, large intestine, and kidneys (see Figure 16.8).

The lungs remove carbon dioxide from the blood; and other waste products of metabolism, such as ketone bodies (acetone), are removed by the respiratory system. The salivary glands excrete various salts, particularly sodium chloride. The sweat glands produce water, salts, amino acids, vitamins, and other materials that are carried from the body and deposited on the outer surface of the skin. Excretory functions of the liver include phagocytic action and the removal of bile pigments. The large intestine, following its principal function of water absorption, removes solid waste materials as feces.

Urinary System

The two principal functions of the urinary system are the excretion of wastes and the regulation of the composition of blood. Blood composition must not be allowed to vary beyond tolerable limits, or life will be lost. Regulation of the composition of the blood involves not only the removal of waste products but also the conservation of water and metabolites in the body.

The urinary system consists of two kidneys that secrete urine; the ducts leading from them, the ureters; a urinary reservoir, the bladder; and the tube from it to the surface of the body, the urethra.

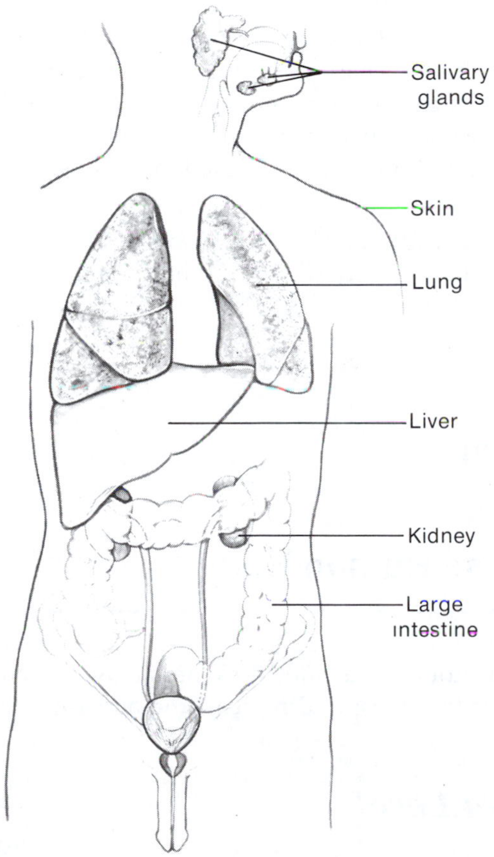

FIGURE 16.8 Organs of the Excretory System

Kidneys

The *kidneys* are deeply embedded in the abdominal cavity in the lumbar region (Plate 15 and Figure 16.8). Both are protected at the back by the last two pair of ribs. They are surrounded by a layer of fat; in front they are covered by renal fascia, the *capsule.*

A kidney is a dark red, bean-shaped organ about 11 centimeters (4.5 in) long, 6 cm (2.5 in) wide, and a little over 2.5 cm (1 in) thick. An adult kidney weighs about 5 ounces.

One of the first organs to receive oxygenated blood is the *kidney.* The kidneys work in much the same way as a screen does in separating rocks from sand. The waste products of cell and liver metabolism are "screened out" by the kidneys, stored in the bladder, and excreted as urine. Through filtration, the kidneys control body fluids and maintain a stable fluid environment. Of the 180 quarts of blood filtered by the kidneys each day, only one to two quarts are excreted as urine. Every twenty minutes the entire volume of the blood passes by a set of molecular filters in the two million glomeruli of the kidneys. Many vital substances, such as salts, minerals, and vitamins, are retained and recycled by the kidneys.

Health Problems of the Excretory System

Some of the problems encountered with the urinary system include cystitis (inflammation of the bladder), gout, and nephritis (inflammation of the kidney). A problem relatively common in young females is urinary reflux, wherein urine is pushed from the bladder back into a ureter and perhaps a kidney. Surgery may be required to rectify this problem.

Implications for Elementary and Middle-School Teachers

Summary Issues

1. The two principal components of the skeletal system are the axial skeleton and the appendicular skeleton.
2. The skeletal system is uniquely linked with the muscular system to produce movement. Skeletal muscles are our action muscles.
3. Our nervous system provides smooth, instantaneous coordination of our movements via messages to our musculoskeletal system.
4. Our endocrine system, like our nervous system, is a means of communication within the body. Hormones are the chemical messengers of the endocrine system, which coordinates the functions of many other body systems (cardiovascular, reproductive, digestive, lymphatic) and responses (immune and stress).
5. The cardiovascular system and respiratory system are united to distribute nutrients and oxygen throughout all the other body systems as well as to eliminate several waste products.
6. The lymphatic system drains all body systems except the nervous system.
7. The digestive system is "put on hold" by our nervous system during times of fight or flight and is obviously important for distribution of food for the functioning of all body systems.
8. The reproductive system is important to the perpetuation of all other body systems.
9. The excretory system removes the waste produced by every cell in the body, which is essential to our survival.
10. Our body systems are interdependent.
11. Our body systems are influenced by both internal and external environments.

Teacher Ramifications

In regard to the body systems, a teacher should:

1. Be cognizant of the common medical problems that afflict the body systems of children
2. Comprehend the interaction among body systems, especially as it relates to the health of children
3. Be able to explain the role of each of the content chapters in this book (Chapters 6–15) on each of the body systems (e.g., the effects of drug use, nutrition, physical activity, mental health, violent and abusive behavior, etc.)
4. Identify the *Healthy Children 2000* objectives that correspond with or have an impact on the body systems

SECTION III

Teaching Strategies for the Human Body

The strategies in this section are divided into grade K–4, 5–6, and 7–8 levels. In addition to strategies that can be used in the classroom, home activities are included. A home activity is designed for student-parent interaction. It is a way to engage the home in school-student learning, and parents can sign a slip of paper to confirm that an activity was completed. Evaluation of all strategies through the use of the National Health Education Standards and performance indicators is indicated. Teachers may also choose to write corresponding learning assessments.

K–4 Level

Strategy One

Objective: Students will associate specified organs with some of their primary functions.

Activity: On a poster board, have prepared a large drawing of the human body with major body parts labeled. Write various activities on index cards (e.g., thinking, breathing, walking). Students are to pick a card and match the activity with the organ primarily associated/responsible for the activity (thinking—brain; breathing—lungs). Difficulty may be increased by listing more specific organ systems that contribute to the accomplishment of an activity (e.g., throwing a ball—skeletal, muscular, and nervous).

Integration: Language Arts

Related Health Content Areas: Growth and development, diseases

Health Education Standard and Performance Indicator: 1(3)

Strategy Two

Objective: Students will find the location of various organs in the body.

Activity: On a flannel or bulletin board, put up a life-sized outline of a human body. Using a variety of colors, cut out the shapes of the major organs of the body (heart, lungs, liver, stomach, etc.). Have students take turns putting the organs up on the board in their correct place. You may also want to have them tell one thing they know about that organ. This could also be made into a game, using teams instead of individuals.

Integration: Science, Language Arts

Related Health Content Area: Growth and development

Health Education Standard and Performance Indicator: 1(3)

5–6 Level

Strategy One

Objective: Students will be able to identify major components of the human body systems. Students will be able to describe how the various organ systems work.

Activity: Separate students into heterogeneous groups and assign to each a particular body system to study (skeletal, muscular, nervous/sensory, endocrine/lymphatic, digestive, circulatory, respiratory, or reproductive/excretory). Then follow these steps:

1. Using pieces of paper about five feet long and three feet wide (bulletin board paper is ideal), have one student in each group lie down in the center of the the paper. (The groups can also choose their own "model.") Other students in each group are to outline the body of the "model" on the paper.
2. Each group is now to illustrate their assigned body system within the outline. Students should be encouraged to be innovative in the choice of materials used to depict the system (e.g., Red Hots candy and small white breath mints may be used for red and white blood cells). Completion of these illustrations may take three or four days.
3. Students are to research different aspects of their body system in order to explain it to the class. Teachers may wish to have students write reports instead of giving verbal explanations to the class.
4. Depending on the time available, students can rotate through different groups, cross-teaching each other on their body systems. If this is done, it is helpful to have handouts depicting the various body systems that students can use to write down information on.

Note: This activity may be used as the centerpiece of an entire unit lasting two weeks. But the teacher can also shorten the length of the activity or unit if appropriate.

Integration: Science, Language Arts, Art

Related Health Content Areas: Growth and development, illness and disease

Health Education Standard and Performance Indicators: 1(1,3)

Strategy Two

Objective: Students will demonstrate competency by solving the puzzle in Figure 16.9.

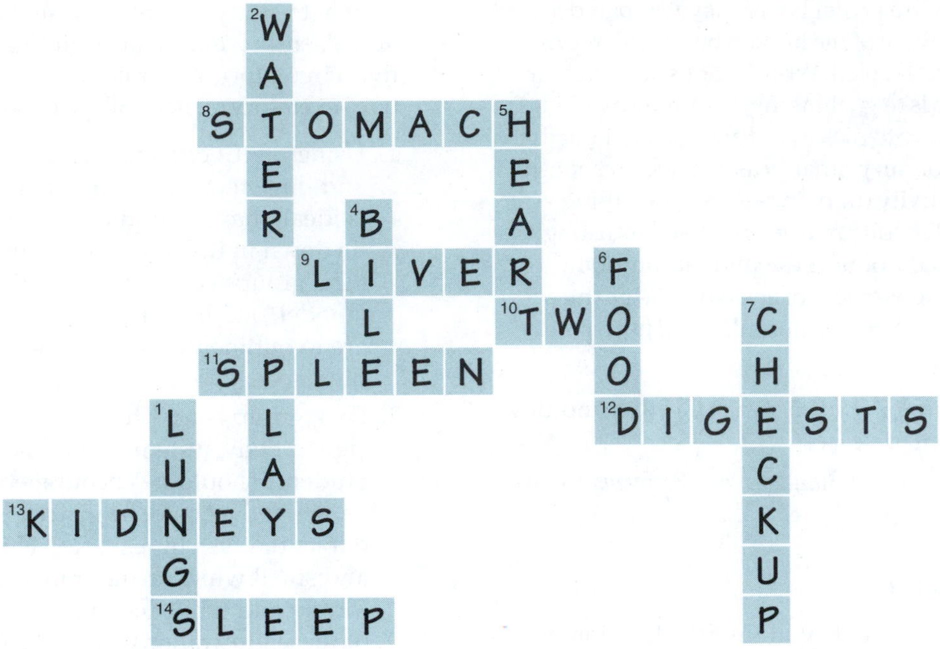

Directions: Each sentence below contains a missing word. Fill in the blank space with the words provided. Then place the word in the crossword puzzle space with the same number, either down or across.

DOWN

1. L ___ ___ ___ ___ are shaped like balloons.
2. Your body needs 4–5 glasses of W ___ ___ ___ ___ daily.
3. You should P ___ ___ ___ outdoors.
4. The liver secretes B ___ ___ ___ .
5. The H ___ ___ ___ ___ is the size of your fist.
6. The right F ___ ___ ___ is good for your body.
7. You need a health C ___ ___ ___ ___ ___ ___ ___ once a year.

ACROSS

8. The S ___ ___ ___ ___ ___ ___ ___ can hold one quart of food.
9. The largest glandular organ is the L ___ ___ ___ ___ .
10. The heart has T ___ ___ pumps.
11. You can live without your S ___ ___ ___ ___ ___ .
12. The stomach D ___ ___ ___ ___ ___ ___ food.
13. The K ___ ___ ___ ___ ___ ___ are shaped like beans.
14. You need plenty of S ___ ___ ___ ___ and rest.

Use these words:

Water	Check-up	Sleep	Liver	Kidneys	Heart	Digests
Food	Play	Bile	Spleen	Two	Stomach	Lungs

FIGURE 16.9 Crossword Puzzle on Body Organs

Activity: The puzzle may also be used as a review activity.

Integration: Science, Language Arts

Related Health Content Area: Growth and development

Health Education Standard and Performance Indicator: 1(3)

7–8 Level

Strategy One

Objective: Students will demonstrate how all body systems are interdependent and necessary for activity.

Plate 1

THE SKELETAL SYSTEM (front view)

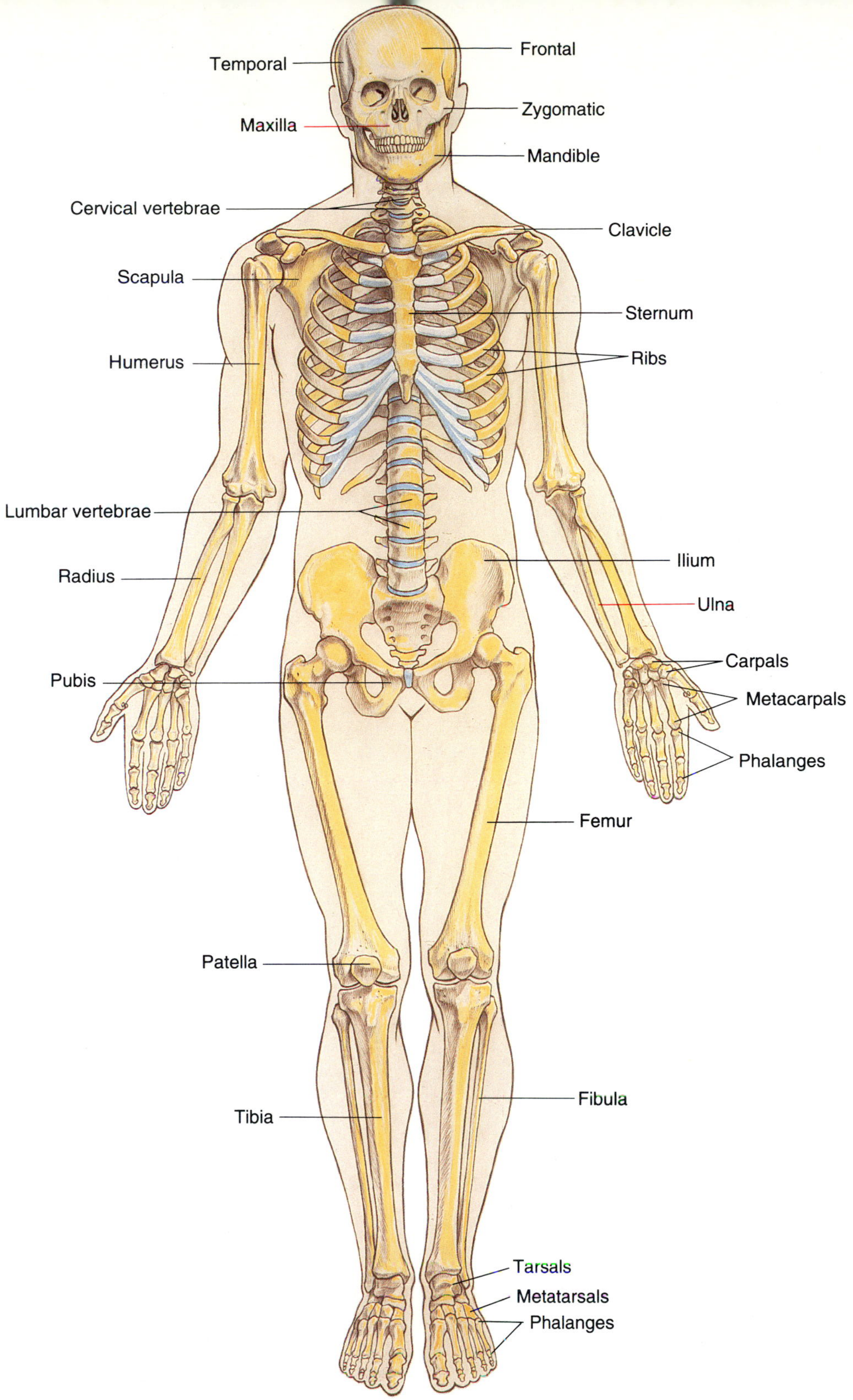

PLATE 2

THE SKELETAL SYSTEM (side and back views)

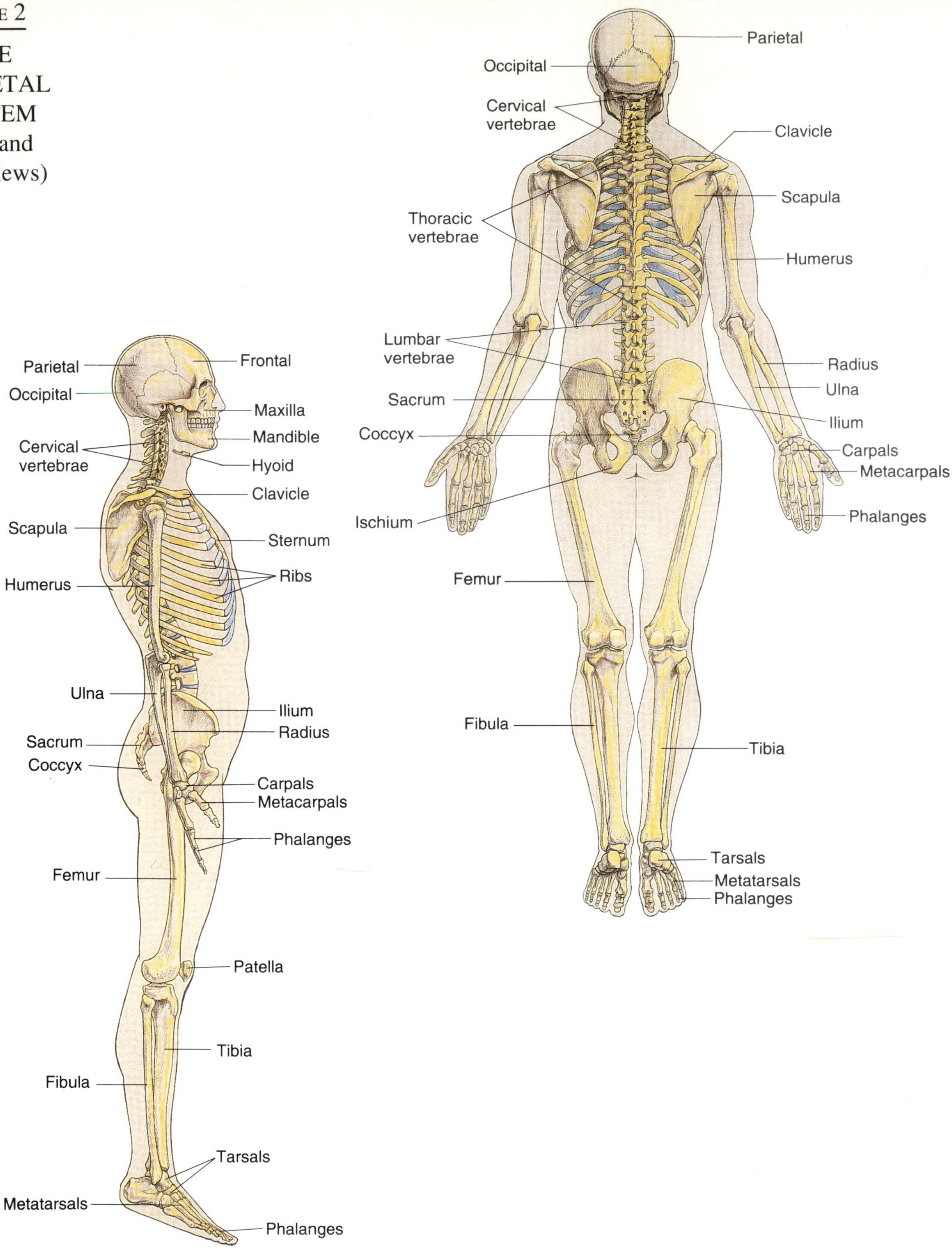

PLATE 3

THE MUSCULAR SYSTEM (front view)

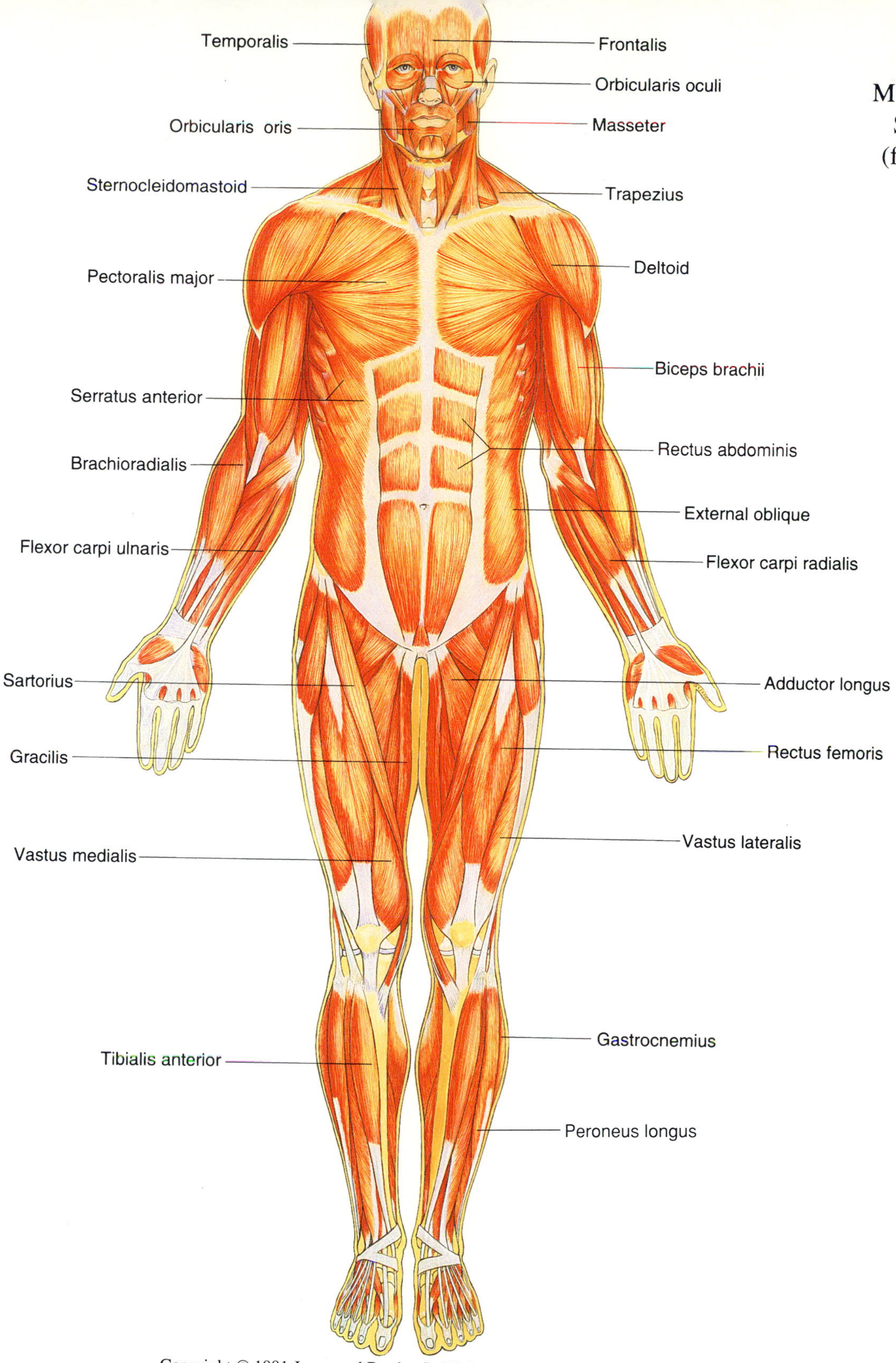

PLATE 4

THE MUSCULAR SYSTEM (side and back views)

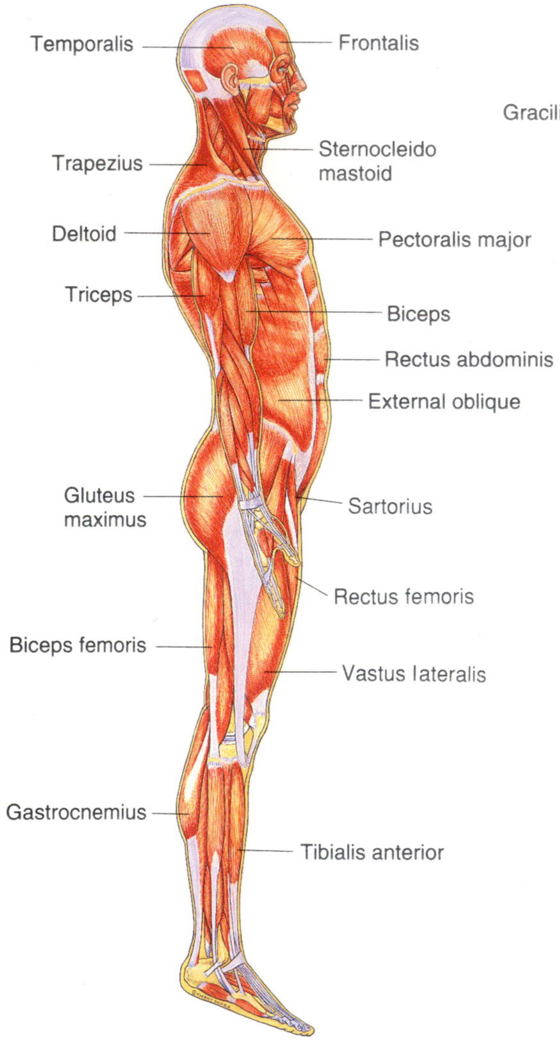

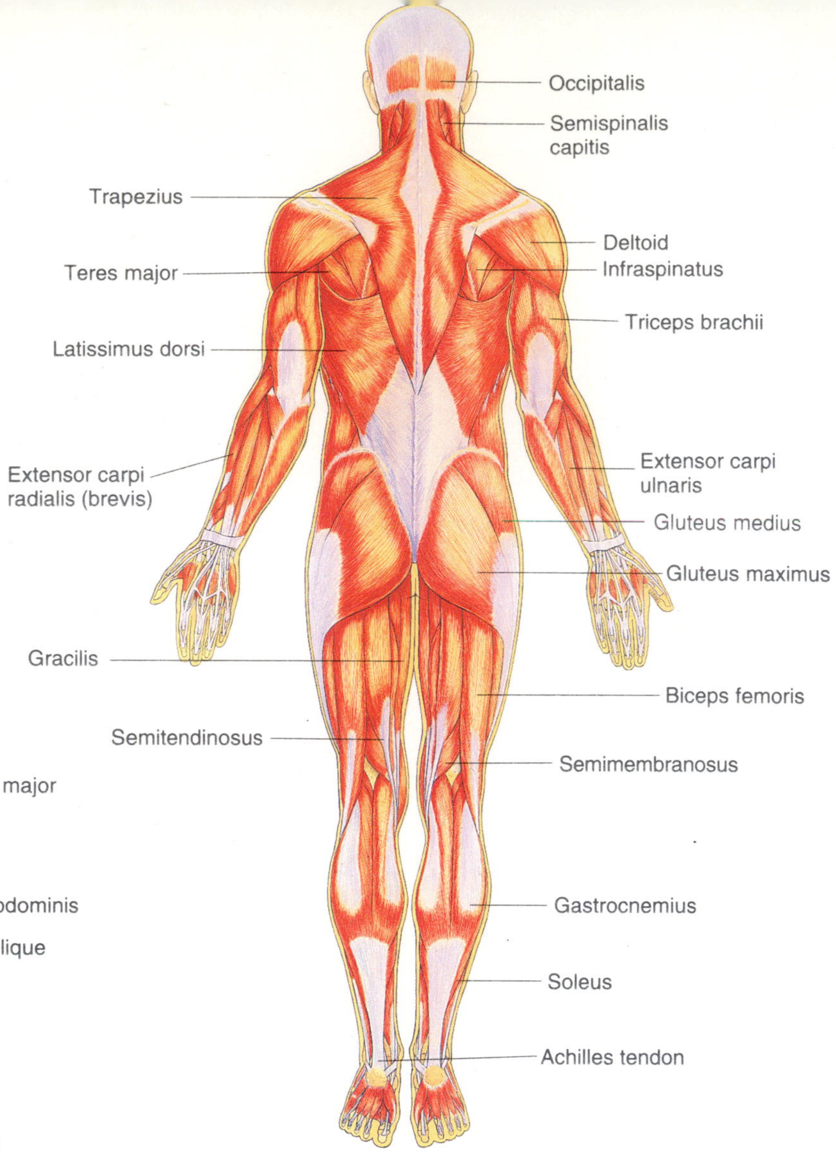

Plate 5

THE SKULL and MUSCLES OF THE HEAD

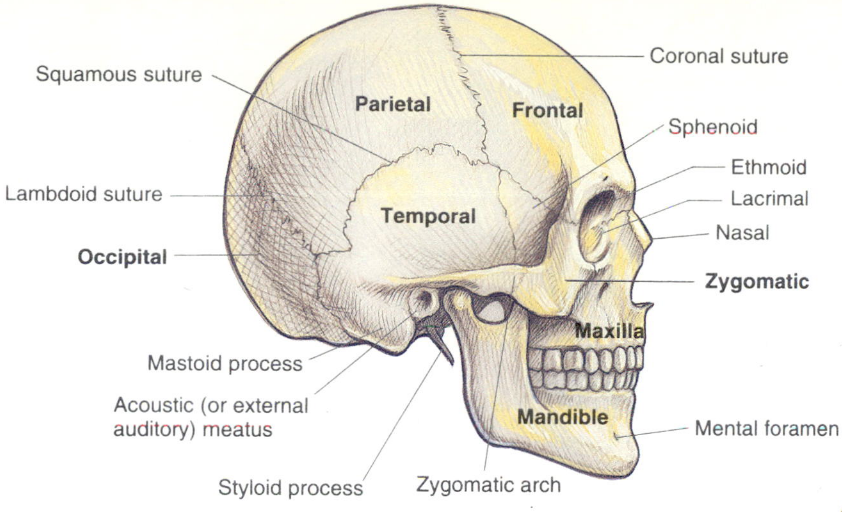

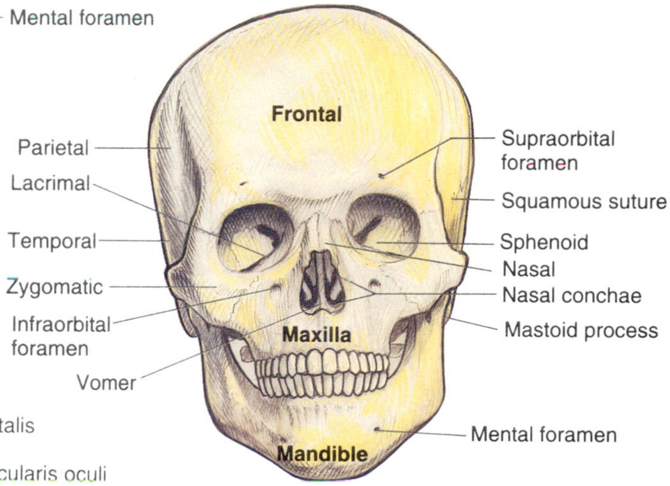

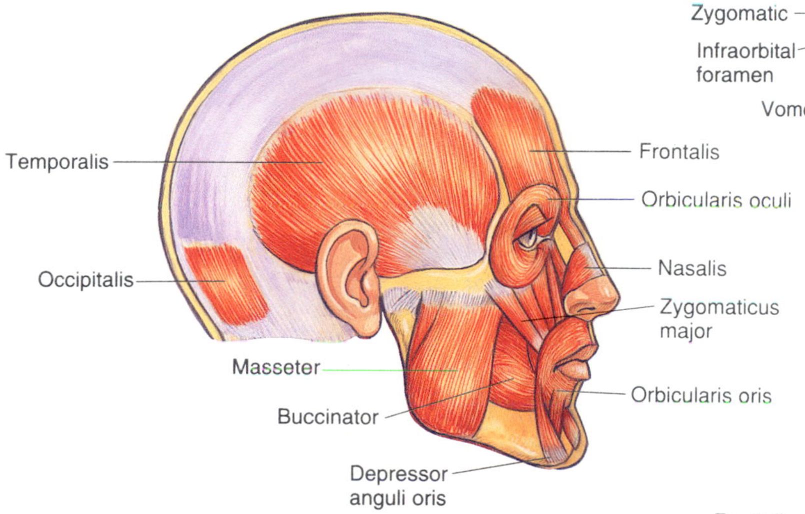

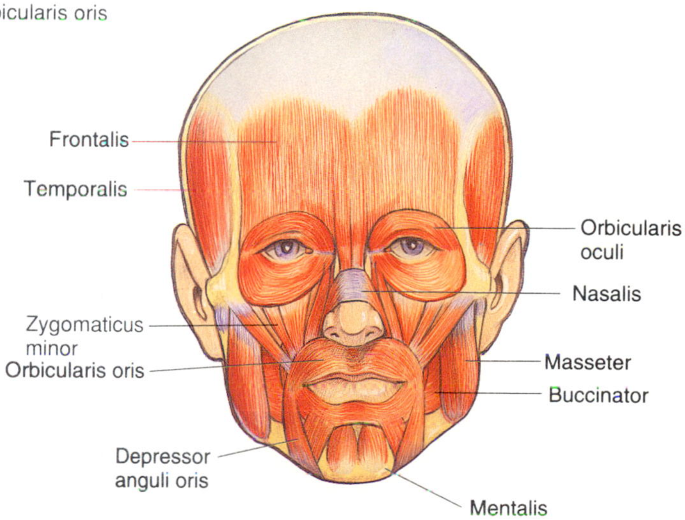

Plate 6

THE ARTERIAL SYSTEM and THE VENOUS SYSTEM

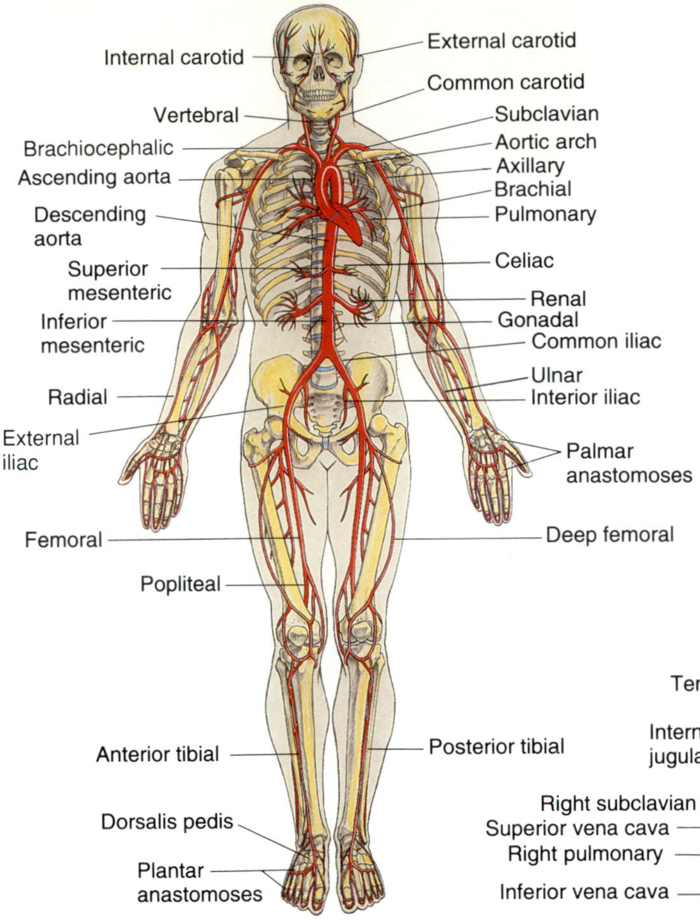

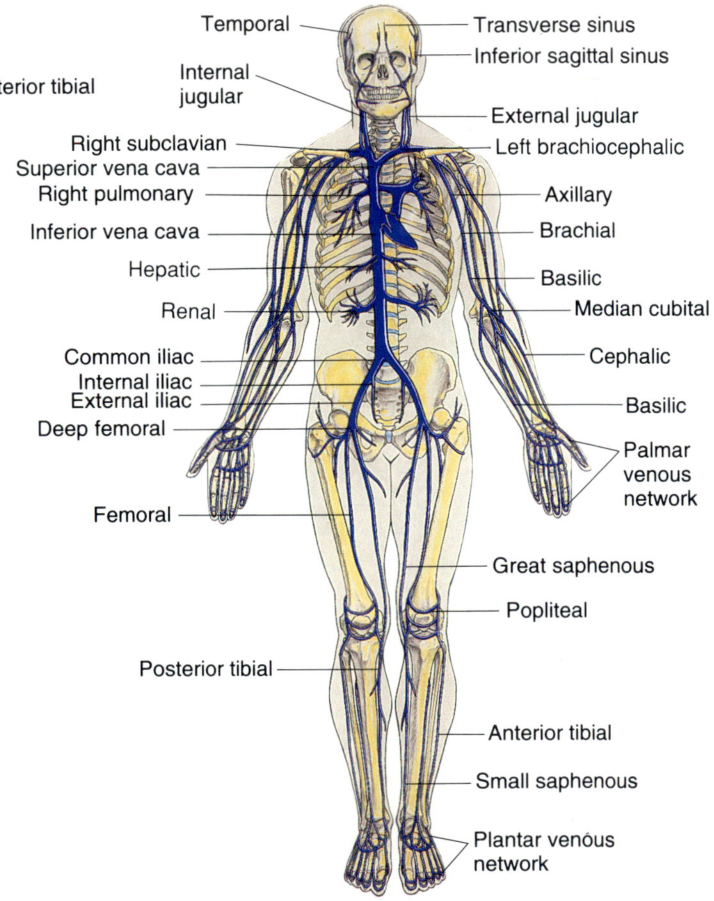

THE ARTERIAL-VENOUS SYSTEM

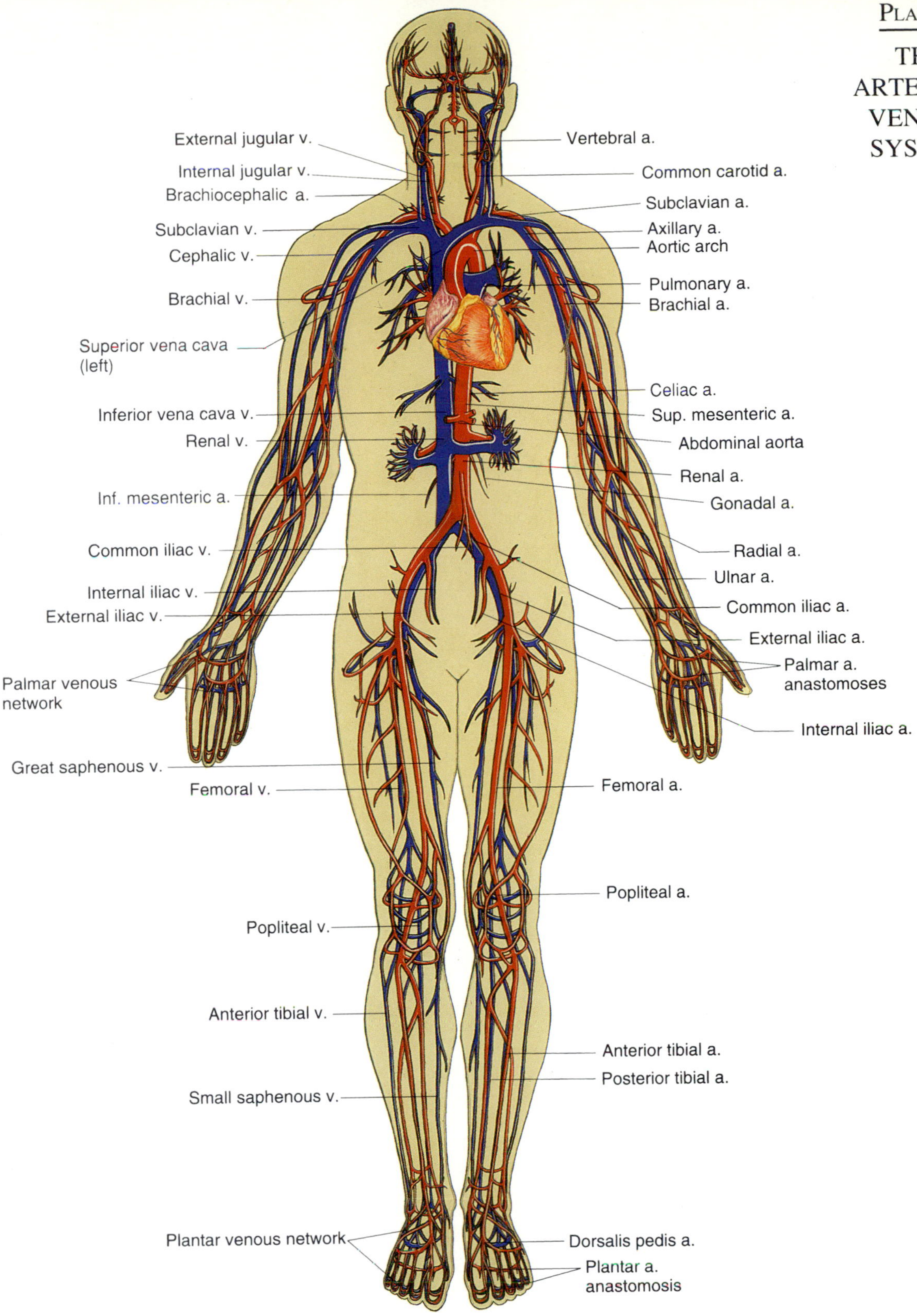

PLATE 8

THE HEART and BLOOD CIRCUITS

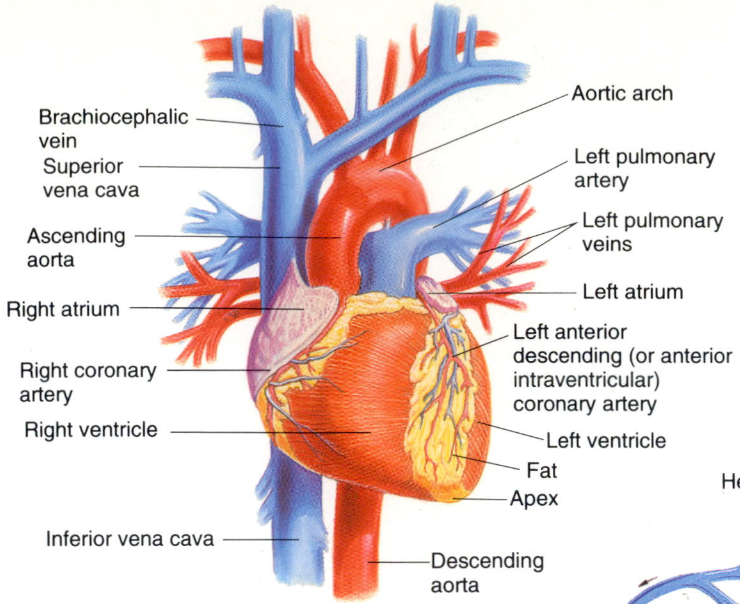

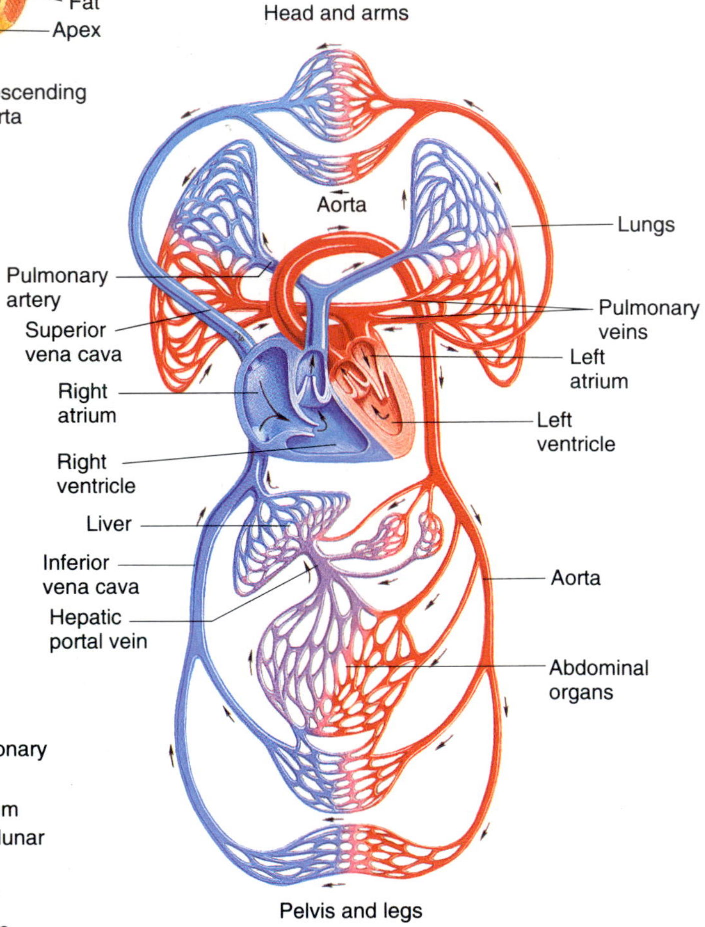

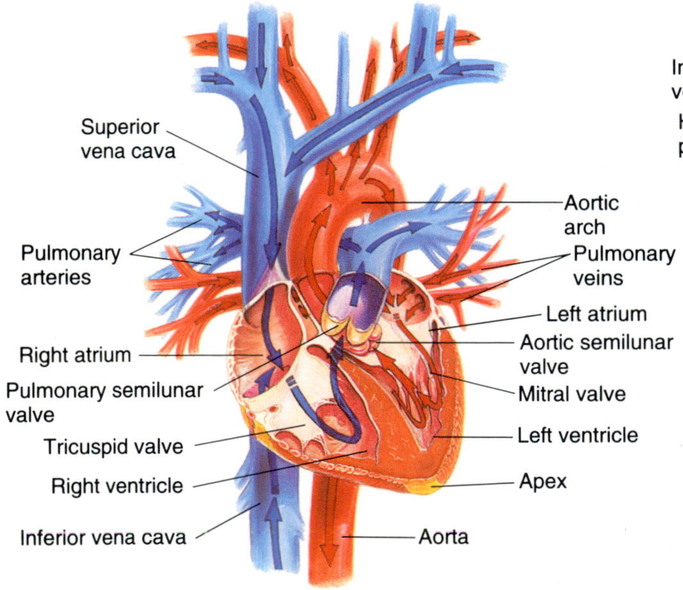

THE ENDOCRINE SYSTEM

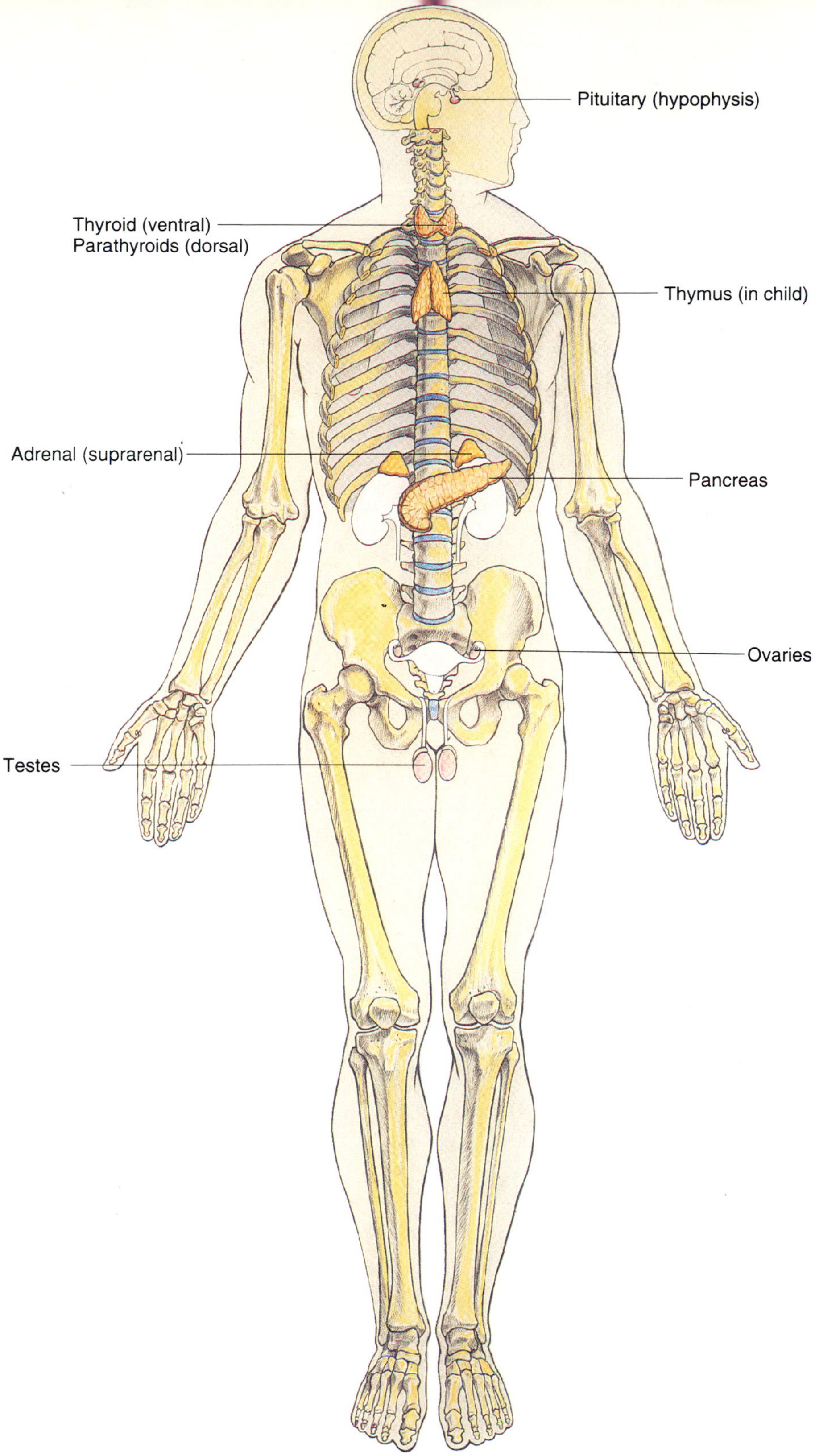

PLATE 10

THE LYMPHATIC SYSTEM

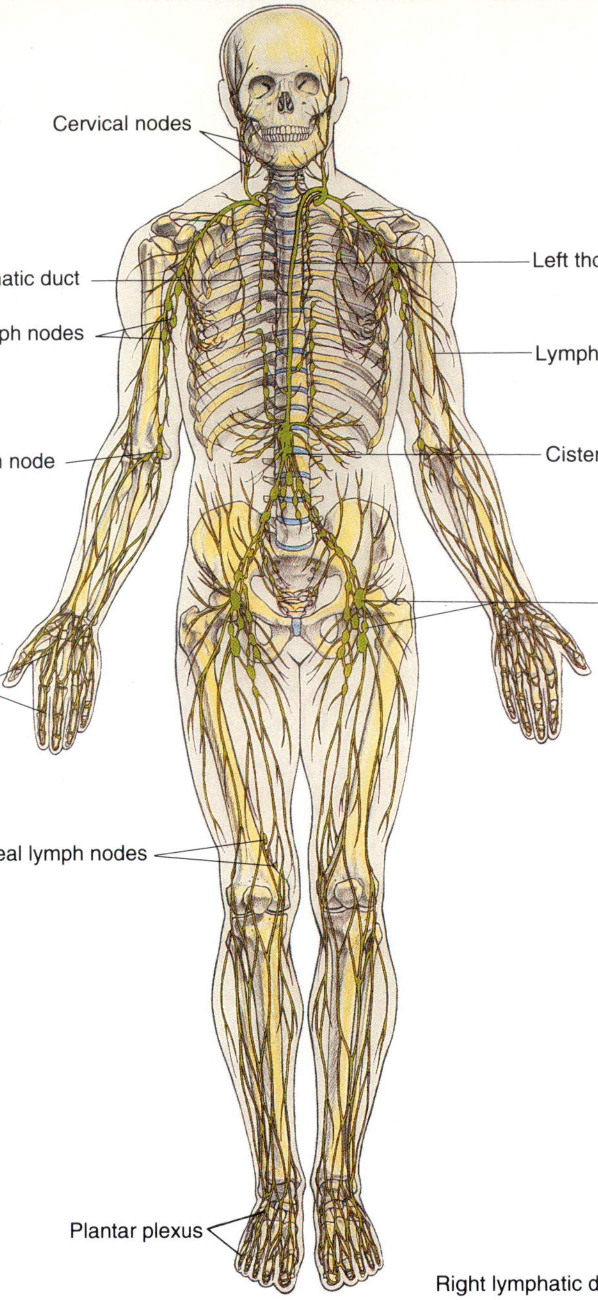

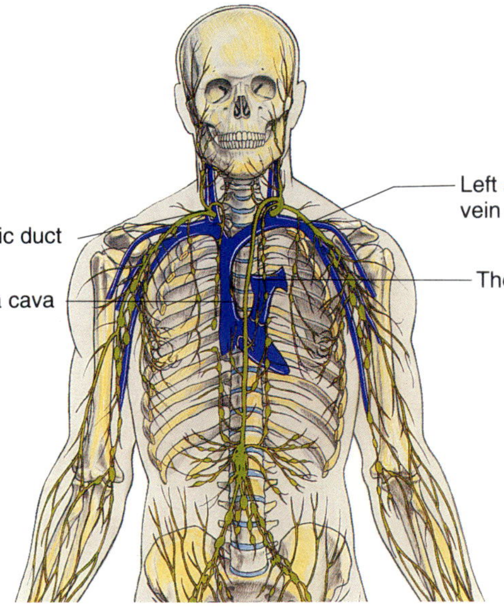

PLATE 11

THE NERVOUS SYSTEM and THE BRAIN (surface and midsagittal views)

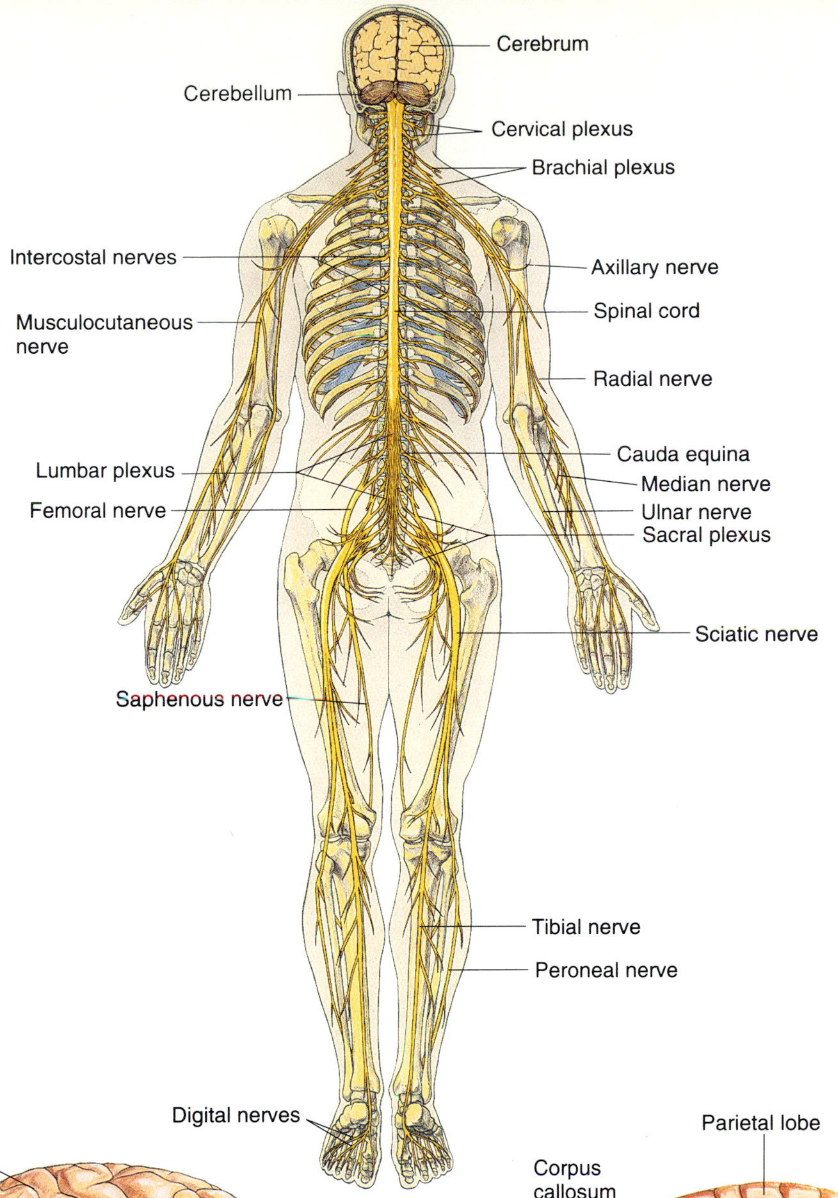

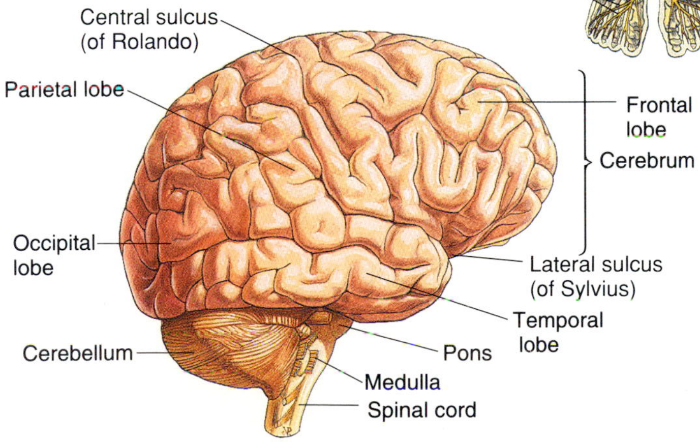

Surface View of the Brain

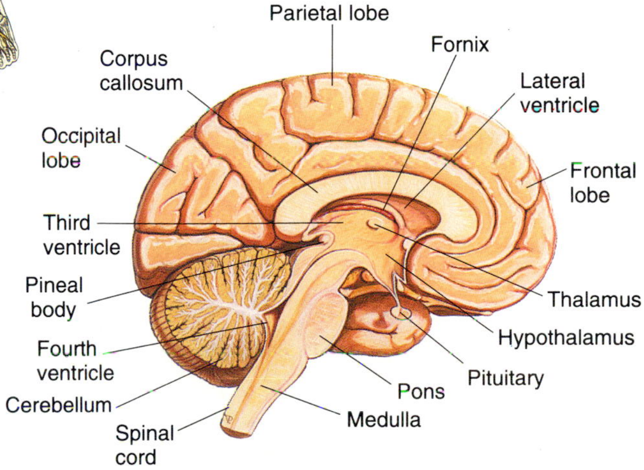

Midsagittal View of the Brain

PLATE 12

THE VISCERA

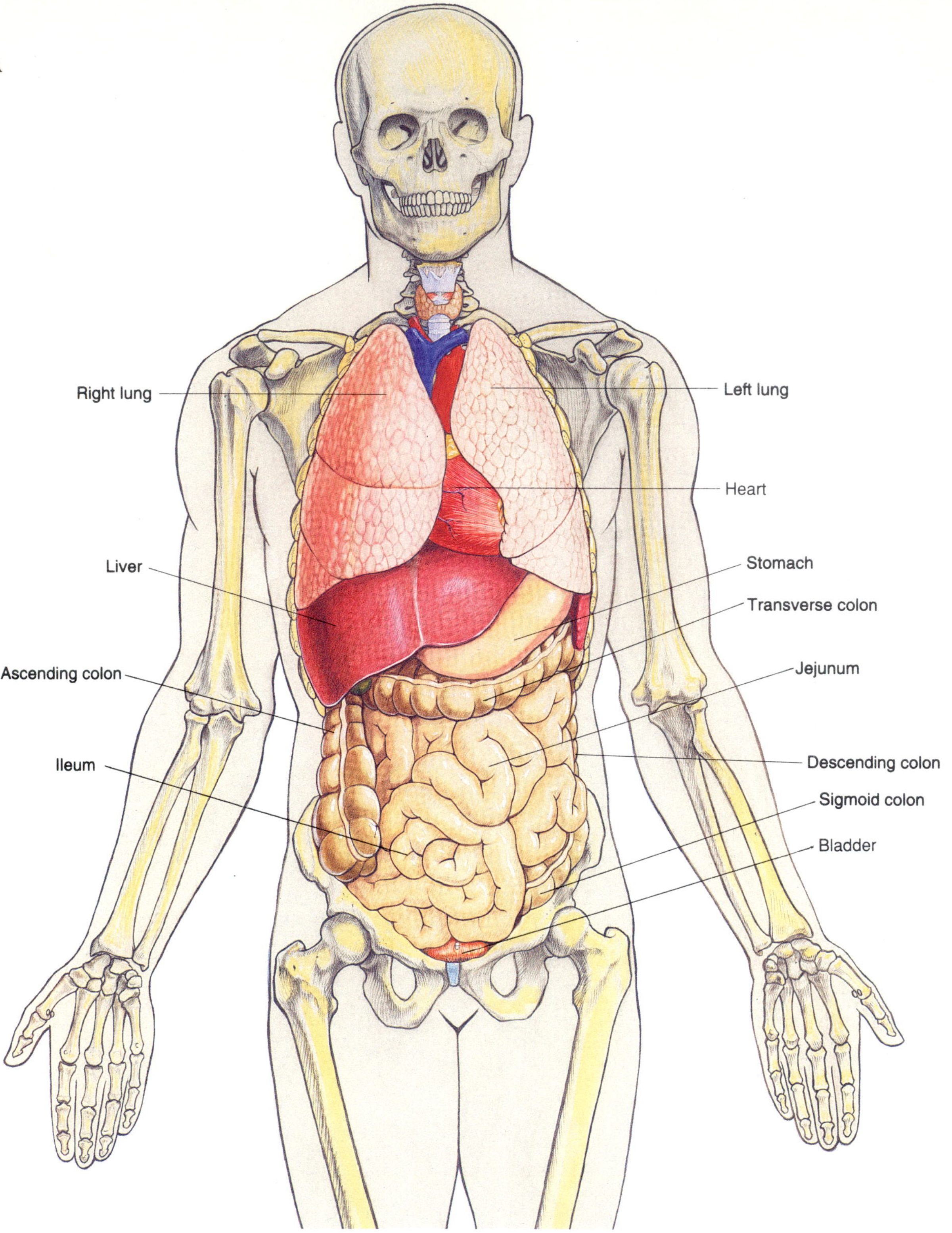

THE RESPIRATORY SYSTEM

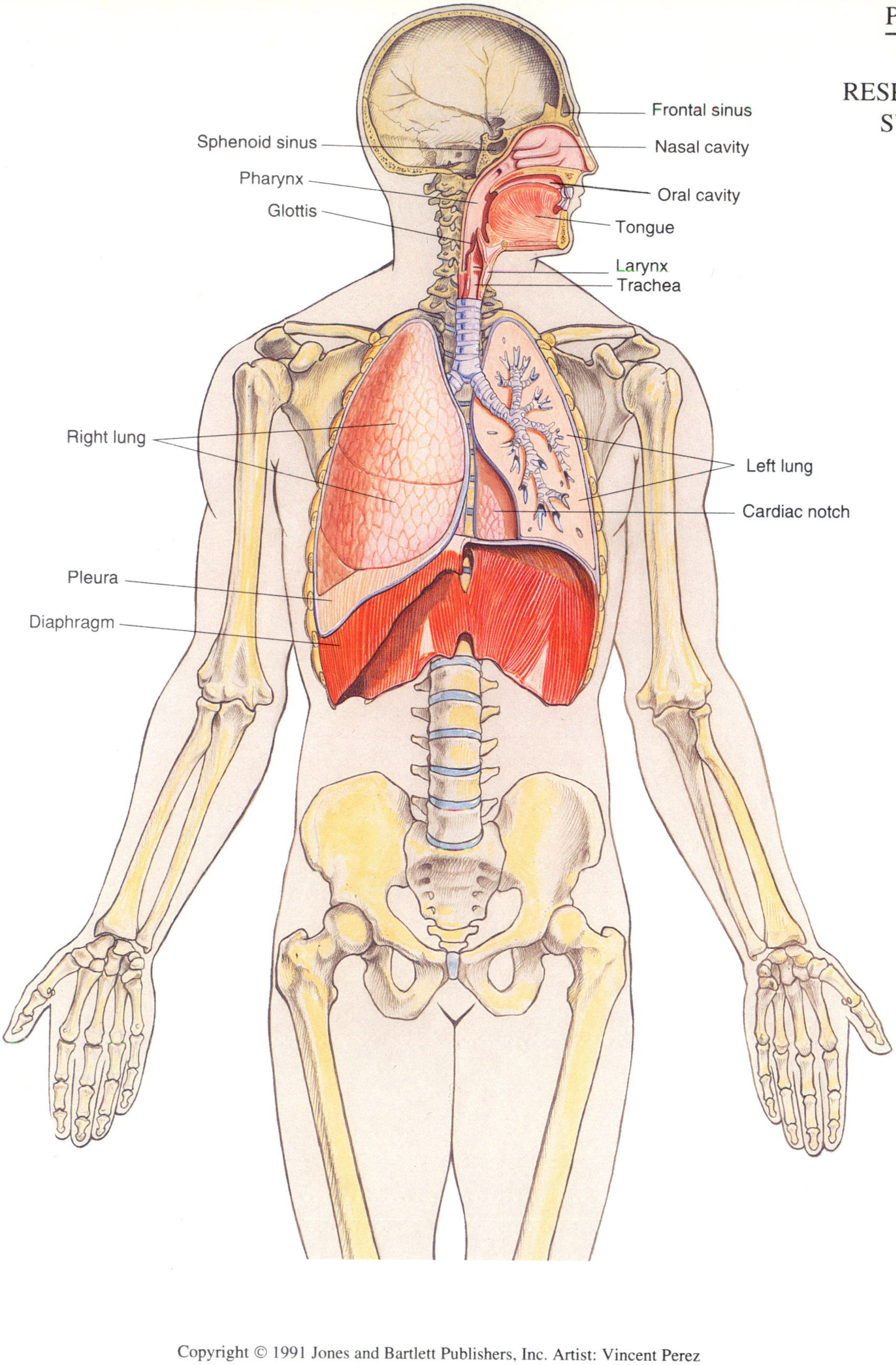

Plate 14

THE DIGESTIVE SYSTEM

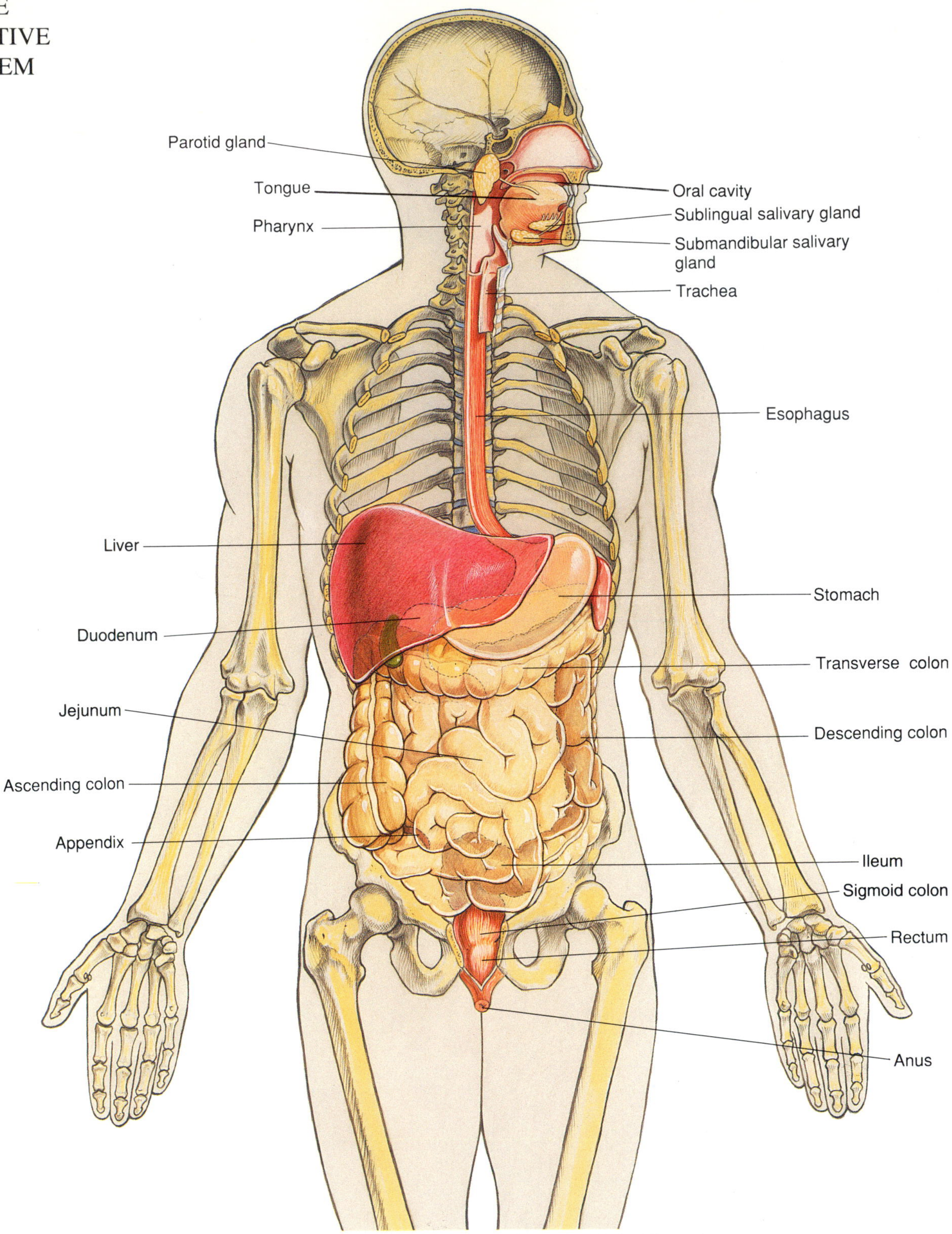

PLATE 15

THE URINARY SYSTEM and THE FEMALE AND MALE REPRODUCTIVE SYSTEMS

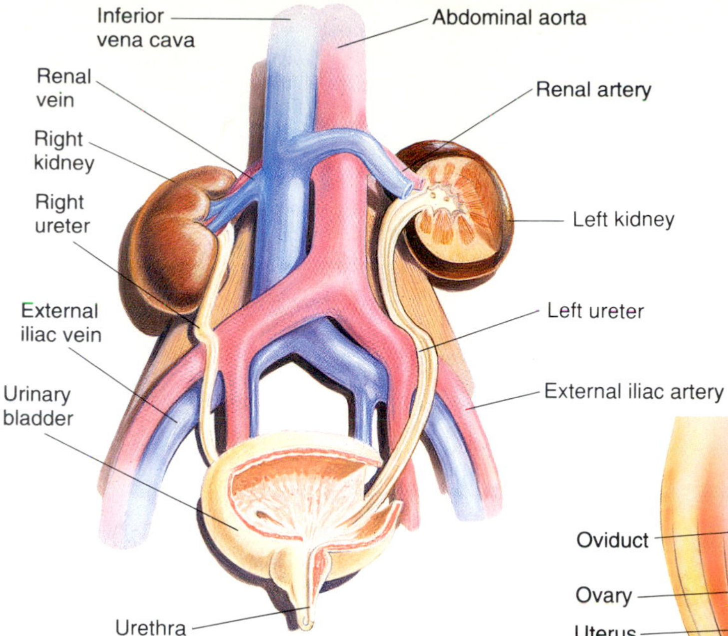

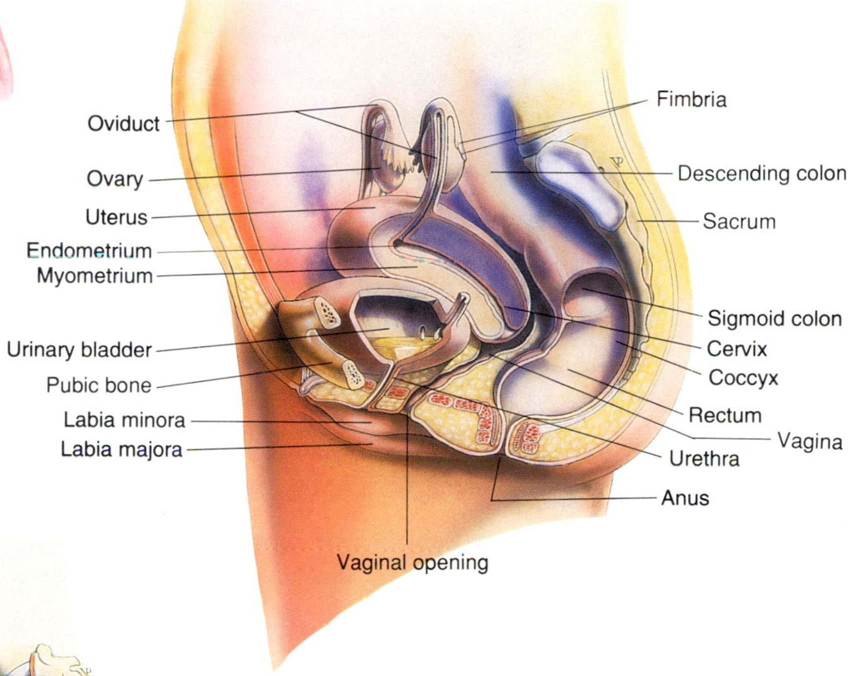

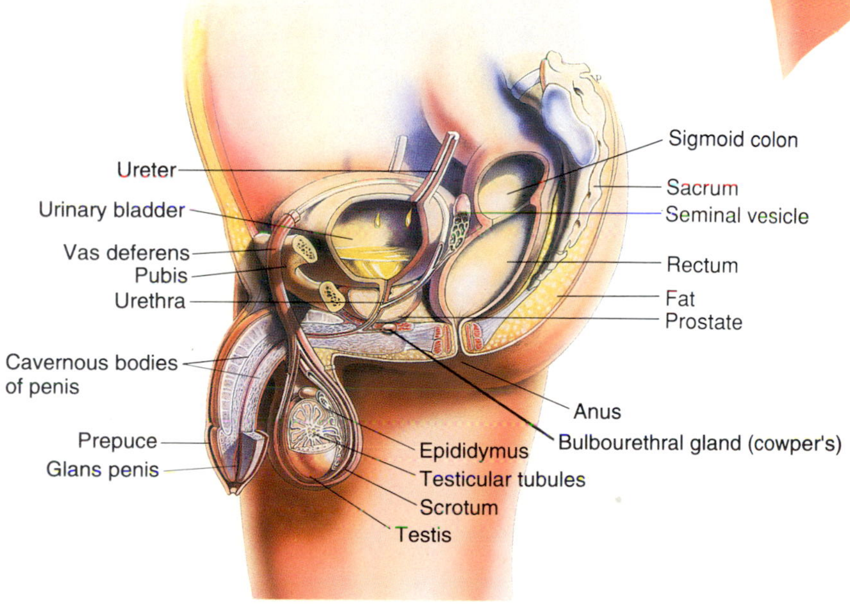

Plate 16

THE SENSES

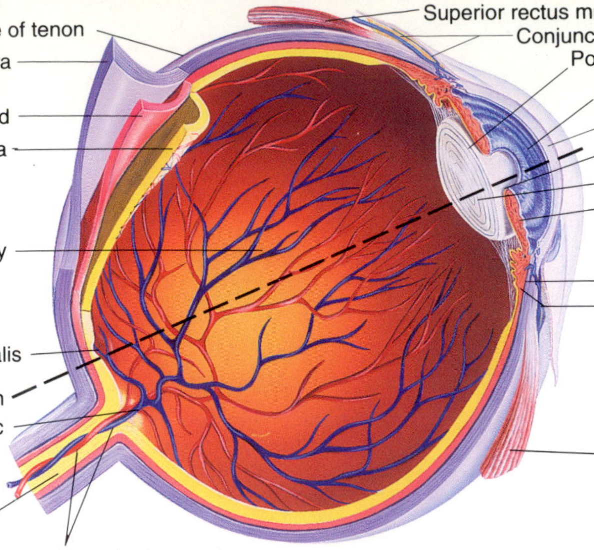

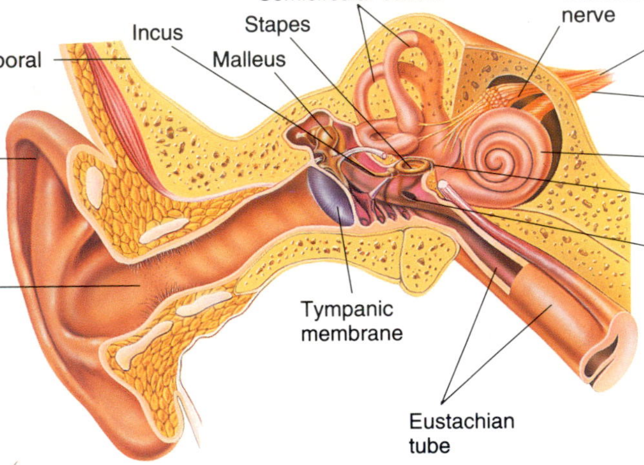

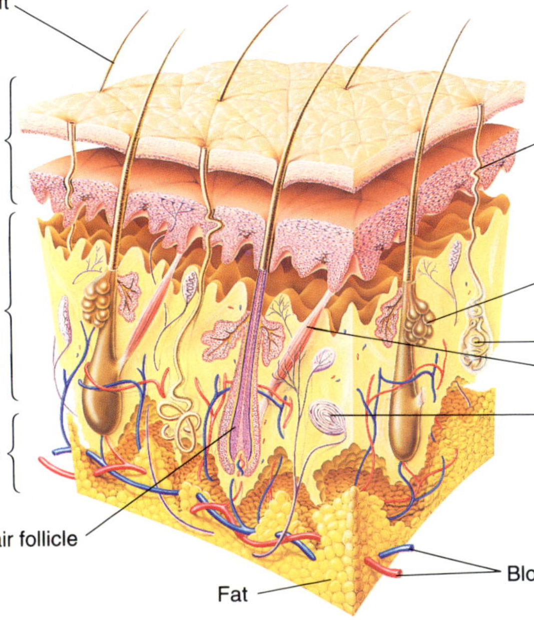

Activity: Divide students into groups of four and five. Give each group an activity (e.g., playing basketball). Students are to describe how each body system contributes to a person's ability to complete that activity (sensory—eyes and touch, brain, muscles, etc.). Students will need to have access to a variety of references. To illustrate what they discover, have the students draw a "cycle" diagram or use graphic organizers.

Integration: Art, Language Arts, Science, Physical Fitness

Related Health Content Area: Growth and development

Health Education Standard and Performance Indicators: 1(2,8)

Strategy Two

Objective: Students will demonstrate comprehension of the connection between body systems and organs and their functions.

Activity: Have students play a game of matching organs and their functions (see Table 16.1). Using the television program "Jeopardy!" as a model, ask students to identify either the correct body function or organ.

Integration: Science

Health Education Standard and Performance Indicators: 1(2,3)

Strategy Three

Objective: Students will be able to identify and describe how various diseases affect different organ systems.

Activity: Provide students with a list of diseases and diagrams of the human body. Have students work in cooperative groups to determine which disease primarily affects which organ system. Students may then discuss how each disease would affect other organ systems. This activity may be a multiday lesson.

Integration: Science

Related Health Content Area: Illness and disease

Health Education Standard and Performance Indicators: 1(3,7)

Home Activities

Strategy One

Objective: Students will investigate and analyze the issues involved in organ donation.

Activity: Problem-based activity (see Chapter 4) as follows:

Allison's mother, who is dying, told Allison that she wanted to be an organ donor; she even expressed these wishes on her driver's license. Allison's father has agreed, but her maternal grandparents are against it. Allison wants to talk to her grandparents to find out their objections and has asked Jamie, her closest friend, to help her.

- What is the major problem facing Allison in this vignette?
- What information should she have about organ donation?
- How does this information apply to Allison's problem?
- What would you do if you were Allison? Jamie?
- How might Allison evaluate her decision?

Integration: Science, Social Studies

Related Health Content Areas: Diseases, emotions, consumer health

Health Education Standards: 4,6,7

Strategy Two

Objective: Students will examine organs of animals for their similarities to those of humans.

Activity: Parents are to visit a slaughterhouse with their child, or obtain organs from a slaughterhouse or butcher to use at home. Intestines and hearts from pigs; liver, kidneys, and eyes from cattle; and so forth may be used. Bones may also be obtained. Students and their parents are to examine the organs visually, or dissect the organs. Then discussion can take place regarding how various parts work together.

Integration: Science

Related Health Content Areas: Nutrition, disease, growth and development

Health Education Standards: 1, 2

Tables 16.1 Matching Organs and Their Functions

Question	Answer (What . . .)
	Skeletal System
Spinal column	Protects the spinal cord
Ribs	Protects the heart and lungs
Femur	Supports the leg
Skull	Protects the brain
Humerus	Supports the arm
	Digestive System
Esophagus	Tube through which food passes from mouth to stomach
Stomach	Digests food into chyme
Small intestine	Further digests food after it leaves the stomach
Large intestine	Removes water from food before it exits the body
Liver	Filters out the blood and produces glucose
	Urinary System
Urethra	Tube through which urine exits the body
Urinary bladder	Holds urine before it leaves the body
Ureter	Takes urine from the kidneys to bladder
Kidney	Filters urine out of blood
	Muscular System
Triceps	Straightens the arm
Biceps	Bends the arm
Rectus abdominis	Helps bend the body forward
Pectoralis major	Supports the shoulders and chest
Rectus femoris	Straightens the leg
	Nervous System
Brain	Controls thinking and movement
Spinal cord	Sends messages to and from the brain
Nerves	Carries messages from the brain to parts of the body
	Circulatory System
Heart	Pumps blood throughout the body
Arteries	Takes blood from the heart to parts of the body
Veins	Takes blood from parts of the body to the heart
Blood	Carries oxygen throughout the body
	Respiratory System
Trachea	Takes air to the lungs
Lungs	Exchanges oxygen and carbon dioxide in blood
Diaphragm	Helps the lungs to take in and release air

References

American Lung Association. *Lung Disease Data 1994.* American Lung Association, New York, 1994.

Farish, D.J. *Human Biology.* Jones and Bartlett, Boston, 1993.

Sloane, E. *Anatomy and Physiology.* Jones and Bartlett, Boston, 1994.

U.S. Department of Health and Human Services. *Healthy Children 2000.* Jones and Bartlett, Boston, 1992.

Appendices

- **APPENDIX A**
  National Health Education Standards for Students (Organized by Standard)
- **APPENDIX B**
  Heath Education Resources
- **APPENDIX C**
  Electronic Resources for Health Education Information

A

National Health Education Standards for Students (Organized by Standard)

Health Education Standard 1: Students will comprehend concepts related to health promotion and disease prevention.

Rationale

Basic to health education is a foundation of knowledge about the interrelationship of behavior and health, interactions within the human body, and the prevention of diseases and other health problems. Experiencing physical, mental, emotional, and social changes as one grows and develops provides a self-contained "learning laboratory." Comprehension of health-promotion strategies and disease prevention concepts enables students to become health-literate, self-directed learners which establishes a foundation for leading healthy and productive lives.

Performance Indicators

As a result of health instruction in grades K–4, students will:

1. Describe relationships between personal health behaviors and individual well being.
2. Identify indicators of mental, emotional, social, and physical health during childhood.
3. Describe the basic structure and functions of the human body systems.
4. Describe how the family influences personal health.
5. Describe how physical, social, and emotional environments influence personal health.
6. Identify common health problems of children.
7. Identify health problems that should be detected and treated early.
8. Explain how childhood injuries and illnesses can be prevented or treated.

As a result of health instruction in grades 5–8, students will:

1. Explain the relationship between positive health behaviors and the prevention of

This represents the work of the Joint Committee on National Health Education Standards. Copies of the *National Health Education Standards: Achieving Health Literacy* can be obtained through the American School Health Association, Association for the Advancement of Health Education, or the American Cancer Society.

injury, illness, disease, and premature death.

2. Describe the interrelationship of mental, emotional, social, and physical health during adolescence.
3. Explain how health is influenced by the interaction of body systems.
4. Describe how family and peers influence the health of adolescents.
5. Analyze how environment and personal health are interrelated.
6. Describe ways to reduce risks related to adolescent health problems.
7. Explain how appropriate health care can prevent premature death and disability.
8. Describe how lifestyle, pathogens, family history, and other risk factors are related to the cause or prevention of disease and other health problems.

As a result of health instruction in grades 9–11, students will:

1. Analyze how behavior can impact health maintenance and disease prevention.
2. Describe the interrelationships of mental, emotional, social, and physical health throughout adulthood.
3. Explain the impact of personal health behaviors on the functioning of body systems.
4. Analyze how the family, peers, and community influence the health of individuals.
5. Analyze how the environment influences the health of the community.
6. Describe how to delay onset and reduce risks of potential health problems during adulthood.
7. Analyze how public health policies and government regulations influence health promotion and disease prevention.
8. Analyze how the prevention and control of health problems are influenced by research and medical advances.

Health Education Standard 2: Students will demonstrate the ability to access valid health information and health-promoting products and services.

Rationale

Accessing valid health information and health-promoting products and services is important in the prevention, early detection, and treatment of most health problems. Critical thinking involves the ability to identify valid health information and to analyze, select, and access health-promoting services and products. Applying skills of information analysis, organization, comparison, synthesis, and evaluation to health issues provides a foundation for individuals to move toward becoming health literate and responsible, productive citizens.

Performance Indicators

As a result of health instruction in grades K–4, students will:

1. Identify characteristics of valid health information and health-promoting products and services.
2. Demonstrate the ability to locate resources from home, school, and community that provide valid health information.
3. Explain how media influence the selection of health information, products, and services.
4. Demonstrate the ability to locate school and community health helpers.

As a result of health instruction in grades 5–8, students will:

1. Analyze the validity of health information, products, and services.
2. Demonstrate the ability to utilize resources from home, school, and community that provide valid health information.

3. Analyze how media influence the selection of health information and products.
4. Demonstrate the ability to locate health products and services.
5. Compare the costs and validity of health products.
6. Describe situations requiring professional health services.

As a result of health instruction in grades 9–11, students will:

1. Evaluate the validity of health information, products, and services.
2. Demonstrate the ability to evaluate resources from home, school, and community that provide valid health information.
3. Evaluate factors that influence personal selection of health products and services.
4. Demonstrate the ability to access school and community health services for self and others.
5. Analyze the cost and accessibility of health-care services.
6. Analyze situations requiring professional health services.

Health Education Standard 3: Students will demonstrate the ability to practice health-enhancing behaviors and reduce health risks.

Rationale

Research confirms that many diseases and injuries can be prevented by reducing harmful and risk-taking behaviors. More importantly, recognizing and practicing health-enhancing behaviors can contribute to a positive quality of life. Strategies used to maintain and improve health behaviors will utilize knowledge and skills that help students become critical thinkers and problem solvers. By accepting responsibility for personal health, students will have a foundation for living a healthy, productive life.

Performance Indicators

As a result of health instruction in grades K–4, students will:

1. Identify responsible health behaviors.
2. Identify personal health needs.
3. Compare behaviors that are safe to those that are risky or harmful.
4. Demonstrate strategies to improve or maintain personal health.
5. Develop injury-prevention and management strategies for personal health.
6. Demonstrate ways to avoid and reduce threatening situations.
7. Apply skills to manage stress.

As a result of health instruction in grades 5–8, students will:

1. Explain the importance of assuming responsibility for personal health behaviors.
2. Analyze a personal health assessment to determine health strengths and risks.
3. Distinguish between safe and risky or harmful behaviors in relationships.
4. Demonstrate strategies to improve or maintain personal and family health.
5. Develop injury-prevention and management strategies for personal and family health.
6. Demonstrate ways to avoid and reduce threatening situations.
7. Demonstrate strategies to manage stress.

As a result of health instruction in grades 9–11, students will:

1. Analyze the role of individual responsibility for enhancing health.
2. Evaluate a personal health assessment to determine strategies for health enhancement and risk reduction.
3. Analyze the short-term and long-term consequences of safe, risky, and harmful behaviors.
4. Develop strategies to improve and maintain personal, family, and community health.
5. Develop injury-prevention and management strategies for personal, family, and community health.

6. Demonstrate ways to avoid and reduce threatening situations.
7. Evaluate strategies to manage stress.

Health Education Standard 4: Students will analyze the influence of culture, media, technology, and other factors on health.

Rationale

Health is influenced by a variety of factors that co-exist within society. These include the cultural context as well as media and technology. A critical thinker and problem solver is able to analyze, evaluate, and interpret the influence of these factors on health. The health-literate, responsible, and productive citizen draws upon the contributions of culture, media, technology, and other factors to strengthen individual, family, and community health.

Performance Indicators

As a result of health instruction in grades K–4, students will:

1. Describe how culture influences personal health behaviors.
2. Explain how media influence thoughts, feelings, and health behaviors.
3. Describe ways technology can influence personal health.
4. Explain how information from school and family influences health.

As a result of health instruction in grades 5–8, students will:

1. Describe the influence of cultural beliefs on health behaviors and the use of health services.
2. Analyze how messages from media and other sources influence health behaviors.
3. Analyze the influence of technology on personal and family health.
4. Analyze how information from peers influences health.

As a result of health instruction in grades 9–11, students will:

1. Analyze how cultural diversity enriches and challenges health behaviors.
2. Evaluate the effect of media and other factors on personal, family, and community health.
3. Evaluate the impact of technology on personal, family, and community health.
4. Analyze how information from the community influences health.

Health Education Standard 5: Students will demonstrate the ability to use interpersonal communication skills to enhance health.

Rationale

Personal, family, and community health are enhanced through effective communication. A responsible individual will use verbal and nonverbal skills in developing and maintaining healthy personal relationships. Ability to organize and to convey information, beliefs, opinions, and feelings are skills which strengthen interactions and can reduce or avoid conflict. When communicating, individuals who are health-literate demonstrate care, consideration, and respect for self and others.

Performance Indicators

As a result of health instruction in grades K–4, students will:

1. Distinguish between verbal and nonverbal communication.
2. Describe characteristics needed to be a responsible friend and family member.
3. Demonstrate healthy ways to express needs, wants, and feelings.
4. Demonstrate ways to communicate care, consideration, and respect for self and others.

5. Demonstrate attentive listening skills to build and maintain healthy relationships.
6. Demonstrate refusal skills to enhance health.
7. Differentiate between negative and positive behaviors used in conflict situations.
8. Demonstrate nonviolent strategies to resolve conflicts.

As a result of health instruction in grades 5–8, students will:

1. Demonstrate effective verbal and nonverbal communication skills to enhance health.
2. Describe how the behavior of family and peers affects interpersonal communication.
3. Demonstrate healthy ways to express needs, wants, and feelings.
4. Demonstrate ways to communicate care, consideration, and respect for self and others.
5. Demonstrate communication skills to build and maintain healthy relationships.
6. Demonstrate refusal and negotiation skills to enhance health.
7. Analyze the possible causes of conflict among youth in schools and communities.
8. Demonstrate strategies to manage conflict in healthy ways.

As a result of health instruction in grades 9–11, students will:

1. Demonstrate skills for communicating effectively with family, peers, and others.
2. Analyze how interpersonal communication affects relationships.
3. Demonstrate healthy ways to express needs, wants, and feelings.
4. Demonstrate ways to communicate care, consideration, and respect for self and others.
5. Demonstrate strategies for solving interpersonal conflicts without harming self or others.
6. Demonstrate refusal, negotiation, and collaboration skills to avoid potentially harmful situations.
7. Analyze the possible causes of conflict in schools, families, and communities.
8. Demonstrate strategies used to prevent conflict.

Health Education Standard 6: Students will demonstrate the ability to use goal-setting and decision-making skills to enhance health.

Rationale

Decision-making and goal-setting are essential lifelong skills needed in order to implement and sustain health-enhancing behaviors. These skills make it possible for individuals to transfer health knowledge into healthy lifestyles. When applied to health issues, decision-making and goal-setting skills will enable individuals to collaborate with others to improve the quality of life in their families, schools, and communities.

Performance Indicators

As a result of health instruction in grades K–4, students will:

1. Demonstrate the ability to apply a decision-making process to health issues and problems.
2. Explain when to ask for assistance in making health-related decisions and setting health goals.
3. Predict outcomes of positive health decisions.
4. Set a personal health goal and track progress toward its achievement.

As a result of health instruction in grades 5–8, students will:

1. Demonstrate the ability to apply a decision-making process to health issues and problems, individually and collaboratively.
2. Analyze how health-related decisions are influenced by individuals, family, and community values.
3. Predict how decisions regarding health behaviors have consequences for self and others.

4. Apply strategies and skills needed to attain personal health goals.
5. Describe how personal health goals are influenced by changing information, abilities, priorities, and responsibilities.
6. Develop a plan that addresses personal strengths, needs, and health risks.

As a result of health instruction in grades 9–11, students will:

1. Demonstrate the ability to utilize various strategies when making decisions related to health needs and risks of young adults.
2. Analyze health concerns that require collaborative decision-making.
3. Predict immediate and long-term impact of health decisions on individual, family, and community.
4. Implement a plan for attaining a personal health goal.
5. Evaluate progress toward achieving personal health goals.
6. Formulate an effective plan for lifelong health.

Health Education Standard 7: Students will demonstrate the ability to advocate for personal, family, and community health.

Rationale

Quality of life is dependent on an environment that protects and promotes the health of individuals, families, and communities. Responsible citizens, who are health-literate, are characterized by advocating and communicating for positive health in their communities. A variety of health-advocacy skills are critical to these activities.

Performance Indicators

As a result of health instruction in grades K–4, students will:

1. Describe a variety of methods to convey accurate health information and ideas.
2. Express information and opinions about health issues.
3. Identify community agencies that advocate for healthy individuals, families, and communities.
4. Demonstrate the ability to influence and support others in making positive health choices.

As a result of health instruction in grades 5–8, students will:

1. Analyze various communication methods to accurately express health information and ideas.
2. Express information and opinions about health issues.
3. Identify barriers to effective communication of information, ideas, feelings, and opinions about health issues.
4. Demonstrate the ability to influence and support others in making positive health choices.
5. Demonstrate the ability to work cooperatively when advocating for healthy individuals, families, and schools.

As a result of health instruction in grades 9–11, students will:

1. Evaluate the effectiveness of communication methods for accurately expressing health information and ideas.
2. Express information and opinions about health issues.
3. Utilize strategies to overcome barriers when communicating information, ideas, feelings, and opinions about health issues.
4. Demonstrate the ability to influence and support others in making positive health choices.
5. Demonstrate the ability to work cooperatively when advocating for healthy communities.
6. Demonstrate the ability to adapt health messages and communications techniques to the characteristics of a particular audience.

B

Health Education Resources

Government

Healthy environment:

Environmental Protection Agency
Forms and Publications Center
Research Triangle Park, NC 27711
919/541–2111

Cardiovascular disease:

High Blood Pressure Information Center
1501 Wilson Blvd.
Arlington, VA 22209
703/558–4880

Several health areas such as safety and first aid, drug use, environmental health, and health careers:

National Archives and Records Service
General Services Administration
National Audiovisual Center
Washington, DC 20409
301/763–1896

Use and abuse of drugs:

National Clearinghouse
on Drug Abuse Information
Room 1056, Parklawn Building
5600 Fishers Lane
Rockville, MD 20857
301/443–6500

Prevention of disease; materials for teachers:

National Heart, Lung and Blood Institute
9000 Rockville Pike
National Institutes of Health Bldg. 31/4 A24
Bethesda, MD 20205
301/496–1051

Safety issues, including alcohol use:

Highway Traffic Safety Administration
U.S. Department of Transportation
Washington, DC 20590
202/426–1828

Mental health issues:

National Institutes of Mental Health
5600 Fishers Lane
Rockville, MD 20857
301/468–2600

Dental hygiene, personal health:

National Institute of Dental Research
National Institutes of Health Bldg. 31/2 C34
Bethesda, MD 20205
301/469–4261

Information on several different health topics:

Public Documents Distribution Center
Department 20
Pueblo, CO 81009

Disease prevention, community health, dental health, safety and first aid, alcohol and drugs, growth and development:

Superintendent of Documents
U.S. Government Printing Office
Washington, DC 20402
202/783–3238

Many different materials regarding health education:

U.S. Center for Health Promotion and Education
Centers for Disease Control
1600 Clifton
Atlanta, GA 30333
404/633–3311

Drugs, personal health, consumer health:

U.S. Food and Drug Administration
5600 Fishers Lane
Rockville, MD 20857

Many different materials regarding health education:

U.S. Office of Health Information
and Health Promotion
Hubert Humphrey Building
200 Independence Ave. S.W.
Washington, DC 20201
202/655–4000

Nongovernmental Health Organizations

Cancer, including statistics and cancer-related materials; National Health Education Standards:

American Cancer Society, Inc.
(national headquarters)
Clyton Road
Atlanta, GA 30030

Nutrition, disease prevention, growth and development, first aid, drugs:

American Heart Association
(national headquarters)
National Center
7320 Greenville Ave.
Dallas, TX 75231
214/750–5300

Disease prevention, growth and development, environmental health, community health:

American Lung Association
(national headquarters)
1740 Broadway
New York, NY 10019
212/245–8000

Safety and first aid, growth and development, consumer health, community health, family life:

American Red Cross (national headquarters)
17th and E St. N.W.
Washington, DC 20006
202/737–8300

Prevention of disease, disease control:

Arthritis Foundation
(national headquarters)
3400 Peachtree Rd. N.E., Suite 1101
Atlanta, GA 30326
404/266–0795

Disease prevention and control:

Asthma and Allergy Foundation of America
1125 15th St. N.W., Suite 502
Washington, DC 20005

Prevention and control of disease:

Epilepsy Foundation of America
4351 Garden City Dr.
Landover, MD 20785
301/459–3700

Birth defects, disease prevention and control, growth and development, drug use:

March of Dimes Birth Defects Foundation
1275 Mamaroneck Ave.
P.O. Box 2000
White Plains, NY 10605
914/428–7100

Prevention and control of disease:

Muscular Dystrophy Association
(national headquarters)
3561 E. Sunrise Dr.
Tucson, AZ 85718
605/529–2000

Prevention and control of disease:

National Association
for Sickle Cell Disease, Inc.
3460 Wilshire Blvd., Suite 1012
Los Angeles, CA 90010
213/731–1166

Alcohol use and abuse:

National Council on Alcoholism
and Drug Dependence
12 W. 21st St.
New York, NY 10010
212/206–6770

Growth and development, safety, prevention of disease:

National Easter Seal Society
for Crippled Children and Adults
2023 W. Ogden Ave.
Chicago, IL 60612
312/243–8400

General safety information:

National Safety Council
425 N. Michigan Ave.
Chicago, IL 60611
312/527–4800

Prevention and control of disease:

United Cerebral Palsy Association, Inc.
(national headquarters)
7 Penn Plaza, Suite 804
New York, NY 10001
212/268–6655

General Resources

Dental health, personal health:

American Dental Association
211 East Chicago Avenue
Chicago, IL 60611

Several health education–related materials, including programs and statistics about adolescent health:

American Medical Association
P.O. Box 821
Monroe, WI 53566

Recent information covering several aspects of health education:

ERIC—Clearinghouse on Teacher Education, Health Education
One Dupont Circle N.W.
Washington, DC 20036

Prevention and control of disease:

Juvenile Diabetes Association
23 East 26th Street
New York, NY 10017

Personal health, growth and development, nutrition:

National Dairy Council
6300 North River Rd.
Rosemont, IL 60018

Alcohol and related drugs:

National Clearinghouse for Alcohol Information
9199 Gaither Road
Gaithersburg, MD 20760

Health careers:

National Health Council
1740 Broadway
New York, NY 10019

C

Electronic Resources for Health Education Information

In addition to the growing amount of software available for health and science education, there are many resources that can be accessed on the Internet.

Libraries	Address
Library of Congress	http://lcweb.loc.gov
National Library of Medicine	http://www.nlm.nih.gov
National Health Information Center	http://nhic-nt.health.org/

Educational Sites	Address
ERIC Educational Resources Information Center (ERIC), AskERIC (selected resources for education and general interest)	gopher ericir.syr.edu 70 http://ericir.syr.edu
Clearinghouse assessment evaluation	http://www.cua.edu/www/eric ae/
Elementary and early childhood	http://ericps.ed.uiuc.edu
Rural education, small schools	http://aelvis.ael.org/~eric/eric.html
SunSITE (University of North Carolina)	http://sunsite.unc.edu
Texas Education Network (has complete listing of education sites)	http://www.tenet.edu/education/main.html
U.S. Department of Education	http://www.ed.gov
WebWorld for Kids	http://www.wentworth.com/classroom/edulinks.htm

Environmental Sites	Address
Environmental Protection Agency	http://www.epa.gov
Hazardous Substances & Public Health Homepage	http://atsdrl.atsdr.cdc.gov:8080/HEC/hsphhome.html

Other Resource Sites	Address
Adolescent Directory Online	http://education.indiana.edu/cas/adol/adol.html
Centers for Disease Control	http://www.cdc.gov
CDC Morbidity & Mortality Weekly Report	http://www.crawford.com/cdc/mmwr/mmwr.html
Global Health Network	http://www.pitt.edu/HOME/GHNet/GHNet.html
National Centers for Health Statistics	http://www.cdc.gov/nchswww/nchshome.htm
National Institutes of Health	http://www.nih.gov
U.S. Department of Health and Human Services	http://www.os.dhhs.gov
World Health Organization	http://www.who.ch
Yahoo (good resources)	http://www.yahoo.com

Web Sites

Topic	Address
Bacterial/fungal disease	http://www.cdc.gov/diseases/bacterial.html
Biomedicine	gopher://inform.uchc.edu/11gopher_root%3a%5b_data04._data0401%5d
Cancer	gopher://gopher.nih.gov:70/00/clin/cancernet/instructions
CDC Aids/HIV Info Page	http://www.cdc.gov/diseases/aids.html
CDC Daily Summaries	gopher://gopher.niaid.nih.gov70/11/aids/cdcds
CDC HomePage	http://www.cdc.gov
CDC Surveillance Data	gopher://gopher.niaid.nih.gov:70/11/aids/csr
Census data	gopher://mail.coin.missouri.edu:70/11/reference/census/us
Comprehensive list of sites	http://www.netgen.com/cgi/comprehensive
Diabetes	http://www.biostat.wisc.edu/diaknow/index.htm
Domestic violence	http://www.interport.net/~asherman/dv.html
Drug-related network	http://hperreal.com/drugs/faqs/resources.html
Duke University Health Devil	http://h-devil-www.mc.duke.edu/h-devil

continued

Topic	Address
Web Sites—continued	
Electronic health journals	http://kuhttp.cc.ukans.edu/cwis/units/Lee/JOURNALS.HTML
E-mail for Health Educators	http://www.siu.edu:80/departments/coe/hedrec
Environmental-Project NatureConnect	http://www.pacificrim.net/~nature/
Go Ask Alice	http://www.columbia.edu/cu/healthwise
Government agencies	http://www.yahoo.com/government/agencies
Health in Perspective	http://www.perspective.com/health/index.html
Heart disease	http://osler.wustl.edu/~murphy/cardiology/compass.html
International Red Cross	http://www.ifrc.org/
Men's health	http://www.vix.com/pub/men/health/health.html
National Institute of Environmental Health Sciences	http://www.niehs.nih.gov/
National Institute of Occupational Safety and Health	http://www.gov/diseases/niosh.html
Nutrition/diet analysis	http://www.yahoo.com/Health/Nutrition
Occupational Safety and Health Administration	http://www.osha-slc.gov
Safer-Sex Page	http://www.cmpharm.ucsf.edu/~troyer/safesex
Stress	http://www.cts.com/~health/stressbus.html
UCHC Library Page	http://cortex.uchc.edu/~libweb/libpg1.html
Viral diseases	http://www.cdc.gov/diseases/viral.html
Women's health	http://sfgate.com/examiner/womensweb.html

INDEX

continued

continued